ALSO BY BILL JAMES

The Bill James Baseball Abstract

The Bill James Historical Baseball Abstract

This Time Let's Not Eat the Bones

The Bill James Baseball Book

The Politics of Glory

The Bill James Player Ratings Book

The Bill James Guide to Baseball Managers

The New Bill James Historical Baseball Abstract

Win Shares

The Bill James Handbook

The Neyer/James Guide to Pitchers (with Rob Neyer)

The Bill James Gold Mine

Praise for Popular Crime

"An intellectual walkabout . . . For true-crime aficionados, this book is a hoot. James has to be the least starchy serious writer I've run across in years. He has the gift of writing the way a person talks—no easy task, believe me—giving *Popular Crime* a folksy, conversational feel."

—*The New York Times Book Review*

"A very entertaining book, and it will instigate arguments even as it scores many important points."

—*The Washington Post*

"An engagingly written history of well-publicized deadly crimes."

—*Pittsburgh Post-Gazette*

"[An] insightfully unorthodox history of famous murders."

—*New York* magazine

"The book is a success, thoughtful and thought-provoking. It is also gruesome, ghoulish and appalling—and utterly fascinating."

—*The Daily Beast*

"A fascinating read . . . well-written, thought-provoking and ungory."

—NPR.org

"James' first, brilliant, fascinating, infuriating foray into the world of popular crime is one of the great—and truly unexpected—books of 2011. It is at once a shock, a delight, an education and an infinitely debatable outrage. And a pleasure to have James applying his hilariously unique skill set to the crimes and scandals that have captured the public imagination."

—*Buffalo News*

"Bill James is an American original who has an original take on everything he writes about, on criminals as much as catchers. You may feel compelled to skip dinner, turning his pages, even when you think he's out to lunch."

—Adam Gopnik

"*Popular Crime* will remind you of just how wonderful a writer Mr. James is. Incisive analysis and encyclopedic knowledge tempered by a sometimes morbid, but never jaded, dose of Americana: it's sabermetrics meets the Coen Brothers."

—Nate Silver, FiveThirtyEight/*The New York Times*

"I would read Bill James on anything. I would read him on the price of burlap in Des Moines. Yet here, as with baseball, he has found a subject worthy of his obsession. *Popular Crime* is the best kind of guilty pleasure: sure to inspire countless bar-stool digressions and brimming with arguments about why these tabloid stories, and the ways we often misunderstand them, actually matter. James may be our foremost forensic historian."

—Ben McGrath

"Bill James brushes aside the clouds of unknowing that have surrounded America's most popular crimes, from the shooting of Jesse James to the murder of JonBenet Ramsey. The chapters on the Boston Strangler, the Kennedy assassination, the Zodiac killer, and O. J. Simpson are models of clarity which should precede any further reading you do on the subjects. But don't start reading *Popular Crime* at bedtime, because you won't be able to put it down."

—Allen Barra, author of *The Last Coach*

POPULAR CRIME

REFLECTIONS ON THE
CELEBRATION OF VIOLENCE

Bill James

SCRIBNER

New York   London   Toronto   Sydney   New Delhi

Scribner
A Division of Simon & Schuster, Inc.
1230 Avenue of the Americas
New York, NY 10020

First Scribner trade paperback edition May 2012

SCRIBNER and design are registered trademarks of The Gale Group, Inc., used under
license by Simon & Schuster, Inc., the publisher of this work.

For information about special discounts for bulk purchases,
please contact Simon & Schuster Special Sales at 1-866-506-1949
or business@simonandschuster.com.

The Simon & Schuster Speakers Bureau can bring authors to your live event.
For more information or to book an event contact the Simon & Schuster Speakers
Bureau at 1-866-248-3049 or visit our website at www.simonspeakers.com.

Designed by Carla Jayne Jones

Manufactured in the United States of America

7   9   10   8

Library of Congress Control Number: 2010036180

ISBN 978-1-4165-5273-4
ISBN 978-1-4165-5274-1 (pbk)
ISBN 978-1-4391-8272-7 (ebook)

THIS BOOK IS DEDICATED TO PHYLLIS MCCARTHY
MY WIFE'S MOST GRACIOUS MOTHER

Contents

———◆———

I.   1

    Plautius Silvanus   1

    L. Pedanius Secundus   2

    Elizabeth Canning   3

    Introductory Comments   6

II.   10

    Elma Sands   10

    Helen Jewett   15

    Mary Rogers   15

III.   23

    Ann McAllister   23

    Missing White Girls   24

    The Yale Murder   26

    Webster/Parkman Case   26

    On American Crime Rates   31

IV.   33

    Boys on the Ice   33

    On Why Certain Crimes Are Chosen for Fame   35

    Charlie Ross   36

    The Wild West   41

V.   43

    Lizzie Borden   43
    Motive, Means and Opportunity Argument   44
    On Weighing Evidence   45

VI.   66

    "Profiting" from Crime   66
    H. H. Holmes   67
    Kansas Charley   69
    William Goebel   69
    Old Man Rice   71
    Griffith J. Griffith   74
    Frank Steunenberg   75
    Chloe Canfield   75
    Erich Muenter, Part 1   75
    Stanford White   76
    Thomas H. Swope   76
    Radicalism and Crime   77

VII.   80

    Clarence Darrow and the McNamaras   81

VIII.   89

    Erich Muenter, Part 2   89
    On the Astonishing Openness of American Society
        a Hundred Years Ago   93

IX.   95

    Old Murder Statistics   95
    Moman Pruiett   96
    On the Evolution of the Legal System   101

X.   106

    Mary Phagan Introduction   106
    A System of Categorizing Crime Stories   106
    Mary Phagan Case   107

XI.   119
    Robert Stroud, Part 1   119
    Grace Roberts   120
    Harry K. Thaw   122
    Sacco and Vanzetti   122

XII.   129
    The Hall/Mills Case   129
    The Oregon Train Robbery   135
    The Snyder/Gray Case   137
    Summary of 1920s Crimes   139

XIII.   141
    Levels of Description   141
    The Lindbergh Baby   144
    Post-Lindbergh Journalism   156

XIV.   159
    The Mad Butcher of Kingsbury Run   159

XV.   173
    Mad Dog Killer Stories   173
    Thalia Massie   174
    The Scottsboro Boys   176
    Robert Stroud, Part 2   178

XVI.   181
    William Heirens   181
    The Black Dahlia   182
    Caryl Chessman   187
    On the Importance of What People
        Choose to Be Interested In   193

XVII.   198
    Sam Sheppard   198

XVIII.   216
    Lowell Lee Andrews   216
    In Cold Blood   217
    Robert Stroud, Part 3   218
    The Onion Field   220
    The Warren Court   223

XIX.   226
    The Boston Strangler   226

XX.   241
    On the Success Rate of the Judicial System in
        High-Profile Cases   241
    True Crime Movies   244
    The Kennedy Assassination   245

XXI.   257
    The Michigan Murders   257
    Definition Creep   261

XXII.   264
    The Zodiac   264

XXIII.   273
    Susan Nason   273
    Katherine Ann Power   274
    Juan Corona   278
    John List   281
    The Burger Court   285

XXIV.   287
    Randall Dale Adams   287
    Ted Bundy   289
    Gary Tison   293
    Fatal Vision   296
    Echoes in the Darkness   297

XXV.   299
  Charles Hatcher   299
  On the Value of Police Sketches   303
  The Yale Murder and the Insanity Defense   305
  Reviving Prison Reform   309

XXVI.   310
  Sid Vicious/Nancy Spungen   310
  Dallas Egbert III   310
  Dean Milo   314
  Chris Hobson   314
  Lawrencia Bembenek   317
  McMartin Preschool   317
  Wayne Williams   318
  John DeLorean   318
  Aside on Car Companies   319
  Jean Harris   319
  Jody Plauché   319
  Bernard Goetz   319
  Kenneth McElroy   319
  Joseph Kallinger   322

XXVII.   323
  Richard Kuklinski   323
  Robert Hansen   327
  Putting the Criminal Justice System Back Together   331

XXVIII.   335
  John Joubert   335
  Charles Sasser   337
  Notes toward a Theory of Injustice   340
  Lake and Ng   342

XXIX   347
  Jon Dunkle   347
  On the Differences between Real and
      Fictional Serial Murderers   351

New Bedford, Massachusetts 352
Richard Grissom 354
Ray Copeland 356
William Lester Suff 358
How Serial Murderers Are Caught 359

XXX. 362
Computer Spy Case 362
Mel Ignatow 363
The Menendez Brothers 365
Pam Smart 367
O. J. Simpson 368

XXXI. 374
On Fictional Elements in Real Crimes 374
Rabbi Neulander 375

XXXII. 387
JonBenet Ramsey, Part 1 387

XXXIII. 409
JonBenet Ramsey, Part 2 409
On Prison Reform 412
On Partisanship and Justice 419

XXXIV. 423
Summary of Recent Crime Stories 423
On False Confessions 435
On Popular Crime 437

Addendum 445

Acknowledgments 475
Index 479

POPULAR
CRIME

I

In Rome in the year 24 AD, the praetor Plautius Silvanus pushed his wife Apronia out of the window in the middle of the night. They hadn't been married very long, or, we might guess, very happily. It was a high window, and she did not survive the fall.

Silvanus was a member of one of Rome's most celebrated and successful families. His father, also Plautius Silvanus, had been consul in 2 BCE. His grandmother, Urgulania, was a close friend of the empress, and a cousin, Urgulanilla, was then married to the man who would later become the emperor Claudius.

Apronia's father rushed to the palace and awakened the emperor Tiberius. Tiberius went immediately to the scene of the crime, where he saw obvious signs of a struggle and the marks of Apronia being forced out the window. Silvanus had no explanation. He claimed that he had been asleep at the time, and that Apronia must have leapt to her death. He was arrested, judges were appointed, and Tiberius presented his evidence to the Roman senate.

A great public scandal arose, in the midst of which Urgulania sent her grandson a dagger. This was taken to be a hint. Silvanus attempted to stab himself with the dagger, and, that failing, apparently enlisted the aid of confederates; in any case, Tacitus records that he "allowed his veins to be opened," and was soon gone.

There was still to be a trial, however. Silvanus' first wife, Numantina, was put on trial on charges of having driven her late ex-husband insane with incantations and potions . . . what we would now call "witchcraft." She was acquitted.

Silvanus' family was destroyed by the scandal. Claudius divorced Urgulanilla, who was believed to have been implicated in the matter in some opaque way. The grandmother disappears from history.

In 61 AD the Prefect of the city of Rome, L. Pedanius Secundus, became embroiled in a dispute with one of his slaves, either because he had agreed to release the slave for a price and then reneged on the deal—the story told by the slave—or because Pedanius and the slave had both fallen in love with the same slave boy who was kept as a prostitute, which was apparently the story circulated in the streets. In any case, Pedanius was murdered by the slave.

Roman law required that, when a slave murdered his master, all of the slaves residing in the household were to be executed—in fact, even if the master died accidentally within his house, the slaves were sometimes executed for failing to protect the master. Pedanius had 400 slaves. The law had been as it was for hundreds of years, Roman law being harder to change than the course of a river, and there had been cases before in which large numbers of slaves had been executed, but now people were losing respect for the old values, and the slaves no longer saw the point in this tradition. Crowds of plebs—rank-and-file civilians, neither slaves nor aristocracy—gathered to protest the executions. Rioting broke out, and not for the first time, incidentally. Rioting had erupted over the same issue at other times through the centuries.

The senate debated the matter, and most of the senators realized that the executions were unjust. They were unable to block implementation of the law, however, and the order was given that the executions must be carried out. Troops attempted to seize the slaves, but a crowd gathered to defend them, armed with stones and torches, and the soldiers were beaten back. By now Claudius' stepson Nero was the emperor, never known for his civility. Nero ordered thousands of soldiers to the scene. The slaves were taken into custody, and legions of soldiers lined the streets along which they were taken to be put to death.

Ordinarily, crime stories sink gradually beneath the waves of history, as proper stiff-upper-lip historians are generally above re-telling them, but street riots are one of the things that sometimes cause them to float. On January 1, 1753, an 18-year-old girl disappeared from a country lane in an area which is now part of London, but which at that time linked London to the village of Whitechapel. Employed as a maid in London, Elizabeth Canning had spent New Year's Day with her aunt and uncle in Whitechapel. As the holiday drew toward evening she headed back to London, and the aunt and uncle walked with her part of the way. With less than a mile to go along the thinly populated lane her relatives turned back, assuming that she would be safe making the last leg of the trek alone in the gathering dusk. In 1753, of course, the streets were unlit, and also, London had no regular police service. She had with her a little bit of money, what was left of her Christmas money, which was called a "Christmas Box," and a mince pie that she was carrying as a treat for one of her younger brothers.

She failed to arrive back in London. What happened then is oddly familiar to us. Her mother immediately raised the alarm, and her friends, relatives and her employers immediately organized a volunteer search. Within hours of her disappearance they were knocking on doors throughout the area, and within two days they had covered much of London with advertisements and fliers asking for information and offering a small reward. Her disappearance attracted the attention of the city. Someone along the lane thought that he remembered hearing a woman scream about the time she disappeared.

The search, however, went nowhere for several weeks. On January 29, late in the evening, Miss Canning suddenly reappeared at her mother's house, looking so bedraggled that her mother, when first Elizabeth came through the door, had not the slightest idea who she was. She had bruises on her face and body, a bad cut near one ear, she was dirty and emaciated and the nice dress she had been wearing at the time she disappeared had been replaced by rags. Her mother screamed, and, in the crowded part of London where they lived, the house filled quickly with friends and curious neighbors.

At this point the system of justice, such as it was, flew into action with unfortunate speed. Her neighbors began peppering her with questions about her disappearance—an obvious lapse of judgment, but what do you expect from eighteenth century peasants? We're lucky they weren't carrying pitchforks. Where have you been? Who took you? Where were you held? When you escaped, where did you find yourself?

Elizabeth, I believe, tried to answer these questions as best she could in her desperate condition. The story that she told, confused and disjointed and somewhat incoherent, is that, walking along the lane on the fateful holiday, she had been accosted by two thugs, who robbed her of her coins and her nice dress, and then pushed and dragged her several miles to a large house. There they turned her over to a group of women who made some half-hearted efforts to force her into a life of immoral trade. Resisting these efforts, she was locked in the hayloft—the attic, we would call it now—and apparently forgotten until she finally managed to escape, injuring her ear in the process. She had lived for four weeks on a loaf of bread, a pitcher of water and the mince pie.

Within minutes, the finger of suspicion had been pointed at the residents of a particular house, a large house filled with gypsies, tramps and thieves. There were some loose women who lived there, and some other oddballs and eccentrics. Yes, said Elizabeth; that sounds like that must be the house.

She was given a day to rest and recover, and then taken before an Alderman, who interrogated her and expressed some doubts about her account, but ultimately issued a warrant for a search of the property in question. A posse of Elizabeth's over-eager friends descended on the house, accompanied by a representative of the Lord Mayor of London and by other officials. All of the residents of the house were arrested. They were arraigned days later before a Justice of the Peace, who happened to be the novelist Henry Fielding. Fielding issued warrants for the detention of two women.

This story, very much like the story of the Duke Lacrosse team, would soon explode into a divisive national controversy with political overtones, occupying the attention of the British people to an extent that is ultimately inexplicable. Elizabeth Canning was destined to become, for a few months at least, perhaps the most famous person in the world. Crime stories of this magnitude make entire cast and crew into celebrities. In this cast we have an old gypsy woman named Mary Squires, with a face like a child's drawing of a witch, and a mistress of the house called Mother Wells, and in the crew we have a man bearing the moniker (I am not making this up) Fortune Natus, and a young prostitute named Virtue Hall.

Mary Squires smoked a pipe and would tell your fortune for a penny. She was the ugliest woman in the history of the world, a skinny old crone with a face full of warts, a nose the size of a pear and a lower lip, said the writers, the size of an infant's arm. Ms. Canning accused Squires and Susannah Wells, who owned the house, of stealing her corsets or, as they were called at the time, her "stays." (They were probably called "stays" because they helped the woman's body stay where it was put.) The underwear was worth perhaps less than Ms. Virtue's virtue, but at that time one could be hanged for theft in

England, and while that was not the usual punishment this was not the usual case. In the early days of the story, due to the great public sympathy for Ms. Canning, her accusations were accepted at face value, and by late February the old gypsy stood in the shadow of the gallows.

The mayor of London at that time was Sir Crispe Gascoyne. Gascoyne became concerned that an injustice was occurring on his watch, and took it upon himself to prevent this. The story told by Elizabeth Canning had serious problems. She had given a description of the house which did not match the suspect dwelling in one particular after another, and she had failed to mention things about the hayloft which, having been locked in there for 28 days, she could hardly have failed to notice. It seemed to many observers inexplicable that, in describing the events before the court, she had failed to give a hint about her assailant's quite remarkable face. Further, Mrs. Squires stated immediately upon being accused that on the first of January she had been a hundred and twenty miles away, and, on investigation, this appeared to be true; once somebody finally bothered to check, she had witnesses.

The trumpet of justice had sounded, however, and Ms. Canning refused to recant. All of England now began to choose sides, the Canningites against the Egyptians (the gypsies being commonly believed to have originated in Egypt). Which side you were on tended to match up with which pub you socialized in. There was a class division, somewhat inaccessible to us now, between domestic servants and lower-class people who lacked a position.

So one pub would decide that Mrs. Squires was guilty and the one across the street would decide that Miss Canning was lying, and occasionally they would meet in the middle of the street and try to settle the matter with fists and stones. Canning's supporters raised large amounts of money to prosecute those she had accused; Squires' defenders raised essentially equal amounts for the other side. A legal battle raged back and forth for a year, bills of indictment being sought and obtained on all sides. Henry Fielding authored a pamphlet, *A Clear Statement of the Case of Elizabeth Canning*, supporting the Canningites; Tobias Smollett was among many publishing on the other side of the issue. Voltaire published a history of the affair (*Histoire d'Elisabeth Canning, et de Jean Calas*). At one point the Lord Mayor—the head of the Egyptians, who opposed Canning—was dragged from his coach and roughed up by a mob of Canningites.

Mother Wells, immediately upon being convicted as a thief, was branded with a red-hot iron, the letter "T" being seared into her skin near her thumb.

This was done in open court in full view of the spectators to the trial. Mary Squires, sentenced to be hanged, was pardoned by the King, outraging Canning's supporters, some of whom lobbed stones at the King's carriage. In April of 1754, a little more than a year after the first event, Elizabeth stood trial at the Old Bailey on a charge of perjury, accused of giving false testimony against Mary Squires. The trial lasted for seven days, making it perhaps the longest trial of a commoner in English history up to that point, and certainly the most avidly followed. She was convicted on a close vote, a unanimous verdict not being required, and was ordered to be transported to America for seven years as punishment.

Elizabeth's opponents insisted that she had made up the whole story as an excuse for some adventure that had gone awry. This is unlikely. Her supporters insisted to the end that she was right about everything except a few details of her account, that Mary Squires' gypsy friends had created a false alibi. This is unlikely. Miss Canning may have suffered exactly what she said she had suffered, but mixed up the details in her confusion, and wound up innocently participating in the prosecution of innocent people. She may have run off to meet a man she knew or thought she knew, and found herself in a horrible situation, which she never came clean about. She may have lied to avoid admitting that she had been raped. Ultimately, we just do not know.

Elizabeth Canning's supporters raised money for her to travel to America in comfort and with a little bit of a purse, to which the British judicial system made no objections. On the ship across the Atlantic she was befriended by a Philadelphia minister and his wife. She met and married a well-off young man named John Treat, the grandson of a former Connecticut governor, bore three sons and a daughter, died before the revolution, and is believed to be buried in Wethersfield, Connecticut.

The modern American phenomenon of popular crime stories is in absolutely no way new, modern, or American. That it is truly a universal phenomenon throughout human history perhaps should not be asserted without a more complete survey, but I know of no society which did not have sensational crimes and huge public interest in them, except perhaps societies which were so repressive that the government was able to quash them.

Crime stories rush by us like oncoming traffic. New crime stories emerge in the national media almost every day. Each one roars by us for a few days, is remarked upon in casual conversation and filed away as something less than a memory. Occasionally a crime story turns and follows us, visible in our mirror for months or years afterward. Each one is important to somebody, and a few of them—something less than 2% of the murders—become books.

We are, not as a nation but as human beings, fascinated by crime stories, even obsessed with them. The Bible is full of them. On your television at this moment there are four channels covering true crime stories, and five more doing detective fiction. And yet, on a certain level, we are profoundly ashamed of this fascination. If you go into a good used book store and ask if they have a section of crime books, you will get one of two reactions. One is, the clerk will look at you as if you had asked whether they had any really good pornography. The other is, they will tell you that the crime books are down the aisle on your left, in the alcove beside the detective stories. Right next to the pornography.

The internet service that I use headlines news stories with links to them. A huge percentage of these are crime stories—yet in the chart attached, where their news summaries are sorted into categories, there is no category for crime. Maybe a third of their top news stories are crime stories; you would think that would rate one category among their 25. Apparently not.

Cable television networks which are financed and organized with high-minded civic purposes—the Biography channel, Arts & Entertainment Network, Discovery Channel—find themselves being swallowed up by crime stories, because when they put on crime stories, people watch. Forensics are a wedge, respectable science applied to dirty little crime.

If you go to a party attended by the best people—academics and lawyers, journalists and school bus drivers, those kinds of people . . . if you go to a party populated by the NPR crowd and you start talking about JonBenet Ramsey, people will look at you as if you had forgotten your pants. If you are a writer and you try to talk your editor into working on a book about famous crimes, he or she will instantly begin hedging you toward something more . . . something more *decent*. Maybe if you included a chapter on Watergate, it would be alright. If you write anything about JonBenet, you need to say how un-important that really was, compared to the attention it drew; that's really the only appropriate thing to be said about that case.

If you try to talk to American intellectuals and opinion-makers about the phenomenon of famous crimes, they immediately throw up a shield: *I will not talk about this. I am a serious and intelligent person. I am interested in politics and the environment. I do not talk about Natalee Holloway.* It is as if they were afraid of being dirtied by the subject.

Of course, no one has a social responsibility to be interested in Rabbi Neulander; that's not what I am saying. What I am saying is that given the magnitude of this subject, given the extent to which it occupies the attention of the nation, there are a series of obvious questions which one might guess would be matters of public discussion, but which are not discussed anywhere because the kind of people who participate in the national conversation are terrified of being thrown out of the boat if they confess to an interest in such vulgar matters. *Why do some crime stories become famous? Why does the Scott Peterson case become a national circus, while a thousand similar cases attract nothing beyond local notice? Why are people interested in crime stories? Is this a destructive phenomenon, as so many people assume it to be, or is there a valid social purpose being served? Who benefits from this? Who suffers from it? Who makes the critical decisions that cause crime stories to explode or fizzle? Are these stories actually significant to the nation, or are they truly as petty and irrelevant as intellectuals tend to assume they are?*

Beyond this roomful of questions there is another room where the questions are yet more important. Does our criminal justice system work well? How could it work better? When it fails, why does it fail? How could this failure have been avoided? Do the rules make sense? What does it take to earn a conviction? What *should* it take?

Crime stories are very often the basis on which new laws are proposed and old ones modified. We have Megan's Law and Sarah's Law and Jeremy's Law and Amber Alerts. This has been true for many years. In the 18th century several new laws sprung from the story of Elizabeth Canning. In the 1930s we had the Lindbergh Laws and the Little Lindbergh Laws. A great deal of our law and of our criminal procedure has *always* been shaped and re-shaped by these very famous crimes that the best people refuse to discuss.

Of course there *is* a national discussion about those types of issues—among the lawyers. When the rest of us try to comment, we are reminded firmly that we are not lawyers and therefore don't know what we're talking about. No one writes about these issues. Name a book by a non-lawyer, published in the last ten years for the general public, which attempts to discuss these issues in a serious way. On truTV, whenever a guest tries to comment on some irrational wrinkle of judicial procedure, some self-important lawyer immediately steps forward to "explain" why the system *has* to work this way, why the system of justice would collapse if a juror were allowed to read a news report about the case or a cop was allowed to mention his prior run-ins with the defendant.

It is not my intention to bash lawyers. It is my belief that the lay public—non-lawyers—should participate actively in the discussion of crime and justice. It is my notion that popular crime stories could be and should be a passageway that the lay public uses to enter into that discussion.

I said that no one writes about these issues, which is not literally true. I am sure that in some corner of the academic world there hides an intellectual who knows vastly more about these issues than I do and has written 208 published articles about them, which none of us have ever heard of, probably because he writes like a troll, or, not to be sexist, she writes like a troll or trollette. I am not here to bash intellectuals, either; I'm just a sarcastic bastard by nature.

This book is about three things. First, it is about famous crimes, and in particular about famous crimes which have happened in the United States since about 1880. Second, it is about *crime*, in a general way, about the kinds of issues I have tried to introduce here.

And third, it is about crime *books*. I am not a lawyer or an academic, nor even a cop or a court groupie. My understanding of these issues is based on what I have read, which includes a thousand or more crime books. There is, to the best of my knowledge, no book about crime books.

The world has lost track of Elizabeth Canning's grave. She lies somewhere in Connecticut, but no one seems to know exactly where. Her story is not a part of proper history, you see; she is just someone in whom the world was so foolish as to take an interest. We know where ancient athletes were born and where they died, and the same for actors and politicians, generals and inventors, musicians and artists, writers and industrialists. Elizabeth Canning was about the same age as George Washington, and was for many years vastly more famous than he was—and yet we have entirely lost track of her, her story sinking gradually beneath the waves.

II

*f this were a British book for a British audience, it would be easy to find the back border of our subject. The story of Jack the Ripper, for the British, casts such a giant shadow that it tends to obscure the rich history of criminal lunacy that preceded it. The British love to write books about Jack the Ripper. Most of these books are written by quasi-academic twits who wouldn't recognize a real serial murderer if he ate their liver, and propound the most fantastic and inane theories of who Jack the Ripper might have been. One of my particular favorites is a book which argues that the Ripper murders were committed by three men—a famous artist, a prominent physician and a member of the Royal family—who went skulking around the East End in an effort to distract attention from an unauthorized Royal marriage. There isn't the slightest bit of evidence which would incline anyone to buy into this preposterous explanation, but the authors declare their theory proven after about 40 pages anyway, and spend the rest of the book saying "And if you *still* don't believe it, what about *this,* huh?"

In America there is no such watershed event to provide an easy marker, and thus there are more crimes that remain more famous from before Lizzie Borden. Let us begin with Elma Sands.

The Ring family was doing very well as the 18th century drew to a close. They were Quakers, Elias and his wife Catherine (Sands) Ring. They ran a collection of businesses at 208 Greenwich Street in New York. Elias had a dry goods store. Catherine had a dress shop that employed as many as twenty women sewing finery and waiting on customers, and together they managed a boarding house, all at the same address. Catherine's sister, Hope Sands, lived there with her and worked at the dress shop, as did her cousin, Elma Sands.

Elma had come to New York three years earlier as a modest young woman. She was 22 years old, not beautiful, but she had a very cheerful manner, regarded by her family as too sprightly for a Quaker. In July of 1899 Levi Weeks, a carpenter, moved into the boarding house, and began pursuing first one female boarder, then another. By mid-August he was spending time with Elma. In another month a yellow fever epidemic swept New York, killing 1500 people—one-fortieth the population of the city. Those who could afford to do so fled the city. Levi and Elma were left more or less alone in the boarding house, hovering in the shadow of death; Elias Ring was still there, but Catherine, Hope and most of the boarders took to the country. Levi began spending the night in Elma's room. When Hope Sands returned in late October Elma confessed that Levi had asked her to marry him, but he had insisted that they tell no one about the engagement for the time being, and she begged Hope not to tell Catherine. Hope waited almost two weeks before telling Catherine. Levi still thought that no one knew.

Aaron Burr had a property development company, the Manhattan Company. The company still exists; it is now called the Chase Manhattan Bank. The Manhattan Company had dug a well in a quasi-rural area about where Broadway and Spring Street intersect today; the closest modern address has been reported as 89 Greene Street. Late in the evening on Sunday, December 22, 1799, Elma Sands left the boarding house, telling Catherine that she and Levi were going away to be married. The next day Levi was still around. Elma was never seen alive again. She had borrowed a muff from a neighbor. A few days later the muff was found by some boys, floating in the Manhattan Well, and there, on closer examination, lay the body of Elma Sands.

The crime rate in New York City had spiraled during and after the revolution. In 1800 it was reported that one of every 129 residents of the city was the victim of a crime—20 times the crime rate in the rest of New York State. Murder was far from unheard of in the small city, and yet despite this and despite the nation's obsessive mourning for George Washington, who had died a week before, the story of Elma and Levi broke through the clutter to become the first big popular crime story of 19th century America. Her body was displayed in the Ring house, but the crowds that came to view it were so large that they overwhelmed the house, and forced the open coffin to be displayed in the public street.

In the public's mind, Levi Weeks was guilty from the word go. Handbills were posted around town accusing him of the murder, and there was a fear that he would never see a courtroom. Weeks was arrested on January 2, 1800, indicted on January 6, and went to trial on March 31.

Weeks was a laborer. He was, however, the younger brother of a wealthy and influential investor, Ezra Weeks. Ezra may have triggered the tragedy by refusing to give Levi permission to marry Elma. In a time when persons accused of murder often stood trial without an attorney, three lawyers were hired to defend Weeks. One of them, Brockholst Livingston, would be appointed to the United States Supreme Court by Thomas Jefferson, and would spend seventeen years on the high court. The other two were Aaron Burr and Alexander Hamilton.

Burr and Hamilton were drawn into the case by their competing political ambitions. They were, of course, the leaders of the two strong political factions in New York. Apparently as a strategy devised by either Brockholst Livingston or Ezra Weeks, they were given a chance to take center stage in a drama that riveted the city, at a moment when they were involved in a war for political power over the city and state. Once one of them accepted, the other could not afford to refuse. Since most of the newspapers of the day were either Republican newspapers (Burr's) or Federalist newspapers (Hamilton's), this gave Weeks' defense spin control. Newspapers which days earlier had flatly stated that Weeks was guilty now began to emphasize the need to reserve judgment.

Weeks was put on trial at the old City Hall, where Washington had been sworn in as the first President eleven years earlier. Inside the courtroom one could hear the hum and bash of the crowds outside, many screaming for Weeks to be hanged. Three of the most powerful men in New York, including the mayor, formed a tribunal to preside over the case and guide the jury toward justice.

There is a 1989 book about the case, *The Trial of Levi Weeks,* by Estelle Fox Kleiger (Bantam Books). It is a factual, faultless and straightforward book, but in some odd way it fails to express the sweep and passion of the story it contains.

The evidence against Levi Weeks was muddled and inconclusive. Witnesses near the well had heard a woman shouting murder and screaming unseen in the dark. There was the track of a single horse-drawn sleigh in the snow, leaving Greenwich Street and circling the well. Levi had borrowed his brother's horse and sleigh that evening, returning them a half-hour later. There were the signs of a struggle in the snow. The couple had been seen together in the sleigh on the way to their mortal appointment, but in dim light by people who did not know them. Weeks looked agitated upon returning to the boarding house. He gave evasive and inconsistent answers when asked what he knew of Elma's departure. Before the body was found he tried to pressure Hope Sands into signing an affidavit stating that he had paid no special attention to Elma, which everyone knew to be a lie. On being told that the body had been recovered, he asked whether it was found in the Manhattan Well.

The court opened session at 10 AM on March 31, and sat without a break until 1:30 AM the next morning. Most criminal trials in this era lasted no more than a day, but the jurors were starting to nod off, and the judge had no choice but to adjourn until the morning.

One of the other lodgers at the Ring boarding house was a man named Richard Croucher. He was a sour, nervous, unattractive man, and he made a poor witness for the prosecution. The defense's original theory, essentially, was that Elma Sands may have committed suicide by leaping into the well, or may have been assaulted by persons unknown. Now, however, they noticed that Croucher had several features that were useful to the defense. He admitted to having had a small quarrel with Elma a few weeks before her disappearance. He could not account firmly for his whereabouts at the time of the murder, at least within the constraints of the trial, and his own account of his whereabouts placed him in the vicinity of the well near the time of the murder. He had participated in placing handbills around town accusing Levi Weeks of the murder, and had gone out of his way to accuse Weeks to acquaintances.

The defense began to insinuate that it was Croucher who had murdered Elma Sands, at one point holding a candle in front of Croucher's severe unlovely face so that a witness could identify him among the throngs gathered in the back of the courtroom. Hours past midnight on the second day of the trial, the judge issued instructions to the jury, speaking for the tribunal, which virtually amounted to an order to acquit. The jury complied in five minutes. It was said to be the longest criminal trial in the history of New York up to that point—two very long days.

The people of New York were outraged by Levi Weeks' acquittal, an outrage perhaps tempered by the newspapers, which mostly told them to accept the verdict. The case remained famous for 50 years afterward or a little more. It is now referenced only in biographies of Burr and Hamilton, by writers who, at least according to Kleiger, rarely come close to getting the facts right.

Levi Weeks moved to Natchez, Mississippi, became a successful architect, and designed beautiful buildings that still stand today. He died in 1819 at the age of 43. The judge who presided over the case vanished from the face of the earth in 1829, his disappearance a complete mystery.

In truth, there are in modern America not an awful lot of people who escape justice through clever lawyering. There was an era in which this was common, but that era passed away.

However, it is my general view that the cause of justice is not well served by hiding facts from the jury. Levi Weeks escaped justice, in part, because his lawyers were able to get Elma Sands' revelations about her upcoming secret marriage banned from the trial as hearsay. This was wrong; it may have been right by the law, but it was wrong in a larger sense. Without the looming portent of a marriage Levi Weeks was without motive to commit the crime.

In my view, whenever a jury is sheltered from the facts, there is a risk of injustice resulting. Denying Levi Weeks' jury access to the true facts of the case enabled Weeks' extremely clever lawyers to create a kind of shadow play, in which the real issues of the case were minimized and ants were projected as monsters. The O. J. Simpson verdict came about not because O.J.'s jury was stupid, but because O.J.'s jurors had been living for months in a meticulously constructed bubble in which they were denied facts about the case that were available to everybody else in the country. This, in the same way, enabled O.J.'s lawyers to create a kind of shadow play in which they conjured a monster out of the racist history of a detective who should have been off the stage in an hour. The mechanics of it were different in 1994 than in 1800, but the principle is the same: blocking out the sunlight increases the ability of the lawyers to play with the shadows.

And, as in the O. J. Simpson case, the prosecution asserted things that it had no real need to assert, and found itself trying to prove things that never happened. While I have little doubt that Levi Weeks murdered Elma Sands, I am not convinced that the horse and sleigh had anything to do with it. The time frame on the horse and sleigh is very short and not exactly right. The murderous errand does not require a horse or sleigh, since the distance was less than a mile and Elma would willingly have gone there with Levi on foot. A witness who scanned the area after the screams saw a man standing at the well, but no horse or sleigh. If we assume that the horse and sleigh is all a mistake, the prosecution loses almost half of its witnesses—for no real reason, since the murder does not require the participation of the horse.

Burr and Hamilton were joined again in the century's next great crime story, of course, the duel of 1804. Brockholst Livingston, the third lawyer in the case, also killed a man in a duel—before ascending to the Supreme Court. I'm thinking if you did that now, it might be an issue in the confirmation hearings.

In 1836 a New York city prostitute named Helen Jewett was murdered in a brothel owned by John R. Livingston, a cousin of Brockholst Livingston, and an old politician himself. The story of Helen Jewett's murder is discussed at length in the addendum to the paperback edition of this book, which begins on page 445, which I presume is at the back of the book.

In the summer of 1841 Mary Rogers was a 19-year-old girl who worked at John Anderson's cigar store at 321 Broadway in New York City. Mary's mother ran a small boarding house on Nassau Street. Her father had long since departed on some seafaring adventure from which he had not returned. Mary was engaged to a man who lived at the boarding house and worked as a cork cutter.

The population of New York City by 1841 was up to 300,000, five times that of 40 years earlier. The fastest-growing profession was publishing. The penny press—the daily newspaper, available for a penny and thus available to almost anyone—was made possible by an 1836 invention, if one can call stapling together a printing press and a steam engine an invention. There were dozens of newspapers, closer in spirit to blogs than to modern newspapers. Nassau Street was Publishers' Row, the center of the business. Anderson's cigar store, near Nassau Street, was a place where men hung around, especially newspaper men.

About 10 AM on Sunday, July 25, Mary knocked on the door of her fiancé's room. Daniel Payne was getting dressed, but she spoke to him through the door, telling him that she was going to visit her aunt for the day—which was apparently a lie—and that she would return on the Broadway stagecoach at 6:00 that evening, which was probably supposed to be the truth. He said that he would meet her where the stagecoach stopped on Ann Street.

It rained hard that afternoon, however, and Payne, figuring that Mary would stay at her aunt's, did not go to meet the returning stage. Her mother, as well, failed to raise an alarm when Mary did not come home that night, a fact from which some people inferred, probably incorrectly, that Mary didn't always come home at night. In any case no one reported Mary missing until Monday night, when Mr. Payne learned that his intended had never arrived at her aunt's house. Her body was found floating in the Hudson River on Thursday, July 29, near the entrance to Sybil's Cave in Hoboken. She had been sexually assaulted, apparently bound and gagged at the time, and then choked to death and thrown into the water.

Hoboken at this time was a kind of pastoral retreat for New Yorkers and those from other nearby cities, with a river walk and a large park known as the Elysian Fields. Inside the Elysian Fields was a cave, Sybil's Cave, leading to a spring from an underground aquifer. Sybil's Cave was so delicately constructed that many people assumed it to be a natural opening, although in fact it had been dug out to reach the water in 1822. The proprietor of the cave sold unfiltered spring water to the beachgoers for a penny a glass. It was located between Eighth and Ninth streets on what is now Frank Sinatra Drive. It was covered over by industry, finally filled in and obliterated in 1937.

The death of the Beautiful Cigar Girl consumed the interest of the New York public as few stories ever have. Hordes of people flocked to Sybil's Cave, a new crowd every day. Every newspaper wrote about it in every edition. When facts were in short supply speculation filled in nicely. In the wake of her tragedy, some newspapers would present Mary as a modest, respectable young girl, while others would present her as a bit of a tease. In all likelihood neither side knew what they were talking about, but it does seem clear that the cigar store employed her for the same reason that Hooters hires Hooters' girls: she brought in the boys.

The investigation pulled up empty hooks for several days. Some of her clothes were missing, and her parasol. For days no one could be found who had seen Miss Rogers alive after she left her boarding house. Finally a New Jersey stage driver stepped forward with information. He had seen someone who fit Mary's description arrive in New Jersey by ferry, accompanied by a tall, well-dressed man over 30 years of age, dark complexioned. She had accompanied him to Nick Moore's House, a roadhouse on the Jersey shore.

Nick Moore's House was run by Fredericka Loss. Well, yes, said Mrs. Loss, there WAS a young woman like that who stopped here on the 25th of July, accompanied by three men. But Mrs. Loss had seen the body when it was taken from the water—she had been summoned by authorities, as were many others, to see if she could identify the body—and she could not say whether it was the same woman. She had thought at the time that it was not.

Several days later, however, Mrs. Loss changed her story under police questioning. It *was* Mary Rogers who had come to her house, she admitted, accompanied not by three men but by one, the tall, dark stranger. They drank a glass of lemonade and then were on their way, toward the Elysian Fields. Shortly after they left, her house was visited by a group of several ruffians, who also had a drink and left in the same direction, along the same path. Not too much later she had heard a woman scream, but she didn't think it was anything unusual at the time.

The police investigation now centered on identifying the mystery stranger. What had become of him? Mrs. Loss popped back into the story in September. One of her sons, she said, had found Mary's missing clothes and her parasol in the field behind their house. She turned these over to the police, who didn't have a clue what to do with them. (In fact, the word "clue," in its current meaning, had not yet entered the English language.) The primary police strategy appears to have been to focus on Mary's suitors and ex-suitors, and arrest them and charge them one after another, hoping some evidence would turn up. It never did. This continued until the police gave up on it, which appears to have happened in a matter of months, rather than years, as the New York police were not at that time organized to sustain a long-term investigation.

Three things happened later which gave the story legs. On October 8, 1841, Daniel Payne (to whom Mary had been engaged) went over to Sybil's Cave, and committed suicide with a lethal amount of laudanum. He had been living a dissolute life since the tragedy, drinking heavily. He left a suicide note, but it contained no new information about Mary's death.

Second, in November, 1841, Edgar Allan Poe published a story about the case, a fictionalized version of it called "The Mystery of Marie Roget," which moved the case to Paris and proposed a solution. Poe, living in New York City at the time of the Helen Jewett murder, had been fascinated with that story and the interest that it generated. When the Mary Rogers story exploded five years later he was living in Philadelphia, but he published his fictionalization as a way of pushing himself into the market. The story is considered a cornerstone of the detective story genre, and is still widely read today. Poe's imitators and rivals followed by issuing a number of *other* fictionalized versions of the tragedy. The detective story genre, then in its infancy, grew in substantial measure out of these Mary Rogers stories—although we should also point out that, many years before, there had been fictionalized versions of the story of Levi Weeks and Elma Sands. One of Helen Jewett's favorite novels was *Kenilworth*, by Sir Walter Scott—which is a fictionalization of a famous crime that occurred in 1560.

Then, on October 24, 1842, Fredericka Loss was accidentally shot by one of her sons. She lived for two weeks, and gave a deathbed confession, one final effort to clean up her story. Her third and final version of the tragic day was that Miss Rogers had come to Nick Moore's tavern on July 25 in "company with a young physician who undertook to procure for her a premature delivery." Miss Rogers had died during the procedure, and, after a hurried consultation, it was decided that one of Mrs. Loss' sons would take her body out into the river and tie a stone to it, sinking it so that it would never be found.

The scandalous and unsolved death of Miss Rogers became a pivot point of cultural and political debate, making Miss Rogers a central figure in the history of New York in the mid-19th century. The New York police force was re-organized top to bottom in 1845, substantially due to shortcomings which were exposed to public scrutiny during the Rogers investigation.

Moralists and social reformers, preachers and poets and politicians all stood upon the Rogers affair to broadcast their platforms. In the years 1843–1845 (and since, in many quarters), the botched-abortion theory became the most commonly accepted explanation for Mary's death. Abortion was not illegal in New York in 1841. Killing someone in a botched abortion was illegal, but abortion itself was not. It became illegal in 1845, in large part because of the death of Mary Rogers.

The importance of the Mary Rogers' murder in the early history of abortion legislation has turned her story into a kind of obscure feminist battleground where people use phrases like "the misogynist politics of antebellum journalism." The irony is that there is not the slightest reason to believe that Mary Rogers was ever pregnant. Mrs. Loss' story is nonsense. The New Jersey coroner who performed an autopsy on Miss Rogers, Dr. Richard Cook, reported very specifically that a piece of lace was tied around her neck, that there were ligature marks on her wrists, that there were evident marks of manual strangulation, that there were extensive abrasions and contusions on her back where she had been held down and raped, and further, that there was no indication she had ever been pregnant, and that he believed she had been a chaste woman until the mortal assault.

Dr. Cook overstated what he could have known, which caused people to pay no attention to him, even when he was talking about things that he very probably did know. The coroner's statement that the marks from the fingers of the person who choked her to death could be clearly seen around her neck may have seemed far-fetched to 19th century readers, but readers of modern crime books will know that this certainly does happen, and in fact, it almost always happens when a person is choked to death. The story of her being abused post-mortem and thrown into the river to cover up what really happened is physiologically impossible. Strangling a dead person doesn't leave bruises; the dead don't bruise. In order to believe that she died in a botched abortion, you have to totally discount the coroner's examination, not on one point but on many points. Having thrown that aside, one must then give credence to a story told years later, which has few earmarks of the truth, and which was the third account given by Mrs. Loss.

There are at least six competing explanations:

1. That she was murdered by her fiancé, Daniel Payne, who discovered her duplicity,

2. That she was murdered by the dark stranger who was never identified,

3. That she was murdered by some rejected suitor,

4. That she was murdered by some unknown assailant or assailants,

5. That she was murdered by one of the roving gangs of thugs which were then active in New York,

6. That she committed suicide by jumping into the water (this explanation being inexplicably popular among a segment of the contemporary public).

Mr. Payne's behavior is in certain respects peculiar. It is odd that, by his own story, he agreed to meet his fiancée at a time and place, and then failed to notice that she wasn't there. It is odd that he degenerated so completely in the following months. Grief is a powerful corrosive on the soul, but guilt is an even more powerful agent. His melodramatic suicide would be more common for a guilty lover than an innocent one.

Adding these facts together, they fall far short of a credible indictment of Mr. Payne. He was extensively interviewed by police, who failed to find anything to tie him to the crime. There is no reason to believe that he was a man of such ill character as to commit an atrocious crime against a woman he loved. While men do, of course, sometimes murder those with whom they are involved, this crime very little resembles most of those crimes. It just does not seem probable that Mr. Payne was anything but a collateral victim of Mary Rogers' murder.

The police played out most of their energy on the secret boyfriend and rejected suitor theories, leading nowhere. The most widely accepted theory in the weeks after the crime was that she was murdered by a roving gang of thugs. There *were* gangs of thugs in New York at this time, sometimes organized around volunteer firehouses, there was a great deal of fear of them, and this murder was a natural outlet for that fear. Further, Dr. Cook, who performed the first autopsy on her, thought that she had been assaulted by six to eight men, and of course Mrs. Loss included a gang of thugs in one of her stories.

While the theory that she was assaulted by one of these firehouse gangs or some other group of ruffians certainly could be true, there are several problems. It is an almost invariable rule that when more than three people are involved in a crime, one of them is eventually going to talk about it. None of them ever did. Dr. Cook thought that Mary Rogers had been sexually assaulted by six to eight men, but it is not clear how he would know such a thing, after she had been dead and in the water for several days. Dr. Cook also reported, much more believably, that Mary's hands had been bound during the assault. A group of six men assaulting a young woman would not likely tie her hands, because they would not need to.

One of Edgar Allan Poe's early anthologists and biographers appended to the story of Marie Roget a footnote which claimed that later events proved that Poe had correctly figured out the clues and worked out the solution in broad terms. This footnote or a similar note was picked up and copied by later editors, becoming almost a part of the Marie Roget story itself; it was still there when I first read the story in the 1960s. The claim is bogus. First of all, no one knows what happened to Mary Rogers, so it is hard to see how Poe could be said to have anticipated the "real" solution. Second, Poe invented or mixed up details of the case critical to his solution of it, making it all but impossible to translate the fiction back into fact in the way that this footnote implies. And third, Poe later bought into Loss' account of Mary's death, and he published versions of his story in which he changed the solution—which means that Poe himself wasn't convinced by his resolution of the case.

The most convincing solution for the Mary Rogers case was put forward by the criminologist Will Clemens in a November, 1904 article in *Era* magazine. Mr. Clemens returned many years later to the area where the crime had occurred, and found a number of elderly residents who had known Mrs. Loss and her family. Every one of them believed that the murder had been committed in the roadhouse by Mrs. Loss' sons, who had also murdered her companion. In support of this theory, consider the following facts:

1) Mrs. Loss had three sons, who were ages 20, 18 and 16 at the time of the murder.

2) These boys lived very near the scene of the crime, and, by their mother's deathbed confession, were at or very near the scene of the crime on the day in question.

3) By way of Fredericka Loss' deathbed confession, one of the sons acknowledged participating in the disposal of the body—a serious crime in which he had no apparent motive to participate.

4) It was one of these same sons who "found" the rest of Mary's clothes, two months after the murder.

5) No one saw Miss Rogers and her companion alive after they entered Nick Moore's House.

6) Mrs. Loss viewed the body and pretended not to recognize it. She later gave two false statements about the crime before the deathbed confession.

7) The deathbed confession was given to a local magistrate, Gilbert Merritt, who was summoned for the purpose. Mr. Merritt later took it upon himself to swear out an affidavit about the matter. Although he lacked any evidence on which to act against them, Mr. Merritt stated that he firmly believed that the Loss boys had murdered Mary Rogers, that they were "worthless and profligate" young men, and that the roadhouse run by Mrs. Loss was "one of the most depraved and debauched houses in New Jersey."

If we assume that the abortion story is patently false, which I am convinced it is, this raises the question: why did Mrs. Loss tell this story? Mrs. Loss was trying to explain how this young girl went into her tavern alive and came out dead, and, when she had some time to think about it, that was what she came up with. Like her earlier statements about the case, it's simply more disinformation. The third try was highly *successful* disinformation, unfortunately; one wouldn't figure that a thing like that would work, but it did.

Mr. Clemens argued that Mary and the tall, dark man were forced into the roadhouse by the afternoon thunderstorm, and were marooned there for some time by the downpour. They never left the house alive.

There are problems with this explanation, but I am inclined to accept Mr. Clemens' theory. It seems to me that Mrs. Loss and her mischievous sons keep barging into the narrative rather too often, telling a series of stories, none of them true. We have persons of bad character who are known to be at the scene of a crime, later telling stories which are not true and withholding and then coming forward with pertinent information—more than once. That's a damaging combination. It is puzzling that the contemporary authorities failed to rigorously investigate the Loss family, but . . . those things happen. I believe that the Loss boys killed Mary Rogers.

I argued before that popular crime stories are much more important in reshaping our culture than we are generally willing to see. I don't mean to overstate the importance of the Mary Rogers story, and I'm not expert enough in all of these areas to be certain that I am not over-stating it, but . . . if you read a history of metropolitan police departments, I am certain that it will reference the significance of the Mary Rogers case in leading to the re-organization of the New York police department in 1845. If you read the early history of abortion law, I am confident that it will reference the Mary Rogers story. If you study the history of the detective story, I feel sure that you will find that the Mary Rogers stories were critical to that genre's breaking out of its narrow early trench, and becoming a part of the culture. If you know anything about the history of journalism, you certainly know that the newspaper business rode on the backs of crime stories for a hundred years, the Mary Rogers case being one of the sturdiest carriers. But if you read a history of America in the 1840s, it is likely that not a word will be said about Mary Rogers.

III

"Compare Yale or Dartmouth, where the regimen is that of 'moderate Calvinism', with Harvard. The state of morals at the latter is, to say the least, not lower than at other institutions. The observation of the Puritan happens in an editorial on 'murder and other capital crimes'. The occurrences at Yale should shut the mouths of Calvinists as to any opinion like that we have here noticed."
—CHRISTIAN REGISTER, JULY 22, 1848

In December, 1841, Ann McAllister was found in a canal in Boston, the circumstances indicating murder. This is sometimes referred to as Boston's Mary Rogers case. McAllister, apparently also a beautiful young woman, cultivated and well-educated, had come to the city in 1835 from Ellsworth, Maine. She was 16 years old at the time, invited by a friend to come to Boston and learn a trade.

The friend died a year after, however, and Miss McAllister began relying on more tenuous friendships. She learned the trade of attending balls and parties, at which she was apparently quite successful, and became engaged to a Boston artist. However, according to some frustrated novelist working for the *Boston Cultivator* (December 11, 1841), "the brute who is supposed to have caused her death fixed his eye upon her, and determined to accomplish her ruin. He whispered false stories in the ear of her lover, and excited his jealousy by various stratagems, until he finally brought on a quarrel between them, and by pretending to take the part of the woman, won her confidence, and gained access to her heart." She "admitted him to her society," reports the would-be Dickens, by which he means that she began having sex with him, and he supported her financially for a time. After a time he cut her off. She began to drink heavily, and eventually wound up in the water. To the best of my knowledge this very sad case was never resolved by the law—making four in a row for us, as the law also failed to finish off the cases of Elma Sands, Helen Jewett and Mary Rogers.

Within a few years Boston would have its own mega case, perhaps bigger than Mary Rogers, but before I get to that there was a point I wanted to make. In the summer of 2005, in the wake of the Natalee Holloway case and several similar, there was a media *contretemps* provoked by objections from minority groups that the media was focusing disproportionately on what they called "Missing White Girl" cases, and ignoring murders that occurred in the black community, murders and disappearances of men, and murders and disappearances of ordinary, frumpy-looking people. As far as CNN knows, you're not missing unless you're cute.

While this is certainly true, what I wanted to point out is that this is not a function (or malfunction) of the modern media. This is the way it has always been. Popular crime stories are of many different types and descriptions, and it is not easy to say why one case becomes famous and another does not. In my view, it is not possible to predict whether a crime will become famous, based on the elements of the crime. What makes a crime famous is not the crime itself but the way the media reacts to it, which depends to a large extent on the contextual dynamics of the media competition. It's like a fire . . . what makes one fire grow huge and another die out quickly is not that there is a difference between one fire and the other; it's the context in which the fire starts.

However, while it is essentially unpredictable which crime story will explode into a media firestorm, there are certain elements that the biggest crime stories tend to have in common. Number one is an attractive victim. It is inherent in the definition of the word "attractive." It means that others pay attention. The murders of children and pretty women are dry tinder, especially children and women of privilege.

Let me suggest a theory, and if I'm wrong, perhaps you will be tolerant enough not to be angry with me. Popular crimes stories are an expression of our impulse to draw a protective circle around ourselves. The interest that we take in a crime is therefore proportional to the sense it creates that our sanctuary may have been violated. If we suspect that our perimeter has been violated, we are immediately concerned to locate, identify, and rectify the problem.

The murders of men tend not to alarm us because, on a certain level, we perceive men as voluntarily accepting risks by leaving the protective bubble of the community to go on hunter/gatherer missions. If you are interjecting here that this perception is sexist and archaic . . . well, that's right, it is. Much of our social behavior is sexist and archaic. When men are murdered, we tend to "think" . . . I shouldn't say think because it isn't really thought. We tend to internalize that as "Somewhere out in the dangerous world, something happened to him." We don't feel threatened by that, at least on the same level as if the crime occurred within our community.

When a pretty young girl is murdered, we tend to internalize that as "somebody is after our women." Somebody has broken into our camp. Women feel threatened by that, and men challenged. We feel that it is our job to protect the women, and we react viscerally to any sense that we have failed to do this.

When a child is murdered by his or her parents, that does not tend to be a big story, because we don't perceive that as a violation of our circle, but rather, as something that happened within some other circle. That was somebody else's cave. When a child is or may have been murdered by outsiders, that is even more likely to become a huge story than is a missing white girl.

The murders of black people tend not to explode as popular crime stories because we tend, on some level, to perceive them as not belonging to "our" group, our camp. If you want to say that this is racist and archaic . . . well, yes, of course it is. Much of our social behavior is racist and archaic. As time passes and our society's racist history recedes, this will become gradually less true. But it will be many, many years before we tend to perceive a crime against a man the same way we perceive a crime against a woman—and society is more likely to eliminate crimes against children than to learn to react to them the same way we react to crimes against adults.

Celebrated murders . . . *what a horrible phrase.* Celebrated murders tend to have other things in common. They tend to happen on Sundays, and on or very near holidays. Elma Sands and Mary Rogers both disappeared on Sundays; Helen Jewett was murdered early on Sunday morning. Elizabeth Canning disappeared on New Year's Day, Laci Peterson and JonBenet Ramsey right around Christmas (and also Elma Sands). Marilyn Sheppard was murdered on the Fourth of July. The Zodiac referred to two of his crimes as the Christmas murder and the Fourth of July murder. These similarities also are trying to tell us something about the nature of popular crime, but I'd better get back to the narrative.

The stage for the Harvard murder had been set several years earlier by a murder at Yale. In late October, 1843, a Yale tutor, John Dwight, stumbled across a group of underclassmen who were amusing themselves by breaking some windows. The hooligans split up and ran, and Dwight and another man took out after them. Dwight, who was 21 years old and athletic, had the misfortune to catch up with his culprit, a sophomore named Lewis Fassitt. Fassitt pulled a large knife and stabbed the tutor three times. The wounds did not appear to be life-threatening, but Dwight developed a fever, and died a few days later. Fassitt, from a wealthy family, posted a $3,000 bond and went back to his home in Philadelphia, and the law essentially kept the $3,000 and dropped the matter. At that time it was so difficult and so expensive to track down and arrest a man out of state that, even though this was a high-profile murder case, they just didn't bother. Ain't that a kick in the pants?

The press chewed over this murder and the failure to prosecute quite a bit; in fact, I found two newspaper articles from the period which referred to "these murders at Yale." When you are researching a crime book a phrase like "these murders at Yale" will get your attention, but I think there was only the one. My father would do that; if there was a break-in at a store downtown and he wished to generalize from it, he would refer to it as "these break-ins downtown."

While it is impossible to predict what makes a crime story explode, the Yale murder had certainly lit the fuse for the furor that surrounded the Harvard case. The president of Harvard, Josiah Quincy, mentioned the Yale murder more than once to make some point or another, and the good scholars of Yale were on record as suggesting that if he were a gentleman he would shut up about it.

So there was a murder at Harvard, finally, and the press ran wild with it. As he was going about his daily business on Friday, November 23, 1849, Dr. George Parkman disappeared from the streets of Boston and from the face of the earth. Dr. Parkman was a man of extremely regular habits, so when he failed to return home for his two o'clock dinner his wife was concerned. When he failed to return home that evening she was distraught, and, by the following morning, frantic. Dr. Parkman's aging father suggested that his son perhaps had wandered off into the woods and had gotten lost. This was more probable than alien abduction, but not much more. Dr. Parkman was a little bit peculiar, and his father, who had a low tolerance for peculiar, sometimes exaggerated his failings.

Dr. Parkman was well known not only among the rich and celebrated of Boston, amongst whom he had nestled since birth, but also among the common folk. He was easily recognized—odd-looking, and he walked everywhere. He was a tall, thin man who walked bent forward at the waist with quick, energetic strides, his long nose, long chin and prominent Adam's apple poking forward like a trident, wearing the top hat and tails that were his generation's best effort at dignity. He refused to keep a horse and he refused to ride in a carriage anywhere that he could walk. If it was the middle of winter and he needed to go to Cambridge, he would walk to Cambridge and he would walk back.

The city marshal wanted to raise an alarm immediately (Saturday morning) but Dr. Parkman's family asked that he wait until the afternoon trains arrived, in case Parkman had just been called away suddenly and someone had failed to deliver a message. By Sunday afternoon the entire city of Boston was looking high and low for Dr. Parkman, and by Monday evening the nation had been alerted to his disappearance.

Dr. Parkman's manservant, new to his position, had reported a visit Friday morning from a man he did not recognize, arranging a meeting at 1:30 that day. On Sunday afternoon the mystery man stepped forward. It was Dr. John Webster, a friend of Dr. Parkman's since childhood. Webster and Parkman had attended Harvard together, and had hung out together in London as young doctors. Dr. Parkman, the word was, had used his influence to help Webster win appointment to the Harvard Medical School.

Dr. Webster was above suspicion, but over the next four days he engaged in a catalogue of suspicious behaviors that would get the ingénue indicted. His manner in reporting the appointment was cold and indifferent. He locked all the doors of his Harvard laboratory, which had never been his custom, and spent long hours locked inside. He built roaring fires inappropriate to the weather. He purchased strong acids. He went out of his way to spread rumors about the investigation, and about Dr. Parkman being seen alive. He claimed to have paid off a large debt to Dr. Parkman just before Parkman disappeared, although it was fairly clear that he didn't have the money.

That, and there was the straightforward fact that George Parkman was never seen again after he was seen on the steps of the Harvard Medical School, on his way to an appointment with Dr. Webster. The caretaker of the Medical School building was Ephraim Littlefield. Littlefield had an apartment on the ground floor of the large, impressive building, built on land given to Harvard by Dr. Parkman. Littlefield cleaned and maintained the building, carried coal for the furnaces, filled water tanks, shoveled sidewalks, signed for deliveries and cared for horses. He had assisted the police in two searches of Dr. Webster's laboratory and office, and had become increasingly suspicious. There was a vault in Dr. Webster's laboratory, designed for the disposal of waste from animal dissections. It was built of brick, several layers lined with copper, accessible only through a small privy lid in Webster's lab. Dr. Webster had asked Littlefield, apparently before Parkman disappeared, whether it was possible to get a light into the vault to see what was there. Littlefield had said that it was not. The air in the vault was so humid and foul, he had learned from experience, that a lamp or a candle would go out immediately if lowered inside.

Littlefield normally fed the fire in Dr. Webster's furnace, but now found himself locked outside while Webster built raging fires, so hot Littlefield feared that he might burn down the building. On Wednesday, five days after the disappearance, Webster surprised Littlefield with the gift of a large Thanksgiving turkey. This was the last straw for Littlefield. He had known Webster for years, and Webster had never given him anything. Now, standing at the center of an inferno, Webster was trying to buy his silence. Convinced that Webster had murdered Dr. Parkman, he determined to break into the vault and see what was there. Squeezing himself sixty feet through a crawlspace under the building, Littlefield chipped away layers of brick and pried through the copper, where he discovered the dismembered remains of Dr. George Parkman.

Webster was arrested that night, Thanksgiving night, was convicted the following March, and was hanged near the Boston Common on August 30, 1850. It was an argument about money. He owed Parkman a few hundred dollars—nothing to Parkman, but Webster couldn't pay. He had secured the loan with a mineral cabinet, containing specimens he had collected from all over the world. He had tried to sell the collection to Harvard for $10,000, but the president of Harvard wouldn't buy. A few weeks earlier, Dr. Parkman learned by chance that Webster had also used the cabinet as collateral to secure another loan. This was, of course, illegal. Irate, Parkman had demanded payment of the debt. Unable to pay, Webster had killed Dr. Parkman.

The best source for information about the Webster/Parkman case is *Murder at Harvard*, by Helen Thompson (Houghton Mifflin, 1971). There were at least a dozen earlier books on the case. It was stupid for Webster to claim that he had paid off the debt, because everybody knew—certainly the bank knew, and his friends and family knew, and Harvard knew—that he didn't have the money. The Webster family had once been as wealthy as the Parkmans. Dr. Webster's grandfather had gotten rich during the Revolutionary War, selling medicines to the army. Webster had inherited a small fortune and had lived for ten years as if he had inherited a large fortune. The money gone, he had been unable to rein in his spending habits, and was desperately in debt.

It is, in a sense, a tawdry, straightforward crime. Dr. Webster's story, when finally he told it, was that he had simply lost his temper when Parkman confronted him about the money, had struck his old friend with a piece of wood, and was immediately horrified and remorseful. Unable to revive Parkman, he had made a panicked decision to destroy the body.

The Harvard murder became one of the most famous crimes of the 19th century not because it *was* interesting, but because it came to light in a way that made it *seem* interesting. Like a good novel, the story kept unanswered questions in front of the reader for the better part of a year. The public learned first that Dr. Parkman was missing, then that there was a massive search for him but he was still missing, then that Parkman had gone to a meeting with an unidentified man, then that the unidentified contact was Dr. Webster, then that Dr. Webster was suspected in the disappearance, then that the body had been found and Dr. Webster arrested. That was the first week; after that the story went on for almost a year through Webster's trial, conviction and execution, and during most of that time Dr. Webster and his friends insisted that he was innocent.

And, like a good novel, the Harvard murder had a fantastic cast of characters. The story directly involved Oliver Wendell Holmes, probably the most famous doctor in America at that time, remembered also as a poet and as the father of a yet-more-famous jurist. Holmes—who occupied the George Parkman chair in the Harvard Medical School—was in the building at the time of the murder. His office was searched. There were dozens of others peripherally involved in the case who were famous not only at the time, but who remain famous today, running on two centuries since. Henry Cabot Lodge was a neighbor of the Parkmans, as had been the late Charles Bulfinch. The Parkmans and Websters were close to John Adams, and John Quincy Adams was among Parkman's dearest friends. His son, Charles Francis Adams, reported that he would often find the former president and Dr. Parkman sitting asleep in their chairs before the fire, having talked things over until the night overcame them. John James Audubon would stay at Parkman's house when he came to Boston. Henry Wadsworth Longfellow visited Webster several times in prison, as did James Russell Lowell. Ralph Waldo Emerson would pop his head into the story, and George Ticknor, and Bronson Alcott, and Daniel Webster. (A British newspaper once mixed up the story and reported that Daniel Webster had been accused of the crime. In fact, Daniel Webster's connection to the story was that John Webster's friends had asked him to be lead counsel for the defense, a task which he eventually declined.) The judge in the case—who himself was among the most prominent American jurists of the 19th century—was the father-in-law of Herman Melville. Melville and wife traveled to Boston and stayed with the judge during part of the trial, probably bringing with them the manuscript of *Moby-Dick*.

There was a remarkable collection of men in Massachusetts at that time, men (and a few women) who had convinced not only themselves but generations of scholars yet to be born that they were smarter than the rest of us, braver, and purer in spirit. Henry David Thoreau, according to F. B. Sanborn, was one of a group of Harvard undergraduates disciplined by the college for setting off (inside a building) a giant sulphur-based stink bomb they had built with chemicals given them by Dr. Webster. Emily Dickinson was nearby, out in Amherst, Hawthorne in Concord (*The Scarlet Letter* was first published in Boston in 1850, by Ticknor, Reed, and Fields). The Abolitionist movement was center stage in America then, and many of the leading abolitionists lived in Boston—William Lloyd Garrison, Julia Ward Howe, Abby Kelley Foster. It was this that really drove the coverage of the crime: that much of the nation was taking unbridled delight in the fact that a petty and vicious crime had occurred in the very center of this group of high-bred citizens who lived on ether and farted perfume. Perhaps it was Edgar Allan Poe's celestial revenge. Poe, who died the month before Parkman's murder, had been born in Boston, and had published his first poem anonymously under the name "A Bostonian." Rejected by the Boston literary elite, Poe had grown to detest these people (particularly Longfellow) and had tried to commit suicide in Boston in 1848. He would have been—or perhaps was—absolutely delighted by the Webster/Parkman furor.

The murder divided Cambridge from Boston, Cambridge almost unanimously believing Webster to be innocent, and Boston unanimously convinced of his guilt. Oliver Holmes, who was close friends with both Webster and Parkman but closer to Parkman, danced around the issue but was probably an exception. Holmes knew Webster well enough to know his faults. But most of Harvard was determined to see Webster acquitted, denying his guilt even after his conviction—and, in their fervor, married themselves ever closer in the public mind to a sinking scoundrel.

There is a small wren called Parkman's wren. Audubon gave it that name, after George Parkman. Charles Dickens visited Boston in 1868, his first trip to Boston since the 1840s. He was greeted by a party of old friends. "What would you like to do in Boston?" they asked. Dickens asked if he could see the room where Webster murdered Parkman. Oliver Holmes gritted his teeth and conducted the tour, Dickens beaming and almost beside himself with excitement.

A great deal had happened by then, of course; an ocean had moved under the bridge before 1868. America during the Civil War—and during the run-up to the Civil War, and during the cooling-off period after the Civil War—had too much crime to take much of an interest in any of it.

When I was a young student, our professors would periodically implore us to ponder deeply why the crime rate in America was so dramatically worse than the crime rate in most of Europe. Any complex phenomenon can be explained in multiple ways, each as true as the others. But one of the true explanations is this: that murder rates in America shot up so fantastically, in the years between 1840 and 1885, that even though they have been generally going down for most of the last 125 years, they remain high today.

The human race is involved in a long, long battle to eliminate murder from our midst, as we are involved in equally long and torturous struggles to eliminate war, famine, slavery, disease and underarm wetness. We will ultimately succeed in this struggle; murder will eventually be all but entirely eliminated, but our gains are so slow and irregular that progress can only be seen by staring back across the centuries.

Murder rates in America even in 1840 were almost certainly significantly higher than they were in England. Between 1840 and 1885, however, four factors combined to drive the murder rate in America sharply higher, at least relative to Europe. First, firearms became cheap. In 1840 relatively few Americans and few citizens of any other country owned a firearm. Between 1835 and 1870, due to the inventiveness of a group of merchants centered in New

England—Samuel Colt, Horace Smith, Daniel Wesson, Oliver Winchester, Eli Whitney Jr. and Richard Gatling, to name a few—firearms became dramatically cheaper, better built, easier to use, and more deadly. Second, the American Civil War led to a widespread breakdown of law, order and justice, which allowed crime to flourish, as it always does in all countries in all civil wars. Third, there was a circle of legitimized violence that surrounded the Civil War, which coarsened the culture. In Lawrence, Kansas, more people were murdered on one day—August 21, 1863—than during all of the twentieth century. There were numerous other murderous raids on Lawrence—and raids by people from Lawrence on other cities, particularly in western Missouri—dating back to the mid-1850s.

One of the most famous bank robbers of the late 1800s was Cole Younger. By the time he was 21 years old, Younger had personally witnessed violent death dozens of times—first, in a series of violent incidents involving his family, second, in the murderous "raids" or rampages of which I spoke earlier, and third, as a soldier during the Civil War. It is not too surprising that he became a violent criminal. He was capable of violence as he was capable of decency. After twenty years as a criminal he spent fifteen years in prison, was released, lived peaceably another fifteen years, and died a Christian. The Civil War set loose in our society an epidemic of rage and violence, and this epidemic scarred the life of Cole Younger as it did the lives of hundreds of thousands of other people.

And fourth, the very rapid expansion of America through the frontier created an impossible problem for the law enforcement community. If you take 10,000 people and put them in one square mile, you can police them effectively with ten cops. If you take 10,000 people and spread them out over an area the size of Nebraska or Kansas or South Dakota or Arizona, you can't begin to police them with 200 cops.

IV

C. R. R.—*Money is ready. How shall I know your agent?*
—PERSONAL ADVERTISEMENT IN *PHILADELPHIA LEDGER*, JULY 22, 1874

The explosive combination of these four punches—the invention of cheap firearms, the disruption of law and order during the Civil War, the coarsening of the culture surrounding the Civil War, and the rapid expansion of the frontier—sent the American crime rate spiraling so high that a century since has not been enough to flog it back into complete remission. In late 19th century America there are two entirely different sets of crime stories. On the one hand, you have the "Wild West" stories of Billy the Kid, Jesse James, The Wild Bunch, the gunfight at the OK Corral, and a thousand others, many of which remain famous today, but which I will pass over as being essentially outside the tradition of popular crime, which centers on villainy, rather than lawlessness.

On the other hand you have the modern urban crime stories, and so I will resume my narrative with a story which is neither of these, neither fish nor fowl, and which actually was never all *that* famous, apart from a few weeks in 1868. On April 6, 1868, a wooden transport ship named the *Arran* sailed from Greenock, on the west coast of Scotland, near Glasgow. It was a mid-sized ship, with a crew of 22 men and two officers, bound for Quebec. As soon as the ship was clear of the port a young boy crawled out of hiding; he had stowed away on the ship, looking for adventure at sea, or, that failing, sustenance. He had no shoes, no coat and only a flimsy pair of trousers.

This was unexpected but not all that unusual, and the ship continued across the Atlantic—but then a second small boy crawled out of the woodwork, and then another, and another. You couldn't open a cupboard on the

Arran without pulling out an urchin. They weren't all that small and some of them had shoes, but by the time the ship was four days at sea the crew had been joined by the remarkable total of seven uninvited guests. Three of them were boys of 11, one was 12, two were 16, one 22.

The captain of the ship was Robert Watt, aged 28, and the mate was his brother-in-law, James Kerr, aged 31. They were large, bearded men who had never raised families, and had neither the inclination nor the time to provide childcare. They had sufficient provisions to make America even with the extras, however, and so they continued on. Watt appears to have been a decent enough soul, but he wasn't strong enough to stand up to Kerr, and Kerr was a bit of a monster. Seasick, the youngsters vomited up their meat. Kerr responded by ordering that they be given no more meat. He assigned them work to do on the icy deck, barefoot and without coats in the wind and rain of the North Atlantic, and when they snuck below deck to get warm he would have them beaten. They slept in filth and were beaten because they were filthy; they stole food to stave off hunger, and were beaten then as thieves.

For several days in early May the *Arran* dodged ice floes, and, on May 10, found herself lodged firmly in an ice pack off the coast of Newfoundland. The officers climbed off the ship and walked around the ice, surveying their situation. The stowaways took the opportunity to grab some food. When Kerr and Watt returned to the ship they were enraged, and ordered the stowaways off the ship.

Although Kerr had been chiefly in charge of the barbarities up to this point, it was Watt, the Captain, who actually ordered the boys onto the ice. Some of the youths, fearing that to be put off the ship barefoot on an iceberg was near certain death, cried and pleaded to be allowed to remain on board. To this, the Captain was said to have replied that they could as well die on the ice as on board, but they weren't going to get any more of the ship's food. Others were by now so desperate that they were ready to take their chances on the ice. They stood on the ice and begged for a little food to take with them. Some biscuits were thrown overboard, one biscuit apiece.

The officers, when finally they came to trial, claimed that they had never intended for the stowaways to perish. There were houses that could be seen in the distance, at least through a spyglass. They pointed the boys toward these unseen structures, five to ten miles away—or, if they preferred, toward another ship, also stuck in the ice, which was perhaps within a mile or two.

Two witnesses claimed that the Captain had told the boys that they could return to the ship if they were unable to reach safety.

As luck would have it, five of the seven stowaways were able to reach land. Two of the eleven-year-olds perished, one abandoning hope and sitting down to await death, the other falling into the icy water while attempting to jump from one ice floe to another. The others walked for about twelve hours, eventually reaching a place where they could see houses across a stretch of water. They tried to ferry across the water on a chunk of ice, using a stick as a paddle. They were spotted from the land, and a boat was sent to rescue them.

When the *Arran* returned to Greenock in July a mob of men stormed the ship, trapping the captain and mate in their quarters, where they defended themselves with firearms for several hours until rescued by the police. The surviving stowaways, who had spread quickly around Newfoundland in search of work and shelter, were rounded up and brought back to Greenock, crossing the Atlantic the second time in comfort and leisure.

Kerr and Watt stood trial in Edinburgh in November 1868. Kerr pled guilty to assault, and the charge against him of culpable homicide was dropped. He was sentenced to four months in prison, which was the time he had served awaiting trial. Watt was found guilty of culpable homicide, but with a recommendation of mercy based on his previous good record. He was sentenced to eighteen months in prison. The courtroom rocked with boos and hisses. Watt, released from prison in mid-1870, went back to work as the captain of another ship, and continued to command ships into the 20th century. Kerr also went back to work as a first mate, but died suddenly just a few years later.

The story of the Boys on the Ice is an unusual crime story, but it is in a certain sense an archetype: that crime stories very often center on entirely remarkable circumstances. It was an amazing thing, to have all of those stowaways on one ship, and it led to a peculiar dynamic on the ship. The two-sided drama of officers and crew became a three-sided conflict—officers, crew and stowaways—and, whereas a single stowaway might have been adopted by the crew almost as a pet, a whole assembly of them presented an entirely different problem. This led, ultimately, to a fantastic loss of judgment on the part of the officers.

A definition of a news story, of course, is Man Bites Dog. Run-of-the-mill crimes involve, as a rule, people who never had any good judgment to begin with. Crime *Stories*, on the other hand, often involve people whose judgment appears sound enough and whose lives appear to be on a successful track, but who for one reason or another lose their moral compass and do things that are frankly difficult to believe. All murders are tragedies in the common sense of the word, but Crime Stories are often tragedies almost as Aristotle defined tragedy—an action which is serious, complete, and of a certain magnitude, in which a person of substance is reduced to ruin by a flaw in his/her character revealed under the tensions of the stage. Robert Watt would never have imagined himself to be a murderer; he was a ship's captain, for Christ's sake. Harvard could not imagine Dr. Webster as a murderer. Fall River could not imagine Lizzie Borden as a murderess.

The two biggest American crime stories of the post-war years were Jesse James and the kidnapping of Charlie Ross. The press never resolved whether it was Charlie or Charley, by the way. A search of newspapers from the era finds almost equal frequency of each spelling, with a sprinkling of Charly.

This fact is an appropriate place to begin the Ross story, as the story of Charlie Ross is perhaps America's most confusing crime story. I will do my best to get the story straight, but there are multiple published accounts of many different parts of the story, and there is no authoritative after-the-fact source that satisfactorily ties up the loose ends. On July 1, 1874, four-year-old Charles Brewster Ross and his six-year-old brother Walter were playing in the front yard of their house in Germantown, Pennsylvania, in the Philadelphia area. Their father was half-watching them while running his business; their mother was in Atlantic City, recuperating from an illness. The Ross family had once been quite wealthy, and their "house" was a mansion on a hilltop. Sometime in the early afternoon two men pulled up in a buggy, and offered to take the boys to buy some fireworks. The two men had been hanging around for several days, giving the boys candy and toys. They were seen by a number of witnesses taking the boys away.

Within a few miles, young Charles was screaming that he wanted to be taken home. His abductors stopped at a store in Philadelphia, and gave Walter a quarter to go in and pick out some fireworks; they said that they were going to try to calm down Charlie. When Walter came out of the store the carriage was gone.

The boys' father, Christian Ross, searched the neighborhood and then went to the police. He asked the police to keep the search quiet, trying to keep word from reaching his wife in Atlantic City; she was not well. He placed personal ads in local newspapers, asking for information and offering to pay for the safe return of his sons. A friend in Atlantic City spotted one of the ads, however, and Mrs. Ross was alerted to the disappearance.

The older boy, Walter Ross, was located in Philadelphia and returned to the family. Asked to describe his abductors, he described a wiry man with a low forehead, a dark tan and an old broad-brimmed straw hat, and his partner, a man with a misshapen red nose, what he called a "monkey nose." Within days Ross had received a nearly illiterate letter from someone claiming to hold Charly; the letter repeatedly misspelled the word "you" but came within one "n" of correctly spelling "annihilation." A later letter from the same source specified an amount to be paid for Charlie's safe return: $20,000.

The pieces of the story now assembled, the abduction of Charlie Ross captured the attention of the nation. The mayor of Philadelphia was recalled from his vacation in California. Negotiations between Ross' parents and the supposed kidnappers continued, eventually reaching 23 ransom notes and some unknown number of cryptic personal ads posted in response. Children who were supposed to be Charlie Ross kept popping up all over the country. This happened so often that it developed its own protocol, with conditions that must be met before the Ross family would dispatch a relative to see whether the child in question was in fact Charlie.

This was the first high-profile kidnapping for ransom in American history, a new crime as far as most Americans were concerned. Copycat crimes now began to appear—in Brooklyn, in Boston, once more in Philadelphia. Christian Ross was assailed in newspaper editorials for his bad judgment in offering to pay for his son's return. This, said the newspapers, was fueling the spate of kidnappings. (In reality, of course, it was the newspapers themselves that were feeding the problem.) One article in the *Reading Eagle* was so vicious, and so clearly untrue, that the Ross family sued for libel—and won an $1800 judgment against the paper in late September, 1874. When Philadelphia citizens learned that Christian Ross was bankrupt and unable to pay the $20,000, a fund drive was organized to raise the money—and a competing fund was organized to advertise a $20,000 reward for the arrest of the kidnappers, specifying that not a penny was to go to the culprits. Police turned Philadelphia upside down, breaking down doors and searching houses without warrant. The Pinkerton agency circulated literally millions of fliers with Charlie's picture and descriptions of the kidnappers, asking for information. People were arrested all over the country on suspicion of involvement in the crime. Two men and a woman were arrested in Odell, Illinois, with a little boy dressed as a girl. The dramatic story of how a private investigator chased this party across the country and finally got the police to make an arrest in Odell was printed in newspapers across the nation before it could be determined whether the boy was in fact Charlie. He wasn't; one of the men involved was from Philadelphia, and the boy had been secretly taken in a domestic dispute, but he wasn't Charlie. Another young boy dressed as a girl turned out, on doctor's examination, to be a girl after all. The Keffer Sheet Music Company of Boston published a song, "Bring Back Our Darling," words by Dexter Smith, music by W. H. Brockway. The song sold in the hundreds of thousands, and copies of the music still exist.

In the middle of this circus, poor Christian Ross stopped eating, stopped working, and grew so weak that he was reported near death. Despite the efforts of the Ross family and those who tried to help them, no rendezvous with the kidnappers could ever be arranged.

Judge Charles Van Brunt, a member of the New York Supreme Court, had been raised in a grand house in the Bay Ridge area of Long Island, and continued to use this house as a summer residence. After midnight on December 14, 1874, two men broke into the house, not realizing that it had been recently equipped with an invention of which they had probably never heard: a burglar alarm that sounded not there, but at the nearby house of Van Brunt's brother, Holmes. Holmes Van Brunt, his son and a man who worked for them grabbed their pistols and went to the house. They could see lanterns moving about inside. They staked out the house, waiting for the burglars to emerge. It was very cold. After a couple of hours they grew tired of waiting, and decided to force the issue. Charging through the doors, they confronted the burglars. The intruders opened fire, and a gun battle ensued. Within moments one of the burglars was dead, and the other, a career criminal named Joe Douglas, was dying. He asked for whiskey, and said that he had something to say before he died. They had stolen Charlie Ross, he said—he and the other burglar, Bill Mosher. He had helped Mosher to kidnap Charlie Ross.

The gunfire had awakened the neighborhood, and there were multiple witnesses to whatever else was said that night. Some people thought he said that only Mosher knew what had happened to the boy. Others thought he said that Mosher's wife knew where he was, and he would be returned now, and others, that he had said that the boy was dead. Douglas didn't live long enough to straighten this out, and he was less than cogent at the time of his confession.

There was a New York City Police Inspector, Washington Walling, who was something of a publicity hound ... somebody should write a book about him. He shows up in dozens of crime stories. A beautiful blonde woman found in a trunk; Inspector Walling is on the case. Anyway, one version of Douglas' deathbed confession reported that he said Inspector Walling knew all about it. Apparently, Walling had suspected for months that Mosher and Douglas had committed the crime, and he and his men had been chasing them and harassing their relatives all along, trying to find them; this, at least, is the story Walling fed to the press in mid-December.

There is no doubt that Mosher and Douglas did in fact commit the crime. They matched the description of the criminals given by Walter Ross and others. Mosher had a red, misshapen nose—the "monkey nose" that Walter had described. Shown pictures of the culprits, Walter confirmed that those were the men who had abducted him. An uncle and various other people in Germantown remembered that the pair had been hanging around in the days before the kidnapping.

Mosher's wife now went on the lam, and the next task of the investigation was to find her. Finally located, she could tell officers nothing about the fate of Charlie Ross. Mosher's brother-in-law and criminal associate, William Westervelt, was arrested and put on trial on a charge of assisting in the kidnapping. He was convicted of unrelated crimes but there was no evidence that he had had anything to do with Charlie Ross.

Christian Ross recovered, wrote a book about the experience, and searched for Charlie until he died in 1897. In February, 1878, he traveled to Baltimore to see a boy who was reported to look like Charlie. He told the *New York Times* that this was the 573rd boy that he had been called to see or had been written about. "My hundreds of failures to identify each waif as my own," he said, "has taught me to entertain no sanguine hope. I suppose I shall continue going to see boys till I die, but I don't expect to find Charlie in any of them." Charlie's mother also recovered from whatever was ailing her, lived until 1912, and she also hoped for Charlie's return and searched for him as long as she lived. The spate of copycat crimes ceased after the deaths of Mosher and Douglas. There wasn't another high-profile kidnapping for ransom in America during the rest of the 19th century (although there were some minor, local kidnapping stories in the 1890s). But for decades later, people would step out of the shadows claiming to be the little lost boy. None of them ever was.

In all likelihood, Charles Brewster Ross was dead before nightfall on July 1, 1874. Later experience has shown that this is what most commonly happens in cases of this type. His abductors do not appear to have made any plans or provisions for his care. Mosher's partner in crime, Joe Douglas, claimed or may have claimed that he did not know what had happened to the boy after the kidnapping. Although Ross' father repeatedly offered to pay for the return of his son, and although money was raised for this purpose, the kidnappers never came through on an offer to return the boy. It is unclear whether the parents were in fact corresponding with the actual kidnappers, or whether the letters were sent by a con man trying to intervene in the crime.

"The details of the abduction of Charlie Ross, and of the subsequent discovery of his kidnappers," wrote the *Chicago Tribune* on December 19, 1874, "excel in romantic interest any story of crime yet conceived by romancer or playwright. The disappearance of the child, the alternations of hope and despair in the hearts of the afflicted parents, as news came from time to time that their boy had been discovered, the various threads of rumor that the officers unraveled only to find that they led to nothing, the pursuit of the real kidnappers for months by the detectives acting under the orders of Inspector Walling, of New York, and the manner in which they avoided them and finally put them off the scent altogether, and the tragical denouement a few days ago, which discovered them, and at the same time brought a swift and terrible revenge upon them, form a series of chapters in one of the most thrilling episodes of crime ever known in this country."

The New York City police were in a very different place in 1874 than they had been 33 years earlier, at the time of the Mary Rogers case. In 1841 the New York police went to crime scenes, responded to emergencies, kept order, sorted out disputes, arrested people, conducted investigations at the direction of the coroner or the prosecutors, and beat the truth out of people they suspected of wrongdoing. They weren't organized to conduct an investigation into a mysterious death or disappearance. In 1841 the concept of a detective barely existed. To the best of my knowledge, the word "detective" never appeared in a New York newspaper until the late 1840s.

By 1874 New York City had squads of detectives, including one which spent a lot of time investigating a crime that had happened in Philadelphia. But even in 1874 there was no police training of any kind for at least 99% of the nation's police. You learned to be a policeman by being a policeman. In order to get Inspector Walling to investigate the abduction, Christian Ross had agreed to pay the expenses of the investigation, a common practice at the time. Further, and more shockingly, it was common, in this era, to hire ex-convicts as police officers. I'm not sure about New York, but throughout the West and in Philadelphia, certainly, there was no prohibition against hiring people with criminal records to work in law enforcement, nor was there any general feeling that this was improper. The police needed to be tough guys; you hired tough guys. If they had done things wrong in the past . . . well, I'd rather have them working for us than working against us.

This policy was, in a narrow sense, enlightened. Modern society causes problems for itself by making it too hard for a young person who makes mistakes to get back into the pathways of success. Even in 19th century America, it was SOP to roust the ex-cons when a crime had been committed, to harass them, to make them the first suspects when you didn't know who had done something. But if a man got out of jail, got a job, stayed clean a few years . . . well, you didn't hold the past against him.

I would argue that in a certain sense, that's an appropriate policy, although obviously not for the police. Throughout the West, there were many cases in which people who had criminal records got hired as police officers, and continued their criminal careers under the protection of the badge. In the 1880s, when the frontier west ended, there was a kind of a sea change, and it was realized then that this was improper.

Jesse James was murdered in St. Joseph, Missouri, on April 3, 1882. Like Charlie Ross, people stepped forward for years afterward claiming to be Jesse James. The last and best-known of the Jesse James imposters, J. Frank Dalton, died in 1951, still claiming that he was Jesse.

The judicial system treated the Wild West bandits with an unusual degree of understanding. Those who surrendered and survived—Frank James, Cole Younger, Emmett Dalton—served a few years in prison and then went on with their lives; people would not have run around claiming to be Jesse James if this was not true. The West was closing up. The cattle drives ended in the early 1880s. Reconstruction ended in the South. Automobiles and movies and telephones and record players and electric lights and unions washed the continent. The world in which these men had murdered and robbed and plundered no longer existed, and no one felt much need to punish them here and now for the crimes they had committed long ago and not merely far away, but in a place that wasn't anywhere anymore.

V

If there's a strange coincidence, you let it pass. If there are two, you can still let it go. When it gets to three, well, in the end you have to say that it's no longer a coincidence.

—ARTURO MINOLITI, QUOTED IN *THE MONSTER OF FLORENCE*

On the morning of August 3, 1892, Abby Borden visited her doctor, who was also her neighbor, and complained that she thought she might have been poisoned. She was ill—so was her husband, for that matter, and the maid wasn't feeling too hot, either. Somebody was trying to poison them. The doctor assured her that it was nothing serious, that nobody was trying to poison her, and she should go home and sleep it off.

Later that morning, Lizzie Borden visited a local drug store, and tried to buy some poison. Lizzie was Abby Borden's stepdaughter, and none too fond of the old woman. She had a sealskin cape, she told the druggist, and the insects were getting into it. She wanted to buy some prussic acid to treat the cape. The clerk refused to sell her the prussic acid without a prescription.

On the following morning, Andrew and Abby Borden were murdered inside their home in Fall River, Massachusetts. To this point, I have avoided using the word "blood" in this book; also the words "angst," "cuspidor," "turquoise," "disgusting," "arachnid" and "rectal thermometer," but you get my point. We can't get past the Borden murders without blood; there was blood everywhere. It was a gruesome murder, each of the elder Bordens being struck in the head a dozen or more times with an axe or a hatchet of some kind. Lizzie discovered the body of her father a little after 11 o'clock in the morning. He was in a downstairs sitting room, probably dozing off at the time he was murdered. Lizzie yelled for the maid, Bridget Sullivan, told her that her father had been murdered, and sent her across the street to summon the doctor. The doctor was away, but she (Bridget) told the doctor's wife what had happened, while Lizzie, waiting anxiously outside, alerted another neighbor. The neighbor and the maid discovered the body of Abby Borden in a room at the top of the stairs. By 11:30 the police, the doctor and an assortment of neighbors, relatives and passers-by were on the scene. By 11:45 they had been joined by seven more policemen and the medical examiner.

The three essential facts about the Lizzie Borden case are:

1) That it is almost impossible to see how Lizzie could have committed the crime,

2) That it is very, very difficult to understand how anyone else could have committed the crime, and

3) That Lizzie made a number of statements about the case that were self-contradictory and in conflict with the testimony of other persons.

It is difficult to see how Lizzie could have committed the crime because there simply was not time for her to have committed the crime, cleaned herself up, and disposed of the murder weapon. The time frame of the murders—we'll spell it out in detail later—is very, very tight. Andrew Borden must have been attacked between 10:55 and 10:58 AM. Lizzie yelled for the maid just moments after 11 AM. These events are pinned in place by a long list of time-stamped observations.

On the other hand, the alternative explanation seems equally improbable—and Lizzie did make a large number of apparently untrue statements about the crime. How do we figure it out?

The police thought it was obvious that Lizzie had done it. After all, they said, only Lizzie had the motive, the means and the opportunity . . .

As a framework for the logic of convincing evidence, the prosecutorial troika of motive, means and opportunity is as useless a set of concepts as anyone could conceivably come up with.

Let us suppose that it was possible to make a mathematical system to evaluate the evidence against a person accused of a crime. I know, I know, I know; this is totally impossible, it's ridiculous, it's absurd, it can't be done, logic doesn't work that way; I understand all of that, I get it. I'm just saying . . . what if? If I could flap my arms and fly to San Jose, which way would I need to go?

My first thought, in trying to puzzle out this problem, was to try to put a "weight" or "value" on each piece of evidence, and thus to weigh the evidence pointing to innocence against the evidence pointing toward guilt. The presumption of innocence, in that system, would be represented as a kind of dead weight that must always be overcome by the prosecution—a 50-point rock, let us say, that is always added to the defendant's side of the scale.

There are three problems with this concept. One is the unoriginal observation that it is often impossible to prove innocence. Suppose that you were required to prove that you didn't murder Chandra Levy. Where were you when Chandra was murdered? Can you prove it? We all understand that you can't prove a negative, and this premise underlies the judicial system.

A more practical problem with that framework for "scoring" the balance of the evidence in a criminal case is that it is in many cases impossible to say where a piece of evidence fits on the scales. There are, in almost every criminal trial, numerous pieces of evidence that are claimed by both sides. How do you deal with these? Split them? Toss them out?

It isn't the evidence *itself* that forms an argument against the accused; it is the story told by the evidence. There is a different story in every case, and this is what makes it impossible to place numerical values on the evidence, or makes it seem impossible. The evidence is a sort of a map. What matters is not how big the pieces of evidence are, but how they are arranged.

The third problem with the "scales of justice" mathematical model is that it provides no guidance as to what to do with cumulative evidence. A great deal of what is said in criminal trials, by both sides, is true and relevant evidence, but bears an uncertain relationship to proof beyond a reasonable doubt. The easiest example is in the O. J. Simpson case, where Marcia Clark opened the prosecution by proving that Simpson was an abusive husband— and then proved it again, and proved it again, and proved it again. The evidence was not irrelevant. It was certainly relevant to the case whether O.J. was or was not abusive. The evidence may not even have been cumulative in the legal sense of the term, that it proved a *fact* that had already been established. Since there were numerous incidents during which Simpson was abusive, the prosecutor was legally entitled to introduce evidence of several of these if she chose to do so. It was cumulative in a slightly different sense: that it proved a point that was already on the scoreboard.

In a "scales of justice" point count system, each incident in which Simpson was abusive might be seen to carry a certain weight. The problem is, ten of these incidents don't weigh significantly more than one. As the jury saw it, proving that O.J. was abusive was some small portion of what the prosecution needed to prove—5% maybe, or 10% at most. The rest of it was a waste of time. Clark thought that she could poison the jury's mind toward O.J. by showing what a bad person he was, but it backfired on her. The jury saw instead a prosecutor who was insulting their intelligence by hammering for weeks on a point already proven, and they turned against her because of it.

My second thought was that perhaps we could contain this "redundant weight" effect by breaking down what must be proven into the categories cited 47 times every day on truTV: motive, means and opportunity. Suppose that what must be proven is 33% motive, 33% means, 33% opportunity. O.J.'s abusive history goes to motive, I suppose, so the limit of the value given to that might be 33 points.

But working with the actual evidence in criminal cases, what quickly becomes apparent is that the real evidence bears not the slightest resemblance to the so-often-cited structure of motive, means and opportunity. The problem with the concept of motive, means and opportunity is that hundreds of thousands of people every year have the motive, means and opportunity to commit crimes that they had absolutely nothing to do with. Suppose that you apply this concept of "proof" to some ordinary event. Let us suppose that the prosecution is trying to prove that you purchased a melon last Saturday. Did you have a motive to purchase a melon? Well, yeah . . . I was hungry and I like watermelon, so I guess I had a motive to purchase a watermelon. Did you have the opportunity to purchase a watermelon? Well . . . sure. There's a grocery right next to my office, and they had watermelons on sale for 49 cents a pound. I guess I had the opportunity to purchase one. Did you have the means to purchase a watermelon? Well . . . sure. What's a watermelon cost, five, six dollars? I certainly can't deny that I did have the means to purchase a watermelon.

The only thing is, I didn't purchase no goddamned watermelon. Motive, means and opportunity have nothing to do with real evidence. Real evidence that I purchased a watermelon is like a sales receipt for a watermelon that has my fingerprints on it, a check that I wrote to the grocery store for that amount on that date, and a videotape of me carrying a watermelon out of the store. There's a half-eaten watermelon in the refrigerator and watermelon rinds in the garbage; you got me. Motive, means and opportunity, you've got squat.

The same applies to criminal cases. There is a place where motive, means and opportunity are useful in understanding a crime. MMO is a kind of "directional arrow" which, very early in the case—in the investigative stages, when the case is in the hands of the detectives—can be used to focus the investigation. There is a circle of fifteen people surrounding the victim. Of those people, maybe four had some kind of grudge against him and two others stood to profit from his death, so that's six of the fifteen. Two of those six have solid alibis for the time of the assault, so there's no opportunity there, four left. There's a bullet hole in the victim and one of those four has been seen carrying a weapon which has now disappeared, bingo.

Motive, means and opportunity are useful in telling the investigators where they should *look* for evidence, at the beginning of the case. But if a prosecutor is arguing at the *end* of the investigation that the accused had the motive, means, and opportunity, what she is essentially saying is that she doesn't have a clue what happened.

OK, so what does work?

Let us begin by asking this question: is there any one piece of evidence, in any case, which is entirely sufficient to sustain a conviction?

No, there is not. A confession? People confess to murders that they didn't commit every day of the year, and sometimes they figure out enough facts about the case to convince people that they actually did it. A videotape? They've got fifteen cameras pointed at a running back every Sunday, and at least thirteen of them won't tell you whether he stepped out of bounds or not. What if it's somebody who looks a lot like me? Didn't you ever know two people who looked just alike? If you have a common face, like mine, there are hundreds of people who can easily be mistaken for you.

The most convincing single piece of evidence that we see in real cases is DNA from semen in a rape/murder. But even that evidence, by itself, is not sufficient to convince beyond a reasonable doubt, because it remains possible that the victim had consensual sex shortly before she died with someone other than the person who murdered her.

But certainly, DNA evidence in a rape/murder case is very, very damning evidence. Suppose that it takes 100 points' worth of evidence to convict a person beyond a reasonable doubt. How many points do you give to the DNA evidence?

The answer is fairly apparent: it has to be about 80 points. It has to be in that range. It doesn't take two or three or four facts of that nature to convict somebody; it just takes one, plus a little bit of a shove. Such a fact is not proof by itself, but it is so close to being complete proof that the rest of the proof must almost inevitably follow like the dirt that comes up with a carrot when you pull the carrot.

On the other hand, a great deal of the evidence which is introduced in crime cases is so tangential that it would be impossible to score at even one point. Crime books . . . and this is really what I am interested in; not the trial, but the crime itself and the whole universe of admissible and inadmissible evidence which surrounds it . . . crime books are normally composed almost entirely of "evidence" that is so tangential that it bears no weight whatsoever. A book about Rabbi Neulander points out that he served shrimp at his wedding reception—an odd choice for a prospective Rabbi. It is evidence against him, sort of. It paints a picture of a Rabbi who is less than 100% committed to his belief system, thus it might be more believable that he went bad, as opposed to Rabbi Leibowitz across the hall, who served whitefish.

This is evidence, I suppose, but one hundred facts of this nature would not be sufficient to convince anyone that Rabbi Neulander was a murderer. Books arguing that Sam Sheppard was innocent or that Richard Hauptmann or Julius Rosenberg was innocent will go out of their way to tell stories about the time that Sam or Richard or Julius stopped to help an old lady with a flat tire. They are essentially arguing that "this is not a bad person; this is a good person. This is not the kind of person who would pass nuclear secrets to the Lindbergh baby."

What do we do with such evidence as this? How do we state the relationship of these alleged facts to the guilt or innocence of the accused?

I would suggest that we can approach this problem by working the evidence in a seven-step process.

1) State the fact itself in a way that is unambiguously true.

2) State that which tends to be proven by the fact, as if this was known to be true.

3) Put the statement of fact proven by (2) in a "standard evidence" form (a statement of evidence, as opposed to a statement of fact).

4) Establish the value of the statement of evidence (3) with reference to a standard set of values for such evidence.

5) Make an estimate of the extent to which statement (3) is unproven.

6) Make an estimate of the extent to which the statement (3) is irrelevant.

7) Discount the value (4) by the extent to which the statement is unproven (5) or irrelevant (6).

We begin by making statements about the case that are unambiguously true. The unambiguously true statement is not that Lizzie Borden attempted to buy poison on the morning before the murders, but that *it is alleged* that Lizzie Borden attempted to buy poison on the morning before the murder.

This is certainly a damaging fact, if true, but . . . why is it a damaging fact? We are moving on to (2) here, trying to state that which is proven by the fact. The fact is damaging because it tends to prove *that Lizzie Borden was involved in a previous effort to murder her parents.*

The range of things that are proven by evidence is much narrower than the range of things that are evidence itself. DNA in semen is devastating evidence, because it proves that the accused had sex with the victim near the time of her death. The same thing might be proven in ten thousand other ways. A bartender may report that he saw you leaving the bar with your arm around the victim. This proves the same thing, only less definitively. The victim's downstairs neighbor may report that she heard noises coming from the apartment that sounded like two people having sex, and 20 minutes later she saw someone who looked kind of like you leaving the apartment. Your fingerprints may have been found on a wine glass in the apartment.

If the court has the accused' DNA as a starting point, none of these other facts add much to the case against him. They all serve to establish the same fact that there was a sexual encounter between you and Hermione just before Hermione died. Whereas the universe of relevant facts (1) is incomprehensibly large, the universe of things proven by those facts (2) is much smaller.

We can make that universe yet smaller (3) by placing the statement in the form of a type of evidence that normally appears in (let us say) a murder case. In this case, *Lizzie Borden was involved in a previous effort to murder her parents* becomes *the defendant had been involved in prior acts of violence toward the victim.*

At this point our protocol calls for us to check the potential value of this statement of evidence against a list of standard values of such statements. Unfortunately, since no such list of values exists, we're going to have to wing it. If the defendant has been involved in prior acts of violence toward the victim(s), what is the value of such evidence, on a scale in which 100 points is proof beyond a reasonable doubt?

This statement of evidence would appear in the table of values as one of a set of three, for which I will suggest values:

50 Bill James

1. The defendant had been involved in prior acts of violence toward the victim(s) (35 points).
2. The defendant had made threats against the victim(s) (25 points).
3. The defendant bore malice toward the victim(s) (15 points).

These three, of course, often appear together, and when they appear together—that is, the accused has made threats against the victim and has also been involved in prior acts of violence toward the victim—they can go a long way toward convincing me that the accused is guilty of the crime. If B is found murdered and there is clear, convincing evidence that A had a long history of violence toward B and had threatened to murder B, I am more than 50% convinced that A is good for the crime. Let us say that the potential value of (1) and (2) combined is about 60 points.

But what is it in this case? First, how certain is it that Lizzie was in fact involved in a previous act of violence (attempted poisoning) directed at the victims?

Not at all certain . . . in fact, it seems unlikely that it is true. Abby Borden told her doctor/neighbor that she thought she was being poisoned, it is true, but

1. The doctor dismissed her comments out of hand, and
2. Thorough and professional autopsies were performed on the victims by the leading experts in the field, finding no evidence of poisoning.

A pharmacy clerk did claim that Lizzie had attempted to buy prussic acid on the day before the murders, it is true, but people come forward in cases that excite the public's imagination and say all kinds of things, many of them untrue—in fact, most of them untrue. The clerk did not know Lizzie before the attempted purchase; he stepped forward in the investigation in response to rumors. He appears to be just an excitable gossip who pushed his way into the case. Think about it this way: setting aside the murders, could you convince a jury beyond a reasonable doubt that Lizzie Borden was trying to poison her family? You couldn't come close. We're not within a mile of clear proof that Lizzie Borden was involved in an effort to poison her family.

The 6th stage of the analysis—relevance—does not apply a further discount in this case. We would discount the fact for relevance if, for example, the previous violence was remote in time from the murder, or if it was of a distinctly different nature than the murder. The 60 points for (1) and (2) combined would apply, for example, if an abusive husband had repeatedly told his wife "if you leave me I'm going to kill you." But suppose that the accused and the victim had once had a shoving match. A shoving match is very different from a murder, so that's more like 10 points than 35. If it was a shoving match that occurred two years ago, if there were no incidents between the victim and accused in the intervening two years, it might be 2 points. In this case, we're talking about murder-on-murder (a poisoning plot vs. a hatcheting, true, but murder is murder) and about events that occurred on the day before the murders. It's entirely relevant, if it's true.

So what value do we place on this evidence? We can't "confirm" that Lizzie was trying to poison the family unless the family was actually being poisoned, which, in my opinion, they probably were not. The 35 points would apply in a case where there was a well-documented history of violence by the accused toward the victim—an exceedingly common feature of real murder cases. We don't have anything like that here. We don't have Lizzie beating up her stepmother, pushing her downstairs, threatening to kill her if she doesn't do this or that . . . we don't have it. We don't have Lizzie being aggressively mean to other people. While it is well documented that Lizzie did not particularly care for her stepmother, the events of the first week of August, 1892, arise out of a blue sky in terms of a documented history of violence. Pondering the massive gap between the actual evidence and the evidence necessary to convince a skeptic that Lizzie Borden was attempting to poison her family, I would discount the charge by about 70%, and score these facts at about 10 to 12 points.

The case against Lizzie can be summarized into thirteen unambiguously true statements:

1) Her stepmother complained, 24 hours before the murder, that someone might be trying to poison the family.

2) A drugstore clerk testified that Lizzie attempted to purchase a poison, prussic acid, the day before the murders.

3) Two other persons confirmed that Lizzie was in the drugstore on that day.

4) Lizzie denied that she was in the drugstore that day.

5) Lizzie did not like her stepmother.

6) Lizzie stood to profit by the crime, by inheriting a substantial fortune.

7) Lizzie's emotional affect after the murders was flat, and seemed to some people inappropriate to the situation.

8) Lizzie burned a dress three days after the murders which the prosecution claimed was the dress she had been wearing at the time of the murders.

9) Bridget (the maid) said that she heard Lizzie laugh from the landing, near where Abby had been murdered, as she unlocked the doors for Andrew Borden at about 10:45 AM.

10) Lizzie said that she was in the barn at the time of the murder, in the hayloft.

11) Two police officers said that there was a thick layer of dust on the floor of the hayloft, and it didn't appear that anyone had been there for some time.

12) The house was locked, and no one else is known to have been in the house, other than Lizzie and Bridget and the victims.

13) No murderer was seen coming or going from the house.

There are a lot of other known facts about the case . . . it would take me several thousand words to summarize them briefly. There's a hatchet with a newly broken handle, the head of the hatchet apparently rolled in ashes. There's a relative who was staying in the house, a sister who was out of town, etc. What we're trying to do is to shrink the universe of facts so that we can get our arms around it. None of those things are evidence against Lizzie any more than they are evidence against anyone else, and I'm going to focus here on the facts that relate to Lizzie. Lizzie's alleged lesbianism is about as relevant as the shrimp at Fred Neulander's wedding reception, and is certainly less relevant than the well-documented fact that Lizzie taught Sunday school.

I earlier evaluated the "poisoning" evidence at about 10 to 12 points . . . let's say 12. I think that these thirteen unambiguously true statements can be summarized into six prosecution contentions, or "statements of evidence":

1) That Lizzie was involved in an earlier effort to poison the family.

2) That Lizzie disliked her stepmother, Abby Borden.

3) That Lizzie stood to profit by the crime.

4) That Lizzie's actions after the murder show consciousness of guilt.

5) That many of Lizzie's statements about the case are untrue.

6) That no one except Lizzie had the opportunity to commit the crime.

Let me back off and answer a question to which I have, to this point, just assumed that the answer was apparent. Why the hell are we doing this?

We are doing this because the evidence in crime cases—like Lizzie Borden's—is often very confusing, and it is often extremely difficult to judge whether the evidence against a defendant is or is not sufficient to conclude that he or she is guilty beyond a reasonable doubt. I have read books about people who were convicted on what seemed to me to be very flimsy evidence, because the prosecutor was much better at selling his evidence than the defense lawyer was. I have read books about people who walked free despite what seemed like overwhelming evidence. These things would happen less often if people thought more clearly about evidence. I am trying to propose a structured system to enable us to think more clearly about the evidence in criminal cases, so that, in theory, injustice might be avoided, and justice might be delivered, a little more often.

A trial is rather like a basketball game at which no one keeps score, but at the end of the game the audience is asked to vote on which team has played better. All games are supposed to be on a neutral court. I am trying to propose, because I am too ignorant to understand that this is impossible, a system of keeping score.

One of the dirty little secrets of crime stories is that some people follow them not because they are morbid and obsessed with the salacious details of horrible crimes, but because they are anxious to see justice. Crime stories are about the search for justice. I am trying here to offer my ideas about how this process could work better. It makes my blood boil when I read about some poor sap being convicted of a crime because he had the motive, the means and the opportunity. I think that somebody should point out that this is, when you think about it, a really stupid concept. The world will reject these ideas; lawyers will scoff at them, judges will ignore them, juries will never hear of them and will probably be legally prohibited from giving them any weight if they happen to hear of them. That's OK; I'm going to say what I have to say. I can live with being ignored.

Now, back to the six statements of evidence against Lizzie, having already dealt with the first:

2) Lizzie disliked her stepmother, or *the accused had malice toward the victim.*

This means almost nothing in my view. We all have people we don't like. If one of the people you don't like is murdered, it is a very long step from "George didn't like Fred" to "Fred is dead; George must have killed him." I would give a well-documented dislike of the victim a potential evidentiary weight of 15 points, but

a) That would be in the case of an unusually clear and well-documented hostility, and

b) These 15 points are not to be a redundant accounting of the values given to threats or prior violence.

While it is well documented that Lizzie did not like Abby Borden, she loved and revered her father, Andrew, and is not known to have spoken ill of him. The Borden house was not a happy one—you have four adult women, ages 25 to 65, living in a relatively small house with a sour old miser—but there is tension of some kind in most families. The animosity between Lizzie and Abby was not of a type or intensity that is normally predictive of violence; they just didn't really like each other. That's fairly normal. You can't convict people of murder based on the normal conditions of everyday life. I would score this evidence at approximately 2 points, giving us about 14 points in the case.

3) Lizzie stood to profit by the crime, by inheriting a substantial amount of money, or *the accused stood to profit by the crime.*

Again, this is nothing in my view. Andrew Borden was a wealthy man, but few people are so greedy that they will kill their parents in order to inherit their parents' money. Those who are that greedy usually give off pretty clear signals of unusual avarice. Lizzie was not in need. She did not have gambling debts or huge unpaid debts at the department store. She didn't have a drug habit to support. She was going to inherit the money anyway. There is no record of her talking a lot about money in the days before the crime.

To say that Lizzie Borden "profited" by the crime is to take a narrow view of the facts. The murders made Lizzie Borden's life a living hell. She was ostracized, ridiculed, was imprisoned for the better part of a year, stood trial for murder and was a social pariah for the rest of her life. To assert that the money was a motive for murder, one must assume that she saw the money coming toward her and nothing else. Certainly some people (and most murderers) are so shortsighted that they do not foresee these "negative side-effects" of the murder, but the money provides a plausible motive for many other people as well. Borden may have been slain by someone who felt that Borden had cheated him in a business deal. On the board of several banks, he may have uncovered wrongdoing by someone involved in one of the banks, or in one of his other businesses. He may have been slain by someone who rented a house or an apartment from him. He may have been slain by some other relative with whom he was less than generous. The simple existence of this money does not indicate, to me, that Lizzie Borden committed the murders.

4) Lizzie's actions after the case show consciousness of guilt, or *the actions of the accused, after the crime, reveal a consciousness of guilt.* This consciousness of guilt is supposedly revealed in three ways:

One) Her emotional affect was flat, and seemed to some people inappropriate to the situation.

Two) She burned a dress on the following Sunday.

Three) She made numerous statements about the case which were untrue or were at odds with the testimony of other persons.

As to the untrue statements, we'll deal with them in a separate category. On (one) above, people react to alarming and horrible events in all kinds of different ways. There are so few people who have an experience like "discovering your father's horribly mutilated body in the moments after he has been murdered" that it is difficult to generalize as to how they behave, even assuming that they would have some general and predictable set of behaviors. It would take a great many facts of this nature to convince me that Lizzie committed the crime.

Lizzie was an emotionally "flat" person by nature . . . that's the way she always was. After the crime, people expected to see her distraught, and she was—sometimes. When she reported the murder to a neighbor she was crying and shaking. During the inquest, when she was read a description of the injuries suffered by her father, she wept until she vomited. During her trial, when the prosecutor carried toward her a hatchet and the skull of her father, she fainted dead away. At other times she seemed to some people to be unnaturally composed, but . . . you can't dial your emotions to a certain tone and hold them there for weeks on end just because that's what people are expecting to see. You go up and down, you go into shock, and you come out at some unpredictable point.

Lizzie was given sedatives shortly after the murder, and was heavily sedated with morphine for several days following that. This can cause the appearance of an inappropriate emotional affect. The *only* things that a person can do after a crime that make them guilty of the crime are

1) To reveal knowledge about the crime,

2) To show consciousness of guilt, and

3) To attempt to profit from the crime.

That's it; otherwise the crime is done. People have inappropriate emotional states all the time. People are depressed at parties. People act giddy and get silly during business meetings, get horny during job interviews and act bored during sex. An inappropriate emotional affect is not consciousness of guilt per se.

The burning of the dress was *the* trigger that caused Lizzie to be arrested and brought to trial, absolutely and without question. The moment the judge and grand jury heard about the burning of the dress, they ordered Lizzie bound over for trial.

But logically, this seems to be much ado about nothing. Lizzie's sister (Emma) testified that the dress in question was faded, that it had been spotted with paint when the house was painted some months earlier, and that she—Emma—asked Lizzie to burn the dress after she was unable to find a nail on which to hang a newer dress. The dressmaker who made the dress confirmed that it had been spotted with paint not long after it was made.

Further, the notion that the dress might have had small spots of blood on it because of the murders is fairly preposterous. It is clear that Lizzie Borden had virtually no blood on her in the minutes after the murders. All of the people who saw her at that time, without exception, stated that there were no bloodstains on her dress at that time. If Lizzie had been wearing that dress while she committed the murders, the dress would have been soaked with blood. She could perhaps, conceivably, have had a wrap of some kind *around* the dress, through which some little bit of blood had seeped, but the police had very thoroughly searched the house before the dress was burned, to the extent of tearing apart a woodpile log by log looking for a murder weapon, and had closely examined every garment in the house, looking for bloodstains. They found nothing. The police had extensive opportunity to seize this dress before Lizzie burned it. They did not do so. Lizzie's burning of the dress is not unusual, is not consciousness of guilt, and had nothing to do with the murders.

5) Many of Lizzie's statements about the case are untrue, or *the accused was not truthful in describing the events surrounding the crime.* While this statement of evidence is in a sense redundant of consciousness of guilt, it appears so often in criminal cases that it probably needs to be treated separately.

In my view, this type of evidence carries very little weight, perhaps a maximum of 20 points in some unusual case in which the accused made obvious misstatements clearly designed to avoid justice. The allegation that the accused has made untrue statements to the police or to others about the crime must appear, I would guess, in nearly 100% of murder cases. I have rarely known it to be convincing.

What happens in murder cases—and what happened in spades in this case—is that the defendant is repeatedly asked questions designed to confuse her and designed to elicit inconsistent statements that can be used against her. A series of events happened that were, at the time, quite trivial—Abby Borden went out, or Lizzie thought she went out, the maid was washing some windows, Lizzie was ironing some handkerchiefs, Andrew came home, Lizzie went out to the barn to try to find some sinkers for a fishing trip. These are not the kinds of events that make you check the clock and take mental notes. All of a sudden, Lizzie returned to the house, found the screen door wide open and her father horribly murdered. Dazed, shocked, and heavily sedated, she was then questioned relentlessly, for days on end and without a lawyer, about this series of trivial events, which had occurred on the other side of the most horrific experience of her life. While undergoing this interrogation she was intermittently accused of the crime. It is virtually impossible to avoid making inconsistent and inaccurate statements under those conditions. Specifically:

a. Lizzie said that she had gone out to the barn and to the hayloft of the barn to look for sinkers, and that she found her father murdered upon her return. Two police officers, however, said that there was a thick layer of dust in the hayloft of the barn, and it didn't appear that anyone had been up there in weeks.

However—second however—a young boy testified at Lizzie's trial that, hearing about the murders, he and a friend ran to the house and attempted to see what was going on. Turned away by the police, they had gone out to the barn, and had watched the spectacle from the hayloft of the barn—within an hour of the murder, and before the police had looked into the hayloft. Thus, it appears to be not Lizzie but the police who were in error about this fact.

b. The maid said that she heard Lizzie laugh from the second floor landing as she was unlocking the door to let Andrew Borden into the house about 10:45. However, Lizzie said that she was in the kitchen at that time, later that she was in her bedroom on the second floor, and later (again) that she was in the kitchen, ironing some handkerchiefs.

The noise that the maid heard while unlocking the door was almost certainly some noise made by the murderer, be that Lizzie or someone else. However, if you think about it as evidence against Lizzie . . . Abby Borden was already dead by this time, probably had been dead for an hour. It is extremely difficult to imagine that Lizzie Borden murdered her stepmother at 9:45, was laughing maniacally ten feet from the body at 10:45, hacked her father to death at 10:55 and yet appeared stunned, pale and shaken when calling for help just after 11.

A laugh, particularly coming from a different area of the house at a different elevation, is a relatively indistinct sound, easily mistaken for some other noise. The scratching of a cat, the creaking of a door, the rustling of cloth . . . any of these can, at times, be mistaken for laughter. The noise that the maid heard was a fairly trivial event at that time . . . she heard a sound, thought "what was that?" and concluded that it must have been Lizzie laughing about something. Maybe it was, but . . . it's an odd circumstance to be laughing, even if she's guilty.

c. Lizzie said that on the morning of the murders Abby Borden had received a note asking her to visit someone who was ill. No such note was ever found. Lizzie said that perhaps she had burned it or perhaps Abby had burned it, but no one came forward to say that she had sent such a note, and it seems extremely unlikely that Abby Borden ever left the house on that morning.

Lizzie's answers on this issue are certainly troubling. Looking at it from Lizzie's standpoint, she may have heard someone at the door, which may well have been Abby, admitting the murderer to the house, and she may have noticed shortly afterward that her stepmother did not seem to be about. She may have put two and two together wrong, and figured that Abby had been called away to visit someone. She did tell the maid, before the murders, that Abby had been called away on a sick visit. Questioned about this later in a dazed and confused state, she may have attempted to give an explanation that fit what she could remember, and may have filled in the gap with a nonexistent note.

The judge at Lizzie's trial, in the process of demonstrating profound bias in Lizzie's favor, speculated that perhaps the note was written by the murderer, who took it with him when he left. However, neither of these is a very satisfying explanation, and Lizzie's lack of forthrightness about this issue is troubling for her defense.

d. A neighbor said that she sat before a window facing the Borden house with a clear view of the back door from 10:00 to 10:55, and saw no one come or go from that door. This conflicts with Lizzie's testimony that she went out to the barn about 10:50, and many people assume that it also conflicts with the "intruder" theory, although in reality it doesn't.

However, an independent witness, a passing peddler, confirmed that he saw a woman crossing the yard, heading toward the barn, just before 11:00. It's not really surprising, I think, that a neighbor would fail to take notice of Lizzie leaving her house and heading toward the barn.

Lizzie was accused by the prosecutors of lying or giving inconsistent statements about dozens of other issues—for example, at one point she said that she had been home all day the previous day, and at another time that she had been out, at one point that she had visited her sister in Fairhaven and at another point that she had not, at one point that she had overheard a conversation between her father and uncle and at another point that she had not, at one point that she had eaten a meal with the family and another point that she had not, at one point that a door was locked and at another point that it was not, and one point that she had gone out to the barn at about 10 o'clock and had stayed for a half-hour and at another point that she had gone to the barn just before 11 o'clock and had stayed only a few minutes. These conflicts, in my view, can only be characterized as normal confusion, in many cases centered on immaterial facts. Lizzie is accused of contradicting herself, for example, because at one point she said she went to the barn looking for a flatiron, and at other times looking for fishing sinkers. But Lizzie, like many people at that time, used the term "irons" for fishing sinkers. The accusation that she had changed her story was, in reality, just a misunderstanding based on the use of an unfamiliar expression.

I will give the prosecution 5 points out of the possible 20 here because Lizzie did make a number of statements that appear to be inconsistent with other testimony. It is my opinion that

1. Evidence which can be created in any case is not real evidence, and

2. These types of conflicts can be and are generated by the police and prosecutors in every murder case.

A favorite police and lawyer's trick in these circumstances is to ask the accused to *characterize* something which has no precise description— and then later, in different words, ask them to characterize it again. One day Lizzie might say that relations between her and her stepmother were "cordial," another day that they were "distant." What do you mean, they were "distant"? Didn't you say yesterday that your relationship was cordial? Was it cordial, or was it distant?

The $64,000 question is, was she lying? Do these mistakes reflect consciousness of guilt? Lizzie Borden was questioned for many, many hours, without a lawyer and under the influence of morphine, by police and by highly trained lawyers who were convinced that she had committed the crime. She never confessed to the crime, she never came close to confessing to the crime, and she never found herself trapped in a maze of lies. She made no truly damaging admissions. She answered every question. She said nothing, in my opinion, which could be described as a clear and deliberate falsehood. If she was hiding something, she was damned good at it. The facts, taken as a whole, are much more suggestive of a consciousness of innocence than of a consciousness of guilt.

By this time it must be apparent that the evidence presented against Lizzie Borden, in my opinion, falls far short of what could be described as proof beyond a reasonable doubt. If 100 points are proof beyond a reasonable doubt, the available evidence against Lizzie is about 20. This was also the judgment of the jury, which acquitted Lizzie after a very brief deliberation, and it was the judgment of most of the press that attended the trial. This is the common judgment of most people who write about the case today—that the case presented against Lizzie was obviously inadequate to sustain a conviction. A 1997 mock trial of Lizzie at Stanford, presided over by William Rehnquist and Sandra Day O'Connor, again led to her acquittal.

The much harder question is, was she innocent in fact? Many people know more about this than I do, many people have studied it more than I have, and I would urge you to give more weight to the opinions of the experts than to mine. But if you want my opinion, I think she was innocent.

First, the scenario by which some outsider may have come into the house and committed the crime is difficult. To believe that, you have to believe seven things:

1) That the intruder entered the house unseen,

2) That he murdered Abby Borden in a gruesome and excessively violent manner without making any loud noises and without attracting any attention from the two other women in the house,

3) That Abby Borden then lay dead in the house for an hour without anyone being aware of it,

4) That the murderer remained hidden in the house for that hour without anyone becoming aware of his presence,

5) That he then attacked and murdered Andrew Borden with equal violence, again without anyone being aware that this was happening,

6) That he then left the house unseen and unnoticed through the busy neighborhood when he was virtually a walking bloodstain, and

7) That he avoided the attention of police and avoided being associated with the crime for the rest of his life.

No one element of that package is all that hard to believe, but the package, taken as a whole, is almost inconceivable:

1) *That the intruder entered the house unseen* is not hard to believe, since there are many possible explanations for this. A door may have been left open for a few minutes as Andrew Borden or John Morse departed that morning (Morse was Borden's brother-in-law, who spent the night with the family). He could have entered the house while Bridget was going in and out, washing windows. He could have been admitted to the house by Abby Borden—in my opinion the most likely scenario. He could have broken into the house during the night by jimmying a door or a window. He could have broken into the house that morning through the basement. The murderer entering the house unseen is really not an obstacle.

2) *That he murdered Abby Borden in a gruesome and excessively violent manner without making any loud noises and without attracting any attention from the two other women in the house* is difficult to believe but is possible, since the time frame of Abby's murder cannot be precisely pinned down. She may have been murdered not long after 9:00; she may have been murdered as late as 10:30. The doctors thought that she had been dead an hour or so before Andrew was killed because her blood had coagulated by the time her body was found, but this is a very imprecise way of timing the death. Since Lizzie and Bridget were moving about throughout the house, there may well have been some few minutes when neither of them was in position to hear the assault or to hear the body hit the floor.

3) *That Abby Borden then lay dead in the house for an hour without anyone being aware of it* seems incongruous but is not actually difficult to believe, since a prosecution witness performed tests which showed definitively that it was almost impossible to see Abby's body from anywhere other than inside the guest bedroom.

4) *That the murderer remained hidden in the house for that hour without anyone becoming aware of his presence* is creepy but not otherwise difficult to imagine. Also, this "hour" may have been only 20 minutes.

5) *That he then attacked and murdered Andrew Borden with equal violence, again without anyone being aware that this was happening* is not

easy to envision, but it is possible if Bridget was up in the attic lying down and Lizzie was out in the barn, which is where they testified that they were.

6) *That he then left the house unseen and unnoticed through the busy neighborhood when he was virtually a walking bloodstain* is very difficult to imagine, although I suppose that it could happen if he had on dark clothes and was well known in the neighborhood, or if it simply happened that none of the people who might have seen him chanced to be paying attention at that moment.

7) *That he avoided the attention of police and avoided being associated with the crime for the rest of his life* is surprising.

The neighbor's testimony about being able to see the back door from 10:00 to 10:55, while writing some letters, does not conflict with the intruder theory, since the intruder was most likely in the house before 10:00 and departed just moments before 11:00. The intruder explanation, taken as a whole, is immensely difficult to swallow. But the alternative explanation—that Lizzie committed the murders—seems even more difficult to believe, if not entirely impossible. First, the time frame:

1) Borden had a conversation with a carpenter who was working on a store that Borden owned downtown. That conversation ended about 10:30.

2) Andrew Borden was seen by numerous people downtown, blocks from his house, just as a 10:35 trolley car departed, and it departed on time.

3) Borden then walked home. He was admitted to his house by the maid at about 10:45, according to her testimony.

4) He then went upstairs and did something in his bedroom, probably dropping off some papers from his morning rounds, while Bridget continued washing windows. He then spoke to the maid, spoke to Lizzie, went into the parlor and lay down to take a rest.

5) Lizzie yelled for the maid just after 11:00.

6) The maid went to the neighbors to fetch a doctor. The doctor was not there, so the neighbor yelled for her handyman, and sent him to run to the police station, about a quarter of a mile away.

7) The police logged the report of the incident at 11:15.

8) By 11:30, many people were in the house.

Lizzie was entirely clean at that time, *and there was no murder weapon in the house.* This seems impossible to explain if Lizzie had committed the murders. The time frame of Andrew Borden's murder absolutely will not expand.

No matter how you look at it, Lizzie Borden has no more than ten minutes to commit the second murder, clean herself up and dispose of the murder weapon. It's impossible. Some people have suggested that she committed the murders while wrapped in protective sheets, and then burned the sheets, but that seems hardly possible. She could cover her clothes, but her hair, her face, her hands, her feet? There was no blood on her *anywhere*. If she had covered herself with a sheet, blood should have seeped through it. Even if she had wrapped herself up like a mummy, she would have gotten blood on her hands and arms when she pulled it all off and put it in the fire—and there is no time. She didn't have time to put her shoes back on; she didn't have time to wash her hands. She didn't have time to build a fire. If that had happened there would have been blood all around the stove and bloodstains forming a path to the stove, and she didn't have time to clean it up—even assuming that she had the remarkable foresight to plan all this out in advance.

In a 1975 made-for-TV movie starring Elizabeth Montgomery as Lizzie Borden it was suggested that she committed the murders in the nude, then washed herself off quickly and re-dressed before calling down the maid. Again, this seems to be virtually impossible. First, for a Victorian Sunday school teacher, the idea of running around an occupied house naked in the middle of the day is almost more inconceivable than committing a couple of hatchet murders. Second, the only running water in the house was a spigot in the basement. If she had committed the murders in the nude, it is likely that there would have been bloody footprints leading to the basement—and there is no time to have cleaned them up. There isn't enough time for her to have washed herself off and gotten back into her clothes, even if that was all she had to do.

Bridget saw Lizzie after the first murder and before the second (if the first murder was committed much earlier, as contemporary authorities believed). She wasn't covered in blood then. She'd have had to clean herself up twice. She couldn't have gone through the house to the basement and washed herself off in the basement while Bridget was washing windows without Bridget being aware of that. And . . . where's the murder weapon? The police tore the house and the property apart looking for the murder weapon. When they couldn't find a murder weapon, they took a broken-handled hatchet out of the basement, its head covered with ashes or dirt, and suggested that perhaps Lizzie had broken off the handle during the assault, then burned the handle in the kitchen stove. This exploded in the prosecution's face when:

1) One of the policemen confessed that the broken-off handle had actually been in the box with the hatchet when they found the hatchet,

2) The prosecution's expert witness testified that there wasn't a trace of blood on that hatchet, that it would have been extremely difficult to have cleaned all of the blood off the hatchet so that it couldn't be found, that the hatchet was dirty and obviously had not been cleaned at all, and further, that the hatchet was dull and rusted, whereas the murder weapon was razor sharp.

Modern re-tellings of the Borden story will sometimes point out that, in the eyes of a modern criminal profiler, the excessive violence of the murders—hacking the bodies far beyond what was necessary to end their lives—indicates that the person who committed the murder had a passionate hatred for these two people, and thus indicates someone who was involved in a close relationship with them. This is true—but what else would the modern criminal profiler say? A modern criminal profiler, looking at these murders without knowing who was accused of the crime, would say that the attacker was almost certainly male, over 30 years of age, probably had a documented history of violence, probably lived or worked in the neighborhood, probably was well known to the victims, and very likely was a person who was comfortable being covered in blood, such as a butcher, a farmer who did his own butchering (as farmers usually did in the 19th century), or someone who had worked on a whaling vessel.

Leaving the issue of gender entirely out of it, it would be extremely unusual for a person with no history of violence to commit two extraordinarily savage hatchet murders without provocation—or, for that matter, with provocation. Lizzie has no documented history of violence, and these murders were without provocation.

Unusual; I can get by unusual. But the murderous attack probably occurred between 10:55 and 10:58, and Lizzie probably yelled for help about three minutes later. That leaves her essentially three minutes to clean herself up, get her shoes and stockings back on, bundle herself back into her cumbersome Victorian outfit, dispose of the murder weapon and pull herself together. Make it six minutes, make it nine minutes, make it twelve. You can't do it in an hour. Empty a bottle of ketchup all over yourself, over your face, your hair, your shoes, your clothes, and then see how long it takes you to get back to clean and dry—even using the kitchen sink and the shower.

I believe that in a modern investigation, Lizzie Borden would have been almost immediately excluded from suspicion, because a modern investigator would know immediately that the perpetrator would have to be covered with blood spatter. Hitting a person in the head with a hatchet causes blood to squirt everywhere. In a modern investigation this would have been one of the "first facts" of the investigation, and this would have taken the investigation away from Lizzie Borden within a matter of hours.

VI

◆

I left a loose end hanging in Lizzie Borden, which is that I failed to address the question "What is the potential value of the allegation that the defendant stood to profit from the death of the victim?"

It seems to me that this allegation, by itself, is never very persuasive evidence, and I question whether this allegation should ever be valued at more than about 5 points on a 100-point scale. There are some cases in which it seems to be much more. Suppose, for example, that a man buys several life insurance policies on his wife, who then is dispatched into eternity. This, certainly, is fairly persuasive evidence, and I might value that at 35 points, since I would think that three facts of this nature might be sufficient to establish guilt, but two would not.

This, however, is quite different from the Lizzie Borden case, in that the accused there *has taken deliberate steps* to profit from the death of the victim. It might be more than 35 points if we find, for example, that the accused has taken out life insurance policies on the deceased, and the signature of the deceased was a forgery. Then that might be 45 points, since this would be a very bad fact for the accused.

Or suppose . . . this is something that we see often in crime stories . . . suppose that there is a young woman who has a boyfriend who then marries a well-off man in his late fifties. The well-heeled hubby is murdered some months later, and it is then learned that the young widow has been continuing to enjoy Thursday afternoon relations with the old boyfriend, throughout her marriage. Again, the accused has taken deliberate actions to profit from the death, and again there is deceit involved in those actions. Doesn't look good.

Even in the case of Lizzie Borden, I might find her inheritance to be somewhat persuasive, if she was desperate for money, or if she had a clearly demonstrated focus on the money. The Menendez brothers, after all, killed their parents for the money, as have thousands of others. But the Menendez brothers were greedy little bastards who killed their parents and started spending money like it was toilet paper—and even that was nowhere near sufficient grounds to arrest them, until there was other evidence. It seems to me that there might be an array of statements of evidence here, like this:

1) The accused took deliberate actions *involving fraud or deceit* to profit from the death of the victim (0 to 45 points).

2) The accused took deliberate steps to profit from the death of the victim (0 to 35 points).

3) The accused stood to profit from the death of the deceased *and had a demonstrated focus on that potential* (0 to 25 points).

4) The accused stood to profit from the death of the deceased and was in a precarious financial position (0 to 15 points).

5) The accused stood to profit from the death of the deceased (0 to 5 points).

A demonstrated focus on the money means either that the accused had talked about the money he/she stood to inherit in more than a casual way, or that the accused is shown to be an avaricious person or a greedy little bastard. This should not be redundantly charged. In the case of the Harvard murder, for example, Dr. Webster certainly was in a precarious financial position (15 points), but also took fraudulent actions designed to profit from Parkman's death (45 points). But that's 45 points maximum, not 60, because the fraudulent note in that case is certainly not 60% persuasive of Webster's guilt.

I have used the term "profit" to refer to money, but what if the profit is less direct? What if, for example, A and B are rivals for a promotion, and B is murdered? That's an entirely different kettle of fish, and, by the way, to the best of my knowledge there are very few real murders that occur under that scenario; it's something that happens often in fiction, but not so much in real life. But let's move on . . .

There are two outstanding books of recent years about crimes of the same era as the Borden murders. One is *The Devil in the White City* (Erik Larson, 2004, Vintage Books), about the murders by H. H. Holmes in Chicago, which happened in the same time frame as the Borden murders—Holmes murdered some people before, some after. *The Devil in the White City* is about Holmes, but also about the Chicago World's Fair of 1893, and really, more about the fair than the murders. Larson is more comfortable when he is writing about fairs, architects, inventors and inventions than when he is writing about murder, and the story of the Chicago World's Fair is a fantastic story. Some people don't like the book because there's a little bit of that old turn-up-your-nose-at-the-crime-story attitude in Larson's writing. Did you ever know one of those people in college who was a good guy but so responsible that you always wanted to set his shoes on fire? It's 5 o'clock on Saturday afternoon, and he's studying his Latin. Larson is kind of like that. Whereas some other sources blandly assert that Holmes murdered 30 to 70 women—with basically little evidence that he did, but some indications that he might have—Larson goes to the other extreme, the "responsible" extreme: he refuses to speculate *at all* about crimes that Holmes might have committed. Sometimes you want to slap him. He is, however, a terrific researcher and a terrific writer, so I guess I am honor bound to recommend the book.

The truTV Crime Library account of the Lizzie Borden case states, somewhat bizarrely, that the Borden case "was the first nationally prominent murder case in the United States," while the Wikipedia entry on Lizzie Borden at this writing states that the publicity given to the case was "a relatively new phenomenon for the times." Hurray for them; it's hard to be first when you arrive on the scene so late. On the other hand, Larson tells about a drinking establishment created and frequented by Chicago newspapermen of the era, the Whitechapel Club, which celebrated famous murders. They had guns and knives all over the walls that had been used to commit murders, a noose that had actually been used to hang somebody, skeletons and skulls taken from medical schools and a coffin for atmosphere. That gives you a better sense of the true state of journalism in that era. These people wallowed in crime stories like pigs in muck, utterly unashamed. Nancy Grace, by comparison, looks like she's reporting on arms control negotiations. There were probably, I would guess, more famous and more nationally famous murder cases in 19th century America than in 20th century America.

And Holmes was a fascinating criminal, in a way that escapes Larson's best efforts. Compare Holmes with the most famous criminal of them all, Jack the Ripper, who was a contemporary. Holmes built and lived in a sort of handyman's castle, a huge, jerry-built house/hotel on Chicago's south side. Here's the funny part: he didn't really have much money. He conned people into building it for him. He'd hire a contractor to come in, put up some exterior walls, do some foundation work, then he'd find fault with his work, fire him, refuse to pay him what he owed, and hire another guy. The other guy would build some walls, put in some windows . . . Holmes would pay him a little bit, string him along, then fire him. That's a sophisticated criminal, who can con people into building a hotel for him. He had a room or two in there with no doors, no escape . . . a kind of gas chamber with a peephole so he could watch you die. An elevator. That's a *really* sophisticated serial murderer. Jack the Ripper, as much as the British love him, was just some dumb jackass with a knife who ran around slashing hookers. And there are 75 books about him.

The other crime book that I want to recommend is *Kansas Charley*, by Joan Jacobs Brumberg (Penguin, 2003). Charley Miller was a New York City orphan who adopted the sobriquet Kansas Charley, in the manner of a Wild West adventurer, after spending a few relatively pleasant and peaceful weeks on a Kansas farm.

In September 1890 Charley Miller murdered two other young travelers on a train near the border between Nebraska and Wyoming. It proved difficult to deliver justice to Charley Miller, because:

a) nobody was too sure whether the train was in Nebraska or Wyoming at the time of the murders, and

b) Charley Miller was only fifteen years old.

There was a very active movement against the death penalty in the 1890s, and the wisdom of executing a juvenile was a natural flashpoint in that debate. A national debate developed about whether Kansas Charley should be executed, very reminiscent of a similar debate that we have had in America in the last twenty years. Ms. Brumberg's excellent book recounts and illuminates that debate.

In the years after the Lizzie Borden case American crime stories were dominated by a long series of murders of rich and powerful people, sometimes by assassins but more often by relatives, lawyers and other rich people.

On January 30, 1900, William Goebel, due to be sworn in as Governor of Kentucky the next day, was shot five or six times from a window of the state building as he walked across the grounds of the Kentucky State Capitol. It had been widely rumored that an assassination plot was afoot. Kentucky politics were descending into violence, and the state was hovering on the brink of a civil war. Goebel himself had killed a political opponent in a gun battle on the streets just a few years earlier.

The kingpin of the Kentucky legislature, Goebel had "earned" the governorship by a long series of political shenanigans. He had gotten passed a phony election reform bill, the Goebel Election Law, which put his political appointees in charge of Kentucky elections. Finding himself the third-most-popular Democrat at the Democratic state convention in 1899, he had made a deal with the second-most-popular Democrat to unite their votes and drive the most popular candidate out of the race, in part by denying credentials to his voters; Goebel, predictably, controlled the credentials committee. With the leading Democrat forced out of the race, Goebel stabbed the second-most-popular candidate in the back (figuratively) by breaking the agreement and re-entering the contest. This split the Democratic Party and created another three-way contest in November, allowing a Republican, William Taylor, to win the election. Goebel appealed to his political appointees who controlled the election boards. To everybody's surprise they turned him down and affirmed the Republican winner by a two-to-one vote.

Goebel, however, had yet more tricks up his sleeve. Forcing the resignation of the two election commissioners who had voted against him, he claimed that the remaining member of the commission had the right to appoint the other members to re-fill the board. This was patently untrue; the right to appoint members of the board belonged to the governor, who was, by now, Governor Taylor. But with both sides claiming the right to make the appointments the issue went to the Kentucky Supreme Court—which was controlled by Democrats. Goebel won in that venue, and the newly appointed board proclaimed that he had won the election.

Kentucky politics now split into two camps, with two different groups claiming to be the legitimate Kentucky legislature and two men claiming to be governor—one of them Goebel, who survived the shooting for a few days and took the oath of office to be governor. He died on February 3. His death probably prevented civil war in the state, as personal hatred for Goebel was one of the forces driving the state toward madness.

Sixteen people, including the "other" governor, Governor Taylor, were indicted for involvement in Goebel's murder. An agreement was negotiated to abandon all prosecution for the murder in exchange for recognition of the Democratic governor (Goebel's successor), but Taylor refused to sign the agreement and fled the state. One of the others accused was a lawyer and career politician named Caleb Powers, who had been Taylor's Secretary of State. Powers was accused of masterminding the assassination, which was actually carried out by a man named Jim Howard.

Powers was put on trial three times over the next seven years, but the trials were as irregular as the election had been. Powers was tried by judges who had been Goebel's close friends and political soldiers, in front of juries composed entirely of men who had been Goebel's supporters. He was convicted all three times, but the convictions were thrown out by the appeals courts, which were controlled by Republicans who had been political allies of Governor Taylor. Powers and Howard, still asserting their innocence, were pardoned by a Republican governor in 1908. The evidence against them was weak and bewildering, and no one really knows who killed Governor Goebel.

You know the old moral quandary . . . if you were in position to kill Adolf Hitler in 1934, would you have been morally justified to do so? I think almost everyone agrees that you would. The assassination of Goebel may be that very rare case where the murder was morally justified. Goebel was not Hitler (although he was German . . . he was raised in an immigrant family, and spoke only German the first six years of his life). Goebel was not Hitler; he was more like Huey Long. Had he been able to consolidate power, I have no doubt that he would have ruled Kentucky, as Long ruled Louisiana, for the rest of his life. The people of Kentucky did not want him as their ruler, but he didn't care; he was determined to gain power by whatever means could be found. His determination to rule Kentucky, regardless of the will of the people, was driving the state toward civil war. It's easy to pooh-pooh that now, but armed militias were in place on both sides. If the only soldier who died was William Goebel, that may have been the best outcome that we could hope for.

On September 23, 1900, William Marsh Rice was murdered in his apartment in New York City. Born in Massachusetts before 1820, Rice moved west, and made a fortune in Houston before the Civil War. Although he was a slaveholder Rice disapproved of slavery and sided with the North, thus moved back to New Jersey during the war. By 1900 he lived in the Berkshire Apartments, 500 Madison Avenue. He was 84 years old, a widower, and childless except for his stock certificates. He was almost a recluse at the time of his death, living with Charles Jones, who served as his butler, valet, and personal secretary.

Rice's relatives had begun fighting over his money several years before his death, and he had decided to leave his money to a private institute that would bear his name, the William M. Rice Institute. It is today known as Rice University. His wife had other ideas, however; she had left a will dispensing of one-half of the couple's assets, or about $2.5 million, most going to relatives. She died first—unexpectedly—and her will was contested by Mr. Rice, a contest that depended on whether or not Mrs. Rice was a legal resident of Texas at the time of her death. If she was a Texas resident, then she was entitled under Texas law to dispose of one-half of their assets in her will; if not, under New York law, the community property would pass automatically at her death to her surviving spouse.

She hadn't been to Texas in years, but the wife's would-be beneficiaries hired an enterprising attorney, Albert Patrick, to find or invent evidence that Mrs. Rice *intended* to return to Texas, and thus might be considered a Texas resident. This put Patrick at odds with Rice, and a deep enmity developed between the two men. The attorney approached Mr. Jones, Rice's butler and personal secretary, to see whether, at the right price, the butler might be willing to help the litigation come out the right way. Jones was interested, and the two began to work together to pilfer from Rice's fortune.

They conspired for several years as the litigation dragged on, and eventually Patrick spotted a bigger opportunity. Mr. Jones prepared all of Rice's correspondence and could forge his signature passably well, so Patrick had him prepare a new will, naming Patrick as Rice's principal beneficiary, but also setting aside a few hundred thousand to be distributed among Rice's relatives and other interested money-grubbers. The genius of his plan—and this is the kind of thinking that you just don't get unless you have an actual attorney involved in the conspiracy—was that he left the previous will in existence, and made sure that *both* wills would be found at the time of Rice's death. If he had destroyed the legitimate will, then the self-interest of Rice's survivors would have been to prove that the new will was false, since that would mean that Rice had died intestate, and his wealth would be divided among his natural heirs. But by leaving the old will on record and greatly increasing the amount of money set aside for the relatives, Patrick made it in the interest of the relatives to accept the new will as valid. Without asking them, Patrick intended to draw relatives, employees, and even the doorman into his conspiracy.

The original design was not to murder William Rice, but merely to steal his estate when he happened to pass away. But how to explain Rice's decision to leave the bulk of his estate to a man that he hated?

To make this seem plausible, Patrick and Jones created a string of fictitious documents supposedly passing between Patrick and Rice, amicably resolving the previous dispute, and then making Patrick the attorney of record for William Rice. Events began to press upon the conspirators, however, and they took steps to hasten the old man's demise. They got a doctor to prescribe mercury pills for him, and then fed him more than he needed, attempting to weaken his heart.

On September 16, 1900, a fire destroyed the plant of the Merchants and Planters Oil Company of Houston, of which Rice owned 75%. It would cost $250,000 to re-build, and Rice, the old fool, was prepared to wire them the money. Patrick had better plans for that money. Worse yet, a deposition was scheduled in the suit concerning his late wife's estate. If Rice gave his deposition, that would undermine the deception regarding the settlement of the suit. We have to act now, Patrick told Jones. About 7:00 on the evening of Sunday, September 23, 1900, Charles Jones soaked a sponge in chloroform, wrapped it in a towel, and pressed it to the face of the sleeping William Rice.

Doctors hired to say so would later insist that the chloroform did not kill William Rice, that he merely happened to die a natural death at about that time. This sounds pretty stupid to me, but what do I know; I'm not a doctor. Patrick had arranged in advance for a death certificate, signed by a physician, after which Rice's body was to be rushed to a crematorium. They arranged for burial of the ashes on Tuesday morning, and waited until late Monday afternoon to notify the relatives, most of whom lived in Texas, of the death. In the meantime, they worked to drain Rice's bank accounts.

They had overlooked a few details. It took 24 hours to heat the crematorium; they hadn't realized that, and didn't have the time to spare. Their efforts to cash large checks, forged with Rice's signature, drew the attention of bank executives, who called the police. Nobody bought their story. The police arrived in time to order an autopsy. The issue of the relatives supporting the phony will was never reached, since the conspirators were in custody before the will could be filed.

The trial of Albert Patrick became a legal landmark:

> Space forbids any reference to (Patrick's) elaborate and ingenious defense . . .
> Wherever lawyers shall get together, there the Patrick case will be discussed

with its strong points and its weak ones, its technicalities and its tactics, and
the ethics of the liberation of Jones, the actual murderer, now long since vanished into the obscurity from which he came.

—ARTHUR TRAIN, *TRUE STORIES OF CRIME* (SCRIBNER'S, 1908)

Train was the Assistant D.A. who prosecuted the case. Patrick argued, in
short, that in the actual murder there was no evidence against him except the
testimony of Jones, who was allowed to walk in exchange for his testimony
against Patrick. By law, the testimony against his co-conspirators of a person involved in a crime was admissible only if it was corroborated. This was
un-corroborated, therefore inadmissible, therefore there was no case against
him.

Technically, this was probably true. Had Patrick been able to get a jury
of twelve lawyers, he might even have been acquitted. What got him, in the
main, was the paper trail. The string of false documents produced to make
the will seem reasonable had the effect of proving an elaborate conspiracy
between the two men, of which Patrick was the primary beneficiary. Technically, this may have proved only that Patrick committed fraud, not murder,
but in any event he was convicted of murder, and sentenced to die in the electric chair. He fought to save his life with appeals and challenges; in the words
of Arthur Train, this became "the most extraordinary struggle in the legal
history of the State on the part of a convicted murderer." His life was spared
by the Governor of New York in 1906, when his sentence was commuted to
life in prison. In 1912, for reasons that evade my ken but have something
to do either with bribery or doubts about the legality of his conviction, he
was pardoned by the governor, and allowed to leave Sing Sing. He moved
to Oklahoma, where he lived quietly for the rest of his life, at least by the
standards of Oklahoma, where at that time you were considered quiet to the
point of peculiar if you didn't kill somebody once in a while.

There is a book about the case, *The Death of Old Man Rice*, by Martin
Friedland (New York University Press, 1994), but I have not seen the book,
and can't tell you whether it is worth reading. And I don't dislike lawyers, or
Oklahomans; I'm just having a little fun with them.

Colonel Griffith J. Griffith was a wealthy Los Angeles mining and real estate
investor who several years earlier had given the city Griffith Park, and who

would later add the funds for the Griffith Observatory. On September 3, 1903, Col. Griffith, in a drunken rage, forced his wife to kneel in front of him and then shot her in the head. She survived, lost an eye, got a divorce. Col. Griffith got two years in prison and a reputation so sullied that the next time he tried to give the city of Los Angeles a few million dollars they actually turned him down. Griffith Park remains one of the largest municipal parks in America, and is the home of the famous "Hollywood" sign.

On December 30, 1905, the former governor of Idaho, Frank Steunenberg, was killed by a bomb at the gate of his house in Caldwell, Idaho. A man named Harry Orchard was arrested, and confessed to that murder and many others, saying that he had committed the crimes at the instigation of nationally known union leader Big Bill Haywood. This led to a sensational trial, at the end of which Haywood was acquitted, there being no real evidence against him other than the statements of Orchard. Haywood was loud, aggressive, and violent to the point of being half crazy, but had no clear motive to murder Steunenberg, against whom there was reason to believe that Orchard held a grudge. Harry Orchard, whose life was spared in exchange for his testimony, lived quietly in an Idaho prison until 1954.

On January 27, 1906, Chloe Canfield, a beautiful Los Angeles socialite and philanthropist, was shot dead at her front door by Morris Buck, an ex-employee who had been fired years earlier for beating the horses. Mrs. Canfield's husband, who had co-founded the Midway Oil Company, stated that he would spend millions, if necessary, to ensure that Buck was executed. And he was.

On April 6, 1906, a child was born to a woman near death in Cambridge, Massachusetts. Her name was Leone (Krembs) Muenter, and she was near death because her husband was putting arsenic in her tea. The childbirth was attended not by a regular doctor, but by a couple of young women who were called "faith cure" doctors. Most likely Muenter was trying to make it appear that his unfortunate wife had not recovered from childbirth, but the young women called in real doctors, who prescribed a regimen of medicines and treatment. After a few days the doctors decided that the regimen was not being followed properly, blamed the faith cure doctors for this, and withdrew from the case. A couple of days later—April 16—Mrs. Muenter passed away.

Once she was dead the doctors re-entered the case, performed an autopsy, and removed the stomach contents for analysis. On April 17 her husband packed up his dead wife and his two young children and headed for Chicago. On April 18 an analysis of the stomach contents found the arsenic, but by this time police were unable to find Mr. Muenter.

Erich Muenter had been a lecturer at Harvard, lecturing in German, which was his native language. He was a tall, thin, shuffling psychotic with pale gray eyes, a hook nose and an excitable nature. He had earned a degree from the University of Chicago in 1899, and had taught at the University of Kansas before working his way up to Harvard. He fled to Mexico, it was later learned, where he worked as a cook and an accountant. We will leave Mr. Muenter in Mexico, and he will re-enter our story later on.

On June 25, 1906, world-famous architect Stanford White was murdered on the roof of the old Madison Square Garden, which he had designed. White was murdered by Harry Kendall Thaw, a wealthy young man from Pittsburgh who had married White's former lover, Evelyn Nesbit. This is, of course, the most famous crime of the era, and has been depicted in film numerous times, most notably *The Girl in the Red Velvet Swing* (Joan Collins and Ray Milland, 1955) and *Ragtime* (Howard Rollins, Mary Steenburgen and James Cagney, 1981; Norman Mailer and Elizabeth McGovern play Stanford White and Evelyn Nesbit).

Colonel Thomas Hunton Swope of Kansas City had much in common with Colonel Griffith J. Griffith of LA. Like Griffith, he was a Colonel of uncertain derivation and no known military accomplishments. Like Colonel Griffith he left home as a teenager and headed west. Like Colonel Griffith he built a fortune into a huge fortune by purchasing land in the path of the development of a burgeoning city. In 1896 Colonel Swope gave Kansas City 1,350 acres to make Swope Park. It was at the time the second-largest municipal park in the United States, pushed down the list one year later by Colonel Griffith. Unlike Colonel Griffith, who was born in Wales and had little education, Swope was a Yale graduate. He was modest, polite, soft-spoken and a bachelor.

On October 3, 1909, Colonel Swope died in his brother's mansion. Kansas City public schools were closed so that school children would be free to line the route of his funeral procession. Dr. B. Clark Hyde—an unfortunate name for an accused murderer—was married to Swope's niece, and was in attendance at the time of death. Just two days earlier he had been in attendance at the bedside of another of his wife's old uncles, when he, too, had died suddenly. A few weeks later he was attending his wife's brother when the brother also went off to explore the afterlife.

Dr. Hyde was arrested three months later, charged with poisoning all three relatives in an effort to inherit as much of Swope's money as he could get as soon as he could get it. By murdering his wife's relatives he was cutting down on the number of ways that the inheritance would be split, as well as the number of people that he had to put up with at Thanksgiving. Over the next seven years he was put on trial for these offenses three times. He was convicted in the first trial and sentenced to life in prison, but the conviction was thrown out on appeal. The next two trials resulted in hung juries, in one case because they just couldn't agree and in the other case because a juror lost his mind in mid-trial. A fourth trial was scheduled but was eventually abandoned. Hyde's wife inherited $114,000 from the estate. She divorced Dr. Hyde a few years later, charging cruelty and violence. Dr. Hyde became an eye, ear, nose and throat specialist in Lexington, Missouri.

There were other crime stories in this era, of course, but there is no other era in American history in which the most prominent crime stories are so much the same—the murders of rich and powerful people by others who knew them and envied them. To draw parallels between famous crime stories and cultural history is, as a rule, a dubious effort. Crime stories embody the unusual, not the normal, and despite this they seem much the same across borders and across centuries, and thus tell us more about human nature than about the vicissitudes of the culture.

But in this case I think there is something here; there is a reason these stories dominated that era. Crime stories do not generally involve the rich and famous; they generally involve people lifted out of obscurity by the crime. But America between 1890 and 1915 was driving toward revolution, or toward a second civil war. I always find it amazing how little people understand this, and how little they know about it. It seems to me that, since we didn't actually *arrive* at the revolution, people dismiss the whole concept that this could have happened. One might expect historians to disagree about how close we were to revolution or civil war, but it doesn't seem to me that they do; they just dismiss the whole concept and talk instead about the international conflicts leading to World War I and the revolution in Russia. We weren't at the brink of civil war in 1914, as Kentucky was in 1900, but we were headed in that direction.

I came of age in a pre-revolutionary era, the 1960s, as did many of you. I have thought a lot, over the forty years since, about why that revolution ultimately failed. I should say that I am very glad that it did fail; no sane person would want to live through a revolution, except as a last remedy for the most grievous of social ills. But the revolution of my generation failed, in part, because the leaders of the revolutionary movement had based their appeal on pacifism—meaning that they were rooted to the position that violence is not a legitimate means to an end. This made it impossible for them to justify acts of violence directed against the state. They tried to justify violence as a form of resistance, but they failed. This crippled their ability to mobilize their supporters. It's a trivial and personal story, but I remember participating in an anti-war rally early in the summer of '69. A few leaders of the rally, unknown to us, hijacked the rally for some pre-planned acts of petty violence . . . throwing a few rocks, breaking a few windows. Nothing serious. But the next time those guys tried to organize a protest march, I didn't go; most of my friends didn't go. The leaders of The Movement were more revolutionary than they were pacifist, but the followers were more pacifists than we were revolutionaries. The revolution failed for this reason, that when the head of The Movement sent the body a signal that it was time to move, the body didn't accept the signal.

But the revolutionary movement of the teens, culminating in 1914–1915, was very different; those people certainly did justify murder as an instrument of politics, and did so not only in extraordinary circumstances, like William Goebel, but routinely. The fantastic economic growth of the mid-19th century, which attended the opening of the American West, had created a class of super-rich people, while allowing others to languish in fetid poverty. Mine owners made huge fortunes enabling them to make showy displays of wealth, while miners lived like rodents.

I am always puzzled, in reading modern accounts of the shooting of Stanford White, that modern writers refuse to face what White had actually done to offend Thaw. Modern writers will say that there was a "relationship" between White and Nesbit. In reality, Nesbit's mother had left the sixteen-year-old Evelyn in White's care, and White had gotten her drunk and "seduced" her—even this is a euphemism—converting her more or less into a concubine. Maybe he didn't deserve to be shot for it, but he could certainly have stood to be horsewhipped. It seems to me phenomenal that people writing about the case will buzz over this "relationship" as if there was nothing untoward about it.

And I think that, by refusing to make any moral judgment here, even the most modest one, people are missing something obvious about the time: that there was a revolutionary fervor in that era fueled not by racial injustice, as Doctorow presented it in *Ragtime*, but by hatred of the rich, which was fueled in turn by the fact that rich people were behaving like pigs.

It is a terrible thing to justify murder, for one murder makes justice of the next one, lighting a fire that runs no charted course. For those of you in my generation . . . for decades now we have looked back on our youth with some chagrin. We should be proud or at least relieved, I think, that we never crossed that certain line. When the revolution embraced violence, we abandoned The Movement and got our hair cut. In the minds of the true believers, this made us petty and faint of heart. Indeed we were, my friends; indeed we were. And thank God for that.

VII

A metropolitan newspaper never entirely shuts down, and men were still working in the offices of the *Los Angeles Times*, September's last work shift carrying them into October, 1910. Sixteen sticks of dynamite were hidden in a storage corridor, among barrels of ink. Time fuses were set for one AM. The explosion, at 1:17 AM, October 1, could be heard for miles. It ripped open the gas mains, turning the building into a three-story torch, with a hundred men and women trapped inside. Twenty-one people were killed. Most of the rest were seriously injured.

Within minutes, bombs had exploded at two other locations in the Los Angeles area, those being the Llewellyn Iron Works and the Merchants and Manufacturers headquarters. The *Los Angeles Times* was owned by, and spoke for, General Harrison Gray Otis. General Otis had made the *Times* a leading opponent of organized labor, and for this reason it was immediately assumed that the bombing was an act of political terrorism. The *Times* headline of the following day, rushed to the city through the facilities of a hated rival, read BOMBS EXPLODED BY ENEMIES OF INDUSTRIAL FREEDOM/ FEARFUL LOSS OF LIFE; OTHER CRIMES THREATENED. Within hours, labor leader Samuel Gompers in faraway St. Louis had stated that "we had nothing to do with it. I am reliably informed by men who have studied the matter that it was the result of gas mains exploding, and the deaths were entirely due to the fire caused by this mechanical failure."

Long before anything could actually be known about the subject, then, sides were chosen, with labor men claiming that labor had nothing to do with the explosion, and the spokesmen of commerce asserting blandly that the bomb was the work of organized labor.

The powers of Los Angeles gathered, and asked Earl Rogers to take charge of the investigation. Rogers, who was the real-life model for Perry

Mason, was a defender, not a prosecutor. He had defended Colonel Griffith J. Griffith, earning a light sentence for him; he defended dozens of other murderers, almost all of them guilty, and gotten almost all of them off. He had accepted a handsome fee to switch sides and prosecute the hapless Morris Buck, who had shot Chloe Canfield, but he was remorseful about that, and could never forgive himself for helping lead Buck to the gallows. He was an anti-establishment man, a professional thorn in the side, more inclined to favor labor than management. It was against his nature to take charge of a police investigation, but on the other hand, his office was across the street from the *Times*, and he had been on the scene within moments of the blast. He had seen doomed men appear briefly in windows, and then disappear behind the smoke. He had heard the screams of women on fire. He had seen others leap to their deaths. One of the men killed had been a dear friend. He accepted the charge.

The investigation drew on the Los Angeles police, on the funds of General Otis, the resources, including reporters, of the *Los Angeles Times*, the Burns Detective Agency (also brought into the fight by General Otis) and the experienced cadre of private detectives regularly maintained and directed by Earl Rogers in his defense of his accused. Even so, it took months for the investigators to trace the materials of the bomb to their purchase point in San Francisco.

The dynamite had been purchased by James B. McNamara. J. B. McNamara's brother, John J. McNamara, was secretary-treasurer of the International Bridgeworkers and Structural Ironworkers Union. He was a well known labor official, and a member of a clique of radicals which was centered in Indianapolis, Indiana.

Detectives from the Burns agency located J. B. McNamara and a confederate, Ortie McManigal, in Detroit, and placed them under arrest. McNamara was indicted on seventeen counts of murder. McManigal talked, and the arrest of J. J. McNamara followed two weeks later in Indianapolis. Thus, the bombing of the *Times* had been tied directly to the labor movement.

Labor leaders sent representatives to Los Angeles, or came themselves, to talk to the McNamaras. The McNamaras denied any involvement in the bombing. Labor undertook their defense. Red, white and blue buttons proclaiming "The McNamaras Are Innocent" were worn throughout the country. A socialist candidate for mayor of Los Angeles, Job Harriman, put up billboards all over town, pleading "Save the McNamaras from the Capitalistic

Conspiracy." Hundreds of thousands of dollars were raised for their defense. Clarence Darrow came to Los Angeles to take charge of the case. He said it would take at least $350,000, millions in today's money, to put on a proper defense against the powerful forces arrayed against his men.

From the nickels saved for Tuesday's lunch, from dresses not bought, from trousers worn bald, shoes forced through the summer with strips of cardboard, the money came flowing in. And Clarence Darrow knew all along that the McNamaras were as guilty as sin.

If Clarence Darrow actually did all three things his accusers said that he did, it was an astonishing trifecta of disreputable acts. First, he misled his friends in the labor movement about the facts of the case, begging for money under false pretenses. Second, or so The People claimed, he attempted to bribe a juror to save the McNamaras. And third, when the second failed, he sold his clients down the river to save his own skin.

Darrow may have taken the McNamara case believing his clients to be innocent. More likely he didn't. The war between capital and labor, in Darrow's mind, was exactly that—a War. People got killed. Darrow had no problem with that.

In any case, by mid-summer, 1911, Clarence Darrow was well aware that the McNamaras were in fact responsible for the dynamite at the *Times*. "My God," he said to James McNamara. "You left a trail behind you a mile wide."

On arriving in Los Angeles, Darrow had hired several local investigators to help him sort out the facts. Among these was a former deputy sheriff, Bert Franklin. Franklin, an able, aggressive individual, became Darrow's right-hand man.

Los Angeles chose juries from a rotating "wheel" of potential jurors, which allowed the defense to anticipate who might be on their jury. Darrow, rolling in labor money, had directed his staff to learn as much as possible about all of the potential jurors. He put Bert Franklin in charge of this.

One of the members of the jury pool was a man Franklin knew, another former law enforcement officer. In October, 1911, the ex-cop visited the District Attorney's office with a story to tell. Bert Franklin, he claimed, had offered him money to vote "Darrow's way" on the upcoming case. According to Franklin (said the ex-cop), Darrow was aware of and had authorized the payment. Weeks later, another juror also contacted the police, reporting a similar offer. On November 28, 1911, Bert Franklin met his juror on a street corner in downtown Los Angeles (Third and Los Angeles), and handed him $4,000. Franklin was arrested immediately thereafter.

Clarence Darrow was present when the money was passed. Darrow was not arrested on the scene, mostly because the police who had set up the sting were flabbergasted to find Darrow present in the flesh, and didn't know quite what to do with him.

After months of insisting that the McNamaras were innocent and would be acquitted, Darrow did an about-face. Three days after the arrest of Bert Franklin, both McNamaras pled guilty in exchange for leniency. "Leniency," for J. B. McNamara, meant life in prison. His brother got ten years.

Darrow's critics, including the judge who handled the McNamara case, have alleged that Darrow pleaded the McNamaras guilty in the hope that this would make the bribery case against Clarence Darrow disappear. If so, it was a dreadful miscalculation, as well as a betrayal of his clients. The end of the McNamara case did three things to Darrow's. First, it deprived the Los Angeles authorities of an opportunity to try the McNamaras, leaving them frustrated and angry. Second, it allowed them to focus on the bribery issue, without worrying about the McNamaras.

And third, it drove a wedge between Darrow and labor. Darrow had been the lead attorney for the labor movement, by this time, for about 17 years, since representing Eugene Debs in a civil action in 1894. For a decade and a half, labor leaders had been brought up on charges true and false, and for a decade and a half Darrow had defended them. His victory in the trial of Big Bill Haywood had made him a star.

Darrow, however, had told his supporters that the McNamaras were innocent, right up to the day he pled them guilty. For seventeen years Darrow had seen the money gush in, for the defense of Debs, for the defense of Bill Haywood, for the defense of the McNamaras, for the defense of countless others. Now it was Clarence Darrow under indictment, and he assumed that the money would flow in for the defense of Clarence Darrow.

He got nothing. Labor leaders refused to make any effort to raise money on his behalf. It is a debatable point whether those labor leaders were furious with him, whether they were merely cold toward him, or whether they cut him off in miserly self-interest.

For a modern reader, raised on the image of Clarence Darrow as The Great Defender, it requires an effort to understand the depth of Darrow's peril. Darrow was not a hero to all of the American people; he was a hero to half of them. He was a hero to the labor movement; the other side hated him. Even among social progressives, socialists, anarchists, and civil rights activists, there were many who distrusted Darrow, and many who hated him. He was famous for his tactlessness. He would make anti-Semitic remarks to a gathering of Jewish leaders, vaguely racist comments to African Americans, and engage, at professional functions, in vicious lawyer baiting. In any place and at any time, he would find the most unpopular idea, and advocate it brilliantly. This was his genius.

Now, facing the very real prospect of ending his career in San Quentin, Darrow was abandoned and despised by that half of the public that had previously admired him. By the time he was indicted, he had been in Los Angeles for about eight months, and was well aware who the best attorney in town was.

Darrow asked Earl Rogers to defend him.

Rogers agreed.

Lawyers.

To those involved in the matter, Earl Rogers' acceptance of Darrow's case was as much a betrayal as Darrow's abandonment of the McNamaras. Rogers had been set to lead the prosecution of the McNamaras. He would have been the prosecuting attorney. How, the good people of Los Angeles wondered, could he now defend this despicable scumbag who had been the McNamaras' mouthpiece?

Rogers, of course, didn't see it that way. He had agreed to prosecute the bomb makers because they had murdered his friend. That was over now, and Darrow had nothing to do with it. Darrow hadn't killed anybody. Darrow had been caught in a police trap. Rogers didn't like police traps. Besides, a defense attorney does not make a living defending saints. He makes a living defending sinners. Darrow was no worse than the rest of them.

Johnnie Cochran, in the midst of O.J.'s trial, cited the trial of Clarence Darrow to establish some obscure legal point. It was, he said, the "first 'Trial of the Century.'" The two most famous attorneys in America were now partners in the defense of Clarence Darrow. It was an unhappy partnership. Both Rogers and Darrow had complete contempt for the idea of formal education. Apart from this, they had astonishingly little in common. Rogers was trim and neat, obsessive about fashion. Darrow was overweight, soiled and rumpled, affecting the appearance of the common man. Rogers was precise and surgical; Darrow was broad and forceful. Rogers spoke to the jury box as though the juror was a dinner companion; Darrow spoke to the room, to the world, as though the courtroom was a stage. Darrow was depressed and emotional; Rogers was hyperactive and alcoholic. Darrow would collapse in his seat and weep openly at great length. Rogers found this nauseating. Rogers would go on drinking binges, and disappear for days. Darrow thought this was inappropriate conduct for a defense attorney in the middle of a trial.

Darrow wanted to argue that the case against him was a conspiracy manufactured by the enemies of labor. Rogers refused to put on such a defense, arguing that

a) it simply wasn't true, and therefore would be difficult to prove, and

b) whether it was true or not, he could never make a jury believe it.

Rogers wanted to argue that Darrow had to be innocent, because he couldn't possibly be that stupid. If a smart lawyer had intended to bribe a juror, Rogers argued, he

a) would never have allowed a close associate to carry the bag, and

b) would have been damned sure to be hundreds of miles away when the money was passed.

They argued endlessly and loudly over which defense to use. Rogers, who had taken on hundreds of cases knowing full well that his client was guilty, had taken this case in part because Darrow was one of his heroes, and he had believed that Darrow might be innocent. When he realized (or concluded) that Darrow had in fact initiated the bribery scheme, he was unable to look at Darrow without revulsion.

In any case, working together, sort of, the two men got Darrow off, sort of. Darrow was acquitted of attempting to bribe the ex-cop/potential juror, who had received the $4,000. However, there was another bribery charge pending, from the other potential juror. The case was much weaker, there having been no exchange of money, but it gave the Los Angeles prosecutors a chance to make a second run at Darrow, and they decided to take it.

Rogers bowed out, citing health concerns, and Darrow decided to act as his own attorney in the second case. This decision was very nearly fatal to his career. Darrow used the "frame-up" defense that had been vetoed by Rogers in the other case, and shouted his innocence to the world. Eight jurors voted to send him to prison. Fortunately for Darrow, the other four held out, and he escaped with a hung jury.

Darrow made an agreement with the state. They would agree to drop the prosecution, and he would agree never again to practice law in California. After two long and agonizing years in LA, Darrow was free to return to Chicago.

Was Darrow guilty? Biographer Kevin Tierney's synopsis seems reasonable. "It is as impossible to be sure what happened in retrospect as it was impossible at the time," wrote Tierney in *Darrow,* "but nearly everyone acquainted with the circumstances, or who was present at the trials, thought that Darrow was guilty."

The centerpiece of the evidence against Darrow was the testimony of the bribed juror and the testimony of Bert Franklin, the former deputy sheriff who said that Darrow hired him to make the bribe. But even without the cooperation of those two men, the state could still prove:

a) that the crime was committed,

b) that it was committed by Darrow's employee,

c) that it was committed on behalf of Darrow's client,

d) that it was committed in Darrow's presence, and

e) that it arose from a pattern of activity commenced and directed by Clarence Darrow, that being the extensive "research" on the jury pool.

Arguing against Darrow's guilt is, in essence, only one thing: the sheer inconceivability of Clarence Darrow resorting to jury bribery.

This wall of doubt is perhaps less steep than one might imagine. The legal practices of 1911 were far more aggressive than those of today. Attorneys in important cases would often try to influence potential witnesses, and many times the arrangements that were made with those witnesses were not clearly distinguishable from bribery. Coercion and intimidation of witnesses, up to and including what would now be considered kidnapping, was not terribly uncommon.

Darrow came from a place—Chicago—where these practices were more advanced than they were in Los Angeles. The courts of Chicago at that time were as corrupt as any courts this country has ever had. Another of the most prominent attorneys in Chicago was found guilty of jury tampering in a trial that ran concurrently with Darrow's. In 1903 Darrow quarreled bitterly with his law partner, the poet Edgar Lee Masters, because Darrow wanted to admit to the firm as a full partner another lawyer who had recently been convicted of bribing a jury. Masters wasn't opposed to hiring the other attorney; he just thought it looked bad to start him out as a full partner, a few months after the scandal. Darrow didn't see that as a problem.

Darrow was engaged in a Great Cause, the kind of cause in which "right" is defined as "whatever is done by those on the side of good," and "wrong" is defined as "that which is done by the forces of evil." Victor Yarros, a junior associate of Darrow's, reported that Darrow said to him, years later, "Do not the rich and powerful bribe juries, intimidate and coerce judges as well as juries? Do they shrink from any weapon? Why this theatrical indignation against alleged or actual jury tampering in behalf of 'lawless' strikers or other unfortunate victims of ruthless Capitalism?" Clarence, your soup is getting cold.

The LA *Times* bombing and the McNamara trial were to the radicals of that era what the 1968 Democratic Convention and the trial of the Chicago Seven were to the sixties radicals. In 1968 a group of radical leaders conspired to foment made-for-TV violence at the Democratic Convention. Put on trial for this a year later, the radicals made such complete asses of themselves that the people who had supported them in the past said "Oh, my God," and went off to do other things. The radical movement floundered and drowned, the counterculture disappeared, but the energy that had been bound up in The Movement carried on in other forms, leading to the environmental movement, the gay pride movement, a resurgence of the women's movement, shock troops for consumer-rights activists, and many other causes.

Something vaguely similar happened here. The McNamara trial caused the common people who had supported the radical labor leaders to say "Oh, my God." Before the *Times* bombing the labor movement and the radical left worked so closely together as to be indistinguishable. From the middle of the McNamara prosecution onward they were drifting apart. The labor unions fell under the control of professional labor leaders. Some of the radicals, like John Reed and Big Bill Haywood, wound up in the Soviet Union, trying to prove that socialism would work. Many more of them became reformers— prison reformers and school reformers and the first generation of consumer reformers, putting an end to the sale of rotten meat by unscrupulous butchers and comic-book cancer cures by self-proclaimed doctors.

Clarence Darrow rebounded from professional catastrophe, and even made it work to his advantage. He was famous anyway; his own trial made him more famous. Cut off from organized labor, he was free to pick and choose his cases. Since he was no longer partisan, writers from across the political spectrum were free to admire his passion and oratory without endorsing labor (or worse yet, labor violence). In his mid-fifties at the time of the trial, he would practice law another twenty-five years, becoming a world-renowned figure in the 1920s as a consequence of two cases: the Scopes trial, and his defense of the Thrill Killers, Loeb and Leopold. He defended school-teachers, crooked judges and vicious psychopaths, in cases that were tragic and silly. With the possible exception of F. Lee Bailey, no one else in the 20th century was involved in so many cases that had so much impact on the public imagination.

VIII

— ◆ —

Do you remember Erich Muenter, the Harvard lecturer who poisoned his wife, Leone, and fled to Mexico in 1906? By 1908 he had grown a beard and re-entered the United States. Calling himself Frank Holt, he emerged first as a student and then an instructor at Polytechnic Institute in Fort Worth, Texas, where he met another Leone—Leone Sensabaugh, the daughter of a prominent Dallas minister. From there he moved to what is now called Oklahoma State University, from there to Vanderbilt, and then to Emory and Henry College in Virginia. By 1912 he had a new wife Leone and was back in the Ivy League, lecturing at Cornell.

Later on he would tell people that he was a professor at Cornell, which was not quite true. Unknown to Holt, he had been "made" as Muenter. A colleague at Cornell, who had brushed past Muenter briefly at Harvard, was certain that Holt was Muenter. When he applied for a full-time position at Cornell the colleague whispered his secret to the department head, who said, "Well, he's kind of a nut, anyway ... why don't we wait awhile before we make him a professor?" I am making up this conversation, but in a general way that is how it went down. (Numerous sources say that Muenter in fact *was* a professor at Cornell, but I think the better evidence is that he was not. In that era anyone who taught at a college was said in common usage to be a professor, making it somewhat difficult to tell whether he was *actually* a professor as opposed to a lecturer, an instructor or some other kind of pedantic peon.)

Anyway, by the fall of 1914 Germany was at war. Muenter/Holt, who spoke and wrote French, Italian and Spanish as well as German, spoke in English with a German accent, although he always insisted that he had been born in America. Holt favored the Germans in the war, and, being a pathological liar among his other faults, pretended to be not a German sympathizer but a pacifist. America was neutral in the war, but Americans were not. J. P.

Morgan had loaned about $12 million to the Russians and some unknown ungodly amount of money to the British, and many other Americans were also taking sides in the war. Holt thought this was terrible. He wrote letters to newspapers proclaiming his passionate pacifism. He wrote a letter to the Kaiser. He also posed as a socialist . . . or perhaps he was a socialist; it is so hard to be sure with these people, but in any case he was pretty upset about the fact that J. P. Morgan even *had* hundreds of millions of dollars, let alone that he was using it to fight the Germans or investing in the war or whatever it was that he was doing.

On May 7, 1915, the British luxury steamship *Lusitania* was torpedoed and sunk by a German warship, killing 1200 people including 137 Americans. This created pressure to push America into the war. Holt had accepted a position at Southern Methodist University in Dallas, and his wife had returned to the Dallas/Ft. Worth area to set up housekeeping. Holt went to New York City, where he rented a bungalow under the name "Patton" and purchased (under the name "Hendricks") as much dynamite as he could get his hands on—120 pounds, at least. He began fashioning it into bombs. On July 2 he traveled to Washington, DC, where he entered the United States Capitol building, at that time open to the public without security checks. The Senate was not in session. Unable to get into the Senate chamber, Holt left his package in the Senate reception room, and shuffled off to Union Station, where he bought a ticket on the midnight train to New York.

The bomb went off at 11:23 PM. It didn't kill anyone, and failed to bring down the Capitol building, but it destroyed the Senate reception room, blowing open a door to the Vice President's office which had been barred for 40 years. Holt mailed some letters to the Washington newspapers, which were signed "R. Pearce," taking credit for the bombing and imploring the United States to prohibit Americans from providing munitions for the war in Europe. Should we not "stop and consider what we are doing"? Pearce implored. "I, too, have had to use explosives (for the last time I trust). It is the export kind, and ought to make enough noise to be heard above the voices that clamor for war and blood money. This explosion is the exclamation point to my appeal for peace."

Carrying two handguns and three sticks of dynamite, the disheveled pacifist disembarked in New York in the wee hours of July 3, and made his way to Glen Cove, where J. P. Morgan lived. He had been past the house before, checking the place out. About 9:30 AM—ten hours after he bombed the nation's Capitol building—he knocked on the door of the wealthiest man in America, and introduced himself to the butler as Thomas P. Lester. He had a business card with that name on it. He asked to see Morgan. The butler refused. Holt pulled a .38 from his left pocket and a .32 from his right, and forced his way into the house.

The butler, a courageous man named Stanley Physick, now told Holt that Morgan was in the library, which was on the west side of the house. In fact, Morgan was on the east side of the house, eating breakfast with his wife and kids and the British ambassador. When Holt realized that the library was empty Physick yelled to Morgan to take cover. Morgan, his wife and kids scrambled for the staircase, but Holt chased them down and began firing. J. P. Morgan rushed directly at the man, who fired four shots, hitting Morgan once in the leg and once in the abdomen before the much larger Morgan overpowered the consumptive Holt and pushed him to the ground. The butler hit him over the head with a lump of coal.

They took his guns away and tied him up until the police came. One of the other servants spotted dynamite sticking out of his pocket, grabbed that and placed it in a bucket of water. In custody the man said that he was Frank Holt, a professor at Cornell, and gave a "free and voluntary" statement admitting to the shooting of J. P. Morgan. He had gone to the house, he said, in an effort to force Morgan to use his influence to create a U.S. embargo against weapons sales to Europe.

It was the practice of the day for confessions given to police in serious crimes to wind up in the newspapers, verbatim, usually within a few hours. Holt insisted that he had been in New York for weeks, but as soon as his confession was in the newspapers authorities in Washington recognized the rambling, lunatic pacifism of the "R. Pearce" letters, and began to suspect that Holt, arrested with dynamite in his possession, had left some in Washington as well.

Holt would spend the last three days of his life being questioned by the police from numerous jurisdictions, by psychiatrists (alienists, as they were then called) and by reporters, who at the time were often allowed to question prisoners. He never exactly acknowledged responsibility for the bombing, but he acknowledged that he had been in Washington and that he had written the "R. Pearce" letters. He gave diverse reasons for going to Morgan's house, saying at various times that he had intended to kill him, that he had merely wanted to talk with him, and that he had intended to take Morgan's

wife and children hostage to force the man to stop financing Germany's enemies. "How terrible it all looks now," he wrote in a last letter to his father-in-
law, "and how different from my plans!"

Police, meanwhile, were trying to piece together Holt's history. They
learned three things that most interested them. First, they learned that he
had purchased quite a bit more dynamite than they were able to account
for. Second, they had figured out within a few hours that Holt bore a strong
resemblance to Erich Muenter, the missing Harvard professor who had poisoned his wife back in 1906. And third, they got a wire from the governor
of Texas, who had been informed by local police that Holt had sent a letter
to his wife in Dallas, claiming that he had placed bombs on board a number
of ships headed for Europe. The bombs, he claimed, were due to blow up on
July 7.

In fact, there *was* an explosion and fire on a ship, the Atlantic transport
liner *Minnehaha*, not on July 7 but on July 9. This was not one of the ships
Holt had named in the letter, and no one was clear whether the *Minnehaha*
explosion was actually from one of Holt/Muenter's bombs or something
else. There had been a series of bombs placed on ocean-going vessels, apparently the work of German sympathizers, and police now determined to learn
whether Holt was a member of the gang.

Meanwhile, the press pursued the possibility that Holt and Muenter were
one and the same. His picture was shown to his sister in Chicago, who hadn't
seen him in decades and said that she couldn't be sure whether it was him
or wasn't, and to his former in-laws in the same windy city, who were pretty
sure that it was. People in New York who had known Muenter at Harvard
were located and brought in to look at him. Mostly they thought it was him.
His Minister from Massachusetts, based on a photograph, said absolutely
that it was. Authorities from Harvard stopped just short of refusing to admit
that they had ever heard of Erich Muenter.

The man did not exactly deny that he may have placed bombs here and
there in the cause of peace and justice, but he fervently denied that he was
Erich Muenter or that he had ever done any wife killin'. There was no record
of Frank Holt anywhere before 1908, however, and his wife reported that he
had always claimed he had no living relatives. Muenter attempted to slash
his wrists with a broken pencil, and was placed on suicide watch. On the
night of July 6 a guard, thinking Muenter was asleep, neglected to lock his
cell. Muenter slipped out of the cell, climbed to a second-story railing about

fifteen feet above the ground, and dived headfirst onto the concrete floor, killing himself instantly.

Police, deprived of their best source of information, now scrambled frantically to identify all of the places Holt/Muenter might have sent a bomb. A search of his bungalow turned up more than a hundred sticks of dynamite and various homemade bombs, but there were still at least 50 sticks unaccounted for. Ships were recalled to harbor. Mailrooms were searched on both continents and on the seas between. No more bombs were ever found, and the rest of the dynamite was never accounted for.

The ring which had been placing bombs on ships was busted up in the spring of 1916, and appears to have had no connection to Holt/Muenter, who probably acted alone. Morgan recovered quickly from his wounds, and lived another 28 years.

In the story of Muenter and Morgan, what most strikes me is the astonishing openness of American society at that time. Muenter, suspected in the murder of his wife, was nonetheless able to board a train and leave town, which enabled him to disappear. Re-entering the country with no passport and no legitimate résumé, he was nonetheless able to work his way back into a position at an Ivy League university in a matter of a few years. He was able to buy guns and dynamite with no questions asked, and to board public transportation while armed and loaded. He was able to walk around the nation's Capitol building unescorted after hours. He was able to walk up to the door of the wealthiest man in the country and demand to see him, although Morgan knew very well that his support for Germany's enemies had made him a target. In modern America you couldn't do any of those things.

People will say "Oh, well, they didn't have the security we have now because they didn't have the crime problems we have now," but that's just not true. America then was ramping up to our first big foreign war in a hundred years. Terrorism, as a practical matter, was a far more real threat then than it is now, and there was a great deal of paranoia about terrorism. Although there were no national crime statistics, the national murder rate was certainly much higher than it is now, probably several times higher.

People simply did not choose to protect themselves in the way that we do now. Were people of that era blind to the risks of daily life, or did they consciously choose to live in a more open society?

I think the best answer is that we have more security now because we can afford it. You have to remember: a high percentage of the population was still on the farm in 1915, and a high percentage of the people were still on the farm because they had to be in order to produce enough food. When you have 60% of the workforce devoted to agriculture, there is no way you can have 5% devoted to security. You can't afford it.

What we are doing, in a sense, is making ourselves constantly more aware of the threats and dangers around us, and then erecting security walls as if these threats were closing in on us, when in reality we are pushing them further and further away. Crime stories have the function of making us constantly more aware of crime. I am not saying that this is a bad thing, but neither am I entirely convinced that it is a good thing. Security is a very good thing. Crimes devastate people's lives. On the other hand, openness is also a good thing, and paranoia is not. Is there an endpoint to this game? Or in 50 years, when the real crime rate will be a third of what it is now, will we be passing through magnetic screening devices designed to make sure we are not carrying scissors into the grocery store or little vials of nitroglycerin onto the subway? At some point can we vote on this?

IX

A 2003 study by the National Center for Health Statistics reports that the murder rate in the United States was 1.1 per 100,000 population in 1903, increasing to 4.9 per 100,000 in 1907, then to 6.2 by 1914. This, if true, would make the homicide rate in 1914 essentially the same as it is now, and the rate pre-1905 dramatically lower than it is now. I stand by my statement that the murder rate in fact was many times higher in 1915 than it is now.

There were no national crime statistics compiled early in the 20th century, and the rates reported now are based on those homicides which later researchers have happened to catalogue. A 300 percent increase in homicides between 1903 and 1907, had such a thing actually taken place, would certainly have been a phenomenal occurrence.

In fact, it is remarkably difficult to make an estimate of what the actual murder rates were then, in the modern meaning of the term "murder." Over the last hundred years a large number of events have been re-classified as murder. A hundred years ago, "justifiable homicide" was a term that had very, very wide latitude. A hundred years ago if somebody broke into your apartment and you shot him, nobody was going to give you a hard time about that. Until about 1970 when parents beat their children to death they very often escaped punishment. They would be prosecuted if it was clear and deliberate murder, but if a parent slapped or shook a child and the child died and the parent said the kid fell down the steps, the police virtually never followed up.

A hundred years ago, if a trench collapsed and a worker was killed, that was a tragic accident. Now, it's negligent homicide. Very large numbers of workers were in fact killed on the job—160-plus in the Triangle Shirtwaist Factory Fire in 1911. A hundred years ago if two men were in a fight and one of them died, police would ask whether it was a fair fight. A hundred years ago accused murderers were not infrequently seized by mobs and executed before trial. (In an 1898 newspaper which I tragically failed to make a copy of and now cannot find, I found a story about an accused murderer who was being returned to Ohio, where, according to the newspaper, he *would be lynched* as soon as he arrived.) A hundred years ago substantial numbers of black people were murdered in the South—in fact, I would predict that the murders of southern blacks *alone,* if they could be tallied, might exceed the number of homicides estimated by the NCHS study for the years 1900–1903. Medical malpractice leading to death, a hundred years ago, was never or virtually never investigated as murder. The killing of citizens by police officers was never or virtually never investigated as murder. Frank Hamer, who set up the ambush that killed Bonnie and Clyde, has been reported to have personally killed 65 people in the performance of his police duties. (In the 1920s the Texas Bankers Association offered $5,000 rewards to police officers for the deaths of outlaws. This led to several innocent people being set up and murdered by Texas police officers—a practice which Hamer is credited with having put an end to, busting up the murder ring.) The killing of strikers by hired strike-breakers (such as the Pinkertons) was not generally prosecuted as murder.

When I was in high school, the football coach used to work us hard on hot days and not let us have water. Of course, across the country a few kids every year would die from this practice, but . . . that was just the way it was. Kids still die occasionally from that kind of practice, but when it happens now, it is called reckless homicide. The estimate that there were only 1.1 murders per 100,000 people in the United States at the start of the 20th century is, in my view, utterly preposterous, at least in the modern understanding of the term "murder."

From 1894 into the early 1930s, Oklahoma attorney Moman Pruiett defended 343 persons accused of murder. None of them was executed, and 303 or 304, depending on the source, were acquitted outright, although about the same number were probably guilty in fact. These are truly phenomenal numbers, to a modern reader, and we need to masticate them a moment before we can digest them. Moman—the name was a backwoods corruption of "Morman"—would not uncommonly defend two accused murderers a week in separate trials, sometimes three. Very rarely would any of these scoundrels be convicted, and if they were, Moman took it as a personal affront. He would carry his case to the governor, who would either be a close personal friend or a hated political rival, depending on the state and the season. If the governor could be cajoled or corrupted into issuing a pardon, he would get a pardon. If not, he would work on getting a new trial or getting a new governor, or both. Once, early in his career and before he had any serious connections, he had a client who was convicted and stood to be executed. He went to Washington, DC, knowing almost no one, finagled a meeting with the President, and convinced the President to issue a pardon.

It is hard to say whether Moman Pruiett should be described as a criminal lawyer, or just a criminal. He was both. Pruiett was born in Kentucky in 1872. His mother was a pioneer woman who made up in determination for what she lacked in teeth. Pruiett never went to school, apart from a few weeks one winter, but his mother was determined that he should be a famous orator, and she would occasionally drag him around Kentucky or Arkansas or wherever the hell the family was hunkering, so that he could listen to famous men speak. That was as much education as he got, and in his mid-teens he could neither read nor write, although even then he could talk pretty good.

Twice, as a young man, Pruiett was convicted of serious felonies (forgery and armed robbery) and sentenced to substantial terms in prison. One of the crimes amounted to murder, although Pruiett was not convicted of murder. A man well known to Pruiett was knocked unconscious and robbed, and his residence set on fire. The man died, and Pruiett was convicted of armed robbery.

And both times, after his conviction, Pruiett's mother determined to convince the governor to pardon her son. She would ask for an audience with the governor, and she would plead his case, and when she was turned down she would be back the next week to plead it again, and when she was told to go away she would take up residence in the governor's waiting room, begging for just a moment of his time. By this method she convinced first the governor of Arkansas, then the governor of Texas to issue a pardon for her beloved son.

Before and between his prison sentences Pruiett liked to hang around lawyers' offices, fetching coal and running messages to the court. With a little help from the lawyers he taught himself to read, and he began studying the law books. He used his time in prison well. He got out of prison the second time in 1894, 22 years old, and was admitted to the Texas bar just months later, due to the influence of a judge who took a liking to him, and took the oath enabling him to speak to the United States Supreme Court in 1900.

He was a tall, vigorous, attractive man who dressed well in a Western fashion. He could quote from memory hundreds of long passages of law and legal opinion. He was eloquent, even mesmerizing. He would quote the Bible or Shakespeare or Abraham Lincoln, whatever the occasion called for, and he would do *anything* to win a case. He practiced mostly in Oklahoma, some in Texas, later on moved to Florida. Once, defending a woman who had killed her husband, he learned that the departed had been a member of the Ku Klux Klan, and that several Klansmen were on the jury. Undeterred, Pruiett used Klan code words to hint that he, too, was a Klansman, and put the poor widow on the stand to recite a history of abuse at the hands of the late husband, who she now claimed had been born in Italy. She was free and out of the state before anybody could prove she was just making it up.

One time, figuring out who would be on the jury and guessing correctly who would be picked as the foreman, Pruiett persuaded the defendant's sister to move to Oklahoma, seduce the jury foreman and move in with him, never revealing that she was the accused man's sister. Pruiett played poker with judges, and accepted acquittals to settle debts. His stock in trade, though, was common perjury. A rancher, John Evans, was arrested for killing his wife's lover. He was tracked to and from the scene of the crime by the horseshoes on his horse. Pruiett produced a blacksmith who swore he had not put those shoes on the horse until days after the murder, and a stockman who swore that, on the morning of the murder, the horse had been bred to one of his mares. Oklahoma jurors knew that horses are not shod during breeding, for the same reason you and I don't wear iron gloves during sex. The stockman, challenged to do so, produced a record book and a receipt for the stud fee. John Evans was acquitted.

In some cases, Pruiett probably arranged for key witnesses to be kidnapped and unavailable at the time of the trial. Incredible as this sounds today, that practice was not terribly uncommon at the time; witnesses in trials in that era *frequently* failed to appear, and by no means was it only defense lawyers who arranged this; most of the time it was the prosecutors. At that time there was no federal law against kidnapping, and no one, in 1910, would ever have thought to term the private detention of a potential witness as "kidnapping." They might have recognized it as an unlawful act, certainly, but would not have placed it, as we would, in the same category as "holding a person for ransom."

Some of his clients were no doubt innocent. In 1913 Oklahoma Senator Thomas P. Gore, who was blind and Gore Vidal's grandfather, was accused of attempting to rape a young woman named Minnie Bond. Pruiett defended him, and earned an acquittal that was probably justified by the facts; Gore was a lecher but probably not a rapist. (Thomas P. Gore may have been very distantly related to the family of Al Gore, but there is no clear connection.)

According to numerous possibly reliable sources, Pruiett tried 342 murder cases, resulting in 304 acquittals, 37 convictions on lesser counts, and one conviction for murder, which was subsequently set aside by presidential pardon. While I wouldn't want to bet a lot of money that these numbers are accurate, a modern reader must wonder how they are even possible.

There are uncanny parallels between Moman Pruiett (1872–1945) and Earl Rogers (1869–1922). Both men were remarkably successful lawyers who secured the release of dozens if not hundreds of probably guilty murderers; Rogers' Wikipedia entry claims a won-lost log of 74–3. Both men were nice-looking, extremely well dressed, and usually divorced. Both lived with the boldness of heroes, projecting fantastic self-confidence while undertaking formidable tasks. Both men were political insiders who battled against the establishment on behalf of reprobates and peddled influence inside the establishment on behalf of banks and oil men. Both men were alcoholics who fell near if not actually into the gutter when the bubble of alcoholic courage collapsed underneath them. Both men would do whatever was required to win a case. Although the evidence against Rogers is not as clear as the evidence against Pruiett, Rogers' commitment to victory was absolute, and his string of successes is nearly inexplicable.

Although both men earned very large amounts of money in their legal practice, Rogers by the age of 50 was living in a room in his daughter's house, sneaking out occasionally to get lost and get drunk, while Pruiett died at 73, at the time living in a 50¢ a night flophouse, bumming whiskey from strangers in seedy bars.

And both men became the subject of wonderful books. I thought about drawing up a list of the 100 best crime books ever, decided not to. A consensus pick for number one would be *In Cold Blood,* and I don't quarrel with that; *In Cold Blood* is a remarkable book. But my number two pick, I think, would be *Final Verdict,* Adela Rogers St. Johns' account of growing up in her father's law office. Earl Rogers, as I mentioned, didn't believe in formal education; he thought his daughter would learn more going to the office—and to court—with him. As a little girl and a young woman Adela Rogers was present in person for most of Earl Rogers' fantastic career. Many years later (1962), after a distinguished career as a journalist and screenwriter and finally a novelist, Adela Rogers St. Johns wrote the story of Earl Rogers' career in *Final Verdict*. We have here a skillful novelist with an amazing true-life story to tell.

Not quite as great, but somewhere in the top 25 would be Howard K. Berry's bio of Moman Pruiett, *He Made It Safe to Murder*. The story of this book is a novel in itself. As a young lawyer in the late 1930s Berry became fascinated with Pruiett, by that time on the far downhill slope of his brilliant career, and spent many hours listening to his stories and writing them up, doing some incidental research to associate Pruiett's stories with real cases. Pruiett, predictably, let Berry put the book together and then tried to steal the manuscript and sell it as his own. This led to a lawsuit, and the book was tied up for years in litigation.

The book emerged in 1944 but with a very small print run, under the name *Moman Pruiett: Criminal Lawyer*. Many years later, as an old man, Berry was able to bring the book back out, stronger, under the new title.

Much of the charm of the book is that it is so preposterously dated. Book writers of the 1940s did many things that would never be tolerated for a modern writer who wished to remain respectable. They told stories in vaguely mythic form, without dates and without references, and with the periodic inclusion of details that don't exactly resound with the ring of truth. The writers of that era . . . and, to an extent, this applies to Adela Rogers St. Johns as well . . . believed that their central responsibility was to tell a compelling story. If the story went one way and the facts went the other, they followed the story.

Howard Berry's book is choppy, episodic, vague, amateurish and tinged with BS—and that's what makes it work. His lead character, Moman Pruiett, is a walking contradiction, partly truth and partly fiction, as Kristofferson wrote about Johnny Cash. Berry stares at him in open-mouthed awe for 700 pages. You can't often find a copy of the book for less than $150, but . . . it's worth every penny.

There were other attorneys of the same era who also had fantastic careers. Samuel Leibowitz (1893–1978) was reported to have successfully defended dozens of murder cases without a loss, in a career culminating in his defense of the Scottsboro Boys in the 1930s; the book about him is Quentin Reynolds' *Courtroom: The Story of Samuel S. Leibowitz*. Leibowitz defended Al Capone and numerous other gangland figures whose names were once infamous, like Kid Twist and Pittsburgh Phil.

Pruiett, Rogers, Leibowitz and others defended legions of murderers with hardly a loss. We posed a moment ago the question: How is it even possible that they did these things? Or, stated more accurately from a historical standpoint: How did it happen that these things became *im*possible, since certainly they are impossible in modern America?

I would argue that essentially three things happened to make stories like these no longer possible. First, the bar associations, in the years 1915 to 1940, cracked down on and gradually brought under control such practices as jury tampering, suborning perjury, bribing judges and intimidating witnesses. That wasn't all done between 1915 and 1940, and it wasn't all done by bar associations, but the bar associations in that era were very active at prosecuting and disbarring renegade attorneys.

Second, and most important of the three . . . in my opinion, by far the largest change in American criminal trials over the last 100 years has been the accumulation of layers of pretrial discovery. In a series of landmark cases beginning with *Mooney v. Holohan* (1935) and culminating in *Brady v. Maryland* (1963), the Supreme Court ruled that defendants had the right to know in advance what testimony would be introduced against them at trial.

This, in essence, moved the action of a trial outside the trial, and into the pretrial skirmishing. I am oversimplifying here . . . worse, I am oversimplifying things that I but dimly understand. But a hundred years ago, murder cases resulted in murder trials, plain and simple. You had 100 murders; you had 90 murder trials. This was still vaguely true into the 1960s.

After *Brady v. Maryland* in 1963, the real action moved from the trial to the foreplay, the pretrial discovery. There were always defendants who entered pleas; there was always some possibility of negotiating a plea in return for a negotiated sentence. After *Brady* this process exploded, and the ratio of trials to accused criminals began to shrink. For 100 murders we started with 90 trials, each lasting a day or two days. Eventually we had 15 trials or less for each 100 murders, but trials lasting, at least sometimes, for months. (A study by David Feige reported in the *Boston Globe* says that 44% of murder "cases" go to trial. I am uncertain what is meant by a murder "case," but certainly the number of murder trials in the United States is nothing like 44% of the number of murders. For that matter, it probably isn't anything like 15%, either; I just said 15 to stay clear of the fine edges of the issue.)

The third thing that happened—and I honestly don't think that anyone understands why this happened—was a dramatic shift in the ratio of acquittals to convictions. A newspaper editorial reproduced in *He Made It Safe to Murder* claims that in England at that time (just after World War I), 90% of accused murderers were convicted, whereas in America 80% were acquitted. Newspapers of that era are fantastically unreliable, but obviously a high percentage of persons who were accused of murder in that era were, in fact, acquitted or found guilty of lesser charges. But in America today, according to Feige, 85% of murder trials result in conviction.

How did that happen? How did it happen, and doesn't anyone but me see that as being somewhat remarkable? There have, after all, been dozens of landmark Supreme Court rulings in the last hundred years that were intended to protect the rights of the accused. And yet, a hundred years ago, when there was no Miranda and no Brady, no Gideon and no exclusionary rule, no Escobeda and no *Malloy v. Morgan*, a large majority of accused murderers walked away from the courthouse. Today they are almost all led away in shackles. How did that happen?

The most benign explanation for this change is that prosecutors have become more careful about who they put on trial. In the time of Rogers and Pruiett, prosecutors would file charges first and ask questions later. Now, although certainly innocent people are still accused of crimes, almost all prosecutors will insist that they would never file charges unless they were convinced of the accused person's culpability. There has been a significant change in how prosecutors view this issue, and I think that that does account for at least some of the difference in conviction rates.

Pretrial discovery, since Brady, has created a situation in which people who have some defense that they can offer have the opportunity to negotiate down from the maximum charge. That leaves in the dock only those accused persons who really have no defense, thus have nothing to gain from making a deal; this, at least, is the theory. No doubt that also explains some of the change.

Let me suggest some other things that I think may have contributed. Police officers are much more professional now than they were a hundred years ago. Police officers a hundred years ago were often not respected by juries because, in truth, they very often were not worthy of much respect. They are better educated now; they have better uniforms and better PR guys. This probably causes juries to give them more credence. This is perhaps unfortunate. Professionals lie just as often as amateurs, only more skillfully.

At the same time, I have to wonder whether the high conviction rates of modern America are not due in part to . . . well, cynicism. It's the law of un-intended consequences. In my grandfather's time police officers beat confessions out of criminals, perjured themselves and sprung surprise witnesses who were often persons of low character—and the juries looked upon it with a jaundiced eye, and demanded to be convinced. The Warren Court swung the balance of power toward the accused—and the counterbalance of skepticism moved the other way. Trials were once spontaneous, quick and dramatic; now they are rehearsed, endless and often boring, interminable bullshit from professional witnesses who have practiced their skills at sparring with defense attorneys. The jury looks upon the accused as if he must be guilty, or why would he be here?

I am trying to get to the issue: is this change a consequence of the phenomenon of popular crime? Do the ceaseless stories of spectacular crimes cause so much fear among the American people that juries come into court determined to convict?

Perhaps. I don't think so.

Here's another theory about this change. A hundred years ago, America was rural. Now it's urban.

I grew up in a small town where I knew everybody. I will always remember this: that in my first semester in college I knew every person in any of my classes. I knew their names, their faces, a few facts about everybody, hometowns and hobbies. Years later, I could still remember every one of those people.

Three years later, when I was a second-semester senior, I happened to think back to the previous semester—and realized that I could not remember the name of one single person that I had taken a class with the previous semester. The people I had had classes with as a freshman, I still remembered. The people I had met as a senior, I had never made any effort to get to know.

The difference is this: that a rural person expects to know every person in his world, and therefore thinks of every person as an individual. An urbanized person never expects to know the people he comes into contact with, and therefore rarely focuses on them as individuals.

Stating the same thing in a different way, when you have more *categories* in your mind than *people*, you tend to see the categories as characteristics of the people. Like this:

Jack	Susan	Daryl
Rich	Poor	Black
Tall	Short	Intense
Dumb	Smart	Well-Dressed
Jock	Business Major	Loud
Frat Boy	Dorm Dweller	English Major

But once you have more people in your world than categories, you start to sort the people into categories. Like this:

Frat Boys	Dorm Dwellers	Blacks
Jack	Susan	Daryl
Teddy	Mary	Cliff
Chip	Lucy	Jules
Scott	Alice	Wes
Josh	Marlee	Lonnie

What had happened to me, between the time I started college and the time I finished, was that the number of people in my world had expanded such that it became more practical for me to keep track of the people under the labels than it was to keep track of the labels under the people.

This is just a theory, but I wonder if this surge in the conviction rates wasn't caused by the same phenomenon. In 1915 we were a rural nation. Jurors, introduced to a person charged with a crime, instinctively looked upon her or him as an individual, and demanded to see the proof that he or she was guilty.

But by 2009 we were an urban nation. Jurors tended to look upon a person accused of a crime as . . . well, a criminal. The accused started out underneath the heading "accused criminal."

It's just a theory. I wouldn't want anyone to think I was suggesting that the criminal justice system a hundred years ago was better than it is now. It certainly was not. The criminal justice system of modern America is vastly better than the justice system of a hundred years ago. It is dramatically better than it was 30 years ago.

Trial by ambush was not a good thing. At the same time, the burden of pretrial discovery has added so much weight to modern trials that the trials are in danger of sinking under the load. It seems to me unlikely that the Warren Court, in issuing the *Brady* ruling, intended to force upon the justice system changes that were quite as sweeping as those that actually followed. And it seems to me a defensible position that modern justice could benefit from having trials that were cheaper, shorter, more spontaneous and more common.

X

Mary Phagan was thirteen years old, four feet, eleven inches tall, and worked in a pencil factory in Atlanta. On April 26, 1913, the little working girl went by her factory on a Saturday to pick up a paycheck. It was Confederate Memorial Day, a major Southern holiday at the time, and there was a parade through downtown Atlanta. Mary wore her prettiest homemade dress, lavender with lace trim, and a ribbon in her hair, and carried a silver mesh pocketbook. The factory owed her $1.20 for one day's work—they had shut down the rest of the week, awaiting supplies—and she was going to pick it up on her way to the parade. She didn't make it to the parade. A night watchman found her body about three o'clock the next morning, in the basement of the pencil factory. She had been sexually assaulted and beaten. A couple of nearly illiterate notes were found near her body.

Leo Frank was arrested. Frank was the superintendent of the pencil factory, and for that reason was the last person to whom Mary Phagan could be traced.

Suppose that we were to categorize crime stories. Let us pretend that you and I are academics who wish to study crime stories, and, as a first step in that process, we need to sort them into categories so that we can study groups of like stories. How would we do that?

One key element would certainly be the size of the story, the degree to which it seizes hold of the public's imagination. The murder of Mary Phagan, on a 10-point scale, would probably be a "9" or a "10." It didn't command the nation's attention on the level of O.J. or the Lindbergh baby or the assassination of JFK, but it was right behind them, on the level of the Manson family murders or the Scott Peterson case.

It didn't draw the same level of *attention,* but it generated much more *passion.* Let us take three or four cases from this era—the Mary Phagan murder (1913), the crime for which Sacco and Vanzetti were executed (1920), and the Hall-Mills murder (1922). All of these were huge cases, all "9s" or "10s" on an attention meter—but the attention is of a very different nature. The Hall-Mills case was a media sensation, probably earning more inches of contemporaneous newsprint than any case in American history up to that time, but the Hall-Mills case—like the Snyder-Gray case three years later— was more or less manufactured by editors to sell newspapers. People were *interested* in it, as people are interested in a novel or a soap opera, but on a certain level they didn't really *care* about it, the way they did about Mary Phagan.

And then there is Sacco and Vanzetti, a case that received little newspaper attention at the time of the crime or at the time of the trial, but became famous later on because people at some point began to care about it. Sacco and Vanzetti is essentially a "Dreyfus" story, as I would categorize it, a story about an innocent person's fight for justice.

So we have tabloid cases and Dreyfus cases and . . . what do we call the Mary Phagan case? But the Mary Phagan case has also within it a Dreyfus story, as Leo Frank is a Dreyfus figure. It turns out to be too complicated to categorize stories in that way, as crime stories contain different mixes of elements. There are, for example, celebrity stories like Lindbergh and O.J. There are mystery stories, in which some unknown person has committed a crime, and the nation gets caught up in the effort to find the villain. One of the most famous crime stories in British history, the murder of Julia Wallace in 1931, is a classic mystery. The characters involved are uninteresting and essentially unsympathetic, but the case remains enduringly famous because, despite an abundance of clues, there is no apparent solution; the clues can be used equally well to show the innocence or the guilt of the accused. The Lindbergh case is a celebrity story, certainly, but it is also a mystery. Later writers have tried to convert Bruno Richard Hauptmann into a Dreyfus figure, which is fairly silly, but I guess I am getting ahead of myself.

I think that there are at least eighteen elements that characterize crime stories—probably more, but eighteen I can pin down.

1) *Tabloid elements,* which involve soap opera–like stories and are media-driven.

2) *Dreyfus elements,* in which an innocent person pursues justice.

3) *Celebrity elements,* which involve persons who were famous before the crime.

4) *Mystery stories,* which are essentially driven by the effort to identify the killer.

5) *Political elements,* which are driven by the perception that an issue of political significance is involved. The assassination of JFK is a political story, obviously, as are stories involving police corruption. Spy stories are political. The case of the Rosenbergs is a political story as well as a Dreyfus story. The LA *Times* bombing, the terrorist acts of Erich Muenter and the assassination of ex-governor Steunenberg in 1905 were all political stories.

6) *Bizarre elements* cause stories to stand out from the mass of criminal events by gruesome, grotesque and extremely unusual features. Jeffrey Dahmer is a Bizarre story, as is Charles Manson and Winnie Judd, the Trunk Murderess (1931). Any story involving unusual amounts of cruelty could be called a Bizarre story.

7) *Killer on the Loose stories* receive attention due to the public's perception that they may be in actual danger. The Beltway sniper was a Killer on the Loose story, as were John Dillinger, Bonnie and Clyde, and Charles Starkweather. The story of Michael Swango, the doctor/poisoner, is a Killer on the Loose story because of the perception that the refusal of the medical establishment to deal with a sociopathic doctor represents a threat to the public.

8) *Organized Crime elements* are an essentially different phenomenon. I haven't really dealt with Organized Crime in this book, in that I regard Organized Crime as fundamentally outside the tradition of Popular Crime.

9) *Innocent Victim elements* appeal to us because of the desire to see justice for an innocent victim. Of course, JFK is an innocent victim as well, and Nicole Brown Simpson, and all of the people killed by the Beltway snipers and Charles Starkweather. They are innocent victims, but this is not why their cases became famous. The average crime story consumer can't name one person killed by the Beltway snipers. Some cases are about the victims, and some cases are about the killers.

10) *Literary elements* are cases that become famous because of the *quality* of journalism invested in them, not the quantity. The murder of the Clutters (*In Cold Blood*) is a Literary case, as is the 1963 murder of Los Angeles police officer Ian Campbell (*The Onion Field*) and the case of Robert Stroud (*Birdman of Alcatraz*). In these cases it is neither the killer nor the

victim who makes the case famous, nor is it the amorphous and competitive press. Rather, it is a single identifiable skilled journalist or author or some small set of journalists, dramatists or moviemakers, acting together, who make the case famous.

11) *Justice System stories* are stories that are fundamentally about the system of justice itself, such as the Duke Lacrosse Non-Rape story, the story of Moman Pruiett or the 1976–77 battle to execute Gary Gilmore.

12) *Fraud elements* involve stories of deception and highly organized deceit.

13) *Money stories* are stories about extremely wealthy people or about money itself.

14) *Adventure stories* are stories about disturbing things that happen to people while they are out in the world on some adventure, which seems to attract the attention of the media.

15) *Violence stories* are stories about sudden eruptions of unplanned street fighting, involving multiple combatants.

16) *Missing Person stories* are about people who suddenly go missing for no apparent reason.

17) Stories that demand our attention because of the *Number of Victims* involved we will call "Number" stories.

18) And there are, finally, *Sexual Violence stories.*

Eighteen elements. Alphabetically:

A—Adventure Stories

B—Bizarre Elements

C—Celebrity Elements

D—Dreyfus Elements

F—Fraud Elements

I—Innocent Victim Elements

J—Justice System Elements

K—Killer on the Loose Stories

L—Literary Elements

M—Missing Persons Stories

N—For "Number"

O—Organized Crime Elements

P—Political Elements

Q—Mystery Stories

$—Stories about Money

T—Tabloid Elements
V—Violence Stories
X—Stories of Sexual Violence

Money, Mystery, Mass Shooting and Missing Person all start with "M," so I used the dollar sign for money, "N" for stories which involve many victims, and "Q" (Question Mark) for Mystery. I tried using an actual question mark, but it just didn't fit.

We could categorize crime stories, then, by the two or three most prominent elements of the case from the list above, and by the degree of public interest on a 1 to 10 scale. We would need to spell out exactly what distinguishes a "6" from a "7" in terms of media interest. "1" would be a case that receives little notice from the local press and no national interest. "2" would be a case that receives some degree of local interest, characterized perhaps by 1 to 5 front-page stories in the local newspapers.

That's enough of that; I can see you yawning. The trial of Clarence Darrow, then, might be categorized as CJP 9—a celebrity story involving the justice system, with political significance, very big. The story of Erich Muenter would be PB 7—a political story with a somewhat bizarre twist, attracting strong short-term national interest. The murder of Stanford White by Harry K. Thaw was CT 9—a Celebrity/Tabloid story, very big. The murder of little Mary Phagan, on the other hand, would be IDQX 9—an innocent-victim sex crime with a Dreyfus angle and a mystery subplot, attracting huge and enduring national attention, eventually becoming the subject of many books.

The death of Mary Phagan engaged the passions of the American public to a greater extent than any other crime, ever. There have been other stories as big, and some bigger. There has never been any other crime story about which so many people cared so much.

I broke into the narrative to try to figure out why this was true. I believe that this happened, first, because the two kinds of crime stories that people care most about are Innocent Victim Stories and Dreyfus Stories. The Mary Phagan case combined both of those elements at a very high level. All really big crime stories have some element of mystery in them, and most big crime stories have some political overtones. Again, the Mary Phagan case has these. The case combines the elements that tend to make a case *big* with the elements that make people genuinely care about it, to a degree that I think is without parallel. Let me recap the chronology quickly:

Mary disappeared on April 26, 1913.

Her body was found by a night watchman at about three o'clock in the morning on April 27.

Leo Frank was arrested and charged with the murder on April 29.

His trial began on July 28, 1913, in downtown Atlanta.

He was convicted and sentenced to death on August 26, 1913.

On June 21, 1915, his sentence was commuted to life imprisonment by the governor of Georgia, John Slaton.

On August 17, 1915, a group of citizens calling themselves the Knights of Mary Phagan seized Frank from the prison farm where he was incarcerated, drove him back toward Atlanta, and hanged him.

On a certain level these events are unremarkable. The murders of young girls by lecherous men have been unfortunately common throughout history. In the first quarter of the twentieth century it was not uncommon for those murders to be avenged by extralegal executions. What made the Mary Phagan story remarkable was the quite extraordinary level of public engagement in the process. At the time of the trial tens of thousands of people surrounded the courthouse in Atlanta. Large rallies protested the conviction of Leo Frank in almost every Northern city, often attended by thousands of protestors. Hundreds upon hundreds of newspaper editorials were written on both sides of the case, Northern newspapers urging Frank's acquittal, Southern newspapers urging his conviction. When the clemency appeal for Frank was on Governor Slaton's desk he received more than 100,000 letters urging him to do one thing or the other.

Leo Frank was an innocent man—Jewish and a Yankee, yes, but innocent of the crime. The murder was committed by Jim Conley, a janitor at the pencil factory, who was Frank's chief accuser at the trial. This has been the conclusion of almost everyone who has written about the case in the last sixty years, and in my view there is no reasonable doubt that this is correct. I would argue that Conley's guilt is not only clear, but obvious, based on the facts as they are now known:

1) Several crudely constructed letters were found with the body, letters purporting to be in the hand of Mary Phagan, but obviously written by someone else. Conley acknowledged writing the letters.

2) Conley was at the scene of the crime, by his own testimony, hiding out in a dark area near Leo Frank's office.

3) Crimes of this nature are normally committed under the influence of alcohol. Conley was drunk at the time. There is evidence from various sources that Conley was drunk when he reported for work at eight o'clock on the morning of the crime, and had continued to drink throughout the morning until he ran out of alcohol and money.

4) Conley was a man of extremely bad character, arrested and incarcerated many times throughout his life for many different types of crimes.

5) Conley told a story in which he was pressured by Leo Frank to assist Frank in covering up the murder. He thus acknowledged participating in the staging of the crime scene, including writing the notes, but insisted he had done so at Leo Frank's direction. The story told by Conley is clearly untrue.

6) Alonzo Mann, a 14-year-old office boy for Leo Frank, came forward many, many years later, when he was near death, and confessed that he had seen Jim Conley with an unconscious Mary Phagan in his arms. He said that Conley had threatened to kill him if he told what he knew. Mann's mother ordered him to keep quiet, his father re-enforced the order, and the police never asked him what he knew. The story told by Alonzo Mann appears to be true.

In any case, the story told by Jim Conley is quite certainly false, and should have been seen at the time to be false. Mary Phagan ate a lunch of cabbage and bread about 11:30 to 11:40 on the day of her death. The cabbage and bread were found in her stomach during her autopsy, largely undigested, indicating that she had died within an hour of her last meal. Leo Frank reported giving her pay envelope to her at 12:05. She was never seen alive after that.

But in Conley's story, Frank asked him to help dispose of Mary Phagan's body much later in the afternoon, sometime around 4:00. It has to be that late, because a prosecution witness saw Frank step out of his office at about 12:30—about the time that Mary Phagan actually died—and Frank's time is well accounted for most of the afternoon. He was seen by dozens of people doing different things in that time period. The prosecution's case simply ignored the actual time of death, even though that time of death could be well established.

In Conley's story, Frank committed the murder on the second floor of the pencil factory, and Conley assisted him in moving the body to the basement, using the elevator. There were two ways of getting into the basement—

the elevator, and a trap door with a ladder beneath it. Conley said that they moved the body with the elevator, but there are four facts indicating that the body was moved through the trap door:

1) Blood smears on the trap door,

2) Drag marks from the ground under the trap door to the place where the body was found,

3) Persons working in the factory near the elevator, who would have heard the elevator had it been used during the afternoon, swore that the elevator was turned off and was never used during the day,

4) Conley acknowledged that he had defecated into the elevator shaft on the morning of the murder. The elevator went all the way to the ground, and jarred to a stop when it hit bottom. When police investigating the crime rode the elevator to the basement the elevator car smashed the excrement and released the odor from it, indicating that the elevator had not been to the basement since Conley had used it as a toilet.

So the story Conley told in court is wrong about the time and the place of the murder, and is also clearly wrong about innumerable other facts. He said that the notes found with the body were written in Frank's office, but they were written on discarded paper that was stacked in the basement, near where the body was found. Conley said that Mary Phagan was strangled with a strip of bed tick torn from a discarded mattress, but there was no such mattress and no such cloth in the factory. When other people write that Conley committed the murder, skeptic that I am, I look for an escape hatch to suggest some other solution, but there simply isn't one. Conley quite obviously committed the murder.

How, then, did the police, the prosecutors, the jury and the public get it so fantastically wrong? Why did almost everybody in the South, including Mary Phagan's family, choose to believe a filthy, drunken, semi-literate black criminal telling a story that doesn't match the known facts in one particular after another, rather than a clean, white, sober, upstanding and respectable factory supervisor whose only real story was that he had no idea what had happened?

The short answer is that our emotions, once engaged, have a powerful capacity to pull us toward the explanation that we choose to believe. The nation's passions were engaged in the Mary Phagan story to an extent that they have never been engaged in any other crime story. I suggested before two factors that contributed to that, but also, the nation's passions were already enflamed at that time. As I argued in a previous chapter, we were drifting toward civil war. We were not near civil war, but we had begun to drift in that direction about 1890, and by 1913 we had moved a good distance. The basic schism was rich against poor, capitalists against labor. It was an era of genuine, deep, widespread hatred of the rich. Leo Frank represented one side of that divide. Mary Phagan represented the other.

Onto this volatile stage stepped four people: Mary Phagan, Leo Frank, Jim Conley and Hugh Dorsey. Hugh Dorsey was the Fulton County Prosecuting Attorney. He stepped into the investigation of the crime at a very early stage, and personally prosecuted the case. After winning the case he stepped outside into a jubilant mob that thrust him into the air and passed him over their heads several hundred feet to his office, his feet never touching the ground. He was elected Governor of Georgia on the sole basis of the popularity he gained through the Phagan/Frank case.

Some people have painted Dorsey as a cynical man who prosecuted Frank for his own political gain. I doubt that that is accurate. I think that he sincerely believed that Frank was guilty.

Do you remember the Duke Lacrosse Non-Rape story? In that case the highest elected official connected with the case, Mike Nifong, entered the case very early, made a decision about who to believe very early, *and committed himself to that view, in the press and in full view of the public*, at a very early stage, before the facts of the case emerged. The same thing here; Dorsey entered the case very early, which was somewhat unusual but not entirely unusual and not improper, and committed himself in the press to Frank's guilt.

Nifong became so convinced that the Duke players were guilty that he lost all judgment, and began to say things that were just frigging stupid in defense of the proposition that a rape had occurred. But in the Duke case the police didn't get emotionally invested in the case. As soon as the case against the lacrosse players began to fall apart the police cut Nifong's legs off, and the press tore him to shreds—as they should have done; his actions were irresponsible, and very dangerous.

But in the Mary Phagan case the police followed Dorsey headfirst into hell, and carried the local press with them. Within seven days of the murder the Atlanta public was thoroughly convinced that Frank was good for the crime—a not unusual thing. In high-profile cases the police very often try to relieve the pressure on themselves by leading the public toward an early decision that the guilty party has been identified.

Dorsey focused on Frank essentially because he misread his eyes. He saw nervousness in Frank, and he misread it for guilt. Perhaps Frank *did* feel guilty about something. Perhaps he was embezzling a little bit from the company, or perhaps he was involved with a young girl who worked there. Perhaps he had been attracted to Mary Phagan. Perhaps he was just a nervous young man with some limits to his social skills. God knows what it was, but in any case Dorsey came to an early and mistaken belief in Frank's guilt.

A month passed before the investigation focused on Jim Conley. Conley was first interviewed by the police a few days after the crime. He told police that he could not read or write, and the police wrote him off because they assumed at that time that the murderer was the author of the notes found with the body.

A month later the police learned that Conley could in fact read and write. On comparing his previous letters to the murder notes, it was obvious that he had written the notes—but by that time the police, the prosecutors and the public were deeply committed to the theory that Frank had committed the crime. When Conley said that he had participated in moving the body and staging the crime scene, at the behest of and at the direction of Leo Frank, this simply re-enforced their belief in Frank's guilt. When Conley told a story about these events that didn't make any sense, the police pressured him to re-construct his story to fit the scenario that they had developed. There is no doubt that this occurred. The police testified that it occurred. They testified to it like "When Conley finally confessed to being involved he told us a pack of lies about how things had happened, but after we leaned on him for a couple of days he finally told us the whole truth."

There was a powder keg, and there was a match, and the match was thrown into the powder keg, and then gasoline was sprayed into the fire. The powder keg was the intense emotions of the moment, which were national in scope. The match was the very emotional nature of this case, which was both an innocent-victim case and a Dreyfus case. The act of throwing the match into the powder keg was Dorsey's premature commitment to the guilt of Leo Frank.

And the gasoline was the Northern press. The national press, entering the story later and from a much greater emotional as well as literal distance, immediately saw through the prosecution's case. By the time the Northern press took an interest in the case more facts had emerged. But you now had a Southern press corps that was absolutely convinced of Frank's guilt, and a Northern press that was certain of his innocence.

It was 48 years since the end of the Civil War. Many, many of the witnesses at the trial had lived through the War, and most of the adult population of the South still stung from the humiliations of the South that took place in the reconstruction era. The Northern press patronized the South, writing about the people of Atlanta as if they were a passel of ignorant slobs who had no interest in seeing justice. Amazingly enough, this did not cause the Southerners to back off and take a second look at the evidence against Frank. Belief in Leo Frank's guilt became a touchstone of Southern loyalty. Alonzo Mann had witnessed Conley with Mary Phagan's body in his arms. When he tried to tell his fellow soldiers during World War I that Frank was innocent, he was beaten up by angry comrades.

Modern writers about the case, many of them Jewish, have tended to lean heavily on anti-Semitism as an explanation for what happened. While not denying that there was a strong anti-Semitic streak in America at that time or that this may have been worse in the South than elsewhere, I believe that the same fate might well have befallen Frank had he been an Episcopalian. One of the things that contributed to Frank's conviction was that Jim Conley was extremely convincing on the stand. He told a story that was complex, nuanced, intricate and rich in detail. He stuck to that story through days of intense cross-examination by excellent lawyers. He was a fantastic liar.

To the people of the South in that era, nurtured in the belief that blacks were congenitally stupid, it was inconceivable that a black man could outsmart the police and the jury. Yes, he was an alcoholic. Yes, he was lazy and dishonest. Yes, he was a career criminal. Yes, he was uneducated. Yes, he lived normally in filth and squalor.

But he was also clever. To people taught since birth to see blacks as inferior and of limited intelligence, it was inconceivable that this drunken, filthy, nearly illiterate black janitor could be smarter than most of them—but he was. Leo Frank was condemned more by boomerang racism than by anti-Semitism.

Governor Slaton was a Southern aristocrat, a genteel man whose wife had made her social debut under the sponsorship of Robert E. Lee's daughter. He was leaving office just as Frank's appeal for clemency came to his desk. He knew that if he passed the matter on to his successor Frank would hang. He knew that Frank was innocent. He knew that if he signed the order he would be hated throughout the South, a pariah for the rest of his life. Before he signed the commutation he gave orders for Frank to be secretly moved to a prison farm on the far side of the state, as far away from Atlanta as one could get within the borders of the state. He called out the militia to surround his house, and signed the order commuting Frank's sentence to life in prison. A mob marched on his house, perhaps a thousand strong. The militia turned them back. He left office a few days later, and left the state for many years, returning quietly to Atlanta in the late 1920s.

A fellow prisoner stabbed Leo Frank in the neck, saying later that he had done so because he feared that the mob that came to kill Frank would kill them all. Frank survived that, and was on the road to recovery when he was seized by a group of orderly, determined men who invaded the prison camp on a paramilitary mission. They intended to hang him from the town square in Marietta, near where Mary Phagan had lived. Daylight caught up with them, and they had to stop a few miles short of Atlanta.

A carnival atmosphere swept the site of the hanging. The people who hung him made little effort to conceal their identities. Photos were taken of Frank's body hanging in the air, with other people easily identifiable in the photos. The photos were printed on postcards, which were sold until the 1950s. No one was ever prosecuted for that crime. The Knights of Mary Phagan believed that they had done a good thing. They had delivered justice to the murderer of an innocent young girl. A few weeks later, many or all of the same men re-organized themselves and applied for a charter from the state of Georgia in the name of a long-dormant Southern organization, the Knights of the Ku Klux Klan.

Leo Frank had been president of the B'nai B'rith in Atlanta. The B'nai B'rith had been discussing the formation of an Anti-Defamation League. The murder of Frank led directly to the foundation of the Anti-Defamation League—as it did to the 20th century revival of the Ku Klux Klan—and the Anti-Defamation League was committed from its inception to the effort to stop lynching.

Thus, the Mary Phagan case led very directly to the alliance between Jewish civic leaders and African-American civil rights leaders. That alliance remained strong into the late 1960s, and helped to shape many subsequent crime stories, including the Scottsboro Boys and the 1964 murders of

Chaney, Goodman and Schwerner. Its influence went far beyond that. The support of Jewish leaders for African-American civil rights, organized after the death of Leo Frank, was pivotal throughout the civil rights era. The alliance between Jewish and African-American leaders began to crumble in the late 1960s, for reasons beyond my understanding.

XI

On March 26, 1916, Robert Stroud, incarcerated for an earlier murder, killed Andrew Turner, a guard at the federal prison in Leavenworth, Ks.

A prisoner, as a rule, has limited resources to mount a defense. In 1916 a convicted murderer who killed a prison guard was a good candidate to be executed, probably within weeks. In this case the defendant's mother, Elizabeth Stroud, made great sacrifices to raise a fund for Stroud's defense.

Stroud pleaded innocent, claiming "insanity and self-defense." He was convicted and sentenced to hang. His attorney found an error in the judge's instructions to the jury, however, and the case had to be re-tried.

Now the authorities were really mad, so in the re-trial the prosecuting authorities went to unusual lengths to get a conviction. At this time prisoners were prohibited from testifying in federal court (as well as in most state courts). Most of the witnesses to Stroud's murder of the prison guard were, of course, prisoners. Prosecutors solved this problem neatly enough by arranging to pardon half a dozen prisoners literally as they entered the courtroom, thereby making them no longer prisoners, thus eligible to testify. Stroud's defense witnesses, if he had any, remained prisoners, thus unable to testify on his behalf.

Stroud was convicted again, and sentenced to life in prison—not a bad sentence under the circumstances. Gambling, he decided to fight it out again, and the case went to the Supreme Court. The Supreme Court found unconstitutional the law prohibiting prisoners from testifying, and set aside Stroud's conviction.

Now the authorities were really, *really* mad. For the third time, Stroud went on trial for murdering Turner, and for the third time he was convicted. For the second time, he was sentenced to hang.

By now it was 1920. Once more the Strouds went to battle, and once more the case reached the Supreme Court. This time Stroud lost. The Leavenworth authorities prepared to hang him.

Elizabeth Stroud, however, would not be defeated. Since her only recourse was for the President himself to commute the sentence, she started a letter-writing campaign, imploring the President to save her son. President Woodrow Wilson was bedridden following a stroke, and his wife was conducting the affairs of his office. Moved by Mrs. Stroud's plight, she handed her husband the order commuting the sentence to life in prison, and suggested that he sign. Robert Stroud's sentence was commuted to life in prison.

Frustrated and angry, someone within the prison system ordered that Stroud should serve his life sentence in solitary confinement. Although this order had no legal standing, it became the basis for one of the most remarkable prison stories in American history. We will check in on Robert Stroud—The Birdman of Alcatraz—a few decades down the road.

She liked to be called Grace Roberts, although her true name was Maizie Colbert, and upon her death the newspapers immediately reverted to calling her that. It depended on the newspaper; some called her Maizie, some Grace. She was the daughter of an unskilled laborer, born and raised in a small mining town in northwestern Pennsylvania. At the age of 17 she moved to Philadelphia, where she got into the business of modeling lingerie and modeling for artists. She became known as "The Onyx Girl" and "The Silk Stocking Girl"—onyx, for the black ink that represented her stockings in the engravings that appeared so often in the newspapers. She was said to have the most famous legs in America.

She was in her mid-twenties when she died, hit in the head with a flatiron in her apartment in West Philly and then, ironically, strangled with a silk stocking. She left bloody fingerprints on the walls and curtains as she tried to escape. It was December 30, 1916. She didn't answer phone calls for several hours, and her sister asked the janitor to crawl through a window into her apartment. Her body had been covered with a bed sheet, and a rubber tube from the gas jet put into her mouth in a crude effort to stage a suicide.

It was a nice apartment, upscale. A week earlier she had pawned some of her jewels to buy Christmas presents for her family. Her apartment was stocked with letters and cards from the most prominent men in Philadelphia, politicians and lawyers, actors and businessmen and athletes. Valuables in plain sight ruled out burglary; this was an act of passion. All of those men had to be questioned. One by one the police approached them, delicately, and struck them from the list.

The building superintendent remembered that on the previous day, early Friday morning, he had been pulled from his bed by an irate cab driver who had left a fare near the Wilton Apartments, where Maizie lived, in the middle of the night. The fare told him to wait, but had never returned. The cab driver was owed $19.60.

Police located the cab driver, who gave them a description of the scofflaw, as well as a name, "Bernie." The driver had picked up a handsome young man and two ladies at the Bellevue-Stratford Hotel, and had driven the girls to their home in Germantown, then taken Bernie to the Wilton, where he had disappeared.

Police found a picture signed "Love, Bernie" in Maizie's apartment. The cab driver ID'd the man, who turned out to be Bernard M. Lewis of Pittsburgh. The girls from Germantown, the Kyle sisters, confirmed the identification. They were schoolteachers. Lewis had begun recently to court one of them.

Like Harry K. Thaw, who had murdered Stanford White in 1906, Bernard M. Lewis was the spoiled son of a wealthy Pittsburgh family. Bernie and Harry had known one another back in Pittsburgh, years ago. Lewis' father had made a fortune in coal. Bernie attended Yale from 1897 to 1899, dropped out to begin spending his money in earnest. By 1916 it was gone. He had been arrested in New York City for swindling a woman, and sued in Pittsburgh for bilking a theater promoter. He was separated from his wife, and had dated Grace Roberts a few times, but then who hadn't?

Lewis was registered at the Hotel Adelphia, but had skipped out on his bill before the police arrived. On January 4, 1917, Lewis phoned the Kyle sisters. They were being interviewed by a reporter at the time of the call. Lewis complained that his "business" was being ruined by the Maizie Colbert investigation, and said that he had never met Miss Colbert. They urged him to surrender to police. He said that he would.

Police traced the call back to Atlantic City, where Lewis' family had a summer home. A woman in Atlantic City called police, and told them he was staying at a hotel a few blocks from the summer home. He had borrowed $10 from a hotel maid that morning, and had used it to buy a .22 rifle equipped with a silencer.

On January 5, 1917, one week after the murder, police knocked on his door. They heard a sound inside, like the banging of an inner door. They thought Lewis was headed out of a window. They broke into his room through a bathroom that was shared with an adjoining room. Bernard Lewis was hanging over the edge of the bathtub, his hand still on the trigger of the .22, his brains all over the walls.

One of Maizie Colbert's handkerchiefs was found in the room, caked with dried blood. Lewis' hands and arms were scratched and bloodied, as if Ms. Colbert had fought for her life.

Harry K. Thaw was back in the news. In the murder of Stanford White he had been found innocent by reason of insanity. Declared sane and released in 1915, he had been arrested in the first week of January, 1917—perhaps the day Lewis died—for assaulting a teenager in New York. Thaw was so upset by Lewis' death that he attempted suicide himself, slitting his throat. He was convinced that police had hounded Lewis to his demise. Thaw seriously injured himself in the attempt, but did recover, and went on with his nutty life.

It is my view that the events surrounding the execution of Sacco and Vanzetti represent the American radical movement flaming out. Exploding. Bursting into a million little red-hot pieces like an exploding firework, each fading quickly. I'm not a real historian; there are people who know more about this than I do, so if you're really interested, take their word rather than mine. My view is that the American radical movement began to fall apart at the seams in 1912–1914, around the time of the trials of Clarence Darrow. Prior to that time the radicals had broad and consistently growing public support, and a realistic chance to bring on the revolution they desired. But, in the same general way that the radical movement of the 1960s had broad and growing support until 1968, but became a hollow shell after that, the radical movement of fifty years earlier began to degenerate some years before the revolution in Russia and America's involvement in World War I, then, finding itself marginalized after those events, flamed out violently from 1918 through 1922.

The violence of that era was much more widespread than the violence that accompanied the decay of the 1960s revolution. There were dozens of incidents involving the deaths of scores of people—the anarchist bombings of 1917–1919, the Palmer raids, a race riot in Chicago in 1919, Matewan (1920), a horrific race riot in Tulsa in 1921. There was a large labor strike in

Seattle in 1919, a police strike in Boston leading to the firing and replacement of the entire Boston police force, and there were strikes in many other places. Gary, Indiana, was put under martial law due to a progression of violent incidents.

These events may not be connected by anything more than the *zeitgeist*, something in the wind. The violence of this era was much greater than the violence at the end of the 1960s revolution for three reasons:

1) The nation was more violent,

2) The grievances of the underclass were much more tangible, involving more real suffering and less self-indulgent whining, and

3) The radical leaders of the earlier era were much more accepting of violence as an agent of change than were the 1960s radicals, who were half revolutionaries and half pacifists. The radical leaders of the 1910s were also pacifists, at least in the sense that they wanted nothing to do with the war in Europe, but they were . . . well, *violent* pacifists.

Luigi Galleani was born in Italy in 1861. By age 17 he had adopted the worldview that he was to champion for the rest of his life. He was an anarchist, a revolutionary, and a dedicated opponent of whatever government he happened to live under. He fled Italy in his late teens to avoid prosecution for radical activities, was expelled from France, kicked out of the University of Geneva, arrested back in Italy, escaped from prison, fled to Egypt, left there under threat of extradition, went to England, and finally, in 1901, to New Jersey. Indicted for inciting a riot in New Jersey, he fled to Canada, and was quickly kicked out of Canada. He snuck back into Vermont, settled in Massachusetts and started a newspaper, *Cronaca Sovversiva*, which is Italian for *Subversive Chronicle*.

An excellent writer and a spellbinding speaker if you like that sort of thing, he developed a following in the Italian-American community. His followers were small in number, but they had lots of bombs. *Cronaca Sovversiva* sold a 46-page booklet entitled *Health Is In You!*, which was actually a detailed description of how to build a bomb. In 1916 one of Galleani's followers, a chef named Nestor Dondoglio, poisoned 200 people at a banquet in Chicago. Fortunately he used too much arsenic; everybody vomited up the soup and nobody died, but I'm told that it totally ruined the banquet.

Sacco and Vanzetti were Galleanisti. The Galleanisti had been sending bombs to people that they thought needed bombs since at least 1914. *Cronaca Sovversiva* advocated violence against the rich and powerful, sold

25¢ pamphlets on bomb making, and printed the home addresses of famous capitalists and government officials.

At the outbreak of the First World War Galleani urged his supporters to flee to Mexico, rather than registering for the military draft. Sacco met Vanzetti in Mexico in 1917, at the Galleanist camp. The camp in Mexico was such a miserable hellhole that almost everybody filtered back into the United States after a couple of months. In June, 1917, Luigi Galleani was arrested for conspiracy to obstruct the draft. Outraged, Galleani's supporters began sending bombs to powerful people whom they perceived as their enemies, including J. P. Morgan, John D. Rockefeller, Oliver Wendell Holmes, the U.S. Postmaster General, and the United States Attorney General, A. Mitchell Palmer. On June 2, 1919, a bomb blew out the windows of Palmer's house and his neighbors' houses all up and down the block, killed the bomber, and terrified Palmer's wife and children—not to mention Franklin and Eleanor Roosevelt, who lived across the street and were walking near their house when the bomb went off. Several other bombs exploded the same day in other cities.

The bomber who died planting a bomb at Palmer's house was an editor of *Cronaca Sovversiva*; it was a small publication, and the employees had to double up on their duties. Palmer reacted by ordering a series of aggressive and sometimes extra-legal raids, the Palmer raids, aimed at shutting down the Galleanisti and any other radicals with bombs.

Palmer has received heavy criticism in history for the Palmer raids, but realistically, what would you expect the man to do? The American public overwhelmingly supported the Palmer raids—as they would now under the same circumstances. Do you want him to say, "Go ahead, kill the rich people, kill the Supreme Court justices, kill my wife and kids; this is just the price we pay for our respect for civil liberties"? I don't think so.

The Palmer raids, at some cost to civil liberties, sent the Galleanisti scurrying for cover. Many of them left the country. Galleani himself was deported. It seems an astonishingly moderate penalty under the circumstances. Sacco's alibi for the day of the murders was that he was at that very moment visiting the Italian consulate in Boston, trying to get his papers in order for his return to Italy.

There were several payroll robberies around Boston, and in one of these, down in South Braintree, two payroll guards were killed. The police tracked the car which was involved in the fiasco. They found the car—Mario Buda's car—being held by a third party. Sacco and Vanzetti were among a group of men who tried to pick up the car for Buda. The man holding the car stalled, and the group dispersed. Sacco and Vanzetti were both carrying concealed handguns at the time of their arrest, and pled guilty to carrying concealed weapons. Vanzetti was tried and convicted of an attempted payroll robbery at a shoe company in Bridgewater, Massachusetts, on December 24, 1919, and Sacco and Vanzetti were tried and convicted for a completed payroll robbery at a shoe company in South Braintree, Massachusetts, on April 15, 1920—the crime involving the two dead payroll guards.

Vanzetti's first trial, for the Bridgewater robbery, drew little attention from the media, and attracted only a minimal show of concern from their colleagues on the left. After that first conviction, however, a few leading radicals organized the framework of a defense for Sacco and Vanzetti, bringing in a high-profile activist lawyer named Fred H. Moore.

It was 1920, but Fred Moore could party like it was 1999. Like Earl Rogers and Moman Pruiett, he was an alcoholic, usually divorced, who would go on binges and disappear for days, sometimes in the middle of a trial. Moore, however, was a purposeful partier. He was a public relations savant who invited into his home night after night journalists, radicals, artists, bohemians, and people who could bring booze and broads. With no rules of evidence and no one there to cross-examine the witnesses, he peddled his story unhindered: Sacco and Vanzetti were simple, peace-loving, immigrant peasants who were going about their daily lives when they were jerked rudely off of a streetcar and persecuted for their political beliefs.

On one level this was a total crock; the Nicola Sacco and Bartolomeo Vanzetti of 1919, who saw themselves as cutting-edge revolutionaries, would either have been amused or annoyed to see themselves portrayed as simple men swept up in an onrushing tide of events. It was rather like Che Guevara and Fidel, arrested and put on trial, finding themselves portrayed by their lawyer as Gilligan and the Skipper. At the same time there *is* something to the defense, as it is not really clear that the revolutionaries had anything to do with the South Braintree debacle. I simply do not know whether the South Braintree robbery was a part of Galleani's armed insurrection, or whether the police had half of a case against the anarchists, and they had an armed robbery with two people dead, and when they put them together and added some spackling and pounded it flat, it all sort of fit together. In my view there are solid arguments and serious problems on both sides of the issue.

On September 16, 1920, a car bomb exploded at the corner of Wall and Broad streets in lower Manhattan; actually it was a horse and buggy bomb, but the same concept. The bomb killed 33 people, and is often cited as the worst terrorist act on American soil until the 1990s.

It is now generally believed that this bomb was built and delivered by Mario Buda. Buda's car had been used in the robbery—or so the police claimed—and Buda had gone on the lam after the robbery, sending his friends to pick up his car.

Buda was never found by the American police, eventually re-surfacing in Italy, and it was not until years later that enough facts emerged to make it fairly clear that the Wall Street bomb was Buda's doing, in revenge for the indictment of Vanzetti a few days earlier. Thirty-three dead people. To express his great and righteous anger at the indictment of his friend, he killed more people than Ted Bundy.

There were, then, two very different campaigns being waged on behalf of Sacco and Vanzetti: a campaign of terror, which was a hapless effort to intimidate the government into backing off the prosecution of the anarchists, and a PR campaign, which was an exceedingly clever effort to paint Sacco and Vanzetti as warm and fuzzy day laborers with an unpopular philosophy. Had it been known at the time that the two campaigns were intimately connected, of course, neither could have succeeded.

It is the opinion of many people who have written about the case that Fred Moore might have served his clients better had he paid less attention to the PR campaign and more attention to the boring lawyer stuff. He didn't, in any case, and, on July 14, 1921, Sacco and Vanzetti were convicted of murder. There was no immediate outcry from the public, which still had only a passing interest in what was at that time a local crime story.

Gradually, however, Moore's public relations offensive began to pay off. Finding the American mainstream media unresponsive, Moore peddled his narrative to the fringe and foreign newspapers. There he received a better hearing; the French, after all, think that Leonard Peltier is innocent, and Jerry Lewis is a genius. Like a saucepan of water, the Sacco and Vanzetti story began bubbling at the outer edges of the media, and continued to heat up until a rolling boil had engulfed the whole. The Sacco-Vanzetti defense committee, given seed money by leftists and eccentric dowagers, was eventually pulling in substantial resources, sufficient to fund not only Fred Moore's legal defense but his ever-expanding partying, and eventually his drug habit.

Sacco hated Fred Moore, and Vanzetti wasn't crazy about him, either. Eventually Moore got fired, replaced by a lawyer who was more into the nuts and bolts of the case. Moore whispered to writers, after the executions, that Sacco was guilty in fact. Felix Frankfurter entered the case, eventually becoming the accused' most visible defender.

Sacco and Vanzetti were executed on August 23, 1927, to a chorus of international protest so loud that it has yet to stop echoing. What may safely be said about the case, looking at it strictly as a criminal event, is that no one should be executed on the basis of evidence such as that which was presented at trial against these two men . . . that looked like him, that looked like his car, that looked like his gun.

Cases like Sacco and Vanzetti tend to draw us away from the central focus of our book, which is popular crime. *(We are trying to have a serious discussion about Trash here. Stop distracting us with serious topics.)* Political crime stories tie us into social issues like a ground wire, yet in the way that most people think about famous crimes they are a part of the same subject, and we can't really ignore them. One of my arguments is that crime stories— not political crime stories, but popular crime stories—are much more central to American history than most people understand. When we dismiss these stories as trivial distractions we blind ourselves to the real and serious consequences of these events.

The *political* story surrounding Sacco and Vanzetti, which is the story of the effort to save them from a probably unjust execution . . . that story is often told, and that's the story that people assume is the important one. But the *crime* story, which ended in 1920, may actually have been of more significance to the country. The Galleanisti were a small group of nut cases very much like the Palestinian terrorists of today. Mario Buda is credited with inventing the car bomb. But the violence of the Galleanisti contributed heavily to the anti-immigrant sentiment that culminated in the Johnson-Reed Act of 1924, sharply curtailing immigration. The sudden cutoff of immigration caused a rapidly growing economy to slam into a wall a few years later, helping to bring about one of the central traumas of twentieth century America, the Great Depression. Thus, this little group of violent loonies which included Sacco and Vanzetti contributed very directly to one of the greatest afflictions of the century.

Crime stories are one thread in a dense net that we spread over ourselves in our effort to be safe. They are like doors, locks, security cameras, doormen, police, security guards, banks, courts and prosecutors, jails, fines, probation officers, handguns in a safe by the bed, sign-in procedures and calling your mom when you get there. By propagating crime stories and by taking an interest in them, we are trying to figure out how we can defeat the criminal population.

Dreyfus stories, on the other hand, are almost the opposite: they are about protecting ourselves from our own security apparatus. A Dreyfus case is one in which an innocent person's foot is caught in the net, and he finds himself suddenly dangling from the canopy of the judicial jungle. This reverses the poles. The cops and prosecutors who were previously heroes become persecutors. Our friends become our enemies. People who are above taking an interest in crime stories become interested.

In the American political structure the right advocates Law and Order—thus advocating that more resources be put into the security net—while the left is perennially convinced that our rights are being strangled by the security net. All of this is immature thinking. Pulling the net tighter does not make us more secure; making the net stronger does not make us less free. Exposing the flaws in the criminal justice system does not weaken the criminal justice system. All of that nonsense is just gut-level thinking. Sacco and Vanzetti's innocence does not justify their philosophy; the violence of their friends and associates does not justify their execution for crimes of which they were possibly innocent.

XII

At 8:30 on the evening of September 14, 1922, Eleanor Mills and the Reverend Edward Hall left their respective families in New Brunswick, New Jersey, and headed for a rendezvous in the woods. About 10:15 three or four shots were heard on the outskirts of town. No one paid much attention; it was hunting season. The bodies of Reverend Hall and Mrs. Mills were discovered on the following Saturday, September 16, lying side by side under a crab apple tree.

Reverend Hall, 41 years old, was the pastor of the Episcopal Church of St. John the Evangelist in New Brunswick, a large and successful church. He had married money. In 1911 he had married Frances Stevens, a proper, sturdy woman several years his senior. She was related to the founders of Johnson & Johnson, the Band-Aid makers. The couple lived in a grand house on the finest street in town with Mrs. Hall's brother, Willie Stevens, and several servants.

Eleanor Mills, 32, was a member of St. John's choir, and also was married to the sexton of the church, James Mills. A "sexton," if you were wondering, is kind of a caretaker. A janitor and handyman.

The murders of Hall and Mills exploded immediately into the biggest news story in the nation.

• Within hours, the crab apple tree where the bodies had been discovered had been stripped of its bark by souvenir hunters. Within days, the tree had been completely demolished.

• The scene where the murders occurred was mobbed by so many people that eight to ten vendors set up tents on location, selling popcorn, peanuts, candy and soft drinks to the Lookie Lous.

• Mrs. Hall's brother Willie, a defendant in the subsequent trial, became so famous that his peculiar looks and odd hair would be a touchstone of common reference for people of that generation. A writer of the 1920s would say that a person "looked something like Willie," and people would know that that meant Willie Stevens, just as a 1990s writer might say that somebody "looked a little like Kato."

• Several years after the murders, during a quiet period in the prosecution, a rumor arose that Mrs. Hall was aboard a ship leaving for Europe. Twenty-five to 30 New York reporters stormed the port, searching the ship top to bottom for Mrs. Hall.

The interaction of the media as a part of the story, which many commentators are convinced was invented for the O. J. Simpson trial, was far more overt in the 1920s than it is now. When the case eventually went to trial one newspaper hired Mills' teenaged daughter to "report" on the proceedings. Several reporters were called as witnesses, and numerous items of evidentiary value, including Mrs. Mills' love letters to Hall and a business card of Reverend Hall's which was found next to the bodies, had either been sold or given to newspapers before the case went to trial.

As to why the public became so obsessed with the murders of a philandering New Jersey clergyman and his paramour:

1) Newspapers of the time often chose certain crimes, and exploited them shamelessly, and

2) There was a "competitive panic" among newsmen that drove the selection of stories.

Some newsmen are obsessed with what other newsmen are doing. They are afraid of "missing the story." When one newsman broke furiously for the scene of the crime, that defined it as a major story for the next newsman. When two newspapers headlined the crime, it became crucial for a third to participate. Timing, luck, the absence of anything else to write about on that particular day—it simply happened. Within hours of the discovery of the bodies, editorial decisions were made which caused the murders of Hall and Mills to emerge as the Crime of the Century, at least until the next big case came along.

According to Rex Stout, the investigation which followed showed "a record of sustained official ineptitude, surely never surpassed anywhere." Police failed to secure the scene of the crime, which was ravaged by newsmen and souvenir hunters. The investigation went nowhere for several weeks, until a rural neighbor named Jane Easton or Jane Gibson came forward with a story about having witnessed the crime.

Her story was palpably false—improbable on its face, at variance with several of the known facts, and belatedly introduced by a woman who was such a notorious liar that it proved impossible to figure out what her name actually was. Still, it was the best hoss the prosecutors had, so they rode it. The press took to calling Mrs. Gibson the Pig Woman, in part because she kept pigs, but also, wink wink, because she kind of looked like a pig. The Pig Woman alleged that, on the night of the murders, she had heard someone on her property. Since she had been troubled by thefts, she grabbed a shotgun, saddled up her mule, and set off in pursuit. She lived half a mile from the murder scene. As she drew near to the area she heard voices. Tying up her mule, she crept close. Hiding in the shadows, she saw two men and a woman—Mrs. Hall and her two brothers—murder the lovers.

She retreated to her house but, not content with the first performance, returned to the clearing in the middle of the night. Amazingly enough, she claimed, so did Mrs. Hall. Mrs. Gibson saw her back there again about 12:30, wailing at the corpse of her departed husband. Prosecutors took the Pig Woman's story and the rest of their "evidence" to a grand jury, which refused to indict.

And there the case lay, for several summers. In 1926 a man named Arthur Riehl filed for annulment of his marriage. His wife had been a maid of the Halls at the time of the tragedy. Riehl alleged in his annulment petition that the girl had had a sexual relationship with the minister and had knowledge of the murders, which she had concealed from him at the time of their marriage.

These fanciful allegations were withdrawn before they could be tested in court. It is believed that a newspaper had paid Mr. Riehl to say ridiculous things for the purpose of re-starting the story. They succeeded. The governor of New Jersey, embarrassed by years of inaction and ineptitude in the sensational case, appointed a Special Prosecutor to pursue the matter. The Special Prosecutor, Alexander Simpson, took it back to a grand jury. This grand jury went along with the game, and Mrs. Hall and her brothers were brought to trial on November 3, 1926.

More than 100 reporters covered the trial. The Pig Woman had a stroke in the middle of the trial, and was carried in to testify from a hospital bed. There was no real evidence against the accused persons, and they were acquitted after a long and painful trial, one of the sorriest spectacles in the history of American justice.

William Kunstler, emerging as a national figure, wrote a book about the case in 1964. His book, *The Minister and the Choir Singer,* became a major best seller, and re-introduced the case to another generation of Americans. The book is fairly good, although I couldn't really explain why it sold as many copies as it did.

Kunstler proposes a solution to the mystery, which is that the KKK did it. Kunstler was the lead attorney for the civil rights movement, personal lawyer for Martin Luther King, and his explanation is obviously a product of his own experiences, having nothing to do with the facts of the case. Kunstler argues that the KKK was responsible for a series of crimes with many elements in common with the Hall-Mills case.

But first, "organizations" do not commit murder. To say that the KKK committed the murder, even if it was true, is not really a solution. Individuals commit murder, sometimes within organizations. And second, the "pattern crimes" that Kunstler cites have almost nothing in common with the murders of Hall and Mills. The crimes were mostly committed against black people living hundreds or thousands of miles from New Jersey. Kunstler's theory has *nothing* going for it.

The suggestion that Mrs. Hall and her relatives committed the crime ranks, if anything, even lower on a probability scale, having been tried in court and decisively defeated. The state devoted vast resources to the attempt to prove that these people committed the crime. They failed not merely to win conviction, but to discover any real evidence against those they had accused. Most of the case the state put on is so far-fetched and improbable that it should never have been introduced in court.

So what does that leave? Essentially two possibilities. First, the murders may have been committed by a thief or thieves. Reverend Hall had $50 or more in cash on him; this money disappeared, as did a valuable gold watch. Kunstler dismisses the theory that the murders were committed by thieves because

a) the bodies appeared to have been carefully arranged after death,

b) Mrs. Mills' throat had been slashed, apparently after she was dead, and

c) the valuable gold watch never surfaced.

I don't think that the theory of a robbery/murder can be dismissed. The autopsy work, like everything else connected with the investigation, was poorly done, and I wouldn't bet big money that Mrs. Mills' throat was cut after she was dead. She may well have screamed (there is some evidence that she did), and a thief may have sliced her throat to shut her up, seconds before his partner shot her. It is not certain that the bodies were "arranged" at all; they may simply have fallen back, and the thieves may have pulled their arms out while searching the bodies for valuables. The gold watch was certainly stolen, but it never surfaced regardless of who took it, so I can't see how that indicates one scenario rather than another.

The Hall-Stevens defense team suggested during the trial that more attention should have been paid to the dead woman's husband, James Mills. We will never know who committed the crime, but the three most obvious indicators of whom we should suspect all point to Mills, rather than the Hall family, as the more likely assailant.

First, Reverend Hall was killed by a single bullet to the head, while Mrs. Mills' body showed the marks of excessive and redundant violence. In a modern investigation this would direct attention to James Mills, since this is a sign of anger toward one victim, as opposed to the other.

Second, the letters which were found scattered near the body had been written by Mrs. Mills, it is agreed, *but had never been mailed.* According to Kunstler, the letters "were written by Mrs. Mills to Hall while he was on vacation . . . during his four-week absence Eleanor assuaged her loneliness by writing letters which she never intended to mail. On the night of September 14 she had decided to deliver them to her lover."

That's possible, but Hall had returned to New Brunswick a month earlier, and the couple had arranged numerous meetings since that time. The last known place where the letters were was in the Mills' house. How did they get to the murder scene? It is equally plausible that James Mills found them in his house, boiled into a rage, committed the murders, and threw the letters over the bodies.

Third, Edward Hall's parting from his house was, according to all accounts, peaceful. He said he had to go see Mrs. Mills about her medical bills, in his role as her pastor, and he left. The parting of Mrs. Mills from her husband was accompanied by sharp words, overheard by a neighbor.

"Where are you going?" asked James Mills.

"Follow me and find out," responded Eleanor.

James Mills was interviewed by the police several times, and interviewed for several hours. He withstood the interrogation, and never became a prime suspect in the case, in large part because he didn't strike anyone as a killer. Damon Runyon described James Mills as "a man bullied by his children and by all the world, a man anybody could push out of their way without protest from him, a harmless, dull little fellow." William Kunstler dismissed him as "a man of extremely limited talents, who looked upon the world about him with dull and uncomprehending eyes, [and who] was thoroughly dominated, first by his wife and then by his daughter. It is highly likely that not only was he completely unconcerned by his wife's romance with Hall, but that he welcomed the limited economic benefits it brought."

Well, let's take a little multiple-choice test here. First question, which do you find more believable,

a) that James Mills truly appreciated the fact that his wife was screwing the minister, because it enabled him to hold on to his piddly little job as a sexton, or

b) that James Mills, despite his outward acceptance, seethed quietly at his wife's infidelity?

Second question, which is a better principle on which to build an investigation,

a) ignore any potential suspects who seem too timid to have committed such a horrible crime, or

b) pay close attention to the evidence of the crime scene?

Is there some sort of law that mousy, ineffectual people don't commit murder in New Jersey? Mrs. Hall called the police the morning after the murders to ask if there had been any reported "casualties." The state tried to use this fact against her at her trial. But James Mills *didn't* contact the police. He said that it was common for his wife to disappear for a couple of days at a time—a remarkable claim for which there is no corroboration.

Mills initially denied knowing that his wife was involved with Mr. Hall, but a neighbor of the Millses, whose telephone they routinely borrowed because they didn't have one, told newsmen that the affair had been the subject of frequent loud arguments between the couple, several of which she had overheard.

Mills has an alibi, sort of. He was seen on his porch by another neighbor, about 9:00, working on some window-boxes. He was seen there again by his son, about 10:30.

The neighbor, however, means almost nothing, because that's 75 minutes before the crime, and he was only a twenty-minute walk from the scene of the crime. The event she witnessed—Mills on his front porch, working on a window-box—didn't become significant until at least two days later, and the event itself is so trivial that it would normally be difficult to say for sure whether such a thing happened on Wednesday or Thursday or a week ago last Tuesday.

That leaves Mills' presence on the porch depending on the story of Mills' son, who was

a) a relative, and

b) twelve years old at the time.

Danny Mills was visiting his aunt on the evening of the murders, and recalled that he got home about 10:30. But who knows whether it was really at 10:30 or 10:45 or 11:00? The time of the crime, for that matter, is not tightly fixed. Although shots were heard in that area about 10:15, the couple may well have been murdered later in the night. For all practical purposes, James Mills doesn't have an alibi.

Mills doesn't have an alibi, but the state also doesn't have a case. Everything followed from the failure to secure the crime scene, but some crimes are destined never to be solved. Even if the police hadn't made a terrible mess of it, there's no guarantee they would ever have found the culprit.

Roy and Ray D'Autremont were twins, born in 1900 in Oregon. Ray was sent to prison in his teens for some sort of labor union violence. When he first got out, Roy and Ray went to Chicago to try to get in on the bootlegging which was making power brokers of common thugs. Finding themselves unwelcome and unable to horn in on the action, they slunk back to Oregon and enlisted their younger brother in the implementation of a clever plan that Ray had worked out while he was in prison. It is often described as the last great train robbery of the American West.

There was a tunnel on a mountain near where they had lived as children, near Ashland, Oregon. The trains labored slowly up the side of the mountain, and then were required to test their brakes before the downgrade. The plan was to board the train on the brake-stop, then to force it to a more permanent stop by setting off dynamite in the tunnel in front of it. The rumor was that the train carried $500,000 in gold.

What the twin masterminds had failed to consider was that when you set off a lot of dynamite in a tunnel, you have so much dust and debris flying around that you can't see your hand in front of your face. Also, you can't get the train out of the tunnel. Also, there apparently wasn't any gold; apart from those things it was a very clever plan. They panicked, killed the four men who were the crew of the train, and escaped without a penny.

The blast from the dynamite was heard miles away—yet another attribute of their plan that the criminal geniuses had failed to anticipate. A railroad crew thought that the engine had exploded, and a rescue crew rushed to the scene, where they discovered the bodies of the crewmen and various items left behind by the overplanned robbery—a revolver, a battery-powered detonator, a pair of burlap shoe covers soaked in creosote that had apparently been intended to prevent dogs from tracking their scent, and a neatly folded pair of overalls that someone had apparently intended to escape in.

Months passed. Local and state police, unable to do anything with the clues, finally sent the overalls to a man named Edward Heinrich, who was in charge of the forensic laboratory in Berkeley, California. Heinrich, in a landmark of forensic research, reported to the astonished locals that the overalls belonged to a left-handed lumberjack in his early twenties, about 5'10", 165 pounds, light brown hair, very meticulous in his personal habits—left-handed, because of the wear and tear patterns in the pockets and the way the overalls had been buttoned; a lumberjack, because the overalls were embedded with tiny fragments of wood and because the grease found in the left-hand pocket turned out to be the natural residue of fir trees; 5'10", 165 pounds because the overalls would fit a man of that size; light brown hair because of hairs found on the overalls; early twenties because of the condition of the hair; and careful in his appearance because of fingernail clippings found trapped in the seams.

He also reported that the man rolled his own cigarettes, and there was a scrap of paper found in a pocket. It was squashed up and had been washed blank and didn't appear to be useful, but when Heinrich stained it with iodine and put it under exactly the right spectrum of light, it turned out to be a mail receipt for a package that had been delivered to a Roy D'Autremont of Eugene, Oregon.

Roy D'Autremont turned out to be a left-handed lumberjack in his early twenties, 5'10", 165 pounds, light brown hair, rolled his own cigarettes, very careful about his appearance. He also had not been seen since the train robbery—nor had his brother Ray or his other brother, Hugh.

Arrest warrants were issued and a high-profile investigation followed, but enough time had passed to allow the D'Autremonts to establish themselves under new identities. They remained free men until 1927, when a sergeant in the United States Army identified Hugh D'Autremont as a soldier serving in Manila. From there they were able to find the brothers, working in a steel mill in Ohio. All three confessed, and were sentenced to life in prison. Roy went crazy in prison, and a lobotomy was performed on him in 1949. Hugh developed stomach cancer, and was paroled shortly before his death in 1958. Ray's sentence was commuted by the governor of Oregon in 1972, and he lived peacefully, painting and writing, until his death in 1984.

In the third week of February, 1927, as they lay abed in the Waldorf Hotel, Ruth Snyder and Henry Judd Gray formed a plan to dispose of the lady's husband.

They decided on a sash weight.

Ruth and Albert Snyder worked together in the art department of *Motor Boating* magazine. He was the art editor, fourteen years her senior; she was his assistant. They had a nine-year-old daughter, a house on Long Island, and a bad marriage. At 32, she liked to get out on the town. He didn't. They fought. According to Ruth, Albert had threatened repeatedly to throw her out of the house.

She was introduced to Henry Gray at a fashionable New York City restaurant. They violated the Seventh Commandment and the Eighteenth Amendment with equal energy. As Henry would tell it, he drank heavily almost every time they were together—in Kingston, in Schenectady, in Albany and Amsterdam, in Watertown and Syracuse, in Booneville and Gloversville, at the Snyders' home in Queens Village. A traveling corset salesman, he knew every gin joint and cheap hotel in the Hudson Valley. She once arranged to make a ten-day trip with him, and try them out.

She began to talk about offing the old man. Snyder was insured for a small fortune, with a double indemnity clause in some of the contracts. Henry kept saying it was up to her. She had tried several times to do the job, once with sleeping powder, once with bichloride of mercury. She tried gas; she tried tampering with the brakes. Nothing easy seemed to work.

They decided on a sash weight. A window weight, you know; one of those heavy things that was used to balance a window. They had backup plans.

On March 4 Henry went to an out-of-town hardware store, and bought a sash weight and some picture wire. He ventured out to Long Island on March 7, murder in mind; Mrs. Snyder sent him away, saying that the time was not right. (This incident provided the basis for the double images in one of the classic fictionalizations of the Gray/Snyder murder, *The Postman Always Rings Twice*.)

On the evening of March 19, 1927, a Saturday night, Mr. and Mrs. Snyder went to a party given by some neighbors. The hostess remembered that Mrs. Snyder had hardly anything to drink, but was careful to see that her husband was well lubricated. She had left the front door unlocked, and a side door as well, should that prove to be more handy. Gray hid in a spare bedroom.

Ruth had left a small bottle of whiskey for him. He drank that, then looked around for more. He found another quart, and drank most of it.

Sometime about midnight the Snyders came home. Albert fell asleep on his bed. Mrs. Snyder met Gray in the spare room, and kissed him. Gray set upon Snyder with the sash weight.

Here their stories begin to part. Gray said that after he struck one or two initial blows, he passed the hardware to his woman, who belabored him with it. This was his term—she belabored him with the sash weight. She denied this. In any case, Mr. Snyder sat up in bed, and the three began a drunken, mortal combat. Gray had a handkerchief soaked in chloroform, which he pressed to Snyder's face until the unfortunate man passed out. One of them put the picture wire around his neck and wound it tight, to ensure that he would not recover.

Afterward they went downstairs and drank some more whiskey, and talked about the perfect crime. They pulled out some drawers and dumped stuff on the floors to fake a robbery. Gray walked to the railway station a little before dawn, where he caught a taxi back to Manhattan, leaving Ruth bound with tape. When her daughter came downstairs in the morning Ruth sent her next door to summon the police.

The police had a million questions, seemed like obvious questions to them. How had the burglar entered the house? What were all these empty liquor bottles doing around, and isn't that whiskey on your breath? Did he tie you up first, and then go commit the assault, or the other way around? Did you scream? Is that blood? What's this railroad ticket we found in the spare bedroom? Was your husband insured? Where did the picture wire come from? Was the burglar carrying chloroform and picture wire with him?

They had more questions for the neighbors. The neighbors had some stories to tell. Within hours, Ruth Snyder and Henry Judd Gray were both under arrest, both singing like troubadours, and each blaming the other for the series of events which had swung tragically out of control.

They were put on trial about a month later. It was probably the most pub-licized murder trial in American history up to that point, surpassing even the Hall-Mills case, setting a standard not to be unsettled until the Lindbergh baby trial. One hundred twenty newspaper reporters arrived on the first day of the trial, many of them with secretaries; there were also "novelists, preachers, playwrights, fiction writers" and miscellaneous celebrities. The case captured the imagination of New York theater crowd, and many of the most prominent actors, directors, writers and producers of the day attended the trial.

The case was, essentially, the Amy Fisher affair of its time. As in the Amy Fisher case, two lovers had an inconvenient spouse who became the target of violence. As in the Amy Fisher case, there was no real mystery to be resolved; the case appealed more as a soap opera than as a puzzle. The "mystery" of Snyder/Gray was in sorting out the charges and counter-charges of the culprits, the chronology of villainy, the balancing of blame between two people neither of whom was clothed by a wisp of innocence.

The jury deliberated less than two hours, and sentenced them both to the electric chair. They were executed on January 12, 1928. A newspaper reporter—one of twenty witnesses selected from 1500 applicants—smuggled in a tiny camera, strapped to his leg, and took a picture of Ruth Snyder at the moment the electricity surged through her.

James M. Cain's *Double Indemnity*, a popular novel that became the basis of another classic film noir, was also based very directly on the Snyder/Gray case. Damon Runyon covered the trial for King Features Syndicate. He wrote brilliantly, at the peak of his powers, though on occasion his descriptions seem over the top. His articles about the trial were put together by Richard Glyn Jones for the 1987 anthology *Solved* (Famous Mystery Writers on Classic True-Crime Cases), and these provide the most readable account of the crime that is, or might be, still in print.

No other crime has been so often retold and re-invented by Hollywood. The 1981 film *Body Heat*, although a seventh-generation copy of the original, bears an unmistakable debt to the Snyder/Gray phenomenon. Ruth Snyder was not quite a beautiful woman, but she was handsome; a movie star could play her. Judd Gray was not quite William Hurt, but he suited the part of the rogue lover. That frantic, bloody struggle in the middle of the night, a small girl asleep in a nearby room—that was everything the movies made it out to be, and something awfully more.

The four most famous crimes of the 1920s, in order of their contemporary news coverage, were 1) the Snyder/Gray case, 2) the Hall/Mills case, 3) the

Loeb/Leopold "Thrill Killing," and 4) the Sacco and Vanzetti case. I have nothing to say about Loeb and Leopold, and perhaps you'll forgive me for skipping that one. There was also the Scopes Monkey Trial, but . . . that's not a real crime story.

Setting aside Sacco and Vanzetti, there is something fantastically light-weight about these stories. It is not that America lacked serious crime. Organized crime was dramatically more organized in 1929 than in 1920. There were 72 mob murders in Chicago in 1928. On February 14, 1929, seven men were lined up against a wall and gunned down in a garage in Chicago—the St. Valentine's Day Massacre. In New York City Albert Anastasia organized Murder, Inc. It has been estimated that in their ten years of operation Murder, Inc., killed 400 to 700 people.

Those were serious stories, but I am trying to write here about the serious consequences of the trivial events, the tabloid stories. Tabloid stories have been around at least since 1700 and are omnipresent around us today, but in some sense they reached their apogee in the 1920s, culminating, of course, in the Lindbergh case in the early 1930s. It was the golden age of something horrible. All of the big cities in 1920 had multiple daily newspapers. These newspapers competed with one another to nakedly exploit horrific human tragedies for their own profit.

The great crime stories of the 1910–1920 era were vitally connected to the struggle for the nation's soul. They had to do—almost all of them—with rich against poor, with labor against capital, with radicals against the establishment, with the South against the North, with the pacifists against the militants at the time of the Great War, with immigrants against natives. By 1922, somehow, most of that had simply vanished, at least from the crime stories. Looking back on it from 90 years later it seems almost like a miracle, as if all of these rifts were somehow suddenly healed by the nation's prosperity. Things somehow jumped into packages. Labor split off from radicalism; fiery labor agitators were replaced by tough labor union professionals. Crime became organized and professional and horribly lethal, while "journalism" learned to package and market cheap, tawdry stories of cheating wives and spoiled rich kids who murdered for fun. The bomb makers and the bomb throwers were brought under control, not to resurface until the 1990s. I wish I could tell you what happened to America in 1921, but the truth is that I do not understand it, and I haven't seen the evidence that anyone does.

XIII

T he descriptions given to police in criminal investigations could be sorted into six levels.

A **Level One** description is a description that would eliminate 90 to 99% of the population, but might include 1 to 10%.

You may ask why we start at 90%. If it doesn't eliminate 90% of the population, it's not even a description. Just saying "it was a black female" . . . that eliminates 90% of the population, since only about 7% of the American population is black females. Just saying "it was a tall young man" eliminates 90% of the population, since only 50% of the population is male, 70% of the males are either children or men too old to reasonably be described as "young men" and only half of the remaining men can reasonably be described as "tall."

A Level One description is of use to the police in certain limited situations, given some other information. Suppose, for example, that a crime is committed by a tall young man in a parking lot, and we can surmise that it may have occurred in a dispute over a parking space. If the police can get a record of the cars in the parking lot, they can find those cars belonging to tall young men. It might give them ten candidates to have committed a crime, rather than fifty.

In general, however, a Level One description is of little or no use in a police investigation, and there is almost no such thing as a situation in which a Level One description is helpful in a trial. A Level One description would include 100 to 1,000 people, even in a small town of 10,000.

A **Level Two** description is a description that excludes 99 to 99.9% of the population, but includes somewhere between one person in a hundred, and one person in a thousand. A Level Two description is often of some use in a police investigation, but is still of very limited use in earning a conviction. Suppose, for example, that the person running from the scene is a black teenaged male, short and very overweight. That's a Level Two description. Black Americans are 12–14% of the population. Teenagers are something less than 20% of that, thus 2–3% of the entire population. Half of those are male. Divide that by half again, to represent those who are shorter than average, and by half again, to represent those who might plausibly be described as overweight . . . you're in the middle of the range, 1% to .1%. But at the same time, there are too many short, black male teenagers for the police to identify them all and question them all.

Suppose that you know that the crime was committed by a white male about 30 years of age, short, in very good condition, with a moustache and acne. Again, that's a Level Two description. About 40–45% of the population is white males. Roughly 10% of those are people who could plausibly be described as "about 30 years of age," so that gives us 4–5% of the total population. Probably half of those are in good condition, so that is, let us say, 3% (we always estimate on the high side). Something less than half of those are men with moustaches, and something less than half of those have acne. You're probably talking one person in 300, one in 500, who could meet that description.

That gives the police somewhere to start, but again, you can't really convict someone of a crime because he matches a Level Two description. On the 100-point scale that I outlined before, matching a Level Two description might be counted for one point. It's there and you can consider it, but . . . it's not really anything.

Why are we doing this, you might ask? It is my experience, reading crime books, that people don't think clearly about this issue. I have often seen cases in which the police got carried away with the fact that someone matched a Level Two description, and used that as a basis to start building a case around a suspect. I have occasionally seen cases in which there were very good descriptions of a suspect, which nobody paid any attention to because, apparently, nobody stopped to think through the issue of "How specific is this description?" I have often, in crime books, seen very good descriptions dismissed by the writer as loose or general descriptions. It seemed to me that it might be useful to sort descriptions into "Levels of specificity" in order to think more clearly about descriptions.

A **Level Three** description, then, would be a description that excludes 99.9 to 99.99% of the population, but includes between one person in a thousand and one person in ten thousand. These would be examples of Level Three descriptions:

• Suspect was described as a Caucasian male, 50 to 55 years of age, tall, athletic, blue eyes, gray hair, driving an older model pickup truck.

• Suspect was described as a Caucasian female, 20–23 years of age, brown hair, brown eyes, about 5'7", large breasted, extremely attractive, piercing in the nose and large tattoo on lower back.

• Suspect was described as a Hispanic female, 45 to 50 years of age, extremely short, somewhat overweight, perhaps 4'11" and 130 pounds, bushy eyebrows, wears glasses, blue painted fingernails.

She wears glasses and paints her fingernails, but what if she switches to contacts and pink paint?

Some elements of a description are "hard," meaning that they can't readily be changed, and some are "soft," meaning that they can easily be altered. It's a Level 3 (Soft) description, or a Level 2 (Hard) description, meaning that it's a Level 2 description based on the things that can't easily be changed.

A Level Three description is often of some value to police, and is sometimes of real consequence in a trial. Still, a person can't reasonably be convicted of a crime because he or she matches a Level Three description. On a 100-point scale, matching a Level Three description is perhaps worth 3 to 5 points toward a conviction.

A **Level Four** description is a description that would exclude 99.99 to 99.999% of the population, but might still include between one person in ten thousand and one in a hundred thousand. These would be examples of Level Four descriptions:

• Male Caucasian, 40–45 years of age, 5 foot 2 to 5 foot 5, thin, long, sandy-colored hair, large glasses, large, square face, smokes cigarettes. Looks a little like John Denver.

• African-American male in his 20s, average height, muscular build, shaved head, several gold teeth, gold earring in left ear, prominent scar on his neck. Very deep voice with perhaps a trace of a Jamaican accent.

A Level Four description should be enough, in most cases, to bring the police to your door, but should not be enough to convict you, absent other information. If there's a Level Four description of a criminal and you match the description, that's probably 20% of what is needed to convict—thus, 20 points on a 100-point scale.

A **Level Five** description is a description that would exclude 99.999% of the population or more, and would include one person in 100,000 or less. A Level Five description *can* be built out of a long string of elements such as those above, but more often contains one element that is fairly unique—a missing finger, a tattoo of a horse, a white streak in the hair, one green nipple, something like that. I remember reading a story about a basketball player who tried to hold up a grocery store in a small town in the Midwest, wearing a mask, and was recognized by the clerk.

"Leonard?" asked the clerk.

"How'd you know it was me?" asked the puzzled post player. He was seven foot tall.

Even a Level 5 description, by itself, isn't or shouldn't be enough to convict you of the crime, but it puts you on the defensive. If you match a Level Five Hard description, you're going to need an alibi.

A **Level Six** description is a description that applies to only one person. Your fingerprints are a Level 6 description. Your DNA is a Level 6 description. If you are seen at the crime scene by a person who knows you and recognizes you, that's a Level 6 description. A Level 6 description is an identification.

A police investigation, in many cases, starts with a Level One or Level Two description, and tries to build onto it until it becomes a Level Six description, a positive identification.

Charles Lindbergh was the most famous man in the world, or if he wasn't, at least I have copious references for the error. The first generation of airplanes had made local heroes of local fliers. In 1927 Lindbergh, alone, took a flimsy airplane across a great ocean, and by so doing became a hero on both sides of the Atlantic. The feat required intelligence, imagination, and tremendous courage, as several men had perished in similar efforts. Lindy didn't, and the world adopted him. Every stride of his shoes was tomorrow's news.

And he married Anne Morrow, and they had a baby, and somebody stole the baby, took the baby into the cold night and murdered him. March 1, 1932. A late-winter drizzle was falling in the Sourland Mountains of New Jersey, where Lindbergh had built a retreat, hidden close to New York City on 500 acres of private land. A few minutes past nine o'clock, Lindbergh heard something crack. "What was that?" he asked his wife. She had heard nothing.

He had heard, it is thought, the breaking of a ladder. Someone used a makeshift ladder to climb into the nursery on the second floor. As the kidnapper was leaving, or perhaps as he was entering, a rung snapped. A note was left in the nursery:

Dear Sir

Have 50000$ ready 25000$ in 20$ bills 15000$ in 10$ bills and 10000$ in 5$ bills After 2–4 days we will inform you were to deliver the mony We warn you for making anyding public or for notify the police The child is in gut care Indication for all letters are singnature and three holes

The blue-and-red three-hole design, kept secret through the negotiations, would identify the kidnappers. A homemade three-part extension ladder was recovered near the house. Four things were initially surmised about the kidnapper(s):

1) They had used the ladder to enter the nursery.

2) The kidnapper was either German, or pretending to be German. He wrote the dollar sign after the amount of money, as the Germans do, and used the German word "gut" instead of the English "good."

3) The crime was not the work of a sophisticated criminal enterprise. An experienced group of criminals would have asked for more than $50,000. They probably would not have left a handwritten note. They probably would not have abandoned evidence at the scene.

4) The kidnapper(s) may have had inside information. They apparently knew where the nursery was. They apparently knew that the Lindberghs would be there on that evening. The Lindberghs normally spent Tuesday evening at the home of Anne Morrow's parents, closer to New York City; they had changed their plans at the last moment.

Suspicion fell immediately upon the household staff. A follow-up note—we will call it the second note—was delivered with the mail on March 4; it raised the ransom demand to $70,000.

There followed an awful roar from the nation's media, which descended on Hopewell, New Jersey, in almost unimaginable numbers, and a terrible stillness from the kidnappers. For several days, while uncounted words were published in speculation, nothing was heard from the men who held the baby.

Enter John Condon, stage left. Dr. Condon was a seventy-two-year-old physical education instructor; he lectured at Fordham on pedagogy, which at that time was not a criminal offense. Dr. Condon was a physical marvel, a tower of strength and energy, an inveterate writer of letters to the editor, and an incurable blowhard. When the Lindbergh baby was kidnapped Dr. Condon got very exercised about the subject, and decided to let off steam in his traditional way: he wrote a letter to the editor. He offered to act as an intermediary between the kidnappers and the Lindberghs, and also to put up his life savings—$1,000—to augment the reward. The *Bronx Home News* printed the letter as they had printed several of his previous efforts.

To the astonishment of everybody, the kidnappers answered. They sent him a note; OK, you can be the intermediary, signature with three overlapping holes. Condon was dumbfounded, didn't know what to do at first. After a few hours he called the Lindbergh estate. It was agreed that he would act on behalf of the Lindberghs throughout the negotiations with the men who held the baby.

They built a special box in which to send the money to the kidnappers, a box that could be easily recognized. Before the money was ready a note came, delivered by a cab driver, directing Condon to a rendezvous in a cemetery. Condon went, without the money. The cab driver provided the first description of a suspect in the crime. The man Condon met in the cemetery fit the description: light complexioned, German or Scandinavian. The man gave his name as John—Cemetery John, they began to call him. Condon had taken the pins, by which the baby had been fastened to the bed. He asked Cemetery John what they were. The man recognized them immediately. Then he asked a curious question.

"Would I burn if the baby is dead?"

The baby was not dead, he assured Condon. The baby was in good hands, gut hands. He presented himself as a go-between, a part of a large and well-organized plot. Condon demanded to see the baby. John said he couldn't allow that, but would send the baby's sleeping suit.

The garment came in the mail, and was identified by Colonel Lindbergh as the genuine article.

The $70,000 was put together. A series of tense messages was sent back and forth, Condon sending his messages through the *Bronx Home News*. He used the code name Jafsie, from his initials, JFC. A second rendezvous was arranged for Saturday, April 2. Condon again met John in the cemetery. Lindbergh stood nearby in the shadows; he heard the man call out "Hey Doctor." A pause. "Hey Doctor, over here!"

Condon demanded the baby. John said he couldn't deliver the baby until he had the money. Condon said $70,000 was too much; Lindbergh could only raise $50,000. John agreed to accept fifty. An exchange was made; John got $50,000; Condon got a set of directions, where he could find the baby.

The directions proved worthless.

Directing the investigation for the state of New Jersey was Colonel Norman Schwarzkopf, the father of the man who would direct American troops against Iraq. There was at least one other line of negotiations still open, with another group claiming to hold the baby. Schwarzkopf investigated the other line of negotiations and pronounced the information there worthless. Lindbergh, desperate to recover his son, continued to pursue the alternative negotiations.

On May 12, 1932, the baby's body was found less than two miles from the Lindbergh house, half-buried in the spring mud.

The household staff had been subject to relentless police scrutiny. Every one of them, everyone they knew, everyone they had contact with became a potential subject of the investigation. Violet Sharpe, a maid of the Morrow family (Anne Lindbergh's family), had had a date with a mysterious stranger the evening of the kidnapping, a man she seemed to know almost nothing about, and a man that the police were at first unable to identify and interview. It was a double date, she said; she had gone out with some friends and this other guy. She wouldn't say who the friends were. This was naturally regarded as suspicious, and Violet Sharpe was questioned repeatedly by the police, and told that she was suspected of involvement in the crime. Informed that she was to be questioned again on June 10, she committed suicide on the evening of June 9, 1932.

At the time, this seemed likely to break the case open, and her circle of friends and acquaintances was investigated even more intensely in the following days. Eventually, however, the friends and the date were identified, and it turned out that her story was true. She had refused to talk about it because a) she was engaged to another man, and b) the date may have been a little more interesting than she wanted to talk about. It is painful to have one's secrets exposed. It is painful to see one's relationships crumble. It is stressful to be a suspect in a criminal investigation. It is stressful to be at the epicenter of a media storm. Putting it all together, it was more than the high-strung woman could deal with. Numerous other people associated with the case also committed suicide over the next decade.

Brief digression. On June 30, 1860, a four-year-old boy named Saville Kent was taken from a wealthy family in England, near Trowbridge. Like little Charles Lindbergh, the boy was taken from his crib and brutally murdered in the middle of the night; it is one of the most famous crimes of 19th century England.

Charles Lindbergh's nursemaid—to whom he was reportedly more attached than his own mother—was a woman named Betty Gow. Saville Kent's nursemaid, to whom he was similarly attached, was a woman named Elizabeth Gough. The two names are really the same; "Betty" is a nickname of "Elizabeth," and "Gow" and "Gough" could be variant spellings of the same name. Like Betty Gow, Elizabeth Gough was suspected of the crime and was mercilessly harassed by police and by public speculation, in both cases for no real reason other than her proximity to the crime. It seems so odd, that these two women who really have the same name play identical roles in somewhat similar crimes.

At this point (returning to New Jersey) the narrative of the Lindbergh kidnapping breaks into a myriad of small strands, forming a kind of medieval tapestry with a mind-boggling array of storylines. There were extortion plots playing off the kidnapping, some more famous than others. There were false arrests, many of them making headlines. There was the exceedingly strange story of Ellis Parker, a famous private detective who commissioned a band of thugs and kidnapped an innocent man, holding him prisoner until he confessed to kidnapping the Lindbergh baby. Parker and his cohorts went to jail, but no information about the crime was produced.

There have been dozens or hundreds of books and thousands of magazine articles written about the Lindbergh kidnapping and/or related subjects. The case was so famous in its time that everyone who was touched by the case became something of a celebrity, his life changed forever after. If a cop worked on the investigation in some meaningful capacity, that fact alone was enough to make the memoirs of his career publishable after he had retired. If a journalist covered the trial, and hundreds of journalists did, that made his or her memoirs publishable. The maze of issues into which the case divides, as it moves forward in time, is almost without limit.

Seventy-five years later, this remains true: No other police investigation in the history of the country was ever so extensive. Maybe the 9/11 investigation. Massive resources were invested in solving the Lindbergh kidnapping, by the New Jersey State Police, the FBI, the Treasury Department, every local police department, county sheriff, every cop on the beat, every ambitious private detective with a spare moment, by the press, and by the public. The story never really died down, even in the two years when nothing happened; it required but the faintest aroma of a breakthrough to pitch it back onto the front page.

One of the most clever things was the work of Arthur Koehler, an expert on wood, to trace the materials of the ladder; I'll sketch that story later. The main focus of the investigation was the money, the bills that had been turned over. All of the serial numbers had been recorded. Better yet, the money was in gold certificates, which were being taken out of circulation. The serial numbers of the ransom bills were distributed throughout the nation, posted on the walls of hundreds of thousands of small shops and large banks, where clerks from Miami to Seattle could routinely check the numbers on any bill that came across their counter.

Ransom bills surfaced on a fairly regular schedule, one or two a week, and Treasury agents tried to trace each one back to its source. Often this proved impossible, as the bank would not be able to say where a bill had come from. As fewer and fewer gold certificates remained in use, however, it gradually became easier to spot the Lindbergh money. On numerous occasions police did trace a bill back to the business where it was used—almost always in the New York City area—and were able to get a description of the customer who had brought in the gold certificate. Many of these descriptions meshed: a man of average height, about 5'9", clear blue eyes, high cheekbones, wide, flat cheeks, a small mouth, strong German accent.

This description, submitted independently by twenty or more clerks, matched Dr. Condon's description of Cemetery John. Treasury agents began a program of urging all clerks in the New York area who received gold certificates to get some form of identification from whoever brought in the bill. Knowing that the kidnapper had to have an automobile, they particularly emphasized that service station attendants should note the license plate number of anyone using a gold certificate.

On Saturday, September 15, 1934, a man bought 98 cents' worth of gasoline at a service station at 127th and Lexington, and paid for the purchase with a $10 gold certificate. The clerk stood behind him as he pulled away, and wrote his license number on the edge of the bill.

The bill was deposited in the bank on the following Monday, September 17. On Tuesday, September 18, the head teller identified the gold certificate as a part of the Lindbergh ransom money. Checking the deposit slips in the same stack, Treasury investigators concluded it had come from one of three filling stations. The manager of one of those stations confirmed that he had written the number on the edge of the bill, and that it was, in fact, a license plate. He remembered very clearly the man who had given him the bill.

It was Cemetery John.

Bruno Richard Hauptmann was taken into custody the next day. Treasury and FBI agents had decided to arrest him, if possible, away from his home, speculating that he would be carrying one of the bills with him, which would be incriminating. He was, in fact, carrying one of the ransom certificates. He said it was the only one he had. Police, searching his garage, found $14,000 of the ransom money hidden there.

Dr. Condon and Joseph Perrone, the taxi driver, both identified Hauptmann as the man they had met two years earlier.

Handwriting analysts testified that Hauptmann had written the ransom notes, all of them.

Arthur Koehler testified that one of the rails of the ladder found at the crime scene had been made from a board taken from Hauptmann's attic.

Several people testified to seeing Hauptmann in the vicinity of Lindbergh's estate in the days before the kidnapping.

A bookkeeper reconstructed his finances, and claimed that Hauptmann had $50,000 of unexplained income. Hauptmann never confessed, but was convicted of the crime on February 13, 1935, and was executed by the state of New Jersey on April 3, 1936.

The governor of New Jersey, Harold Hoffman, was uncertain whether Bruno Richard Hauptmann was guilty, and tried unsuccessfully to save his life. Hoffman's doubts, in time, have fueled an industry. In the last thirty-five years, numerous books have been written claiming that Hauptmann was framed.

Hauptmann was not framed.

Hauptmann was clearly and absolutely guilty of the crime.

The trial of Richard Hauptmann had several serious flaws, owing mostly to the very great attention that was focused on the case. Attention creates pressures that lead to abnormal actions. If you and your colleagues at work were to get together in the morning and decide that all of tomorrow you will pay a great deal of attention to Marcia, the clerk in the corner, the extremely predictable outcome of that would be that, by the end of the day,

Marcia would be acting in some extremely atypical manner, and probably would do inappropriate things. Attention creates pressure; pressure distorts behavior.

The trial of Hauptmann had one central defect, and the prosecution case against Hauptmann had one major problem and a series of minor problems. The central defect of the trial was the pervasive intrusion of the media. The major flaw in the prosecution's case was that Hauptmann was convicted of carrying out the crime alone and un-aided, when there is a substantial possibility that he had confederates.

Beyond those problems, the case against Hauptmann had the following substantial errors:

1) An old man named Amandus Hochmuth was allowed to testify that he had seen Hauptmann near the Lindbergh estate days before the kidnapping, when in reality he almost certainly had not.

2) Other persons also testified to seeing Hauptmann near the Lindbergh home. This testimony is unconvincing, and there is little reason to believe that any of them actually saw Hauptmann there.

3) Accountants reconstructed Hauptmann's finances, attempting to account for the remainder of the ransom money by showing unexplained income. This was speculative, and does not really rise to the level of "evidence."

4) A timesheet from Hauptmann's employer, which was used to attack his alibi for two critical dates, suggests the possibility of tampering, and probably should not have been entered into evidence.

These are not trivial failings. On the other hand, setting all of that aside, there is much more than sufficient reason to believe that Hauptmann was guilty.

1) Hauptmann was found in possession of the money. He was noted passing a bill, was arrested carrying a bill, and denied having any more of the money, but $14,000 of the money was found hidden in his garage.

2) Police had developed a Level Five description of Richard Hauptmann, based on descriptions from numerous people, before they had identified Hauptmann as the suspect.

3) Numerous experts identified the handwriting of the ransom notes as Hauptmann's, and Hauptmann himself acknowledged very directly that the handwriting of the notes was identical to his.

4) Dr. Condon, who had met with the kidnapper three times and had

handed the money to him, positively identified Hauptmann as the man who took the money.

5) Joseph Perrone, the taxi driver who had been instructed to deliver a letter to Dr. Condon's house, also positively identified Hauptmann as the man who sent the note.

6) Dr. Condon's phone number was found scribbled on a piece of wood inside the Hauptmann house. Hauptmann acknowledged writing the number there, explaining that he was "a little bit interested in the case."

7) Hauptmann quit his job essentially the day the ransom money was delivered to the kidnappers.

8) Hauptmann had a long criminal history in Germany, and had come to the United States (illegally) after escaping from jail in Germany.

9) While the precise accounting of his income is questionable, Hauptmann clearly had more income in the early 1930s than any other itinerant carpenter in the country.

10) Arthur Koehler, the wood expert, had traced the wood used in the construction of the ladder to the exact lumberyard where Hauptmann regularly did business, and had done so long before Hauptmann was identified as the suspect.

11) One rail of the ladder was a piece of wood obviously previously used, and taken from some other source. This wood perfectly matched a board taken from Hauptmann's attic, and had, in fact, been sawed off of that board.

These eleven facts, taken as a whole, form an extremely solid foundation for the prosecution of Hauptmann. The "Hauptmann Is Innocent" writers of the last thirty to forty years have used three techniques to try to confound the public about this issue. First, they exaggerate the real and substantial failings of the Hauptmann trial. Second, they try to take your eye off the ball by warbling on for hundreds of pages about issues entirely irrelevant to the case. And third, they allege—with absolutely nothing to support them—that everybody who participated in the prosecution lied about everything.

There are really two books that are central to the belief that Hauptmann was innocent. Those books are *Scapegoat,* by Anthony Scaduto (G. P. Putnam's Sons, 1976), and *The Airman and the Carpenter,* by Ludovic Kennedy (Collins, 1985). I'll deal with *The Airman and the Carpenter* first because we can deal with that more quickly: This is the most dishonest book that I have ever read, bar none. Virtually every word of the book is a lie, a con, or a deception of some sort. You can pick up the book, flip open to any page, point at some sentence at random, and it will, at a very minimum, shade the truth. The title is a lie; it should have been called *The Airman and the Petty Criminal*. The only books I can think of that come close to it in terms of persistent dishonesty are Caryl Chessman's death row fictionalizations, but Chessman, after all, was trying to con his way out of the gas chamber; Kennedy just seems to enjoy pulling the wool over the readers' eyes.

Scaduto's book is different; Scaduto's work I certainly respect, while I entirely disagree with him. I respect Scaduto because he has done very well something that I could never do: investigative journalism. *Scapegoat* was written in the aftermath of Watergate, when investigative journalism was getting a little carried away with itself. *Sixty Minutes* was barging into boardrooms, ambushing people with television cameras and no fair opportunity to prepare for the interview.

These books started to come out in the 1970s, in large part, because they couldn't come out until the people who remembered the case had died and been replaced by a public that was unfamiliar with the time and the facts of the case, thus could be told tall tales without spotting the obvious fallacies. A couple of simple examples: Hauptmann quit his job the day the ransom money was handed over. Hauptmann tried to explain this by claiming that he quit the job in a dispute or disagreement over how much he was to be paid. Well, it was 1932. People were standing in breadlines. Carpenters didn't quit jobs because of little disputes and live off of their investments. People in 1935, at the time of the trial, understood that, and they reacted to Hauptmann's claim with deep skepticism. People in the 1970s didn't quite catch it. He didn't like what he was being paid; he quit the job, so what?

Of course, even if we assume that he *did* have a dispute over the money, it's still quite a coincidence, but it plays different if you understand the context. He quit his job, and incidentally never worked again. Another thing is the "Rail 16," the one rail of the ladder that was a different piece of wood, which had nail holes showing that it had obviously been used before for some other purpose. The "wood expert," Arthur Koehler, demonstrated very convincingly that this piece of wood was sawed off of a board in Hauptmann's attic.

Scaduto and Kennedy pooh-pooh this whole theory, Scaduto arguing—falsely—that many pieces of wood have similar grain patterns and markings. But the thing is, if you look at two pieces of wood that have been sawed apart, you can *tell* whether they fit together. Anybody can. Take an old piece of wood that's been used somewhere, saw off a piece of it, put them together and ask the jury "Did these used to be part of the same piece of wood, or not?" If they weren't, it will be obvious for 25 reasons—the age and color of the wood, the finish, the shape, usage patterns, dimensions, type of wood, the width and pattern of the grain, etc. You couldn't fake a match like that, any more than you could switch somebody's dog with another dog or their shoes with somebody else's shoes. It would be obvious.

Men of the 1930s, who almost universally had worked with wood as a part of the common experience of growing up early in the twentieth century, would have known that. Having the wood in front of them would re-enforce the concept. But to people reading about it in a book forty years later, when working with wood was no longer part of the common experience of life, Scaduto's argument seems as if it might be plausible.

Scaduto claims that Condon's phone number was written on a board inside a closet in Hauptmann's house by a reporter to manufacture a news story, and this claim has entered the apocrypha of the case, now assumed by many who write about the case to be true. But

1) Hauptmann acknowledged to police that he had written the number, and attempted to explain why,

2) There isn't *any* background documentation for Scaduto's claim, which emerges from a cesspool of rumor forty years after the fact, and

3) The discovery of the phone number was reported simultaneously by multiple newspapermen, none of whom was the man Scaduto alleged to have written the number there in order to manufacture an exclusive news story.

The Freedom of Information Act was passed into law in 1966. It was originally assumed to apply only to a fairly narrow range of documents. Over the next few years, lawsuits successfully expanded the range of documents which could be accessed by journalists under the Freedom of Information Act. Scaduto was the first man to realize that the Freedom of Information Act could now be used to pry open the files of the Lindbergh investigation, and he did so.

If Scaduto's reading of the old documents "proved" that Hauptmann was framed, he had a book. If the papers merely proved that Hauptmann was guilty, he had nothing. Still, I don't doubt that, when he began his investigation, Scaduto sincerely believed in Hauptmann's innocence. But he lost all judgment and perspective, and would use any information, no matter how clearly it pointed to Hauptmann, to try to prove that Hauptmann was framed.

Joseph Perrone (the taxi driver) provided the first eyewitness description of Hauptmann. According to Scaduto, one of the things that he most wanted to find, in his investigation of the investigation, was Perrone's first description of the suspect, long before Hauptmann's name surfaced.

And he finds it. You've got to respect that, right? That's good investigative journalism.

The only thing is, it turns out to be an uncannily perfect description of Bruno Richard Hauptmann. "German or Scandinavian, about thirty-five, one hundred seventy to one hundred eighty pounds, blue eyes, brown felt hat, brown double-breasted overcoat." Let's see . . . he's a white male, so that's 45% of the population. Let's assume "German or Scandinavian" (meaning German or Scandinavian accent) is one-tenth of all the white males—in reality it is probably more like 1%, but let's say—that gives us 5%. About thirty-five years old is maybe 10% of those people, so that's one-half of one percent. He nailed Hauptmann's weight precisely; let's say that a fourth of the German or Scandinavian men of about 35 years of age are somewhere close to that in weight, that gives us a little more than one-tenth of one percent. Blue eyes cuts that down a little more; we're under one-tenth of one percent. *It's a Level Three description of Richard Hauptmann!*

But Scaduto, rather than admitting that Perrone has nailed Hauptmann to a T, lifts out of context one line from a *different* description of the man, given by Perrone at a different time and in a different place, and uses that to argue that Perrone must be describing somebody else. At that moment the astute reader may conclude (I did anyway) that Scaduto knows perfectly well that Hauptmann is guilty, but has committed himself to the "scapegoat" theory and is going to run with it no matter what. On some level this sophistry seems preferable to Ludovic Kennedy's self-delusional ranting.

Condon said that the kidnapper/contact had "wide almond-shaped eyes," so Scaduto predictably argues that Hauptmann's eyes were not almond-shaped. But anyone looking at photos of Hauptmann can see that he does, in fact, have wide-set, almond-shaped eyes. Scaduto depends on his readers being so uncritical that they won't make the minimal effort to look at a photograph and draw their own conclusions about this.

Scaduto's book is not a failure; it's a success. He succeeded in putting together a readable and entertaining book. He succeeded in making some money off the book, God bless him, and he succeeded in convincing a generation of gullible readers that Hauptmann was framed. This has devolved into popular culture, and now some halfwit is running around arguing that the Lindbergh baby was murdered by Anne Morrow's sister.

The only thing is, the whole premise is nonsense. On a scale on which 100 points are necessary to convince a skeptic that Hauptmann was guilty beyond any reasonable doubt, I would score the evidence against him at about 213 points:

40 points for the fact that the money was found in his possession,

35 points for the fact that his handwriting matched perfectly the handwriting of the ransom notes,

35 points for the fact that one rail of the ladder was made from a board taken from his house,

30 points for Condon's definite identification of him as the man he had met with in the cemetery,

15 points for Hauptmann's previous criminal convictions,

15 points for the fact that Hauptmann was a perfect match for the Level 5 description which had been built up of him before he was arrested,

13 points for the fact that he quit his job on or about the day the ransom money was handed over,

10 points for the fact that Hauptmann had been a regular customer of the lumberyard to which Koehler had already traced the wood used to build the ladder,

8 points for Joseph Perrone's positive identification of him,

5 points for the fact that Hauptmann never had a job or attempted to get a job after receiving the money, but continued to live comfortably,

4 points for the fact that Condon's phone number was found written on a board inside his house, and Hauptmann acknowledged writing it there,

2 points for Lindbergh's identification of Hauptmann, based on a quick viewing and on hearing Hauptmann shout the words "Hey Doctor" to Condon, and

1 point for the fact that Hauptmann was a regular reader of the *Bronx Home News*, the small newspaper that had played a key role in the transfer of the money.

After the Lindbergh case (and the Massie case in Hawaii, which was a contemporary case that we will get to a little later) . . . after those cases there would not be another case as big for many years. Well, there wouldn't be another case as big as Lindbergh until the O. J. Simpson case in the 1990s, but there wouldn't be another case as big as Massie or the Hall-Mills case or the Snyder-Gray case or the Loeb and Leopold case; there wouldn't be another pure crime megastory like that until Sam Sheppard in 1954. There was the Black Dahlia case in the 1940s, which was big then and is huge now, but there was no contemporary media circus surrounding that that was in any way comparable to these other big cases.

For fifteen years the coverage of crimes had spun in an ever-widening orbit, ratcheting up to a new level and a new level and a new level. The Lindbergh case, said H. L. Mencken, was the biggest news story since the Resurrection. After Lindbergh there was no new level for a long time. I've thought a lot about why that happened, and I'm not sure that I understand it, but I'll give you the best explanation I can. There were five factors:

1) *The criminal justice system stopped playing along.* The bull-in-a-china-shop intrusion of the media into the process of justice was curtailed by judicial reforms after the Hauptmann trial. The Hauptmann trial was frequently interrupted by newsmen taking photographs, which in that time meant flashbulbs. Reporters interviewed witnesses before and after they took the stand, and sometimes asked them to repeat their testimony for the newsreels. This was entirely improper. The media was elbowing the system of justice out of the way so that they could get their story. After the Lindbergh case the courts said, "We can't let this happen. This is *our* system; we can't let the news media take it over and run it." Many reforms were adopted in direct response to the Lindbergh trial circus, including the banning of cameras from the courtrooms.

2) *World War II, of course, changed everything*—but America didn't enter World War II until almost seven years after Hauptmann's trial.

3) *Burnout.* Do you remember how tired a lot of people were of the O.J. case by the time it was over? The wall-to-wall O.J. coverage, even though the country was really into the case, eventually started to turn people's stomachs.

I think that something similar happened here, perhaps a little more so. By the end of the Lindbergh case, the American people were sick of it, and they didn't want another case like it.

4) *Newspaper consolidation.* New York City about 1850 had . . . nobody knows, maybe 140 daily newspapers. The rapid consolidation of newspapers from the mid-1930s into the mid-1950s reduced the competitive pressures on newsmen, and reduced somewhat the tendency of newspapers to try to

increase circulation by splashing sensational stories—often crime stories—across the front page.

5) *Journalistic ethics.* The newsmen of 1880 were not "journalists"; they were just newsmen. They didn't go to college and study journalism. They didn't go to college at all, overwhelmingly, and colleges didn't teach "journalism." The first school of journalism was founded in 1908 at the University of Missouri.

As educated and professional journalists gradually took over the field, many of them looked askance at the tawdry spectacles of crime reporting. It wasn't *eliminated* from newspapers, but it was gradually controlled.

In the teens and twenties there were in most larger cities "scandal sheets," which were in truth little more than fronts for blackmail operations. A scandal sheet might have two reporters on staff, one of whom would hang around the police station and pay a cop to tip them off about a local politician arrested naked in the back seat of a Packard with a sixteen-year-old girl, for example, or a leading clergyman whose wife made a habit of falling down the stairs. These rags had an audience—there is always an audience for that sort of thing—but they really made their money from the stories they agreed not to print. "Councilman Johnson, we have this story. You buy some advertising from us, we don't print the story." They would also agree to print stories for money. When Councilman Johnson was being opposed for re-election, he might come up with $200, in return for which a story would run accusing his opponent of cohabiting with a woman with a drug habit, or being a silent partner in a gin room, or what have you. By the late 1920s the scandal sheets were being driven out of existence by better ethical practices of policemen and prosecutors, with whom they were in bed, as well as by the opposition of reputable journalists.

XIV

Euclid Beach is toward the eastern side of Cleveland, on the south shore of Lake Erie. On September 5, 1934—fourteen days before Hauptmann was arrested—a young man strolling along Euclid Beach came across the partial remains of a dismembered young woman. The pathologist said she had been in the water for several months.

The woman was never identified, and the crime was never solved.

Less than three weeks later, two headless corpses were found in Kingsbury Run, their bodies complete except for the heads and genitalia. A serial murderer was at work in Cleveland.

He would never be caught.

Kingsbury Run is the bottom land on the east side of the Cuyahoga River, where trains slip into and out of the city. There is a rough, undeveloped area there, the railroad yards and the cliffs beside them, which had become a squatter's camp during the Depression. The delta, where the river makes ready to meet the lake, was Cleveland's red-light district, the Roaring Third.

Between September, 1934, and August, 1938, an unknown person murdered and dismembered thirteen or more victims. As a rule, he abducted hoboes from the squatters' camps or prostitutes from the Roaring Third district, and dumped their bodies in Kingsbury Run. This is a generalization; not all of the victims were tramps or prostitutes, and not all of them were dumped near the tracks. In fact, since only two of the thirteen victims were ever positively identified (an astonishing fact in itself), any statements about who the victims were are largely conjecture.

After the sixth murder, the crime spree became the biggest ongoing story in the Cleveland papers, and began to consume more and more of the time and energy of Cleveland's director of public safety, Eliot Ness. This story is told in *Torso: Eliot Ness and the Hunt for the Mad Butcher of Kingsbury Run,* by Steven Nickel (Avon Books, 1989). It's a good book, careful and intelligent, though at times Nickel lacks historical perspective.

The last bodies of the series were discovered on August 16, 1938. Criticized for his inability to find the culprit, Ness ordered two extraordinary measures to bring the Butcher's run to an end. First, police conducted a series of raids on the shantytowns of Kingsbury Run, trampling and burning the pitiful possessions of the men who lived there. When this brought even harsher criticism raining down upon him, Ness ordered a house-to-house search of the Roaring Third, using the pretext of fire safety investigations to avoid the necessity for search warrants.

Nickel suggests (and I am inclined to agree) that the investigators may have missed the monster's "lair" because they were expecting something obvious. They were looking for blood-spattered walls, blood-drenched mattresses, bloody axes and blood-soaked clothing. Eliot Ness had once expressed the opinion that the murderer's "laboratory" must be very elaborate. Subsequent experience with murderers from William Heirens to Jeffrey Dahmer has demonstrated that the murderer could very well have committed the crimes in an ordinary apartment, and left no obvious evidence after the fact.

In any case, they didn't find him. Cuyahoga County authorities had for three years refused to get involved in the case, arguing that since the murders were committed in Cleveland, it was Cleveland's problem. As the crimes continued, pressure mounted on the county sheriff, and the sheriff retained a private investigator to work on the case.

On July 5, 1939, the private eye and an associate arrested a bricklayer named Frank Dolezal on suspicion of being the Butcher. Hanging around the Roaring Third, the investigator had identified a bar that was patronized by the only two victims who had been positively identified, as well as a third missing person, tentatively identified as a victim. Dolezal was also a patron of that bar. He was a powerfully built man, as the killer surely must have been, and was tied to the crimes by a web of circumstance. He had been seen in the company of one of the known victims shortly before she disappeared. He had once worked in a slaughterhouse, as police suspected the killer might have done. He lived in the Third District, within half a block of where one of the bodies had been dumped. He had had long periods of unemployment, which coincided to a degree with the periods of the murders. He carried knives, and police had reports that he often threatened to use them. An acquaintance claimed that he had once thrown a knife at a woman.

On July 7, 1939, Dolezal confessed to the murder of Flo Polillo, one of the known victims.

Immediately thereafter, however, the case against him began to fall apart. Cleveland police, embarrassed at being beaten in the investigation by a part-time johnny-come-lately private detective, set out to discredit the arrest. Blood found in Dolezal's apartment was discovered not to be blood at all. Details of the confession were found to be in error, while others were discovered to have been coached. His first confession, it was learned, had come after 50 hours of constant questioning and sleep deprivation. Though he repeated his confession numerous times, always adding details, his stories were strange to the point of being unbelievable, he refused to confess to any of the other murders, and he repeatedly failed the crucial test: adding original material which could be verified by further investigation. Like, what did you do with that woman's head?

On July 12, Dolezal retracted his confession. On August 24 he committed suicide, hanging himself in his jail cell. An autopsy revealed that he had recently suffered six broken ribs, lending credence to his lawyer's claim that the confessions had been beaten out of him.

The case against Dolezal had disintegrated, but there were no more murders—none after he died, none for a year before then. As Nickel wrote, "the mere fact that no more bodies turned up in Cleveland prompted some to suggest that Dolezal really had been the killer . . . But most people knew better. As Coroner Samuel Gerber later declared, 'The arrest of Frank Dolezal didn't stop the murders; they had already stopped.'"

While the murders had stopped in Cleveland, there were numerous similar murders, or somewhat similar murders, committed in the region over the next few years.

Now, to go back in time and fill in the story. In 1923 and 1924, six bodies were found in a swamp near New Castle, Pennsylvania. Well, some bodies were found, and some heads that didn't all match up. Altogether, there must have been six people there before somebody started separating the heads from the bodies.

On July 1, 1936, another headless corpse—a new one—was found in an abandoned boxcar near the swamp in New Castle. By this time the search for the Butcher was in full swing, and New Castle is just across the line from

Ohio, within a hundred miles of Cleveland. Eliot Ness sent a team of detectives to New Castle, where they met with the local sheriff. The sheriff took Ness's men out to the murder swamp and, according to Nickel, "shared his theory that the remains were those of victims of gang murders and that the swamp was used as a dumping ground by mobsters. [The Cleveland police] could not argue . . . it was infinitely more plausible than believing that the twelve-year-old killings had been the work of the same maniac now terrorizing Cleveland."

For much of the twentieth century, "gang-related murder" was a kind of policeman's code, which could be roughly translated as "I don't have a chance in hell of solving this crime, and I'm not going to worry about it." Taken literally, the theory that these were gang-related murders is stupid. Organized mobsters do not decapitate their victims, put the bodies in the trunks of their Oldsmobiles and transfer them out to some small city in the middle of nowhere. It's just not how it's done.

On the other hand, the theory that this was the work of the same maniac, as Nickel argues later in the book, has a great deal going for it. The pattern killings have much in common, including

• The decapitation of the bodies, a relatively rare feature among serial murderers, and extremely rare in garden-variety crimes.

• The dumping of the bodies, nude, in the open.

• The use of railroad right-of-way or land beside railroad right-of-way to dump bodies.

• The discovery of old newspapers underneath the bodies.

• The fact that both murderers, if indeed they were separate, were astonishingly successful at abducting victims who would never be missed and could never be identified.

In opposition to the theory that the killings were all the work of the same man appears to be only the separation in time and space. The distance between New Castle and Cleveland is utterly insignificant, since the killer could obviously transport easily between the two. The dumpsites are united by a single rail line. The separation in time is more significant, between 1923 and 1934, but hardly a prohibitive barrier, particularly since another New Castle murder was committed in 1936. Many serial murderers are known to have committed murders separated by more than fifteen years, and many have had inactive periods because of incarceration and/or confinement in a mental hospital.

And, as the murders may not have started in Cleveland, they may not have ended there, either. On June 30, 1939 (one week before Dolezal's confession), the bones of a dismembered woman were found in a dump near Youngstown, Ohio, which is halfway between New Castle and Cleveland, on the same rail line. On October 13, 1939, a nude, headless man was found resting on an old newspaper, in the weeds, near the train tracks in New Castle.

On May 3, 1940, three decapitated bodies were found in an abandoned train in McKees Rocks, Pennsylvania. From various evidence, it was determined that the victims had been murdered while the cars were in a yard in Youngstown in December, 1939.

The remains of a headless woman, dead about a year, were found in the New Castle swamp in 1941.

A headless man was found near a train track in Pittsburgh in 1941.

Do the murders go on? The pattern breaks up, leaving Cleveland, leaving the area, winding into a rat's nest of could-bes and look-alikes. A headless man was found near the railroad tracks in Cleveland on July 22, 1950. Old newspapers were found with the body.

I have as much respect for the tradition of the literary detective as you have (none whatsoever), but this is a situation that cries out for the treatment. While the identity of the Butcher of Kingsbury Run is unknown, there are a few things that may be safely inferred about him:

- He was a man of impressive physical strength.
- He had a house.
- He had a car, or had access to a car.
- He lived in the area.

The police investigating the case thought that the Butcher unquestionably had an automobile, and this became a key to their investigation. I wonder if a more accurate summation might not be that the evidence shows that the murderer had *limited* access to an automobile. Some of the bodies were dumped in places that almost certainly argue for the use of an automobile, it is true—but many of the dumpsites suggest nothing of the sort. Several victims were dumped within blocks of where they were last seen. There is no consistent description of an automobile, consistent from one case to another. Various vehicles are described in places possibly associating them with various bodies. The murderer can be more conclusively tied to trains than he can to automobiles.

In the case of Andrei Chikatilo, in Russia, the police concluded, based on similar evidence, that the murderer had to have an automobile. They then wasted a vast amount of time and effort tracking down automobiles, when in fact Chikatilo did not drive—which, since they were at one point calling him the "Railway Station Killer," they might actually have guessed. Something similar may have happened here.

I would bet that from 1934 to 1938 the Butcher lived within one mile of the intersection of Broadway and Carnegie, in eastern Cleveland. (If you plot the bodies in a serial murder case on a map and draw a circle around them, the murderer normally lives somewhere near the center of the circle. Also, since several victims were found within a few blocks of the place from which they disappeared, it seems very unlikely that the murderer would have taken the victims out of the area, then put their corpses in his car and driven them back to where he picked them up.)

This much was relatively evident to the men who investigated the crime, but by standing on the shoulders of Robert Ressler, John Douglas, and the others who developed criminal profiling, we can see a little more. For one thing, it seems extremely apparent, from the work of Ressler, that the individual in question had killed before the first definitely "known" victims, the two headless corpses found in Kingsbury Run on September 23, 1934. This is apparent for several reasons. It is enormously unlikely that an inexperienced offender would begin by killing two people almost simultaneously, then ceremonially placing their bodies on a hillside. This is the act of an experienced murderer, in control of his actions. The victims found in Kingsbury Run

a) had been decapitated by a single blow from a long, heavy knife, and

b) had been mutilated by an individual showing knowledge of human anatomy.

Either of these factors would be uncommon in an inexperienced criminal. The placement of the bodies reveals what I think Ressler would describe as "extremely advanced staging" of the crime scene. The murderer washed the bodies, drained the blood from them, carried them to the scene, placed them down carefully, spread out on the ground as if sunning themselves, wrapped their heads in their clothes and left the package somewhere in the area, in a paper bag. Ressler argues that the "staging" of the crime scene reflects the experience of the criminal. A first-time murderer dumps the body and runs. An older, more experienced criminal takes his time, savoring his experience and arranging the scene the way he wants it to be found. This was very advanced staging, as if the killer had committed numerous previous crimes.

We might also infer from this, from the unusual extent to which the murderer was in control of himself and in control of the situation, that he was not too young. Most serial murderers begin killing in their mid-twenties; this guy may have been in his mid- to late thirties.

This brings us back to the New Castle murders, and to the question of whether the Kingsbury Run crimes were a distinct crime spree, or the work of the same man. Leaving aside the silly idea that the New Castle murders were mob-related, there really are only two possibilities:

1) That the crimes were all related, or

2) That there were two separate serial murderers, using similar methods in an overlapping time frame.

The second thesis should not be hastily rejected, as there have been numerous times when police confused the crimes committed by different serial murderers, to the detriment of a solution. Nonetheless, the first thesis, that the crimes are all related, is

a) much more tenable on its surface, and

b) even more so if we accept the proposition that the Cleveland police were dealing, from the beginning, with an experienced murderer.

Let us assume, just to see where that takes us, that the crimes were all committed by the same individual. If so, the individual would likely have been born between 1895 and 1900. (Most serial murderers begin killing in their mid-twenties. This man began killing in 1922 or 1923. If he was born before 1895, he would have been almost 50 by the end of the crimes to which he is tied, which is less likely.)

One of the most striking things about the Butcher, which so far as I know no one has ever commented on, is that he never dumped a body in a rural area. Most serial murderers dump their bodies in isolated areas, for obvious reasons, and isolated areas often mean rural areas. The Butcher never used rural areas; he always dumped his bodies in brushy, isolated areas in or near cities, or towns of some size. He is never known to have killed anyone in a rural area, or a truly small town.

From this, we can infer two things. First, the Butcher almost unquestionably grew up in a city or a town of some size. Serial murderers dump their bodies in places where they feel comfortable. The Butcher felt uncomfortable out in the country, as city people often do. He felt exposed, vulnerable.

This is significant, because 80% of our population lived on farms or in small towns in 1900–1920. The Butcher didn't. This takes the focus away from a large portion of the persons we might otherwise be inclined to look at.

Second, this supports the argument that the Butcher may *not* have been a driver. He may have used a vehicle on occasion, but probably not routinely. He wasn't accustomed to getting behind the wheel and hitting the road. He didn't know where the isolated rural areas were. He wasn't comfortable putting a body in the trunk, and heading for the hills.

The Butcher was most likely raised in New Castle, Pennsylvania, although he may have been born in Pittsburgh, Youngstown, or Cleveland. (New Castle was growing fairly rapidly in that era. Most serial murderers have unstable childhoods that involve moving from place to place. The Butcher may have moved to the town early in his life. Had the murderer not had strong ties to the New Castle area, he would not have remained there through a series of killings in 1922 and 1923, but would probably have moved on after the first crime. Even more markedly, had he not had strong ties to the New Castle area, he would not have returned to New Castle to commit additional murders later on, during his most active period.)

After committing several murders in New Castle in 1922–23, the individual was probably arrested for some unrelated crime, a serious crime such as burglary, arson, assault, assault with a deadly weapon, rape, murder, or attempted murder. He was given a substantial prison sentence, and was in prison until late 1933 or early 1934.

(He would not have become inactive from 1923 to 1934 unless he was confined. While it is certainly possible that he was confined to a mental hospital, I regard this as less likely. Highly Organized Murderers are not obviously insane. They're not people who rant, rave, bite off their tongues and burst out laughing at funerals. They recognize that their private fantasy lives are forbidden, and conceal them effectively.

On the other hand, virtually 100% of serial murderers are thieves. They always steal things, anything. Often they are also arsonists. Since the Butcher was a large, powerful man who may have had a deep-seated hatred of his father, he might at any time have gotten drunk and beaten the hell out of somebody. It must have been a serious crime, because he wouldn't have been locked up for ten years for running a red light, but there is a large range of crimes that such an individual might have committed in New Castle in 1923 or 1924, without being associated with the bodies in the swamp.)

Upon being released from prison in late 1933 or early 1934, the individual moved to Cleveland, and resumed his killing within a period of months. (Subsequent experience with serial murderers who are incarcerated in the middle of their run, such as Arthur Shawcross, Charles Hatcher, Ted Bundy, Larry Eyler, Kenneth McDuff and Robert Hansen, shows that they virtually always resume killing within months of their release, and in many cases within hours of their release. The Butcher probably was obsessed with murderous fantasies while he was in prison, and probably left Pennsylvania as soon as he got out because he knew that if he returned to New Castle and resumed killing there, he would, as an ex-con, immediately be associated with the crimes.)

By his own peculiar lights, the Butcher was getting his life back together. He moved to Cleveland, got a job, got a house, perhaps got a car, and got back to killing people. During this four-year period he killed with impunity, gradually beginning to feel that he was invincible, that the police would never catch him. Ressler describes this phenomenon in *Whoever Fights Monsters*, that organized serial murderers, if uncaught, become increasingly bold, and may begin to dump their bodies in more and more incriminating places, almost as if to taunt the police. The Butcher's last two victims in 1938 were dumped together by the side of the lake, a ten-minute walk from Public Square in downtown Cleveland, almost within view (perhaps literally within view) of the city and police office building where Eliot Ness had his headquarters.

After this crime, however, came the Raids, the raids for which Eliot Ness was so harshly criticized. Ness and his men made a house-to-house search of the Third District, where the Butcher almost certainly resided. They must have come to his house, seen something suspicious, and perhaps taken him to the police station for questioning, as they took in dozens of others. This shattered the Butcher's conviction that he was invulnerable, and prompted him to pick up quickly and run, probably within hours after being questioned by the police.

(This is another reason why I believe that the Butcher must have been in a prison, rather than a mental hospital, from 1924 to 1934. The police must have interviewed the Butcher in August or September, 1938, but without discovering his secret. If the Butcher had had the telltale signs of an unstable personality—the nervous eyes, the excessive hand gestures, the high, cracking voice—the police would have recognized these, and might have focused upon him. Instead, the Butcher came away from the interview un-scored upon. He realized how close he was to being caught—but the police did not realize how close they had come to catching him.

An almost equally good possibility is that the Butcher may actually have been arrested at this time, and may have served a short prison sentence in late 1938 and early 1939.)

Leaving Cleveland, he may have vowed that he would kill no more, that he would "regularize" his life. The vow didn't hold, and he resumed his murderous ways in Youngstown in 1939. His health probably began to fail him in the early 1940s, and he was probably dead by the early 1950s.

The killer certainly lived alone in Cleveland, although he may have been married from about 1919 to 1923. He was probably about 6'2" tall, and weighed 210 to 225 pounds. (A bloody footprint was found on the "murder train" in 1940; it was of a size 12 boot, indicating a large but not exceptionally large man. He was extremely strong, as is evident from many of his actions, such as carrying two bodies several hundred feet down a steep hill to stage their discovery on a hillside. A man of ordinary size and strength could not have accomplished this, and an obese man could not have accomplished it.)

The killer was intelligent, and he could read and write. (Old newspapers were found with many of the bodies, indicating not only that the Butcher read newspapers, but that he kept them around.) However, the suggestion that he may have been a doctor or have had some medical training is without merit, and should be disregarded. (This suggestion, as many readers will know, was quite common in pre-1970 serial murder cases in which victims were dismembered or eviscerated. The suggestion was often made by coroners or medical examiners, but it derives from an obvious fallacy. The coroner observes the dissection of the body, and realizes that the killer has some anatomical knowledge. "I have this kind of anatomical knowledge," the medical man realizes, "because I am a doctor. Therefore, because the killer knows the same kind of things that I know, he must also be a doctor." But this is a fallacy, because it assumes that the killer must have acquired this specialized knowledge the same way that the doctor has acquired it—while in reality, he may have acquired it in numerous other ways. Like cutting up bodies.)

The Butcher had a trade, working with his hands. He may have been a machinist, a mechanic, a heavy-equipment operator or a carpenter. He may even have been a butcher. (Although he opened the decade in prison, by the mid-1930s he had a house or secure apartment to use as his base of operations. He may have had a car. This was the Depression, and many, many people were homeless—therefore, the killer must have had something significant he could rely on, as a source of income.

Organized serial murderers in our time are very often small businessmen. Serial murderers are never wealthy or extremely successful, except in fiction, because they are never highly motivated. Their obsession drains away enough energy to prevent them from focusing on significant work objectives. They are, however, very often intelligent people who hold decent jobs and work hard at them.)

All of this is speculation, of course, but I think it's all fairly safe. That is, IF the Butcher of Kingsbury Run and the murderer of the New Castle Swamp were indeed the same man, then we know a great deal about him, and we can reasonably infer more. Let me now go one step further, and speculate about what might also be true. It might also be false, of course, but I am trying to push the envelope so that, if a couple of the guesses I make here turn out to be correct, and if someone else will follow through on the investigation, and if we get tremendously lucky, we might yet be able to actually identify this madman.

If the killer was born about 1895–1898, and if he was a big, strong, healthy man, then where does that place him? That places him right smack in the middle of World War I. If your grandfather was born in 1898, and if he was a big, strong, healthy man, then your grandfather was in World War I.

And what was World War I noted for?

Bayonet fighting. Mustard gas, land mines and bayonet fighting.

The Butcher, I would suggest, may have been in World War I. He may have observed or participated in bayonet warfare, and may indeed have killed enemy soldiers with his knife or with his trenching tool. Many American soldiers did do this.

But while most of those soldiers were sickened and appalled by the War, the Butcher may have had a different reaction. He may have thought that it was the most exciting thing that had ever happened to him. He may have had an unexpected sexual climax after decapitating an enemy soldier, accompanied by a feeling of great power and force, and may have spent the rest of his life attempting to recapture that feeling.

If he was young and inexperienced in 1917–18, a man from an unhappy and abusive home (as he probably was), then the War may have been the first "successful" experience of his life. He may have had his first sexual experiences in Europe during the war. He may have won medals for his courage. It may have been the first time in his life that he had been singled out for praise and honor.

Without knowing who he was or where he was, it is impossible to be any more specific about the War experiences that he might have had. But if he did have this experience, and if he did find it thrilling, then he might have attempted to keep it alive in his mind through reading about it, fantasizing about it, and re-enacting it. He probably would have read books and articles about war, particularly those emphasizing its most gruesome aspects. He probably read the *Police Gazette* and/or any similar publications, which featured stories about violent crimes.

This, then, would explain what is otherwise one of the most puzzling aspects of the crime. One of the three victims found on the train at McKees Rocks in May, 1940, had the word "NAZI" carved into his chest. When I first read this, I thought "Well, that's not the same man." It seemed unlikely that a veteran serial murderer, more than twenty crimes into his career,

a) would begin carving words on the victims, not having done so before, and

b) would choose to carve into the victim's chest something taken from current headlines. The Nazis had just invaded Poland, just weeks before this murder was committed, but I was surprised that a current news story would re-shape long-established behavior.

But if he was in World War I, and had been re-enacting it in his fantasies, then of course it makes all the sense in the world that he would label his victim a German soldier. The War in Europe broke out in September, 1939. The Butcher, inactive or nearly inactive for a year before then, killed four people in late 1939.

There is another distinction between these murders and the crimes in Cleveland, which helps to explain the change in pattern. In Cleveland the Butcher had a house. After he fled Cleveland he apparently did not have a secure place to take his victims, either because he was homeless or, more probably, because he was living in a rooming house or a walkup apartment, or (conceivably, although it is unlikely) because he had re-married. The victims on the train in McKees Rocks had been murdered on the train, where their bodies were discovered months later.

In the Cleveland murders there were inconsistencies in what was found. Sometimes entire corpses were found, no longer intact, but other times parts were missing. It may well be that the Butcher *did* carve words into the torsos of some earlier victims, but that he was canny enough to dispose carefully of those body parts, so that the police would not have the evidence of what he had written.

My final guess is that the Butcher probably was dead by the early 1950s. There are several reasons for saying this. First, leaving aside ridiculous speculation such as that tying the Butcher to the murder of the Black Dahlia, there is little evidence that he was active after 1941 (although the 1950 murder, mentioned earlier, of Robert Robinson does appear to be either a genuine extension of the pattern or a copycat crime).

Second, single men die earlier than any other class of persons—earlier than single women, earlier than married men or women. Single men are inclined to indulge their bad habits. While many single men are exceptions to the rule, because they do discipline themselves, it does not seem likely that this individual would have been among the self-disciplined minority. The Butcher almost certainly hung around bars and consorted with prostitutes. It is probable that he had self-destructive personal habits.

Third, when the victims were found on the train in 1940, "on a plank a few feet away was a circular mark in blood. Lawmen theorized that it might have been left by a peg leg or the heel of a woman's shoe." (Quote is from *Torso.*) I doubt seriously that there was a woman there with high-heeled shoes, and the Butcher did not have a peg leg, either earlier in his career or in 1939. There is, however, something like a peg leg that is much more common: a cane. The Butcher, in December, 1939, may have been walking with a cane, which may suggest that he was recovering from an injury, or even that he was developing a permanent disability.

There is another theory that suggests itself here. The Butcher's last known victim was in 1941. The United States entered World War II in December, 1941. Could the Butcher have re-enlisted at that time, packed his bayonet and gone back to Europe?

There's no absolute reason he couldn't have. He would probably have been about 43 years old at that time. Many hundreds of World War I veterans did re-enlist at the outset of World War II. Despite his prison record, the army probably would have welcomed him back, if he was just reasonably healthy, and might have started him out as a Sergeant, since he had previous combat experience. Such an individual might very possibly have requested assignment to Europe, and may have died there during the War.

So that's my biography of the Butcher—born in Cleveland, Youngstown, Pittsburgh or New Castle about 1895–1898, spent his childhood in New Castle, went into the army about 1917, mustered out in 1918 or early 1919, may have been married in 1919 to a New Castle woman. In 1922 he suffered a major stress, possibly the breakup of his marriage.

In 1924 or 1925 he was convicted of a serious crime, and sent to prison. Released in 1933 or 1934, he moved to Cleveland, and lived in Cleveland's Third Ward. In 1938 he was interviewed by the police, and fled Cleveland, taking up residence in Youngstown, where he continued to murder people. He was a large man with a trade, he could read and write, and he was of above-average intelligence. He may have died as early as 1942 or as much as 12 years later.

This biography is specific enough that it is statistically very improbable that there would be a "random match" to it—thus, if we can identify an individual who matches this biography, we have probably identified the Butcher of Kingsbury Run. The place to start looking, if anybody takes a notion, would be newspapers and police records for New Castle, Pennsylvania, in 1923 and 1924. I would guess that there would be no more than 50 to 100 persons convicted of serious crimes in that time. Only a handful of those would fit the general description of the Butcher (a large World War I veteran, in his mid- to late twenties). Another place to start would be military records.

The downside is that it might be nearly impossible to prove that such an individual was in Cleveland from 1934 to 1938, even if he was. The Butcher probably was taking active steps to minimize his visibility within the community. He probably did not have a phone, and he probably did not own the house where he lived. He may have used a false name. He did use an automobile, so there is a possible source of records, but it is equally likely that he was a mechanic or auto body worker, or that he had access to automobiles for some other reason. He may also have simply stolen a car when he needed one.

It is a general rule that serial murderers reflect the patterns of those they kill. Ted Bundy and John Norman Collins, who killed beautiful co-eds, were handsome college students themselves. Wayne Williams, who killed black children, was a child-like black man.

The Butcher killed nameless people, people who were impossible to identify despite the vigorous efforts of the Cleveland police. Despite our best efforts, it is unlikely that we will ever be able to put a name on him.

XV

The 1930s were the high water mark of the "Mad Dog Criminal at Large" type of story. The essence of the Mad Dog Criminal at Large type story is that "there is this person running around killing people. We know who he is, we know what he looks like and we know who he has killed, but we don't know where he is right now and we don't know who he will kill next." This story has a long history, and it still crops up occasionally—for example, the 1997 story of Andrew Cunanan, who killed Gianni Versace and others, was a Mad Dog Criminal at Large story. It's a sub-genre of the "Killer on the Loose" story.

There were many such stories in the 1930s, the biggest of which was John Dillinger, but others included Bonnie and Clyde, Machine Gun Kelly, Baby Face Nelson, and Ma Barker and her boys. Guns were out of control—you could get a machine gun pretty easily in 1930—times were tough, and these people saw themselves as romantic desperadoes battling against a system that was trying to destroy them. The press, up until about 1934, cooperated in portraying them as romantic desperadoes. And then, about the same time as the Hauptmann trial, something changed, and I don't really know what. Some idea swept the newspaper industry, some vague realization that "we are promoting human tragedy to sell newspapers, and we should be ashamed of ourselves," and they stopped doing it. Mostly. For a while.

Crime stories in the 1930s can be divided into three groups: the Mad Dog stories, the Organized Crime stories (of which Al Capone was the largest), and the traditional crime stories, which focused not on *criminals* (like Dillinger and Capone) but on *crimes*. The biggest crime stories of the 1930s, focusing on crimes, were:

1) The Lindbergh kidnapping,

2) The Massie case,

3) The Scottsboro Boys, and

4) The Winnie Judd "Trunk Murderess" case.

I'll try to summarize these very briefly . . . if you need more, you know where the internet is.

Thalia Massie was the wife of a Navy Lieutenant stationed in Hawaii. She was twenty years old, had grown up well-off and spoiled, and she still had a lot of growing up to do. On September 12, 1931, she had a fight with her husband at a party, threw a drink on somebody and stormed out. This was not the first time such a thing had happened.

She didn't show up at her house until some hours later, and when she did she was covered with cuts and bruises. She reported that she had been raped by five men, native Hawaiians.

Police investigated, and arrested five men—probably not the right ones— who were duly put on trial. Remember, at this time Hawaii was not a state; Hawaii was an American territory, with a diverse population and remnants of a system of royalty. The arrest of the five locals was unpopular with the native population, and pitched the island nation into high tension and occasional turmoil. The jury was unable to agree upon the guilt of the accused, and a mistrial resulted.

Ms. Massie's mother was a strong-willed, high-born woman named Grace Fortescue. Mrs. Fortescue and Mr. Massie and two other sailors went looking for the accused men, and found one of them, a young man named Joseph Kahahawai. Mr. Kahahawai's body was later found in the back seat of Mrs. Fortescue's car.

This flipped the story up to another level, and then, as if that wasn't circus enough, Clarence Darrow entered the case. He was the lawyer for Grace Fortescue and those accused with her. By now, we're using terms like "international incident" and "riots in the streets." The aging Darrow, in his last big case, put forward the theory that this was an "honor killing," not a murder but an honor killing. An honorable murder. In modern parlance he was asking for jury nullification.

The jury didn't buy it, thinking perhaps that murder in general is dishonorable, but the governor did. The defendants were convicted of manslaughter and sentenced to ten years in jail, but the governor, Lawrence Judd, commuted their sentence to one hour. Thalia Massie never really recovered. She divorced Massie two years later, attempted suicide then and periodically over the next three decades, and died in 1963 of an overdose of barbiturates, circumstances suggesting suicide.

There is a very good 1966 book about the case, *Something Terrible Has Happened,* by Peter Van Slingerland (Harper & Row). Van Slingerland was a Harvard graduate and an experienced screenwriter, and he knew how to tell a story, although this book appears to have been the only major success of his publishing career.

Something Terrible Has Happened is the best title ever for a crime book; that actually is what I was going to call this book until I realized the title had already been used. Those exact words appear in countless crime books; it is what one says to prepare a loved one for a life-altering revelation. Those words turn the "crime story" inside out by exposing the human beings standing on what otherwise appears to be a vast and grisly stage. Something has happened to us which is so big that our lives will not be the same anymore. Something has happened which is so foreign to us that before I can tell you about it, I must first prepare you for the possibility that I will tell you about it. There is a seriousness and an urgency in those words that forces the reader to look for just a second at the vulnerable souls flung suddenly into a vicious carnival.

It's a good book, but Van Slingerland has a slant that I don't quite get. Van Slingerland is convinced that the accused men were innocent, which is probably true, but only probably. His argument—like my argument in the case of Lizzie Borden—rests heavily on the time frame. Joseph Kahahawai couldn't have committed the crime, he argues, because he was—I think this is my favorite alibi in the history of crime—he was at that very moment almost a mile away, assaulting some other woman. There's a police report showing that he was, a road rage incident. The time frame of the Massie assault is locked in place by the observations of a dozen or so people, almost all of whom were drinking heavily or were thugs, or both. Two of the five "innocents" accused had prior convictions for attempted rape—not including the man who was, at the moment, beating up another woman. It strikes me as an odd coincidence.

Van Slingerland makes constant references to the "alleged" rape, and there is a lengthy discussion about the lack of "evidence" of an actual rape. Well, no one questions that this very attractive young woman was abducted off the streets in the middle of the night—there were witnesses—and there is no question that, when she turned up an hour or so later, she had cuts and bruises, torn clothes and a broken jaw. She said she had been raped. What's your theory? Contents of her purse, broken, were recovered from the place where she said she had been taken. So the doctors failed to do an appropriate medical examination. So what?

Because Van Slingerland is the major source of information about the case, his curious lack of clarity about this issue colors almost everything written about the Massie case going forward from 1966. People now write about Thalia Massie as if she was a manipulative bitch who was probably making the whole thing up. She wasn't, and this seems to me inappropriate.

On March 25, 1931, a large number of people, some black and some white, had hopped a freight train as it left Chattanooga, bound for Memphis. A fight developed on the train, between a group of young black men and a group of young white men, and the white youths—outnumbered about fifteen to six—were forced to jump off the train. The white youths told their story to a stationmaster shortly after their departure. The stationmaster telegraphed ahead, and a group of white men, acting either as a posse or a klavern, grabbed their guns and stopped the train in Paint Rock, Alabama, where they pulled nine black youths off the train and placed them under arrest. Several other black men, probably including those most active in the fight, had wisely exited the train before it got to Paint Rock.

Two white women were among those who had hopped the train. They had lived hard lives, and they had some cuts and bruises. Perhaps under pressure from the "posse," these women now alleged that they had been raped by several of the black men after the fight.

It is the consensus of those who have studied the case that no such crime had occurred. The allegation was toxic, however, and for two days it appeared nearly certain that the accused, ranging in age from twelve to nineteen, were about to be lynched. The governor of Alabama sent the National Guard to move them to a marginally more secure prison in Scottsboro, Alabama, which was only a few miles away.

By April 9, 1931—two weeks after the fight—the nine Negro youths had been indicted, brought to trial, convicted, and sentenced to death. All nine of them, including the twelve-year-old. At this point the NAACP and the International Labor Defense Fund (commies) entered the case, and began to fight for the accused. This battle went on for many years, through trial after trial after trial. None of the accused was ever acquitted, and none was ever executed. Most were in prison for many years. The Scottsboro Boys became the most famous American Dreyfus figures between the execution of Sacco and Vanzetti in 1927 and the execution of the Rosenbergs in 1953.

With the passage of time the Scottsboro case has become more famous than the Massie case, and, as they have several components in common, modern writers have begun to overlay the Scottsboro Boys onto the Massie case. The cases are very different. Hawaii was not Alabama. Those accused in Hawaii were not convicted, and those convicted in Alabama were not murdered. Thalia Massie was not a lying, manipulative, scheming prostitute like Victoria Price, who was the chief accuser of the Scottsboro Boys; Thalia Massie was a shy, socially awkward, immature young woman who liked to read and listen to good music, and who would have been much happier if she had gone to college rather than getting married at sixteen.

On October 16, 1931—six months after the Scottsboro incident, five weeks after the rape of Thalia Massie—two women were shot to death in a duplex in Phoenix, probably by their ex-roommate, an attractive 26-year-old woman named Winnie Ruth Judd. Their bodies were packed into two trunks—one of the bodies had to be hacked up to accomplish this—and shipped to Los Angeles; don't ask me why, since Phoenix at this time was a small city surrounded by hundreds of miles of empty desert. By the time they got to Los Angeles the trunks smelled to high heaven and there was blood oozing out of the bottoms, attracting the attention of the railroad.

Winnie Judd was the daughter of a Methodist minister from Indiana. At age 19 she married a doctor in his early 40s. She never actually divorced him, but he didn't do much of a job of supporting her, and by 1931 she was living in Phoenix, on her own, had a decent job, and was involved with the owner of a local lumberyard, a man named Jack Halloran. On the evening of the murders Halloran failed to show up for a date with Winnie. Angry, Winnie went to visit her two ex-roommates, who apparently had what was sometimes referred to as a Boston marriage. Some sort of argument developed, and Winnie shot them. Somebody—Halloran, we would guess—helped Winnie box up her dismembered friends and get a ticket to LA, sending the trunks ahead of her.

Winnie was convicted of the murders on February 8, 1932 (three weeks before the Lindbergh kidnapping), and was sentenced to death. Before execution, however, she was adjudged to be insane. Locked up in what might very loosely be described as a "hospital" for the criminally insane, Winnie escaped from custody seven times over the years—twice in 1939, once in 1947, once in 1951, twice in 1952, and once in 1962. Generally she was re-captured after a day or two, but after the 1962 escape she was loose in San Francisco for six and a half years, being finally re-captured in June of 1969.

By 1969 Winnie Judd was just a sweet old lady who wasn't bothering anybody. In theory she was still in line to be executed if adjudged to be sane. With the help of Melvin Belli (a very famous attorney of the time), Ms. Judd was judged sane and paroled by the state of Arizona in 1971. She lived peacefully another 27 years, and died in her bed at the age of 93.

Enjoy it; that may be the only story in our book that has a happy ending.

We last saw Robert Stroud, a two-time murderer, at the start of Chapter Eleven. Spared the death penalty by first lady Edith Wilson, Stroud was ordered to spend the rest of his life in solitary confinement. As a practical matter this was impossible. Locked in a dark hole without anyone to talk to, without anything to read or write, without anything to give shape to the ramblings of the mind, a few months in solitary confinement would reduce almost anyone to madness. The order called for cruel and unusual punishment, besides which few if any prisons actually have a place to lock a man in solitary for a period of years.

In practice, "solitary confinement" became "isolation," a segregated section of the Leavenworth prison reserved for discipline problems. In his first years behind bars, Stroud had established a small business making hand-painted greeting cards. He was a capable enough artist with time on his hands, so he would paint or draw cards, give them to his mother, and she would sell them, making a little money to contribute to his defense fund.

Sometime in the summer of 1920, alone in the yard at Leavenworth, Stroud found a nest with a pair of baby sparrows in it. He smuggled it back to his cell, and made the birds into pets. This wasn't news; other prisoners at Leavenworth had been allowed to keep pets.

Having established the right to keep birds, Stroud asked for permission to get a canary. The authorities said OK. He got a couple of canaries, and began breeding them. He subscribed to some small newspapers that covered bird care and breeding. He got a few more birds, and began making his own cages, cardboard ones at first. He ordered birdseed. Advertising in small newspapers, he sold a few of his birds.

He branched out from canaries to more exotic breeds. He got permission to have his own letterhead printed. Eventually he got enough birds that he started ordering birdseed in bulk. He got several varieties of birdseed, tested them on his birds, sifted and mixed the ingredients, and began to market his own line of bird food. Most of the people who bought birdseed from Stroud had no idea that they were ordering from a prison.

In an institution where all letters were re-typed before being given to the recipient, where men had to request permission to write a letter, Stroud was running a small business. More important than the business was the research. When some of his birds took sick and died, Stroud began studying avian diseases. He made copious notes about the appearance and behavior of his birds, the time and date of each symptom. He performed autopsies on them after they died, gently tearing apart the flesh with his fingers, since he was not allowed to keep a knife.

He began writing a column on bird diseases in one of the small papers serving the needs of bird fanciers. He ended up, twenty years later, as the world's expert on the care and feeding of pet birds. In the 1930s he wrote and illustrated a book, *Diseases of Canaries*, the first book on the subject published in more than 40 years. Ten years later he added a second and more impressive book, *Stroud's Digest on the Diseases of Birds*. He claimed to have developed cures for more than twenty avian diseases, saving the lives of hundreds of thousands of birds. He sold a medicine, "Stroud's Specific," out of his cell.

In a horribly overcrowded prison, with men sleeping on the floors of hallways, Stroud had two cells with a doorway cut between them. The two cells were crammed top to bottom with birdcages, birdseed, cleaning solutions, chemicals, tables, hot plates, a file cabinet, beakers, test tubes, a microscope, a microtome, thermometers, slides, books, magazines, government bulletins, a typewriter, typewriter ribbons, correspondence, envelopes, buckets of dirt, a manuscript and stacks of illustrations, metal, wire, and the tools used to build bird cages.

The situation, from the standpoint of the prison, was out of control.

Stroud's explanation was that he simply did things, without asking, and then depended upon the argument of the status quo, that he had always been allowed to do this in the past. It would be equally true to point out that the warden of the Leavenworth prison was a progressive administrator who believed that prisoners should be given the opportunity to contribute to society in any way that they were capable of contributing. Faced with a thousand or so career criminals who had nothing to contribute and one Robert Stroud, he made Stroud into the showpiece of his reform program, the star attraction of every prison tour.

Stroud's remarkable sentence, life in solitary, put him in a different class from the other prisoners. This was used to justify his unusual treatment.

Jolene Babyak, in a 1994 biography of Stroud (*Bird Man: The Many Faces of Robert Stroud*), argues that almost all of Stroud's research on bird diseases was lacking in merit. Although Stroud worked very hard at analyzing bird diseases, she argues, he had no grounding in scientific methods, and no real understanding of them. He classified all diseases by their symptoms, which created no reliable diagnoses, since many different diseases can create similar symptoms (molting, diarrhea, convulsions, etc.). A modern reader, reviewing Stroud's work today, would be unable to ascertain exactly what diseases he was describing. His cures, most of them, are of little value, and might in many cases be lethal.

I am inclined to think that she misses the point. The point is, he did it. He started the research. He studied the subject as thoroughly as he could, developed treatments, and wrote books describing the results. He took his subject seriously. When no one else was interested in the problems of pet birds, he demonstrated that there was a need for such a text. If later researchers could do the job better (with more education and better facilities), power to them. If you had canaries in 1950 and you wanted to know how to take care of them, Stroud was what you had. Nobody gave that to him.

XVI

On June 3, 1945, a middle-aged woman was found murdered in her apartment in Chicago. The woman had been stabbed repeatedly and her throat had been cut, but bandages had then been wrapped around her neck, apparently in a belated effort to save her life. The victim had not been raped, but police found evidence that the killer had remained at the scene for some time following the crime, masturbating in various parts of the apartment.

Six months later, on December 10, a woman who had been a soldier in World War II (a WAVE) was found dead in her apartment, her body stabbed and mutilated in a similar manner. The killer had written on the wall, in lipstick, "For heaven's sake catch me before I kill more I cannot control myself." This vivid incident had a lasting effect on the imagination of the post-war public, and was copied in movies until it evolved into a cinematic cliché.

The message had been left, and the women murdered, by William Heirens, a sixteen-year-old student at the University of Chicago. He had also committed numerous "fetish burglaries" in the area, stealing items whose value was that they excited him. Kill again he did. On January 7, 1946, a six-year-old girl, Suzanne Degnan, was abducted from her bedroom. Although a ransom note was left at the scene, Heirens murdered and dismembered the little girl before dawn, dropping the body parts in sewers around the area. At the time, this murder was not connected to the earlier crimes.

Little Suzanne's murder outraged and terrified the Chicago area in the months that it went unsolved. In June, 1946, Heirens was arrested during a burglary attempt. A routine check of his fingerprints put him in the middle of the Degnan investigation. Heirens admitted knowledge of the crime, but attributed this (and other murders) to a friend, George Merman (or Murman). Merman, police concluded, existed only in Heirens' mind.

Under the influence of sodium pentothal, Heirens confessed to the three murders. This endangered the investigation, as the Chicago police seemed surprised to learn that giving a juvenile truth serum and interviewing him without an attorney present might possibly taint the resulting confession. A deal was worked out, under which Heirens would plead guilty to the three crimes, but would avoid the death penalty.

Heirens was sentenced to life in prison, and as of this writing, he is still working on it. Heirens became the first person in Illinois history to earn a college degree while incarcerated, and has also done graduate work. Now in his early eighties, Heirens has been a model prisoner, and has battled hard for his release. In the early 1950s he tried to get his case reviewed in the courts, but was eventually turned down by the Illinois Supreme Court (1954). In April, 1983, a federal judge ruled that Heirens had been rehabilitated and must be released from prison, but this was overturned on appeal. Heirens, who now denies the killings, is probably the longest-serving prisoner in the nation.

Elizabeth Short—the Black Dahlia—was murdered in Los Angeles in January, 1947. Accounts of her life always insist a little too forcefully that Ms. Short was not a prostitute, by which they seem to mean "yet." An attractive young woman from Medford, Massachusetts, she had come to Hollywood to break into movies. For several months she had been crashing with friends, dodging from apartment to rooming house to seedy motel. Her teeth were cracking, and she was growing desperate. On January 9, 1947, she was dropped off by an acquaintance near the Biltmore Hotel. In the pre-dawn hours of January 13, her dismembered body—she had been cut in half—was carried from a black car, and deposited in an empty lot.

This has become, in a sense, the American Jack the Ripper case—in this sense: that whereas the British have an apparently limitless appetite for books accusing some random citizen of being Jack the Ripper, Americans have somehow developed a healthy appetite for books accusing some random person of murdering the Black Dahlia. I have read all of these books, and I will tell you with absolute certainty that no one who is accused of being the murderer by any of these books had anything whatsoever to do with the crime, with one possible exception. The one book about the case that you should probably read, if you haven't, is *The Black Dahlia Files: The Mob, the Mogul, and the Murder That Transfixed Los Angeles,* by Donald H. Wolfe (ReganBooks, 2005).

Wolfe's research about the case is very, very good. His explanation of the murder, his "who done it," is the same sort of malarkey that all of the other books have to peddle. He names five people who he says committed the crime, and he claims that he has some good, hard, police locker room gossip to tie them to the case, which he got from this old cop who's been dead for years now, but who told him all this good stuff before he died.

The one exception is a guy named Jack Wilson, also known as Arnold Smith, and, I would guess, by quite a number of other names. If the things that Wolfe says about Wilson/Smith are true,

a) That would be nice for a change, and

b) Then in my opinion there would be a substantial likelihood that the man may have been involved in the crime, or may have committed it by himself.

What seems to me fairly obvious, in the same sense that it is obvious that the world is flat, is that Elizabeth Short was probably murdered by an unidentified serial murderer. You have to understand . . . and it's really difficult to wrap your mind around this concept, but it's true nonetheless . . . police in that era did not believe in serial murderers. The *term* "serial murderer" did not exist. There was no parallel term in use. "Mass murderer" or "crazed killer," perhaps, but those terms referred to a particular type of multiple murderer.

Serial murderers have existed in fiction for many years, but police until about 1980 absolutely insisted that they were exactly that: fiction. Oh sure, they would say, there is a case or two or record of crazy people who ran around murdering for excitement, but experienced policemen all "knew" that almost all "real" crimes were committed by persons who knew the victim.

All the experienced policemen knew this, but the only problem was that it wasn't true; there were just as many serial murderers around then as there are now, only they mostly were never caught because the police refused to look for them and didn't know how to look for them anyway. Within a month of the murder of Elizabeth Short, and about seven miles away, police found the nude body of Jeanne French. The letters "B.D." had been written on her body, but, according to Wolfe "it was obvious to [the police] that there was no relationship between the two cases. The MO was totally different." It was one of those vast, incalculable idiocies to which the human race is prey, like "women are not intelligent enough to handle the affairs of the world," which vast numbers of men believed just a generation ago. Our ability to misunderstand the world is without limit.

Most murders, of course, are *not* committed by serial murderers, but there are a few obvious hallmarks of a serial murder victim. The Black Dahlia has all of those hallmarks. She was an attractive young woman, who would be a natural target for sexual sadism. She was not a prostitute, at least yet, but she was a woman down on her luck who could be easily persuaded to climb into a car with a man she did not know. Her body was found nude, obviously dumped somewhere other than where she was killed. She had been the victim of horrible abuse, and had been dismembered. Her body was placed in the wee hours of the morning in a location isolated enough to allow the murderer to drive away unseen. All of this is suggestive of a serial murderer at work.

Whoever killed Elizabeth Short was an advanced sexual sadist. A killer does not leap to that condition; a person develops those traits and habits as he develops any others: in stages, and by degrees. It seems extremely likely, to me, that the murderer of the Black Dahlia had numerous previous kills, which had become progressively more gruesome.

The essential problem with Wolfe's thesis is this. The people of Los Angeles in 1947—as any other city—could be divided into those who live well-documented lives, and those who live undocumented lives, understanding of course that we don't mean that they are *entirely* undocumented. In the one group you have civic leaders, rich and powerful people, sports heroes, media figures, famous mobsters and writers and, this being Los Angeles, movie stars. In the other group you have everybody else, the guys and dolls who get up at 6:30, take their kids to school at 8:00 and go anonymously to work.

For every famous somebody there are several hundred undocumented lives. As a starting point for the discussion, it is overwhelmingly more likely that the murder was committed by a member of the undocumented hordes, rather than the privileged minority. If you have a bag of groceries and you ask "Who bought this bag of groceries," 99.9% of the time the answer will not be "Clark Gable" or "Mickey Spillane"; it will be somebody you never heard of. Same thing here . . . it *could* be a famous person, but most likely it isn't.

However, if you back away from the murder scene a great distance, sixty years or so, and you then ask "Who in Los Angeles could have committed this murder?" you are inevitably pushed toward those people whose lives you know something about—the famous people. We *know* what Bugsy Siegel was doing on January 12, 1947; it's in his FBI file. We *know* what the movie stars were doing; it's in the gossip columns. We have no idea what Jack Stanton was doing that day, or Darrell Lum, or Jerry Carpenter, or any of the other phone book full of phony people I could make up by mixing and matching names. They are disappearing quickly into the mists of time, and we have no way to tie them to the crime. If you're trying to figure it out at that distance you work with the documents.

The way that we perceive the event from across acres of time is very different from the way it really was. We should start with the presumption that the crime was probably created by an anonymous nobody, and, in my view, we should be very skeptical of efforts to link the crime, decades later, to members of the well-documented elite.

Wolfe—and this is a wonderful book that I recommend highly—but Wolfe alleges that Elizabeth Short was pregnant, a claim which is not well-substantiated, and further alleges that a rich and powerful man would be the father, a claim for which there is no evidence at all. He then argues that the pregnancy provides a motive for the crime. Well, Elizabeth Short was tortured, probably over a period of several days, before she was murdered. It seems overwhelmingly likely, then, that she was murdered by some sick bastard who enjoyed hurting women. Asking what his "motive" was is silly. He enjoyed it.

Wolfe argues that Short was murdered by, among others, Bugsy Siegel and Harry Chandler, of the *Los Angeles Times* Chandlers. Wolfe has extensive documentation about the lives of the people he implicates in the murder, but all he has that ties them to Elizabeth Short is just rumors, gossip, innuendo and coincidences, a bridge held up by toothpicks and spider webs. He ties Harry Chandler to the Biltmore Hotel; he ties Elizabeth Short to the Biltmore Hotel—but how many thousands of people could be tied to the Biltmore Hotel? Elizabeth Short was murdered by a psycho nut case, and Benny Siegel was a psycho nut case—but how many thousands of anonymous psycho nut cases are there in a major metropolitan area?

Wolfe thinks that the murder was never solved because the police covered it up. That's possible. It is more likely that the crime was never solved because:

a) Stranger-on-stranger murders are extremely difficult to solve, and generally are not solved, even today, and

b) These crimes are especially difficult to solve if you assume that the murderer was someone she knew, which was the universal working assumption of police in that era.

But read the book—*The Black Dahlia Files*, by Donald Wolfe. In time, Wolfe's improbable explanation for the murder may become the dominant explanation, simply because Wolfe's research is much better than the research of the other people who have written about the case. But I'm voting to acquit.

In each generation, due to indigenous journalism, some part of the country becomes the source of a large share of the nation's crime stories. In our time it is Florida. In the 1970s and 1980s it was Seattle. In the late 1940s it was Los Angeles.

On January 3, 1948, two men and one .45 caliber automatic robbed a haberdashery in Pasadena.

Ten days later, a gray 1946 Ford coupe was stolen from a Pasadena street.

At 4:35 AM on January 18, someone driving a 1947 Ford coupe (the 1946 and 1947 Ford coupes were almost indistinguishable) used a flashing red spotlight to pull over a couple driving near Malibu Beach. Pretending at first to be a policeman, the lone assailant pulled a .45 automatic and relieved them of their valuables.

Later in the day that crime repeated itself near the Rose Bowl: someone using a red spotlight approached a couple in a parked car. Thinking he was being approached by a cop, the man lowered his window and asked the cop what he wanted. This time the woman was struck in the face, for no real reason. The driver believed the car to be a 1946 Ford sedan.

The crime spree took a turn for the worse on the evening of January 19. A couple was parked in West Pasadena, in the hills overlooking the Rose Bowl, when a gray Ford coupe with a red spotlight pulled up behind them. The driver of the coupe approached, his hand on a revolver, and asked for identification. The man produced his license. The cop produced a .45. After robbing the couple, he took the woman back to his car, where he forced her to perform oral sex.

The newspapers had begun to follow the crimes, dubbing the unknown assailant the "Red Light Bandit," and anxiety about his attacks sharpened after the rape. The next day, January 20, a couple parked on Mulholland Drive was robbed in a similar manner, although the woman was not assaulted.

Two days later, the Red Light Bandit established a new standard in his violence. Approaching a couple driving slowly down Mulholland Drive (they were returning from a church dance), the Red Light Bandit pulled them over, robbed them both, then took the woman, an innocent seventeen-year-old girl, back to his car. The boyfriend drove off, trying to get the police; the bandit followed, attempting to force the other car off the road into a canyon. He told the girl he would kill her boyfriend if she didn't do what he wanted. When she acquiesced, he pulled off into a secluded area by the side of the road, where he forced her to submit to oral and anal rape.

Pulling together reports from all over the area, two detectives from the Hollywood Bureau compiled an APB, released shortly after five o'clock on January 23, alerting police to be on the lookout for a tan or gray Ford coupe. An hour after the APB was issued two men with a handgun robbed a clothing store in Redondo Beach. An hour and a half after that, two patrolmen spotted a suspect car in North Hollywood. They pulled up behind it. The car fled, initiating a high-speed chase, which ended as they generally do. Caryl Chessman and David Knowles were in custody by nine o'clock. It had been less than three weeks since the crime spree began.

There is no murder here; the Red Light Bandit had committed no murder. The two most famous crime stories of the twentieth century which do not involve a murder both occurred at the same time: the Caryl Chessman case, and the Julius and Ethel Rosenberg matter.

The case of David Knowles would be adjudicated and resolved, making a little bit of legal history along the way. Caryl Chessman would become perhaps the most famous criminal of the 1950s, and one of the pivotal crime figures of the twentieth century. His case would go to the Supreme Court sixteen times. Chessman would write at least four books while in prison, spending many, many weeks on the best-seller lists, and would become the subject of numerous other books and films. His execution by the state of California on May 2, 1960, was protested by Eleanor Roosevelt, Pablo Casals, Aldous Huxley, Albert Schweitzer and the Queen of Belgium, among millions of others.

But back to 1948 . . . Showing his resourcefulness quickly, Chessman elected to act as his own attorney—and then immediately filed a motion challenging his competence to act in that capacity, on the grounds that he might be insane. The judge ruled that he wasn't insane and could act as his own attorney if he wanted to.

After a trial lasting about the same length of time as the crime spree, Chessman was convicted on 17 of 18 counts. Under the provisions of California's so-called Little Lindbergh Law, Chessman faced the possibility of a death sentence. The Little Lindbergh Law held that:

1) Whenever an individual was taken from one place to another against his will, that was kidnapping, and

2) If the kidnapping victim was harmed, it was a capital crime.

Since two women were taken back to the Red Light Bandit's car and physically harmed, it was a capital case.

The Little Lindbergh Law broke down during the prosecution of David Knowles. Knowles, apparently Chessman's partner in the clothing-store robberies, had not participated in the sex crimes. Still, using the spurious argument that clerks were "kidnapped" when they were forced into a back room, Knowles was also charged and convicted under the law. In 1950 the California Supreme Court threw out the conviction, ruling that this was an impermissible abuse of the law. Prosecutors were using the law to get a life sentence or even a death sentence for armed robbery. This was never the intention of the legislature, but once it became a standard practice that shifted the ground of the argument, forcing legislators to go against the law-and-order sentiment in order to correct the law. The California Supreme Court finally told them they had to. The law was amended during the 1951 legislative session.

Chessman's description of this, in *The Face of Justice* (p. 58), was that "the anomalous result was that Chessman had been tried, convicted and sentenced to death for technical 'kidnapping' for the purpose of robbery, an act that apparently would no longer be punishable at all under the clarified law." This is a preposterous description of the matter. The acts committed by the Red Light Bandit have been serious crimes everywhere in the civilized world since the time of Hammurabi, and always will be.

A few weeks after Chessman's trial the court reporter suddenly died. He had transcribed only one-third of the record of Chessman's trial; the rest was in shorthand notes, which, when referred to an association of court reporters, were initially described as "completely indecipherable." When the judge sentenced Chessman to death, the absence of a complete trial transcript became a stumbling block, which would trouble the case until its resolution twelve years later.

At this time, people sentenced to death were normally executed in a matter of weeks. Into the 1940s, the law in many states required that a person filing an appeal must pay for the preparation of a trial transcript. Preparation of the trial transcript was expensive, and this made it impossible for most convicted criminals, even those facing death sentences, to appeal their crimes. "If you're broke and can't afford to have a transcript prepared," the law said to the convicted, "that's tough luck, but we're going to execute you anyway."

Many death sentences were never appealed, because of this barrier and others, but even when they were appealed, the appeals were normally resolved within a matter of some months. California, a little ahead of the nation, had reformed the law to this extent: that when a man facing a death sentence filed an appeal, the state was required to produce a transcript of the trial. The court reporter's death made it extremely difficult for the state of California to meet this obligation.

Building upon that small strand of good fortune, Chessman began to pursue appeals with great vigor. As his own attorney, Chessman was what might be called "constructively incompetent." Having no training in the law, Chessman of course made many procedural mistakes. Whenever one of these was found, Chessman would seize upon it to try to block the process: See, I should never have been allowed to act as my own attorney (he would argue). Look what I did here—this might have changed everything that happened from that point on. At the same time, he was a brilliant and resourceful advocate, constantly pursuing different lines of appeal in different courts. When one appeals court would turn him down, he would appeal the issue to a higher court. When one avenue of appeal was closed to him, he would open another one, entangling them if possible, so that it became impossible to actually execute him, since the state could never reach the point where all of the legal issues in his case had been resolved.

Later, of course, this became standard operating procedure for a death-row inmate, and later still the higher courts clarified the law to limit appeals. But it hadn't happened before. Chessman largely invented it. Although condemned prisoners in his time were guaranteed access to legal representation, this representation was often perfunctory. Chessman, fighting for his life, declined the help of court-appointed attorneys. He faced an almost-impossible task. He had to figure out, as the process was happening, how to stop the state from executing him—a task roughly equivalent to taking the court against the Los Angeles Lakers with an untrained team, figuring out the rules of a basketball game as the clock is running. He did this job so well that he invented a small industry, the death-row attorney's game.

In 1954 Chessman published his first book, *Cell 2455 Death Row* (Prentice-Hall). He was an amazing writer. The book vaulted to the top of the best-seller list, and stayed there. By the time the book was published Chessman claimed that he had already established an American record for the length of time spent on death row, six-plus years.

The publication of *Cell 2455* gave him two important weapons in his fight with the state: money, and attention. There had been an active movement to abolish the death penalty for a hundred years before 1950. Several states had abolished the death penalty before or about the turn of the century, but most had gradually reinstated it. Caryl Chessman became the poster boy for the anti–death penalty movement. After he hit the best-seller list with his first book, everything he did was news. If he disobeyed a prison directive and was confined to quarters, that was in the papers.

Now Chessman could command the attention of good lawyers, committed to keeping him alive, and he began to accept their assistance. They helped him to invent more ways to frustrate the government in its efforts to carry out the sentence.

Chessman wrote four books from death row. The later books were not as well written as the first, and his popularity as a writer gradually waned.

Chessman spit out arguments about his innocence at a machine-gun pace. He succeeded in convincing hundreds of thousands of readers that he was indeed innocent, and this is still apparent today. In Frederick Drimmer's book *Until You Are Dead,* Drimmer writes that "To the very end, Chessman insisted he was not guilty—and to this day the evidence he presented seems so persuasive it is hard to understand why he was ever convicted and executed. But that is reckoning without the power of the circulation-hungry California press, which whipped up a campaign against him that would not be stilled until his life was."

Drimmer follows this with a seven-page account of the Chessman case, during which he gives hardly a clue as to what the "evidence" was that he found so persuasive. Descriptions of the Red Light Bandit "were conflicting," writes Drimmer. "A few of the people who'd been robbed identified Chessman; others, however, couldn't."

Well, the crimes for which Chessman was executed were committed at night, in dark and isolated places. The bandit parked behind the victims and walked toward them through his headlights. He covered his face with a handkerchief and stood behind their door(s), as a cop would in writing a ticket. He shined a flashlight in their faces. *Of course* not all of his victims could identify Chessman as the assailant. That's not evidence that he was innocent.

On the other hand, both rape victims gave strong, positive that-is-the-*man* type of identifications. A man who was with one of the rape victims, and who also got a good look at the assailant, was equally certain that Chessman was the perpetrator. This pair of victims happened to drop by the police station at the time Chessman was being interviewed. Without being told that their assailant was anywhere around, they spotted Chessman and rushed up to him, accusing him of the crime.

As to the "conflicting descriptions" of the criminal, when were there ever not conflicting descriptions of a criminal, if there were multiple witnesses? I've certainly never heard of such a thing. In fact, though, the APB issued for the Red Light Bandit on the evening of January 23, 1948, put together a composite description of the criminal, based on all of the witnesses. Even leaving out the 1946 Ford sedan in which he was captured, it seems an obvious description of Caryl Chessman: "Male, Caucasian, possibly Italian, swarthy complexion, 23–35 years, 5'6" to 5'10", 150 to 170 pounds, thin to medium build, dark brown wavy hair, close cut, dark brown eyes, crooked teeth, narrow nose with slight hump on bridge of nose, sharp chin, possible scar over right eyebrow." Chessman was Jewish, not Italian, but looked Italian. The suspect is described as 5'6" to 5'10"; Chessman claimed to be six foot, but was probably 5'10" or 5'11".

Also, the APB describes a subject with a "narrow nose"; Chessman had a huge nose. However, why the APB says this is something of a mystery, since several witnesses had specified that the attacker had a large, broken nose.

Frederick Drimmer's other arguments in favor of Chessman focus on essentially irrelevant points. Chessman was tried before a judge who "reportedly had sentenced more criminals to death than any other in the state's history." I don't doubt that he was a hanging judge, but what does this do to prove that he hung the wrong man? Chessman, says Drimmer, made "some grave mistakes" in defending his case. "The worst was in choosing the jury. One man and eleven women were selected—four of them with daughters the same age as the bandit's female victims." One of the Bandit's rape victims was a teenaged girl; the other was a woman in her thirties. But even if this was true, why should it cause us to believe that Chessman was innocent?

As I see the case, there is every reason to believe that Chessman committed the crimes for which he was executed. Apart from the eyewitness identifications and the fact that Chessman matches the description of the Red Light Bandit, we should consider:

• Chessman was arrested driving the stolen car described in the APB.

• Stolen property from the Redondo Beach robbery, committed 90 minutes earlier, was in the car at the time of his arrest.

• Chessman initially denied the clothing-store robberies as well as the sex crimes, and offered an implausible explanation of how he came to be driving the stolen car.

• Chessman, throughout his criminal career, had several times used the pretense of being a police officer to gain the element of surprise before committing a robbery. The jury which convicted him of the crimes did not know this.

• Chessman was alleged by police and eyewitnesses to have made incriminating statements during a police lineup—for example, when an officer attempted to help him place a handkerchief over his face, he said "I know how I wore it." Chessman denied making such statements.

Chessman's basic defense, the one he returned to again and again and again after he abandoned the pretense of complete innocence, is that he was "just" a thief. Economic circumstances had forced him, at an early age, to steal, so he argued—but he was not a pervert. He was not a sex criminal, never had been, never would be.

This argument, however, is so weak that I wonder if I need even rebut it. All of Chessman's previous convictions, it is true, were for theft—but how does this prove that he *didn't* commit the crimes with which he was charged? Criminals have been known to change the types of crimes they commit, you know, to start out in one area and escalate gradually toward more serious criminal behavior. This happens in . . . oh, I don't know, 95% of all crime stories, give or take a few.

What's more, the crimes for which Chessman was executed *did* start out as economic crimes; the Red Light Bandit began by pulling a gun on lovers in remote places, then taking their money and valuables. It's just that, as he found himself in control of young women who were afraid to resist him, he began to grow bolder, and began demanding sex acts as part of his price. There is nothing in this that is inconsistent with Chessman's prior history.

It is, of course, a terrible thing that a brilliant and multi-talented man like Chessman was executed for crimes that fell short of murder. By no means do I minimize the crimes that he committed. His second (known) rape triggered a nervous breakdown in the victim, from which she never recovered. She was in a mental hospital for many, many years after the crime.

But when people write about the Chessman case today, there is a tendency to assume that the battle focused on the appropriateness of executing a man convicted of rape and kidnapping, but not murder. In fact, it did not; perhaps Chessman should have chosen to fight that battle, but he didn't. The battle was focused on the questions of Chessman's guilt, and on questions of due process. Since Chessman was in fact guilty and had in fact received a fair trial, it was perhaps inevitable that the story would end with his execution. He was one of the last people in this country to be executed for a crime less than murder.

Julius and Ethel Rosenberg were executed on June 19, 1953. I am going to stiff you on Julius and Ethel, but there was something related to them I wanted to say.

One of the arguments made against popular crime stories—probably the most common one—is that they distract the public from more serious news. In my view, this argument is without merit.

First of all, as I see it, no one has any ability whatsoever to figure out what is going to be important to people. I look back on my own life. When I was in high school I had two habits that greatly irritated my teachers; actually, many more than two, but let's focus. One was writing funny notes to my classmates, trying to make them crack up in the middle of class. The other was spending hours of valuable study time making mystifying totals from the agate type in the sports pages. I was called on the carpet any number of times and told to stop doing this stuff and pay more attention to What Was Really Important.

As I look back on those years, the two most useful things that I was doing, in terms of preparing me for my career, were

1) Writing humorous notes to my classmates, and
2) Making mystifying totals from the agate type in the sports pages.

By writing amusing if vulgar notes to my classmates, I was learning to write—not learning to write in a way that would please English teachers, but learning to write in a way that would hold the interest of people who had no reason to read the note, other than the expectation that they would enjoy reading it. That's much, much closer to writing books than writing insipid research papers to please bored English teachers. The adults in charge *thought* they knew what was important, but in retrospect they were just completely wrong.

In the 1960 election cycle, the island nations of Quemoy and Matsu emerged as central issues. In essence, Nixon charged Kennedy with being unreliable on national defense, and Kennedy defended himself. Kennedy was asked, "If you were to learn tomorrow that Quemoy and Matsu—American allies—were under attack by communist forces, would you commit American forces to defend them?" Kennedy insisted that he would, and this dispute became a central issue in the race.

The intellectuals, the commentators, the smart-money crowd ridiculed that. "Why are we spending all of this time talking about Quemoy and Matsu?" they demanded to know. "Why aren't we talking about the real issues in this campaign?"

And yet, in retrospect, that turned out to be precisely the defining issue of the following years. The name of the obscure ally that we had to decide whether we wanted to defend with blood and treasure was "Vietnam," not "Quemoy" or "Matsu," but the principle was the same. The smart people who thought they knew what was "really" important turned out, in retrospect, to be just entirely wrong.

Third example . . . psychology. Since the 1960s, when trendy psychology burst onto the scene, it has been common to ridicule it, and in particular to ridicule popular psychology by contrasting it with serious workaday psychology.

And yet in retrospect, at least as it seems to me, a huge percentage of what was mainstream psychology in the 1950s and 1960s has now been discarded. Freudian psychoanalysis turned out, in retrospect, to be a useful plot device for *The Sopranos* and several Woody Allen movies, but otherwise almost entirely a waste of time. Nobody really does that stuff anymore, because nobody will pay for it, and the insurance companies won't pay for it because there is no actual evidence that it does much good.

On the other hand, pop psychology, at least in my view, has turned out to have great value to our society. Popular psychology has created an entire lexicon of internal-dialogue concepts that we all use every day to try to think through our problems.

When I was a senior in college I was taking a class in which we read a number of Charles Dickens novels, in regard to which the professor made this argument. "In Dickens' time the serious novelists wrote for public consumption," he said, "and many of these writers had huge audiences. Whereas now, anybody who is *really* 'serious' about writing novels writes for a very small audience composed mostly of other writers."

"Dr. Worth," I objected, "what is your definition of 'serious'? Why would any serious person waste his time writing to an audience of a few hundred people?"

"That is the way it is done now," he replied.

I wrestled with this exchange for weeks following. Dr. Worth's definition of "serious" was "people like Dr. Worth." People like me, who have PhDs, we are serious people, and we only write to other serious people. But is that really serious?

I would argue that it is *not* serious. Writing academic novels to be read by a few dozen or a few hundred other academics is not "serious" writing; it's literary masturbation. The people who do that are amusing themselves, without engaging the society in serious discussion.

This is the way I see it:

1) The world is vastly more complicated than the image of the world that we all hold in our heads, therefore

2) Nobody really has any idea what will be important to society or to individuals in society in the future.

That which is symbolically significant, like the Super Bowl and Michelle Obama's sleeves, often turns out, over time, to be of far more real importance than that which is tangibly significant, like Middle East policy and economic reform. Sophisticated Frenchmen, a hundred years ago, were appalled to see France tearing itself apart arguing about the Dreyfus case. It was a symbolic issue, justice for one man. In retrospect, what was going on in France at that time that was more important?

Bob Costas once had a contract to fill in for Larry King on CNN. Costas thought he had made it clear, in negotiating that contract, that he was not going to do "stories" that exploited personal tragedies. But as soon as the contract started, he found himself being maneuvered into interviews that he felt he should not be doing. Finally, pressured to do an interview about the Natalee Holloway case, he refused to do the interview, and walked away from a lucrative contract.

I certainly admire Costas for having the courage to stand up for his values. I also think that he was right—but not because the Natalee Holloway case was not important. The problem with doing another hour on Natalee Holloway was that there was simply nothing to be said. Several cable shows were spending hours a day, at that time, "covering" Natalee Holloway. There was no actual news; it was just stupid speculation, masquerading as news. I respect Costas for saying, "I'm not going to take part in that."

But at the same time, I do not believe that the serious news issues favored by grave and enlightened commentators are any more likely to be of real importance to society than . . . the Natalee Holloway case, to pick one at random. I think the whole idea of popular crime stories diverting attention from serious news is just complete nonsense.

Now, back to Julius and Ethel and their commie friends. Popular crime books normally run 100,000 to 150,000 words, or 250 to 400 pages, more or less. Books about the Rosenbergs—and there are dozens of them—start at 600 pages and go up. These God Damned things go on forever.

Why?

Because the authors are so "serious" about their work—in the same sense that academics are serious about their precious academic novels. The authors of the Rosenberg works are trying to communicate to us, through the vastness of their literary output, how serious they are about their subject. "This is not a lightweight amusement about Ted Bundy or Darlie Routier or the Manson family," they are saying. "Oh, no. This is A Serious Book containing Serious Academic Research about A Serious Subject."

My view is that if the people who write these Rosenberg books were *really* serious people, they would

a) figure out what it was that they had to say,

b) say it, and

c) shut up.

They won't do that, for the most part, because they're operating out of a paradigm of what constitutes a "serious" subject that they've never really questioned, and which they couldn't defend.

At one point I was very interested in the Rosenberg case, and I actually bored through six or seven of those interminable texts that constitute the

Rosenberg bookshelf. For younger people who may be mystified by the reach and impact of the Rosenbergs, I would say that in many respects the Rosenberg case parallels the 1991 battle between Anita Hill and Clarence Thomas. In both cases, there was a small, tightly knit group of people who were

a) ethnically distinct,

b) highly political, and

c) quite remarkable people.

Within this small group of very bright, highly motivated political activists, there was a betrayal, one member accusing another of an act which the other vehemently denied. Because it lay so close to a national nerve, unraveling the exact nature of that betrayal became a coast-to-coast obsession. What was at stake in one case was whether two people would die; what was at stake in the other was whether a man would go onto the Supreme Court. But in both cases, the entire nation picked sides in this dispute, based on their own philosophical predispositions, because in each case, the issue defined the fault lines of America's politics at that moment. If you believed that there were communists hidden among us, you believed that the Rosenbergs were guilty. If you believed it was all a witch hunt, you believed they were innocent.

In an ordinary trial, the issue is whether the accused committed the crime. O. J. Simpson may or may not have killed Nicole, but there is no question that somebody did. In the Rosenberg case, as in the Anita Hill/Clarence Thomas affair, the central issue is whether the crime ever occurred. If you want my take on the case, it is

1) That a crime of espionage certainly did occur,

2) That Julius Rosenberg almost certainly was involved in that crime,

3) That Ethel Rosenberg probably had some knowledge about the crime, but that

4) Nothing really happened here that required that anybody be executed.

The Rosenbergs were executed because of paranoid and exaggerated perceptions about the seriousness of the crime. They were executed to make the point that one could be executed for supporting the commies. This was wrong. It's not really a Popular Crime story.

XVII

Anyone experienced in interrogation learns to recognize the difference between a man speaking from life and a man telling a story that he either has made up or has gotten from another person.

—F. Lee Bailey, *The Defense Never Rests* (p. 151)

Sometime after midnight on the Fourth of July, 1954, Marilyn Sheppard was bludgeoned to death in her bed in a Cleveland suburb. Her husband, Dr. Sam Sheppard, called a neighbor about 6:00 in the morning; the neighbors rushed over and then called the police.

Sam's story was that he was sleeping on the couch, downstairs, when he heard his wife scream. Middle of the night; he doesn't have any idea what time it is. Groggy, he gets to his feet and rushes up the stairs. Near the top of the stairs he can see a faint form in a light-colored shirt inside Marilyn's room, but as he reaches the top of the stairs somebody clubs him from behind, and the lights go out.

The lights go out, figuratively; the lights were out anyway, but now Sam is unconscious in the dark. He remains that way for some time. Eventually he comes to, goes to Marilyn's bed, checks her pulse and decides that she must be dead. He goes to his son's room, checks on his sleeping son, and then hears something downstairs, somebody rustling through stuff. He races downstairs, and sees a figure heading out the back door, toward the lake. He chases the figure out the door, down a set of outdoor steps that lead to the beach. At the bottom of the steps somebody jumps him, perhaps from behind, and begins choking him. He loses consciousness again. When he comes to he is lying in the water at the edge of the lake, and dawn is breaking.

He returns to the house, and checks again on his wife. She is still dead.

He checks again on his son, Chip, sleeping in a nearby room; Chip is still fine. Woozy and disoriented, Sam wanders around the house for some time, wondering whether this might be a nightmare. He decides it is not a nightmare. He tries to remember a phone number . . . this is twenty years before 911 services. The phone number he remembers is of a friend and neighbor, Spencer Houk, incidentally the mayor of Bay Village. Then he passes out.

After the neighbors called police they also called Sam's brother, Stephen Sheppard, also a doctor, and Stephen called the rest of the family, his father and other brother also being doctors; even the family dog was a part-time veterinarian. The brothers arrived soon after the police, examined Sam quickly, and rushed him off to the hospital that was run by their family.

The police for the rest of the day ran back and forth from the house to the hospital, harassing the medicated, lawyerless and sometimes nearly comatose Sam to get his story on record. His story, as they got it, seemed to them to be full of holes, and the police never believed a word of it. They didn't find any evidence that anyone had been in the house, other than Sam and his late wife and the kid and the dog. The doors hadn't been broken in, and there hadn't been any real burglary, just some lame efforts to fake a burglary, and there hadn't been any serious attempt at a sexual assault. This looked to them like a domestic murder.

Unfortunately, they couldn't prove it, as there wasn't any real evidence that Sam had killed his wife, so the case sat idle for the next three weeks. The Cleveland newspapers began running daily stories about the case, with headlines like "Someone Is Getting Away With Murder," "Why Don't Police Quiz Top Suspect?" and "Why Isn't Sam Sheppard in Jail?"

What sometimes happens is that a police officer becomes convinced that he knows who done it, and lays out his story for prosecutors, who tell him that he doesn't have a case that will hold up in court. The police officer refuses to accept that he doesn't have a case, and begins leaking information to the newspapers in an effort to force the prosecutor's hand. No sources say so, but I would bet that this is what happened here: a police officer or the coroner was feeding information to the newspapers in a deliberate effort to force the prosecutors to file charges.

Dr. Sheppard was arrested on July 30, 1954, and was convicted of murder on December 21, 1954. Over the following years numerous books and articles were written claiming that Sheppard had gotten a raw deal, and pointing to flaws in his trial, specifically:

1) The court's failure to distance or isolate itself from a hysterical media onslaught,

2) Too much attention being paid to Sheppard's marital infidelities,

3) The failure to deal with forensic evidence which tends to argue his innocence, and

4) The dismissal, in his original trial, of other evidence that tends to exonerate him.

And there are other issues, kind of petty issues . . . I guess I'll deal with the petty issues first; the case is so famous that many of you probably know all of the issues. The Cleveland coroner, Dr. Samuel Gerber, was probably the nation's most famous coroner at that time. The Sheppards were D.O.s, Doctors of Osteopathy. There is a long history of distrust between the osteopathic community and the medical establishment, and there were allegations that Gerber had expressed hostility toward the Sheppards, who were highly successful osteopaths.

In the trial, Gerber—who obviously thought Sheppard was guilty, and had to a large extent engineered the prosecution of him—testified that a bloody imprint on a pillowcase had apparently been made by some kind of surgical instrument. This was untrue, and this was used by journalists in the years after the trial, and eventually by F. Lee Bailey, in court, to make it appear that Gerber was out to get the Sheppards all along.

But I don't think he was, and I don't think that whole angle amounts to anything. Gerber thought that Sheppard had committed the crime, and was out to get him in the same sense he was out to get any other murderer. He said the murder weapon was a surgical instrument of some kind because he thought it was. He was wrong about this, and he shouldn't have said it, but it was a few words out of a long trial in which both sides said things they probably shouldn't have said. I don't think it had anything to do with Sheppard being convicted. A juror insisted that this was never mentioned in jury deliberations.

A witness reported seeing a bushy-haired man outside the Sheppard residence that night, probably just before the attack, and another witness saw a man walking away from the house later, probably after the attack. The jurors, for reasons known only to them, paid no attention to this testimony.

After the trial was over Sheppard's attorneys arranged for Dr. Paul Kirk to examine the crime scene. Dr. Kirk was the nation's leading criminologist, crime scene investigator; he is to that field what Einstein was to physics. (In modern terminology he would probably be called a criminalist.) Dr. Kirk found evidence in the blood spatter that the murder weapon had been wielded left-handed, that the death blows had been struck by a man swinging something—a lead pipe, a flashlight, something like that—full throttle left-handed. Dr. Sheppard was right-handed.

From my standpoint, it is almost impossible to understand how Dr. Kirk could be wrong about this. Play along with me here. Stand up, and brace your knee against the desk, or against the chair you are sitting in . . . whatever. Face the desk/chair, and pretend that you are beating the living hell out of something sitting in the middle of it, left-handed. Pretend you have a billy club in your hand, and you are swinging it full force at the skull of a person lying in front of you.

Now, look at where the blood would fly off your club as you draw it back and swing it forward time and again. Look at the ceiling, the wall, the furniture . . . look where the blood would fly to.

Now do the same thing right-handed, and ask yourself: studying the blood pattern, could you make a mistake about whether this was done right-handed or left-handed? You can't. The difference between the blood spatter pattern if the murders were committed left-handed as opposed to right-handed is unmistakable. Sheppard was right-handed; the murder was committed left-handed.

Dr. Kirk also claimed that the forensic evidence clearly showed that Marilyn Sheppard bit her attacker's hand, and that the murderer would have had injuries to his hand in the days after the murder. He based this on Marilyn Sheppard's broken teeth, which were not broken in, but pulled out as if she had bitten her attacker very hard, and also on the analysis of certain of the blood spots in the bloody bedroom, which he said had characteristics inconsistent with Marilyn Sheppard's blood, although they were of the same blood group. Dr. Sheppard had no such injury to his hand on the day after the murder.

This information certainly should have been introduced at the trial, but the onus of that failure is on Sheppard's defense team. Sheppard's attorneys argued that the police locked up the house in which the murder occurred and denied them access to it until after the trial, and also that the dog ate their brief in which they were going to demand access to the house.

What happened, I think, is that Sheppard's lead attorney, William Corrigan, thought that he could beat the case without taking on those issues. He thought, correctly, that the police didn't really have much of a case against Sheppard, and he thought, incorrectly, that he could beat them. When he lost, he went into CYA mode, calling in Dr. Kirk to do what should have been done before the trial. The appeals courts ruled—correctly, in my view—that this was *not* newly discovered evidence in the legal meaning of the term, since it could have and should have been discovered by Sheppard's defense before the trial, and that Corrigan was simply trying to use this tactic to get a do-over. Sheppard's defenders have claimed, in response to this, that the police had locked up the crime scene and denied them access to it until it was too late. That's ridiculous. The police commonly and appropriately lock up a crime scene until the case is resolved, and they obviously could not have denied Sheppard's defenders access to the scene had access been demanded. The failure to demand access was an incredible blunder by Sheppard's attorneys, and one that kept him in jail for many years.

The court's failure to insulate itself from the Cleveland press coverage, which created what an appeals court described as a Roman circus, was certainly a blatant and serious failing of the trial.

The prosecution argued that Sheppard wanted Marilyn out of the way because he was having really fun relations with a knockout named Susan Hayes. This also did not sit well with Sam's defenders. "The Susan Hayes matter," wrote Margaret Parton of the *New York Herald Tribune* in the middle of the trial, "was blown up way beyond its importance." Lawyers like to say that it is one thing to commit adultery, a very different thing to commit murder. Evidence that a man has committed adultery does almost nothing to prove that he is capable of murder.

I see this a little differently. To me, it seems an extremely relevant issue, for this reason: that a man who is involved with another woman is dozens if not hundreds of times more likely to murder his wife than is a faithful husband. As anyone who follows crime stories has to know, men who kill their wives in cold blood are almost *always* involved with another woman, so much so that it is hard to come up with an exception. *Cherchez la femme.* Where there is a Scott Peterson, there is always an Amber Frey.

Set it up as a story problem:

A. What percentage of husbands are at any one moment involved in extra-marital affairs?

B. What percentage of husbands who kill their wives in premeditated plots are involved in extra-marital affairs at the time?

C. Knowing "A" and "B," how much more common is it for a cheating husband to kill his wife than for a faithful husband?

Using any kind of reasonable assumptions, it is apparent that for a philandering husband to kill his wife has to be at least twenty times more common than for a faithful husband to kill his wife, at a very minimum. In reality, the number is probably much larger than that. So, to me, it seems *very* relevant whether or not a suspected husband has been recently faithful to his late wife.

In any case, over the years the pendulum of public opinion swung gradually in Dr. Sheppard's favor. In 1954 virtually everyone in Cleveland was convinced that Sheppard was guilty. The newspapers had said so several times a week for months. Paul Holmes wrote a book about the case in 1961, *The Sheppard Murder Case*, essentially arguing that Sheppard had not received a fair trial. Other books followed, including two more by Holmes.

Beginning in 1963 there was a TV show—a really good TV show—called *The Fugitive*, which used the story of Sam Sheppard as a framework for the story of a heroic doctor, fleeing justice and saving lives on a weekly basis. *The Fugitive* grafted onto the outline of Sam Sheppard's tragedy the image of a doctor who was modest, sensitive, selfless and honorable, and hadn't been banging the nurses. This improved Sheppard's public image immensely.

Paul Holmes was a lawyer as well as a journalist. As a consequence of his books he became a participant in the story. About 1963 Holmes introduced a young attorney, F. Lee Bailey, to the Sheppard family, and after that acted as an aide to Bailey.

Bailey discovered new avenues of appeal, and eventually landed his case in front of the Supreme Court, the big one in Washington. The Supreme Court ruled that the trial court had failed its responsibilities by making minimal efforts to protect the trial from prejudicial publicity. This became an important precedent, laying out for the first time a court's responsibility to make a trial stand clear of flying journalistic debris. They ordered a new trial for Dr. Sam, or else that he be set free.

The city of Cleveland didn't really have their heart in the new trial, but they decided to go through the motions anyway. They dropped the Susan Hayes angle altogether, leaving Sam with no apparent motive to murder his wife. In the first trial the prosecution had claimed that Sam's injuries, suffered on the night of the murder, were trivial and/or fake. They got beat on that issue, so in the re-trial they just dropped it, and allowed Sam's lawyers to claim without challenge that his injuries were more serious than they probably were. They (the prosecution) came up with an entirely new and entirely improbable theory of how he had sustained these injuries. Although they had had eleven years to review Dr. Kirk's analysis of the crime scene and prepare to rebut it, they didn't seem to have a clue what to say about that, probably because most of what Dr. Kirk said was true, and they would have looked stupid trying to prove that it wasn't.

In spite of all this, the re-trial was not quite a slam dunk; on first ballot, four or maybe five jurors still thought Sheppard was guilty. Unable to point to any facts supporting his guilt, their position weakened as the jury debated, and eventually the jury voted to acquit Dr. Sheppard, but *The Fugitive* was cancelled anyway, and did poorly in re-runs.

I have read four books about the Sheppard case, which are *The Sheppard Murder Case,* by Paul Holmes (McKay, 1961); *Retrial: Murder and Dr. Sam Sheppard,* also by Holmes (Bantam, 1966); *Mockery of Justice,* by Cynthia L. Cooper and Sam Reese Sheppard (Onyx, 1997); and *The Wrong Man,* by James Neff (Random House, 2001).

There are at least three books about the Sheppard case which I have not read, which are *Dr. Sam: An American Tragedy,* by Jack Harrison Pollack (1972); *Endure and Conquer: My Twelve-Year Fight for Vindication,* by Sheppard himself (1966); and *My Brother's Keeper,* by Stephen Sheppard and Paul Holmes (1964). There is also information about the Sheppard case in many other books, including *Murder One,* by Dorothy Kilgallen (Random House, 1967), and *The Defense Never Rests,* subtitled, "Man, I Was Hot Shit," by F. Lee Bailey and Harvey Aronson (Stein & Day, 1971).

Holmes' first book about the case is a lucid, straightforward account of the matter as it stood in 1961, seven years after the original events. It's the best starting point if you want to read about the case; the other books assume too much knowledge, and tend to be confusing.

Mockery of Justice is the story of Samuel Reese Sheppard, the little boy who slept through the murder, and his lifelong efforts to blame everybody but his father for what happened. This book *assumes* that Dr. Sheppard is innocent, as a starting point, and advances the theory (among many others) that the real murderer may have been Richard Eberling, a man who washed windows at the Sheppard house and was convicted of murdering an elderly lady in the 1980s.

Sam Reese Sheppard endured a tragedy almost beyond comprehension. It is not reasonable to expect that he would get over this and move on with his life, and he never did. But the book is essentially whining. *Mockery of Justice* never engages the evidence against Dr. Sam, but instead simply re-writes the facts to fit one theory and then another. Their re-telling of Dr. Sam's story makes it appear that he gave a description of an assailant who could well have been Richard Eberling—ignoring entirely Sheppard's actual story at the time, or the fact that, years after the murder, Sheppard was still suggesting that he thought there probably were multiple assailants, one of them a woman.

There is a simple theory to explain what happened in the Sam Sheppard case which seems to me to accommodate *all* of the facts which can be clearly established. That theory is that Richard Eberling did in fact murder Marilyn Sheppard—at the behest of and with the aid and assistance of Sam Sheppard.

All of the books about the Sheppard case argue that he was innocent—but none of them deal fairly with the real reason that he was convicted, which is the rank implausibility of Sheppard's story. Bluntly stated, Sam Sheppard's account of the night Marilyn was murdered just doesn't make *any* frigging sense. It didn't make sense to the police who investigated the case, it didn't make sense to the prosecutors, it didn't make sense to newspaper guys, it didn't make any sense to the judges, and it doesn't make any sense to me. If you read between the lines of the court opinions which rejected Sheppard's appeals throughout the second half of the 1950s, that's really what they're trying to say: *this guy's story doesn't make any sense.*

What is wrong with his story? Well, first of all, is there one intruder or two? Sheppard never exactly said for sure, either because he didn't know or because he was keeping his options open, but in the main, he suggests that there were multiple intruders—first, because he thinks the intruder is wearing a light-colored shirt in the upstairs bedroom and a dark shirt on the beach, second, because the intruder seems to be simultaneously in the bedroom with Marilyn and attacking Sheppard as soon as he reaches the top of the stairs, and third, because the fleeing suspect immediately gains the advantage on him as soon as he reaches the bottom of the stairs down to the beach.

Over the years that followed, Sheppard became more and more explicit in suggesting that there were multiple intruders—an intruder, he says, and (I swear I am not making this up) an "intrudress." Sheppard never actually *says* that there are two intruders . . . it's just that it is dark, and he is groggy, and he never sees anything clearly, and he doesn't have any clear idea what's going on.

OK, fair enough; it's dark, he's groggy, he doesn't know. I'll accept that. Let's assume on first look that there is one intruder, because

a) There is no evidence of a second intruder,

b) Sheppard's defense witnesses, who claim to have seen a bushy-haired man outside his house at 2:30 and 4:15 in the morning, both reported seeing one man, not two,

c) It's really irrational behavior for two people,

d) If we assume that there were two perpetrators it becomes much more likely that one of them would later have told the police about it,

e) Sheppard's modern defenders have settled on Richard Eberling as the culprit, rather than Richard Eberling and his grandmother Ethel, and

f) It's just the sort of thing one usually does alone. I mean, personally, whenever I break into my neighbor's house and beat his wife to death in the middle of the night, I always do that sort of thing alone.

Anyway, the second question which arises is, "What was this guy who broke into the house after?" Did he break into the house *intending* to kill Marilyn? If so, why? Was he a burglar who was surprised by Marilyn's awakening and screaming, and over-reacted? Did he start to commit a sexual assault, and get carried away in violence when Marilyn screamed? Why did this happen?

From Sheppard's account of the crime, none of the answers make sense. If he was a burglar, why didn't he take anything of significance? If he was a burglar and Marilyn woke up and discovered him, why didn't he just hit her on the head with his lead pipe or whatever it was and get the hell out of there?

If he was there to commit murder, why did he rifle through some drawers downstairs before or after the crime? If he was there to commit murder, why did he let Sam Sheppard alone after knocking him out with his first blow? Why didn't he kill Sam, too—either then or later, when he had him unconscious again on the beach?

If he was there to commit a burglary, and we assume that he must have had a flashlight with him to find his way around, how did he not notice Sam Sheppard asleep on the living room couch? Or *did* he notice Sheppard there, and decide to go upstairs and murder Sheppard's wife anyway?

The essential theory advanced by Sheppard's defenders is that the intruder was a burglar—had to be, because drawers were rifled through—who discovered Marilyn, thought she was alone, attempted to assault her sexually, and went berserk when she woke up and screamed. The intruder is kind of a little bit of a burglar and a little bit of a would-be rapist, but the only thing he *really* does is commit murder—and he does that really well. He's thorough about that one.

But again, I'm 100% willing to give Sheppard a complete pass on these puzzling questions, because

a) Criminals often do things that we don't understand, as do life insurance salesmen and football coaches, and

b) It's not the victim's responsibility to explain the conduct of the criminal.

It might make perfect sense if we had better knowledge of what had happened.

But now we get into the nitty-gritty of the crime: the sequence of events. Did the rifling of the drawers downstairs occur *before* the murder, or after?

Well, obviously it seems massively unlikely that it could have occurred after the murder, for three reasons:

1) There would be blood all over the drawers,

2) By this time the burglar quite certainly knows that there is a man in the house, and that that man knows that he is in the house. He would have to assume that the police may have been called, and

3) He would have to be one cold son of a bitch to go downstairs and start calmly looking through drawers after having beaten a woman to death. Even hardened criminals aren't *that* cold and dispassionate. When they kill somebody, they mostly get out of the house as fast as possible.

So the theory that the dumping of the drawer contents occurred *after* the murder is totally untenable, while the theory that the dumping of the drawers occurred *before* the murder is largely untenable as well. It is difficult enough to believe that the intruder enters the house, pokes around in the front room in the dark with his flashlight, doesn't make any noise, finds the steps and tiptoes upstairs without Sheppard waking up or his dog barking. If the rifling of the drawers occurs before the murder, that increases the time that the burglar is in the house, and it increases the noise that he has to make. Three things that seem improbable have to happen there:

1. That Sheppard doesn't wake up when this man breaks in, when he looks around, when he goes into the study, when he dumps stuff on the floor of the study, when he comes back out, or when he climbs the stairs right next to where Sheppard is sleeping,

2. That the intruder doesn't notice Sheppard sleeping on the couch, and

3. That the dog doesn't bark.

It's not *impossible*, but it's a reach.

Does the savage beating of Marilyn Sheppard occur *before* Sheppard awakens, or after?

It can't occur *before* Sheppard awakes, because he hears Marilyn's scream. According to Sheppard, he hears Marilyn scream, gets up and immediately races up the stairs, where he is knocked senseless by the intruder.

If Marilyn had been struck one blow, two blows, three blows . . . no problem. She was struck twenty-five to thirty-five times . . . blood flying everywhere. The majority of these blows can't have been struck before she screamed, or she would have been dead at the time she screamed. Most of them have to have been struck afterward. Sheppard doesn't report hearing repeated, bone-crushing thuds while he is racing up the stairs, nor is there time for that to have happened, since the intruder, having heard Sheppard running up the stairs, goes over to meet Sheppard at the top of the stairs.

Then, apparently—by now certainly alerted that there is a man in the house—the burglar/rapist/murderer returns to the bedroom, and completes his vicious assault on the unconscious woman, who by now can certainly not be either a threat to him or a potential rape victim. What kind of sense does it make?

When I first read Sheppard's account of the crime, what most bothered me about it is that he is just *sooo* vague about the details. We expect him to be out of it . . . it's the middle of the night, he's asleep, it's dark, and he's hit on the head. We expect him to be foggy on the details—but he is *so* vague on the details that one can't avoid the feeling that he is being deliberately evasive. He doesn't know what time the assault began, nor when it ended . . . doesn't have a clue. He doesn't know *anything* about the assailant . . . doesn't know whether it was a man or a woman, two men, three men, an armada . . . he doesn't know. He doesn't have *any* description of the assailant . . . no height, weight, shoe size, hair, clothing, nothing (the famous description "bushy-haired man" was introduced into the case later by other people, and Sheppard sort of vaguely signed onto it). In his first interviews with police he is apparently not even sure that the assailant is human; he keeps describing it as "this form" . . . I was chasing this form down the stairs toward the lake. I guess it must have been a human if you say so. (An appeals court judge, years after the crime, ridiculed Sheppard's lawyer for refusing to say that the murderer was human.) Despite two brave physical confrontations with the murderer, he is unable to get *any* information about him. Despite losing his own shirt under conditions which he is unable to explain, he is unable to rip a shred of cloth off the murderer that might give us a hint about the clothes he was wearing. If he was wearing clothes.

When you break it down into parts, you see that Sheppard has four reasons why he doesn't know anything:

1) He is asleep when the event begins,
2) It is dark,
3) He is knocked unconscious, and
4) He is later choked into unconsciousness.

Being knocked out *twice* during the assault is . . . well, it ties the record. I know of a lot of crime stories in which a witness is knocked unconscious; I can't really think of another one in which he is rendered unconscious *twice*, having gotten up in between and chased the intruder several hundred feet. But this list of explanations for his inability to observe anything about the murderer understates the case. It's not just that he is asleep, he is *really* asleep. He is so soundly asleep that he doesn't wake up when the murderer breaks in, pokes around the house, dumps the contents of a few drawers on the floor, and then walks up a staircase *which is two feet from where he is sleeping*; the day bed backs up against the staircase.

And it is not just that it is dark, it is *really* dark *because he keeps running by light switches without turning on the light.* This bothers everybody about his story . . . why doesn't he turn on the light? He's sleeping, he hears Marilyn scream, he knows something is wrong, the light switch is right there, it wouldn't cost him one second to turn it on; he doesn't do it. Why? Wouldn't you? Later he wakes up, he's chasing this guy through his house . . . no lights.

And the intruder doesn't have any trouble seeing everything! The intruder has no trouble with the lights or with the layout of the Sheppard house. The intruder is able to bash Marilyn twenty-five or more times in the head—in the dark. Although it is pitch dark, the intruder, hearing Sheppard running up the stairs, is able to go right to the top of the stairs, find Sheppard and punch his lights out—in the dark. The intruder is able to find the drawers and dump them on the ground, find the medical bag which he takes a little ways from the scene of the crime. The intruder, racing through Sam's house in the dark being chased by the doctor, is able to find the back door, run outside, find the steps leading down to the lake, run down them in the dark, apparently without falling, and then gain the advantage on Sam once more as soon as Sam reaches the bottom of the steps.

(The preceding paragraphs are printed here exactly as they were written after I had read Paul Holmes' first book on the Sheppard case, *The Sheppard Murder Case*, but before I looked into *Retrial: Murder and Dr. Sam Sheppard*, also by Holmes. In the second book, Holmes piles on yet another explanation for Sheppard's inability to remember anything that might help identify the intruder(s). In a lawsuit filed against the state of Ohio, Sheppard claims that "as a result of (his) injuries, (he) suffered traumatic amnesia, and still so suffers; as a result of said amnesia (he) is unable consciously to recall the identity of the person or persons causing the said murder, even though (he) did observe said person or persons." He wants a hypnotist allowed into the prison to help him free the details from the darkened basement of his mind.

The first book, written seven years after the crime, never suggests that Dr. Sheppard's failure to describe the assailant(s) has anything to do with amnesia. This issue arises only in the second book. I don't know how this looks to you, but imagine how it looks to me. Having already ridiculed Dr. Sheppard for offering an improbable array of reasons for not remembering anything, I now find that, years after the crime, he comes forward with yet *another* explanation. It makes a total of five: sleep, darkness, two concussions and now amnesia as well. He is damned lucky he can remember that he was ever married.)

It is a genuinely stupid story that Sam tells, and *nobody* believes it—not the police, not the judges, not the jury, not the media, not even his friends and neighbors, who line up to testify against him. The only people who believe him are his family and his lawyers and a couple of newspaper guys.

And yet, the forensic evidence *does* tend to acquit him. Blood spatter analysis was in its infancy in 1954, and the police did not make any effort to analyze the blood spatter patterns in the room where the murder occurred. After the trial, however, Dr. Paul Kirk examined the murder room, and concluded that the murder had to have been committed by a left-handed man.

In 1959 Cleveland police arrested Richard Eberling for burglary. Eberling made a living washing windows and doing odd jobs; he had washed the windows at the Sheppard house a few weeks before the murder. He was arrested when it was learned that he was stealing from the houses where he worked, sneaking in and going through drawers.

Eberling was a large, powerful man—right-handed, unfortunately, but you can't have everything. During the questioning after his (1959) arrest, the police for some reason started talking to Eberling about the Sheppard murder, and one of them asked Eberling if he could explain why his blood was found at the scene of Marilyn Sheppard's murder. The cop was bluffing, but Eberling somewhat stunningly produced an immediate explanation as to why his blood was at the scene: he had cut himself on a window while washing windows there, and had dripped blood all around the house before he got it bandaged up.

By this time more than 25 people had confessed to murdering Marilyn Sheppard, and the police were pretty well inured to such confessions. The police had zero interest in proving that they had screwed up the Sheppard case, and in any event, Eberling never confessed. The incident passed quietly. Eberling was never mentioned in Paul Holmes' classic 1961 book about the Sheppard case, and was never mentioned at Sam Sheppard's re-trial in 1966.

In the 1980s, Richard Eberling murdered an elderly woman, beat her to death. Public interest in the Sheppard case was such that there were still people trying to figure out what had really happened, and some of those people now turned their attention to Richard Eberling. In 2001, after Eberling's death, James Neff wrote a book essentially arguing that Eberling had committed the murder.

In the late 1990s Sam Sheppard's son, Samuel Reese Sheppard, sued the city of Cleveland for wrongfully prosecuting his father, when they could have and should have known that the evidence pointed strongly toward another man. Attorneys for the city of Cleveland elected to defend the case by in essence re-trying Sam Sheppard for the murder once again, arguing that Sheppard *did* commit the murder, and that it was the *second* trial, the 1966 trial, which was the miscarriage of justice.

Cleveland won. The jurors once more found Sheppard's story unbelievable, and sided with the city of Cleveland.

My theory is that Richard Eberling did indeed commit the murder—and that he was hired to do so and assisted in the act by Sam Sheppard. I am not aware of any clearly established fact in any of the books about the case that is inconsistent with this theory. The bushy-haired man seen hanging around in front of the Sheppard house at 2:30 that morning and seen walking away from the scene about 4:15 was in fact Richard Eberling. At 2:30 he was waiting in Sheppard's front lawn for Sam Sheppard to come quietly to the door and signal for him to come in. This also would explain many of the nagging problems with the case:

1. Why there was no sign of forced entry, leading to a dispute about whether the Sheppards habitually locked their front door.

2. Why Sam Sheppard chose to sleep on the couch, although his guests the previous evening reported that he and Marilyn appeared to be getting along well that night.

3. Why Sheppard's jacket was reported by the first police officer on the scene to have been neatly folded in the middle of the day bed.

4. Why the "break-in" occurred on a night when the Sheppard's houseguest, Dr. Lester Hoverston, happened to be absent. Dr. Hoverston had been staying with the Sheppards for several days, but happened to be away that night.

5. Why Sheppard "fell asleep" while entertaining guests the previous evening.

Sheppard knew nothing at all about the murderer because he knew everything about him, knew exactly what he looked like and knew who he was.

He slept on the couch so that he could get up in the middle of the night and let Eberling in, and he put the plan in motion on that day because he knew that Dr. Hoverston was out of town.

The police could find no evidence of a break-in or robbery because there wasn't any break-in or robbery.

The police could find no real evidence showing that Sheppard committed the crime because he didn't commit it in person.

The police didn't find Eberling at the time because they didn't look for him. They knew that Sheppard was lying through his teeth, so they didn't look any further.

Sheppard had bruises on his face after the crime, as if he had been struck by a left-handed man. He had been. He had instructed Eberling to make it look good. (Eberling was not left-handed, but his right hand had probably been disabled by Marilyn's bite.)

Sheppard's night shirt/undershirt was missing after the crime because, when Eberling whacked him across the back of the neck with the lead pipe or whatever it was, he left a recognizable blood pattern on the shirt, in Marilyn's blood. Sheppard threw the shirt in the lake to get rid of evidence that might have helped the police piece together what had actually happened.

On reading about the case, it bothered me that Sheppard fell asleep on the couch the previous evening while friends were still visiting. *Mockery of Justice* tries to make it appear that this was not unusual behavior for Sheppard, but I'm skeptical. I don't know about you, but if I fell asleep on the couch while we were entertaining friends, my wife would kill me.

If the neighbors had stayed too late this would start to interfere with the murder plot. Once the neighbors leave, Marilyn has to put a few things away, go on upstairs, get ready for bed, maybe take a bath, perhaps read a few minutes or relax in bed before she falls asleep—and she needs to be soundly asleep before you can commence to killing her. You need 90 minutes there. If the guests stay until 1:00 and Eberling is planning to come about 2:00, that's a problem. What do you do? Sheppard fell asleep on the couch—or pretended to—a little before midnight, thus clearly signaling to the neighbors that it was time to go home.

Cooper and Sheppard, in *Mockery of Justice*, report on the 1993 discovery of a 1954 police report which reports finding spots of blood on the steps down into the basement, apparently a continuation of a blood trail leading from the scene, and also finding traces of blood on and inside a red leather chair in the doctor's study. Police now know—only Dr. Kirk knew at the time—that the blood trail had to come from an open wound, since blood dripping from a weapon or from bloody clothes would congeal too quickly to leave such a blood trail.

Cooper and Sheppard interpret this, of course, as evidence of Sheppard's innocence. To me, it seems like obvious evidence of Sheppard's complicity in the crime. If, in fact, the killer went down to the basement to wash himself off after the crime, as Sheppard and Cooper suggest that he did, and if he sat in the red leather chair in the study after committing the crime, this, to me, powerfully suggests that he had no fear of being discovered. He had no fear of being "discovered" because the witness was a co-conspirator.

Sheppard had known Eberling, according to Eberling's 1980s recollection, since October of 1953. Sheppard, looking for someone to kill his wife, somehow realized that Eberling was a criminal. Many times, probably most of the time, when a man tries to hire a hit man to murder his wife, he winds up negotiating with an undercover cop wearing a wire, or he talks to some guy in a bar who comes forward after the crime and says "Sam Sheppard offered me $2,000 to run over his wife with a pickup truck." Sheppard was either smart or lucky, or maybe both. He was smart enough to pick the right guy to talk to, smart enough to get Eberling to talking about things he'd be willing to do for money before mentioning what it was he had in mind. He was lucky, in a perverse meaning of the term, that the police assumed that Sheppard had committed the crime himself, and never really looked for an accomplice.

It could be asked why Sheppard hired someone to commit the crime, rather than do it himself, but this is very common behavior for a murderer, and doesn't really need to be explained. Sheppard would have known that, if he committed the murder with his own hands, the police could prove he committed it. What he didn't anticipate was that, even though he didn't commit the crime with his own hands, the prosecutors could prove he did, anyway.

It could be asked why Sheppard didn't arrange the murder, if he was going to arrange the murder, at a time when he was out of the house, as he was often called away in the middle of the night. (In 1954 small hospitals didn't operate emergency rooms. Doctors made emergency house calls.) But a) he had to arrange the murder on a day when Les Hoverston would be out of town, and b) Sheppard never knew in advance when he would be called away. And c) for Marilyn to have been murdered an hour after Sheppard was called away from the house in the middle of the night would have been extremely suspicious, and would immediately have led police to search for an accomplice.

One final thought. Did you ever look at how similar the Sheppard case and the 2002 Scott Peterson case really are? In both cases, a very attractive young wife was murdered. In both cases, she was pregnant. In both cases, the murder occurred on a major holiday—the Sheppard murder on the 4th of July, the Peterson murder on Christmas Eve.

Both cases erupted immediately into major national stories. In both cases the husband was the primary suspect from the outset of the investigation. In both cases the husband was soon learned to have been involved with another woman.

In both cases the husband was fairly quickly convicted of the murder. In both cases the husband was convicted, in my judgment, largely because he acted like a creep and said things that didn't make sense, rather than because of the evidence. There was little or no physical evidence against Sam Sheppard and, in my view, there is essentially no physical evidence against Scott Peterson.

In the case of Sam Sheppard, the nation began, years later, to question whether he had in fact committed the crime, and eventually public sentiment turned in his favor. This has not yet happened to Scott Peterson, and perhaps it never will, unless the Lifetime channel is able to put together a successful series about a heroic fertilizer salesman on the run from the police.

I am not suggesting that Scott Peterson is innocent. It is my view, however, that if he is guilty, the actual evidence against him is astonishingly thin. No one saw him commit the murder. No one saw him transport the body. No one heard him make any threats against his wife. No blood was found in his house or in his car that would suggest a murder scene. No one knows where the murder was committed. No one knows what the murder weapon might have been. He had no marks or bruises on him that would be consistent with a struggle. There are no fingerprints or gunshot residue, no bloody footprint or speck of blood on his shoes—nothing. He had not purchased a million-dollar life insurance policy on her, or met with a potential assassin in a bar.

That's not that easy to do, you know, to commit a murder without *any* real evidence, other than some coincidences and the fact that he was a first-class heel who fouled up the role of a grieving husband. Not saying he is innocent; it just bothers me a little.

Although there have been hundreds of movies inspired by real-life crimes, *The Fugitive* may be the only episodic television show in the same genre. If there are others, it was certainly the best. There was a 2000 re-make of the series—which was also quite a good show although it did not succeed—and there was a 1993 Hollywood hit starring Harrison Ford and Tommy Lee Jones, which I think is an extremely good movie. The general theme of an innocent man on the run has also been adapted into countless other TV shows following *The Fugitive*'s lead, such as *The A-Team*.

XVIII

owell Lee Andrews was an honor student at the University of Kansas. He weighed 300 pounds, had a pasty complexion and wore thick, unfashionable eyeglasses.

On November 28, 1958, Andrews was home from school for the Thanksgiving holiday. Home was Wolcott, Kansas, a town about the size of your living room. After supper he finished reading *The Brothers Karamazov*. After that he murdered his family—mother, father, sister. He shot them all with a rifle, firing some extra bullets into them from a revolver.

He ransacked the house, faking a robbery; the guy who invented that one must be collecting some massive royalties. Then he drove back to Lawrence, where the university is, a 40-mile drive on icy roads. There he talked to his landlady, picked up a typewriter, went to a movie, chatted to the ushers a minute so that they would remember he was there, and headed back to Wolcott.

No one had discovered the murders, so he called police, reporting a break-in. When the police came Andrews was sitting on the front porch, petting the family dog. The police asked what had happened. He gestured for them to go inside.

Under the M'Naghten Rule a man was innocent by reason of insanity only if he was unable to understand the nature of his actions. Doctors at the Menninger Foundation, anxious to challenge this rule, found an ideal test case in Andrews. Because Andrews had taken pains to establish an alibi, he was unquestionably sane under the M'Naghten Rule. On the other hand, the kid was obviously nuts. He was so dissociated from the events, so un-attached to the world around him, that he was obviously schizophrenic.

So the doctors argued.

They lost.

Lowell Andrews was executed on November 30, 1962.

In June and July, 1959, Floyd Wells and Richard Hickock were cellmates in the Kansas State prison. Ten years earlier Wells had worked for Herb Clutter, a well-to-do farmer in the western part of the state. Wells and Hickock got to talking, as captive men will, and Wells told about the Clutter farm. Hickock was enthralled. Was Clutter rich, he wanted to know? Yes, he was rich. Did he have a safe on the property? Did he keep money there?

Hickock wanted to know everything about the Clutters. He got Wells to draw a map of how you got to the place, and a diagram of the house and where the safe was. He talked often, from then on, about robbing the Clutters. He said that he would leave no witnesses.

November 14, 1959, was a Saturday night with a full moon. A little after midnight, Richard Hickock and Perry Smith pulled into the driveway of the Clutter residence. They parked in the shadow of a tree, some distance from the house. The front door was unlocked. In theory, they might have found the safe and left the house unseen. There was no safe, however, and in truth it was more about murder than it was about money. Hickock and Smith were there to prove themselves to one another, to show each other that it wasn't all just talk. They woke up Herb Clutter, demanding that he show them the safe. The rest of the family stirred. The murderers escaped with $40.

Truman Capote was casting about for something to write about, and a news item about the inexplicable slaughter of a peaceful family on a quiet farm seized his imagination. He packed lightly, took along his friend Harper Lee, and headed for Kansas.

The book project was, in a gruesome way, blessed. It seemed odd to other writers that Capote, a foppish eastern author with standing in the literary community, would be attracted to this earthen event, and because it seemed odd, they wrote about it. Capote promoted his "non-fiction novel" brilliantly, and so the book, *In Cold Blood,* was enormously famous two years before it was published, and became a monster best seller when it finally appeared.

The book is outstanding. The story that Capote had stumbled onto was genuinely interesting—a real-life mystery involving subtle and complex personalities, yielding to another kind of story, about the trial and incarceration, and building to a definitive resolution.

I am a Kansan, born and bred, and known to be hyper-sensitive about the way Kansas is portrayed by alien journalists. Capote, however, came out here and lived with the story until he understood. He wrote about the area without condescension or caricature. His reports on the last days of the Clutter household are so detailed and so natural that the reader almost lapses into the assumption that he was there, taking notes.

The killers had driven out from eastern Kansas. In a sense, eastern Kansas is closer to Philadelphia than it is to Dodge City. Capote grasped this at once, and made it central to his story—the invasion and destruction of an honest, almost noble clan of westerners, by creatures of a different world. In later life Capote became a cartoon character, a lisping, mincing, preening old queer, posing for every camera, but no hint of that can be seen here. Capote's writing is rich without being contrived, graceful without being delicate.

The book became the basis of a pretty decent movie, *In Cold Blood*, and of course years later there were twin movies made about the writing of the book. The first movie catapulted Robert Blake to minor stardom as Perry Smith. To get back to the story . . . Hickock had talked about the perfect crime, about leaving no witnesses. Floyd Wells received the news of the Clutter killings as a sledgehammer to the gut, and knew immediately what had happened. He contacted prison authorities, and the search for Hickock and Smith was soon underway. They were arrested in Las Vegas two months later, and were executed on April 14, 1965.

In Cold Blood was required reading at Shawnee Mission North High School in Mission, Kansas, in the early 1970s. One day a young man was so affected by doing his homework that he dropped the book to the floor, and staggered out of the classroom in a daze. He had figured out, from reading the book, something that his family had never told him. His father was Richard Hickock. He was a baby at the time of the crime. His mother had long since re-married, and he had been adopted many years earlier. But he knew his grandmother, and he pieced the facts together after he saw her name in the book.

Back to Robert Stroud, the Birdman of Wherever, whom we last visited with in the 1930s (page 183). On December 16, 1942, Stroud's possessions were seized without warning. It had been learned by authorities that Stroud was using his unusual privileges to smuggle uncensored letters out of the prison, and to conceal contraband within his cell. He was placed in handcuffs, and his cells were cleaned. He was being transferred to Alcatraz.

Although known to the world as the Birdman of Alcatraz, Robert Stroud was never allowed to keep birds, or anything else of consequence, while he was in Alcatraz. Through the first ten years of his stay there, he slipped gradually toward obscurity. On the night of April 27–28, 1946, Stroud began yelling about stomach pains. Two visits from a medical technician failed to quiet him down, and Stroud's complaints eventually triggered a full-scale riot in D Block, the isolation wing of Alcatraz, where Stroud was held with a select group of the most dangerous criminals in America. Although no one was hurt in that incident, enormous damage was done to the prison by fire, water, and broken ceramic plumbing.

Four days later, on May second, three prisoners from D Block broke into the gun gallery, containing keys to most of the prison, as well as a few guns and some ammunition. This set off another wild 24-hour skirmish, in which hundreds of rounds of heavy ammunition (including many grenades) were fired into D Block in the effort to bring the rebellious inmates to heel. Three convicts and two guards were killed in the escape attempt. Two other convicts were later executed for murdering one of the guards.

Alcatraz officials regarded Stroud as an agitator, and held him largely responsible for both events, the riot of April 27 and the escape attempt of May 2. Authorities moved Stroud to a ward in the prison hospital, where it was possible to hold him in an even more restrictive confinement, and redoubled their efforts to keep him in prison for the rest of his life.

In 1955 Thomas Gaddis published a book about Stroud, *Birdman of Alcatraz*. Gaddis had never actually met Stroud, until years later, was denied access to his prison records, and was prohibited from corresponding directly with him. He picked up the book project from another writer, who bailed out after realizing that Stroud was perhaps not someone who should be celebrated in print. Gaddis was given access to hundreds of letters written by Stroud to his family over the years, got involved with the birding community, and listened to the gossip about him in a community of people who had never met him, either.

Gaddis imagined Stroud to be a kindly, good-natured old man, sort of a country bird doctor, paying a heavy price for his youthful indiscretions. This is the Robert Stroud that he created in his book, and this is the Robert Stroud that Burt Lancaster won an Oscar nomination for portraying in the 1962 film *Birdman of Alcatraz*.

Unfortunately it bears not the slightest resemblance to the actual Robert Stroud, who was a vicious sociopath. Stroud, among his other charming qualities, liked to write violent pornography in which he fantasized about abducting, raping and murdering small children. Alvin (Creepy) Karpis, a famous criminal from the 1930s who was confined with Stroud at Alcatraz, wrote in his account of life on Alcatraz that Stroud talked constantly about raping and killing children, and insisted that he wasn't bluffing; if he had gotten a chance, he would have done it. This led to a Kafkaesque scene at a parole hearing for Stroud in 1962. Outside the building protestors marched, holding placards demanding the release of the kindly bird doctor portrayed by Burt Lancaster in the movie, while inside the hearing parole officials dealt with a distinctly disturbed old man who mumbled about getting out of prison soon because he had a long list of people he wanted to kill and not much time left to kill them.

There was a much more accurate book about Stroud written forty years later by Jolene Babyak, *Bird Man: The Many Faces of Robert Stroud* (Ariel Vamp Press, Berkeley, California, 1994). Her research is extremely good. Her writing is uneven. About Stroud's prison friendship with Morton Sobell (involved in the Rosenberg conspiracy), Babyak writes (p. 234) that "Sobell, an engineer with two master's degrees, was almost as equally famous as Stroud."

Babyak quotes frequently from Stroud's writing, including liberal quotes from unpublished manuscripts. This is disconcerting, as Stroud's writing is trim and graceful, while Babyak's is harsh and blocky. Stroud was a remarkable man—brilliant, resourceful, determined and courageous. If you want to read a compelling story that uses his name a lot, read Gaddis'. If you want to know what the man was really like, read Babyak's.

About 10 o'clock on the evening of March 9, 1963, a Saturday night, officers Ian Campbell and Karl Hettinger stopped two men in a car. They were patrolling Hollywood, and they stopped the two men because they looked like hoodlums, using a missing rear license light as a specific, legal excuse to make the stop.

One of the hoodlums, Gregory Powell, pulled a gun on Campbell, took

Campbell's weapon, and forced Hettinger to surrender his. They drove them to a county road in the San Joaquin Valley, between two onion fields, where Powell murdered Officer Campbell. Hettinger broke and ran. His glasses fell off. He ran blindly through the onion fields, pursued by the two armed men who had just murdered his partner.

Powell was arrested leaving the area in a stolen car. His partner, Jimmy Smith, was apprehended in Bakersfield the next day. They confessed to the crime, were convicted, and were sentenced to die in the California gas chamber.

Hettinger, however, had escaped into a personal hell. Police Inspector John Powers, described as the General Patton of the Los Angeles Police Department, drafted an order known as the Hettinger Memorandum, which second-guessed Hettinger's decision to surrender his weapon, and ordered all members of the force never, ever, to do anything like that again. Hettinger, who felt tremendous guilt over the death of his partner, was pushed further into depression and despair. He began to steal things, shoplifting, and was forced to leave the police force.

Meanwhile, the prosecution of Powell and Smith got caught in the backwash of the Supreme Court decisions that rocked the criminal justice system in the mid-sixties. On the day that Ian Campbell was buried, police in Phoenix, Arizona, arrested Ernesto Miranda, a young man whose name would enter the language. Between June 22, 1964, and June 13, 1966, the Supreme Court issued three decisions about the rights of prisoners—the Escobedo, Dorado and Miranda decisions.

The police officers who questioned Smith and Powell in custody had treated them like gentlemen, eliciting confessions from them by a few hours of friendly questioning. They clearly informed Smith and Powell that anything they said could be used against them in court, and also that they had the right to an attorney. Still, the Supreme Court decisions made it all but inevitable that Smith and Powell would receive new trials. Various courts had required—a year after the fact—not only that these warnings be given, but that specific language be used, and that a paper trail be maintained to ensure that those protections were in place.

Since the confessions of Smith and Powell had been obtained without "qualified" Miranda warnings, the confessions were thrown out, and the police had to start from scratch. Their opponents were two career criminals. By now, those criminals had already spent several months on death row, and were very much aware that they faced the gas chamber if they confessed again.

Powell and Smith came back into court with new lawyers, including the infamous Irving Kanarek, who specialized in making such a circus of a courtroom that it became almost impossible to conduct a trial. (Kanarek later defended Charlie Manson. If Manson's prosecutors could have executed one or the other, Manson would have gone free and Kanarek would have hanged.) Without confessions, their prosecution rested almost exclusively on the testimony of the surviving officer, Karl Hettinger. Since Hettinger, riddled by guilt, had developed into a kleptomaniac and been dismissed by the force, the defense bore down upon him, forcing him through an interminable series of psychological evaluations and re-evaluations, trials and appeals and penalty hearings which forced him to re-live that pitiless night again, and again, and again. The transcript of the trials (alone) would eventually run more than 45,000 pages, at the time a California record.

Joseph Wambaugh wrote a brilliant book about the case, *The Onion Field*, and in 1979 the book was made into a movie, starring a young Ted Danson as Ian Campbell, James Woods as Gregory Powell and John Savage as Karl Hettinger. I must have seen that movie a dozen times. If it is on TV, I have to watch it. Gritty and depressing, the movie was not a box office hit. It is probably the best movie ever made about a crime. Made on a low budget, it was the breakthrough movie for two stars, Danson and Woods, but the most memorable performance is by Franklyn Seales, as Jimmy Smith.

All generalization is dangerous. The Los Angeles police brought about some of their own headaches with Smith and Powell by trying too hard to send them both to the gas chamber. While Gregory Powell was a despicable punk whose actions surely merited a cyanide capsule or two, Jimmy Smith was a follower. He had never intended to kill Campbell or anyone else; it was his misfortune—and his bad judgment—to be Powell's partner when Powell chose to murder a cop. As far as the law was concerned they were equally guilty, since they were partners in the commission of a felony that led to a murder. The police were determined that they should both pay the ultimate price for this offense. That isn't justice. Smith *may* have fired four shots into Campbell as he died, but the prosecution couldn't prove it. I believe in protecting police officers, too, but it's not right to execute a man because his partner does something stupid. The prosecutors complicated the battle for justice by pushing for something more than justice.

Still, for anyone who wants to understand the explosion in crime rates in this country between 1964 and 1976, there can be no better explanation than to read *The Onion Field*. The Supreme Court decisions of the mid-sixties, though carrying no inevitable harm, established in the minds of lower courts the idea that the primary object of the process was not to deliver justice, but to protect the rights of the accused. The lower courts for ten years thereafter competed to see who could force the police to jump through the most hoops in the process of trying to convict a criminal. The California Supreme Court, the Rose Bird court, ruled that the police had violated the cop killers' rights by being friendly with them so as to earn their trust so that they would confess. Such "psychological devises," they ruled, were condemned by the U.S. Supreme Court in *Miranda v. Arizona*.

The best book about crime in the late 1950s/early 1960s is certainly *In Cold Blood*—but the book which can help you to truly understand America's prevailing attitudes about crime in that era is *Birdman of Alcatraz*. And the book which can help you to understand the transition that followed, how we got from Burt Lancaster to Charles Manson in just seven years, is *The Onion Field*.

We look back on the 1950s as a "conservative era," the Eisenhower era. We look on the era in that way because the radicalism of the 1960s followed close behind it, and the mind contrasts a thing with that which stands next to it. The dominant American attitudes about crime and criminals in the late 1950s were far more liberal than those which prevail today. *Birdman of Alcatraz* assumes a culture that believes in the humanity of the convict. "A man may have done terrible things," the book argues implicitly, "yet he remains a man." The book argued for the proposition that all men are within the realm of redemption. This is admirable—yet the book was also romanticized, vague, one-sided and false.

Birdman of Alcatraz and numerous other movies of that era (*The Wrong Man*, 1956, *I Want to Live!*, 1958, and *Compulsion*, 1959) portray criminals as complex personalities capable of normal emotions, and often caught in a cruel and inefficient system of justice. I do not wish to demean the members of the Warren Court by presenting them as weepy eggheads who saw *Birdman of Alcatraz* and went out determined to make the world do better by these poor suffering wretches, but there is a close connection between the worldview encapsulated in these movies and the court decisions of the

mid-sixties. That a man may commit a crime, yet he remains capable of dignity; that the prison walls contain more victims than truly evil people; that
our society is responsible for its reprehensible treatment of the accused and
convicted—these were, at the time, not liberal views. These were mainstream
positions, widely accepted by common people in the 1950s, and up to the
mid-1960s.

The Onion Field portrays actual policemen, dealing with the judicial
swamp created in the backwash of this prevailing attitude. The irony is that
these principles, simply stated, are undeniably true. A man may commit a
crime, yet remain capable of dignity. Our society *is* responsible for the reprehensible treatment of its incarcerated. What is hard to accept is that these
statements are one thing when stated as principles—and something entirely
different when converted into judicial fiats. The careless application of the
principles of prisoner's rights empowered the worst that the human race
has to offer, from Gregory Powell to Charles Manson. The sympathy generated by Burt Lancaster on behalf of Robert Stroud became a tool with which
Gregory Powell could battle the world.

Even today, old liberals try to explain the explosion of violence in this
country between the mid-1960s and the mid-1970s in terms of demographic
shifts. These explanations are logically preposterous. The damned foolish-
ness of the Warren Court unleashed upon us a torrent of criminal violence
which pitched the nation backward into atavistic attitudes about crime and
punishment. We have yet to regain our footing. We will not regain our footing, I would argue, until Liberals stop making excuses for the Warren Court,
and accept responsibility for the tragic consequences of the Warren Court's
runaway enthusiasm for essentially good ideas.

There was, before 1965, a long tradition of activism for criminal reform.
That activism had led to the abolition of poorhouses (debtor's prisons), to the
end of the practice of cutting off hands and fingers of criminals, to the end of
public hangings and to the virtual abolition of executions, to the end of the
practice of shackling prisoners to the walls of madhouses, to the end of chain
gangs, to the end of the practice of selling prison labor as slave labor. Prison
reformers got job training programs into the prisons, and, for a brief time,
meaningful access to psychological counseling.

And then, with the Warren Court, prison reform slammed into a wall
and was killed on the spot. By 1980 prison reformers were outcasts in the
corrections system; the very term "reformer" became a joke and a pejo-

rative. Since 1975 we have allowed the evolution of huge, horrific prisons ruled by prison gangs. We have to move past that, and toward a vision of a punishment and reform system based on an effort to salvage those lives that can be salvaged. We will not move forward until we take ownership of our failings.

XIX

◆

There are two statements that seem to appear in every online account of the Boston Stranglings, at least one of which cannot be true. One is that most of the murders occurred in the Back Bay section of Boston. The other is that most or all of the murders occurred in rundown apartment buildings. There is a problem here. The Back Bay is not exactly a slum.

As it happens, both statements are untrue. Of the fourteen murders that weave the narrative of the Boston Strangler investigation, only three occurred in the Back Bay, and most occurred in buildings that were then—and are today—very decent.

The series of crimes which are united now under the Boston Strangler label began on June 14, 1962, with the murder of a 56-year-old woman who lived just behind the Boston Symphony Orchestra, on Gainsborough Street.

A similar crime occurred two weeks later, out by the Chestnut Hill Reservoir—four and a half miles from Gainsborough Street—and a body was found up in Lynn, Massachusetts, two days after that. Lynn is twenty minutes north of Boston. The *Boston Globe* implicitly united the three crimes, and referred to them as "the Silk Stocking Murders."

There was another murder nine days later at a cheap hotel out in the Dorchester area, and two more a month after that. By late August, 1962, there had been six murders in just over two months, all but one within a five-mile radius of the first, similar victimology and similar staging of the crime scenes. Media attention started with the third murder, and would roar a little louder with each event over the next sixteen months.

One in October, back over near the symphony, but this was a young woman, and black, and murdered in the street. The eighth murder, in December and a block away from the seventh, was another young black woman.

The ninth, later in December, was a young secretary, murdered in her apartment near Kenmore Square.

The victimology disintegrated first, and then the geography. The first murders were of white women with white hair. That pattern broke up, but the press kept counting. Then the murders, which started in a tight geographical knot, moved out of town. Lawrence, Massachusetts, is 25 miles northwest of Boston; Belmont is next to Cambridge, six to eight miles from downtown Boston. In March, 1963, two elderly women were murdered, one in Lawrence, one in Belmont. The Belmont murder was quickly "solved" with the arrest of a handyman, and until years later was not generally connected with the series.

The eleventh murder was in May, in Cambridge, a college student. In September, 1963, a 58-year-old woman was murdered in Salem, up north of Lynn. In November, just after the death of President Kennedy, a young woman was murdered in Lawrence. In the opening days of 1964 a young woman was murdered in a low-rent apartment near Beacon Hill.

Fourteen murders, fourteen women in nineteen months strangled in and around Boston, by persons unknown. In early January, 1964, Massachusetts Attorney General Edward Brooke, later Senator Edward Brooke, moved to take over the investigation. There had already been many investigations into the killings, of course, but Brooke now proposed to organize a massive state investigation, sparing no effort to find the end of it.

Brooke placed in charge of the operation an old buddy from law school, John S. Bottomly, who was selected for the job, according to Brooke, "because he had no experience in criminal law per se." If this seems a head-scratching explanation, let me point out the striking similarity between this and the almost simultaneous appointment of the Warren Commission to examine the assassination of President Kennedy. The Warren Commission took the investigation of the President's murder out of the hands of police officers, and turned it over to . . . lawyers; bright, energetic lawyers with stunning résumés, but little or no experience at investigating a murder. They made a hash of it, staging an overproduced investigation with tunnel vision, and emerging from it with a too-pat explanation for what happened, which ultimately failed to satisfy the public precisely because it was *designed* to satisfy the public.

What happened in Boston was the same: Brooke took the leadership of the investigation away from police officials, and turned it over to a group of very bright lawyers who didn't have a clue what they were doing. The Boston police continued their own investigation; over time the parallel investigations became increasingly competitive, and increasingly frustrated. The killings stopped just before the state investigation started, and the investigation ran into dead ends and blind alleys. A long year passed, with several public embarrassments for the Bottomly team, but no solution. The investigation was consuming mass quantities of police resources, and its failure was stalling careers.

So they did what the Warren Commission had done: they made up a pat explanation, and told the public that they had the whole thing figured out, go to bed now, we've got it all figured out.

At least, that's one theory.

In March, 1965, Albert DeSalvo began telling people that he had committed the murders. DeSalvo was insane; in fact, he was locked up in the Bridgewater Loony Bin at the time he began to talk. He was, however, a certified sex criminal, and he was able to get the attention of F. Lee Bailey. Bailey, just emerging as a superstar lawyer, had another client in Bridgewater, George Nassar. DeSalvo told his tale to Nassar—a murderer of some standing himself—and Nassar persuaded Bailey to come hear what DeSalvo had to say.

Bailey decided that DeSalvo was telling the truth. He could tell. He had magic ears. Once Bailey decided that DeSalvo was the Boston Strangler, then, he had a very interesting situation. He had a client who was making a credible claim to be the most wanted criminal in America—and the police had never heard of him.

Well, actually, they had *heard* of him; they had just never connected him with the Stranglings. Bailey's problem, anyway, was how to accommodate DeSalvo's need to confess, and the public's need to keep him out of old women's apartments, without getting him executed.

Bailey handled this brilliantly. He says so in his autobiography.

Repeatedly.

Bailey tried to negotiate a deal with the Bottomly commission: I will bring you the Boston Strangler, he told them, if you will agree not to use the information we volunteer to prosecute him. You prosecute him for the things you already have him in jail for, and I will plead him innocent by reason of extreme nuttiness. To show the court exactly how nutty he is, we will tell the court all about the murders, even though he is being prosecuted for something else. You agree to allow him to be certified as insane, and we will put him away in an asylum. You can tell the public that you've solved the case, Albert won't be prosecuted for the murders, and I can sell the rights to his story for a book and a movie and make a lot of money. Everybody wins.

Probably he didn't talk about the money.

Bailey—who genuinely was (or is) a brilliant man—was a lawyer in the Perry Mason mold. He had worked his way through law school by operating a private-eye business, employing several detectives. When the movie was finally made Bailey had disappeared from it, apparently unable to make a deal with the producers. Meanwhile, back in real life, there remained the problem of convincing the nice folks on the Bottomly staff that a) Albert had actually committed the crimes, and b) they should accept the deal because they couldn't prove it otherwise. There is a dispute about whether any bargain with the Bottomly investigation was ever reached, and there is a dispute about how eager the Bottomly investigation was to believe the confessions. DeSalvo had quite a bit of information about the crimes, it is true, but

a) A substantial amount of information about the crimes had appeared in the newspapers over the years,

b) Albert, fascinated by the murders, had absorbed and retained all of it,

c) He was, after all, incarcerated in a psychiatric hospital that was teeming with violent criminals, and

d) By the time DeSalvo got to court, several of the top investigators on Bottomly's staff had resigned from the investigation and were working for Bailey.

When doubts about DeSalvo's confessions first surfaced, in the 1980s, many people suggested that DeSalvo may have been fed information about the crimes by another inmate, who was the actual murderer. George Nassar is prominent in this theory.

Another theory is that the police themselves may have fed DeSalvo information about the crimes to bolster his credibility, thus allowing them to declare victory and go home. In any case, the investigators on Bottomly's staff bought into the confessions. DeSalvo, on trial for serious crimes, talked to psychiatrists about the Stranglings, and Bailey acknowledged in open court that DeSalvo was the Boston Strangler. He was gambling on an insanity verdict.

He didn't get it. DeSalvo was found guilty of the sex crimes, and sentenced to life in prison. Bailey declared victory, claiming that he had saved DeSalvo from the electric chair. An alternative interpretation is that he had allowed a small-time hood to talk himself into a life sentence. In either case a writer, Gerald Frank, was brought in to talk to DeSalvo, and to write the inside story of the case. Bottomly allowed him complete access to the case files. Shortly after the trial the *Boston Record* began printing excerpts from the book. A couple of murders were taken out of the account, because DeSalvo said that he didn't commit them, but another murder was thrown in, because DeSalvo said that he did.

A movie was made from the book, starring Tony Curtis as DeSalvo and Henry Fonda as Bottomly, and the public bought into the story lock, stock, and barrel. As an avid reader of crime books and crime stories, I never heard anyone, from 1967 until the 1980s, question that DeSalvo had in fact committed the crimes. The person who really changed that—and, in a sense, the hero of our story—was Susan Kelly.

You have to remember: in 1964 there was no such term as "serial murderer," and there was very little in the way of organized discussion of them. In the late 1970s Ted Bundy and Robert Ressler and John Wayne Gacy and John Douglas and some other people changed that. By the early 1980s serial murderers were red hot.

In 1981 Ms. Kelly was researching a novel about a serial murderer. Much of her research consisted of talking to Boston policemen. To her surprise, Ms. Kelly kept running into old Boston cops and prosecutors who categorically didn't believe that Albert DeSalvo was the Boston Strangler, or the Boston Strangler's brother, or the Boston Strangler's uncle, or the Boston Strangler's drinking buddy. They didn't think he had anything to do with the murders. In April, 1992, Ms. Kelly wrote an article for *Boston* magazine, laying out the case against DeSalvo's guilt as best she understood it at that time. By 1995 she had built this into a book, *The Boston Stranglers* (Birch Lane Press).

Ms. Kelly's research is outstanding. Her thesis is that the murders which came to be united under the Boston Strangler flag were in fact the work of several different men, none of them DeSalvo. This is a credible enough thesis; it is very likely or certain that several of the crimes were copycat crimes, and not the work of the original Strangler. What I think that Ms. Kelly doesn't quite get is that the old cops that she talked to, in the 1980s and 1990s, had been trained in the 1950s and 1960s to believe that virtually all murders were committed by someone in the victim's life, and that the random crazy stranger was just a storybook boogeyman. What these cops told

Ms. Kelly is what cops from that era *always* believed: there's no monster on the loose here, these are unrelated crimes. We know who committed these crimes, it was the brother or the uncle or the drinking buddy. We just can't quite prove it yet.

But here is another way in which 1995 was very different from 1965. In 1965 there were very few books written by ninnies claiming that Jack the Ripper was Thomas Hardy, the Lindbergh baby was stolen by Secret Service agents working for Eleanor Roosevelt, Errol Flynn was secretly Batman and the Black Dahlia was murdered by my Uncle Harry. By 1995 there were many such books.

When I first heard that someone had written a book claiming that Albert DeSalvo was *not* the Boston Strangler, then, I thought, "Yeah, yeah, right; I'm sure you have a better candidate." By 1995 I had accepted for thirty years that Albert DeSalvo was the Boston Strangler, and it was not easy for me to move away from that.

But when you finally reach the point of asking, "OK, what is the evidence against DeSalvo?" it is quite astonishing how thin the case really is.

First, Albert DeSalvo was never charged, indicted, accused or prosecuted by any court for any action in connection with the Boston Stranglings.

Second, there appears to be absolutely no physical evidence of any kind tying him to the crimes. Gerald Frank, who was convinced of DeSalvo's guilt and wrote the book convincing the rest of the nation, repeatedly makes this point in *The Boston Strangler*: that there is an absolute void of evidence tying DeSalvo to the crimes.

Third, there is no eyewitness testimony from anyone placing DeSalvo at or near any of the crimes to which he confessed. In several of the Strangler cases, a person in a neighboring apartment reported a man behaving suspiciously just before a murder was committed. This man or these men were seen by numerous witnesses—none of whom thought that DeSalvo was the man.

There was a survivor of one attack that may have been by the Strangler. That survivor said it was not DeSalvo.

There was a palm print left on a television at one scene, police thought perhaps by the Strangler. It was not DeSalvo's.

Dr. James Brussel, who had earned fame ten years earlier by drawing up what was widely reported to be an uncannily accurate profile of the Mad Bomber, George Metesky, also drew up a profile of the Boston Strangler. DeSalvo bears basically no resemblance to that profile.

F. Lee Bailey was certain that DeSalvo's story was true, but Dr. Ames Robey was a psychiatrist at Bridgewater who knew DeSalvo much better than Bailey did, and who was much better trained to make that determination. About a month before DeSalvo began confessing to the crimes, Dr. Robey testified under oath that DeSalvo was delusional and was mentally incompetent to stand trial. Dr. Robey was always convinced that DeSalvo was lying, and that he had nothing to do with the murders. Thomas Troy, the attorney who represented DeSalvo after Bailey, did not believe that DeSalvo had committed the crimes, and Francis Newton, who represented DeSalvo after Troy, didn't believe it, either. DeSalvo's wife didn't believe that he was the Strangler, and thought that it was just another of DeSalvo's endless Big Lies.

On the other side of the ledger there are essentially only two facts:

1) That DeSalvo said that he committed the murders, and

2) That some of the cops and some of the prosecutors believed that he was telling the truth.

And some didn't.

The Bottomly commission believed that DeSalvo was guilty, they said, because he knew things that only the killer would know. Ms. Kelly disputes this. Ms. Kelly argues that DeSalvo's confessions, of which transcripts survive although the tapes themselves are missing, were so rife with inaccuracies that, in reality, they make it fairly apparent that he *didn't* commit the murders.

Ms. Kelly savages the Bottomly commission with the theatrical outrage established by Anthony Scaduto in *Scapegoat* as the tone of the genre. I think it is unlikely that the Bottomly commission investigators were as inept as Ms. Kelly presents them, but this merely gets us to the issue of the evidence. What, ultimately, do you believe?

Albert DeSalvo was a very sick man. Ms. Kelly thinks he was too gentle to be a murderer, but, despite his easy charm, he carried a great deal of anger in a disorganized mind. I wouldn't dismiss the possibility that he did commit some of the crimes, particularly the later murders committed north of Boston, in Lynn, Lawrence and Salem.

But no one seriously believes that one man committed *all* of these murders. As noted by Kelly and most everyone else who has written about the crimes in the last twenty years, there are obvious indications that un-related murders were staged as Strangler murders to try to throw the police off the scent. DeSalvo confessed to all of these murders.

I don't *know* what happened, and I'm not expert in any of this; I hope you understand that. My knowledge of the case is based on my reading of five books and numerous magazine and online articles, the five books being *The Boston Strangler* (Gerald Frank, 1966), *The Defense Never Rests* (F. Lee Bailey and Harvey Aronson, 1971), *The Boston Stranglers* (Susan Kelly, 1995), *Search for the Strangler* (Casey Sherman, 2003), and *A Death in Belmont* (Sebastian Junger, 2006). Frank and Bailey think that DeSalvo was guilty, Kelly and Sherman think that he was just making it up, and Junger is on the fence but leaning toward guilty.

It seems to me massively unlikely that Albert DeSalvo committed the "original" Strangler murders, the first batch of murders that started the Strangler panic. For four reasons:

1) There is no evidence that he did, other than his confessions.
2) The credibility of his confessions is tarnished by the fact that his confession consolidates murders that were almost certainly committed by different people.
3) His confessions, on several levels, lack the ring of truth.
4) DeSalvo, if he was in fact the murderer, is an exception to many of the things that we now know about serial murderers.

Massachusetts police interviewed 25,000 people in connection with the Boston Strangler homicides—but had never associated Albert DeSalvo with the crimes until he confessed. This is *possible*, certainly, but it is contrary to the usual experience of serial murder investigations. The normal experience of serial murder investigations is that the killer's name surfaces early in the investigation, and his name appears in the files numerous times before he becomes the focus of the investigation.

Sebastian Junger says that DeSalvo's "initial loss of control was the worst and most savage, resulting in four murders in two weeks. Subsequent binges of violence were limited to pairs of people and then, finally, to one person at a time." But this is the exact opposite of the pattern normally described by experts in the field. The pattern which is normally described involves a gradual loss of control beginning long before the actual murders, breaking through in an isolated event, then culminating in more and more frequent attacks and more and more reckless behavior, until ultimately the killer commits suicide or begins killing people closer to him, people to whom he can be linked.

The Strangler victims were grouped together because the staging of the crime scenes was ornate and grotesque, women with big bows tied around their necks, left displayed to the world in gruesome ways. What seems most likely to me is that there were earlier murders that were not tagged to the Strangler because they were less ornate and grotesque. The murderer, when he committed his first murder, probably panicked and fled the scene immediately. Later, when he had committed two or three murders, he began lingering around the crime scene after the murder, enjoying what he had done, and celebrating what he had done by elaborately staging the crime scene.

The eminent Dr. James Brussel—who had drawn up the "profile" of the Strangler, which turned out not to resemble DeSalvo at all—nonetheless testified for DeSalvo in DeSalvo's sex crimes trial, testifying that DeSalvo was insane. He, too, had left the investigation to go to work for F. Lee Bailey. "It would start the night before with a burning up inside, like little fires, little explosions," according to Brussel by way of Sebastian Junger's *A Death in Belmont*. "And he would get up in the morning feeling hungry, yet he would not eat and he did not want to eat. And he would get in his car or truck and drive, sometimes not knowing where he was going, and on occasion he would suddenly look around and find that he was in Connecticut or Rhode Island and ask himself, What am I doing here? He would drive to an apartment house or a multiple dwelling that he knew, and he would go inside."

That's an account of DeSalvo's sex crimes, for which he was on trial. But the Stranglings are entirely different. DeSalvo *did* drive all over hell and creation, committing sex crimes in random places hundreds of miles from his home—but the Stranglings—the ones that were probably the work of one man—were predominantly concentrated in Boston, forming a little "walking circle," the center of which is somewhere near Coolidge Corner.

DeSalvo's sex crimes were scattered over several states and hundreds of miles. Doesn't it seem likely to you that if DeSalvo had in fact "graduated" to murder as his advocates claim, that the murder victims would also be scattered over several states and hundreds of miles?

Dr. Brussel describes a syndrome that starts the night before the crimes, and he volunteers the information, based on his interviews with DeSalvo, that "it would be early morning frequently" when DeSalvo acted out his aggressions. But the Strangler attacks almost all occurred in mid-afternoon; one occurred on a Sunday morning, and one about 6:30 in the evening, but for the most part they are tightly bunched in the mid-afternoon.

Of course, some people doubt that DeSalvo actually committed many of the sex crimes to which he confessed, either. It could be that he didn't; he was a maddeningly prolific confessor. But if you lose the sex crimes, you lose all credibility for DeSalvo as the Strangler. The fact that he was a convicted sex criminal is one of the very few points in favor of the theory that DeSalvo was the Strangler. If he falsely confessed to the sex crimes, then he's a very poor candidate to be the Strangler. If he did commit the sex crimes, then we have to expect the elements of those to parallel the elements of the murders to some extent. They don't; the sex crimes were committed against young women, in the mornings, spread out across three states. The murders were committed against old women (primarily), in the afternoons, within walking distance of one another.

F. Lee Bailey reports in *The Defense Never Rests* that he asked DeSalvo whether the police should look for his fingerprints at the crime scenes. DeSalvo shakes his head dismissively, and says, "They're wasting their time."

But DeSalvo was never a clever criminal. DeSalvo had been arrested countless times over the years, mostly for MSMCF (Making Stupid Mistakes in the Commission of a Felony). How did he get to be, when it came to the Stranglings, this fantastically clever criminal who didn't make *any* mistakes, and was identified only because he confessed?

While I am not a psychologist, it is difficult for me to see that the crimes of which DeSalvo was found guilty and the Stranglings would be natural products of the same psychosis. DeSalvo groped, fondled and eventually sexually assaulted attractive young women. Oversimplifying, that sounds like extreme sexual frustration, hyper-sexuality, immaturity and poor self-control. The Strangler murdered and sexually humiliated older women. That sounds more like extreme anger, hatred of authority and sexual confusion.

Extreme anger and sexual frustration are not radically different things, and it is not impossible that one psychosis could contain both, in the same way that it's not impossible to believe that a fire broke out on the third floor of an apartment building and an unrelated fire broke out about the same time on the first floor. It's not impossible; it's just unusual. It is not a common thing for a murderer to make leaps of that nature.

Sebastian Junger's *A Death in Belmont* is a serious and intelligent book about a murder case which has many of the hallmarks of the Strangler murders, but which was not included in the Strangler case because it was quickly

Elizabeth Canning, whose testimony against an old gypsy woman divided 18th century England into Canningites and Egyptians.

A fanciful, if stunning, depiction (1850) of Mary Rogers, who was murdered by persons unknown on July 25, 1841.
(Photo © Mary Evans Picture Library/The Image Works.)

Clarence Darrow during the Scopes Monkey Trial.
(Photo © Hulton Archive/Getty Images.)

The house/hotel—the so-called Murder Castle—constructed by H. H. Holmes of Chicago.
Holmes was executed in 1896. This photo was taken in 1937.
(Photo © Topham/The Image Works.)

Harry K. Thaw of Pittsburgh. Does this man look like a murderer to you? *(Photo courtesy of the Library of Congress, Prints and Photographs Division.)*

Inside the United States Capitol building, 1915. The bomb was left by Erich Muenter, also known as Frank Holt, Thomas P. Lester, R. Pearce, and numerous other names. *(Photo courtesy of the Library of Congress, Prints and Photographs Division.)*

Robert Stroud—the Birdman of
Alcatraz—who was never allowed to keep
birds at Alcatraz, but never mind.
(Photo © Archive Photos/Getty Images.)

The site of the Hall-Mills murders. Within days, the crab apple tree under which the bodies
were found was stripped of its bark and chipped down to slivers for souvenirs.
(Photo courtesy of the Franklin Township Public Library Historical Collections.)

Charles Augustus Lindbergh Jr. would now
be 79 years old (2011), were he still alive.
*(Photo © Scherl/SV-Bilderdienst/The Image
Works.)*

The execution of Ruth Snyder.
*(Photo © Tom Howard/New York Daily News
Archive via Getty Images.)*

A newspaper headlines the acquittal of
those accused in the murders of Reverend
Edward Hall and Eleanor Mills. A caption
in the original states that Prosecutor
Simpson would seek a new trial, although
how that was possible after an acquittal
I do not know. The legal interpretation
of the constitutional prohibition against
double jeopardy may have been a little
different at that time.
*(Photo: New York Daily News, December
4, 1926. Courtesy of Franklin Township
Public Library.)*

Thalia and Thomas Massie, 1932. Thalia Massie's paternal grandfather was Teddy Roosevelt's uncle. Her maternal grandfather was Charles Bell, who was the first president of Bell Telephone Company. He was a cousin of Alexander Graham Bell. *(Photo courtesy of the Library of Congress, Prints and Photographs Division.)*

Samuel Leibowitz and the Scottsboro Boys. Truman Capote was 8 years old, Harper Lee 6 at the time that the story was most in the news. The story is thought to have inspired *To Kill a Mockingbird*. *(Photo © New York Daily News Archive via Getty Images.)*

Richard Hickock. Everybody liked James Dean, but nobody liked him as much as the criminals did.
(Photo courtesy of the Kansas State Penitentiary.)

This photo, which shows Caryl Chessman acting as his own attorney at his 1948 trial, was taken six years before he became a national figure.
(Photo © Archive Photos/Getty Images.)

Albert DeSalvo holds up a necklace—a "choker"—that he made while he was incarcerated in Walpole, Massachusetts. DeSalvo—who almost certainly was not the Boston Strangler—enjoyed having people think that he was.

(Photo © Hulton Archive/Getty Images.)

Sid Vicious and Nancy Spungen. The name Sid Vicious was suggested by his band mate, Johnny Rotten, after Rotten was bitten by his pet hamster, who was named Sid.

(Photo © Steve Emberton/Getty Images.)

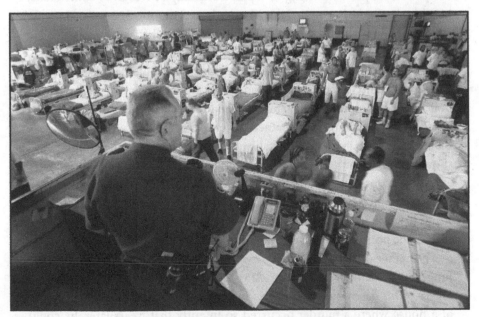

Deuel Vocational Institution in Tracy, California.
(Photo © Tony Avelar/The Christian Science Monitor/Getty Images.)

"solved" by the conviction of a black man who had been working at the house on the day of the murder. As fate would have it, Albert DeSalvo is now known to have been near the scene of the murder on that day, because he was working at Sebastian Junger's house; it is actually the *only* Strangler-related murder for which there is any independent evidence that DeSalvo was in the neighborhood—if one accepts as evidence the 40-years-later recollections of the Junger clan.

Junger starts with the premise that the man convicted of the murder may have been an innocent auxiliary victim of a crime committed by Albert DeSalvo, but he is intelligent enough, and honest enough, to realize that there are serious doubts about whether DeSalvo was actually the Boston Strangler—thus, the fact that he was nearby when this Strangler-type crime occurred may be simply a weird coincidence.

Junger argues that if the Strangler killings were "the work of several men, it is almost certain that some of them would have been caught." But this is fallacious, because the murders that are identified as the Strangler killings are picked from the list of unsolved murders. Any similar murder that was solved was simply stricken from the list.

Some of Albert DeSalvo's confessions, at least as edited and released by the police, may have the ring of truth. But many of DeSalvo's confessions, in all honesty, don't sound right. They're based too much on visual recall. All of the books about DeSalvo note this visual recall at least in passing. He would "close his eyes," wrote F. Lee Bailey in *The Defense Never Rests* (p. 151). "Then, *as if he were watching a videotape replay,* he would describe what had happened" (emphasis mine). Two pages later, Bailey recounts DeSalvo telling police that, at one victim's apartment, he had knocked a pack of cigarettes to the floor beside a bureau. He named the brand of the cigarettes. At this, says Bailey, the police investigator "grabbed his briefcase and pulled out a photo showing the bureau and a pack of cigarettes just as Albert had described it."

My reaction, on reading that, was "that sounds like DeSalvo had seen the same photograph that the cop had." I did not know, at that time, that Dr. Ames Robey had been claiming for years that that was exactly what had happened: the police showed DeSalvo photographs of the crime scenes.

"Whether or not DeSalvo had ever been at the Goldberg house," wrote Junger in *A Death in Belmont* (p. 223), *"the newspaper photo was clearly the source of his description"* (emphasis mine). DeSalvo had studied the photo of a house where a murder occurred so intently that, years later, he could still describe in detail what the photo contained—square drainpipes, shades pulled down. He remembered the outside of the house from studying the photo in the newspaper.

"I went into number 77," said DeSalvo in supposedly recounting the first of the murders. "I remember it said that on glass over the door in gold letters." It doesn't sound right; to me; it doesn't sound like he was really there. It sounds like he had seen the pictures.

I don't get into visiting crime scenes, but I lived in Boston during most of the time I was writing this book. I noticed that one of the Strangler murders occurred at 515 Park Drive, and I would often catch the T at St. Mary's Square, on the Green Line. 515 Park Drive is just about a one-minute walk from St. Mary's Square. It is close enough that, if you came out the door of 515 Park and saw the train, you might be able to catch it before it left.

Then another time my wife and I were going to the Boston Symphony, and we were a little early and walking around the neighborhood, and we happened to walk past 77 Gainsborough Street, where the first of the Stranglings occurred. I noticed that it's just a block or two off the Green Line. Two of the later murders, which occurred within a quarter-mile of the first, are actually on the other side of that Line, so that the three murders crowd around one stop on the Green Line.

And then one time I was walking out near Boston College, just getting a little exercise, and I realized that I was near another of the murder scenes, at 1940 Commonwealth Avenue, so I took a moment and looked at that building. And there, not thirty feet from the door of 1940 Commonwealth, was a T stop. It's the Green Line.

Another of the murders occurred at 1435 Commonwealth. It's another stop on the same spur of the same line.

There's more to it than that. The Green Line has several spurs. 515 Park Drive, which is about a one-minute walk from the C spur of the Green Line, is also about a two-minute walk from the B spur; it is near the place where they split off from one another, so that one can get quickly to either line.

From that point the B and C spurs of the Green Line diverge, being at one point separated by more than a mile. Then they converge again. You know where they almost meet again? 1940 Commonwealth, where the second of the murders occurred, is right on the B spur—and a five-minute walk from the C spur. That's where they come back together. The closest point is 1940 Commonwealth.

77 Gainsborough Street, where the first murder occurred, is just off the E spur of the Green Line—but that's not how my wife and I got to the Symphony. We got there on a different spur, which is a short walk away.

The T system in Boston is good, but it does *not* have fantastic coverage of the city. There are substantial portions of the Boston area where you can't really use the T, because it takes too long to get to it.

Several of the Boston Strangler's murders occurred not only right on the T system, but in areas that were served by *multiple lines* of the T system—as if perhaps the murderer had thought ahead, "I might have to come out of here and go this way, or I might have to go down that way. I need to be able to get out of this area as quickly as I can no matter which way I'm heading."

Albert DeSalvo, in his "confessions" to the crime, claimed that he *drove* to the murder scenes. I wonder. Where did he park? Why didn't anybody find a parking receipt? Why did he drive, one time after another, into areas that are notoriously difficult to drive to? The murders up in Lawrence and Lynn and Salem . . . somebody may have driven to those. The "original" Strangler murders, the ones that started the panic . . . I'd be willing to bet that whoever committed those murders got there and left on the T.

There's actually more to it than that. We lived not in Boston but in Brookline, which is an independent city so close that you could walk from our apartment to the Boston Common. It's a couple of miles. "Did any of the murders occur in Brookline?" my wife asked.

Well, no, not quite. 515 Park Drive is in Boston—but if you cross the street, you're in Brookline.

1940 Commonwealth is three miles away from there, in the Brighton Section of Boston, near Newton—but you can throw a rock from there back into Brookline.

1435 Commonwealth is in Brighton—but it's a four-minute walk from Brookline.

4 University Drive, where one of the victims lived, is in Cambridge—but it's not a half-mile from Brookline.

The Green Line of the Boston T system serves Brookline (and other areas); one spur goes down the north and west sides of Brookline, another along the east side, and a third goes through the heart of the little city.

In serial murder cases, if you plot the crime scenes on a map and connect the dots, very often they will form a sort of circle, and very often the murderer will live near the center of that circle. This is well known now, although it wasn't recognized until about 1980. If you draw a circle on a map which is a one-mile radius from Coolidge Corner, it doesn't include any of the murder scenes. But if you draw a circle which is a three-mile radius around Coolidge Corner, it includes virtually *all* of the murder scenes in Boston and Cambridge—all but one—and there are murder scenes at all points of the compass.

I am not saying that this is *true*, but it is possible. It is possible that the Boston Strangler lived in Brookline, perhaps between Coolidge Corner and Brookline Village, and that he deliberately left Brookline to commit his crimes, knowing that Brookline has its own police force, and that it might be in his best interests not to have his local police force looking for him.

Actually, there are two circles here—one that is formed by the murders in Boston, and a much larger circle formed if you include the murders in the northern towns. DeSalvo lived nowhere near the smaller circle, the "walking" circle—but he was near the center of the larger circle. I don't know what to make of it. It seems odd to me that this killer came in from several miles to the north and committed these murders that accidentally trace a neat pattern around the edges of Brookline. If the real Strangler did live near Coolidge Corner, and if he did use the T to move around, he could have been back in his apartment ten minutes after leaving most of the buildings where the crimes were committed.

Why did DeSalvo confess? He was crazy, to begin with, and was notorious for telling self-aggrandizing whoppers. According to Bailey, the very first thing that he heard from DeSalvo, by way of Nassar, was "would it be possible for him to publish his story and make some money with it?" The *last* thing anybody heard from DeSalvo was, he was suing people because the money he had been promised disappeared before it reached his pockets.

One can see that, if the police knew that DeSalvo had not really committed the crimes but wanted to take credit for them, then they might allow him to take "credit" for the murders in the public's eye, but never charge him in connection with them. That way, if and when the real murderer was discovered, there would be no impediment to prosecution. If the police had actually *charged* DeSalvo with the murders,

a) they would have had to present some sort of corroborative evidence, which they did not have, and

b) they would have been in a difficult position if the series of murders resumed and the murderer was caught.

The way it worked out was good for the police—in fact, it was great for the police. The police had an excuse to call off the time-consuming, frustrating and fantastically expensive investigation, they got the public to believe that they had solved the crimes—but all of their options were still on the table if the real murderer re-surfaced.

The Belmont murder—Sebastian Junger's case—was never officially associated with the Strangler crimes. Junger, clinging to the belief that DeSalvo may have been guilty, works this into a theory (pp. 258–59) of why DeSalvo, confessing to the crimes, never confessed to *that one* while he was in the process of coming clean. The logic is tortured and unconvincing. But if one assumes the opposite tack, that DeSalvo was being fed information by the police to clean up the crimes so that they could move on, then it becomes very obvious why DeSalvo didn't confess to that crime: the police didn't want him to. They had already hung that one on somebody else.

These arguments present as coherent and logical the outcomes of a judicial process that was, in reality, chaotic and confused. "The police" and "the prosecutors" included people who had opinions all over the map. Some wanted to prosecute DeSalvo for the Stranglings, some wanted to investigate further, some thought he had nothing to do with the case, and some wanted to disbar Bailey for the way he had represented DeSalvo.

My opinion. F. Lee Bailey was a publicity-hungry young attorney who was building a name for himself by getting involved in high-profile crimes, and the Boston police played him. Albert DeSalvo wanted to confess to these crimes, and some of the police went along with it for their own reasons. Bailey was then able to present himself to the public as the clever lawyer who had cut a deal to end the Boston Strangler case, keeping his client off the streets but out of jail.

Everybody got what they wanted out of the deal. The police got rid of an unsolvable case that was draining money and blocking careers. DeSalvo, although he grew unhappy with the deal, got to be a famous important criminal rather than the anonymous lowlife that he really was. Bailey, who was already somewhat famous because of the Sam Sheppard and Carl Coppolino cases, became a lot more famous; he wound up with his own TV show.

The only thing was, no one got to the truth.

XX

F. Lee Bailey was involved in four of the most famous cases of the 20th century, and other very famous crimes as well, but four of the twenty most famous cases of the century. While many other lawyers had multiple associations with famous crimes, only one other lawyer—Darrow—is equally prominent in the *most* famous cases.

Looking back on it, it is my belief that Bailey helped to cause the system of justice to fail in all four cases. In the case of Sam Sheppard, Bailey cleared the name of a man who probably *was* involved in his wife's murder. In the case of the Boston strangler, Bailey sold the entire nation on the story that Albert DeSalvo was the Boston Strangler, which he probably was not.

Patty Hearst was a young woman who was dragged violently from her room in the middle of the night, raped and terrorized into joining her captors in their further misadventures. Bailey's defense of her allowed her to be convicted in 1976 and sentenced to 35 years in prison, a miscarriage of justice later limited by Jimmy Carter, who commuted her sentence, and Bill Clinton, who pardoned her. And in the case of O. J. Simpson it was Bailey, not Johnnie Cochran, who set the N-word trap that turned the trial of O. J. Simpson into a trial of Mark Fuhrman, thus helping a murderer to walk free.

If you were to evaluate our justice system based on how well it performs in high-profile cases—popular crime cases—you would conclude that our system was a disaster. The system failed in these four cases; it has failed, at least so far, in the JonBenet Ramsey case, it failed in the assassination of President Kennedy—allowing the accused to be murdered—it failed in the case of the Black Dahlia. In cases like Ted Bundy, John Wayne Gacy and Jeffrey Dahmer, the system "succeeded" only after many people were dead. In the cases that the tabloids live for, the system of justice fails a huge percentage of the time. Why is that?

Which way does the cause and effect work? Does the system of justice fail, in these cases, because there is something about the types of crimes that become most famous that makes them difficult for the criminal justice system? Or is it the fact that these cases are so famous that causes the system to fail?

It's both. Sometimes it's one; sometimes it's the other; sometimes it's both. In the O. J. Simpson murder case, the system failed in substantial measure because of the attention given to the case. In the JonBenet case, I think the same is true: that had the press never gotten interested in the case, it is more likely that the investigation would have been handled properly.

If that were generally true, it would be an important indictment of the popular crime phenomenon. But more often, I think, it works the other way: that these cases become famous *because* they are hard cases. And in some cases, crimes are solved only because of the attention given to the case by the media.

I'm not a Pollyanna. I am not suggesting that the phenomenon of popular crime does no harm. It *does* do harm. It gums up the machinery of justice. It coarsens the culture. It creates pressures in the justice system that cause distorted allocations of resources. Worse, in some cases it promotes the spread of crime.

The phenomenon of "spree killers," who kill as many random people as they can in a single outburst of rage, has now killed hundreds of Americans. This phenomenon was launched in 1966 with the nearly simultaneous stories of Richard Speck and Charles Whitman. On July 14, 1966, Speck killed eight student nurses in Chicago. Less than three weeks later (August 1, 1966), Whitman—who, like Speck, had been born in 1941—shot fourteen people from a tower in Austin, Texas.

There was little precedent for such crimes in America before 1966. It is the view of the author that people have a ubiquitous tendency to imitate the actions of others, and that this is true without regard to whether those actions are condemned or condoned by society. When these two incidents were given great publicity, other people—not sane people, but people who were troubled—began to imitate these actions, and a wave of random killings was launched. It is my view that, had we somehow been able to suppress publicity about the first incidents, some of the later incidents most likely would never have occurred, and hundreds of lives might have been saved.

But in the case of Andrei Chikatilo, the Russian serial murderer of the

1970s and 1980s, the Soviet police, for the most part, kept his crimes out of the newspapers. The authorities thought that publicizing his crimes made them look bad. This enabled Chikatilo to keep going back to the same places over and over, and grabbing more victims. He was convicted of murdering 52 people. It seems extremely unlikely that he could have killed so many without the implicit cooperation of the police, who covered up his crimes.

I am not suggesting that we say, "Oh well, in a free society these things happen; when we decide to have a free press, we take the costs with the benefits." That's a sloppy way to think about it. Free societies regulate and control all sorts of things; we can damned well regulate and control some elements of the coverage of crime stories without invading our basic freedoms, if we choose to do that. But let me ask you this: Have you ever seen it happen that, in the case of an unsolved crime, the family of the victim will reach out to the media, and try to generate media interest in the case?

Of course you have; it happens all the time. But think about what it means. Does this not suggest that the attention of the media is sometimes a *benefit* to the victims of the crime? If it is not a benefit, then why do people pursue it?

On June 21, 1964, three civil rights workers were murdered in Mississippi. This crime—and this is relatively unique in American history—became a huge popular crime story, largely because an organized group of people was prepared to jump on it and make it a huge crime story. Southerners had been lynching blacks (and sometimes whites) from time out of memory. One of the tools of the civil rights movement was to focus attention on these crimes, so as to induce sympathy, bring about justice, and deter such crimes in the future. Murders such as those of Emmett Till in 1955 and Willie Edwards in 1957 (and others) were publicized by civil rights advocates as a part of a strategy to end lynching.

The murdered civil rights workers—James Chaney, Andrew Goodman and Mickey Schwerner—were involved in a project to register black voters in the South, under the title of "Freedom Summer." The organizers of Freedom Summer anticipated that their workers would be the targets of violence, and were prepared to call as much attention as possible, as quickly as possible, to any attacks on their volunteers.

In my view, Chaney, Goodman and Schwerner were among the greatest of American heroes. They were courageous young men who lost their lives fighting for a better America—as were our soldiers, but the civil rights workers did so without the solace and support of an organized military. They fought monsters with their bare hands. In any case, news of the disappearance of the three young men spread nationwide, and reached to high levels of the government, before the men were even dead.

This is relatively unique, this manufacturing of public interest in a crime for the purpose of creating a shield, but it re-enforces the fact that publicity about a crime *does* contribute to the safety net that surrounds us all.

In 2009 there was a Liam Neeson movie, *Taken*, the premise of which was that beautiful young American girls were being kidnapped in Paris and sold into prostitution. While young Americans *are* sometimes forced into prostitution overseas, the premise of the movie is absurd, and impossible. Remember the Natalee Holloway story? How many beautiful young American girls do you think can be kidnapped in Paris without creating an international incident?

Well, the answer is: none. The phenomenon of Popular Crime makes these events impossible—and thus serves to protect us all. Sometimes black Americans complain that this is a racist phenomenon, that crimes against black Americans go unreported and un-cared about. Yes, of course this is true, and yes, of course it is wrong.

What I am trying to get to is this: that the phenomenon of Popular Crime does not *have* to be a wild animal roaming the streets. It can be caged; it can be used for good purposes. The actions of over-aggressive journalists, intruding into the private lives of crime victims, can perfectly well be regulated, should we choose to do that. And, on the other end, the attention of the media does not need to be focused relentlessly on missing little girls; it can perfectly well be focused, by deliberate actions, on drive-by shootings or other crimes that plague the inner cities. There is a toxin in it that can be controlled; there is good in it that can be used. We tend to do neither.

In a movie based on the Boston Strangler, there is a wildly fictionalized scene in which John S. Bottomly—who in the movie was Henry Fonda, but in real life was a wimp—leaps across a table to slap the out-of-control serial murderer back in his place. Nothing remotely like that ever happened.

In a movie based on the murders of the three civil rights workers, there is a fictionalized scene in which the heroic FBI agent, who in the movie is Gene Hackman but who in real life didn't exist, reaches the end of his patience with the local rednecks, and begins to slap one of them around. Neither of these is a particularly good movie; they're both moderately skilled, competent emotional manipulations. But the question I would pose is, what does this tell us about True Crime, as opposed to fictional crime, that, in order to make True Crime sexier, the movies feel the need to inject phony police violence?

Which then is worse for the soul: True Crime, which exploits horrific events for popular amusement, but which also tells real human stories, or Fictional Crime, which creates imaginary horrific events for popular amusement? I don't know the answer to that, but the worst parts of the True Crime movies are the fictionalized parts.

President John F. Kennedy was assassinated on November 22, 1963. Obviously it is beyond the scope of this little book to sort out the facts of the Kennedy assassination. If you were to read one book a month about the Kennedy assassination, you could read them all in about twenty years—you could, at least, if the assassination buffs would stop writing them. The two books that I would recommend to you—not having read them all, obviously—are *Case Closed*, by Gerald Posner (Anchor Books, 1993) and *Mortal Error*, by Howard Donahue and Bonar Menninger (St. Martin's Press, 1992).

Posner's book is a systematic rebuttal of the specious material which forms the bulk of the other 200-plus books. His main points:

1. *Lee Harvey Oswald was a hyper-political lunatic.* Oswald's behavior over the previous years was absolutely consistent with that of an assassin. He was moody, abusive, erratic, and didn't get along with anybody. He promoted his incomprehensible politics night and day. He had earlier attempted to assassinate another national figure, General Edwin Walker. He was everything that you would expect an assassin to be.

2. *The specific, legal evidence against Oswald, on that particular day, is overwhelming.* He was seen going into the book depository, by people who knew him. He was seen coming out of the book depository. He was seen in the book depository, in the window where the shots came from. The gunshots and the bolt action of the weapon were clearly heard by three men only a few feet away, looking out the window below him. An eyewitness to the shooting, across the street, flagged down a policeman and gave a description of Oswald. He was seen fleeing the scene.

He was seen carrying a long package, which he claimed was curtain rods, into the building before the shooting. His rifle was found hidden in the building after the shooting. Repeated ballistics tests have proven that this weapon fired at least one of the shots which struck the President. His fingerprints were on the weapon. His palm print was on the box which was used to steady the weapon.

His behavior before and after the event was strange, even for him. He left almost all of his worldly money out on the TV at his wife's place, and left her a kind of good-bye note. When a policeman stopped him an hour later, he murdered the policeman. What more evidence could you possibly want?

3. *Jack Ruby was an unstable man prone to acts of violence.*

4. *There is no credible evidence of a conspiracy.* Any event which is prominent in the news will tend to draw the attention of imbalanced people. Whenever there is a highly publicized murder, hundreds if not thousands of people will push forward, wanting to get involved, to be witnesses or participants or psychics or pretend journalists or pretend detectives.

The Kennedy assassination, the biggest news story of the decade, inevitably attracted an unusual number of these people. Given this attention, given these many thousands of persons who actually were involved in the case in some peripheral way or who desperately wanted to be, it is inevitably possible to find "evidence" of limitless plots and counter-plots, if one loosens the standards of what is evidence.

New Orleans D.A. Jim Garrison was willing to do that. An intelligent man with a responsible public position, Garrison was as desperate as anyone to be a part of the story—and observed no ethical restraints as to how he would pursue that goal. He manufactured a sort of case. Though a jury laughed at it, it had its hour in the sun.

And then, paranoia swept the neighborhood. As we lost confidence in our government, we began to suspect that any politician might be Richard Nixon with a better shave. The publishing industry discovered a market for paranoid books about the Kennedy assassination. But using real standards of evidence—what do we actually know that we could prove to a skeptic—what evidence is there of a conspiracy?

None.

Ruby did not know Oswald.

There is no credible evidence that anyone conspired with Oswald to commit the crime.

5. *The conspiracy theorists have abused the truth in the most horrible ways.*

Each of the first four points, in my opinion, Gerald Posner establishes very clearly. In establishing that Oswald was a walking time-bomb, I would score his material at 10 on a scale of 10. On analyzing the details of the fateful day, I should give him at least a nine. On the background of Jack Ruby, I might give him a seven; on the weakness of the conspiracy evidence, another "10" seems warranted.

But if these are solid hits, it is in pointing out the abuses of the conspiracy experts that Posner goes over the top. Taking the list of supposed "mysterious deaths" connected to the Kennedy case, Posner reviews them one by one, and demonstrates how ludicrous it is to suppose that these "mysteries" are a key to some sinister conspiracy. Will Griffin was one of dozens of FBI agents assigned to take witness statements for the Warren Commission in 1963 and 1964. He died of cancer in 1982, and the conspiracy theorists added him to the list of 100+ "suspicious deaths" supposedly connected to the Kennedy assassination.

I think it's a wonderful book, and I feel that Gerald Posner has accomplished a public service in putting it together, granting that in my case he is preaching to the choir. But although I have the highest regard for *Case Closed,* and a genuine appreciation for Posner's effort in writing it, that book ultimately does not win the contest to convince me. It finishes a strong second. The winner is *Mortal Error,* by Bonar Menninger, which is based on the work of Howard Donahue.

Howard Donahue was a Baltimore ballistics expert who became involved in the JFK investigation when he was called by CBS in the spring of 1967. CBS had constructed a mockup of Dealey Plaza, complete with a little track which pulled a moving target repeatedly through the "Plaza" at 11 miles per hour. CBS was trying to see whether they could find anybody who could hit the target three times in 5.6 seconds. Donahue fired three shots into a three-inch circle on the moving target in 5.2 seconds—and became fascinated with the weapons-and-ballistics aspects of the assassination.

Donahue's theory, developed over the following twenty years, is that Lee Harvey Oswald did in fact fire two shots at the President that warm November afternoon, with or without the assistance of a vast array of unknown conspirators. He missed with the first shot, although a fragment ricocheted up and hit the President in the neck. His second shot hit Kennedy and Governor John Connally, and his weapon jammed when he attempted a third shot. Unfortunately, a Secret Service man, George Hickey, grabbed a weapon and jumped when he heard the first shot. Hickey's weapon accidentally fired, and that bullet, from Hickey's gun, mortally wounded the President.

On first hearing this theory, almost no one believes that it could be right. It sounds like just another helium balloon by someone who watched too many *Mission: Impossible* re-runs as a child. But I have read *Mortal Error* carefully, and I have to tell you, if there's a flaw in his argument, I don't see it. Unlike the conspiracy theories, which are almost universally based on conversations which took place in Russia in 1961, in New Orleans in 1962, or in Tampa in 1972, the Donahue analysis is based primarily upon a detailed, careful study of what happened in Dealey Plaza on November 22. The key points of his argument can be sorted into three classes:

1) Ballistics.

2) Circumstantial observations of the critical ten seconds.

3) Circumstantial observations after the fact.

Donahue is a ballistics expert who has testified in many criminal cases in that role. His ballistics arguments include:

1) The trajectory of the fatal bullet, plotted very carefully based on the entrance and "exit" wounds and the position of Kennedy's head at that moment, traces a line behind Kennedy, and directly back to the Secret Service car which was following at a distance of about five feet.

2) The bullet which hit Kennedy in the head disintegrated after impact, which a bullet fired from Oswald's rifle would not have done, but a bullet fired from a AR-15, carried by Hickey, would have. According to Menninger, "The Carcano round [Oswald's round] simply did not have the velocity—either rotational, from the rifling in the gun barrel—or linear, from the gunpowder charge in the skull—to completely shred the thick metal jacket and disintegrate the lead inside upon impact . . . the startling fact was that the bullet that hit Kennedy's head had not behaved like a full metal-jacketed round at all."

3) A Carcano round, fired at the distance between Kennedy and Oswald at the moment of the fatal shot (believed to be 261 feet), could not have transmitted as much energy as the fatal round obviously did.

4) A .223 bullet, as fired from an AR-15 (Hickey's gun), creates a little "lead snowstorm" in its target, as some of the lead actually melts on impact, then cools again in the tissue. A Carcano round has no similar effect. According to Donahue, exactly such an effect was described to him by Dr. Russell Fisher, a member of the pathologists' panel which reviewed the autopsy results in

1968. (The President's brain disappeared from the National Archives shortly after that, making it impossible to confirm this allegation.)

5) The bullet fired by an AR-15 is 5.56 millimeters in diameter. A Carcano round is 6.5 millimeters in diameter. The entrance wound in the back of the President's head was only six millimeters wide—making it seemingly impossible to put a 6.5 millimeter round through the hole.

This material, on first read, is stupefyingly dense, and for that reason has little power to persuade. In establishing the trajectory of the fatal bullet, there's a 3 degree slant of the road, a 16 degree angle of descent from the window to the car, a 25 degree turn to the President's head, a 40 degree tilt to the President's head, a 6 degree left angle from the Secret Service car, an angle of the road from true north, an angle from the grassy knoll, a path to be followed from the book depository to Governor Connally . . . add in muzzle velocities, Zapruder frame numbers, the widths and weights of bullets and bullet casings, and you've got a story problem that would boggle the mind of the Great God Texas Instruments.

So on first reading, my reaction to the ballistic stuff was "Well, he could be right, he could be wrong, I'm not a ballistics expert, and I don't see how anybody can really claim to know." Later, however, after reading Posner's book, after watching a couple of documentaries which include copies of the Zapruder film, I returned to the analysis, and my reaction was different: not merely that Donahue could be right, but that he actually was.

The situation is not as complicated as the language in which it must be stated. If you can wade through the math until you get an intuitive feel for what the argument is about, you can figure things out. Let's start with the fact that, to quote from Posner, "the fatal shot entered the rear of the President's skull and exploded out *the right side* of his head," emphasis mine.

But Oswald was positioned to the right rear of Kennedy, behind him and to the right. That should mean, on the surface of it, that a shot from Oswald should have exited the left side of Kennedy's head. Put down the book, take your fingers and point; you'll see what I mean.

Not only that, but Oswald was way up in the air. The Warren Commission reported that the fatal shot was fired at a downward angle (from the sixth floor of the book depository) of 16 degrees. But, also according to the Warren report, the fatal bullet, as it exited, blew a hole in Kennedy's skull about two inches from the top of his head—above the hairline. Why does a bullet fired at a downward angle of 16 degrees, entering behind Kennedy's ear, exit through his skull? A descending bullet should have created an exit wound through Kennedy's face, about the height of his nose—not through his skull.

The Warren report defenders avoid this quandary by supposing that Kennedy's head, at the moment of impact, is turned sharply to the left (25 degrees) and tilted sharply forward (40 degrees). The problem, based on my own observation of the film, is that they are simply wrong. Kennedy's head *was* turned to the left and tilted forward at the moment of impact—but not nearly enough to explain the anomalous location of the exit wound. Donahue says that in order to cause the actual wound with a bullet descending at 16 degrees, the President's head would have had to have been tilted forward about 60 degrees. In fact, it was tilted forward by about 10 to 11 degrees. On the other hand, the exit wound is exactly where it should be if the fatal bullet was in fact fired from Agent Hickey's weapon.

So Donahue is right on that issue—or at least, he convinces me. Rent one of the documentaries which includes an enhanced version of the Zapruder film, and reach your own conclusion. Watch the film frame by frame (as hard as that is), and ask yourself does this bullet come from

a) the high right rear, or

b) a position on the same level and slightly to the left.

I think that almost anyone would conclude that the answer is (b). *The Men Who Killed Kennedy,* by the way, is a silly documentary and a dreadful disservice to the truth, but it does include a good, clean version of the Zapruder film.

Donahue's other four points, as I have summarized them, involve the disintegration of the bullet, the amount of energy transmitted by the bullet, the "lead snowstorm" in the President's brain, and the size of the entry wound. On none of these issues am I able to get beyond the point of saying that Donahue's argument is reasonable, as opposed to right. On the issue of how a bullet 6.5 millimeters in diameter could pass through a wound 6 millimeters in diameter, the Warren report says, "The dimension of 6 millimeters, somewhat smaller than the diameter of a 6.5 millimeter bullet, was caused by the elastic recoil of the skull which shrinks the size of an opening after a missile passes through it." This is theoretically possible but, since pathologists routinely assume that an entrance wound must be larger than the bullet which causes it, not a very strong argument. The other defense for the anomaly is that the measurement, which is based on an X-ray, may not have been precise. On each of these four supporting points of his ballistic argument, I am inclined to believe that Donahue is probably correct.

Let us deal, then, with the circumstantial observations of the critical seconds. It was this material which, in first reading, persuaded me that Donahue might indeed have unraveled the century's greatest mystery. Donahue's research has concluded that:

1) Secret Service agent George Hickey carried an AR-15, which is the civilian version of the M-16, the rifle used by U.S. military ground troops in the Vietnam era. Numerous eyewitness reports state that Hickey had grabbed this weapon and was waving it around within seconds of the first shot.

2) One eyewitness, S. M. Holland, told a Warren Commission interviewer that "just about the same time the President was shot the second time, he (Hickey) jumped up in the seat and was standing up . . . now I actually thought when they started up, I actually thought he was shot, too, because he fell backwards just like he was shot, but it jerked him down when they started off." Holland also observed that agent Hickey had his weapon in his hands at that moment.

3) Special Agent Winston Lawson was in the first car of the motorcade, the car ahead of Kennedy's on that day. His job was to look steadily backward at the President, maintaining constant visual contact. In a statement written December 1, 1963, agent Lawson wrote that:

As the Lead Car was passing under this bridge I heard the first loud, sharp report and in more rapid succession two more sounds like gunfire. I could see persons to the left of the motorcade vehicles running away. I noticed Agent Hickey standing up in the follow-up car with the automatic weapon and *first thought he had fired at someone.* (emphasis mine)

4) Secret Service agent Glen Bennett, seated next to Hickey in the follow-up car, says that when the second shot hit Kennedy he yelled "He's hit," and reached for the AR-15 on the floor of the vehicle—only to realize that Agent Hickey already had it. Secret Service agent Emory Roberts, who was in charge of the agents in the follow-up car, reported that just after the shooting he turned and saw Hickey with the rifle, and said "Be careful with that."

5) While the sound reports from the scene are confusing, many earwitnesses thought that one or more of the shots had originated from near the President. Austin Miller, watching from the overpass, thought that the

shots had come "from right there in the car." Royce Skelton, also watching from the overpass, said that he thought the shots came "from around the President's car." Mary Elizabeth Woodward, standing just in front of the grassy knoll, described the third shot as "a horrible ear-shattering noise."

Agent Lawson, in the 1990s, was outspoken in condemning Donahue's conclusions. But doing no more than re-wording his contemporary statement, Lawson says that what he actually saw led him to believe that Agent Hickey had fired his weapon—but that later events caused him to abandon or re-interpret this recollection.

6) Several individuals who were part of the President's motorcade reported smelling gunpowder. Mrs. Earle Cabell, wife of the mayor of Dallas, was riding in an open convertible, four cars behind the death car. She saw the barrel of the rifle projecting through the open window, and immediately after that reported smelling gunpowder. Other people riding in the motorcade also reported the smell of gunpowder, including Tom Dillard, a journalist who was riding in an open car about a block behind the President, and Senator Ralph Yarborough, who was in the car immediately behind Agent Hickey's.

This, to me, is probably the most persuasive element of Donahue's argument. If in fact the only shots fired that afternoon were from Oswald's rifle, six stories in the air and inside a building, I have a very difficult time understanding why numerous witnesses would smell gunpowder at ground level and in the path of the presidential limousine.

Posner's version of this is in a footnote. "Others *near the School Book Depository* also thought they smelled gunpowder," writes Posner, emphasis mine. He starts with Mrs. Cabell and lists two others, both of whom were riding in open convertibles behind the President. His explanation for why these people smelled gunpowder is that "a stiff north-south wind did blow the odor of gunpowder further into the plaza."

But this doesn't wash. A stiff north-south wind would disperse the smell of gunpowder, not pass it along intact. Although Posner himself does not believe in the Donahue thesis, all of the persons that Posner reports smelling gunpowder were in the cars which immediately followed Agent Hickey's. This seems to me a weighty coincidence. To say that they were "near the School Book Depository" is disingenuous; they were near the Book Depository when the motorcade went by the depository.

Menninger/Donahue reports on another person who smelled gunpowder, that being Officer Earle Browne, who was stationed on the Triple Over-pass. This makes sense, however, since the Secret Service vehicle would pass right underneath Browne's feet a few seconds after the shot. The smell of the gunpowder would obviously be carried along with the vehicle. According to Menninger/Donahue (p. 90):

> Oswald was sixty feet above the street and most of the windows in the book depository were closed. Bullets don't emit or trail gun smoke. And what about Officer Browne on the highway overpass? He was a considerable dis-tance upwind from Dealey Plaza, and the wind was blowing briskly that day. Any gun smoke produced in Dealey Plaza could never have reached him.

There may be a disagreement here about which way the wind was blow-ing. Leaving that aside, I submit that you can go there today and fire three shots inside that book depository, and nobody down on the street is going to smell gunpowder four seconds later, regardless of which way the wind blows. So if Donahue is wrong, explain it to me. Why did so many witnesses in the path of the motorcade smell gunpowder, if no gun was fired in that path?

From there on, what we have in support of the Donahue thesis is a series of after-the-fact observations, culled by Donahue from dozens of other Ken-nedy books.

1. Jim Bishop, in *The Day Kennedy Was Shot*, reported that Secret Service agent Clint Hill phoned the White House from the hospital. "There's been an accident," he reported, apparently overheard by the reporter.

2. According to *LBJ: The Way He Was*, by Frank Cormier, Lyndon John-son hated to have Secret Service agents tailgating him, and once, on a hunt-ing trip, threatened to shoot out their tires if they didn't keep a safe distance. Another time, Johnson told Cormier that "If I ever get killed, it won't be because of an assassin. It'll be some Secret Service agent who trips himself up and his gun goes off. They're worse than trigger-happy Texas sheriffs."

There are others, but none of the after-the-fact observations, really, can be taken to mean very much. Johnson's comment is intriguing, but as we get further away from the actual event, the circle of material which can be reviewed for supporting "evidence" becomes almost inconceivably large, and for that reason it becomes possible to find support for any theory, no matter how far-fetched; this is the basis of the Assassination Industry.

Donahue's research is somewhat inaccessible. It isn't sexy. It doesn't satisfy our natural paranoia. It relies on some understanding of ballistics, which is a very difficult field for a lay reader to plow through. But to a responsible adult reader who isn't paranoid, much of this reveals not the weakness of Donahue's argument as contrasted with other accounts, but the strength of it.

The best thing that can be said about many of the competing accounts—*High Treason, Contract on America, Reasonable Doubt,* the film *JFK* and the documentary *The Men Who Killed Kennedy*—the best thing that can be said about them is that they are childish. Body-snatching, duplicate Oswalds and duplicate Jack Rubys, reconstructive surgery to disguise the corpse, manufactured photographs and assassins visible in the shadows of grainy Polaroids—who believes this stuff?

As to the conspiracy theories, my personal experience is that the maximum number of people who can successfully conspire to do anything is two. If you get three people involved, one of them is going to talk. If you have two, one of them will probably talk, but it's possible that they'll carry it off, if the deception is small and of no particular interest. Successful conspiracies involving as many as eight or ten people might be theoretically possible, but I wouldn't want to bet on them.

But these vast, international conspiracies involving the FBI, the CIA, the Secret Service, Jack Ruby, the United States Army, the Warren Commission, the mafia, two hospitals—it's crazy. Hundreds of people involved in a plot stretching over twenty years, and yet none of them ever talks about it, except some drug dealer who is imprisoned in Jamaica or someplace. Hundreds of books written about the subject, incalculable man hours invested in researching the case, and yet no document ever surfaces to reveal the conspiracy. It is childish to believe that such a thing is possible.

Donahue's theory is that *nobody* intended to kill the President, other than Oswald; it was an accident. It was an accident which happened to occur in such a manner that it was very unclear, to the persons on the scene, what had happened or what was happening. Once this terrible accident had occurred, very few people would have to have any knowledge of what was going on. It is quite possible that Agent Hickey himself did not realize what had happened.

And those few people who did, faced with a *fait accompli,* have a powerful incentive to keep quiet about it. Look at what happens if they talk:

1. Agent Hickey's life is destroyed.

2. All of the agents involved are professionally destroyed.

3. The Secret Service, a governmental agency with an annual budget of many millions of dollars, is seriously compromised.

There have been other incidents of men being accidentally killed by their own bodyguards—indeed, a book argues that this is what happened to the Kingfish, Huey Long. Ross Perot argued during the 1992 presidential campaign that the Secret Service was a vast waste of money, that it was used for political purposes, that it was used to disguise perquisites of office, and that it should be disbanded. There is much truth in his argument; certainly no journalist close to the President would deny that the Secret Service is routinely used to enable the President to "stage" events.

If, in addition to these abuses, it became known that the Secret Service had accidentally shot President Kennedy, do you think the public would still be willing to shell out millions for this "protection"? I'm not an investigative reporter; I'm just a guy who reads lots of crime books. To me, *Mortal Error* remains the most persuasive account of the tragedy in Dallas.

It is a conventional wisdom that the assassination of President Kennedy represented the loss of America's innocence. In popular history the death of JFK marks the end of the sheltered, prosperous post-war era, and the beginning of the cynicism and alienation which culminated in the anti-war movement. The movie *JFK* sells this point of view, but so do countless other movies, from *Forrest Gump* to *Mermaids*, with Cher.

I don't buy it. Again, I'm not claiming any special expertise here, but I was a child of the sixties, too, and I think my perceptions of the time are probably as accurate as the next person's. If I were to make a list of 50 factors which contributed to the schism in society which rocked the sixties, I'd list things as diverse as the invention of LSD and the "modernization" of small schools into large, impersonal school districts, which put teenagers into contact with hundreds of other teenagers but isolated from adult society, and thus created a youth culture. I'd list pop psychology, rock music and the maturation of the radio market, which caused young people, for the first time, to be listening to different radio stations than their parents. I'd list the civil rights movement and the popularization of the 1950s Beat culture. I wouldn't list the Kennedy assassination among the 50 factors.

Why? It just doesn't ring true in my experience. I wasn't a full-blown hippy, but most of my friends were. We talked incessantly about why we were the way we were; hell, we were the most insufferably self-conscious generation in American history. People talked about their parents, about the police, about the irrelevance of the academic curriculum to the lives we all expected to lead. Some people talked an awful lot about how wonderful sex was, and how terrible it was for all of those previous generations to have repressed their sexuality. We talked about the Kennedy assassination twice a year, when we were bored. What the sixties were about was Sex and Race and War. Our parents were irreparably damaged, as role models, because they were racists and believed in war as an instrument of national policy. We couldn't be like them, we all thought; hell, they're racists.

Sure, the assassination of Kennedy was a shock, but you know what? We had all heard about murder. We had all heard of lunatics. Nobody was under the illusion that a bullet wouldn't kill the President as it would kill anybody else. And almost nobody, at the time, thought anything other than that one of those lunatics had gotten a bullet to the President.

I have no empirical evidence to support what I'm saying, but go to the library, and look up magazines from 1965 to 1968. You'll find volumes of essays about the "generation gap," the split of society into young and old. Very, very few of those articles will make any mention of the assassination of JFK. It's an easy, after-the-fact dividing line between the generations, but it's just not true.

On the other hand, the cultural impact of the Manson murders is enormously *under*-appreciated. The murder of Sharon Tate rocked the nation when the counterculture was just past its peak. The arrest and trial of Charles Manson and his followers delivered to young Americans a simple message of enormous impact: that evil men, adorned with flowers, would look much the same as saints. A culture based on categorical trust and unconditional acceptance was a balloon waiting to burst, and Charles Manson was the needle.

We didn't ask ourselves what evil lurked beneath the skin of strangers, so long as they dressed like us. Evil belonged to the other generations, to the hard cases among our generation who would not open their hearts. Was this naïve? It was preposterously naïve. We were younger than young. The sixties weren't cynical, and they certainly didn't come about after the loss of the nation's innocence. They were innocence personified, innocence run amok. They could not co-exist with personified evil.

XXI

◆

On July 10, 1967, a student at Eastern Michigan University in Ypsilanti went out to get some air. A few minutes later she was seen walking on a nearby street. A gray Chevy stopped, apparently offering her a ride. She rejected the ride; it stopped again, menacingly. She wandered out of sight. She was never seen alive again. Her body was found near an abandoned farmhouse in early August.

Police were baffled by the crime.

On June 30, 1968, a second EMU co-ed disappeared. She was seen getting into a red coupe with a black vinyl roof, going to visit a friend. She never got there. Her body was found by construction workers five days later. She had lived only blocks away from the first victim.

Police were unable to identify the killer.

On March 20, 1969, a female law student from the University of Michigan, only a few miles away, was reported missing. She had posted a note on the board at the student union, asking for a ride home. Someone had answered, apparently with an alias, and had then abducted and murdered her. Her body was found just hours later, dumped in a semi-rural graveyard.

The police, to this point, had downplayed the suggestion that the murders were linked, and were investigating them as separate crimes. Apparently they were at least partially right about this, as a killer will be identified here shortly, and, many years later (2005), a different man was convicted of this last murder. At the time, it all fed into the same community fear. Less than a week later there was a fourth victim, a troubled sixteen-year-old who hung around the campuses. She had disappeared while hitchhiking. Her body was found resting in the woods, a few hundred yards from where the second body had been discovered. This was virtually an announcement that a serial murderer was at work, and persuaded the police to re-direct their efforts toward identifying the killer.

Not that they got anywhere.

On April 16, a fifth young woman was found murdered in a semi-rural area north of Ypsilanti. On June 9, 1969, a sixth victim was found. Her body was dropped in the same area. The pace of the carnage was accelerating, and police remained unable to solve the crimes.

While the Michigan Murders did not fire the public's interest on the same scale as the Boston Strangler, each body, after the fifth, was a national news story. Peter Hurkos, a famous psychic, flew in from Los Angeles to participate in the search—as he had meddled in the Boston Strangler investigation, at the invitation of the Bottomly commission, and with the same result. He was a waste of time.

About one o'clock on July 23, 1969, a young woman named Karen Beineman stopped to pick up a hairpiece, a "fall," from a wig maker's shop in Ypsilanti. She told the clerk that she was having an amazing day. She was doing two things that she never thought she would do in her life: buying a wig, and accepting a ride on a stranger's motorcycle. The clerk, reminding her of the murders, urged her not to go with the stranger, even though he looked alright. She went anyway. She was reported missing later that day.

This gave the police a description of the murderer, who had been seen by several clerks and, as it turned out, several other women whom he had also approached. The task force caught a break, and they were able to make use of it because they had done something smart: they had added a kid to their staff. A young man named Larry Mathewson, who had been a part-time patrolman at EMU while a student there, had been added to the task force, in part because he was young and able to talk to the students. The familiarity turned out to be critical. Mathewson remembered that at about the time in question, 1:00 P.M. on July 23rd, he had seen a young man he knew, John Norman Collins, out riding his motorcycle in the same area, dressed similarly to the suspect—a yellow-and-blue striped pullover shirt. He remembered this because Collins had been talking to a striking blonde girl at the time; Larry remembered the blonde. (We all remember the blondes.) Well, he thought, maybe John saw something. Maybe, if he was out riding around at that time wearing those clothes, he would have noticed somebody else, out and around, wearing similar clothes. He thought he'd ask.

Collins turned defensive in mid-interview. Mathewson looked at him in a different light. Not only was Collins in the same area riding a motorcycle at the time in question wearing similar clothes, Mathewson realized, but he matched the description of the suspect. He lived right across the street from one of the victims.

Mathewson got the name of the blonde, wondering if she would confirm the time, place, and Collins' clothing. As he was leaving, he wrote down the numbers off Collins' motorcycle. Collins became angry.

The blonde girl confirmed the time, date, and the shirt. She also had a picture of Collins. Mathewson took the picture to the clerks at the wig makers. Two of them thought it might be him, might not; fuzzy picture. The third one dropped her sandwich in her lap when she saw the picture.

Carefully, almost gingerly, the young officer typed up a report. What Mathewson didn't know, but his commanding officer did, was that Collins had been investigated in connection with the death of Joan Schell, the second victim. He had been seen by a former fraternity brother, and a date, in the company of Joan Schell on the night she disappeared the previous year. Collins had been questioned at that time, but had said that it wasn't him.

John Collins became the subject of round-the-clock surveillance. The background investigation began turning up markers. Collins had been asked to leave his fraternity after he was suspected of theft. In an unrelated incident, someone had stolen a wallet, then used the stolen ID to rent a trailer, then stolen the trailer. The cop investigating that one had realized that the composite sketch of the trailer thief looked a great deal like the composite sketch of the murderer, which didn't do much good without a name. When Collins' name was thrown into the hopper, it was learned that he had made a trip to California just after the trailer had been taken—and the man from whom the trailer was stolen positively ID'd the photo.

Collins was a handsome young man who had been extremely successful with the opposite sex. One of his former girlfriends said that he had once told her, mischievously, that he might be the co-ed killer, and she shouldn't be alone with him.

He had worked in the same building as the first victim at the time she disappeared. He had worked in another office, right across the hall from her.

He spent a good bit of time in a tavern near where the fourth victim had disappeared.

He had once beaten up his sister, badly enough to put her in the hospital.

Collins' uncle, David Leik, was a Michigan state trooper. Collins was close to his uncle, and had been given a key to his house, to keep an eye on things while the uncle was on vacation. When the family returned, there were splotches of paint on the basement floor. When Leik was informed that Collins was a suspect in the investigation, he mentioned the paint splotches to a friend. The friend suggested that maybe the paint was covering up something else. They decided to check.

Blood.

Actually, it wasn't blood. It was a red varnish that looked like blood. Somebody had painted it over, apparently thinking it was blood.

Collins was arrested. That made the national news, and the California police called within a few hours. On June 30, a month earlier, a young girl had been murdered in California. An unknown Michigan college student—unquestionably Collins—had become a suspect in that investigation.

Collins admitted nothing, ever, for which reason many things about the case remain unknown. In August, 1970, he was convicted of the murder of Karen Beineman. He was never tried for the other crimes, although it might have been possible to make one of the cases. From prison, he continues to this day to deny the crimes.

Like almost all serial murderers, Collins was a thief. He had stolen vehicles, motorcycles and motorcycle parts for years, and for the last eighteen months had been burglarizing homes and apartments, although he didn't need the money. He was just doing it for the kick.

It is the California murder which keeps at bay the nagging fear that the murders were hung around a convenient target. Much of the case against Collins is of the type which might be accidentally manufactured by an intense police investigation, focusing on a flawed and unlucky petty criminal. He lived across the street from one of the victims . . . but hey, who didn't? You've got seven murdered students in a small city. Looking hard enough, the police would inevitably find someone who matched the description of the perpetrator. Looking closely enough at that person, they would no doubt find a hundred little links between that person and the murders. Most of the evidence is of that nature.

But how does one explain that that unlucky suspect took a two-week trip to California, and wound up as a key suspect in an unrelated investigation of an extremely similar crime? The only reasonable explanation is that he was a serial murderer. He was Ted Bundy before Bundy was. And the California case against him was strong, perhaps stronger than any of the Michigan cases.

The book about the Michigan Murders is *The Michigan Murders*, by Edward Keyes (Simon & Schuster, 1976). The book is good—well-researched, written in clear, unpretentious, journalistic prose without undue padding. Keyes worked out the sequence of events carefully, and put every detail exactly where it belongs. He used pseudonyms for everybody *including Collins*, which is pretty silly, but the case itself is interesting, and the book is recommended.

In the endless effort to make the law work, here is a problem that nobody talks about. Definition creep.

In the 1930s "Little Lindbergh Laws" were passed by many states which made kidnapping a capital offense. The problem is, what is kidnapping?

"Kidnapping" is seizing a child and holding him or her to force the payment of a ransom, but what if the child is seized not for ransom but for some other reason?

Well, sure; that's still kidnapping.

What if the person seized is not a child, but an adult; is that still "kid" napping?

Sure.

Well, what if the person is seized by a non-custodial parent, a person who feels that they have the right to see the child, but is legally limited for some reason. Is that still kidnapping?

Still kidnapping.

The Little Lindbergh Laws failed to say what *wasn't* kidnapping, and this allowed prosecutors to seek a death penalty for a wide range of criminal activities. By 1950 prosecutors had established that anytime a criminal pointed a gun at someone and forced them to move from one place to another—even, let's say, into a back room—that was kidnapping, and the criminal could be sentenced to death. Of course this was never meant to be "kidnapping," but once prosecutors had established that the law could be applied that way, then it could be applied that way again and again. That's definition creep. The words of the law start out meaning one thing; they wind up meaning another.

Take "premeditated" murder. When laws were first passed to distinguish "premeditated" murder from acts of passion—in cold blood, as opposed to hot—"premeditated" murder meant that it was actually premeditated. It was thought through in advance. "All murder is heinous," the law intended to say, "but to murder someone in cold blood is *especially* heinous, and so we will give a harsher penalty for that." The law, however, failed to say how much premeditation was enough. Prosecutors immediately began arguing that *any* premeditation was the same as actual premeditation. One second's premeditation was enough.

And, of course, the prosecutors won; the law very soon was taken to mean that one second's premeditation was enough. The problem was that the intended distinction was entirely lost. Once prosecutors succeeded in getting the law to "read" that one second's premeditation was enough, then the higher penalty applied to all murders.

We have "three strike" laws now; three crimes of violence, and you get a life sentence. In principle, I'm on board; hell, I don't understand why it takes three crimes of violence to lock somebody away. If you're talking about a real, serious crime of violence—rape, or aggravated assault, or murder—I would certainly think that two was what my father would have called a God's Green Plenty.

But we had these laws before, the "habitual criminal" laws. The Big Bitch, they used to call it; three felony convictions, you're locked up for life. Most states had habitual criminal laws from the 1940s into the 1970s.

Those laws failed because of definition creep. The original meaning of the term "felony" was that a felony was a crime for which the penalty was the loss of life or the loss of a bodily part. Now, anything can be a felony. You steal something worth $1,000, that may be a felony. If you're caught with enough marijuana to host a frat party, that's a felony.

What happened to the habitual criminal laws was that they relied on the definition of a "felony," when damned near anything can be prosecuted as a felony. So prosecutors would get on somebody's case, and, boom, he's got three felonies before he can get to the bathroom. This was never the intention of the habitual criminal laws, so those laws gradually collapsed.

Then, ten years later, we started re-passing the same laws, only calling it "three strikes and you're out." It started out with three *violent* crimes, but . . . what's a violent crime? If you use a gun, is that a violent crime?

Sure.

What if you don't use the gun, but you wave it in the victim's face? Is that a crime of violence?

It is.

Well, OK, what if you don't wave the gun in his or her face, but you have a gun on you?

If you have a gun, that's still a violent crime.

Sexual predator registries were intended to let people know if a child molester was living next door, which I am all in favor of—but sexual predator registries in practice are overrun with 28-year-old men who, when they were 18, had sex with their 16-year-old girlfriends, and guys who got drunk and left the house naked and got arrested for indecent exposure, and former teachers who lost track for a moment of how inappropriate it was to tell a dirty joke in front of their students.

It sounds like I am arguing on behalf of criminals here. I'm not. I'm arguing on behalf of laws that work.

Did you ever start on a three-day business trip with one small suitcase, only you started stuffing more and more things into the one suitcase until you wound up with a busted zipper? Prosecutors, by their nature, are zipper-busters. They chronically overstuff the suitcase. In order to have laws that work, you have to stop prosecutors from busting the zippers.

XXII

On December 20, 1968, a teenaged couple parked on a lonely road near Vallejo, California, was shot to death by an unknown person.

On July 4, 1969, another young couple parked in the same area was ambushed and shot repeatedly. The woman died; the man survived.

On September 27, 1969, a young couple enjoying a picnic in an isolated area near Lake Berryessa, north of Vallejo, was attacked by a knife-wielding man in a hooded costume. Both were stabbed several times, and the woman died.

On October 11, 1969, a cab driver named Paul Stine was shot and killed near the Presidio, in San Francisco.

Five murders in ten months.

After the second in this series of crimes, the killer began contacting police and the media to claim credit for his kills. Within an hour of the July 4 attack (the second crime) he called the police to say where the bodies could be found, although in fact they already had. At the end of his phone call, just before hanging up, he added the words "I also killed those kids last year."

He wasn't bluffing; he had. In the first days of August, 1969, letters were received by the *San Francisco Chronicle,* the *San Francisco Examiner* and the *Vallejo Times-Herald* from someone claiming to have committed the murders. The letters, all substantially the same, gave details of the July 4th crime not known to the public. Each letter also contained one-third of a cipher, a coded message. The letter stated that the cipher contained the killer's identity.

It didn't. The cipher, de-ciphered by a high school teacher and his wife after all the really smart code-breakers had failed, read "I like killing people because it is so much fun it is more fun than killing wild game in the forrest because man is the most dangeroue anamal of all to kill something gives me the most thrilling experence it is even better than getting your rocks off with a girl the best part of it is thae when I die I will be reborn in paradice and the I have killed will become my slaves I will not give you my name because you will try to sloi down or atop my collectiog of slaves for afterlife." At the end of this there was a string of nonsensical letters, representing a scrambled name or, more probably, just a string of nonsensical letters.

Between August 7, 1969, and March 15, 1971, eleven more letters were written to newspapers, newsmen or, in one case, the lawyer Melvin Belli. The killer had signed the August first letter with a symbol, a circle with crossed hairs. Beginning with the August 7 letter he began calling himself "the Zodiac"; his letters began with the phrase "this is the Zodiac speaking." With the third attack, at Lake Berryessa on September 27, the killer wrote the dates of the three events (involving four murders) on the car door of his victim, and also drew his symbol, the Zodiac's symbol. The killer also called police, in November ("This is the Zodiac speaking"), and demanded to speak to Melvin Belli—on television. He specified a morning show; Belli went on the show and sat there for a couple of hours, waiting for the Zodiac to call.

The Zodiac wrote in long strings of one-syllable words, of which in some letters a very high percentage were misspelled, although in other letters his spelling was almost perfect. The murderer was seeking publicity—and he was continuing to kill, continuing to commit crimes. He committed at least two murders after he began writing to the newspapers about them. This unusual interaction between killer and public created a frenetic swirl of speculation and comment. The vortex of speculation began to suck in other crimes and other communications. People began to speculate that the Zodiac had committed this murder or that murder, or had written this letter or that letter, or had made this phone call or that one.

This speculation swelled the scope of the Zodiac story to unmanageable proportions. The discussion of the Zodiac that continues today in books and on the internet involves dozens of crimes and dozens of alleged Zodiac communications. It is impossible to know for sure which of these other crimes and other communications are in fact the work of the Zodiac, and which are the result of people seeing Zodiacs in their breakfast cereal.

There are three names that have become central to the Zodiac debate: Graysmith, Toschi, and Arthur Allen. Robert Graysmith, a cartoonist for the *San Francisco Chronicle* at the time of the murders, has written two books about the crimes, *Zodiac* and *Zodiac Unmasked*. Portrayed in a movie by Jake

Gyllenhaal, he is the most successful of the dozens of amateur researchers who write about the case.

Dave Toschi was the detective in charge of the Paul Stine case, and thus in charge of San Francisco's Zodiac investigation. Toschi was a colorful, charismatic cop. Elements of his style and personality were adapted by Steve McQueen for the movie *Bullitt* and by Clint Eastwood for the *Dirty Harry* movies. He was haunted by his inability to identify the Zodiac, and his name also pops up in many other crime books.

Arthur Leigh Allen was a man who, although never charged in any of the crimes, was publicly linked to the crimes before his death, and gave interviews denying that he was the Zodiac. Graysmith, in *Zodiac Unmasked*, argues that Allen was the Zodiac.

Whereas almost all serial murderers kill from some concoction of sexual sadism, misogyny and anger, the Zodiac appears to have been driven by satanic beliefs and a desire to create terror. In June, 1966, a college girl had been murdered in Riverside, California, which is down by LA . . . 500 miles from Vallejo. Her murderer or someone convincingly pretending to be her murderer wrote a long letter to the police about the crime. Someone also sent rude eight-word notes to the local newspaper and to the victim's father, and a "poem" celebrating the murder was found scratched into a library desk. In late 1970 an anonymous letter was sent to Paul Avery of the *San Francisco Chronicle*, suggesting that he check out the parallels between the Riverside murder and the Zodiac.

From my standpoint, there appears to be little reason to link this murder to the Zodiac. The murder occurred two years before the first Zodiac murder, and hundreds of miles away. The Zodiac had not (up to this point) included it on his list of murders. The handwriting of the "poem," although it is routinely described as being eerily similar to the Zodiac's, is in fact vastly different. The Zodiac makes a "W" with pointed bottoms—a double V—and with the left half of the W small and cramped, the right half much larger. The Riverside killer makes a "W" with rounded bottoms—a double U—and with two halves of equal size. The Zodiac makes a "d" with a "loop" on the staff, and normally tilted sharply to the left. The Riverside killer makes a two-stroke "d" with no loop. The "o's," "b's," "g's," "r's," "n's" and even the "i's" are obviously different between the two.

Of course, carving letters into enamel on a library desk is different from normal handwriting, and one might expect some differences, even if the Zodiac *had* written the poem. But that isn't the issue. The issue is the absence of any meaningful link between the two cases. The fact that the handwriting is different doesn't prove anything, but that's the point: there is an absence of proof.

The eight-word note mailed to the Riverside newspaper is printed in all caps. The Zodiac never did this (and rarely used capital letters, even when it would have been appropriate to use them).

The eight-word note mailed to the victim's father capitalized each word but not each letter, but the printing seems to bear no resemblance to the Zodiac's. It has, again, the rounded-bottom "w," an "h" made with three strokes when the Zodiac uses one, etc.

There was, in the Riverside case, a letter mailed to the police. But that letter is as much like the Zodiac's as Brahms is like Megadeath. The Riverside letter is coherent, and uses standard punctuation. Zodiac's sentences are short, blunt and cold. The Riverside murderer's sentences are long, elaborate and passionate—passionate about murder, unfortunately, but passionate. "Her breast felt very warm and firm under my hands, but only one thing was on my mind." This guy reads romance novels. Zodiac never writes anything remotely like that.

The Riverside killer is forthright in saying that he has attacked this woman (and will attack others) out of sexual frustration. This *may* be true of the Zodiac as well, but he would certainly never admit it. The Zodiac claims that he kills people because he enjoys it even more than sex, and he thinks this will make them his slaves in the afterlife.

The only handwriting we have from Riverside is the letters mailed to the newspaper (months after the event) and to the victim's father, and the envelope in which these were sent. I studied copies of these as best I could, to evaluate the handwriting. I was looking for common words, words that appear in both the Riverside documents and the Zodiac documents. I noticed the word "die" in the Riverside letters, so I thought I would compare this to the word "die" in the Zodiac letters. And you know what?

It never appears. The Zodiac, in ten to fourteen communications totaling thousands of words, never uses the word "die." The Riverside killer, on the other hand, uses the word "die" constantly; it's his favorite word. In the "poem" scratched on the desk, the word "die" is used twice in 46 words, plus the word "death." In the eight-word postcards mailed to the father and the newspaper, one of the words is "die." In the longer letter mailed to police (about a page and a half) we have "dead" twice, "die" once and "died" once. The Zodiac never uses any of those words . . . die, died, dead.

Why? Dying is what the victim does. The Zodiac's victims weren't real to him. He uses the words "kill," "killed," "murder," "murdered" . . . he uses those all the time, because those are about *him*, about what *he* had done. Shot, shoot, stab, stabbed, pick off, wipe out . . . all kinds of active words about what the Zodiac has done or will do.

The word "die" does appear once, not in Zodiac's handwriting but in the translation of his cipher. When it is decoded, the word "die" appears—but he is talking about *his* death. When *I* die, these people I have killed will be my slaves in the afterlife. And the word "death" does appear twice in the Zodiac letters, but both times in the context of the Zodiac's "death machine"—my death machine, once, and the death machine the other time.

The Riverside case has become a standard, quasi-official part of the Zodiac story. The back cover of Graysmith's *Zodiac* says, "The official tally of his victims was six. He claimed thirty-seven dead. The real toll may have reached fifty." To get six victims, whoever counted was including Riverside.

But here's my real point. Including the Riverside murder in the Zodiac story gives us more information about the Zodiac, but unfortunately it is bogus information, as the Zodiac did *not* commit that murder. Dave Toschi in the early 1970s made public statements certifying as legitimate certain letters which are, in the view of the author, obvious forgeries and/or cases of mistaken identity. Toschi said that the Zodiac wrote letters that, in fact, he very clearly did not. Most likely he did this because he was trying to

a) jerk the Zodiac's chain, and

b) keep the investigation alive.

Toschi claimed that his document examiner had certified as legitimate what is known as the Exorcist letter, and what is known as the Badlands letter. The Exorcist letter, which is the basis of the statement that the Zodiac claimed 37 victims, is, in my opinion, a forgery—but at least it *pretends* to be from the Zodiac, and imitates his handwriting. The Badlands letter makes no claim to have been written by the Zodiac, makes no reference of any kind to the Zodiac murders, uses vocabulary and sentence construction massively inconsistent with the Zodiac's, and was mailed to a newspaper four years after the murders definitely linked to the Zodiac had ceased. Nonetheless, at least according to Graysmith, Toschi claimed that it was a Zodiac letter, and claimed that his handwriting expert had identified it as such.

There has never been a handwriting expert in the history of the world who was incompetent enough to say that that was a Zodiac letter. If in fact Toschi did say that, he was lying. He was trying to poke the sleeping story with a stick.

But the inclusion of the Exorcist and Badlands letters in the Zodiac oeuvre gives us yet more information about the Zodiac—unfortunately, yet more bogus information. One of the things that the experts "know" about the Zodiac is that he was a movie fanatic, and the experts know this because of the Exorcist letter and some other jigamarole. It is an accepted part of the Zodiac's legend, mentioned frequently by Graysmith and other writers, that the Zodiac is a huge movie fan. Graysmith quotes Toschi as saying that "Of course, this guy is a real nut on movies."

But in all of the legitimate communications from the Zodiac, he never mentioned any movie—none, nada, zero, zilch. Nothing. For all we know, the Zodiac never saw a movie in his life. The myth of the Zodiac's interest in movies sprang from the passions of the people who were investigating him, projected onto the Zodiac. In the Zodiac's first cipher, he refers (apparently) to the famous story "The Most Dangerous Game." Toschi, Graysmith, and others investigating the case take this, inexplicably, as a reference to an obscure 1932 *movie* based on the story.

Well, what kind of sense does that make? Let me ask you two questions:

1) Do you know the story of "The Most Dangerous Game"? and
2) Have you ever seen that movie?

Everybody in my generation knows that story. The story was included in high school anthologies, and was read by virtually every high school student in America in the 1940s, 1950s and 1960s. The popular radio series *Suspense* adapted the story as a radio drama three times, once with Orson Welles and Joseph Cotten and once with Orson Welles and Keenan Wynn. To suppose that knowledge of that *story* is evidence of an interest in movies is like assuming that knowledge of a Bible verse is evidence of an interest in the Mel Gibson movie.

The Zodiac *is* an extremely interesting case; the Zodiac murders, in my view, are probably the most interesting unsolved serial murder case in American history. But by including in the Zodiac's story crimes that he did not commit and letters that he did not write, the people who write about him have made of the Zodiac a monster more fiction than fact. The *most* bizarre thing that people say about the Zodiac, of course, is that he is some kind of genius. Ted Kaczynski, the Unabomber, was in San Francisco at this time, and there are numerous sites that speculate on the possibility that Kaczynski was the Zodiac, because, you know, Kaczynski was a genius, and the Zodiac was a genius.

The notion that the Zodiac was a genius is based on four misunderstandings.

First, people assumed that, in order to commit numerous murders and avoid arrest, he must be some kind of super-criminal.

Second, people assumed that the Zodiac was a man of superior intelligence because of his construction of codes that have not been broken.

Third, people credited the Zodiac with intelligence because he could design bombs.

And fourth, people over-estimated the Zodiac's intelligence because they lumped together his actions and his letters with the letters and actions of fifteen other people. Of course, if you credit him with the skills of several different people, it makes it look like he is very capable.

But none of this stands up to a rigorous review. The nation's worst serial murderer, Gary Ridgway, was often imagined by police, in the 25 years that they hunted for him, to be a criminal mastermind. When finally caught, he turned out to have the IQ of a Labrador retriever. Many serial murderers who get by with several crimes turn out, when finally caught, to be men of very limited intelligence, because it is just extremely difficult to identify an assailant who kills someone he's never met before.

There is nothing about the construction of a code, or even the construction of a *difficult* code, that requires intelligence. It requires that you have some understanding of codes or that you have a book about codes, and it requires that you put a couple of hours into it. That's all. If the code isn't broken, all that means is that the person who created the code failed to deliver the message that he was trying to deliver. Any idiot can create an unbreakable code, because any code is unbreakable if you don't give the audience enough material to work with.

The Zodiac's handwriting has been analyzed at length by people who are determined to avoid the obvious conclusion: that the Zodiac didn't actually write many of the letters attributed to him. Graysmith and others try to come to terms with the inconsistencies in the "Zodiac's" handwriting by making him a super-genius who can re-construct his own handwriting to confuse the police.

People associated the fact that Zodiac could design a bomb with superior intelligence. But (a) building a bomb does not actually require great intelligence. The task has, after all, been mastered by hundreds of poorly educated Middle Easterners, many of them persons of limited other accomplishments. And (b), his bomb didn't work.

I absolutely believe that the Zodiac did in fact build this bomb, and that he fully intended to kill a busload of people with it. It's not like he mentions this once and then drops it; it is a theme that runs through several letters. He says he is going to build a bomb, he shows us the diagram, and then he tells us that he is having trouble with the trigger mechanism (misspelling "trigger" and skipping the word "mechanism"), and then he tells us that his bomb got wet when his basement flooded, and then he tells us that his bomb was a dud and draws up a new bomb diagram. Why would he make these things up? He's not trying to portray himself as a blustering fool; he is trying to portray himself as a powerful master of the fates.

But you know why I am absolutely convinced that he did in fact build the bomb? Because he uses the term "ammonium nitrate fertilizer"—and he spells it correctly. The Zodiac can't spell "machine" or "Christmas"; there is no way in hell he could spell "ammonium Nitrate Fertilizer." He couldn't spell ammonium or nitrate or fertilizer; I'll guarantee you, on his own, he would have misspelled all three words. He spelled them correctly because the words were staring right at him as wrote them. He had bags of ammonium nitrate fertilizer in his kitchen.

The Zodiac was *not* as stupid as the people who taught him in school thought that he was. This, really, was what the murders were about: it was the Zodiac's effort to prove how smart he was. That's just my opinion; could be right, could be wrong. I think the Zodiac was a man who had failed at everything, who had been told all of his life that he was stupid, and he started killing people as a way of getting even with the world, and showing everybody how smart he really was. That isn't the way he rationalized it to himself. He told himself that this was fun, and that he was collecting slaves for the afterlife, but what it was *really* about was showing us all that he was smarter than we were.

I don't mean to speak with too much confidence about the Zodiac. It is possible, in my view, that the Zodiac crimes were committed by two or three people, acting in concert and sharing resources, and acting very possibly as a satanic cult. In some communications there are indications that the Zodiac was an older man, past thirty; in other communications there are indications that he is younger. In some communications there are constant misspellings, whereas the Stine letter—over 100 words—contains only one spelling error.

But my view of the Zodiac is that he was, for the most part, exactly what he seemed to be. He misspelled things because he couldn't spell. He used small words and repeated them over and over because he had a very limited vocabulary. His handwriting is the handwriting that he shows us. When he said he was building a bomb, he was building a bomb. When he said he had killed 13 people, my bet would be that he had killed 13 people.

And when he said that he was going to go on killing people, but just stop telling us whom he had killed, I believe that that most likely is what he did. I don't believe that the Zodiac ever wrote a letter to a newspaper after March, 1971, and perhaps not after July, 1970. At some point he was probably arrested or killed or died off, and I have another theory about him that maybe I'll introduce in another book. What his name was . . . I don't know. I don't think it was Arthur Leigh Allen.

XXIII

On September 22, 1969, Susan Nason disappeared from her home in Foster City, California. She was eight years old. This was five days before the murders at Lake Berryessa and an hour's drive away, but I am not associating this with the Zodiac; I am on to another story here. Her body was found ten weeks later, abandoned in a trash pile on public land. Despite massive police efforts, the crime went unsolved for twenty years.

Eileen Franklin was Susan Nason's best friend. Twenty years later, in January of 1989, she was overwhelmed with a terrible memory: she had witnessed the crime. Her father, a brutal, abusive alcoholic, had raped and murdered the little girl in her presence, and then threatened to kill Eileen if she ever told. She had repressed the memory and kept silent for twenty years, but when the scene returned to her mind she told her husband, who contacted the police.

George Franklin had not been a key suspect in the investigation, and there was little independent evidence to tie him to the murder. The police decided that Eileen Franklin's story was credible, and that her account of the murder was consistent with the crime-scene evidence. The latter is a debatable point; almost everything useful to know about the crime scene had made it into the newspapers, and Eileen's confirming memories were vague.

Still, the prosecution had evidence that Franklin was a despicable man who had raped and beaten his daughters. Franklin's wife in 1969, Leah, said that she had always believed that Franklin had committed the crime, and one of his other daughters had once called the police, as an adult, to report that she was convinced Franklin had committed the murder. Since she had no evidence, the police had put her report in the circular file. Franklin's only son defended his father, although he had not spoken to him for several years before the accusation, lived many miles away from him, and still slept with a baseball bat under his bed for fear that his father would show up in the middle of the night.

The jury deliberated for only eight hours. When a monster is on trial, it is easy to vote guilty. The conviction was reversed on appeal, the appeals court ruling that the "repressed memory," with little or no supporting evidence, was insufficient to sustain a conviction.

There are two books about the case, *Sins of the Father*, by Eileen Franklin and William Wright, and *Once Upon a Time*, by Harry N. MacLean. *60 Minutes* also did a segment on the case, as did countless other shows.

It might occur to the reader that a man so depraved that he would rape and murder a small girl in the presence of his daughter might well have committed other, similar crimes, without an audience. This thought has also occurred to the California police, but the passage of time has apparently left it impossible to make any other charges against him.

He is a free man at this writing. While it is unfortunate that Franklin cannot be prosecuted for the things he actually appears to have done, it does seem apparent that repressed memories are an insufficient basis for criminal prosecution. The author is far from convinced that Franklin was guilty of the murder of Susan Nason.

On September 23, 1970, three men and two women held up the State Street Bank and Trust Company on Western Avenue in Brighton, Massachusetts. (For you Bostonians, that's over by the Harvard football stadium.) The three men were all ex-convicts. The two women were Brandeis University honor students. They escaped with $26,000, but in getting away one of the cons shot and killed a policeman, Walter Schroeder. He left a wife and nine.

The unlikely gang split up that night. Two of the ex-cons were arrested in a matter of hours. Susan Saxe, Katherine Ann Power, and the third ex-con, Stanley Bond, headed south to Atlanta. When the other two were arrested police got positive identification of Saxe, Bond and Power, who became fearful of traveling together. Bond gave Power and Saxe each an envelope containing hundreds of dollars, and they agreed to meet up in Detroit.

Bond also gave Power a suitcase, however, which contained a loaded shotgun. The shotgun went off on a baggage carousel at the airport in St. Louis. Power fled the airport, got on a bus, and made her way to Detroit, where she rejoined Saxe. Bond was arrested in Colorado; all three of the career criminals were now in custody.

Kathy Power drove the getaway car for the bank job. She had been assigned to drive the getaway car because, during an earlier crime, the holdup of an arsenal in Newburyport, she had become violently ill, unable to handle her assignment.

I wish I could explain the sixties radicals to you, but you kind of had to be there. They were good people, intent on making the world a better place. But, in their intense desire to make the world a better place, a few of them had trapped themselves in a paranoid fantasy about the world in which they actually lived. Few of them had ever suffered anything very much, and, as they were focused on the suffering of the oppressed, they needed suffering to feel authentic.

Most of us can get past the things that are done to us, but vicarious suffering is different; it's harder to set aside. I can forgive you for the things you have done to me, but who forgives the things that were done to my people a generation ago? Some of the radicals had slipped inside a prism of unforgivable injustices, and they saw the world through that prism. The rays of the sun turned left when they passed through the radical rainbow, and nothing they said or did made any sense when you got outside their bubble.

Anyway, Power and Saxe began life on the run. They had been roommates at Brandeis. Saxe, who graduated *magna cum laude* in the spring of 1970, had been a radical activist for several years. Power got involved with the radicals when she transferred to Brandeis from Syracuse in 1968. At Brandeis she met Bond (Bond . . . Stan Bond), who was a Vietnam vet and a friend of Albert DeSalvo; the two had been locked up together at one time. Bond had arranged to do a work-release study program at Brandeis, had been adopted by the radicals, and had begun to date Power, among others. When the deranged debutantes' society started chattering about undertaking radical actions to strike at the heart of fascist Amerika, Bond introduced them to experienced criminals who knew how to do these things.

After the bank robbery went bad and they found themselves on the FBI's most-wanted list, Saxe and Power traveled together for four years, living for a while in a feminist commune in Connecticut, moving in 1973 to Lexington, Kentucky, where Power attended a chef's school. In 1974, disagreeing about how to remain invisible, and probably just generally tired of one another, they split up. Susan Saxe was arrested in Philadelphia in 1975, and served eight years in prison for her part in the crime.

Power, on the other hand, got to be pretty good at the fugitive dance. The paranoia that characterized and defined the radicals was very useful to a life in the underground: it gave her a hair trigger that Richard Kimble would have envied. Suspicious of everybody and everything, she dropped her life and ran at the slightest provocation, accumulating few possessions, changing her name constantly, working at the kind of jobs and living in the kind of places where nobody asks for references.

From 1974 through 1977 she hid out in the New York/New Jersey area. In 1977 she acquired the birth certificate of a dead baby who would have been about her age, and began to live as Alice Metzinger. She moved to Oregon, where she gave birth to a son in 1979, and met a man named Ron Duncan in 1980. They hopscotched around Oregon together for a few years.

In the mid-1980s, as her son entered the school system, their life began to settle down. The FBI took her off the list. She began to get better jobs, building a résumé. Power and Duncan bought a house, and eventually (1992) got married. She helped to start a restaurant in Eugene; the restaurant became a big success.

Although Power/Metzinger gave the outward appearance of a cheerful, upbeat person, she was deeply depressed most of the time. She had grown up in a large, happy family, and had not seen anyone from that family in many years. She would burst into tears at the mention of the word "mother" or "brother" or "family." In May, 1992, she entered therapy. Her therapist convinced her that she would never be happy as Alice Metzinger, and Power decided to face the music. A series of intermediary attorneys negotiated a plea bargain, and Power surrendered to authorities in Boston in September, 1993. She had been on the lam just short of 23 years, the entire second movement of her life.

She was sentenced to eight to twelve years in prison. At a parole hearing in March, 1998, the family of the murdered policeman showed up to protest her possible release. She was so moved by their testimony that she withdrew her request for parole, and asked to complete her sentence. She was returned to prison, but was released in 1999 to complete her sentence on probation.

There are four famous cases here that involve large elements of the same story, but acted out in different costumes. Those four are Sacco and Vanzetti, the Manson Family, the Katherine Ann Power story, and the kidnapping of Patty Hearst.

A half-century earlier, a small group of anarchists had staged a payroll heist in the Boston area—Braintree—perhaps intending to fund their revolutionary activities with the proceeds. In that crime two persons were killed. Sacco and Vanzetti were unquestionably radical activists, although it is unclear whether they were actually involved in the robbery. Anyway, they were convicted of being involved, and, protesting their innocence every step of the way, were accorded the status of demigods by the left. The crimes are eerily similar—a gang of about the same size, of similar composition (half radicals, half ordinary crooks), both crimes committed in broad daylight, in both cases taking a similar amount of money ($15,776 in 1920, $26,000 in 1970) and committing murder in the process. In many ways Katherine Power is a similar person to Vanzetti—highly intelligent yet simplistic, courageous in her convictions but blind to the consequences of the actions in which she participated.

Yet the fates of the participants are as different as night and day, for while Sacco and Vanzetti became revolutionary heroes by denying their guilt, Katherine Power was horrified by what had happened—and became a nonperson. Was there something about 1970 as opposed to 1920 that caused this different reaction, or was it simply the way it all came down?

In the three cases ca. 1970 (Manson, Hearst and Power), career criminals, a few years older than the baby boomers, adopted the guise of revolutionaries in order to seduce young women—seduce them sexually, but also to seduce them into becoming accomplices, to seduce them into a life sustained by violent crime.

Charles Manson worked with society's least-favored, with young girls who had run away from dysfunctional families, or who had been driven away by physical and sexual abuse. He adopted not the central ideas of the revolution, but the marginalia—the clothes, the hair, the music—and used these to build a "family," a cult of people who had abandoned normal life in order to do whatever Charlie wanted. This cult he then used as a weapon against a bourgeois society that he felt had humiliated him, intending nothing except to cause pain, to cause harm.

Donald DeFreeze, like Manson, was a career criminal who was born in Ohio. He was superficially different but profoundly the same. He escaped from Vacaville prison in March, 1973, and became involved with Patricia

Soltysik, who was for all the world like Susan Saxe, except on the West Coast. DeFreeze and Soltysik co-founded the SLA, the "Symbionese Liberation Army," which was a small band of losers who kidnapped Patty Hearst to draw attention to themselves. Most of them were killed when the house they were in burned down during a battle with the police in 1974.

Manson, DeFreeze and the Brandeis radicals all believed that a race war was imminent in America, and that they could trigger that war with a few well-timed acts of violence. I don't think that was a central idea for sixties radicals; I don't remember it that way, anyway. I think it was more of a prison-culture idea that, in these three cases, crossed over into the counter-culture. None of these three men (Manson, Bond or DeFreeze) had any genuine interest in what was then called The Movement. They used it as a TV huckster uses the Bible. But, more than anyone else, it was these three men who brought it to an end. Being a hippy had had its day; by 1969 it wasn't really cool to be a hippy, but there were millions of them, and the movement could have stumbled on peacefully for generations. These three men, more than anyone else, made it profoundly un-cool to be a hippy, and thus, more than anyone else, brought the 1960s radical culture to an end.

On the morning of May 24, 1971, a man who owned an orchard near Yuba City, California, noticed a hole in the ground on an isolated part of his property, a hole about the size and shape of a shallow grave. When he passed the same spot later in the day, after dark, the hole had been filled. The man called the police, who sent someone out the next day to investigate.

Numerous sources say that the orchard owner called police because he thought someone was illegally burying trash on his property. This seems really unlikely. If I saw a grave-sized hole on my property and then was walking by there at night and saw that it had been filled in, my first instinct would be to pee in my pants. Also, anybody who thinks that you can complain about somebody burying trash on your property and the police will rush out to investigate has been dealing with different policemen than I have.

Anyway, police found a grave, and, looking around, found others. They found a total of 25 graves.

Juan Corona was arrested on May 26. Three things focused the investigation on Corona. All of the bodies had been hacked and chopped in an unusual way with a specific pattern of injuries. When information about this was relayed over police networks, police in Marysville sent information that a man attacked in a bar in 1970 had suffered (but survived) a similar wound pattern. (Marysville and Yuba City are twin cities, one lying on either side of the Feather River, 70,000 people between them.) The chief suspects in that investigation had been the owner of the bar, Natividad Corona, and his brother, Juan.

Juan Corona ran the work crews of migrant laborers on the two farms where the bodies were discovered. He could come and go freely over those properties, and had been seen there on the day the bodies were discovered.

On May 21, 1971, Juan Corona had purchased meat from a Yuba City butcher, signing a receipt, then folding it and placing it in his pocket. On May 25, that receipt was found in one of the graves. The discovery of this receipt led to Corona's arrest.

On June 4, 1971, nine days after Corona was arrested, the 25th grave was found. This one contained numerous items that could be connected to the Corona house, including another receipt with his name on it. Blood was found in his vehicle, in all of his vehicles, blood from all four of the major blood groups (A, B, AB and O). Human blood was found on his boots, on his knife, on a machete that he kept under the driver's seat of his van. Corona was convicted of the crimes on January 18, 1973.

Many questions about the case were never answered, and many things about it remain unknown. The investigation fell upon the Yuba City and Sutter County police and prosecutors without warning, and found them utterly unprepared. Without an hour's notice, there they were out in that orchard digging up body after body after body, with newspaper and television reporters descending upon them like mosquitoes in a swamp. Perhaps inevitably, the evidence was badly handled—bodies were confused, evidence was lost, injudicious statements were made. Even when the evidence itself was maintained, the chain of evidence was smudged. The prosecutors were handed a nightmare, and then, too, they were just small-town lawyers, whose training and experience had never prepared them to deal with anything this big.

With all of these handicaps, it is to the credit of the prosecutors that they were able to obtain a conviction for these horrible crimes. Juan Corona went to trial, his first trial, on September 11, 1972. He was charged with 25 counts of murder. The case as presented by the prosecutors in the first trial was badly confused, almost un-intelligible. Corona's attorney, believing that the jury had no basis to convict his client, elected not to put on a defense. Most courtroom observers were also convinced that the burden of proof had not been met, and were surprised when the jury returned with a guilty verdict. On the second day of deliberations the jury had voted 7–5 to acquit, but had gradually swung around toward guilty. One of the jurors, a dotty woman named Naomi Underwood, told reporters immediately after the case that she had been pressured to go along with the verdict, but did not agree with it in her heart. Juan Corona launched a series of appeals based on these circumstances, and eventually the state of California was forced to put him through another lengthy and expensive trial, with the same result.

Juan Corona has never admitted his guilt, and maintains his innocence to this day. He blames the murders on his brother, Natividad, who died in 1973. Natividad was a homosexual. Juan, who had a wife and four adorable little daughters, was sexually conflicted. It appears that he raped his victims or had sex with them, then murdered them immediately as a way to avoid coming to terms with his sexuality.

Corona, born in Mexico in 1934, had entered the United States in 1950, and had a green card that enabled him to bounce back and forth across the border. There was a flood in the Yuba City area in December, 1955, in which 38 people were killed. Corona, who knew several of the flood victims, had a mental breakdown, and was diagnosed as schizophrenic in January, 1956. Corona was intelligent, assertive, and he was a hard-working man, but he drank heavily, had what we would now call anger management issues, and had been committed to a psychiatric hospital as recently as May, 1970.

He killed 25 people in a period of six weeks—a rate of more than one murder every two days. This is unparalleled in American history—not the number of victims, but the pace of the killing, killing 25 people in 25 separate events over a period of weeks. Newspaper stories about the Corona murders often said that the victims, like Corona himself, were Mexican migrant workers. In fact, the victims were almost entirely Anglo; only one or two may have been Hispanic. Most (but again, not all) were derelicts, down-and-out alcoholics, with a high incidence of mental and physical debility. Many of them had been employed by Corona as migrant workers.

Victor Villaseñor wrote an outstanding book about the case, actually about the deliberations of the first jury in the case (*Jury*, Little, Brown, 1977). Villaseñor interviewed all of the jurors, most of them several times, some of them many times, and painstakingly reconstructed the eight days of deliberations that led to the conviction of Corona. The book, which is reminiscent of the classic 1957 movie *12 Angry Men*, is written in a careful, understated way, with a minimum of interpretation and just enough factual support to avoid leaving the reader disoriented. The jury was disturbed for several days because they had confused the time sequence, and thus had Corona still burying one victim while the police were digging up the others, but you have to figure this out for yourself; Villaseñor doesn't explain it to you. I recommend the book very highly.

John List's life had caved in around him. A few years before he had been a high-salaried executive with a beautiful wife, a stunning home, and three wonderful children. Now he was almost un-employed and almost un-employable, thousands of dollars in debt, with a wife who drank, a nagging mother who lived upstairs, and a brood of surly teenagers. He had looted his mother's savings to stall creditors; now that was almost gone. It was a matter of time until the bank called the mortgage, until the daughter got pregnant, until the mother discovered the thefts.

On November 9, 1971, John List did the only thing he could think of to do: he killed them all.

John List was a deeply religious man. I realize that, in view of his actions, this statement must seem deeply bizarre, but I'll get back to that. List had called the kids' school and told them that the children would be leaving town. It was weeks before their bodies were found, rotting in their large and beautiful house. List, having left notes "explaining" his actions, fled to Colorado, where he established a new life for himself under the name of an old classmate, Bob Clark. Like Kathy Power he learned to cook and became a professional chef, and like Power he was on the run for almost twenty years. He was finally captured after *America's Most Wanted* did a story about him. The story featured a bust of John List, developed by a Philadelphia artist to show what List would look like after all these years. The bust occupies a central role in most re-tellings of his capture. The bust, which now sits in John Walsh's office, is pictured on the front cover of *Death Sentence*, Joe Sharkey's book about the case, and Walsh frequently tells reporters what an unbelievably good likeness it is.

What strikes me is that the bust

a) is not particularly good, and

b) actually played no role in List's capture.

John Walsh is my hero; I'm sorry to piss him off, but that's just the way it goes. List had a little "bulb" on the end of his nose. As time passed this bulb grew, making one of the most notable changes in List's appearance. The sculptor completely missed this, and presented List with a sharper nose at age 60 than he actually had at 40. His guess on the hairline is all wrong, and he gave him a wrinkled, prunish face that not only doesn't much resemble List, it doesn't much resemble anyone. The only thing he really got right was the glasses; he guessed correctly what kind of glasses List would be wearing.

List was caught because the *America's Most Wanted* show prodded into action someone who had identified "Bob Clark" as List two years earlier (and had attempted to convince Clark's wife of this), but had vacillated about calling the police. When she saw the program about him she knew that she wasn't wrong, Clark *was* List, and his crimes were so horrible that she had to act. She was in Denver and he was in Richmond, Virginia, but she had his address from a letter. She made the call.

An FBI agent made preliminary inquiries, hoping to avoid having to check out the report, but concluded that the man named Bob Clark had enough in common with List to warrant a look. By this time Clark was working again as an accountant. He drove to Clark's address, fully expecting the trip to be a waste of time. He had done this a hundred times; it had never amounted to anything. Within a half-hour he had called his office, and told them to make arrangements to arrest Clark. Comparing recent photographs of Clark to the old photos of John List, he realized that they seemed to be the same man.

"Is your husband from Michigan?" he asked Delores Clark, List's wife in his new world.

"*Yes,*" she replied.

"Is he an accountant?"

"*Yes.*"

"When did you meet your husband?"

"*1975.*"

"Have you ever met his family?"

"*No.*"

"Does he have a mastoidectomy scar behind his right ear?"

"*Yes.*"

"Does he have a scar from a hernia operation?"

"*Yes.*"

There is no precise point where circumstances move beyond coincidence; this is why the Lord gave us fingerprints. List was returned to New Jersey, where, after a brief trial, he was convicted of five counts of first-degree murder.

Much of the information in this article is based on *Death Sentence*. Sharkey did a good job of researching List's early life, making a three-dimensional image of him, rather than portraying him as a one-dimensional criminal. This is not unusual; people who write crime books often do a good job of developing the background of the assassin. It contributes more to the book in this case because List's life is not the familiar recitation of abuse and failure which is common among violent men. The criminal's life is normally researched through parole officers, psychiatrist's pre-sentencing reports, and the odd interview with a relative or an early victim.

List, on the other hand, was perhaps a little too beloved, and too well-behaved. He was a mama's boy, but there were many things about him that were admirable. He had genuine accomplishments before frustration and madness took control of him—and some after. Most murderers are but marginally able to hold a job. List rose to become head of accounting for Xerox.

Compared to the typical criminal, John List fell off the opposite edge of sanity. He was everything that murderers usually are not. Criminals are usually men who never learned the value of self-control. John List's obsessive self-control cut off his options and constrained his vision, trapping him in an ever-diminishing box. He was the anal-retentive murderer. He was polite to the point of being obsequious. He was neat to the point of being peculiar. He was obsessed with order, consumed by details. Once, after agreeing to purchase a house, he called back repeatedly to amend the contract. At one point, he wanted to have the contract amended to specify that the previous owners would leave the shelf paper in the pantry.

Sharkey's book is quite good, and I'll recommend it (if I haven't already). But I want to argue with him about one point, because he makes a mistake which I think is common in crime books, and which is commonly damaging to them, although more so in this case.

Crime books often write sympathetically about the criminal at many points in his life . . . well, hell, you can't avoid it. Violent criminals are often people who are beaten senseless and dumped on a trash heap at age three, and if you don't feel something for them, then you don't really understand. But because crime writers must write sympathetically about the criminal at some points, they confront a later problem: how to convey to the reader that their sympathies are not with the criminal, but with the victim and the police. The good people in the story.

To get this message across, Sharkey begins to turn on John List, and to tell us repeatedly that List was a liar, that his religion was a charade, that he didn't really believe the things that he claimed to believe. The problem is that, in my opinion, List believed *exactly* what he claimed to believe. He was not a liar, but a literalist. His set of beliefs was so rigid that it was a prison, and so deeply held that he could not escape from it.

List believed, according to the notes he left behind in 1971, that only by killing his family could he protect them from a dismal future. Without money, they would be forced to leave their beautiful home, to find lodgings in a trailer park or a cheap apartment. The family would be forced to go on welfare, causing them enormous shame. He, the father, would be exposed as a failure and a petty thief. Their place in the church would be forfeit.

His wife was within a year or two of death anyway, in the final stages of a long and painful illness. By killing her, he could end her pain. If he killed his wife, he knew, his mother would not want to live through the shame that would follow in the wake of the crime. She was in her mid-eighties anyway, and she was ready to meet her maker.

And as for the children . . . well, the children faced the bleakest future of all: they would lose their faith. His children, he believed, were still Christians. Faced with the trials of poverty and disgrace, they would fall prey to the temptations of a Godless society. They would face eternal damnation. By murdering them while they still believed, he could save them from an eternity of anguish. Of course, the church proscribed murder, and he himself would be damned to the fires of hell for his actions, but at least the children would be saved. He could sacrifice his own soul to save the souls of those he loved—and then later, he could repent, and go back to being a Christian. God would understand, and God would forgive him.

This set of beliefs causes no problems if one does not truly believe it. Sharkey calls it a rationalization, but a rationalization is used to make actions seem reasonable. List's reasoning made no sense to anyone except John List. The problem was, he had no doubt that it was true. He had zero doubt that his children would move on to a better life—and from this lack of doubt, terrible consequences followed. As Bertrand Russell wrote in "Philosophy for Laymen," "What philosophy should dissipate is certainty, whether of knowledge or of ignorance . . . when you act upon a hypothesis which you know to be uncertain, your action should be such as will not have very harmful results if your hypothesis is false. Suppose you meet a Muggletonian, you will be justified in arguing with him, because not much harm will have been done if Mr. Muggleton was in fact as great a man as his disciples suppose, but you will not be justified in burning him at the stake, because the evil of being burned alive is more certain than any proposition of theology." The average man understands this intuitively, and moderates his actions to allow for the possibility that he is wrong—but List did not. List was the complete accountant. Everything added up perfectly in his own mind.

List was like Katherine Ann Power in this way: that their crimes derived as much from confused reasoning as from psychological disorder. Power reasoned from a belief system based on pacifism to a conclusion that she should help criminals steal guns and rob banks. List reasoned from a belief based on Christianity that he should kill his children. They were locked in to ways of seeing the world that twisted and spun upon themselves.

And, because List was so exceptionally literal, he had no ability to see options. The problem, in short, is not that he was a liar, but that he was crazy. His thinking had been disconnected from first principles. The tragedy of John List is that he was absolutely true to what he believed.

John List died in prison on March 21, 2008; he was 82. Robert Blake, who had played Perry Smith in the movie *In Cold Blood*, also portrayed John List in the 1993 made-for-TV movie *Judgment Day: The John List Story*. He was studying for his role as a murderer. Blake was an excellent choice to play Perry Smith, but a very poor choice for John List. He was too macho. List was a brainy, nervous man, not normally someone who would get into a shoving match at a bar, let alone someone you would think would kill five people.

Stanley Bond, Katherine Ann Power's murderous boyfriend from Brandeis. On June 24, 1972, he was attempting to build a bomb, which he hoped to use to facilitate his escape from prison. The bomb went off, and his remains were carried out of prison later in the day. So that worked out well.

Five days after Bond set off a bomb in his own face, the Supreme Court did the same. On June 29, 1972, the Supreme Court attempted to finish off the American death penalty. The effort blew up in their face, and brought the death penalty back to life.

By 1972 the death penalty had been in decline in America for four decades, and was near to extinction. The same was true of abortion laws; both had been in decline in America for decades, neither had the benefit of any organized public support, and both, in the view of the author, would have died a natural death before 1980 had the Supreme Court simply stayed out of it.

Unfortunately the Court, now led by Warren Burger, couldn't do that; they had to weigh in on the issue, and make a hash of it. In *Furman v. Georgia* (1972) the Court issued a 5–4 decision which can be summarized as "we sort of think the death penalty is mostly unconstitutional, at least as it is now." Black Americans were executed for murder, statistically, at a much higher rate than white Americans convicted of similar crimes. The Supreme Court stopped short of saying that the death penalty was unconstitutional, but invalidated all existing death penalty laws. As the death penalty was near extinction anyway, the Supreme Court was trying to gently put it to sleep, but one or two votes short of being able to state clearly that it was unconstitutional.

For those of us who would like to get rid of not only the death penalty but the endless arguments about it, this was the worst possible outcome. Americans like to think of themselves as a democratic country, and they resent . . . we resent, as I should include myself in this . . . we resent being told by judges what we can and cannot legislate. *Furman v. Georgia* was interpreted by conservative Americans as an effort to dictate to us from the bench, and as such it engendered resentment, leading to resistance.

At the same time—mostly as a result of the earlier carelessness of the Supreme Court—murder rates in America were rising at a horrific pace, feeding a fear of crime. In 1962 there were 8,530 murders in the United States. In 1974 there were 20,710. The combination of the fear of crime and resentment of the Supreme Court's heavy-handedness created a pro–death penalty movement, which would ultimately bring execution rates back to levels unseen in decades.

XXIV

At 12:30 AM on Sunday, November 28, 1976, Dallas Police Officer Robert Wood was shot and killed during a routine traffic stop. Detectives had almost nothing to work with, and the investigation stalled for a month.

David Harris, a gregarious 16-year-old from Vidor, Texas, began to brag to his friends about killing a cop. Word of this reached the police, and Harris was interviewed about the crime. He switched his story quickly. He had been a passenger, he said; this other guy had shot the cop.

This Other Guy was arrested and charged with murder. A young man from Ohio, working in Dallas just a few days, Randall Dale Adams had met David Harris on Saturday morning, about fourteen hours before the crime. His car had run out of gas; Harris had stopped to offer him a lift. The two had spent the day together, along with Adams' brother, drinking beer and smoking pot. Harris and Adams had gone to the movies and then split up. Adams claimed he was home in bed at the time of the crime, didn't know anything about it.

And, in fact, he had been. It was Harris who had shot the cop. In retrospect, there is every reason why the police should have known this. Adams, 28 years old at the time, had never been in any trouble. Harris had been involved in criminal activity all of his life. On the day of the shooting he had stolen a neighbor's car, taken his father's pistol (without permission) and gone into Dallas, where he met up with Adams. The pistol was taken in Vidor by Harris, and was in Harris' possession until recovered by police. The car was also stolen in Vidor by Harris, and was also in Harris' possession until recovered by police. The description provided by the officer's partner, though vague, fit Harris better than Adams. She had seen only one man in the car.

Before the murder of the cop was "solved" by the arrest of Randy Adams,

Harris had been arrested again, for holding up a convenience store, and was suspected in a string of burglaries and break-ins. He was in custody when first interviewed by the police, and he had told many people that he had committed the crime.

It is anyone's guess why the police and prosecutors chose to believe the wrong man. Harris was a personable young man, telling a superficially credible story. The system wanted to burn somebody. Adams, an adult, was subject to the death penalty for shooting the policeman, while the teenager would not have been. If the police believed Adams they had nothing, since Adams didn't know anything about the crime. If they chose to believe Harris, they had the foundation of a case.

Based on the testimony of Harris, the edited testimony of the policeman's partner, and the last-minute surprise testimony of three passers-by, Randy Adams was convicted of the murder. The passers-by had apparently been induced to testify by a combination of reward money and the dropping of criminal charges against them.

A psychologist nicknamed Dr. Death interviewed Adams for fifteen or twenty minutes, and testified in the penalty phase of Adams' trial that Adams was a dangerous sociopath who would be a menace to society for the rest of his life. He often made this recommendation; it was his specialty, and much appreciated by the Texas prosecutors. Adams received the death penalty.

By 1980 Adams was within three days of execution, when a stay of execution was ordered. The Supreme Court later ruled, by an 8–1 vote, that jurors were improperly screened in the penalty phase of his trial, and eliminated the death penalty for him. The governor, faced with the options of re-trying Adams or commuting his sentence to life in prison, chose to commute the sentence. Adams still faced life in prison.

In 1985 David Harris murdered a man named Mark Mays during a burglary in Beaumont, Texas. Meanwhile, an independent filmmaker, Errol Morris, set out to do a documentary on Dr. Death, and acquired Adams' case file as a part of his background research. Reviewing that case (among many others), Morris was astonished to discover that a man was facing life in prison based on such flimsy evidence. Switching horses in mid-stream, he made the documentary about the Adams case, the documentary entitled *The Thin Blue Line*. His film left little doubt about what had really happened. On December 5, 1986, Harris essentially confessed to the crime in a tape-recorded phone conversation, which became the climax of the movie.

On March 1, 1989, about two years after the film was released, the Texas Court of Criminal Appeals ruled unanimously that Adams had been the victim of serious misconduct by the prosecutors, including suppressing evidence and knowingly using perjured testimony. Adams' conviction was set aside, and he was freed a few weeks later. He had spent thirteen years in prison for a crime that had occurred while he was home in bed.

On June 30, 2004, David Ray Harris was executed for the murder of Mark Mays.

Ted Bundy is one of the pivotal figures in the history of American crime, one of the dividing lines. As I have mentioned numerous times in this narrative—and have probably failed to convince you—police forces until about 1980 all "knew" that stories about strangers who ran around killing people as a kind of mad sport were just that—stories. It happens in fiction; it has happened a few times in real life. But it's basically just something that only happens on TV and in the movies.

If you don't accept this I probably can't convince you, but let me give you a few for-instances all the same.

• When the LaBiancas were murdered in Los Angeles the day after the murders at the Sharon Tate house, the police at first refused to believe that the crimes were committed by the same persons, although the word "Pig" was written in blood on the walls of both houses. A copycat crime, said the police, although how such a copycat would have had knowledge of the first crime scene, at that time, is unclear. It wasn't until three months later that police finally began to believe what had seemed immediately obvious to the media—that the crimes were linked.

• Between 1974 and 1977 the killer known as BTK (Dennis Rader) murdered seven people in and around Wichita, Kansas. The crimes had several "signature" elements, such as the cutting of phone lines outside the house, and Rader wrote to police and newspapers to claim the crimes—but police officials insisted that the crimes were not linked, pursued separate lines of investigation in every case, and expressly forbade lower-ranking police officers from speculating that the crimes might actually have been committed by the same person.

• Beginning in 1977 someone began strangling prostitutes in Kansas City, leaving their bodies in city parks, shoeless, with paper towels stuffed in their mouths, and with ligature marks on their necks. He eventually killed thirteen women—but for at least the first eight of those, police insisted that the crimes were not linked, and that they had identified good suspects in each case. In 2007 a man named Lorenzo Gilyard was convicted of the murders, based on DNA evidence.

• In 1980, after discovering the bodies of 21 murdered children, the Atlanta police said they were not certain that they had a serial murderer on their hands.

This is a constant theme. If you checked out 50 serial murderer cases before 1980, I would bet that in 45 of them, the police would be quoted in the newspapers insisting that the crimes were not linked, even as the newspapers suggested that they were.

The capacity of mankind to misunderstand the world is without limit. The external world is billions of times more complicated than the human mind. We are desperate to understand the world; we struggle from the moment of birth to understand the world—but it is beyond our capacity. We thus sign on to simplifications of the world that give us the illusion of understanding. Experts are not *less* inclined to sign on to these simplistic explanations than outsiders; they are *more* inclined to sign on to them. They have more need of them. Thus, an explanation like "real homicide investigators know that virtually all murders are committed by someone well known to the victim" can gain currency among professionals, and become something that everybody "in the business" knows.

There were a series of events that changed this. The term "serial murderer" is often credited to FBI profiler Robert Ressler, although, according to David Frank Schmid in *Natural Born Celebrities* (University of Chicago Press, 2005), the term had actually been used sporadically for decades before Ressler went to work with it.

In any case, the gradual acceptance of the term "serial killer" helped enormously in getting police and prosecutors to accept that the phenomenon was real and serious. According to Schmid (p. 69), "once a serial killer became a type of person, a new form of behavior became visible, along with a typical perpetrator of that behavior, in ways that had been previously impossible. Judges, prosecutors, defense attorneys, doctors, psychiatrists, psychologists, and the police could now 'see' serial killers in a way they could not have done before because the serial killer was now a recognizable, legible type."

That's all true, but there's another part of it. History was swarming. I don't know how many serial murderers there were in America between 1960 and 1980, but I would think it had to be at least 100, and that their victims had to total more than a thousand. I have written about a few of these, but I have passed by many more—Edmund Kemper, the 6-foot, 9-inch, 360-pound genius from California, and the team of Dean Corll and Elmer Wayne Henley in Houston, who killed dozens, and Richard Chase, and Gacy, and Randy Kraft, and Randy Greenawalt, and Sharon Kinne, and Jerome Brudos, and Joseph Kallinger, and the Hillside Stranglers, and many, many more. Santa Cruz, California, had three serial murderers active at the same time in the early 1970s; it took police forever to sort out their crimes. The Michigan Murders may be the work not only of John Norman Collins, but of Collins and someone else not connected to him. You can pick almost any major American city in that era, and find two or three serial murderers—often including ones who have never been included in any of the books summarizing lists of serial murderers.

As more and more of these incidents came to light, it became more difficult for the police to dismiss them as aberrations, so uncommon as to be practically insignificant. Ted Bundy was, in a sense, the straw that broke the camel's back—but there is more to it than that, too.

In the time frame when Robert Ressler and John Douglas and others were attempting to convince the police to flip their thinking about this issue, Ted Bundy was committing a series of very much in-your-face murders. Most serial murderers try to kill people without making waves. They kill people whose disappearance will cause little notice, often prostitutes and drug addicts. Dean Corll and Gacy killed large numbers of teenaged boys, whose disappearance should have set off alarms, but people wrote them off as runaways, and Corll and Gacy both buried their victims, so that bodies were not turning up all around town.

Ted Bundy was killing people whose disappearance could not possibly be written off or marked down. He was grabbing college girls and leaving their bodies where they would be found. It was hard to ignore.

Further, Bundy, when identified, seemed to be such an unlikely murderer. He was nice-looking, clean and articulate. (Like Obama. Sorry, Joe.) He denied having anything to do with the killings. When he broke out of prison in Aspen, Colorado, in 1977, people printed up T-shirts saying "Run, Ted, Run." It was difficult to get people to understand that, despite his appearance, he was a savage and brutal murderer who had killed dozens of young women, and would kill several more after a subsequent escape.

The narrative of Ted Bundy started as several local stories—a local story in Washington state, and a local story in Utah, and a local story in Colorado, and a local story in Florida. As police—and journalists; perhaps more importantly, journalists—pieced together the full horror of what he had done, Bundy and his crimes became the subject of immense public fascination. Many books were written about him, and additional material about him appeared in literally hundreds of other books. There were made-for-TV movies about him, and—later, once the market was organized—uncounted true-life TV crime shows.

Bundy went on trial in Florida in June, 1979. At that time he and his crimes had received little national publicity. In the five years following that, Bundy became America's most famous murderer. At the time of their crimes, no one really wrote books about people like Ed Gein and Earle Nelson and Albert Fish and Harvey Glatman and the Lover's Lane Killer and the New Orleans Axeman. There had been the odd, occasional book about a killer, and there had been many books about Jack the Ripper, but almost all of the books that you see about serial murderers from before 1980 were written *after* the Ted Bundy phenomenon, after the obsession with Bundy had established that there was great public interest in this material—not just Bundy, but Bundy and Gacy and the Son of Sam, more than anyone else. They were written after John Douglas and Robert Ressler—and Ann Rule—had "sold" this concept, the "serial killer."

Ann Rule was a friend of Ted Bundy's, while he was out there killing people, and she was a crime writer. Rule, of course, didn't know that Bundy was killing people; she knew that *somebody* in town was killing people, but she didn't have any idea it was her friend Ted. Crime writing wasn't a big deal then; there were just a handful of detective magazines, and they'd pay you $150 or $250 or maybe once in a while $1,000 to write up a story about some criminal. Rule, divorced with children, was struggling to keep bread on the table writing for these publications.

After Ted Bundy was identified, Rule wrote a series of books about other serial murderers—The Want-Ad Killer, the Lust Killer, the I-5 Killer. These were virtually the only books of that type in the early 1980s, and they played an enormous role in establishing that there was a public appetite for books of that nature.

Later, after Rule became famous, she stopped writing those kind of books and started writing about a different kind of true-crime case. She started writing about real-life gothic soap operas, dream-come-true husbands who turn out to have a dark past and crap. I don't have any interest in those crimes or those books, which I think are written for women, and I haven't been able to read anything she's written in 25 years, although I keep trying. But her early books—the pulp press quickies about serial killers—those were seminal publications. They were the founding monuments of the serial killer publishing industry.

And then, of course, there was cable television. Cable television, although it had a pre-history, began to gain traction in the late 1970s—about the same time as Bundy was arrested and identified as a monster. I am not saying that Ted Bundy changed the world, but he was a catalyst in the change. Robert Ressler, John Douglas, Ted Bundy, John Wayne Gacy, David Berkowitz, Ann Rule, Ted Turner, Bill Kurtis—these people and a few others changed the way that the world of crime was understood by—and sold to—the lay public.

On July 30, 1978, Gary Tison broke out of the Arizona State Prison with the help of his three sons. They took another murderer with them, in case they had any heavy killin' to do, and headed for a hideout in the small desert town of Hyder, Arizona.

Apart from the name, Hyder was a lousy place to hide. It was little more than a squatter's camp, where migrant workers slept in the harvest season. It was barely habitable in the desert summer, probably worse than being in prison. Their plan, which perhaps could more accurately be described as a fantasy, was that Tison's wife would get an airplane, somewhere, and a pilot, somehow, and meet them near Hyder. They would fly to Mexico, fifty miles to the south.

When the plane failed to materialize, they decided to drive in a large circle and drop in on Tison's brother. The old car they were driving split a tire. One of the sons stood on a desert road, near midnight, a day and a half after the breakout. A motorist stopped to offer help. His name was John Lyons. In his car were his wife, a two-year-old son, and a fifteen-year-old niece. The Tisons surrounded them with drawn weapons, and forced them into the brush.

Tison had been serving life for killing a prison guard during a previous escape. He had also committed at least one murder in prison, a hit for the Arizona mob. Yet he could not have been known, prior to the escape, to be what one might call a mad-dog killer.

With the Tisons was Randy Greenawalt, who is believed to have murdered four truck drivers in cowardly attacks, shooting defenseless men with a high-powered rifle. Greenawalt, however, was not in charge; Tison was giving the orders. Why he decided to kill the Lyons family will remain a mystery, but kill them he did, herding them into the back seat of the disabled vehicle, where Tison and Greenawalt opened fire. Discovering the two-year-old child still moving, Tison leaned in through an open window, and shot him in the head.

Before they blundered into a police roadblock three weeks later, Tison and Greenawalt would kill two more people, for the same ostensible reason: to steal their vehicle. The book about the Tison/Greenawalt crime spree is *Last Rampage*, by James W. Clarke (Berkley Books, 1990). A cover quote from a reviewer says that we should "Place this fascinating book alongside Joseph Wambaugh's *The Onion Field* or Joe McGinniss's *Fatal Vision*."

Last Rampage is a far better book than *Fatal Vision*. Mr. Clarke is a professor of political science at the University of Arizona. The book is exhaustively researched, without the flaw which so often accompanies exhaustive research: exhausting detail. Clarke's writing is sound, careful, and intelligent. The story has a thrilling and dramatic climax. Mr. Clarke is so meticulous about concealing the outcome that in reading the climactic chapter, I genuinely had no idea what was about to happen. This is extremely rare—in fact, I don't believe I've read any other crime book that *doesn't* let the alert reader figure out where we're headed, in broad outlines, by the middle of the book.

Some of the Tisons' relatives were deeply religious, and Clarke attempts, inexplicably, to make the place of religion in the life of a sociopath into a theme of the book. In all other aspects, Clarke scrupulously avoids speculation. When the subject turns to religion, he loses all discipline. Since none of the principal actors in the book was at all religious, I am at a loss to understand the theory of this. In practice it becomes a series of snide little comments about fundamentalist Christianity:

> The members of these tiny, too brightly lit, starkly furnished churches practiced a demanding faith. Notions of right and wrong, heaven and hell, and

redemption through unquestioning obedience to God were rigidly cast in the most unyielding scriptural terms. (p. 299)

I would suggest that there is a rule which should apply here, like "there are no funny jokes about AIDS," or "never pick your nose on a first date." You don't denigrate people's religion for no real reason.

There's another problem with the book. Clarke says repeatedly that Gary Tison is highly intelligent, and on a certain level it is essential that the reader believe there is something to the man. The problem is, Tison's crimes—all of his crimes, from his youth through his last rampage—are just incomprehensibly stupid. Tison served as editor of the prison newspaper, but Clarke never quotes anything that he wrote, apart from a few sentences written to flatter the Warden.

I'm not saying that Tison *wasn't* an intelligent man; I am saying that Clarke failed to document that he was, to the detriment of his book. If you or I had escaped from prison, it would be obvious to either of us that absolutely the last thing in the world we would want to do is kill somebody. Your number one goal would be for the story of your escape to die down and get out of the newspapers as quickly as possible. If you kill somebody, that's going to increase ten-fold the intensity of the police manhunt.

Tison, despite his intelligence, utterly failed to perceive this. He killed six people who represented only the most obscure and indirect threat to his continued freedom. How do we explain this? What was Tison thinking? What are the principles that should guide an escaped criminal, in his efforts to remain free, and what are the principles that guided Tison's irrational actions?

I would suggest, based on my experience as a faithful viewer of almost every episode of *The Fugitive*, that the principles which should guide your thinking in this situation would be

1) Disguise yourself,
2) Get out of the area,
3) Have no contact with anybody who might know you, and
4) Don't do anything to draw attention to yourself.

These were the things that John List and Katherine Ann Power did in 1970–1971, as a consequence of which they were able to remain free for twenty years. Tison didn't do any of these four things: he didn't disguise himself, stayed in the area by driving in large circles, made repeated efforts to contact his relatives, and murdered six people, thereby directing the attention of the entire state toward his capture.

Tison's thinking was dominated not by reason, but by fear and ego. The police have limited time and limited resources to deal with many potential threats. If you go about your own business and don't bother anybody, within a few weeks there might be a couple of guys assigned to try to find you, or there might not. It might be years before you happen to brush up against the law.

But Tison was so obscenely self-centered that the idea that he might disappear into a mass of humanity was simply not comprehensible to him. What? *Me* become invisible? The police stop looking for *me*? He saw himself as the epicenter of a world dominated and controlled by police authorities. Thus, since he assumed that he was already the focus of interest for all lawful authority in the known world, he perceived the persons whose vehicles he stole as being terrible threats: they could tell the police where he was, or if not actually where he was, at least where he had been a few hours ago.

Fatal Vision, cited above, was Joe McGinniss's story about Jeffrey MacDonald, a military doctor convicted of murdering his wife and two daughters on February 17, 1970. MacDonald tried to blame the crime on an East Coast franchise of the Manson family. *Fatal Vision* was a very successful book that a lot of people like, but the problem with it is that you could edit out 75% of the book without losing a single fact or insight. The TV mini-series based on the book is better than the book, mostly because the great Karl Malden played MacDonald's father-in-law, Freddy Kassab, who crusaded for almost a decade to bring MacDonald to justice.

That said, *Fatal Vision* does have a major virtue. McGinniss is genuinely obsessed with his story . . . with that story. That's the flaw of the book; McGinniss is so obsessed with his material that he doesn't know when to shut up about it. But it is also the positive of the book, in that McGinniss understands his material at a level that only obsession can give you.

It is common, in crime books, to propose an "author's solution" at the end of the narrative. Ninety-nine times in a hundred, this doesn't work. William Kunstler, at the end of *The Minister and the Choir Singer,* proposes a solution that comes at you like a train that is not merely off-schedule, but miles off its track. P. D. James wrote a very good 1987 book about a series of crimes in England two hundred years ago, *The Maul and the Pear Tree,* but at the end of the book she proposes an author's solution that is so off-the-wall that you can't even figure out what the hell she is talking about.

Fatal Vision has the most convincing "author's solution" ever published. At the end of the book, McGinniss tells you what he thinks really happened, and you say to yourself, "Damn, that's right. He's nailed it." That's very rare.

Another successful crime book that I don't much like is Joseph Wambaugh's *Echoes in the Darkness,* about the 1979 Pennsylvania murders of Susan Reinert and her two children. That case involved an "uh-oh" about the intrusion of the media into the crime. Wambaugh apparently paid a police investigator $50,000 for information, particularly evidence that would implicate a certain suspect (Dr. Jay Smith). Dr. Smith was arrested, tried, and convicted, but his conviction was set aside due to the inappropriate conduct of the investigator.

That issue is between Wambaugh, his conscience and the law, but the problem with the book is that Wambaugh tries to tell Susan Reinert's story more or less as it happens, in a style similar to that used for *The Onion Field,* which is obviously influenced by Truman Capote's *In Cold Blood.* The style doesn't fit the story. The disappearance of Ms. Reinert and her children is fundamentally a mystery, a case so convoluted that one detective worked on it almost full-time for seven years—but as Wambaugh tells the story, in chronological order, we have known in broad outlines what happened to Susan Reinert for several hundred pages before it actually happens. The journey is long and tedious, and the portion of the story after the arrests, when Wambaugh is just trying to convict the bad guys, is positively excruciating.

The story would have worked a lot better, for me at least, if Wambaugh had introduced Bill Bradfield as simply a person, an acquaintance of Susan Reinert's, then brought him forward as a suspect, then began to develop him as a strange, imbalanced personality with a peculiar hold over some women. Instead, he starts beating us over the head with Bradfield's strangeness on page one. By the time Susan Reinert disappears, we believe him but we don't care.

The TV mini-series based on that book starred Robert Loggia as Dr. Smith, Peter Coyote as Bradfield and Stockard Channing as Reinert. That, too, was better than the book, but suffered from the same problems—the absence of real mystery, the lugubrious character development. In the movie it is hard to feel much sympathy for Susan Reinert because she's such a sap, and it's hard to feel anything for her kids because they almost don't exist, mere phantoms in the shadow of Bradfield and Smith. There are also several other books about the Reinert case.

You know, I stopped watching these TV crime dramas decades ago. Maybe I should go back to them; I seemed to like them better than the books. There was one about the Tison escape, too, starring Robert Mitchum as Gary Tison. He was too old for the part, and, because I liked the book, I naturally rejected the movie.

XXV

On May 26, 1978, Eric Christgen was abducted from a shopping area in St. Joseph, Missouri. Christgen (pronounced "Christian") was the four-year-old son of a wealthy family. A babysitter had taken him shopping, and had allowed him to play on a small slide while she ran into a store. When she came out he was gone.

Because of the family's wealth, police suspected a kidnapping for ransom. This suspicion lasted less than 30 hours. Eric's body was found on the following day. He had been raped and strangled.

Months passed.

A frantic search for the killer gave way to a slow, grinding police investigation. Melvin Reynolds, a 25-year-old gay man who lived and worked near where Eric was abducted, was interrogated nine times between May and the following February. Anxious to accommodate, he never asked to have an attorney with him while he was questioned. During one lie detector test he was asked whether he had killed Christgen. "No," he said, "but I'll confess if you want me to." On February 14, 1979, he confessed to the murder. Although he quickly recanted the confession, he was convicted of the crime in October, 1979, and was sentenced to life in prison.

In retrospect, it is easy to say that the police should have known they had the wrong man. Two witnesses had seen Christgen being led to his death. Reynolds resembled the man they had seen about as much as Oprah resembles Bill O'Reilly. The FBI had provided a profile of the man who might commit such an atrocity. Reynolds bore no more resemblance to the profile. The other evidence against him was, obviously, of a type which could have been manufactured. I take this to be apparent from the fact that an innocent man was convicted.

But this also should be kept in mind: that much of the evidence which police deal with in any case will turn out to be false or misleading. One cannot expect the police to drop a prosecution whenever they are confronted by contradictory evidence, because they are virtually always confronted by contradictory evidence. In any case, in July, 1982, the peaceful city of St. Joseph, Missouri, was once more stunned by the disappearance of a young child, 11-year-old Michelle Steele. She was found about 30 hours later on a river bank, less than a mile from where they had found Eric Christgen, and in the same condition.

Charles Hatcher had been seen by a number of people in the area where Michelle's body was found, drunk and behaving more or less as one might expect a psychopath to behave. After being stopped and questioned a few times he had turned himself into a nearby psychiatric hospital, shortly before the little girl's body was found. He asked the attendant to stop the voices. Hatcher could be tied to the murder of Michelle Steele by forensic and circumstantial evidence and eyewitness testimony. There was never any doubt that he had committed this crime. But what about the other one?

After the Christgen slaying, the two witnesses who saw Eric with his abductor had talked with a police artist, who had made a sketch based on their descriptions.

It was an oddly perfect drawing of Charles Hatcher. And Charles Hatcher was a very unusual-looking man.

Despite this, police and prosecutors refused to admit that they had convicted an innocent man in the death of Eric Christgen. Hatcher, it turned out, had been murdering people for more than twenty years. In 1961 he had stabbed to death a fellow inmate at the State Penitentiary in Jefferson City, Missouri. By that time he had been in and out of prison for 14 years. In 1959 he had threatened a newsboy with a knife and attempted to run over a police officer, earning him some serious prison time. In 1961 the warden had determined, by process of elimination, that Hatcher had to have been the man who murdered another inmate, but lacked enough evidence to convict him.

God gives something to every man, and to Charles Hatcher he had given an extraordinary talent for faking insanity. Hatcher, I suspect, was legitimately insane—but he was also a wizened and experienced thug, who worked very hard at exploiting the insanity morass which perpetually gums up the work of the law. Whenever arrested, Hatcher would give a false name; in his career he was booked under dozens of aliases. If the charge was serious, he would then go into his act. At times he would refuse to speak, sometimes for months on end. If speaking, he would ignore questions, grunt, scream, and talk randomly about voices and violence. He would roll his eyes around in his head, expose himself, run around in small circles, and bang his head against whatever was handy. Although many psychiatrists were certain that he was faking, it was nonetheless almost impossible to put him on trial. He would not cooperate with his defense attorney. He wouldn't answer questions. He wouldn't sign anything; he wouldn't say anything about who he was or where he had come from.

He simply made it impossible for the law to give him a fair trial. What does the system do when a crazy man decides to act crazy?

Then, when the process of justice had ground firmly to a halt, he would become sane, or sort of sane, and begin to sue for his freedom. You can't hold me, he would argue; I'm sane. I haven't been convicted of any crime. And, before you know it, he'd be out there killing people.

How many people he killed is not and can never be known. After the murder of Michelle Steele, he went into his shtick. The evidence against him this time, however, was too strong to let him out after a few months of acting crazy, and after a year or so he decided to unburden his conscience. He asked to speak to the FBI, although actually he wasn't speaking at the time. Communicating through notes, he gave the FBI directions to where they could find a body, near Davenport, Iowa.

They found it.

How many people have you killed? asked an agent.

Hatcher rolled his eyes back, visualizing them one at a time, and began counting on his fingers . . . one, two, three. He ran out of fingers. Finally he wrote down an answer. Sixteen, he wrote. "Sixteen total that I know for sure . . ." He was haunted by the 1969 murder of a young boy in Antioch, California, as Albert Fish had apparently been haunted by the murder of Grace Budd. This, he thought, had been his sixth or seventh murder, but different from the ones before, the murder of someone who was loved by someone.

A day or two after the murder in Antioch, he assaulted a five-year-old boy in San Francisco, a vile and disgusting attack which would unquestionably have ended in the boy's death, had not a stranger happened across them in a secluded area, and quickly summoned the police. Hatcher, giving his name as Albert Price, went into his act. He was held in custody for four years, during which he was classified and re-classified sane and insane innumerable times, as authorities fought to qualify him for trial. "It is most unusual," wrote a prison psychologist, "to find an individual with the kind of memory defects that Mr. Price has. This is the first time I have interviewed someone who did not remember the name of his high school or the year that he graduated."

Although authorities never found out who he really was and never linked him to the murder in Antioch, they did eventually convict him of the attack on the five-year-old boy, and he was sentenced to one year to life in prison. He was released in May, 1977.

In custody, both in mental hospitals and in prisons, Hatcher was so abusive that he terrified those around him. Realizing that it was difficult to put him on trial without an attorney, Hatcher would terrorize his court-appointed attorneys. One young attorney, refusing a court's order to continue in Hatcher's defense, said that if his choices were to defend Hatcher or give up the practice of the law, he would abandon the law.

Yet as horrible as he was, some faint reed of conscience still sung within him. His murders bothered him, some of them, and it bothered him that another man was in prison for one of his crimes, because he could relate to that. For a few months he communicated with lawmen in his strange, elliptical way, apparently trying to let the authorities clear up the crimes for which he was responsible, but without exposing himself to renewed prosecution. He stayed with this until Melvin Reynolds, the man who had been wrongly convicted of Eric Christgen's murder, was set free, and then the mad silence with which he tormented the law settled around him once again. He had two sealed envelopes, apparently giving the details of his most serious crimes; he carried these with him at all times. And then he destroyed the envelopes, and then he killed himself. On December 7, 1984, he was found hanging in his cell at the Missouri State Penitentiary.

In the aftermath of Hatcher's suicide, investigators debated what to make of Hatcher's claim to have killed sixteen or more persons. Only five of the victims can be accounted for with reasonable certainty (the 1961 prison murder, the 1969 murder in Antioch, California, the two child killings in St. Joseph, Missouri, and the body found by the FBI in Davenport). The basic argument against the supposition that Hatcher may have killed the other eleven was that he had been out of prison only a few months, here and there, since 1947.

What do I think? Well, serial murderers are fantastic liars—all of them—and you can't believe anything they say. In Hatcher's case, there's a good chance he killed sixteen or more persons. Hatcher was an unbelievably violent person. If I had to choose between spending a week with Hatcher or a week with John Wayne Gacy, I'd choose Gacy in an instant. Most serial kill-ers are not particularly dangerous to you unless you turn them on. I'm not saying that you would want to get comfortable with them, but they're not usually violent from moment to moment. Hatcher was never more than ten minutes away from killing somebody. Anybody. Eleven unknown murder victims in a few months unaccounted for?

No trouble at all. Hatcher was arrested in Minneapolis on July 27, 1977, in a police dragnet organized after a 13-year-old boy had been molested and strangled. The crime was never solved.

Hatcher was arrested for crimes against children which didn't end in murder at least a half-dozen times, and most of those didn't end in murder only because fate intervened. Also, he escaped from prison or from mental hospitals, in his career, at least five times. If I were a lawman assigned to make an account of every murder to be put on his score, I would take very seriously the possibility that he might have escaped from detention on some occasion, killed somebody, and then returned to custody before his absence was officially noted. It is exactly the sort of thing that he would have done. He was canny. He knew enough, when he committed a murder, to get the hell out of town within an hour, before the body could be found. The murder of Susan Nason (Chapter XXIII) seems indistinguishable from crimes Hatcher is known to have committed—and occurred within days and within a few miles of a crime for which Hatcher spent several years in custody. If I have the chronology exactly right, Hatcher was in custody at the time of Nason's murder, but it strikes me as worth noting.

Repeatedly sentenced to long prison terms, he was repeatedly released by a judicial and medical establishment which knew for a certain fact that he was a violent psychopath.

This concludes the Charles Hatcher story, but if I could digress here to make a point . . . I am often struck, in reading crime books, by how little good normally comes of police sketches. Police sketches are the public face of a criminal investigation—here is the man we are looking for—but for some reason, at least in my reading, they seem to accomplish little in these kinds of investigations. A few examples:

In this case, the police sketch was a remarkably good likeness of the actual criminal. Hatcher had an unusual physiognomy—a sunken, wrinkled, mus-cular face and upside-down almond eyes—and the witnesses had remem-bered it, and the artist had captured it. The witnesses had also described a crooked left arm and an extremely stooped shoulder, both of which Hatcher displayed. This bit of good luck did nothing to prevent a miscarriage of justice. No one who saw the sketch recognized Hatcher, even though, in retrospect, it is difficult to understand how they could not have. The fact that Melvin Reynolds bore absolutely no resemblance to the sketch did not prevent him from being coerced into a confession.

In the case of Ted Bundy, Seattle-area police produced and circulated a sketch of "Ted" which is an excellent likeness of Bundy. Several people called police hot lines to report there was this man, Bundy, who was named Ted and who looked very much like the sketch—yet nothing came of that, either. Bundy had no record of sexual assault. The police there had set up a system to attract loose information, but had not constructed mechanisms to manage the flood of information that this generated. Bundy moved on.

In the case of the Boston Strangler, the sketch circulated by police looks very little like Albert DeSalvo, and did nothing to convict him if he was guilty, and nothing to clear him if he was innocent.

In the case of the Son of Sam, New York police mixed up two or more suspects, and compiled a composite drawing which combines features of both men. The man eventually convicted of the crimes, David Berkowitz, was apparently one of the men whom the witnesses had described, but bears little if any resemblance to the drawing (though several books blithely state that he does). It played no role in his capture or conviction.

In the case of the Yorkshire Ripper, Peter Sutcliffe, Sutcliffe looked so much like the drawing that his co-workers jokingly called him The Ripper (nyuk nyuk). Nonetheless, Sutcliffe was interviewed by police at least five separate times before they began to focus on him as a suspect (he had bumped up against the investigation in a variety of different ways, although some of these were before the drawing was circulated). Even after he became the chief suspect, that investigation jumped the tracks when police mistakenly believed that an audio tape mailed to the investigators was genuine. The drawing played no real role in identifying or convicting Sutcliffe.

In the case of Thomas Luther, a suspected serial murderer who operated in Vermont, Colorado and West Virginia from the late seventies until the mid-nineties, one woman who survived an attack worked with a police artist to produce a drawing which is unmistakably Luther. The drawing was published in the Denver newspapers, but had no impact on the investigation (although it was helpful in convicting Luther when the case finally came to trial).

In the case of Richard Ramirez (the Night Stalker), police made an excellent sketch of Ramirez from witness recollections, and several sources mistakenly credit the drawing with his capture. In fact, however, Ramirez was identified through fingerprints he had left in a stolen car. The drawing, once more, actually played no role in identifying Ramirez.

I can think of only a few cases in which an artist's sketch played a critical role in bringing a serial killer to justice. A composite drawing based on hypnotizing a twelve-year-old girl was helpful in identifying Jon Dunkle, 1980s serial killer. We'll get to it.

I don't question that artists' drawings are helpful to police in *other* investigations. My point here is only that, based on my reading, they don't seem to do very much in investigations of this type.

It is a general thesis of this book that the law is too important to be abandoned to the lawyers. You may remember the Yale murder (1843), in which the young man who was charged with the crime posted bond and then went back to Pennsylvania, at which point Connecticut prosecutors closed the case.

In the view of the lawyers involved in the case, this was an appropriate resolution. That's the way things were done. A bond is posted to ensure that the defendant appears at trial. If the defendant doesn't appear for trial, he forfeits the bond, and the books are closed. It *has* to be done that way, the lawyers argued. Otherwise, what is the point of posting bond?

The press had a different take. As the press saw it, the failure to prosecute the murderer because the murderer was wealthy enough to forfeit the bond was an outrage. The lawyers thought that the reaction of the press was ignorant. These people just didn't understand the process. The press brought to it a different perspective—and the press was right, and the press won. The practice of abandoning warrants when a defendant posted bond and fled the jurisdiction was gradually curtailed.

This, I believe, is one of the best justifications for the business of popularizing crime: that it exposes the narrow logic of the legal profession to a broader concept of justice. The legal profession always argues—and you can see this every day of the week on truTV—that this is the way things are done because this is the way things have to be done because this is what the law requires. Lawyers will believe this no matter how unreasonable it is. Their profession trains them to understand why the law is the way it is. Lawyers are trained in the logic of the law, and sometimes, once in a while, they lose sight of the bigger picture.

In the years just before John Hinckley shot Ronald Reagan, there developed a cadre of whore psychologists who made a living convincing jurors that defendants were insane. Almost everybody has some psychological disorder, if you choose to look at it that way, and a person who commits a terrible crime . . . well, he *always* has a disorder. Many psychologists were willing to so testify. By trial and more trial, defense attorneys found a group of these people who were articulate enough and affable enough that juries tended to like them and believe them. These traveling psychologists would testify to the insanity of anyone who had the money to buy their testimony.

In one sense it was appropriate—people who commit crimes *are* almost universally suffering from psychological defects—but in a broader sense, it was an outrage. Lawyers couldn't or wouldn't see that it was an outrage. This was the way the law was; this was the way the system worked. But once the public caught on to it, the jig was up. After Hinckley was acquitted you could be as crazy as a bedbug in orange socks, and you weren't walkin'.

But actually, in the way I just stated that, I undersold my case. Hinckley shooting the President, after all, is not really a popular crime story. That's hard news. But it wasn't actually Hinckley's acquittal which brought about this change; it merely happened at that time, and commentators fell into the habit of attributing it to that. The public's tolerance for irregular psychological defenses was wearing thin years before Hinckley—and it was tabloid crime stories that were the grindstone. The critical case in this process was not Hinckley, it was Dan White.

On November 27, 1978, Dan White, a struggling San Francisco politician, assassinated the mayor of San Francisco, George Moscone, and a member of the San Francisco Board of Supervisors, Harvey Milk. Several highly respected whore psychologists testified that White had had a psychic break—a brief vacation from a long career of mediocre sanity. One psychiatrist pointed out that White, who had normally been a fitness fanatic, had been pigging out on Twinkies and Coca-Cola in the days before the murders, and the bad diet could have contributed to his loss of judgment. Although this was a minuscule part of the testimony of one witness, the popular press portrayed this as "the Twinkie defense." White was found guilty, but not of murder; the jury ruled that he had diminished capacity at the time of the crime, and sentenced him to less than eight years in prison.

The public hated that. Also of significance was a similar defense used successfully in the trial of Richard Herrin, convicted of Not Murdering Bonnie Garland, in what was also called The Yale Murder. As in the case of Dunkin' Danny White, Herrin was a high-functioning individual (due to graduate from Yale in a few months) who took a half-hour break from sanity to kill somebody, in his case his girlfriend. She was breaking up with him. As in the Twinkie case, he was found guilty but with diminished capacity reducing the charge to manslaughter, and drew a sentence of 8 to 25 years. In *The Killing of Bonnie Garland* (Simon & Schuster, 1982), a respected psychiatrist (Dr. Willard Gaylin) picked apart the testimony of the psychologists who testified in the trial (from both sides), and pointed out in a scholarly, deliberate way that the things that these psychologists said during the trial didn't bear any resemblance to the things that psychologists say during the normal conduct of their profession. A prosecution psychiatrist, for example, had insisted that there was "absolutely no" indication of psychosis in Richard Herrin. This would be a fairly remarkable thing for a psychiatrist to say about somebody who *hadn't* beaten his girlfriend to death with a hammer. Psychologists in the case had offered diagnoses of Herrin that were patently absurd, and had done so in terminology unrecognizable within the profession. "The criminal law as it now stands," wrote Dr. Gaylin, "is using false and, perhaps worse for legal purposes, indefinable psychological concepts."

Dan White was released from prison in 1984, and committed suicide in 1985. Richard Herrin was released from prison in 1995, and has lived in almost total anonymity since then. But the cases of White and Herrin, among many others, convinced the public—not the lawyers; the public—that the time had come to pull the plug on the concept of temporary lunacy. White's example made the emotional case for this, and appealed to the masses. Dr. Gaylin made the rational case, and appealed to opinion makers. The pincer movement snapped shut quickly after the acquittal of John Hinckley.

Dr. Gaylin wrote (p. 255, *The Killing of Bonnie Garland*) that "the insanity defense is increasingly used and increasingly effective." Within months of the publication of his book, the insanity defense almost entirely stopped working. There was a sea change in the public's attitude.

As Dr. Gaylin pointed out, until the mid-1970s a person who was found not guilty by reason of insanity would probably spend more time in "prison" than a person who was convicted of the same crime, the only real difference being that the prison was designated as a psychiatric hospital. But in the 1970s, federal courts issued a series of rulings making it difficult to keep a person involuntarily confined in a psychiatric hospital. A New York City policeman named Robert Torsney, apparently sane moments before, shot and killed a citizen for no reason whatsoever, in the presence of many witnesses, and kept walking forward as if nothing had happened. He appeared not to process what he had done. He was found not guilty by reason of insanity, and was locked up for treatment. The psychiatrist in charge of treating him, however, insisted that he appeared to be perfectly sane, and that there was no treatment for him. A court then ordered that Torsney be released, since a person who was not receiving psychiatric treatment could not be confined by the state for psychiatric treatment.

There was a brief period of time—roughly 1977 to 1982—in which persons were frequently acquitted by juries because they were insane, then released months or weeks later by psychiatric hospitals because they were not insane. The Hinckley case ended that period—but it had to end, and it would have ended anyway, even if Hinckley had stayed in Hawaii.

Two progressive reforms collided with great force, and one of them had to shatter. More and more people who committed serious crimes were being ruled insane. This was progress, because these people were in fact insane, and it was appropriate for the law to recognize this. But at the same time, persons involuntarily confined in psychiatric hospitals were acquiring the right to challenge their confinement and walk away. This also was progress, I suppose. But simply putting those two sentences together, more and more people who committed serious crimes were being given the right to challenge their confinement and walk away. This was not progress.

In this collision, the public more or less vetoed the insanity defense. This was not progress. This cycle of reform will come again. Once more, somewhere in the future, people who commit crimes in states of diminished responsibility will begin to be sent somewhere other than to prison. That will be a good thing. But this cannot mean that they are sent to some place from which they can quickly and un-safely be returned to society. That is the true lesson of the pre-Hinckley era.

In the past generation—in my lifetime and in yours—liberal ideas about the treatment of prisoners have by and large collapsed, and prisons have fallen back into barbaric conditions. I am trying to talk honestly here about how this happened, and how progress can be restored. These liberal ideas did not fail because conservatives opposed them or because conservatives stopped them. They failed because they proved unworkable, and this led to very negative outcomes for society. In order to restore progress, we have to understand why the progressive penal reforms of the 1940s and 1950s ultimately failed.

What happened *essentially*, in my view, is that progressives got to driving too fast. The Supreme Court had a lead foot. They wanted society to make progress. They were impatient. New sets of reforms were ordered before the old ones were understood. New sets of reforms were implemented on the heels of old. Too little thought was given as to how this set of reforms would mesh with that set of reforms.

I wish to point out that I am not bashing the Court here to advocate a conservative position. While I am, no doubt, a very bad liberal, I am at the moment bashing the Court in the advocacy of a liberal position: that criminals are human, that they should be treated with humanity, given every reasonable opportunity to return to the mainstream of American life. In 1930, in 1940, even in 1960, this was what educated and sophisticated Americans generally believed. It no longer is. Our prisons are horrible places, much worse than they were fifty years ago, and by and large the American people are fine with that. Prison reformers in America lack the power or the cachet of lawn trimmers.

I'd like to see America start back toward having prisons that try to help people figure out how to live a decent life. We have to understand what went wrong. The operating beliefs of any nation are held together with something like the consistency of taffy. What you believe, your neighbor tends also to believe, but not exactly; there is a spectrum of belief. If you pull on one end of it the other end moves, and, if necessary, it stretches—unless you pull on it too hard, in which case one end pulls away, the center weakens into nothing, and pulling on one end of the taffy no longer moves the other end at all.

In my view, what happened to America's belief in a certain set of liberal values—including decent treatment for criminals—is that the Warren and Burger courts pulled so recklessly on the end of the taffy that it broke loose from the main part, and no longer bore any relevance to the society. Humane ideas became irrelevant to the prison system.

XXVI

—◆—

On October 12, 1978, punk rock star Sid Vicious, a member of the group the Sex Pistols, stabbed to death his 20-year-old girlfriend, Nancy Spungen. Vicious himself died of a drug overdose a few months later, awaiting trial for the murder. Spungen's mother, Deborah Spungen, wrote an account of her daughter's painful life, *And I Don't Want to Live This Life*, which is excellent—very moving, very honest.

Nancy Spungen was a "blue baby"—google "cyanosis"—and was never really normal. Her severe emotional and psychological problems, beginning in infancy, placed a destructive pressure on the Spungen family. Although Deborah Spungen is angry at Vicious for murdering her daughter, she realizes that Nancy was dead to her long before she was dead in fact. Nancy Spungen had never hoped and never expected to live to the age of 25. There was a nameless agony within her which had resisted the best efforts of trained psychologists. She saw death as the only release from that agony, and had pursued her own death not only in the hours before Vicious killed her, but from an early age, and with increasing abandon. Her time with Sid Vicious fulfilled the destiny that she had chosen for herself, and provided for her the closest approach to happiness that she was ever to know.

It is now believed by some people that Spungen was killed not by Vicious but by a comedian or a drug dealer who visited their room about the time of the fatal incident. It's hard to see that it matters. Nancy, Sid, and most of those in their milieu were racing toward death. *And I Don't Want to Live This Life* (Villard, 1983) is highly recommended, but is not a traditional "crime book," and was published before the alternative theories about Nancy's murder began to surface.

James Dallas Egbert III was sixteen years old and a sophomore at Michigan State when he disappeared one afternoon.

When Dallas Egbert was twelve years old, the computer system at Wright-Patterson Air Force Base broke down. Dallas was called in to fix it. That was 1975, before home computers; there weren't computer stores on every corner, and very few people had any understanding of programming. It wasn't only computers which came naturally to him, but all forms of math and most other sciences, in particular chemistry.

Dallas Egbert was a genius, and Dallas Egbert was profoundly unhappy. His mother was always pushing him, pressuring him to do more, do better, work harder. He graduated from high school in 1977, and entered Michigan State on a gifted-student program. He was only 14, but Michigan State assured his parents that they knew how to take care of exceptional children. They assigned him a dorm room, gave him a class schedule, and forgot he existed. Within months Egbert was playing *Dungeons & Dragons* for days at a time, taking drugs, and involved with the university's gay rights organization.

And he had no friends. At sixteen, when life revolves around peer groups, Egbert's peers were the other gay sixteen-year-old geniuses at Michigan State: none. He was living among older kids who had nothing in common with him, and who didn't particularly like him. He was regarded as an irritating little twerp. He was sixteen but looked twelve. The guys he played *Dungeons & Dragons* with told him to get lost; he was too intense, too weird, too into the game. He got involved in numerous campus activities and groups, each of which devised a new kind of rejection for him. His personal relationships, we must suppose, were of the most difficult kind, since even those partners who had come out of the closet could hardly be seen spending time with a juvenile.

The people in the dorm had their own lives. He manufactured drugs in his dorm room, giving some away to anybody who would share them with him, and all the time studying, studying, studying, afraid to report to his mother anything less than a perfect grade.

Large steam tunnels, providing heat to almost every building, lay underneath the Michigan State campus. There are eight miles of tunnels—insufferably hot, slimy, rat-infested, and seeded with thousands of little vents which blast steam without warning. A few sessions of *Dungeons & Dragons* had been played in there, although this was never common (as was represented in some news reports). On August 15, 1979, Dallas Egbert wandered into the tunnels. He left a cryptic note and an even more cryptic map, nothing more than some push-pins on a cork board.

He went into the tunnels, apparently, to make a final choice among his options. There was a little "room" or alcove in the steam tunnels where the heat was not so intense. He sat in Dante's living room, nibbling crackers and debating his course: to be, or not to be. He had brought a quantity of home-made Quaaludes which he believed would be sufficient to cause his death. Depression overcame him, at length, and he decided that he would never be able to make friends, or convince his mother to get off his case, or do any of the other things which make life worth living at sixteen.

Egbert had miscalculated the dosage—barely. The drugs knocked him out for more than 24 hours, and left him sick as a dog when he awoke. He managed to get out of the tunnel and stumble and crawl to the home of a "friend" near campus, passing out from the pain several times along the way; he estimated that it had taken him about eight hours to travel a little less than a mile once he got out of the tunnels. The friend, a man in his early twenties, nursed him back toward health, fed him drugs, and had sex with him.

After Egbert had been missing a few days his family became alarmed. Dallas had an uncle who lived in Dallas. The uncle was acquainted with William Dear, probably the nation's best-known private investigator at that time. Dear agreed to take the case, and dispatched three operatives to Michigan.

It appears that Dear's men must have talked to the individual who was "holding" Egbert, or the man with whom he was staying, within hours of arriving in East Lansing; either they talked to the man, or they talked to someone within his circle of friends. Realizing how things "looked" to an outsider (someone who didn't give children drugs and have sex with them), the "friend" panicked, and arranged to get Dallas out of his house as quickly as possible. He passed him to another man, an older man whom Egbert scarcely knew.

The investigation exploded into front-page news. Within days Bill Dear had guessed that Egbert had gone into the tunnels, although he had not the slightest idea what had happened to him once he got in there, and so Dear determined to search the tunnels. Michigan State authorities insisted that the tunnels could not be accessed by the students—an obdurate and baffling contention, since one could simply walk into the tunnels from three places, and many students knew how to obtain access from other locations. The battle between Dear and Michigan State over access to the tunnels (in the midst of a missing-persons case) was soon on the front pages of newspapers from coast to coast. Dear obtained permission—and assistance—to search the tunnels.

Meanwhile, Egbert was being passed surreptitiously from one house to another, a fact which was apparently well known within the East Lansing gay community. What you have, then, is this: a sixteen-year-old genius, homosexual, capable of manufacturing drugs, is being held by a group of men who are afraid to release him, while the nation's news media roams the campus searching for information. This is not fiction. Each house to which he was passed was further lost in sin than the one before. Dallas was ill treated, and warned constantly how dangerous it would be for him to surface. He became subject to mind control, obeying the orders of his captors even when they were not physically present.

Although of course we do not know exactly what was happening within that damned community, it appears that Dear's group, without fully realizing it, was working its way up the back end of the chain, talking to people who knew not necessarily where Egbert was, but certainly where he had been. Somebody gave Dallas a few dollars and put him on a bus, told him to get to New Orleans. The phone number he had been given to contact somebody in New Orleans was out of operation, and Egbert was on the streets of New Orleans for several days. He attempted suicide again, this time with homemade cyanide, but his cyanide was like his Quaaludes: not actually strong enough to kill him, but certainly strong enough to make him wish even more sincerely that he was dead.

Again he turned to an older man, asking for help, and this time his luck was marginally better. The man took him to Morgan City, Louisiana, where he found a dump to live in and, improbably enough, a job working as an oilfield roustabout.

For the men who had held Egbert, it was a near thing whether it was more dangerous to set him free, or to kill him. It is not entirely clear which they chose—nor, in the end, is it entirely clear which they accomplished. The central plan, apparently, was to get him out, as far as possible away from those who had held him, and also to get Bill Dear out, get him back to Texas, and then to arrange for Dear to find Dallas.

Dallas continued to call back to Michigan for counsel, as he had been ordered to do. Finally he was told to call Dear and, a little before 1 AM on September 13, 1980, he did. He had been missing for 29 days.

There followed a joyous reunion, and a tragic denouement. The Egberts were overjoyed to recover their son. He enrolled at Wright State University in Ohio, closer to home. The problems which had enveloped him at Michigan State proved ultimately intractable. His depression returned and, eleven months later, his third suicide attempt was more successful than the others. On August 11, 1980, a gunshot wound to the temple left him mortally wounded. He died five days later. He was seventeen.

The article above is based largely on the book *The Dungeon Master,* by William Dear (Houghton Mifflin, 1984). Bill Dear missed his moment. Had he been born 25 years later, he would have become the star of his own reality television series, like Dog the Bounty Hunter or those horribly ugly people who re-possess automobiles for the entertainment of the public.

Dear was—I think still is, although he must be in his seventies by now—an utterly shameless self-promoter. It is quite unusual to read a book in which the author talks repeatedly about how handsome he is, and compares himself, with a straight face, to James Bond. At the same time the book *The Dungeon Master* is quite good; another book by Dear, about the murder of Dean Milo, is also quite good. One can't avoid the conclusion that Dear was using the book publishing industry to build his reputation as an investigator, but the books will stand on their own feet.

On April 17, 1980, Chris Hobson disappeared from his home in Overland Park, Kansas. Chris Hobson was a thirteen-year-old boy; Overland Park is a sprawling, wealthy suburb of Kansas City.

Hobson had disappeared in the evening; his parents, or one of them anyway, thought he was out playing, around the neighborhood. When he didn't come home they called the police, who assumed that Chris had run away.

A couple of weeks later his wallet was found in a shopping mall. A senior detective recognized the implications of this immediately. "You're going to have to cover your ass," he told the younger man assigned to the case. The investigation began in earnest. Kansas City media was saturated with Hobson's picture.

The boy was dead before the police were ever called. Paul Sorrentino, a likeable, open high school senior who cut classes more often than he attended, was bragging about the crime to his friends. He had always wanted to be a mafia hit man; this was his entree.

One of his friends went to the police. The police, skeptical, had her make a taped phone call to Sorrentino, who made incriminating comments. The police didn't know what to think. They knew Sorrentino well: he was a police informant, who had been given a pass on numerous felonies because he liked to talk. Was Sorrentino just talking now, or had he actually participated in the boy's murder? Was the boy even dead?

Hobson's body was found May 3 by two other high school kids, out fishing. Sorrentino had described the location of the body, not well enough to enable police to find it, but well enough to leave little doubt that he had been there. Actually, he was lost at the time of the murder, and didn't know where he was.

Sorrentino's arrest unraveled a family soap opera. Hobson was a member of a five-person crazy-quilt family: two marriages, two divorces, children stashed around here, there, and yonder for several years, then another marriage, unstable children from widely varying backgrounds brought together into one house.

Sueanne Hobson should have grown up to be the governor. She was an attractive woman from a comfortable background, trim, neat, always well-groomed. She was intelligent, witty, articulate, and generous to her friends. She had tremendous energy, boundless energy, and phenomenal force of will.

Unfortunately, she was self-centered beyond belief. Ms. Hobson apparently felt that if you spent money fast enough it was the same as being rich. She was a manipulator, which somehow doesn't say it. She was a manipulator in the sense that Michael Jordan was a basketball player, in the sense that Louis Armstrong was a trumpet player. She transcended the genre.

She had married Hobson's father sixteen months before the murder. The son and the stepmother had engaged in an unfettered war for the father's affection. Sueanne had tried to convince Hobson Sr. that Chris should be sent to a military school, and, that failing, to a psychiatric hospital. When Mr. Hobson would not yield, she had tried poisoning Chris with drugs.

Living with them was her seventeen-year-old son, Jimmy Crumm; she had brought him into their home after not seeing him for several years. She leaned on Jimmy to kill Chris, telling him repeatedly that "if you loved me, you would do this one little thing for me." Jimmy listened and stalled; he could not kill his stepbrother, whom he saw as a harmless little dork. Sueanne decided that she needed professional help, and ragged at Jimmy to find somebody to do the job. Jimmy found Paul Sorrentino. Jimmy was to get a car. Sorrentino was to get $350, to get his motorcycle fixed.

They let Chris think he was going with them on a big drug deal, took him out in the country, had him dig his own grave, and shot him. Chris had thought he was digging a place to stash some drugs. Both of them shot him, Sorrentino and Jimmy Crumm.

Convicting Sueanne Hobson was to be no easy task. Jimmy broke as soon as he was arrested, but refused to testify against his mother. Paul Sorrentino had already given the police enough information to convict himself, but he had never met Sueanne; his only contact was through Jimmy. Jimmy Crumm and Sorrentino were both sentenced to life in prison, although both are out now and still alive. Sueanne Hobson and Jimmy's father were divorced and then, in a dramatic testimony to her ability to turn the world inside out, re-married a few months later. Finally, Jimmy's lawyer told him that he should testify against his mother, and he did. In May, 1982, at the conclusion of a complex and difficult trial, she was found guilty of conspiracy to commit murder, and was sentenced to life in prison.

There are two books about the case, *Crazymaker,* by Thomas J. O'Donnell, and *Family Affairs,* by Andy Hoffman. O'Donnell taught English literature at a fine university, and upholds an appropriate standard in his prose. He makes the place, Overland Park and the Hobson house, come alive as a character in his work, although frankly I would have enjoyed the book twice as much if it had been half as long. Hoffman, a newspaper reporter, cuts to the chase with less ceremony.

Sueanne Hobson is now eligible for parole, although she keeps getting turned down. Her husband is determined to get her out, and the prosecutors seem fully engaged in the battle to keep her where she is.

How many criminal cases are there in which your sympathies are with the accused? It's not common, but it happens. The Duke Lacrosse players . . . obviously innocent. Martha Stewart . . . in my mind, her prosecution was a misuse of power. The people who prosecuted Martha Stewart were the people who were supposed to be watching the bankers. They let the bankers lose billions of dollars of your money and my money while they were playing gotcha with Martha Stewart.

In the 1980s there were a string of cases in which the sympathies of the sensitive and intelligent observer (that would be me) tended to lie at least partially with the accused, for a variety of different reasons. The simplest of those were cases in which the accused was innocent or possibly innocent: Lawrencia Bembenek, the McMartin Preschool case, the Little Rascals day care case, Wayne Williams.

OK, I'm not arguing that Wayne Williams is innocent. I'll get to that in a minute.

Lawrencia Bembenek—Bambi to those of us who love her—was a nicely contoured Milwaukee policewoman, a former Playboy bunny, who was accused of murdering her husband's ex-wife on May 28, 1981. The case against her is either specious or doesn't travel well, but Bembenek was convicted of manslaughter. In 1990 she escaped from prison and fled to Canada. The Canadians said they wouldn't give her back unless Wisconsin conducted a judicial review of her case. After the review her conviction was set aside due to a variety of serious problems with the investigation, and in lieu of a re-trial Bambi was allowed to plead no contest to a charge of manslaughter, sentenced to time served (which is to say, released) but told that she was now too old to pose naked. As if this story isn't goofy enough already, in 2002 Bembenek jumped out of a second-story window, breaking her leg so badly that it had to be amputated below the knee. She claimed that she jumped because she was being held against her will by the producers of the *Dr. Phil* television show. I always suspected as much.

In 1983 charges of ritual sex abuse were lodged against several members of the staff of the McMartin Preschool in Manhattan Beach, California, triggering a wave of paranoia that ran coast-to-coast and resulted in the arrest, imprisonment and financial ruin of dozens of innocent child-care providers. In the McMartin case, by the spring of 1984 it was being alleged by a group of highly organized nitwits who had been called in to investigate that 360 children had been sexually abused at the school, as a part of a program of satanic worship. This led to a long series of very expensive trials, at the end of which no one was convicted. Thank God.

A similar case was the Little Rascals day care case in Edenton, North Carolina. In that one several people were actually convicted of large numbers of highly improbable felonies, the convictions later being thrown out, and all charges dropped finally in 1997. There were other, similar cases around the country, such as the Wee Care Nursery School in Maplewood, New Jersey, and the Fells Acres case in Malden, Massachusetts. There are people in some of these cases who are still in jail today—and who knows, some of them might actually have done something. It's possible.

Wayne Williams was convicted of murdering two young adult men in January, 1982, but is widely believed to be responsible for a series of child murders that rocked Atlanta between 1979 and 1981. My problems with the case against him are similar to the complaints lodged about the trial of Richard Hauptmann. In the Lindbergh/ Hauptmann case, people complain

a) That the publicity surrounding the case was out of control, and made the trial a circus,

b) That the prosecution put on a string of witnesses whose reliability is suspect,

c) That the scientific evidence is out on a limb, and

d) That defendant's legal counsel was in over their heads in a case of this magnitude, and provided a defense that was, if not actually incompetent, certainly not what *you* would want if you were on trial for *your* life.

All of those things are true of the Hauptmann trial except the third (the scientific evidence against Hauptmann was actually very good), but it doesn't bother me, because there is much more than sufficient reason to conclude that Hauptmann was guilty of the crime. But it seems to me that these things are *more* true of the Wayne Williams trial than the Hauptmann trial. I'm not saying I would like to see Williams released, but I'd like to see him get a better trial.

Returning to the general point of "cases in which our sympathies were with the accused" . . . John DeLorean, like Martha Stewart, was a victim of a gross misuse of the power of the government. DeLorean was a rich GM executive who had founded his own car company in the mid-1970s. Working in Ireland to take advantage of incentive financing, DeLorean produced 9,000 cars over the period of a couple of years before his resources were exhausted in November, 1982.

Attempting to re-start his dream company, DeLorean had a series of meetings with a former drug distributor, James Hoffman, who, as it turned out, was working for the FBI. Hoffman talked about moving some cocaine in order to raise investment money. DeLorean mumbled and nodded a lot in front of hidden cameras. After a long, highly publicized and expensive trial, DeLorean was found not guilty, it being the conclusion of the judge and the jury (and the author) that the FBI had manufactured the crime for the purpose of entrapping DeLorean.

After that prosecution failed the government went after DeLorean again, the same federal prosecutors pursuing DeLorean in Detroit on fraud charges related to the financing of his company; DeLorean was supposed to have siphoned off for personal use $9 million raised for his company. Once more he was acquitted, and the prosecutors were ordered by a judge to leave him alone. Fighting numerous lawsuits after the collapse of his company, DeLorean was forced into bankruptcy in 1999, and died in 2005.

Drifting afield just a little bit, as I write this the American car companies are gasping for breath, trying to avoid going under for the third time, and people are asking "can America sustain three car companies?" My attitude is, whaddaya, nuts? America should have 250 car companies, or 300, or 500, or more. We sell 16,000,000 new cars a year in this country. If you divide that among 250 companies, that's 60,000+ cars per company per year—many more than are needed to sustain a company. If we had a large number of local companies producing a wide variety of automobiles, those cars would be cheaper, safer, more fuel-efficient—and also more fun, more beautiful, and with a wide variety of features as yet undreamed of. The market would react automatically and seamlessly to the demands of the public. Innovation would run at a hundred times its current pace. If companies didn't produce cars that people liked, they'd go out of business—and quickly.

It is therefore my view that the American government should do whatever it can to encourage and support competition within the automobile industry. Instead, the last two times a competitor to the big car makers has arisen—DeLorean and Tucker—the government has stepped in to crush the upstart with allegations of vague or imaginary crimes. I think it's totally backward, and I think it's a misuse of the power of government.

Another 1980s case in which the sympathies of the public were largely with the accused was the murder of Dr. Herman Tarnower by Jean Harris. Dr. Tarnower was the author of a famous diet book, *The Complete Scarsdale Medical Diet*; Jean Harris was the headmistress of a ritzy girl's school in Virginia. They had been lovers since 1965; Harris shot the 69-year-old Tarnower when he took up with a younger woman. A 2005 movie about the case starred Annette Bening and Ben Kingsley. Although I don't endorse the sentiment, a lot of people felt frankly that Tarnower had it coming.

The other three cases that divide our sympathies are the "vigilante" cases— Bernard Goetz, Jody Plauché, and Kenneth McElroy. In February, 1984, a man named Jeffrey Ducet (also spelled Doucet and Doucette . . . I am unable to sort out the correct spelling) abducted and sexually abused a Baton Rouge eleven-year-old student in his karate class, Jody Plauché. Arrested in Anaheim on March 1, 1984, Ducet was being returned to Louisiana to face criminal charges when Plauché's father, Leon Gary Plauché, stepped out of a phone booth and shot him in the head, in full view of rolling television cameras. Charged with manslaughter, Plauché pled no contest, but the jury refused to convict, and Plauché went free.

On December 22, 1984, Bernard Goetz shot four teenagers on a New York City subway. There had been 13,000 felony crimes reported on New York City subways in 1984; Goetz, who had been mugged and badly beaten three years earlier, was about to become 13,001. Goetz didn't kill any of the four youths, but did cause very serious injuries.

New York City mayor Ed Koch, who had said hardly a word about any of the previous 13,000 subway felonies, was horrified. It was bad enough that citizens were regularly beaten, robbed and stabbed with screwdrivers on the New York City subways, Koch said in effect, but when citizens started to defend themselves, that was going too far.

Goetz was charged with four counts of attempted murder, and aggressively prosecuted by New York District Attorney Robert Morgenthau. Public sentiment—initially favorable to Goetz—swung gradually against him, and he was convicted of carrying an unregistered firearm. He served eight months. In 1996 he was ordered in a civil judgment to pay $43 million to one of his victims or assailants, who was permanently disabled in the incident. Goetz has been forced into poverty and bankruptcy. In 2009 a judge ruled that, despite the bankruptcy, Goetz still owed his victim the $43 million.

There is, finally, the Skidmore case. On July 10, 1981, a crowd of people surrounded Ken McElroy on a public street in a small town in Missouri, and somebody shot him. They had cause; McElroy had been terrorizing the town for years. He had been accused, among other things, of running prostitutes, burglary, theft, rustling livestock, and assault. Lots of assault; he was big on assault. He had fathered children with more than one under-aged girl. He had been indicted 22 times for various crimes, and had recently been convicted of attempted murder for shooting a 70-year-old grocery store owner.

Convicted, but he was still walking the streets until they shot him. He stayed free by a combination of intimidating witnesses and hiring skilled and aggressive lawyers. After the posse shot him nobody would tell the police anything about it, and no one was ever prosecuted for the shooting, but then, nobody was ever given a reward for it, either.

OK, I won't defend Bernard Goetz, exactly, but I will rise to the defense of the people of Skidmore. The modern, enlightened way to think about this case is that vigilante action is terrible, all vigilante action is terrible, justice must be left to the system of justice, and any effort to take the law into your own hands pushes us backward toward anarchy, or, if you like anarchy, toward Bloody Anarchy. Nobody likes Bloody Anarchy.

This is, I would argue, a biased and primitive way to think about the issue. Yes, of course society must not be allowed to fall back into anarchy—but what do you do when the lawful authorities refuse to act? Here is a story about Ken McElroy; it comes from *In Broad Daylight*, by Harry MacLean (HarperCollins, 1984). A County Sheriff's officer saw a car racing through the night on dirt roads, obviously speeding. He stopped the car to write a ticket, but as he approached the car he realized that it was McElroy. McElroy had a gun in his lap. Facing a dangerous, armed criminal without backup, the cop tiptoed back to his own car and drove away.

How does the system of justice get so messed up that something like that can happen? You may buffalo a cop in the middle of the night in a situation like that, but the next morning there are going to be 75 cops on your lawn, and you're going to jail. McElroy had sued the police and prosecutors for harassing him, and had obtained court orders instructing the cops not to go out of their way to pick a fight with him. They didn't know what to do anymore, and they were just letting him walk all over people.

My argument is that there is more than one way for society to fall back into Bloody Anarchy. If the police stop enforcing the law and allow a criminal or a set of criminals to abuse the public, is that not anarchy? Is that not at least a step toward anarchy? Is it not the responsibility of citizens to organize and prevent society from slipping back into anarchy?

I think it is. To assert the opposite, it seems to me, is essentially to argue that the forms and customs of the law must be given precedence over the need to protect the citizenry, *even if* those forms and customs have been demonstrated to be an empty suit. I think that insisting that the Skidmore incident must be condemned as vigilante action is just name-calling.

I couldn't actually read *In Broad Daylight*; it gave me nightmares. In all my years of reading grisly murder stories in the moments before drifting off to sleep, there are only two books that have ever given me nightmares: that one, and *The Shoemaker* (Simon & Schuster, 1983). *The Shoemaker,* by Flora Rheta Schreiber, is a book about Joseph Kallinger, a mid-1970s cobbler-cum-serial murderer in the Philadelphia area. *The Shoemaker* gave me nightmares because Ms. Schreiber so successfully drew the reader into the murderer's disturbed mind. People who write crime books often try to draw you into the mind of the murderer, but Ms. Schreiber had done such a good job of it that it gave me the creeps.

The only other thing I remember about that book—which I read twenty-five years ago and am *not* going to re-read just so I can write this paragraph more accurately—was that, while Mr. Kallinger was evaluated at length by several psychologists and psychiatrists who pronounced him perfectly sane while he was regularly killing people, there was one psychologist who inter-viewed him informally for just a few minutes and picked up the fact that he was a paranoid schizophrenic. The psychologist asked Kallinger whether he had ever been walking down the street and thought that he heard someone call his name. Kallinger vehemently denied that this had ever happened to him. In reality, of course, it happens to everybody. The psychologist real-ized that Kallinger over-reacted to this innocent suggestion because he was hearing voices in his head, but, knowing that hearing voices in one's head is considered crazy, was loudly denying that he had ever done so.

XXVII

New Jersey

On July 1, 1981, Louis Masgay took almost $100,000 in cash to a meeting with a business associate. Masgay failed to return.

Despite the pleas of Masgay's family, police were inclined to believe that Masgay must have taken the money and fled with a comely companion. They believed this until his body was found in September, 1983, wrapped in several layers of garbage bags. At first concluding that he had been dead only a few hours before he was found, police re-considered when they realized that

1) He was still wearing the clothes he had been wearing when he disappeared two years earlier, and

2) His insides were frozen.

Whoever had killed him had apparently put him in a freezer, hoping to let the trail get cold, and also to confuse the police about when the crime had occurred. If the killer(s) had gotten a little lucky, this would have succeeded, but the body was found quickly after it was dumped, so that the autopsy was performed before the carcass was fully thawed, thus exposing the ruse.

This focused attention on the business associate whom Masgay had gone to meet, Richard Kuklinski. For the next three years that attention would grow constantly more intense. As it turned out, Masgay was not the only man to disappear from the face of the earth after carrying a large amount of cash to a meeting with Kuklinski. There were at least three others of those, and then, too, other investigations had tended to lead in his direction.

Richard Kuklinski got into crime by way of Walt Disney. Working at a studio where copies of films were made, he discovered that he could turn a quick buck by making bootleg duplicates of Disney cartoons. He sold these out of the trunk of his car for a while, a few copies at a time, but then decided there was more money to be made at the other end of the spectrum. He started doing the same with pornography.

He got a loan from a loan shark to expand his business. When he missed a couple of payments, the shark sent an enforcer. The enforcer and his friends beat the crap out Kuklinski, but it wasn't easy. The enforcer, Roy DeMeo, also noticed that Kuklinski had certain attributes which were useful in his business. Kuklinski was a great big dude, scary-looking, fearless, and naturally mean. As a matter of fact, Kuklinski by this time had already killed several people, if you can trust his later statements, not for any financial reason but just because he didn't like them. He had killed out of anger.

DeMeo—connected to the Gambino crime family—made Kuklinski a part of his crew. Kuklinski was useless as a leg-breaker, because he was just too mean, so DeMeo started using him for heavier work. Eventually Kuklinski got his own group together, got into stealing cars off of used car lots, knocking off convenience stores, and collecting debts for the mob. He apparently became—although some sources dispute this—one of the leading hit men on the East Coast. His biggest profits, in any case, came from luring businessmen into shady deals. The businessman would buy things from Kuklinski at cut-rate prices, things like blank videotapes or pharmaceuticals. Eventually, the businessman would show up with $20,000 or $50,000 or $100,000 in cash, expecting to purchase a large quantity of whatever it was he had a way to retail. Kuklinski would make him disappear.

In the early eighties, after the discovery of Louis Masgay's body, police began to close in on Kuklinski. Kuklinski attempted to seal himself off by murdering everyone who could connect him to his crimes. He murdered the men who worked for him, who had been his crew. He claims to have murdered Roy DeMeo (and if he didn't, somebody did). He murdered Robert Prongay, another mafia hitter who had been his partner in a number of crimes. It was Prongay, apparently, who had helped him to kill Masgay, and whose idea it was to freeze the body to confuse the police. Prongay was full of those kinds of inspirations.

At the time that these murders occurred, very similar things were happening in the branch of the Gambino family with which Kuklinski was associated through DeMeo. The FBI, the IRS and other law enforcement agencies were closing in on Roy DeMeo and his criminal cadre. DeMeo's associates started murdering one another to seal themselves off from the investigation. Similar things were also happening at the same time in the Lucchese crime family, many of whose members were also known and connected to the Gambinos. These many murders make it impossible to evaluate the veracity of Kuklinski's later claims to have killed his associates. Kuklinski, facing life in prison, may have been trying to project as large a shadow as possible to scare people away from him.

The murders, in any case, slowed the advance of the investigation, but eventually an undercover policeman, Dominick Polifrone, was able to lure Kuklinski into an arms plot by selling him some fake cyanide, and dangling in front of him the possibility of making several hundred thousand dollars on a deal with the Irish Republican Army. Apparently intending to kill Polifrone, Kuklinski talked a little too freely about some of his past crimes. A tape recorder was running. Polifrone was the point man for a large combined force, involving state, local, and federal police, who moved in on Kuklinski after he purchased the fake cyanide.

They had enough on him to convict him of two murders, and he pled guilty to two more to get the feds to stop hassling his family. In prison, he agreed to talk to an independent filmmaker, Jim Thebaut, who hired the renowned psychiatrist Dr. Park Dietz to interview him. The first documentary about Kuklinski was shown on HBO in 1991.

Kuklinski was intelligent and articulate. As a murderer, he was virtually an artist. He killed people with rifles, handguns, automobiles, fists, knives, ropes, dynamite and cyanide. He was equally creative in disposing of bodies, although of course he didn't dispose of the body unless there was some *reason* to, unless he could somehow be traced to the victim. He was patient. Although he was filled with hatred and contempt for almost everybody he met, he learned to control his anger until the time was ripe, until he could *profit* by the commission of the crime. By his own estimate, he killed about a hundred people. While no one can confirm this number, nobody who knew him wanted to argue about it, either.

Thebaut's first documentary, most of which is simply Kuklinski talking about his crimes, is riveting. Kuklinski was a frightening man, a thug's thug, a murderer among murderers. His underworld associates used to refer to him as "the devil himself." Yet on a certain level, one can't help but identify with him, as we must identify with anyone who faces frankly what he is and can explain it in a way that makes some sense. As a child Kuklinski was beaten regularly by his father, and also by neighborhood toughs. As a teenager, he killed one of the neighborhood toughs—and, by luck, got by with the crime. This changed his relationship to the world. He began to take control of his life. He married, started a family, and, although he was abusive, he truly loved his family. He drew them around him as a shield. He provided for them.

But no one else was real to him. He made a decision, simply enough, that he would love that woman and those children—but that nobody else in the world meant anything. The people he killed, he says, were mostly just scumbags. While the law does not regard the "scumbag defense" as a justification for homicide, this does appear to be literally true: most of the people he killed *were* scumbags. He also killed one guy just because the kid cut him off in traffic.

The first film was called *The Ice Man*, which is also the title of a book about Kuklinski by Anthony Bruno. Bruno's book is also quite good. It's a B+ book, not a work of art but a thorough, well-organized, easy-to-read explanation of the crimes, the criminal, and the investigation which brought them to light.

Later, because Kuklinski's interview was such riveting television, HBO went back to him and made two more documentaries in the same style. After he had been in prison a few years Kuklinski started telling stories that are obviously not true, and this undermined his credibility, which made his story less interesting. But then, all serial murderers are compulsive liars; it is just the nature of the beast.

For me, an unanswered question about Kuklinski is to what extent he was the model for Tony Soprano. James Gandolfini, who played Tony Soprano, looks very much like Kuklinski and talks like Kuklinski; Edie Falco, who played Carmela Soprano, looks very much like Kuklinski's wife Barbara, who was a strong woman and was interviewed for the HBO documentary. Kuklinski, like Tony Soprano, was a very large man who was physically intimidating. Soprano dresses like Kuklinski dressed, lives in the area where Kuklinski lived, and commits some crimes that are similar to Kuklinski's crimes. Kuklinski was interviewed by a psychiatrist, with whom he had obviously established a bond; Soprano is shown in almost every episode talking to his psychiatrist. David Chase developed the Sopranos series for HBO after the Kuklinski interview had drawn very high ratings on HBO.

I don't mean to diminish David Chase's genius in creating *The Sopranos*. I think he may have used Kuklinski as a template, but he also used Roy DeMeo, the Gambinos, the Luccheses, and other criminal gangs. There was a richness of invention that drove *The Sopranos,* borrowing from many sources. Kuklinski died in prison on March 5, 2006. His death was officially considered a suicide, although he was scheduled to testify against a Mafioso in an upcoming trial, and he may well have been murdered.

How many serial murderer stories can you stand? In the world of popular crime, the 1980s were the decade of the serial killer. The stories of serial murderers are repetitive and gloomy, but I will tell a few of them and then meet with my editor to decide which ones to throw out, and the ones we throw out I will throw up on the internet.

Robert Hansen was a serial murderer who operated in and around Anchorage, Alaska, from 1971 to 1983.

Hansen was born and raised in Pocahontas, Iowa, the son of a Danish immigrant who ran a small-town bakery. An indifferent student, Hansen graduated from high school in 1957, spent a little time in the Army Reserve, and hung around Pocahontas working in the bakery and getting into trouble. In 1960 he set fire to the barn which housed the local school buses.

Out of prison in a year and a half, Hansen married, took some classes in baking and cake decorating, and moved to Minnesota. A true kleptomaniac, Hansen stole thousands of things, and was arrested for theft several times between 1965 and 1967.

He and his wife moved to Alaska in 1967. They had children. Hansen was a hunter, a big-game hunter, and in Alaska his skills with a bow and bullet flourished. The Pope and Young record books list records for the largest animals of each type brought down, like the 17th-largest Hereford steer ever killed with a tire iron and stuff. Hansen came to be listed in these record books several times, and held a world record: the largest Dall sheep ever killed with a bow and arrow.

On November 15, 1971, he was arrested for assault with a deadly weapon, an attack against a woman. Free on bail, he kidnapped and raped a woman on December 19, but released her, even though she knew enough about him to identify him. On December 22, 1971, an Anchorage woman was kidnapped, assaulted and murdered by an unknown assailant. When that murder hit the newspapers, the December 19 victim went to the police, and Hansen was arrested again.

He was sentenced to five years in prison, and served three months before being released to a halfway house. Let us pause the story for a moment, and look at the pattern. Hansen by the end of 1971 had committed hundreds of crimes, most of them petty thefts, but including at least three very serious assaults against women in the closing months of 1971 (later investigation made it clear that there was at least one victim who never came forward). But in court:

a) All of the stuff that had happened in the lower states in earlier years—the thefts and arson—apparently never surfaced. This was before computerized records. The earlier crimes were a long time ago and a long way away, and it was a different kind of crime.

b) One victim never reported the crime.

c) In one case—the murder—Hansen was suspected but couldn't be tied to the crime.

d) One victim, the December 19 rape victim, was attacked so aggressively by Hansen's lawyer that she broke down in court and became unable to testify, causing that charge to be dropped.

e) Hansen was sentenced on the lesser charge (assault with a deadly weapon), but, hey, he was a family man with a good job. He got five years.

f) Five years became three months due to parole. He behaved well in prison.

Magical math—there are dozens of crimes, but only five of them make it to the level of prosecution, the prosecutors do triage and cut that to the best three, one falls away and the other two are pleaded down into one. Happens all the time.

Out of jail, Hansen appeared to be on good behavior for a time. He added to his family, got his own bakery, bought his own house, his own boat, his own airplane. He resumed his big-game hunting.

In July, 1973, Hansen is believed to have murdered a teenaged girl. He was never associated with that crime until many years later.

He was found in possession of stolen property in 1973, but the police who investigated that incident didn't discover that he was a criminal or was on parole, and weren't sure that they could prove their case. His parole ended a few months later because of his good behavior.

He raped an Anchorage teenager in September, 1974, but she didn't go to the police until many years later, when Hansen was in custody.

In July, 1975, another murder.

In October, 1975, he abducted a dancer from an Anchorage nightclub. He released the woman, who went to a rape crisis center, talked to the police, and positively identified Hansen from a photograph. Hansen admitted to being with the woman, but told the police she was a prostitute who had tried to extort additional money from him. The woman fled the state in terror of Hansen, leaving police unable to prosecute.

Five more serious crimes—more likely ten—have completely disappeared from the court dockets.

In November, 1976, Hansen was arrested for stealing a chain saw. A psychologist who tested him at that time wrote that his evaluation "indicates the disintegration of personality to a highly potential psychotic level or high schizophrenic scale, high manic scale, and high antisocial scale." Hansen pled guilty to the theft. The judge, pointing out that this was Hansen's third felony conviction and aware of some of the other allegations against him, sentenced him to five years in prison.

But.

Hansen appealed. He argued that a) the first felony conviction, the arson, was a long time ago, when he was a kid, and b) the circumstances of the second case were unclear, and c) the theft of the chain saw could have been charged as a misdemeanor, and d) he had been diagnosed as having a mental illness which could be controlled with medicine, which he promised he would take.

He won the appeal. He argued, in essence, that each of these events was less than it appeared. The police and the judge who sentenced him knew that the truth was just the opposite: that there was much *more* here than met the eye. The Supreme Court of Alaska didn't know that, and ordered the Superior Court to re-sentence him.

The Superior Court judge, furious at the decision, stated that "for the record, I'm absolutely convinced that Mr. Hansen is going to commit additional crimes. I don't think that's even an open question." Hansen was released on parole, and there were to be strict, court-ordered guidelines for his supervision—for example, periodic checks that he was taking his medicine.

The guidelines were never issued. There was no follow-up supervision of any kind.

He was released in late 1978. Between then and 1983 he would murder at least seventeen women, most of them prostitutes and/or dancers in seedy clubs. Hansen was a classic serial killer, a sexual predator who abducted young women and left their bodies in remote areas of the Alaskan wilderness. In some cases, he let the women run, and then hunted and killed them.

The system had other chances to stop him. There were other assaults on women who escaped, but the attacks were not tied to Hansen.

In January, 1981, he reported a fraudulent burglary as a part of an insurance scam. The insurance company suspected that the claim was fake, but it was cheaper to pay it ($13,000) than to prove it was false.

Bodies were occasionally found in very remote areas, far from roads. In retrospect, the police investigating the murders might have realized earlier that the killer had to have access to an airplane, which might have focused the search. I'm not blaming the police; sometimes things that seem obvious later on are hard to see at the time.

Hansen burglarized isolated hunting cabins. A victim of one of those burglaries, a layman with no police experience, was smart enough to track it to Hansen. Realizing that the thief had to have an airplane, the cabin owner walked in circles around his cabin until he found where the airplane had landed, photographed and measured the tire tracks, and then went to nine airfields, looking for the plane with the matching tires. It was Hansen's.

The police said that was insufficient evidence for a warrant, and refused to pursue the case.

Most of the victims had no strong family ties, and their disappearances caused little notice. As time passed, however, enough bodies were found and enough families became involved in the searches that the police eventually realized that they were dealing with a serial murderer.

On June 13, 1983, Hansen made an agreement with a prostitute to get her into his car. Once he had her, Hansen pulled a gun, took the woman to his home and raped her several times, then took her to his plane, where she was able to escape.

Hansen hastily arranged an alibi with a friend who owed him a favor. When the police came Hansen denied the whole thing and provided the alibi. The victim was credible and provided specific detail about Hansen's house and plane, but she was, after all, a prostitute. When she skipped town a week later, the police closed the case with no action.

A junior policeman who had responded to the call, however, felt strongly that

a) Hansen had committed the assault,

b) Hansen had intended to murder the woman, and

c) Hansen very possibly might be the serial murderer for whom a special force was searching.

Defying orders, the young cop sent the case file to the task force which was searching for the serial killer. The task force quickly focused on Hansen, and within a month of receiving the file had assembled enough information to raid his house. He was arrested on October 27, 1983, and has been in custody ever since. In February, 1984, he confessed to several murders.

Hansen has never talked freely about his crimes, answering questions only when he could negotiate something in exchange for the information. One of the things he has negotiated for is protection from publicity, and for this reason he is not as well known as many comparable criminals. There are at least two books about him—*Fair Game,* by Bernard DuClos (St. Martin's Press, 1993), and *Butcher, Baker: A True Account of a Serial Murderer,* by Walter Gilmour and Leland E. Hale (Penguin, 1991). DuClos is a native of Pocahontas, Iowa, who became interested in the case for that reason, and did a solid, workmanlike job of writing a book about it. (Hansen's mother's name was DuClose, but I don't know whether that is a connection or a coincidence.)

The judge who sentenced Hansen at the end of his rampage said that "I can't think of a bigger indictment of society than what we have here. This gentleman has been known to us for several years. Yet, we've turned him loose several times knowing that he had the potential to kill."

In response to this, let me say that first, this is not an indictment of "society," it is an indictment of the criminal justice system. And second, of course it is, but . . .

In this respect, the Robert Hansen story is like that of Westley Allan Dodd, or Charles Hatcher, or Larry Eyler or many others—men who did everything but drive to the police station and write their names in their victim's blood, but who nonetheless were turned loose on society repeatedly until the full picture of their depravity became evident.

I have been writing this book for more than twenty years. The article above, about Robert Hansen, was written more than fifteen years ago. By nature I am an optimist. I tend to see the good in everything—but at the time that I was writing stories like this one, I was very negative and depressed about the American judicial system. "What kind of country are we living in," I wondered, "where people like Robert Hansen can be turned loose repeatedly by a justice system that has every reason to know that they are responsible for dozens of violent crimes?"

This was the time, also, in which the criminal population of America passed one million persons, and there was a hue and cry about that from the left. *"Do you realize that there are more than one million Americans now living under the control of the justice system?"* the left would thunder, to which my response was, "Do you mean to tell me that there are only one million people in prison in America? Jesus Christ; no wonder crime is out of control." A million people in America . . . that's nothing. That's one person in 300.

Think about any group of 300 people that you can relate to . . . the people in your high school graduating class, or the people who work for your company. It's easy for me, because I grew up in a town with a listed population of 309. Answer honestly the question: how many criminals were in that group? How many people were there in that group of 300 who would steal from you, or beat you up, or who were so over-the-top reckless that they were a constant danger to those around them? It's not one in 300; it's more like two or three percent. In a country the size of America, the idea that only one million people would be in prison is absolutely terrifying.

Robert Hansen was the end product of a criminal justice system that really didn't *want* to convict people, a criminal justice system that had lost track of its responsibility to protect the public. But you know what? That was 30 years ago, when Hansen was running wild and nobody would step up to stop him. It was a long time ago. It isn't that way anymore. The system has, to a large extent, healed itself.

America ignored the people who were whining about one million Americans being locked up—and rightly so. We went to two million.

In the mid-1970s I taught a junior college class at the Kansas State Prison in Lansing—the same prison where Hickock and Smith had been executed just a few years before. I had a guy in my class who had been sentenced to life in prison for murder, and had been there about two years. In the middle of the semester he made parole.

What?

It turned out that, at that time, "life in prison" generally meant four to six years. The maximum sentence for murder in Kansas was *called* life in prison, but it was actually fifteen years to life. After fifteen years, you were eligible for parole.

You were more than eligible for parole; you were legally *entitled* to parole, unless you had "bad time." There was "good time" and "bad time." "Good time" meant that you had not been convicted of any violations of the rules of the prison, and good time was counted at two-to-one, which meant that you were eligible for parole, actually, after seven and a half years.

What was "good time"? Well, *all* time was good time, really. At the time the policy was adopted, prison officials would take away a prisoner's good time for violations of prison rules. The theory was that this would give prison authorities more control of the inmates, if they had the ability to let prisoners who behaved themselves out earlier. Some prisoner had sued arguing that his loss of "good time" was keeping him in prison when he should be out, however, and he hadn't been convicted of doing anything wrong inside the prison; it was just the judgment of the staff that he had violated prison rules. The result of that lawsuit was a policy that a prisoner could not be denied his "good time" credits without a hearing. You had to have a trial, with the prisoner represented by a lawyer, to *prove* that the prisoner had been found in possession of a knife, or had assaulted another prisoner, or had thrown urine at a guard, or whatever it was; if you didn't prove it in a hearing, you couldn't violate the prisoner's good time.

So basically, all time was good time. There was one case I was aware of in which the prison authorities were fairly certain that a prisoner had killed another prisoner, but they couldn't actually *prove* it, so they couldn't violate his good time. So fifteen years to life, in practice, meant seven and a half years.

But somebody was held in prison for seven years, seven months waiting for the next session of the parole board, so he sued. The result of that lawsuit was a policy that a prisoner had to be granted a parole hearing *no later than* the moment that he was theoretically eligible for parole, which meant 7½ years, if he was doing life. The parole board met every six months. That meant that, if your earliest parole date was anywhere in those six months, you got to go before the parole board—and, unless you had been convicted of a serious crime while you were in prison, you were legally entitled to parole.

So 7½ years meant, really, a little less than 7½ years—but. To count to the 7½ years, you had to include the time the prisoner was in custody while on trial or awaiting trial. Very often, in a murder case, the criminal might have been held in custody for two or three years before the case came to trial. By the time he got to the state pen, he might be four to five years away from parole.

But wait a minute; it gets worse. Sometimes people who were awaiting trial in a murder case couldn't make bond—but most of the time they could. Very often, like Ken McElroy, a prisoner would be able to make bond even *after* he was convicted. If the accused could post bail, he could remain free while awaiting trial or awaiting sentencing or awaiting appeals, *and it still counted as time in custody.* Because he was free on bond, he was still theoretically under the supervision of the corrections system, therefore he was theoretically in jail, therefore his time had to be counted in calculating his parole eligibility date—and had to be counted double, since it was always good time. A murderer who knew that he was likely to be convicted, then, would delay his trial and stay free on bond as long as he could. If he could stretch his pre-trial and pre-sentencing time to four years, then by the time he was convicted, he was only three years away from parole.

It was a fantastic system. It enabled prosecutors to go before the press and announce that they had obtained a life sentence for A. J. Killer, but it allowed A.J. to walk quietly out of prison five years later—sometimes less.

But you know what? It's not that way anymore. The system has, to a large extent, healed itself. Parole has either been eliminated or sharply curtailed in most jurisdictions. Where it exists, it is no longer an entitlement. More of the very worst criminals are sentenced now to life without the possibility of parole. The revolving door doesn't revolve the way it used to. I'm not saying that there aren't *any* Robert Hansens out there anymore, killing scores of people, but America is not the way it was.

XXVIII

J ohn Joubert was an Eagle Scout and a serial murderer, not necessarily in
that order. He became an Eagle Scout in 1981. In August, 1982, at the age
of 19, he killed an eleven-year-old boy in Portland. Joining the Air Force
almost immediately thereafter, he was stationed in Omaha, Nebraska, where
he murdered two more young boys—Danny Joe Eberle, a thirteen-year-old
newsboy abducted off his route (September 18, 1983), and Chris Walden, a
twelve-year-old abducted on his way to school (December 2, 1983).

Even as a Boy Scout, Joubert had attacked a number of young people with
knives, although none of those attacks ended in death. Other than the swift-
ness of his moral descent, the only thing noteworthy about Joubert is the way
in which he was caught. A county sheriff, Pat Thomas, went on TV and said
that Joubert was "a coward who could only kill children . . . If he were a real
man, he would stop picking on children and start picking on someone his
own size." Joubert rose to the bait, and attempted to abduct an adult woman.
She escaped, and got his license plate number. That brought the police to his
door, where they found incriminating evidence. He confessed a few hours
later.

Trying to goad the killer into varying his pattern by taunting him through
the media is, of course, a classic device of crime fiction; you've probably seen
cops do this on television a dozen times—but in this case, it actually worked.

The book about the Joubert case, from which most of these facts are taken,
is *A Need to Kill*, by Mark Pettit (Ballantine Books, 1991). Pettit was a TV
reporter who became interested in the case at the time of the second murder,
that of the Eberle boy. *Whoever Fights Monsters*, Robert Ressler's book about
his work for the FBI, has a chapter on Joubert, and gives a somewhat different account of his capture, which gives the impression that Joubert may not
have intended to abduct the adult woman, but merely to prevent her from

reporting the fact that he was hanging around the front of a school. Pettit's book is OK, short and to the point, although it is punctuated with regrettable sentences such as "The teenager gasped at the red-hot streamer of pain that lanced through his body" (p. 18).

John Joubert was executed in Nebraska in 1996. Pettit's editor is still at large.

> Joubert's eyes were a cold, gray color. Uncaring, piercing eyes. Like the eyes of a shark.
>
> —MARK PETTIT, *A NEED TO KILL*

> But then he turned around and looked at me and I saw his eyes. They were flat. Dead eyes. Shark's eyes. It was exactly like looking into a shark's eyes.
>
> —ANN RULE, *THE I-5 KILLER*

> His eyes reflected no more feeling than a shark, or a doll. Not like he was crazy, or anything like that. Just empty.
>
> —JAYE SLADE FLETCHER, *A PERFECT GENTLEMAN* (ABOUT MICHAEL LEE LOCKHART)

> It was his eyes that really got me. I'll never forget them. They were like those of the shark in the movie *Jaws.* No pupils, just black spots. These were evil eyes that stayed with me long after the interview.
>
> —ROBERT K. RESSLER, *WHOEVER FIGHTS MONSTERS* (WRITING ABOUT RICHARD CHASE)

> Equally disturbing to Freeman were the man's piercing blue eyes; there was something dangerous and forbidding about his stare. Deep inside Garrow's cloudy pupils was a faint glow, like that of a dying light bulb.
>
> —TOM ALIBRANDI, *PRIVILEGED INFORMATION*

> It was as if his eyes had no connection with any emotion he expressed. Whatever his mood—whether he was angry, jovial, or anything in between—his eyes remained the same. Empty . . . his stare was riveting, unsettling, with a malign intensity. What people remembered most about Gary [Tison] were those cold, hard eyes.
>
> —JAMES W. CLARKE, *LAST RAMPAGE*

Gail's heart thumped in her chest. She thought she would faint when Tom
turned his eyes on her. They glinted like marbles.

—CHARLES W. SASSER, *HOMICIDE!*

"He's got dead eyes," Assistant District Attorney Charles Butts, 45, told his
colleagues . . .
"There was no sense of remorse," Butts told his colleagues during the trial. "I
can tell, because he has dead eyes."

—BOB STEWART, *NO REMORSE* (ABOUT KEN McDUFF)

"When I looked in his eyes it was—you hear of people who are chilled to the
bone, well, I was chilled to my soul . . . I looked into his eyes and it was like,
'I want to get out of here,' and I felt chills down to my very toes—it was just
'This is the guy.'"

—PAROLE OFFICER RICHARD WOOD, QUOTED ABOUT DAVID CARPENTER
IN *THE SLEEPING LADY*, BY ROBERT GRAYSMITH

Guys, knock it off. There is absolutely nothing about the eyes of a serial
murderer that is any different from my eyes or your eyes. If you could look
at a guy's eyes and see that he was a serial killer, women wouldn't get into the
car with them. It's magical thinking, that somehow you can look in a person's
eyes and see into their soul, and it's dangerous, because it encourages people
to think that they can identify sociopaths just by looking at them.

In the early 1980s, three women were murdered in Tulsa, Oklahoma, in the
space of a little more than a year. The investigation into the deaths, which
were apparently the work of a serial murderer, was assigned to Charles W.
Sasser, who would

a) Never catch the killer, and
b) Write a book about his life as a homicide detective.

The book, *Homicide!*, was published by Pocket Books (Simon & Schuster) in 1990 (not to be confused with David Simon's *Homicide: A Year on
the Killing Streets*). *Homicide!* is essentially the story of the destruction of
a man's soul by the demands of police work. Wading in filth and evil, dealing constantly with the dregs of humanity, and perpetually compelled to be
tougher than the vicious world he inhabits, Sasser finds himself becoming

progressively more cynical, more dishonest, more vulgar, and less sensitive. His family is disintegrating, and he is drifting toward alcoholism. Sasser has lost faith in the criminal justice system within which he works, seeing that system manipulated by lawyers without conscience and judges without courage. This loss of faith in the system spikes his moral descent. He is aware of these changes within himself, and he despises them—yet he is unable to let go of the policeman's world, in large part because he cannot accept his inability to solve the case of the three murdered women. The book is pretty good, and I'd recommend that you read it.

Sasser was an exceptionally good detective, at least if we can believe his own account of his career. But the book is as interesting for what Sasser *doesn't* understand as it is for what he does. The key sentences in the book occur on page 54, at the beginning of Chapter Eight:

> Every cop knows most homicides are committed by someone the victim knows—wife, husband, son, uncle, friend, neighbor, the local grocer or bookie. That's true even in sex killings like Martin, Rosenbaum and Oakley. There is often a connection between the victim and the perpetrator, however remote. I kept searching for that connection as I probed society's dirty underbelly . . .

The assumption that even killings like these were probably committed by someone the victims knew is, of course, absolutely, totally, and unquestionably false. These killings have the clear signature of a sexual predator, and it is overwhelmingly likely that they were committed by someone who had no connection whatsoever to the victims before the fatal encounter. This mistaken assumption tragically underlies the long, painful years of the investigation. This is one of four points on which Sasser's investigation is clearly misdirected:

• Sasser believes, with no evidence, that the killer has remained in Tulsa. When other policemen challenge him on this point, urging him to accept that the guy may have left town, he brushes them aside, saying maybe he's left town; maybe I'll catch him tomorrow. In retrospect, it seems likely that the killer left Tulsa shortly after the murder of the third victim.

• A psychologist, commissioned by a Tulsa newspaper, drew up a profile of the killer in which he suggested that the murderer was a man "probably with no criminal record." Sasser doesn't specifically endorse this view, but he fails to show any awareness that this is in error. For a man to emerge as a full-blown serial murderer with no history of criminal behavior would be rare—indeed, I can come up with only two such cases, Ted Bundy and Dennis Rader (BTK). It is far, far more likely that the Tulsa killer had a record of sex crimes, arson, malicious behavior, theft and criminal violence stretching back to the time he was twelve years old.

• Sasser works the case of the serial murderer, whom he calls Jekyll and Hyde, *along with his regular caseload of unsolved homicides,* and using essentially the same investigative method. This simply isn't how you catch a serial murderer. If you're serious about catching a serial murderer, you establish a task force, dedicated to the job. The task force doesn't work the victims; they work the criminal population. They look at everybody associated with sex crimes, everybody released from jail about the time the crimes started, every person who assaults another person, and they ask about each one, "Could he be our man?" They identify the leading candidates within the criminal community, and then look for links between the candidates and the crimes.

Sasser, in *Homicide!,* describes a world in which he is burrowing toward death, beating his head against a wall trying to catch a particularly reprehensible killer. What the sophisticated reader knows, but Sasser doesn't, is that the author is beating his head against a wall using an antiquated investigation model utterly inappropriate to the crimes, trying desperately to catch the scent of a killer who has long since left town. Sasser doesn't know this in 1987, when he is killing himself in his work, and he doesn't know it in 1990, when he has quit the job and is writing the book. And this, in short, is why research is sometimes as valuable as experience. Experience has taught policemen to look for a killer in the victim's life. A student of crime would have known that this case was an exception to the rule.

There is another external level on which this book is also intriguing. Could the Tulsa crimes perhaps be the work of a major undocumented serial murderer? Could they be the work of a known serial murderer, but not previously attributed to him?

One of Sasser's victims was found with a pair of black, military-type socks knotted around her neck. Based on this, Sasser believes he is looking for a man in his thirties, since

a) There's no military base nearby, and

b) Young people don't wear those kind of socks.

The work of John Douglas and Robert Ressler gives us, in the late 1990s, a second reason to believe that the killer was in fact an older man. There's no panic here, no hasty retreat. The killer took his time raping his victims and mutilating their bodies. He cleaned up afterward, and, in the first two cases, disposed of the bodies carefully, in a place where they would not be found for days afterward. He concealed the bodies in places he had no doubt picked out earlier, and registered as possible dumpsites.

So if he had done this before, where? The BTK murders were committed in Wichita, mostly in the mid- to late 1970s. It is less than three hours from Wichita to Tulsa; however, the BTK murders and the Tulsa homicides are not very similar, and I think it is quite unlikely that they were connected. Faryion Wardrip, another serial murderer, was then in his early twenties and living in Wichita Falls, Texas, three and a half hours to the south of Tulsa. I doubt that it was him, either, but you never know.

The third Tulsa homicide is very different from the other two. In the first two Tulsa attacks, the killer abducted women in the middle of the night, took them to an unknown place, and dumped their bodies at secure locations. The third attack was much, much riskier, a young woman murdered in broad daylight while jogging through a park, her body obviously left where she was attacked.

But that may explain why the killer left Tulsa at that time. The newspapers, after the murder of Susan Oakley, were on the story like paint. The best detective in town—Sasser—was assigned to the case. The risky daylight attack would have left the killer wondering about witnesses and about evidence left behind.

The Tulsa killer killed young women who were essentially innocent, just attractive young girls who were going about their business. This puts him among a minority of serial murderers, most of whom attack prostitutes. He may have just stopped killing at that point; he may have moved on. Between the two, I'd be inclined to bet on the latter. Since we don't know who he was, we have to wonder. But Sasser made a career out of trying to find that answer, and it nearly killed him.

And, while we are in Oklahoma in the 1980s . . . I have been re-reading Robert Mayer's *The Dreams of Ada*, and then reading John Grisham's *The Innocent Man*. Each book is about a case in Ada, Oklahoma, in the 1980s in which a young woman was murdered by persons unknown. After some years two young men were arrested, one because somebody said he was involved and the other because he was a friend of the man who was said to be involved. Dragging from the young men quasi-confessions extracted under duress, the police loaded the case with jailhouse snitches, fringe witnesses drawn to the drama of the investigation and half-assed experts with convenient interpretations of the forensic flotsam. They succeeded in convicting the two entirely innocent young men, who then spent years in the Oklahoma prison system, fighting execution.

Not one case; two cases . . . the two books deal with different cases, but that is what happened in both cases. Some of the same prosecutors and policemen extracted phony confessions in the two cases, and succeeded in ruining the lives of four young men, two of whom remain in prison as of this writing. An unfortunate use of the power of the law.

(Ada, if you are wondering, is 120 miles from Tulsa. And yes, the crimes all occurred in the same time frame. Don't make too much out of that; there are a lot of unidentified murderers out there.)

Books about cases of injustice inevitably decry the police and prosecutorial misconduct that led to the miscarriage of justice. (By the way, if somebody deliberately *causes* a miscarriage of justice, shouldn't that be called an abortion of justice? Just wondering.) In individual cases it is no doubt appropriate to name the names and kick the behinds of the people who caused the system of justice to abort. My point is that we *always* do this; there is probably no such thing as a book about the prosecution of an innocent person that does not seek someone to hold responsible.

That creates the impression that the system of justice fails *only* when the police are sloppy or insensitive, only when the prosecution is overzealous, only when the judge winks and the defense attorney nods. The system of justice fails because human beings must operate it. Human beings lack the sophistication of understanding that would enable us to figure out, in every case, what has actually happened. We're simply not that smart.

It is exactly this that causes us to be fascinated with crime cases and detective stories: that we are pushing our understanding beyond its natural limits. In the same way that athletic contests fascinate us because they show us athletes pushing their bodies to and beyond the natural limits of the human form, investigations fascinate us because they show us investigators pushing their minds to and beyond the natural limits of deductive reasoning. By working

together for the last 150 years, we have pushed the envelope of criminal investigation inconceivably beyond the intuition with which we began in 1850—
and yet this remains profoundly true: *we do not have the ability to figure out
what happened in every case.* Sometimes we will try, and sometimes we will fail.

I believe that if you think about that, you must accept that this is true. Let
me then ask another question: *Is it wise to construct a judicial system upon
the premise that the pursuit of justice can be perfected?* It seems to me that
this is what we have done . . . or, since it goes on, what we are doing. We
tinker relentlessly with the machinery of justice—changing the rules of evidence, requiring more discovery or less discovery, admitting this and barring
that, requiring that more be done to ensure an adequate defense. Does this
not rest upon the assumption that trials can be perfected?

The real problem is not that trials are imperfect, but that we declare them
to be perfect. Upon the word of a jury, we will take a man's life, sometimes
suddenly and more often by the days. If the jury says "not guilty," we close the
door and walk away; the jury has spoken, the fact of innocence is perfect and
can never be assailed. If the jury says "guilty" we embark on a painful process
to make certain that it was a perfect trial—but if it was, we may feel justified
in taking the life of the guilty person. Is this not an assumption that the trial
has delivered a perfect outcome?

Judges and law professors stand within the circle of the law to study and
debate the perfection of trials. I am stepping outside the circle of the law
to ask a more difficult question: was this a smart idea to begin with? The
"beyond a reasonable doubt" standard pushes the system toward the pretense of certainty, rather than allowing it to recognize the reality of doubt.
Should we perhaps have started with a different assumption: *in many cases
we simply do not know what happened.*

In the world of crime and punishment, the greatest enemy of justice is often
the certainty that justice has already been delivered. I visualize lawyers and
politicians lining up at my doorstep to tell me that the system of justice could
not function without finality, that what it needs is not less certainty but more;
I can see the line forming out my window as I write. Perhaps. I think not, but
serial murderers are awaiting us, and we will save that debate for another day.

A little before noon on Sunday, June 2, 1985, an Asian man entered a hardware store in South City, California, which is on the southern loop of the

San Francisco/Oakland area. He was wearing a parka, in June, which drew the attention of a clerk. The clerk saw the man slip a vise into the folds of the parka. He asked a customer to follow the man, and called the police.

When the customer followed the shoplifter from the store the man bolted, fleeing the area. A large man with a beard approached the clerk, explaining that his Oriental "friend" was simple-minded, didn't know any better. He offered to pay for the stolen item.

A cop arrived, and immediately recognized a familiar scam. Shoplifters not uncommonly work in pairs. When one of them is caught, the partner will spring into action, offering to pay for whatever the simple-minded brother/friend/nephew/jogging partner has carried off. The cop walked the bearded man to his car, and spotted what he thought was a gun under a seat.

He ran the plates. The car's license plates belonged to a different automobile. This gave the police the right to search the car, and take a look at the gun.

The gun had a silencer attached to it. Silencers are illegal.

The bearded man was taken into custody. Within minutes of arriving at the police station, the man could be tied to several different missing-persons cases. The license plates were traced to a man who had disappeared, with his entire family, two months before. The vehicle itself belonged to another missing person. The suspect presented identification belonging to a third missing person, and his pockets yielded receipts given to a fourth.

"Do you want to know who I *really* am?" asked the bearded man. "I'm Leonard Lake, a fugitive from the Feds."

He grabbed a cyanide capsule from under his collar, and swallowed it in a second. He never spoke again, and died some days later.

The automobile yielded bloodstains, bullet holes, and identification cards belonging to yet another missing person. One of the most grisly crime sprees in American history was beginning to come to light.

The Asian man who had fled the scene was Charlie Chitat Ng, pronounced "Charlie Cheetah Ing." Ng is a British citizen of Chinese origin, from a family of some means. He fled to Canada, where he was arrested a month later, again arrested while shoplifting.

Lake and Ng were serious murderers, as opposed to serial murderers. They wiped out entire families, not just once, as Hickock and Smith had done, but at least twice, probably a third time, based on unidentified remains, and for all anyone knows, more. The full extent of their crimes is impossible to ascertain, but it seems safe to say that they killed more than twenty people, although this total may include some crimes committed by Lake without the assistance of Ng.

The next three paragraphs contain perhaps the most unpleasant accounts in the book, and you may wish to skip them. Lake and Ng used a cabin in the woods near Wilseyville, California. A bunker sat near the cabin, a windowless building about the size of a two-car garage. Lake and Ng would gain control of a person, or a couple, or a family, by using some pretext for normal interaction. In one case they called a man who had placed an ad offering to sell a car. The man went to show someone the car, and was never heard from again. Ng brought co-workers out to the forest, offering them odd jobs. They never came back. In one case the murderous pair simply invited their neighbors over for dinner. Lake sometimes stayed in a halfway house in Haight-Ashbury. Three people disappeared from that house in February, 1985. The body of one of them was found in Wilseyville. This is all that is known about the matter. In some cases it is unknown how they made contact with the victims.

In any case, all of the victims came to terrible ends. The men were the luckiest: they were quickly and unceremoniously shot. The women were held prisoner in the bunker and used as slaves for a period of days or weeks. They were assaulted, beaten and tortured before meeting their deaths, all the while pleading for their babies to be brought to them. Lake and Ng took videotapes of themselves abusing the women. The babies were murdered, and may also have been sexually exploited before death.

The bodies were disposed of in all different ways—burned, chopped up into small bits and spread around the property, or buried whole. This made it very difficult to ID the victims, or even to prove that a given victim was actually dead, or even to assemble a list of who all the victims might have been. Then they would loot the victims' property—steal their cars and jewelry, their furniture and cameras, their credit cards and miscellaneous ID.

They would have garage sales, and sell off some of their victims' belongings.

Truman Capote wrote about Hickock and Smith that probably neither man would have committed the crime for which they were executed, but that they created a third personality out of their interaction, and that this third personality committed the crime. Ng and Lake were different. *Both* of them were homicidal, and either of them was entirely capable of killing somebody. Joining forces made them deadlier not because it made them more wicked, but because it made them more effective.

After Ng was arrested in Canada the jurisdiction which was holding him refused to return him to California, citing a long-standing Canadian policy of refusing to grant extradition when the person involved faced the death penalty upon his return. Canada held Ng for four and a half years while the issue was fought out in Canadian courts, becoming a political issue of national interest. Eventually the Canadian Supreme Court ruled that Ng could be returned to the United States if the Justice Minister agreed. The Justice Minister gave permission to the warden of the prison which was holding him, and the prison got rid of him as fast as they could; he was back in California within hours after the Canadian Supreme Court had ruled, before the political opposition had a chance to rally.

Ng went on trial in California in October, 1998, and was convicted of eleven counts of murder on February 24, 1999.

The book about the case is *Eye of Evil*, by Joseph Harrington and Robert Burger. I say this with sadness, but it's a terrible book. It saddens me to say this because

a) The case itself is quite extraordinary,

b) Burger and Harrington are perfectly capable of writing a good book,

c) They did a solid job of researching the case, operating within the confines of a long-standing gag order, and

d) I believe they approached their subject honestly and in good faith, giving a full effort to tell the story of the crimes without sensationalizing or pandering.

They failed, however, for two easily identifiable reasons. First, they invented a reporter, a Nancy Drew–, Brenda Starr–type character named Tomasina Boyd Clancy, or T. B. Clancy for short, who intrudes relentlessly into the narrative. They spend half the book telling us what this fictional foldout was doing and thinking at every stage of the investigation, the delay, and the pre-trial hearing. From Chapter 22:

> Tomasina Boyd Clancy sat on a raised stucco planter box in the Government Center's courtyard. The sun had come out. The rays from that distant star warmed her face.

Yes indeed, she might have done that, if only she had been a real person. I cannot imagine what in the hell Burger and Harrington were thinking of when they invented this bimbo, or what the editor was thinking of when he let her slip through, but in any case it couldn't possibly be more annoying.

Second, Burger and Harrington tell the story in careful chronological order—beginning at the moment when the crimes came to light. The better part of a hundred pages are devoted to a chronological account of a pre-trial hearing. They make not the slightest effort, however, to unravel the chronology of *the events themselves,* the disappearances and assaults. The investigation constantly refers back to one crime or another in a piecemeal fashion—to a piece of identification found buried in a Tupperware container on the property, or to a minor traffic accident involving one of the stolen automobiles, or to the weapons which could somehow be linked to one of the crimes or another.

Clancy nodded. The timing of all this seemed to be Ng's only weapon.

Burger and Harrington seem to understand, on some level, that the chronology is critical to the story—yet they don't lift a finger to help the reader put it together. This is bewildering. The crimes are repetitious, involving a large number of common elements. Burger and Harrington offer the reader no list of the victims or possible victims, no chronology, no sub-section reviewing the events in the order they happened. The victims are never developed into three-dimensional or even two-dimensional persons; they're just names. Although the locale is as critical as the timeline, there are no maps and no diagrams.

The crime spree of Lake and Ng could easily have been ended several murders earlier, had the police system not been in such a mess at that time. Several of the disappearances could easily have been traced to Ng and/ or Lake, if a more timely effort had been made to follow up on a missing-persons report. When two of Ng's co-workers disappeared from the face of the earth in January, 1985, that might have set off alarm bells—and those disappearances could have been traced to Ng. At the time, it just didn't seem important enough to chase down. These people were missing, but there was no evidence that they were dead, so it was a low priority compared to solving the current homicides.

The police were also unlucky in this case. *Some* of the disappearances were taken seriously by the police and were rigorously investigated, but they happened to be the ones which could not be easily solved.

Charlie Chitat Ng remains on death row.

XXIX

—◆—

Jon Dunkle was an affable doofus who lived in the early 1980s in Belmont, California, south of San Francisco.

On Saturday night, November 7, 1981, John Davies disappeared from his Belmont home. Davies was a fifteen-year-old boy. Dunkle, 21 years old by the calendar but more like 14 emotionally, was a friend of the Davies family, almost a member of the family, addressing the parents as "Mom" and "Dad." The Davies prided themselves on keeping an open house, the door always unlocked and the rules so liberal they couldn't quite be considered rules. If the boys drink at home, they figured, they won't have to go somewhere else to drink. The boys drank a lot. They smoked a lot of pot, and they did a fair amount of LSD. The flaw in the theory: if you give them permission to drink at home, you're giving them permission to drink. The scary part is that their mother was a school principal.

Anyway, Dunkle more or less joined the family to get the permission to drink. His own father was strict, and would beat the hell out of him if he came home drunk. This doesn't work either. Dunkle would go over to the Davies house to drink, then sleep it off on their couch.

John Davies disappeared in the middle of the night—and all of a sudden, Jon Dunkle was nowhere to be seen. The Davies thought this behavior odd: he just cut them off, beginning at the moment their son disappeared. The cop initially assigned to the case talked to Dunkle and cleared him of any involvement in Davies' disappearance.

On October 2, 1984, a Belmont 12-year-old was murdered, stabbed with a knife and left in the bushes. Police worked up a composite drawing of a suspect in that case, and carried it around town. Jon Dunkle was identified as some-one who matched the drawing, and so police began trying to arrange a meet-ing with him. Dunkle left town and tried to gracefully dodge the meeting—at which point a cop working the new case and a cop working the old case, the Davies disappearance, realized that they were both trying to get in touch with the same man. At that point, they decided that they *really* wanted to talk to Jon Dunkle.

Dunkle lied to the investigators about peripheral issues, and recited a canned alibi which didn't check out. The cops realized that Dunkle was a serial murderer, and set to work to build a case against him. This proved to be a hellish task. Dunkle had severe dyslexia, resulting in a low measured IQ, but he was cagey. He had left no clues in either murder. Interviewed repeatedly, he confessed to nothing and made no usable incriminating statements. He was open, friendly, and helpful, but gee whiz, he just didn't know anything about either case.

Belmont police sent a cop undercover to work with Dunkle, flipping hamburgers. Dunkle by this time was living in Sacramento, more than a hundred miles away, so this was a difficult thing to do—a small-city police force running an expensive undercover operation in the middle of the state. Sacramento police cooperated and assisted in the investigation. Dunkle and the cop became friendly, so friendly that Dunkle would introduce her as his girlfriend. They hung out together, drinking heavily. Dunkle enjoyed being the chief suspect in the death of the Belmont 12-year-old, bragged about being suspected, and encouraged people to believe that he was involved—but drunk or sober, he avoided giving anything away, except that he did tip off his involvement in another case, a hit-and-run attempted murder.

The undercover assignment aborted when Dunkle left his cop/girlfriend as a lookout while he broke into an occupied house in the middle of the night. Astonishingly, and tragically, that wasn't enough to get him sent to prison. The police by this time could place Dunkle at the scene of one murder, knew that he was a close friend of the missing John Davies, knew that he had DUI convictions, had him on tape confessing to an undercover officer that he had run over another youth and left him for dead, knew that he was stealing knives from work, had him on tape talking in a general way about killing young boys, and had actually witnessed him breaking into a house, where he had grabbed a pair of scissors and dragged the blanket off the bed of a sleeping seven-year-old girl. None of that was considered sufficient to hold him awaiting trial, and he was released after a few days in custody.

Near Sacramento on July 2, 1985, Jon Dunkle viciously murdered a 12-year-old boy named Sean Dannehl, a virtual replay of the previous murder. Sacramento police focused on Dunkle immediately, and quickly determined that Dunkle had been at the park where Dannehl was murdered at the time of the crime—and yet, once more the investigation stalled at that point. Dunkle had left nothing behind, had been seen by no one making actual contact with the victim, and could not be coerced into making any incriminating remarks.

By this time police all over California knew almost for certain that Dunkle was the worst of the worst of the worst, a serial murderer who preyed upon children—and yet all they could convict him of was burglary.

In prison, fortunately, Dunkle began to tell his cellmate what he would not tell the cops, what he would not acknowledge even to the cop who had been pretending to be his girlfriend. The cellmate, also a murderer, talked to authorities, not in exchange for anything, but simply because he was appalled by Dunkle's crimes. Encouraged by police, the cellmate was able to con Dunkle into making a full confession to the three murders he is known to have committed, as well as two other attempted murders.

After stalling for several years with Marsden motions (firing his attorney) and feigned insanity, Dunkle was eventually convicted of two murders. He was sentenced to death, but has not been executed and probably will not be, since he has either genuinely slipped the bonds of sanity or has become so good at feigning madness that psychologists are unable to say for sure whether he is or is not psychotic.

The book about the case, *The Boy Next Door*, by Gretchen Brinck, is readable but un-remarkable. There was also a made-for-TV movie, *In the Company of Darkness*, starring Helen Hunt as the cop who pretended to be his girlfriend. The book has an interesting relationship to the police investigation. Most crime books portray the investigators as either:

a) Heroic knights, or

b) Bungling screw-ups.

Ms. Brinck has chosen the cops-as-heroic-knights model, but has to implicitly acknowledge that, for a bunch of heroic knights, they screwed up a lot of things real bad. The Belmont police initially wrote off John Davies' disappearance as a runaway, didn't investigate it seriously, didn't follow through in a timely fashion, and didn't really even look at Jon Dunkle, despite the suspicions of the victim's family. They persisted in these things until they had thoroughly alienated the Davies family. But in all fairness, having done that, they did make a truly heroic effort to recover.

Apart from that, there are two things about the case which are unique, or nearly unique: Dunkle's personality, and the technique of having a woman undercover cop befriend him. On a chart, Dunkle had many or most of the common traits of a serial murderer: he was a nobody, a loser, he had no close friends, he had a kind of intelligence but had never found anything to which it could be suitably applied, and so he had never been successful at anything. He came from an abusive and dysfunctional family. He drank heavily and had a long history of petty crimes.

What was different about him, however, was his affect—the gee-whiz, boy-next-door, shuck-and-grin act which had completely fooled the first investigator of the Davies murder. There are, I suppose, other serial murderers who have projected similar personalities, but it is certainly not common.

Attempting to nail a serial murderer by getting a cop to pose as his girl-friend is, so far as I know, unprecedented. I don't mean to be unkind, but I don't think this practice is going to make it into the FBI manual. I admire the Belmont cops' determination to put the bad guy away, but the decoy investigation was tremendously expensive, since the decoy had to be backed up and tape-recorded at every moment. The effort was dangerous, and it didn't produce very much. It did not prevent him from murdering again.

The real problem, however, is that having a cop acting as a friend and cohort of a serial murderer presents a feast of ethical, moral and legal perils. Can you spell En-Trap-Ment, boys and girls? It's not entrapment on the surface of it, but almost anything the cop does in the role of confidant presents the risk of crossing the line. Suppose the cop buys the serial murderer a few drinks, drops him off at home, and the murderer then goes out the back door and kills a neighbor boy. Is that entrapment?

It very well might be, yes. It is entrapment if the crime would not have occurred, but for the actions of the police. Dunkle committed his crimes under the heavy influence of alcohol, as do most men who kill children. If the police buy the alcohol, one can certainly argue that that's entrapment.

What if the cop gives the murderer a small present? Could that be entrapment? Dunkle was sexually and socially immature, but if the murderer grabs the policewoman's breast and she doesn't resist, is that entrapment? If the murderer grabs a breast and she *does* resist, an argument ensues, and he commits a murder an hour later, while still angry at the police woman, is that entrapment?

In the actual event, Dunkle left the cop standing watch while he broke into an occupied home which had a child's toys in the back yard. He didn't kill anybody while he was in there, but what if he had? That would be a pretty story, wouldn't it—rabid killer slashes the throat of seven-year-old while two cops meander around in back of the building, knowing full well that

a) he is a child murderer, and

b) he is plundering these people's house.

If you think through the idea of a cop befriending a serial murderer in this way, you realize that it's just full of nightmare scenarios.

On the differences between real-life and fictional serial murderers . . .

In fiction, serial murderers are usually rich. In real life, they most often live at or near the poverty level. I would guess that 50–60% of serial murderers have little or no money, about 30% are middle-class working people, about 15–20% are small businessmen with some resources (like Gacy), and something less than 1% are persons of means.

In fiction, though, they're almost always well-off. In real life they are complete nobodies, nearly invisible in society. In fiction they are usually prominent people.

The *biggest* difference between real-life and fictional serial killers, however, is in the extent to which they are organized. Serial murderers are traditionally divided into "organized" and "disorganized" offenders not because this is a productive way to think about them—it usually isn't—but because *that's the thing you can see at the crime scene*. If you start with a group of serial killers and break them down by their characteristics, "organized" and "disorganized" in truth are barely recognizable generalizations after the fact. But if you have to start with the crime scene and have almost no information, that's something you can "see," so that's how they are usually divided.

But it's useful here. Not only are serial murderers in fiction vastly more organized than serial murderers in real life, but *there is almost no overlap between the groups*. One can *almost* say accurately that *every* serial murderer in fiction is more organized than *any* serial murderer in real life.

I remember a 1970s made-for-TV movie about a serial killer; somebody is strangling women, and the police are trying to figure out who. They look for what the women have in common, and eventually they find it: they all had the same doctor when they were born, 20 years ago. They go after the doctor, only it turns out it isn't the doctor, it's the doctor's wife. She gave birth to a baby girl who was born dead about that time, strangled on the umbilical cord, and she is psychotically re-enacting this tragedy with her murders.

It's too rational, too organized. Real serial murderers don't have a clearly identifiable *reason* for their crimes. In *The Silence of the Lambs* Thomas Harris creates a serial murderer, Hannibal Lecter, who is 50 times more organized, more in control of his actions, than any real-life serial murderer. But even Harris' backup serial murderer, Buffalo Bill Gumb, kills women for an easily identifiable reason: he wants their skin. Sexually confused, he is trying to make a "woman suit" for himself by trapping large girls, starving them so their skin is loose, then killing them and using their skin to make a suit in which he can be a woman. It's too logical, too organized. Real serial murderers aren't that organized. Alfred Hitchcock's *Psycho* is closer to real life.

When people speculate about unsolved serial killings or unsolved murders, they tend to give the murderers the characteristics of fictional serial murderers, rather than the characteristics of real ones. If you look at the people accused by various authors of being Jack the Ripper, they're mostly well-off, successful people, prominent in the community, and very often they're committing the murders for some reason. If you look at the books accusing Tom, Dick and Harry of killing the Black Dahlia, same thing; it's usually prominent people being accused, and often they are attributed some "motive" for the murder. It's not the way it happens in real life.

Speculation about unsolved grisly crimes always includes "evidence" that the killer may have been a doctor; Jack the Ripper may have been a doctor, and whoever killed the Black Dahlia was a doctor, and the Butcher of Kingsbury Run was a doctor. They're all doctors.

In real life, there have been many doctors who killed their patients—but they're all pharmacists, not surgeons. They poison their patients; they don't run around stabbing hookers and dissecting them in secret laboratories.

Between April and early September, 1988, someone abducted and murdered eleven women in New Bedford, Massachusetts. Most or all of the women were prostitutes, and all were drug addicts.

The book about the case is *Killing Season*, by Carlton Smith, who also wrote a book about the Green River Killer. The book is quite good in parts, in other parts prone to long-winded, repetitive speculation that does nothing to move the story.

Smith's thesis is that "there was an ample amount of physical evidence; the pool of potential victims was relatively small, and quite close-knit." Why weren't the cases ever solved, then? "The answer, as I hope this book demonstrates, was not so much an absence of evidence, but rather the result of an inability of police and political officials to set aside their own personal agendas and instead focus methodically on the facts."

Except that he's dead wrong. Smith has it in for District Attorney Ron Pina, whom he sees as a publicity-hungry non-cop who is out of his league commanding this investigation. He hammers Pina relentlessly, essentially laying the failure to solve the crimes at his feet, or microphone.

But while I agree that Pina's performance in command of a serial murder investigation was not good, a more balanced reading of the facts is that

1) Nothing in Pina's experience prepared him to lead the hunt for a serial murderer,

2) This was generally true in that era. *Most* people who found themselves leading a search for a serial murderer, before the late 1990s, had no meaningful preparation for the task,

3) Serial murder cases are by their nature very difficult to solve,

4) This guy was good,

5) The cops weren't all that good, and

6) The murderer just beat them.

Let us take, for example, Smith's claim that "the pool of potential victims was relatively small, and quite close-knit." Yes, but. The last victim was abducted on September 4, 1988. Only two of the women's bodies had even been discovered by November 7, 1988. Most of the victims were never reported missing to the police. It is overwhelmingly likely, therefore, that the murderer had left the state two months before anyone realized (or could reasonably have realized) that a serial murderer was at work. So what is the value in having a relatively small, close-knit pool of potential victims? The implication is that because the pool of potential victims was small and close-knit, it should have been possible to protect them. But how? You can't act to protect someone from a serial murderer at large unless you have some reason to believe that a serial murderer is at large, which no one did. How do you protect somebody in November who has been dead since July?

Smith criticizes the investigators because, after one of the victims disappeared, they failed to make a timely investigation of her apartment. She lived in a drug-infested housing project. After she disappeared somebody else moved in, began stealing her welfare checks and using all of her stuff. Eventually, the victim's sister and daughters broke in, cleaned out the apartment, and just threw away everything that didn't belong to the victim.

According to Smith, "without knowing who the clothing and other articles actually belonged to, the possibility exists that some items found in Nancy Paiva's apartment might have belonged to other victims of the Highway Killer." This, apparently, is a substantial portion of what Smith refers to when he says that "there was an ample amount of physical evidence," and he also says that this act was preventable, and that it "may have made solving the Highway Murders far more difficult."

But I'm not aware that there has ever been a serial murder case in the history of the world which was solved by searching the domicile of one of the victims. It's been tried hundreds of times. When there is a serial murderer around, the police always search the lodgings of the victims, as indeed they should. It's never solved the case yet, and there's no reason to believe that it would have done so here.

Pina's investigation followed the classic pattern of unsuccessful serial murder investigations of that era. Building from the lives of the victims, he tried to develop evidence leading toward the killer. In doing so, he tried to focus on a "super suspect," channeling the investigation prematurely toward a few people that he regarded as hot prospects. These practices work fine in solving ordinary crimes; they don't work at all in pursuing a serial murderer.

But even had he done everything right, all of the crimes were months old before the investigation began. No one witnessed any abductions. The precise time frames of the abductions and murders could not be established. It was a hard case.

When he was sixteen years old, Richard Grissom got a C on his report card. He was afraid to go home with that grade, he said. Instead, he broke into the nearby home of a 72-year-old woman and murdered her, stabbing her repeatedly with a rusty railroad spike. He walked home then, dripping blood through the snow, and confessed when confronted by police.

He served three years in detention, after which he passed the threshold of adulthood, and became, in the legal fiction popular at the time, a different person, no longer responsible for the sins of his youth. He attended college for a couple of years, majoring in burglary, and bounced in and out of prison. Once, at a parole hearing, he pointed out that while on parole he had broken into the homes of at least four women while they were home, but *hadn't* killed the women. He brought this up himself, to show that he was making progress.

Eventually, however, he couldn't stand the pressure, and drifted back into mayhem. Grissom had a thing about keys. He acquired a key-duplicating machine, and structured his work to get keys. He set up a paint-contracting business that serviced apartment complexes. Through this and other scams, he acquired master keys that would open hundreds of apartments.

On the evening of June 6/7, 1989, Grissom is believed to have entered the Wichita, Kansas, apartment of Terri Maness, who was found brutally murdered the next day. On June 12/13, 1989, he entered the Kansas City apartment of Michelle Katf, and attempted to forcibly abduct Ms. Katf. She fought him off, but on the following weekend, June 18/19, Grissom abducted and murdered another woman from the same neighborhood, Joan Butler. These were beautiful young women, all of them. Clean, hardworking young women.

Grissom took Joan Butler's car. Her family, with no idea what had happened to her, organized a search, one element of which was distributing fliers describing her car. A student at Kansas University spotted the car in Lawrence, Kansas, and called police. A policeman stopped Grissom entering the car, and attempted to walk him back to his apartment to check out his ID. The cop had no idea that it was a murder case; all he knew was that the man seemed to be driving somebody else's car. Grissom, once a member of a college track team, broke and ran, escaping from the officer.

Grissom's fingerprints were all over Butler's car; he was identified from the prints. Calling a friend, Grissom got a ride back to Kansas City, picked up his own car, and grabbed his kill kit and his key rings. That evening (June 25/26) he abducted two young women, Theresa Brown and Christine Rusch, and forced them to drain their bank accounts. Like Joan Butler, their bodies were never found, but Grissom was eventually convicted of their murders.

Grissom, half black and half Asian, was a handsome man, intelligent, articulate, always composed. He was able to gain the trust of those around him, a trust which he abused without conscience. Like almost all serial murderers, Grissom was a thief of immense magnitude.

The book about the case is *Suddenly Gone*, by Dan Mitrione (Addicus Books, Omaha, Nebraska, 1995). I'd give the book about a D+. The author blurb identifies Mitrione as "a former federal investigator" (OK, Dan, but what did you *really* do?), and the book has that feel about it, that it was written by a cop. Mitrione developed good connections to the investigation, but the cops are the only people in the book that he seems to care about. His writing is dull, and he has nothing to say other than this happened, and then this happened, and then this happened. His research is good, and his intentions are honorable. This book is in no way an exploitation of the crime. But Mitrione has no ability to bring anyone to life, and doesn't seem to have any real interest in the people. Near the end of the book, we learn for the first time, as an aside, that one of the victims was engaged.

Like many serial murderers, Grissom never confessed, although he had always confessed readily to the other crimes with which he was charged, including the juvenile murder. Grissom told a jailhouse informant that he had committed several other murders—a couple of prostitutes in Florida, a hitchhiker here and there—but there is no basis on which to evaluate these statements. On the basis of what we do know, Grissom was sentenced to four life terms plus 361 years.

In October, 1989, it came to light that Ray Copeland, an elderly Missouri farmer, had been murdering his hired help.

Ray Copeland was a mean, nasty young man who had aged into a mean, nasty 75-year-old. He looked like anybody's old farmer grandpa. He was a grouchy old bastard who would steal from his neighbors, cheat you in a business deal, or pay for his groceries with a bad check. When he was younger he'd beat the hell out of you for good measure.

Part of what you have to understand about Ray Copeland is that there is one guy like this in every small town between Pittsburgh and Sacramento, or anyway there's one in every small town that I ever lived in. They're not usually murderers, of course. Copeland was the kind of guy who had been in and out of jail all of his life, but who still figured he was outsmarting the police because they only got him for about a tenth of the stuff he had actually done. He had always stolen and then sold livestock, even when he was a kid. As he matured his schemes to profit by other people's pigs and cows got more convoluted, without getting more sophisticated. In the early 1970s he began using drifters as intermediaries. Rather than establishing a hollow bank account and buying cattle with bad checks himself, he would have his hired help do it for him, then persuade them to skedaddle out of town before the check came around.

At least, we hope that those drifters just hung the paper and ran; nobody really knows. There's no evidence that Copeland was killing people back then, although anything's possible. Anyway, that landed him back in jail pretty quick. In the mid-1980s Ray Copeland had returned to his farm, fighting bankruptcy after a tour of confinement. With some assistance from his wife, Faye, he developed a scheme to stay afloat. He would visit the missions and homeless shelters near him, and bring home a drifter to employ as a farm worker. He would help the drifter to establish a bank account in the area. Then he and the drifter would visit the sale barns and buy cattle at auction, paying for the cattle with worthless checks from the new accounts. Copeland would murder the drifter and sell the cattle.

This is about as stupid a crime pattern as you could come up with if you set out to get yourself executed. If you're going to kill a bunch of people and try to profit by their deaths, probably the last thing you want is for the county sheriff to come knocking on your door every couple of months, asking if you know what's happened to so-and-so. This was an inevitable consequence of what Copeland was doing. He was killing people who had been seen with him at sale barns buying livestock, at the bank, and at the grocery store, people who had been living in his house—and who left unpaid debts behind them. This had to bring the police to his door.

In October, 1989, a drifter named Jack McCormick, lured into the Copelands' clutches, sensed that something was up, and bolted. As soon as he had made it safely out of state (in a stolen car), he called Crime Stoppers and reported that he had seen human remains on Copeland's farm. He was making that up; he was basically right, but he was making up the part about seeing human remains in order to get people to pay attention to him. The sheriff got a warrant to go out to the Copeland farm and poke around. It took a couple of weeks of searching, but five bodies were eventually found. Ray and Faye Copeland were both arrested, tried, convicted, and sentenced to death by the state of Missouri. At least three other men hired by Copeland in 1988 and 1989 had also disappeared without a trace.

Faye Copeland was eventually pardoned. The evidence against her was not all that strong, and at some point it occurred to Missouri officials that it would be unseemly to execute an 85-year-old woman for crimes committed by her husband. Ray Copeland died on death row.

The book about the case, *The Copeland Killings*, was written by Tom Miller, a local reporter. The book is OK, straightforward and inoffensive.

Between January, 1988, and his arrest on January 9, 1992, William Lester Suff murdered at least thirteen prostitutes, perhaps a few more than that, in and around Riverside County, California.

Suff was a pasty-faced, flaccid, dull, long-winded, ineffectual blowhard, in the general class of murderers which would include Robert Hansen and Gerald Stano. He had no particular talent at anything, including murder. He made every mistake a serial murderer can make, and frequently. He abducted prostitutes within miles of his home, and dumped them within blocks of his home. When he moved, in March, 1990, the dumpsites followed him across the county. He left his victims in the open, where they would be found within hours. Many or most of the victims were found within 72 hours of their disappearance, leaving the bodies and dump locations teeming with physical evidence, and allowing friends and associates of the deceased to be interviewed while they still remembered details. He was seen making contact with at least three of the victims, including once by a woman who was so suspicious of him that she had jotted down a partial license plate as he drove away. He allowed at least one potential victim to escape, probably two, providing police with additional opportunities to develop information about him. One time he picked up a prostitute and took her to a McDonald's. She was leery of him, and made a scene at the McDonald's, so that they were seen together by a large number of people. Suff then dropped off that woman— but crossed the street, picked up and murdered her working partner.

He responded to public goading by police. He took personal items from the victims, and gave them to women he knew. In addition to all of this, the man was a convicted murderer, on parole from a Texas conviction for beating to death his own baby daughter.

Suff was able to end the lives of (about) eighteen young women due largely to the fact that the police who were investigating his crimes had no confidence in their ability to catch him—and, having no confidence that they *could* catch him, failed to take obvious steps to bring about his arrest.

The RSO [Riverside Sheriff's Office] didn't believe the killer could be caught.

Evidently, the Sheriff's Office believed the Riverside prostitute killer was another Green River killer: a shrewd criminal who would continue uncaught until he eventually disappeared of his own accord.

The investigation was composed of *and directed by* officers who had never before been a part of a serial murder investigation. Again, this was quite common until the late 1990s.

Suff's *modus operandi* was simple and almost unvaried: he picked up prostitutes who worked along a seedy strip in the city of Riverside. When Riverside City police had developed enough information about the assailant to perhaps recognize him when they saw him, they set up an intensive surveillance of the contact area. When Suff came through and tried to pick up a victim, they caught him. If they had done the same things a year earlier, they would have caught him a year earlier.

The book about the case, from which the quotation above was taken, is *The Riverside Killer*, by Christine Keers and Dennis St. Pierre (Pinnacle Books, 1997). Christine Keers was a detective assigned to the case; St. Pierre was the co-author. The first 50 or 100 pages of the book are so bad that I thought I was going to have to put it aside as unreadable. I think this may be St. Pierre's first book, and by the time he's 200 pages into the effort he has a better idea what he is doing. While I can't recommend the book, if you routinely read books about serial murderers, I'll list it as one that you can read. Their research is good, and their interpretation of the events is generally solid.

On September 25, 1973, Suff beat his two-month-old baby daughter to death. He was convicted of murder by the state of Texas, as was his wife, who probably had nothing to do with the little girl's death, and both were given seventy-year sentences for the crime. He was paroled less than ten years later as part of a court-ordered effort to reduce prison overcrowding. The parole system lost track of him almost immediately. By the time he was identified and arrested in California he had a new wife and a new baby daughter. He was already facing prosecution by Riverside authorities, for beating the new baby nearly to death.

One of the books that I thought I might write, at one time, was a book entitled *How Serial Murderers Are Caught*. We are all interested in how to catch serial murderers, how to catch them quicker. Might it be that one way to learn something about that subject would be to study how previous serial murderers have, in fact, been caught? Why not do a systematic review of the subject? Find as many details as I could about the capture of, let's say, 300 serial murderers, then try to organize that information. What happened, to bring them to the light? And also, knowing what we know about the murderer *now,* after he has been caught, how could he have been caught earlier? If we had tried this, would it have worked?

I still think that this would be a worthwhile project. There are three reasons why I decided not to write that book:

1. The narrowness of the subject provides few opportunities to examine the issues that make crime cases compelling.

2. The question of how, in retrospect, the criminal might have been caught earlier is a question which is difficult for an amateur to ask in reviewing the work of professionals. By posing this question one is taking license to critique the work of the cops who investigated the case. I have no credentials to critique the work of homicide cops. My intention, of course, is quite innocent—to learn something that might help a cop out next time, not to criticize the way it was done last time. It wouldn't come out that way. It would come out as criticism, and many readers would resent that, and would reject whatever I had to say, because they would say "Who is he to say what the cops should have done?"

3. When you start reviewing cases, it quickly becomes apparent that the answer is almost always the same: PVE. Potential Victim Escapes. That is how serial murderers are caught, in fact—a potential victim escapes from the assassin, and alerts the police. That's how police caught Dahmer, that's how they caught Bundy (among other things), that's how they caught Bob Berdella, Gerald Stano, Bob Hansen, Bill Suff, Ray Copeland, and most other serial murderers.

Again, this is less true now than it was years ago, when I was thinking of writing that book. The police now have a better understanding of how to catch a serial murderer without waiting for a break, and a better understanding of how to recognize and capitalize on a break when they catch one. But still, most serial murderers are caught when somebody they are attempting to murder gets loose.

The one other insight that I had about serial killers, when I was doing the rudimentary research for *How Serial Murderers Are Caught,* is this. Do you know how many serial killers are the sons of prostitutes?

All of them.

OK, it's not all of them, and I won't speculate on the exact percentage. It's a huge number of them. I've read probably two to three hundred books about serial murderers. I have never seen anyone make this point, none of the experts on serial murderers—but when you read the books, it seems obvious. It becomes something you expect to see . . . his mother was arrested six times for prostitution; of course she was. It becomes so obvious that it seems puzzling that no one ever comments on it, and I wonder if it is being not mentioned as a form of political correctness.

Let us ask, then, "Why is this true?" It could be as simple as "Prostitutes have exceptionally poor parenting skills." Their children are dramatically more likely to be abused and neglected than are the children, perhaps, of any other population group. It could be, in a certain sense, cognitive: that being the son of a prostitute imbues a child with deep, deep cynicism in a way that nothing else will.

And it could be that some prostitutes—maybe most prostitutes, I don't know—are involved in violent and destructive relationships with men who abuse them. Probably the child witnesses abuse at a young age, when his primary identification is with his mother. As an abused child very often grows up to be an abuser, a child who witnesses his mother being abused at a young age sometimes grows up to take the role of the abuser. I think that this is the most credible explanation for this phenomenon.

I am done with serial murderers. No more of them, I promise.

XXX

In late summer, 1986, an astronomer/computer wizard named Clifford Stoll started a job as systems manager at Lawrence Berkeley National Laboratory in Berkeley, California. His first assignment was to reconcile a set of mismatched books. Seventy-five cents' worth of computer time had been used but not paid for, but no one knew exactly how the discrepancy arose. He was to figure out what had happened.

Stoll realized that someone had broken into his computer, not once but several times. Curious about what the intruder was up to, Stoll set up a system to monitor what the guy was doing when he broke in, creating a permanent record of every keystroke the intruder made on his system, but in such a way that it was invisible to the hacker.

The hacker, he discovered quickly, was using *his* computer, the Lawrence Berkeley Lab computer, to break into other computers—military computers, specifically. The guy was collecting information about missiles, weapons, aircraft . . . anything military and cutting-edge.

Well, thought Stoll, we'd better stop this. Stoll called the FBI. The FBI, he was astonished to discover, could care less. What's the crime, asked the FBI? He stole 75 cents?

Stoll could have stopped the hacker from breaking into his computer any time he wanted to, but, leftist radical that he was, it still bothered him to think that some spook was wandering around breaking into military computers. His boss had instructed him, early on in the battle, to notify anybody whose computer was broken into on down the line. Stoll did, but some of them didn't seem to care, either. Even after being informed that their computers had been broken into, often they did little to secure them.

As Stoll watched the hacker out of his computer, he began to backtrack, trying to find out who he was and where he came from. Was he local? Apparently not . . . he didn't use the local computer lingo. Was he coming from the south? From computers in the American South, sometimes, but where did he enter the system?

It took almost a year to find out. From a computer in Hannover, Germany, the hacker was breaking into a computer at the University of Bremen. From there, he was breaking into the German Datex-P Network, using their lines to cross the Atlantic and break into Tymnet, the American phone carrier for computer networks. From Tymnet, he was breaking into the files of a defense contractor in McLean, Virginia, and from there, into Milnet, the computer network of the American military establishment.

Trained as an astronomer, Stoll had the astronomer's habit of keeping detailed notes of his work. These notes form the basis of *The Cuckoo's Egg,* Stoll's account of his year-long war of wits with an anonymous hacker, who turned out to be a working spy (Pocket Books, 1990). In a book that has more in common with *The Hobbit* than with *In Cold Blood,* Stoll has encounters with a long series of CIA and FBI agents, military systems managers, librarians, roommates, software salesmen, phone service technicians, bosses, scientists, geniuses, bureaucrats and prosecutors, almost all of whom want to see blood or money before they will take any interest in the matter. Stoll is a fine writer, and I recommend the book quite highly.

In the 1990s Stoll became infamous for predicting the failure of the internet, and the complete failure of all forms of e-commerce. Now 59 years old, Stoll is a stay-at-home dad who sells blown glass on the internet. Oh, well . . .

Brenda Schaefer and Mel Ignatow could almost have been considered yuppies. They were bright, attractive, professional people who earned good incomes, living and working near Louisville, Kentucky. Their marriages had failed, and so, at an age when those of us blessed with children are trying to figure out how to coach a kids' basketball team, they were still living with their parents and dating.

Beneath the veneer of a happy couple, Mel was abusive, or so she said, and Brenda was frigid, or so he said. On Sunday morning, September 25, 1988, Brenda Schaefer failed to return from a Saturday night date with Mel Ignatow. She had gone to break up with him, but then, she had done that before. Her car was found on a lonely highway, a nail in the tire and the windows smashed.

It would become the most sensational case in the history of Louisville. Everybody pretty much assumed that Ignatow had killed her, but the evidence was hard to harvest. The police were sure that he was lying to them, but as long as his lies were consistent and couldn't be traced, what could they do? They couldn't disprove the lies because they had no clear idea what had happened.

Police suspected that Ignatow had pressured or co-opted an ex-girlfriend, Mary Ann Shore, to help engineer the disappearance. They leaned hard on Ms. Shore. After sixteen months, she broke. Shore said that she and Ignatow had dug Brenda's grave a month before she disappeared. Ignatow had brought Ms. Schaefer to Shore's apartment, where he had tortured her for several hours before her death, while Shore took hundreds of pictures. She had cooperated, she said, because she was terrified of Mel Ignatow.

Shore led investigators to Schaefer's body, and agreed to wear a wire to a hastily arranged meeting with the murderer. Police recorded some vaguely incriminating statements, and arrested Ignatow.

He was acquitted of the crime. Shore was a poor witness, telling an incredible story with little corroborating evidence. Although Ignatow's house was searched twice, his cars were searched, a storage unit he rented was searched, the photographs Shore had claimed she took could not be found. Police, prosecutors and the Louisville public were shocked by the acquittal, as was the trial judge, who had no doubt about Ignatow's culpability.

Of course, the prohibition against double jeopardy would not permit Ignatow to be put on trial a second time. But the prosecution, led by the FBI, rallied to go after him on perjury charges—which were, essentially, that Ignatow had lied to the FBI, lied to a grand jury, and lied to a federal prosecutor in saying that he had no knowledge of the events leading to Schaefer's death.

On October 1, 1992, as the perjury trial was set to begin, the missing photographs and Brenda Schaefer's jewelry were found in the house that Ignatow had owned at the time of the crime. It was a complete fluke that the photographs were found. To protect his assets in the event of a damage suit, Ignatow had deeded his house to his mother and his children while he was in custody awaiting trial. His mother died, and his children sold the house to pay his legal bills. The new owners decided to change the carpet in the great room, and the carpet layers discovered a secret cache which two police searches had failed to locate.

Ignatow pled guilty to the perjury charges the next day, supplying the information that he had, in fact, murdered Brenda Schaefer. He would serve five years in a federal prison.

The book about the case, *Double Jeopardy*, was written by Bob Hill, a reporter for the Louisville *Courier-Journal*. It's a strong effort, well researched and well organized. Sometimes he tells you more than you really want to know, and he has an unflagging admiration for the police and prosecutors who screwed the case twelve ways from Sunday. The book is recommended.

On August 20, 1989, Jose and Kitty Menendez were shot to death in their Beverly Hills mansion by their sons, Lyle and Erik.

Jose Menendez was a Cuban immigrant who had made a fortune estimated at $14 to $15 million, working somewhere in the back rooms of the entertainment industry. He was a hard-driving, aggressive man who lectured his sons on the virtues of ruthlessness. He may also have sexually abused them, if you believe the testimony of his sons.

The sons, aged 19 and 21, pretended to know nothing of the crimes. They had been to a movie, they said; they returned home to find this awful scene. They knew how to spend the money. They bought a Porsche, Rolex watches, took tennis lessons from the best tennis teachers in the country. In late October, 1989, Erik Menendez confessed to his therapist. The therapist, concerned for his own safety, talked to his girlfriend, and arranged for her to listen in on a therapy session. Menendez talked about the crime—and threatened to kill the therapist if he told anyone. The girlfriend went to the police. Despite the second-hand nature of the evidence, she was able to lead police to where the guns had been purchased. The Menendez sons were arrested in March, 1990.

It was with the Menendez case that America entered the second golden age of yellow journalism. The first golden age ran roughly from 1880 to 1925. In that era almost every American city had multiple morning newspapers and multiple evening papers, and these newspapers competed for market share by nakedly exploiting the local violence. As newspapers consolidated, the more successful ones buying out the less, that gradually reduced competition within the industry. The last big event for the first epoch of yellow journalism was the Lindbergh case.

American journalism began to seek dignity and respect, rather than simply more sales. I say the words "dignity" and "respect" with a noticeable sneer, but in truth I miss them. The morbid spectacle of the Lindbergh case embarrassed the press, which had become self-aware. They never stopped reporting on crime stories, but they were no longer panting audibly between the lines.

Everything changed in the structure of the media between 1925 and 1990. Newspapers continued to be taken over by other newspapers. Television began and then cable television. The role of radio adapted to the opportunities of the moment, although for some reason radio was never a major player in the coverage of crime stories. The internet began. Magazines came and went. The market was never inert.

Yet throughout that era, the American press was largely controlled by a limited number of very rich persons, who by and large did not want to be embarrassed by their ink-stained employees. This was true even in the first fifteen years of successful cable television, 1975 to 1990.

This era ended about 1990, in my view, not because of the internet, not because of the proliferation of cable networks, but simply because the accumulated alterations in the structure of the media reached a critical mass. The tacit agreements made by the media in the wake of the Lindbergh case were no longer relevant. The two biggest Popular Crime cases of the 20th century—Lindbergh and O. J. Simpson—are the bookends of that era.

Anyway, back to the Menendez twerps. They had a criminal history. They had been burglarizing the apartments of their parents' wealthy friends, a series of crimes for which they would have gone to jail, had not their father protected them. Now the father was dead, and Erik had told his therapist why. Police demanded the therapists' notes, which the therapist refused to turn over or at least pretended to, and which courts, once they had the notes, were reluctant to admit into evidence. A long court battle followed over the admissibility of the therapist' notes. Eventually, the California Supreme Court ruled that the notes were not protected by privilege, and could be used as evidence. The boys went on trial in July, 1993.

Their first trial was open to television cameras, and was shown nationally on cable TV. The boys, despite the absence of an immediate threat to their well-being, pleaded self-defense. They had been so traumatized by years of physical, emotional, and sexual abuse, they argued, that they lived in constant fear for their lives. They killed their parents, they argued, because they were afraid their father was about to kill them. To prevent them from talking about the sexual abuse, you see.

The first trial ended in a hung jury—actually, since two separate juries were trying the two young men, in two hung juries. This outcome was widely criticized by judges, lawyers, politicians and commentators, and widely mocked by comedians. The defense theory of the case is hard to explain to a layman. Let's see, you carefully established an alibi, shot your *mother* in the back of the head while she was watching television, shot her five times, went to another room, re-loaded and shot her again because you were afraid that your *father* might harm you sometime? This is self-defense?

In the second trial, the judge

a) turned off the cameras,

b) imposed a gag order on the attorneys,

c) seated a single jury, rather than separate juries, and

d) refused to allow the Menendez defense team to argue that the crimes were committed in self-defense.

On March 20, 1996, six and a half years after the crimes, Lyle and Erik Menendez were convicted of two counts of first-degree murder. They were sentenced to life in prison without the possibility of parole.

On May 1, 1990, Gregg Smart was shot to death in his townhouse in Derry, New Hampshire.

Gregg Smart met Pam Wojas at a New Year's Eve party on the last day of 1986. Until they were married, they got along great. He moved to Florida to be with her while she finished her degree. After graduation she moved back to New Hampshire to be with him. They got married, had affairs, and argued most of the time. They had been married less than a year at the time of his murder.

Pam worked as a "media director" at a high school. In news reports about the case, she was routinely identified as a teacher, but the book about the case, *Deadly Lessons*, emphasizes that this is incorrect; she did not have a teaching certificate, and was never a teacher.

She was 22 years old when she met Billy Flynn, and she was a knock-out. Billy Flynn was 15, an awkward, dopey kid who spent his time smoking pot, listening to rock music, committing petty crimes and investigating the more serious drugs. Pam Smart, for reasons unclear to everyone except Pam Smart, began hanging out with Billy Flynn and his friends, going to the malls, listening to music, sharing the secrets of their tawdry and unpromising lives. On February 15, 1990, Pam seduced Billy. On February 16, she began pressuring him to kill her husband.

Billy was crazy about Pam, but less than enthusiastic about murder. Time dragged. Billy talked to his friends about it. Pam talked to them, too; the whole gang of them, in the weeks leading up to the murder, appear to have talked about little else. Billy made at least two half-hearted efforts to carry out his assignment, contriving to fail. Pam made it clear to him that if he wanted to continue getting regular action, he was going to have to close the deal. His friends agreed to go along and help out.

On May 1, while Pam attended a school board meeting miles away, Billy Flynn and Pete Randall waited in the dark for Gregg Smart to return home. Pam had left a door open for them. They staged a robbery. A third friend, who had borrowed the gun from his father's collection, waited for them a few blocks away. When Gregg got home they jumped him, shot him and ran.

Somebody talked, of course, and they all went to jail. The case became a staple of *Hard Copy, Inside Edition*, and shows of that ilk. CBS made a movie, *Murder in New Hampshire*. The book about the case, *Deadly Lessons*, was written by Ken Englade; that book is the source of most of this information.

The wonderful 1995 movie *To Die For*, starring Nicole Kidman, is a fictionalization of the Smart case. Pam Smart was a study in contrasts—hardworking, but astonishingly immature; compulsively controlled, but fundamentally irrational. She dressed like Barbara Walters, whom she admired greatly, but hung out with teenagers from the mobile home park. She was addicted to having fun, to raucous music, flakey sex, light drink and drugs, yet she was as cold as ice. She spent weeks working out the details of the crime, yet failed to perceive the most glaring weaknesses in the plan. These contrasts create opportunities for humor and irony as well as pathos, and *To Die For* developed those. They changed the names and altered the story a little bit, because they were interested in making a good movie, rather than exploiting a highly publicized murder to make a quick buck. They made it fiction because, in some ways, only fiction can tell the whole truth. The movie, if you haven't seen it, is very highly recommended.

What is there that remains to be said, about the O. J. Simpson case? It was long enough ago now that a few of you won't remember it. It was beyond belief. We didn't have as many cable channels then as we do now, but a lot of people had 30, 40, 50 channels on their TV. When the O. J. Simpson trial was on, there would be live coverage of it on at least five channels, and often on most of the channels. I can remember dealing with a cable system of about 30 channels—of which, at times, 20 would be broadcasting the live feed of the O. J. Simpson trial.

This unmatched level of saturation coverage turned everyone associated with the case into a household name. This was not a new phenomenon; in the late 1930s every informed American knew the names of Henry Breckinridge, John F. Condon, Violet Sharp and Amandus Hochmuth, peripheral figures in the Lindbergh case. In the 1920s, most everybody knew the names of the people involved in the Hall/Mills case.

It was not new, but it was new to us; most people alive in 1994 had never seen anything like it. I think that there are essentially three questions that remain about the O. J. Simpson epic:

1) Were the murders premeditated, or an act of blind rage?
2) Why did the story grow to such phenomenal proportions?
3) Why did the system of justice fail?

On the first issue—did O. J. go to Bundy Drive intending to kill Nicole?— I simply do not know. My intuition is that he did not, but that he went there to spy on her, and something happened that caused the situation to get out of control. I don't have a compelling argument to make on this issue. It seems like there should be some way to figure it out.

On the issue of why the O. J. Simpson case took over the media and dominated it the way no other case ever has, my explanation would be this. If you were to write a formula to predict how much publicity would be given to a particular crime, that formula would use both variables and constants—that is, both stable and predictable elements, and irrational or arbitrary elements. The case of Scott and Laci Peterson, for example, became extremely famous, although no one could reasonably have predicted that it would. There are a thousand cases every year just like it that don't become at all famous; no one can really explain why that one did. It just happened. It's arbitrary.

The notoriety that attached to O. J. Simpson's murder of Nicole Brown Simpson was not arbitrary, because one can look at the elements of the case and predict that it would become very famous. O. J. Simpson was perhaps the greatest running back in the history of football. He can't just murder a couple of people and nobody will say anything.

I would explain it this way: that in the case of O. J. Simpson, both the stable and the random elements controlling the publicity turned up extremely large. It happened mostly because of small details concerning the white Ford Bronco slow-speed chase. On June 17, 1994, O.J. arranged to surrender to authorities—and then didn't. He apparently was thinking about trying to run away, and also contemplating suicide. The news that O. J. Simpson—a fixture on our TV screens as a football star, football commentator, product pitchman and a minor movie star—the news that Simpson had become a fugitive from justice shocked the nation. In the hours after that shock, Simpson's Ford Bronco (being driven by a longtime friend) was spotted by police, and news media began watching the pursuit, which went on for an inexplicably long time. More channels and more channels began to join in the coverage. NBC television, which had paid millions of dollars for the rights to broadcast the NBA playoffs, dropped coverage of the fifth game of the final round to join all of the other networks in watching O. J. Simpson's white Ford Bronco being followed through the streets of Los Angeles by an armada of police cars.

It was that chase that made the case into a national obsession; if you take away that incident, the case would have been famous, but there would have been one network broadcasting the trial, rather than all of the networks. Crime cases increase in fame *when there is continuing action in the story.*

In most crime cases, the continuing action in a story is predictable. A beautiful little girl goes missing. It is predictable that, at some point, her body will be found. At some point, somebody will be arrested. An attorney will be hired or appointed. There will be a trial. There will be a conviction. There will be sentencing. There will be appeals.

All of this is continuing action in the story, but it is largely predictable. When there is an *unpredictable second act* in a case that the nation is already following, that tends to cause the coverage to explode. The Boston Strangler became extremely famous because, after the case was already in the news, there were several *additional* murders. The Zodiac committed additional murders after he had begun writing to the newspapers. Ted Bundy became as famous as he did because, after he was already in the news at a certain level, he escaped from prison and committed additional atrocities. This caused his story to explode. The white Ford Bronco chase, being covered by all of the television networks in real time, was a gigantic explosion within a story that people were already covering.

And the timing was right for it. The number of cable television networks increased substantially in the late 1980s. By the early 1990s those networks were searching for an audience. At the time of Nicole Brown's murder, there was a lot of cable television air time that wasn't strongly committed any-where. It could go wherever it saw an audience. It just happened.

On the third issue . . . why did the system of justice fail in this case . . . there are six culprits who get smacked for it:

The police, who screwed up the investigation,

The prosecutors, who bungled the presentation of the case,

The defense lawyers, who deliberately obfuscated the issues,

The judge, who lost control of the trial,

The jury, who failed to perceive what was obvious to most people, and

The news media, whose intrusion into the story made it more difficult for the machinery of justice to work.

I would allocate the blame as follows:

To the police, about 5%. The police investigation of Nicole Brown's mur-der was *not* bungled; the case was well investigated, the culprit was promptly identified, and much more than sufficient evidence to convict the accused was given to the prosecutors. Some mistakes were made. An inexperienced criminologist was sent to the crime scene. Some evidence was mishandled. These mistakes were minor, and would not ordinarily have been noteworthy.

To the prosecutors, about 35 to 45%. District Attorney Gil Garcetti made a mistake in allowing the case to be prosecuted in downtown Los Ange-les, rather than the Santa Monica courthouse nearer to where the crime was committed. This decision was apparently made as a consequence of a recently instituted policy about where to file cases; Garcetti simply failed to perceive that this very unusual case might not be best handled by routine policy directives. The result of that essentially inexplicable decision was that Simpson, a black man accused of murdering a white woman, would be tried by a predominantly black jury.

Chief Prosecutor Marcia Clark offended the jury by hammering for weeks on prior incidents of domestic abuse, rather than simply presenting that evidence and moving on. She put her case in slowly and deliberately, making it an ordeal for the jurors, who were sequestered and thus unable to live normal lives. Defense Attorney Johnnie Cochran realized that a seques-tered jury would appreciate it if he put on his case as quickly and directly as he could—in contrast to Clark, who sometimes had experts spend four to six hours presenting their credentials. As the case dragged on Clark became progressively more shrill and unlikable. I couldn't stand the woman, myself, and the jury couldn't, either.

Assistant Prosecutor Chris Darden made a huge error in asking O. J. Simpson to try on gloves left at the scene, which had stiffened and shrunk, allowing Simpson to pretend that the gloves didn't fit.

Prosecutors failed to call to the stand several witnesses who could have placed O. J. Simpson near the scene of the crime, but who had damaged their credibility as witnesses by attempting to profit from their story. They failed to fully vet Officer Mark Fuhrman, whose testimony they didn't desperately need, and whose racist history became a central focus of the trial. The prosecution made numerous large errors, and bears substantial responsibility for the failure to convict.

To the defense lawyers, 0%. The defense attorneys did what defense attorneys are supposed to do: they made it as difficult as possible to convict their client.

To the judge, Judge Lance Ito, about 35 to 45%. Ito started well, but lost control of the case. He allowed irrelevant issues to take center stage in the trial. He ruled that the issue of whether Mark Fuhrman had made racist comments at some point in the past was irrelevant and the testimony inadmissible—and then inexplicably allowed the defense attorneys to spend days talking about the matter and presenting witnesses and evidence about the matter. The entire issue had nothing to do with the case, and should never have been allowed to enter the trial.

There was a witness to the murder, an earwitness who heard O.J. shout "Hey!" three times about the time of the murder. The witness reportedly told police that, when he heard the voice, he thought it was O.J., but in the trial, he wasn't allowed to say that; he was allowed only to say that he thought it sounded like the voice of an African-American man. This led to a silly extended debate about whether the witness could recognize a black voice as opposed to a white voice. That issue should never have arisen; the witness should have been allowed to say what he had heard.

I don't think Ito's a bad guy; I think he's a very good guy, and a good judge. People make mistakes. I'm sure that if Ito could do it over again, he would never allow testimony about whether Mark Fuhrman had, at some point in his past, used the N-word. But he did, and he bears more responsibility for the failure of the trial than any other individual.

To the jury, about 2%. The jury was denied information about the case that was available to everybody else in the country—not irrelevant information, not prejudicial information, but valid and legitimate information to which they should have had access. They could have seen through the fog of distortions created by the defense better than they did, but it wasn't really their fault.

To the news media, about 10 to 15%. The media did intrude into the case in ways that were improper, making financial arrangements with witnesses that compromised their testimony. The extraordinary level of attention to the case distorted everything, making it impossible for things to be done in a normal fashion. Some witnesses seemed to be playing for the cameras; other witnesses seemed to be afraid of the cameras. Jurors had to be sequestered for months because everybody was talking about the case all the time, and this led to jurors having a peculiar perspective on the case. If the trial could be run again, it would have a better chance of finding justice if it could be run without being covered by hundreds of reporters.

O.J. is in jail now, where he belongs, and perhaps it doesn't matter for what, or anyway it doesn't matter to me. But the O. J. Simpson case re-ignited the Popular Crime industry. From then until now, people have been looking for the next really big case. I don't know if there will ever be another case as big.

XXXI

O ne of the things that will cause an everyday, run-of-the-mill crime to erupt into a media circus is fictional elements. Fictional elements are things that a fiction writer might put into a story to make it more interesting, but which commonly would not be a part of a real-life crime if you picked one at random. There are four types of elements that distinguish real from fictional crimes:

1) Careful planning. In real life most violent crimes involve little or no planning. An argument breaks out, somebody grabs a fireplace poker and, boom, there's a murder for you. In fiction, however, crimes are often meticulously planned, with alibis carefully established and false clues planted in advance to throw off the police. In real life these things rarely happen.

2) Wealthy and attractive participants, prominent in the community. In real life the people involved in crime stories tend to be poor, anonymous, and notably unattractive—not always, of course, but this is the tendency.

3) A twisting narrative, covering layers of deception. The story appears to be going in one direction, takes off in some other direction, and you discover that nothing was what it originally appeared to be. In real life most often people are exactly what they appear to be.

4) Bold characters. There are characters in real life every bit as rich and striking as those in fiction, but in fiction there are more of them.

The story of Lawrencia Bembenek, for example, is rife with fictional elements. An extremely attractive woman is accused of murder—a fictional element. Studies show that in real life only three-tenths of one percent of accused murderers are red-hot mamas, and these are often cases in which the public takes an interest.

Bembenek was not just *any* pretty woman; she was known to the Milwaukee community before she was accused of the crime. She was an ex-cop, suing the city for firing her and accusing members of the police force of miscellaneous wrongdoing, some of it related to sex. The crime of which she was accused was, in all probability, carefully planned, and evidence was almost certainly planted by other cops to implicate Bembenek. This doesn't happen a whole lot in real life. It happens in fiction.

She escaped from prison, and fled to Canada. Doesn't happen in most cases. She became the subject of an international incident when Canada refused to return her to American authorities. Books were written about her, and she appeared often on television to discuss her case. This is a very unusual case.

I would argue that there is no other case in American history, however, which has *so many* fictional elements as does the murder of Carol Neulander. There are six principal actors in the story of the murder of Carol Neulander—all of them bold characters:

The victim, Carol Neulander,

Her husband, Rabbi Fred Neulander,

His girlfriend, Philadelphia radio personality Elaine Soncini,

The murderer, Len Jenoff,

The murderer's accomplice, Paul Michael Daniels, and

Nancy Phillips, a *Philadelphia Inquirer* reporter who focused on Len Jenoff, and eventually persuaded him to tell his story.

Carol Neulander was beaten to death in her home in Cherry Hill, New Jersey, on November 1, 1994—about five months after the death of Nicole Simpson. Rabbi Neulander was a beacon to his community. He had established and led one of the largest Reformed congregations in New Jersey. He was widely regarded as a charismatic and devoted rabbi.

Carol Neulander, in addition to raising a family, had started a bakery, Classic Cakes, which had done very well. By the time of her death it was reported that she would sometimes carry home thousands of dollars in cash. It didn't take police a long time to discover that Rabbi Neulander had been involved with a number of his congregants in a manner not recommended by the Talmud. For almost two years his main squeeze had been Elaine Soncini. Ms. Soncini, a tall, cultured and attractive woman who had come to Rabbi Neulander for counseling after the death of her husband in December, 1992, had found comfort in Neulander's arms. The two had been carrying on a rather intense relationship, requiring seven-day-a-week trysts. The police found out about this, among other things, and focused their attention on the good Rabbi.

Let us back off, and try to see Fred Neulander as he was seen before all of this came to light. He was intelligent, and, more than intelligent, bright. He sparkled. He delivered a good sermon. He provided wise counsel. He had the habit of walking the room at Shabbat, putting his hands on the shoulders or arms of the worshippers and speaking directly to them. He was not a man who smiled and begged for acceptance; he was a warm, serious, dynamic and energetic rabbi who demanded and got respect from all who came into contact with him. He conveyed compassion at the deepest level. He managed the affairs of the temple with competence and dispatch. He was the kind of spiritual leader that everyone wants to find.

He had a weakness for the flesh, however, and the police focused not on his many successes but on his moral failings. The Rabbi was shocked to discover how easily the police could pull aside the curtains with which he had hidden these failings from his wife and congregation. They were aware of his philandering within hours of his wife's murder. The police invaded his temple with tape recorders and stenographer's notebooks.

Len Jenoff stood out from the congregation like a crocodile in a horse race. An alcoholic and a compulsive liar, Jenoff had lived a life of many failures. Nearing 50, he was living in a halfway house and, when he got out of there, running a private investigation service out of his bedroom. Coming to Rabbi Neulander for help, Jenoff had been embraced by Neulander and drawn into the community. After the murder Neulander hired Jenoff to investigate the case—the actual murderer, hired as a private eye to investigate the murder. A fictional plot twist. Neulander's explanation for this was, the police weren't doing anything, and he couldn't afford top-shelf investigators. The police were just focused on him; they weren't really doing anything to solve the crime. He paid Jenoff a little money to try to get something started.

Fred Neulander's indiscretions hit the front pages of the tabloids. He resigned his position, and lived for several years in the shadows of scandal and speculation. In 1998 he was indicted for arranging his wife's murder. That was 3½ years after the murder, and no co-conspirator had yet been identified. Another two years went by. He was scheduled to go on trial in June, 2000, and as of mid-April, 2000, prosecutors still didn't know who had actually committed the murder.

Nancy Phillips was nosing around the story for the *Philadelphia Inquirer*, trying to get cozy with Len Jenoff for purposes of pursuing the story, and Jenoff apparently became infatuated with her. I might have, too, had I been there; she was the kind of woman one wouldn't mind getting cozy with. Jenoff couldn't resist. He told her the story of the murder.

And what a story it was! It was a corker. Jenoff liked to pretend that he was a character out of a James Bond film, a secret agent for the CIA and such. He was, of course, a transparent poseur. Rabbi Neulander engaged him in deep philosophical discussions about the moral quandaries of his imaginary profession. "If the survival of the state of Israel depended on it, would you commit murder?" Neulander asked him.

"Absolutely," Jenoff responded.

Len Jenoff had not failed in life because he was stupid. He had failed in life because he was weak and immoral, insecure and immature. He was, within a narrow meaning of the word, quite intelligent. Over the weeks that followed, Neulander led Jenoff into an alternate reality populated by the enemies of the Israeli state, reminding him constantly of the dangerous world in which they lived, and of his promise to do whatever had to be done to protect Israel. At last he revealed to him the person who had to be killed, so that Israel could survive. It was . . .

Well, shit, you've figured that out by now; you're not stupid. Jenoff was living at the halfway house with a bunch of people who would scare the pants off of Jabba the Hutt's bodyguards. Jenoff picked out the scariest of these dudes, Paul Michael Daniels, and drew him into his murder plot. Interestingly enough, he didn't tell Daniels anything about this being a secret mission for the state of Israel. He just told him they were going to go to this house and murder this lady. Sure, said Daniels. Why not?

That's the version of the story Jenoff eventually told the jury. The version he first told Nancy Phillips, apparently in late 1999, was quite a bit different. Phillips by April, 2000, was in fear of her life, afraid that Jenoff, having confessed to her in private that he had murdered Carol Neulander, might be getting ready to wipe out the confession.

Nancy Phillips now begged Jenoff to tell his story to the police, and to testify against Neulander—and at the same time, while technically observing her deal with Jenoff to keep his confession private, directed the attention of the prosecutors toward Jenoff. In late April, 2000, Jenoff and Phillips had lunch, and Jenoff began talking in his maudlin, drunken way about the tremendous guilt he carried from the murder, and how near he was to suicide. She told him he would feel better if he confessed. "Why don't you do it right now," she said (wording not exact). "Why don't you let me arrange a meeting right now with the prosecutor who is preparing the case against Neulander?" Jenoff agreed. The prosecutor brought the cop who had been working the case for years, and Jenoff told them all his story—the prosecutor, the cop, and the reporter.

The Rabbi's trial was delayed by a year. He finally went before a judge late in 2001, seven years after the murder. His first trial resulted in a hung jury, and he was hauled back before the bar of justice one year later, in October, 2002. His second trial led to his conviction, and he was sentenced to life in prison.

Almost everyone in Fred Neulander's life has decided that he was guilty. His old girlfriend, Elaine Soncini, testified against him. His son, having finally concluded in 2001 that Neulander was guilty, testified, and called him "Fred" throughout the trial, refusing to grant him any respect. These people know him and I don't, and I do not doubt that they have a better read on the man than I do. If the people who once loved him now know him to be guilty, who am I to argue?

But the legal case against him, to my eyes were I on the jury, falls far short of "beyond a reasonable doubt"—in fact, I would almost argue that the case should have been dismissed for lack of evidence. The problem with the case, to my eyes, is that

1) There is very, very little that ties Fred Neulander into the plot to kill his wife, other than the testimony of Len Jenoff, and

2) It would be virtually impossible to find a less credible witness than Len Jenoff.

Jenoff's entire life has been directed by sick and puerile fantasies. He has lied to everyone he has ever known, about almost everything. He has acknowledged arranging and participating in the murder of Carol Neulander. If you composed a scale for credibility, it would run from George Washington to Len Jenoff.

It is my reading of crime cases that the greatest injustices often occur when prosecutors and juries ignore the independent indicia of credibility, and make a decision about who to believe based on their instincts about who is telling the truth. That is what happened in the case of Randy Adams, mistakenly convicted in 1975 of the murder of a Dallas policeman. That is what happens, in my view, in *most* cases where innocent people are convicted. Cops, prosecutors and juries decide that they know who is telling the truth; they can just tell.

Len Jenoff was very credible on the stand. He's a really, really good liar. He has 10,000 hours of experience as a liar. He's world-class. My attitude is: I don't care *how* convincing he is. You just don't believe what people like this tell you, unless it is supported by other evidence.

Well, what other evidence is there that Neulander was involved? I would say that the case against Fred Neulander can be reduced to ten statements of evidence:

1) That Jenoff said that he committed the crime at the behest of Neulander.

2) That Jenoff has little motive to commit the crime, whereas Neulander did have a motive for the crime.

3) That Neulander did direct some money to Jenoff after the crime.

4) That Neulander had been involved in numerous extra-marital affairs, which, as a spiritual leader, he needed to conceal.

5) That the Neulanders had an argument, in which divorce was discussed, 48 hours before the murder.

6) That Elaine Soncini reported that Neulander had said to her numerous times that "something would happen" that would allow them to be together openly before her 48th birthday, which was seven weeks after the murder.

7) That Neulander's behavior after his wife's death was inappropriate for the circumstances.

8) That Neulander took actions, at the time of the murder, designed to ensure that he was seen and noted by as many people as possible.

9) That one of Neulander's racquetball partners, a gangster named Peppy Levin, claimed that Neulander had spoken to him of his desire to come home some day and find his wife dead on the floor.

10) That Neulander's daughter relayed an incriminating remark, details to come.

I believe that's all there is, acknowledging that I am working from second-hand sources and might well have missed something. I would score this evidence at about 32 points, on a scale on which 100 points are necessary to convict. Taking these one at a time:

1) Len Jenoff said that he committed the crime at the behest of Neulander. I would score this at no more than four points, since nothing that

Jenoff says has any credibility—setting aside the fact that his narrative, in this case, is bizarre. Jenoff was the kind of guy who would go to an A.A. meeting, and, when given the chance to stand up, would talk about meeting with Ollie North and Ronald Reagan at the White House, and pitching the Iran/Contra project to them. His life was simply a long series of ridiculous stories. Nothing he says is meaningful evidence unless it is confirmed by other sources.

2) **Jenoff had little motive to commit the crime, whereas Neulander did have a motive for the crime.** I would score this at zero, since I simply don't think it is productive to get into speculation about unknown motives. Jenoff may have had a thousand reasons to commit the crime that we don't know anything about. One simply doesn't know what someone like Jenoff will do, or why he will do it. Carol Neulander carried cash—reportedly lots of cash—and people commit murders for which they have little apparent motive all the time.

3) **That Neulander did direct some money to Jenoff after the crime.** This certainly sounds like a damning fact, and I was at first inclined to score this one at about 25 points. But reading accounts of the case as closely as I can, I don't see the evidence—other than Jenoff's testimony, which means nothing—that Neulander paid Jenoff any meaningful amount of money. Jenoff sent bills to Neulander's attorneys for his work as a private investigator looking into the case, but the attorneys refused to pay them. Neulander sent Jenoff a couple of checks, years after the murder, totaling less than $1,000. Jenoff *claimed* that Neulander gave him $7500 in cash before the murder and $7,000 in an envelope afterward, but there appears to be no corroboration for this claim. No one can say where that money came from or where it went.

Jenoff and his accomplice/roommate, Paul Michael Daniels, had a third roommate at the halfway house. The third roommate testified that he saw no evidence of Jenoff or Daniels being flush with cash after the murder.

Jenoff's story is that Neulander conned him into committing the crime. Neulander's story is that Jenoff conned him into paying a little money for a phony investigation. I don't see that this is a mismatch. From my standpoint it seems entirely reasonable to believe that Jenoff conned Neulander out of a little bit of money, rather than that Neulander conned Jenoff into committing murder.

4) **That Neulander had been involved in numerous extra-marital affairs, which, as a spiritual leader, he needed to conceal.** This is certainly not a good thing for the defense. Neulander's philandering and his need to

conceal it, to me, lowers the burden of proof against him by some measure—let's say about 10 points. What's worse, Neulander made statements about this that are not believable. Neulander claimed that he and his wife had an open marriage, that they had both had affairs, and that Carol Neulander was aware of his infidelities. I don't believe it, and this makes everything else he says less believable. Let's say 12 points.

This issue is critical to the erosion of support for Neulander among those closest to him. By saying that Carol Neulander had also had affairs and that she had consented to his affairs, Neulander insulted his wife's memory, and deeply offended those who had once loved them both.

5) **That the Neulanders had an argument, in which divorce was discussed, 48 hours before the murder.** But if we believe the prosecution narrative, the murder by that time was long planned and near at hand. If Neulander knew that Carol was going to be dead in two days anyway, why would he argue with her? The normal practice would have been to just agree to whatever she said.

6) **That Neulander's girlfriend, Elaine Soncini, reported that Neulander had said to her numerous times that "something would happen" that would allow them to be together openly before her 48th birthday, which was seven weeks after the murder.** She was threatening to leave Neulander if he didn't leave his wife. Neulander said the sorts of things that cheating husbands say all the time; just hang in there with me, something will happen. I would fall apart if you left me. A few weeks before the murder he reportedly said to her that "I wish . . . I wish Carol was gone. Poof. She could just vanish, just like that. Maybe her car could just go into the river." To which Soncini had replied, "You had better not be thinking what I think you are thinking."

It's an ugly coincidence in the wake of the murder, but

1. We have already gigged Neulander for having affairs, and,

2. We can't convict him of murder simply because he was cheating on his wife.

We can appropriately consider it; it's not nearly enough by itself. The question is, how much *additional* weight do we give to these statements, beyond the already noted fact that Neulander—seeing Soncini virtually every day—obviously regarded his marriage as a nuisance?

Soncini was threatening to leave him—but Neulander was also involved with at least three other women. A man with four girlfriends does not murder his wife because one of them threatens to break it off. And—here's another fictional element for you—by the time the case went to trial, Soncini was married to one of the cops who had been assigned to investigate the crime. I would score Neulander's statements to Soncini at perhaps an additional ten points.

7) That Neulander's behavior after his wife's death was inappropriate for the circumstances. Neulander sat shiva in the room where his wife had been murdered, with bloodstains still visible on the floor (if you looked closely enough). This gave people the creeps, and it seemed very unusual. He was too genial during the shiva, too pleasant—even, at times, making jokes. The ambulance driver called to the house, who said that he had responded to thousands of situations with people in distress, and knew how people react in those circumstances, said that Neulander's actions were unlike anything he had ever seen. (Neulander's son, also an ambulance driver, said the same thing during the second trial—with devastating effect.)

But people do things, in moments of grief, that look odd or inappropriate to others. If your wife or your husband was murdered and the police suspected you of involvement in the crime, you would do something at the time of the funeral or in the days surrounding the funeral that the prosecutors would argue was inappropriate for the circumstances—absolutely and without question. One virtually never sees a case in which this claim is not made. It doesn't carry any weight with me unless it is genuinely unusual or incriminating, which I don't see that this is.

And further, I would argue that if the prosecution really had a case against Neulander, they wouldn't have been making a big deal out of how he sat shiva. The fact that they did make a big deal out of it undermines their credibility in my eyes.

8) That Neulander took actions, at the time of the murder, designed to ensure that he was seen and noted by as many people as possible. At about the time the murder occurred, Neulander barged in on choir practice at the synagogue to ask some questions of the cantor, which was not a normal practice for him, and wandered around the building being seen by everyone there. Prosecutors argued that Neulander had done this to establish his presence at the synagogue at the time the crime was committed.

But there are always unusual things that occur at about the time of a murder; it's just the nature of the murderin' bizness. I can't see that a rabbi interrupting choir practice is genuinely noteworthy or genuinely suspicious.

The action, if indeed Neulander did do this to establish a solid alibi, was *sui generis*, since he was certainly at the synagogue at the time of the crime, and *somebody* certainly could have verified this, even if he had stayed in his office. The whole business of the too-prominent alibi, again, is just an argument that prosecutors make whenever a person is accused of a crime. They're always going to argue either that the accused has no alibi or that he went out of his way to establish an alibi. I don't think it is worth more than maybe one point.

9) **The claim made by Peppy Levin,** that Neulander had spoken to him after at the racquetball court about wanting to come home and find his wife dead on the floor, is in my view bogus, and bears no weight. Levin was a con man, and, according to the testimony of his driver (brought in as a prosecution witness), closely tied to the mob. There was no context for it; it just came up out of the blue—and the story emerged when Levin was under threat of indictment. Whether Neulander is guilty or innocent, I don't believe that this conversation ever happened.

10) **Neulander's daughter relayed an incriminating remark.** Jenoff had come to the Neulander house a week earlier, saying that he had a letter to leave for Fred Neulander. He intended to commit the murder at that time, but backed out. At the time of the earlier visit Carol Neulander had been on the phone with her daughter, and the daughter reported that Carol said that Fred had told her to expect the delivery of this letter . . . get that, the daughter said that Carol said that Fred said. The defense argued that this was hearsay, which I don't care whether it was or not; I'm not a lawyer, and I don't believe in those rules. When Jenoff came back a week later, Carol was once again on the phone with her daughter, and reported that the same man had returned. She was murdered moments later.

If Carol Neulander did indeed say that Fred had told her to expect the delivery of this letter, that ties Fred Neulander into the conspiracy to murder his wife. The problem with this is . . . well, it's tenuous. A phone conversation is remembered from a week earlier; what *exactly* was said?

I score it at about 5 points—5% of what is necessary to convince me that Neulander was involved in the conspiracy—and maybe that's low. But it's the kind of thing, a word out of place has huge consequences. Did Carol Neulander tell her daughter that "Dad told me to expect this letter," or "He says Dad is expecting this letter," or "He says Dad should have told me to expect this letter," or "Dad is expecting this letter" or "I guess Dad is expecting this letter." Even if Carol Neulander said, "Dad told me to expect a letter," that doesn't mean it's the same letter.

Neulander's daughter apparently didn't decide that he was guilty until years after the fact. She testified in his trial about this statement seven years after the fact. It seems to me that if this was a clear-cut incriminating statement, she would have turned on him years earlier. I'd be very reluctant to find somebody guilty of murder based on the memory, weeks or years later, of the exact wording of a telephone conversation, about an incident that seemed trivial until a week had passed.

Getting back to point one, which is the massive unreliability of Len Jenoff. Jenoff told his story to Nancy Phillips under a specific deal that she would not print it or report it to police—which gave Jenoff a pass to engage in his usual, and endless, self-aggrandizing bullshit. But later, as his third marriage was breaking up, as he was drifting back into drinking heavily, and as the gorgeous Ms. Phillips pressured him to confess to the police, he found himself finally agreeing to do so.

But did he do so because he was, for the first time in his life, telling the truth? Or did he do so because, if he didn't, he would be revealed to Ms. Phillips to be a fraud—not a man conned into murder by a clever rabbi, but a man who had committed a cold-blooded murder to steal a little bit of money? I don't know—but I think that, on the surface of it, the second explanation works better than the first. Jenoff's options in life were pathetic—and, by saying that he committed the murder at the behest of the rabbi, he was reducing his own culpability both in the eyes of the law and in the eyes of others, including Ms. Phillips, with whom he was infatuated. He was given a shorter sentence in exchange for his testimony against Neulander. A jailhouse snitch testified for the defense that Jenoff bragged in prison about framing Neulander.

The book about the Neulander case, *The Rabbi and the Hit Man* (Arthur J. Magida, HarperCollins, 2003), is OK. (There is a second book, *Broken Vows*, that I have not read.) Magida's research is good; his writing is decent. He makes a complicated story easy to understand. I have the sense that, on some level, he doesn't catch what is remarkable about his story, and I think he damages his book by being too certain that Neulander is guilty. He gets dragged into other people's research about philandering clergymen. Who cares? Philandering clergymen are unremarkable, and the phenomenon does not call for extended analysis. It's not what makes this story stand out.

This is Magida's description of the meeting at which Jenoff told the story of the murder, in a back booth of a restaurant with a reporter present, six years after the murder:

> The entire situation was so unorthodox—a guy coming forward on his own, six years after the fact, gulping down coffee and puffing his way through half a pack of cigarettes in a family restaurant on a Friday afternoon—that (the district attorney) just kept thinking, "Holy shit! Holy shit!" There was no interrogation, no pressure. In some ways it was too easy.

Yeah, that's what I'm thinking. The world's biggest liar had had six years to work up the story he would tell—and it wasn't quite right yet. Jenoff claimed then that he didn't realize he was killing the Rabbi's wife until he heard it on the radio the next day. He had thought he was killing an anti-Israeli terrorist. Yeah, right. He claimed that he took several thousand dollars from Carol Neulander's purse, and dumped it in a trash bin. Sure you did, Len.

Neulander testified in his own defense at his first trial, but came off badly. Neulander was supposed to be warm and charismatic. No one is warm and charismatic under hostile cross-examination, and Neulander came across as cold and shifty. Seven years of disgrace had corroded the dynamic personality that Neulander had once had. The jury didn't like him, and the decision was made that he should not testify at the second trial.

Elaine Soncini testified again. With an extra year, she was able to remember a couple more devastatingly incriminating remarks that she had forgotten for the first seven years after the murder. Everyone had moved on. Soncini was married. Neulander had found a new girlfriend. His new girlfriend was Ms. Vicki—the same Miss Vicki who had married Tiny Tim on *The Tonight Show* in 1969. Those of you who are old enough will remember it.

A year after the Neulander murder, a very similar murder occurred five miles away, in Voorhees, New Jersey. A woman named Janice Bell was stabbed to death in her home. Her husband came home to find her lying in a pool of blood. He became the chief suspect. Len Jenoff approached the family, offering to investigate the case for a reasonable fee. The Bell family hired him.

A prisoner who was incarcerated with Jenoff claimed that Jenoff told him that he had also murdered Janice Bell. Neulander's jury was not allowed to hear this testimony.

Again, I am not arguing that Neulander is innocent. I am arguing that the case against him is not convincing. I believe that the Neulander case, over time, is likely to become much more famous than it is now, and I believe this for two reasons. First, the case of the Neulanders, containing as it does a very large number of fictional elements, will stand up to repeated re-tellings in various venues, and is likely to have these. And second, the guilt of Fred Neulander becomes less clear as one gets more perspective on the crime. The people who knew him and loved him are convinced that he is guilty, because he betrayed their trust. The actual evidence against him, apart from this betrayal, is thin and unreliable. I think that, over time, he may develop a cadre of supporters.

One final point about the Neulander case. The prosecutor, Jack Lynch, cross-examined Neulander in a very aggressive manner—yelling at him, interrupting him before he could finish his answers, insulting him, confounding him with angles on questions that he could not reasonably react to in the rapid-fire pressure of the cross-examination. The judge, Linda Baxter, allowed this to happen.

I would argue that it was improper—and further, that at some point in the future, the Supreme Court will rule that allowing such cross-examination is improper. The judge should have said, in my view, that Mr. Neulander was not to be interrupted, not to be yelled at, and not to be intimidated. These practices have no proper place in a court of law. A courtroom is supposed to be an organized, thoughtful and unemotional search for the truth. It is not a place for bullying and emotional badinage. It is not the prerogative of the lawyers in a courtroom to beat up on the non-lawyers. When Lynch stepped over the line, Baxter should have torn him a new one—in full view of the jury. At some point in the future, the Supreme Court is going to throw out a conviction because a judge allowed this to happen. And at some point in the future, we're going to look back on this practice and cringe, just as we do when we look back on surprise testimony, all-white juries, all-male judiciary, flashbulbs going off during the trial, the names of jurors being printed in the newspapers, and 200 other discredited trial practices of the past.

(Late note: Len Jenoff now says that Neulander had nothing to do with the murder, which was simply a robbery that went awry.)

XXXII

JonBenet Ramsey and Mary Phagan are both buried in Marietta, Georgia, albeit in different cemeteries. At 5:52 AM on December 26, 1996, police in Boulder, Colorado, received a 911 call from Patsy Ramsey, who lived at 755 15th Street. Mrs. Ramsey had discovered a three-page ransom note, addressed to her husband, claiming that "We have your daughter," and demanding a ransom of $118,000. Her six-year-old daughter was missing from her bed.

The first policeman on the scene, Rick French, arrived within minutes, and quickly searched the house. Although the ransom note threatened that the girl would be beheaded if anyone was alerted about the crime, John and Patsy Ramsey immediately began to phone friends, gathering a support circle around themselves. By 8:10 (when Detective Linda Arndt arrived on the scene), Ramsey had arranged to pick up the $118,000 from the bank, and more than a dozen people were in the house—the Ramseys, four friends, two victim advocates, the Ramseys' minister, and a shifting and uncertain number of police officers.

John Ramsey was the wealthy head of a Boulder computer graphics firm, Access Graphics. Patsy Ramsey was a former Miss West Virginia, and Jon-Benet, active in the little-girl beauty pageant scene, had also won several trophies as a beautiful little girl. The family (parents, JonBenet and a son) lived in a large house, and kept another large house for summers in Michigan. Mr. Ramsey had a son and a daughter from an earlier marriage, and had lost another daughter to a traffic accident. The Ramseys had gotten up early that morning to fly to Michigan on a private plane.

The FBI arrived about 10:30 AM, setting up a wiretap and recording equipment, then retreating to a nearby command center. Phone calls came from various people, but nothing was heard from the kidnappers. The house became more and more chaotic; friends of the Ramseys came and went, police came and went. No one took charge of the case, and no one secured the scene. Police went to lunch, leaving Detective Arndt, alone, supervising a dozen or so adults in the house. Several times she called her office, requesting backup. No help arrived.

A little before 1:00, Ms. Arndt suggested to John Ramsey and one of his friends, Fleet White, that they should search the house "top to bottom," looking for evidence, looking for anything out of place. She was to say later that she was mainly concerned with keeping Ramsey occupied, keeping him from falling apart. In a matter of minutes, however, Ramsey yelled from the basement, and carried JonBenet's body up the stairs.

JonBenet was quite dead, although Ramsey seemed not to register this at first. She had been loosely tied up, her mouth had been taped shut, and a garrote had been fastened around her neck. Her body had been wrapped in a blanket. She had been dead for several hours.

Suppose that you heard about a juggler who had accidentally cut off his hand while juggling six sharp swords. You would have to conclude that he was actually a pretty good juggler; he just wasn't quite as good as he thought he was. The same should be said of the Boulder, Colorado, police department: it was actually a very good police department. They just weren't quite as good as they thought they were.

The likelihood that you will mishandle a challenge increases with the uniqueness of the challenge. If, on Monday morning, you are presented with a problem that is like the problems you deal with every day, it is likely that you will meet the challenge. If, on the other hand, you are presented with an issue that is different from what you normally deal with, then it becomes more likely that the task will give you headaches.

Without warning and with their resources depleted by vacation schedules, the Boulder police department was confronted with what I believe to be the most unusual crime scene in American history. They made an absolutely fantastic mess of it. Not since the Hall-Mills case in 1922 has a high-profile murder case been so badly investigated.

Of course, there is no way to quantify to what extent a crime scene is unusual or to what extent an investigation is scrambled, therefore no way to prove that these statements are true or false. That's how I can get by with making these outrageous claims. But the basic fact of the case is very unusual, the basic fact being that a little rich girl was found brutally and mysteriously murdered inside her large and beautiful home. There are 15,000 homicides a year in America, of which, in a typical year, approximately zero will be little rich kids found mysteriously murdered inside their homes.

In addition, there are several extremely unusual features of the murder scene:

1) We have a body and a ransom note both left at the scene of the crime,

2) We have the longest ransom note in the history of kidnapping (374 words),

3) We have multiple causes of death—ligature strangulation *and* a blow to the head, and

4) We have a demand for $118,000 in ransom—an unusual amount of money to begin with, and an almost trivial amount of money, given the wealth of the family.

Given this unusual premise, the story of the Ramsey investigation then took a number of remarkable turns.

1) The on-scene investigation, in the hours after the crime, made a stupefying number of very basic mistakes.

2) The continuing investigation, in the weeks and months after the crime, was, if this is possible, worse.

3) John Ramsey used his personal wealth to build a private investigation, attempting to wrest control of the investigation away from police and direct it away from the Ramseys.

4) The tabloid press invaded Boulder in overwhelming numbers, creating extraordinary pressures on the investigation.

5) Simmering animosities between Boulder police and prosecutors boiled over under the pressure into an all-out public feud, the likes of which has probably never been seen in this country.

6) The Boulder command structure, from the city manager to the street cop, crumbled and collapsed under the pressure into a group of warring clans.

Taking those one at a time:

1) The on-scene investigation, in the hours after the crime, made a stupefying number of very basic mistakes. Detective Steve Thomas, in his insider's account of the case, spends several pages laying out in rapid-fire succession a long list of mistakes made by the first responders.

At the time of the Hall-Mills murders the New Brunswick police failed to secure the crime scene, allowing journalists and curiosity seekers to trash the scene, but in 1922 the practice of securing a crime scene was not well established. While the idea of preserving the crime scene was developed, I believe, in the 1880s, it often takes many years for professional practices to spread throughout the culture, and by 1922 that practice was far from mature. In 1922 most policemen had no formal training, and many police departments had no action plans requiring that a crime scene be immediately secured. One can understand, to an extent, the failure to secure the Hall-Mills murder scene.

But by 1996 every policeman had grown up in a culture in which securing the crime scene was basic background information. Every police worker, by 1996, had had "securing the crime scene" drummed into him from Day One of his police cadet training—and yet the first responders acted as if they had no idea of this being a crime scene, and it had never occurred to them that they might need to take control of it. This is inexplicable.

At the same time, one might fail to secure a crime scene 100 times, and 95 times there might be limited consequences to the failure. But in this case— and again, this is quite unusual—in this case Patsy Ramsey had begun calling friends as soon as she got off the phone with the police, so that the house was full of people within an hour. The police made a very large number of mistakes in the first hours of the case—*and they didn't get by with any of them.*

It was the Ramseys' own actions—calling friends to the scene of the crime—that initially caused the investigation to run off track. Patsy did this because that was what she did; that was who she was. She was a drama queen. When she had an emotional trial, she automatically invited her friends in to help her through it. It's not what I would do; it's probably not what you would do. It's the way she was.

What the police *should* have done, finding friends, ministers and others gathering at the crime scene, was to get their attention and announce loudly, "You people have to get out of here. This is a crime scene, and I am a police officer, and this is a direct order. Grab your coats and get out of this house right now. I am not negotiating with you and I don't care how you feel about it. Get out."

Instead, what they did is, they invited more people to come over! They called the "victims' advocate" division, and requested victims' advocates to come to the house—which was totally unnecessary, since the Ramseys had already gathered their own support group. This was merely the first of the series of blunders that destroyed the crime scene before basic facts were established.

2) The continuing investigation, in the weeks and months after the crime, was, if this is possible, worse. The man in charge of the case, John Eller, had never before been in charge of a homicide investigation. Eller was given the opportunity to pick and choose whomever he wanted to form an elite investigative unit, and, after some early struggles, he wound up with a squad of six detectives who were fiercely loyal to him, but most or all of whom were young, inexperienced detectives who had never been within ten miles of a serious homicide investigation.

In the early days of the investigation Eller and his boss, Tom Koby, were approached by many other police services—the sheriff's office, the FBI, and Denver homicide, among others—offering to help. They turned them all away, and insisted on investigating the case with their hand-picked team. Like the man juggling six swords, they were certain they could handle it.

One of those detectives quit the investigation after about twenty months, and wrote a book attempting to place the blame for the failures of the case on the shoulders of the District Attorney's office and on Chief of Police Koby. What that book clearly demonstrates, contrary to the intentions of its author, is that the investigation was staffed by people who had absolutely no concept of what they were doing.

3) John Ramsey used his personal wealth to build a private investigation, attempting to wrest control of the investigation away from police and direct it away from the Ramseys. Ramsey—the CEO of a company with sales of a hundred million dollars a month—was entirely knocked off his feet by the crime, reduced for several weeks to something near the level of a babbling idiot. His friends and advisors closed ranks around him, and—with his permission, but with minimal participation from him—hired teams of private investigators, squads of the most expensive lawyers, and also consultants of every stripe—profilers, forensic analysts, and spokesmen.

This backfired on the Ramseys in the worst possible way. The harder the Ramseys worked to force the attention of the investigators away from themselves, the harder the police worked to force the attention of the investigation back on them. This became a battle of wills, during which the police essentially failed to notice that the actions they were alleging on the part of the Ramseys were fairly preposterous.

4) The tabloid press invaded Boulder in overwhelming numbers, cre-

ating extraordinary pressures on the investigation. The case developed immediately into a tabloid sensation, but was ratcheted up to another level in the following weeks by two events:

a) Video emerged of JonBenet singing and dancing in child beauty pageants, and

b) The Ramseys unwisely decided to do an interview with CNN.

There had been cases before which had received as much attention as the Ramsey murder—not many of them, but there had been some. The O. J. Simpson case received even more media coverage, but that was in LA. Los Angeles could absorb the media; they were used to it. The people of Boulder were caught off-guard by the invasion, and were utterly unprepared to deal with it.

5) Simmering animosities between Boulder police and prosecutors boiled over into an all-out public feud.

The Boulder District Attorney at the time of the crime was Alex Hunter, a liberal and progressive D.A. who had held office for almost a quarter-century before the crime, and who would represent the one power center to emerge from the debacle largely unscathed.

The Chief of Police, Tom Koby, was also a positive and progressive newage cop, who led his department with a light touch and a gentle hand. Koby's motto, which he had framed and distributed to his department heads, was "Police unto others as you would have others police unto you." His outgoing phone message talked about it being a lovely day in Boulder, and expressed the hope that it was a lovely day where you were, too.

The head of Koby's homicide investigation unit was John Eller, an old-line, up-from-the-bottom cop, suspicious of the FBI, paranoid about the media, and inclined to distrust people who got too much edjacashun and thought they had the world all figgered out. This is surely an unfair description of Eller, for which I apologize, but Eller is the person most responsible for making the investigation an unmitigated disaster, and he doesn't come off well in the books about the case.

One of Eller's investigators was a detective, Steve Thomas, who would eventually become the public face of the investigation. Koby, Eller and Thomas would be among the many whose careers were derailed by the investigation.

Alex Hunter, District Attorney.

Tom Koby, Chief of Police.

John Eller, head of the investigation.

Steve Thomas, a cop on the investigative team.

As the case began, Koby and Hunter were good friends, the progressive D.A. and the progressive cop. Koby probably respected Eller, or at least treated him with respect. Detective Thomas referred to Koby and Hunter (and their coterie) as "the beads and sandal types," and said that the beads and sandal crowd were in command positions. Eller and those below him did not particularly like Koby and actively disliked Hunter, but it is common for people to have some emotional distance from their superiors, and Eller and Thomas and those like them accepted Koby and got along with him well enough.

As the pressures of the case heated up, Eller became aggressively paranoid about leaks of the case evidence, and this led him into endlessly escalating confrontations with those above him. When tensions between police and prosecutors seemed in danger of getting out of control, a joint war room was set up to which the two sides would both have access. The prosecutors were soon locked out of the war room, and were publicly accused of leaking critical information about the investigation (of which they were almost certainly guilty, except that the information leaked was nowhere near as critical as Eller and Thomas thought it was. And many of the leaks came from those *below* Eller, rather than those above him). Eventually police and prosecutors were ripping one another limb from limb in the newspapers and in magazine articles. The prosecutors hired their own outside investigators. The police responded by bringing in their own outside attorneys. Police called publicly for prosecutors who had leaked information to be arrested.

The feud between police and prosecutors burned through a long series of efforts to control it. Hunter and Koby would constantly say, "We've got to get a handle on this," and would arrange some new and yet more visible show of mutual support—which would be followed, within days or hours, by yet more irresponsible actions on the part of Commander Eller, ratcheting the war up to a yet-more-unimaginable level of hostility.

6) **The Boulder command structure, from the city manager to the street cop, crumbled and collapsed into a group of warring clans.**

Eller fired one of his top assistants, who threatened to sue the department and was paid damages not to sue. Koby concluded that Eller had lied to him about the firing, and forced Eller to retire. Eller and Koby blamed one another for turning away the help that had been offered them at the beginning of the case. Koby was given a vote of no confidence by the police department's rank and file, and was forced to resign. Koby and Hunter's friendship was strained and probably destroyed. The city manager was forced to resign. Many cops left the department in disgust, and there were numerous lawsuits about the conditions under which they had left. Linda Arndt, who had been "in charge" of the crime scene, wound up suing the department.

The Hall-Mills case, 1922–1928, had also degenerated into ugly factionalism pitting police against prosecutors. However, the all-out, all-in warfare of the Ramsey case is, to the best of my knowledge, unprecedented in American history.

My greatest fear, in writing this book, is that I will be unable to convince you that John and Patsy Ramsey had nothing to do with the death of their daughter. The Ramseys, having suffered a horrendous loss, then became the victims of a fantastically botched investigation which spent several years pointing fingers at them, and of public scorn, condemnation and ridicule stemming from that. I feel a responsibility to do what I can to clear their names, and I fear that I will be unequal to the challenge. I will do my best.

Let me begin by re-tracing for you the route by which I realized that the Ramseys were innocent. Nothing about my theory of this case is new or unique to me. I am advocating a position here and explaining how I came to accept that interpretation, but I didn't invent any of this.

Like most people who followed the case only in passing in its first year, I assumed that the Ramseys were most likely guilty. Once books about the case began to appear and I started to read and study those books, I became hopelessly confused about what might have happened. One of the theories about the case is that JonBenet's involvement in child beauty pageants may have made her a target for a pedophile. "OK," I thought. "Let's read the ransom note carefully, and see what it reveals about the writer's knowledge of beauty pageants."

The ransom note contains no reference whatsoever to the world of beauty pageants, but this was not what struck me. Reading the letter carefully with that question in mind, I was stunned to note that the ransom letter actually contains no reference to JonBenet Ramsey whatsoever. It does not mention her name. It does not mention her age. It does not mention, discuss, suggest or refer to her in any way as a beautiful little girl, a cute little girl . . . nothing.

The letter is a diatribe directed at John Ramsey, JonBenet's father, and it contains some information about him. All it really says about JonBenet is "your daughter." The impression one gets, in reading the note carefully, is that the author of the note really didn't *know* anything about JonBenet. He knew that John Ramsey had a little girl, and . . . that was it.

The police theory of the case was that Patsy Ramsey, having accidentally killed JonBenet or participated in her killing, had written the ransom note as part of staging the crime scene. But if that was true, it struck me as quite extraordinary that she had, in the hours after the death of her little girl, apparently suppressed all awareness of her. Yes, murderers do tend to "de-personalize" their victims, but when a parent loses a small child, that child becomes the all-consuming center of their consciousness. Many parents accidentally kill their children and try to cover it up. But ordinarily, those parents can't *stop* talking about the dead child, can't stop weeping about her, can't stop going on and on about what a wonderful child he or she was. Patsy Ramsey's ransom note—if it was hers—had not only limited the significance of the murdered child, but had virtually eliminated any awareness of her.

Does this mean that Patsy Ramsey is innocent? No, of course not; it simply struck me as extraordinarily odd—as many things about the case do.

My next step toward understanding came when it was pointed out to me that the ransom note contains numerous allusions to a certain type of movie. There is a genre of "action" movies in which a villain captures a child, several children or other innocent victims and uses the captives as pawns to gain power over their parents, the police or the community. There are people who believe that the ransom note contains references to several of these movies. I believe this theory may have been created or popularized by the internet writer Jameson.

The murderer of JonBenet Ramsey, so goes this theory, was a person who watched those movies, probably repeatedly, but identified not with the heroic men of action who rescue the children, but with the villains gaining power by seizing control of the innocents. Feeling victimized by his life, he had fantasized about becoming a powerful criminal genius, and was acting out his fantasy at the time that he wrote the note.

When I first heard this theory I thought, as you probably did, "yeah, yeah . . . right. I'll believe that when I see it." But when you follow it through, the movie references are there, and *some* of them are vague and open to interpretation, and some of them are fairly clear.

The police theory of the case, then, was (apparently) that Patsy Ramsey, within two hours of witnessing or causing the brutal death of her young daughter, had sat down and created this "persona," this "imaginary speaker" who was addicted to these type of movies, and who expressed himself in the language of the criminal masterminds of these movies, directing his anger at John Ramsey as these malefactors had addressed it at their targets. With all due respect, that's ridiculous. To create a persona like that, and write from the psychic perspective of that persona, would be the act of a literary genius, re-working his (or her) material through generations of edits. It is not the act of a panic-stricken beauty queen, scrawling on a legal pad in the middle of the night.

Again, does this *prove* that the Ramseys are innocent? Well, no, I suppose it doesn't. There are a lot of things here that I don't understand. It is unlikely that Patsy Ramsey had ever *seen* any of those movies; they're not marketed to middle-aged couples with children. Still, we have to respect the possibilities that lie within the vast realm of what we don't understand, and I suppose it is *possible,* somehow, that Patsy Ramsey could have found that place in her soul where this imaginary person lived, or it is possible that the references to five or six movies of this type are just a weird coincidence.

Third stage of the realization. To believe that the Ramseys were guilty of this crime, you have to believe simultaneously that they were fantastically stupid, and that they were fantastically brilliant. They were not one of these things or the other; they were both.

If you were John and Patsy Ramsey, and you accidentally killed your daughter, and you then decided to try to get by with it, what would you do?

Within a mile of their house were snow-covered mountains. What you would do, if you were even moderately composed, would be to take the body out somewhere to the snow-covered mountains, and dispose of the body in such a way that it wouldn't be found for months, if ever. You would return to the house, you would clean up everything that could possibly be cleaned up, and then you would tell the police that you had absolutely no idea what had happened. You woke up in the morning and a door was wide open and JonBenet was gone.

What you quite certainly would not do, unless you wanted to spend the rest of your life in prison, would be to write a long, rambling phony ransom note, every penstroke of which would become evidence against you. You wouldn't tie the body up, in some bizarre way, with duct tape and rope, because, again, this would be manufacturing evidence against you. You certainly would not put the body in the basement, call the police and invite them to search the house.

And yet, in the theory of the police, the Ramseys were such fantastically accomplished criminal masterminds that they were able to do everything wrong—and yet escape prosecution because they had left the police with essentially no evidence whatsoever!

In my view, it is not all that easy to commit a murder and get by with it. To commit a murder *in which one is the obvious first suspect* and leave no evidence to hang yourself . . . it's damned near impossible. A fingerprint on the duct tape, a drop of blood on your nightgown, a hair, a shred from your coat . . . you're always going to leave *something*.

The crime scene was a virtual riot of clues. The police had rope (or cord), duct tape, a garrote, a footprint, a palm print, a long letter, the note pad on which the letter was written, the marks of a stun gun, a pubic hair, an unidentifiable teddy bear, DNA under JonBenet's fingernails, the same DNA in her underpants, and the same unidentified DNA on the back of her long johns, where a person would normally put their hand to pull them off. The problem is, none of this evidence points toward the Ramseys, except (to an extent) the handwriting of the letter. What "points" to the Ramseys is a lot of generic crap like a bowl of pineapple, which the police want to spin as evidence, but which doesn't give the appearance of evidence on an intuitive level.

Once again . . . is this proof that the Ramseys are innocent? No, I suppose it isn't. I suppose it is conceivable, barely, that the Ramseys could have been both stupid enough to leave so much evidence and clever enough to avoid leaving evidence that could incriminate them. I suppose.

Argument four. The police liked to point out that, when a child is murdered inside his or her home, it is almost always a relative or close associate who has committed the crime. The number we read is 92%.

Yes, that's true. And it is also true that, in virtually 100% of those cases, there is a long history of child abuse before the crime is committed. *Usually,* when a child is beaten to death by the parents, there have been prior accusations of child abuse against the parents, before the fatal event. Sometimes there is no such criminal record before the murder—but in essentially all such cases, prior child abuse can be later documented.

The extent of the abuse of JonBenet on the night of her murder is off the charts. A young child was carried to the basement of her house, sexually assaulted, bound with duct tape, garroted, and hit over the head hard enough to crush her skull. More severe abuse is difficult to imagine. But not only is there *no* documented history of abuse in the Ramsey family, but it is extremely clear that they had never been abusive to their children, at any level. The Ramseys' life has been subjected to quite extraordinary levels of scrutiny by the police and by the press. It is very clear that, other than the allegations about JonBenet, they never abused any of their children to any extent whatsoever.

Is it conceivable that the Ramseys suddenly transformed from loving, supportive parents into off-the-charts psychotic abusers, and then presented themselves as sane and reasonably normal people some hours later?

Well . . . no; it's not conceivable. The *belief* that such a thing is possible rests upon a pervasive cynicism, founded on the statement that "you never know what goes on within the privacy of the home." Decent, upstanding, church-going, high-earning, high-functioning husbands beat their wives and dress up like harlots and molest their children; happens all the time. Ministers and rabbis have affairs and murder their wives, and sweet-faced little old ladies poison their husbands and have carnal adventures with motorcycle gangs; this stuff happens all the time.

Well, I've read a thousand crime books, and I have never, ever heard of people even remotely like the Ramseys committing any crime remotely like this. Yes, apparently upstanding people do commit horrible crimes sometimes—but

a) the vast majority of murders are committed by persons routinely involved in criminal activity, and

b) when *apparently* upstanding people commit murder, there is virtually always a hidden side to their lives which is exposed after the fact.

Show me the case, anywhere in the history of the world, where people like this committed a crime like this. I simply don't believe that it has ever happened.

Well then, what *did* happen? In the four books that I have read about the case, there are three theories advanced. The four books are:

Perfect Murder, Perfect Town, by Lawrence Schiller,

The Death of Innocence, by John and Patsy Ramsey,

JonBenet, by ex-Detective Steve Thomas, and

Who Killed JonBenet Ramsey?, by Charles Bosworth and Cyril Wecht.

There are also numerous books about the case that I have not read, and there are some that I actually don't believe anybody has ever read. Of the four books on which I rely, the Schiller book is easily the best. Although written quickly in the months after the murder, the book is exhaustively researched and impeccably balanced, without going to the extreme of trying to pretend that John Eller knows what he is doing.

John and Patsy's book is unremarkable, and will not convince you that the Ramseys are innocent. It advances the theory that JonBenet was killed by an intruder, and gives the Ramseys' slant on the many controversies that complicate the case.

JonBenet, by ex-Detective Thomas, attempts to convince the reader that Patsy Ramsey killed JonBenet and John Ramsey conspired to cover it up. The book is well worth reading, essentially because it exposes the investigation as a naked emperor. Detective Thomas makes argument after argument about the Ramseys' guilt—all of them palpably false, and most of them ludicrous. At some point the reader realizes that the police investigating the murder simply have no case, but have so convinced themselves of the Ramseys' guilt that they will interpret *anything* as being evidence against them.

The theory that JonBenet was killed by her parents is really two separate and incompatible theories: 1) that JonBenet was killed by the Ramseys in a deliberate and pre-planned act, and 2) that JonBenet was accidentally killed by the Ramseys, who then staged the crime scene.

That JonBenet was killed by her parents in a pre-planned murder is utterly irrational, and no one believes this, including Detective Thomas, who explicitly states that he believes in the other option. Yet having said this, the good Detective then attempts, not once but many times, to sneak into his shopping cart what can only be interpreted as evidence of pre-planning.

To begin with the most ridiculous example . . . the duct tape. The black duct tape found on JonBenet's mouth was not found anywhere else in the Ramsey house, despite an exhaustive search for it. The obvious conclusion is that the tape was brought into the house and carried out of the house by the murderer.

Detective Thomas can't find any evidence that the Ramseys had ever owned, used, or touched this type of black duct tape on any other occasion. He can, however, show that the duct tape was sold at a local store. He can find evidence that the Ramseys shopped at that store (as did everyone else in Boulder). He can find a receipt showing that Patsy Ramsey, several weeks before the crime, bought something at that store for $1.99, and that this store sold the duct tape for $1.99.

The problem is, the $1.99 item purchased by Patsy Ramsey several weeks before the crime could be duct tape, light bulbs, Scotch tape, an extension cord, drain cleaner, scouring pads, pliers, a houseplant, a Christmas knick-knack, or any of hundreds of other items. Not only that, but the store also sold the same duct tape in different sizes at several other prices. That means that, had Patsy Ramsey purchased something at the store for $1.19 or $4.79, that also, in Detective Thomas' mind, could have been taken as evidence that she had purchased the black duct tape. By Thomas' logic, 100% of the people who shopped at that store—which was everyone in Boulder—could be shown to have perhaps purchased a roll of black duct tape. It was evidence against *everybody*.

The information about the duct tape has no value toward incriminating the Ramseys, and yet Detective Thomas returns to it over and over, ranting about the failure of the District Attorney's office to take this "evidence" seriously, and there is some similar nonsense about nylon cord that could also have been purchased at the same store. Or some other store. Page 179:

> Among the dossiers we found . . . were the very things the DA had been blocking us from obtaining: the Ramseys' long-distance telephone and item-ized credit card records . . . I walked around for days thinking of what I had seen on those records from hardware stores and marine supply outlets in var-ious states. Such places sell duct tape and cord like that used in the murder.

The Ramseys shopped at some store that sold duct tape? Wow; what a revelation. But I have not yet touched on the central absurdity of the Detective's argument, which is: that were it grounded in something other than speculation, this would be evidence of careful pre-planning, weeks before the event, of a crime that Detective Thomas explicitly concedes was not pre-planned. And, not to be unkind, but anyone who believes that this is "evidence" has no business being involved in a homicide investigation.

A Vassar Shakespeare professor, trying to establish a field of knowledge we might call forensic textual analysis, wrote a letter to Patsy Ramsey early on in the case stating that, as a result of studying the language of the note, "I know you are innocent—know it absolutely and unequivocally. I will stake my professional reputation on it." Later on the professor was able to push his way into the case, convincing first Alex Hunter and later the cops that he knew what he was doing. The police met with the professor, and brought him over to their way of seeing things. The professor then wrote a 100-page report concluding that Patsy Ramsey clearly *did* write the note, and offering to testify under oath that she had.

Once Hunter learned of the earlier communication, of course, he immediately dismissed the professor. Obviously, in view of the earlier comments, the professor could not testify against the Ramseys. And, again not wishing to be unkind, but anyone who has any difficulty understanding why this is true is not a homicide detective.

Thomas' statement about this—I swear I am not making this up—is "To me, that only strengthened his position, not weakened it, for it showed he had no anti-Ramsey bias. Once the professor had access to the actual case documents, he changed his mind." Page 284 in Thomas' book; I swear he said that.

Almost every page of Detective Thomas' book contains these kind of inane allegations of "evidence." Patsy Ramsey wore a red sweater to Christmas celebrations the day before the crime, and was wearing a red sweater the next morning. *Detective Thomas thinks it could be the same sweater!*

And, if it is the same sweater? She had a new Christmas sweater; it had a lifespan of about four days. She wore it to visit friends on Christmas, and she wanted to wear it to travel in the next day. This is entirely normal behavior, even for rich people who have lots of clothes.

The medical examiner placed the time of JonBenet's death at 6 to 12 hours before she was found, a little after 1:00 in the afternoon of the 26th of December. Since the Ramseys called police before 6:00 in the morning, that pushes the most likely time of death backward—according to Thomas (p. 147)—to sometime between 10 o'clock and 1 AM.

This, of course, is transparently false. It places the time of death between 1 AM and 5:52 AM. Thomas moves the timeline backward, contradicting the evidence, because the earlier time frame fits better with the theory that Patsy Ramsey killed her daughter, whereas a later time frame works better with the intruder theory. If Patsy Ramsey had a conflict with her daughter and lost her temper, that most likely would have occurred shortly after the Ramseys got home Christmas night, about 10 o'clock. If an intruder committed the murder, that most likely would not have occurred until after everyone was asleep.

On the duct tape that had covered JonBenet's mouth, there was found a single hair, a beaver hair. Not a pubic hair; an actual beaver. When Patsy

Ramsey shows up at an interview months later wearing fur-lined boots, the police begin demanding a search warrant to seize the boots, and Thomas—who apparently slept through the class on "probable cause"—is angry that the D.A.'s office will not cooperate with this request.

But the source of the beaver hair should hardly bedevil a good detective. JonBenet was murdered in the basement, right next to where Patsy Ramsey's paintbrushes were stored, and the garrote was fashioned using one of the paintbrushes. Artist's paint brushes are very often made from beaver hair.

Not that the police are entirely to blame for the mess. The Ramseys, as we noted, sealed themselves off from the investigation at a very early date, which made it impossible for the police to check them out and move on with the investigation. And the District Attorney's office, at times, seemed to have grown so antagonistic toward the police investigation that they looked for reasons to meddle.

A neighbor reported hearing a scream about 2 o'clock in the morning of December 26. It is reported on the internet—although this fact does not appear in any of the books I have read—that a houseguest of this same neighbor distinctly heard the sound of a grate scraping against concrete about ten or fifteen minutes later. However—or so it is unreliably reported on the internet—the police never talked to the neighbor's houseguest.

Detective Thomas seems unaware of this report, but he does say something interesting related to it. Subsequent audio tests revealed that, while the Ramseys might or might not have been able to hear a scream from the basement of the house, the neighbor quite certainly could have. The police thus wanted to immediately re-interview the neighbor. The District Attorney's office inexplicably ordered them not to, on the theory that this might interfere with their trial preparation of this witness. This would be odd reasoning if a trial were at hand. Since no trial was ever on the horizon, it seems a stretch. But this lends credibility to the allegation that the neighborhood was not thoroughly canvassed by police.

Detective Thomas says (p. 23) that Patsy Ramsey "changed a very important part of her story," in that she initially told a police officer that she checked JonBenet's bedroom before heading downstairs and finding the note, whereas later she would say that she first went downstairs.

First, only a person determined to find the Ramseys guilty could possibly interpret this as "chang[ing] a very important part of her story," since it makes no conceivable difference.

Second, who is to say whether Ramsey or the police officer correctly remembered the earlier conversation? Whenever two people talk about anything, each will remember details of the conversation differently. It is inevitable that this would happen in this case, and these inevitable small discrepancies cannot be used to substitute for actual evidence.

Detective Thomas says (p. 23) that John Ramsey told three police officers that he had "personally checked the doors the previous night and all were secure," and insists that Ramsey is lying, since Ramsey later would say that he does not remember checking the locks or saying that he had.

Since it seems immensely likely that the intruder was in the house before the Ramseys returned home that evening, it is immaterial whether Ramsey did or did not check the locks. And as to saying that he had, who would remember every word that he said under such bewildering and terrifying circumstances?

Detective Thomas insists (p. 15, and many times subsequently) that, in the tape recording of Patsy Ramsey's 911 call, Burke Ramsey can be heard in the background saying "What did you find" and John Ramsey saying "We're not talking to you." Since the Ramseys have insisted that Burke never woke up during the phone call, Detective Thomas insists that they are lying.

But no one except some corporation in Los Angeles hired by the Boulder police can make anything out of the background noise. The FBI crime labs and the U.S. Secret Service studied the tape, and stated specifically that there was nothing there. I am aware of numerous cases in which police "heard" things on tapes that were later determined to be hallucinations. And assuming for the sake of argument that Burke Ramsey did wake up at this time and the Ramseys somehow blanked out on it, again, what would that prove?

Detective Thomas argues that, if the Ramseys got out of bed that morning at the time they say they got out of bed, they wouldn't have had time to make their 6:30 AM flight to Michigan. But the Ramseys got out of bed at 5:30. The flight (according to everybody but Detective Thomas) was set for 7:15, and according to Google it was an 18-minute drive to the airport. And it wasn't a scheduled flight; it was a private flight, leaving from an airport that was never busy. It would leave whenever the Ramseys got there and were ready to go.

Detective Thomas states over and over that there is no evidence of a stun gun being used in the crime, as if saying this often enough would make it true. In fact—as a court ruled in 2003—there very clearly *is* evidence of a stun gun being used. There are marks on her neck and on her back like those left by a stun gun, which are at the correct spaces to indicate that they are stun gun marks. There are Christmas photos of JonBenet showing clearly that those marks weren't there the day before. Police responded to this by trying to tie John Ramsey to a stun gun, just as they had tried to tie Patsy to the duct tape. They found, at his office, a catalogue that offered for sale a stun gun, but it was the wrong type of stun gun. That failing, they then began to insist that there was no stun gun; those were just bruises.

They don't look like bruises.

Boulder police released a statement that "there were no footprints in the snow," leading away from the house, which is taken to mean that there was no evidence of an intruder leaving the house. Photos taken early that morning show that the sidewalks were clear, and that there was a patchy snow left from two days earlier on the ground. In any case, the duct tape, cord, the stun gun and the murder weapon (whatever it was that JonBenet was hit over the head with) were not in the house at the time of the discovery of the body. If no one left the house, what happened to them?

There was a window near where JonBenet's body was found, with a suitcase sitting under the window, a scuff mark on the wall, broken glass from the window, and a grate outside the window. A crime scene photo taken on the morning of the murder clearly and unmistakably shows fresh vegetation trapped underneath the edge of the grate, as if the grate had been recently lifted and replaced. Police insisted:

1) That the window had been broken months earlier,

2) That the suitcase had been moved under the window, for an obscure and improbable reason, on the morning after the crime,

3) That the window was too small for an intruder to crawl through (which was later shown to be flatly untrue; in fact, a large man could quite easily crawl through the window), and

4) That there were spider webs on the grate, which, in the opaque logic of the police, proved that the grate had not been pushed open recently, despite the fact that it obviously had.

The ransom note is signed "SBTC." Police argue that this is evidence against Patsy Ramsey because she liked to use acronyms. This is also evidence against John Ramsey, because he was once stationed at the Subic Bay Training Center in the Philippines (although the place he was stationed was never actually called the Subic Bay Training Center).

The room in which JonBenet's body was found had been latched shut with a peg on a screw. Detective Thomas wonders (p. 308), "Would an intruder ... have taken the time to relatch the obscure cellar door peg that police and Fleet White found in the locked position?" But had the cellar door been left unlatched, JonBenet's body would have been found at about six o'clock in the morning. Because the door was latched, it was not found until one o'clock in the afternoon. By taking three seconds to relatch the door, the murderer bought seven hours to flee the scene or to collect the ransom.

Detective Thomas can't understand why the killer would write the ransom note in the house, rather than bringing it with him, and *Who Killed JonBenet Ramsey?* refers to "the idiocy of a kidnapper who forgot to bring a ransom note" (p. 327). But had the intruder been arrested breaking into the house, the possession of the ransom note would have been evidence of the intent to commit a far more serious crime, and might well have made the difference between a weekend in jail and a twenty-year prison sentence.

When you break through the clutter and boil off the anger, Detective Thomas' case against the Ramseys comes down to three things:

1) That Patsy Ramsey wrote the ransom letter,

2) That the Ramseys lied to investigators about any number of small points, and

3) That the Intruder theory is highly improbable, whereas the Ramsey case is straightforward.

On the first point, I do agree that the handwriting of the ransom letter is quite similar to Patsy Ramsey's handwriting.

On the second and third points, I think he is simply wrong.

Some weeks into the investigation, mindful of the lack of experience on the police investigative team, the D.A.'s office hired a veteran detective to participate in the investigation, bringing the number of people involved who had some idea how to actually investigate a homicide up to a total of one. Lou Smit was a retired homicide cop who had participated in hundreds of homicide investigations in a long career.

Within days of joining the investigation, Smit realized that it was unlikely that the Ramseys had committed the murder. Over the following weeks he developed a theory of what had happened. This theory, with a little of my own inference and extrapolation, is as follows. As the Ramseys left their house about 5 o'clock on Christmas Day, someone was watching the house. He broke into the house, probably through the basement window, and immediately explored the area where he had entered the house, thus finding the wine cellar where the body was found the next day, which was near the point of entry. He brought with him the cord with which JonBenet was bound, duct tape, and the stun gun.

The killer hid in the house for several hours while the Ramseys were away, and wrote the ransom note on a legal pad that he found in the house while waiting for the Ramseys to return. When the Ramseys returned he hid in the house, probably under a bed in an empty bedroom near JonBenet's room. Once the family was asleep he crawled out of hiding, crept into Jon-Benet's room, and zapped the sleeping girl with the stun gun, immobilizing her. He then bound her wrists, put duct tape on her mouth, and carried the girl down to the basement, to the room outside the wine cellar, where Patsy Ramsey's paintbrushes were stored along with a lot of other junk. He put her down for a moment while he placed the ransom note on the stairs, her head resting against the banister, thus getting the green decorations from the staircase into the girl's hair.

In the basement he fashioned a garrote from a paintbrush handle and the cord he had brought with him. He put this around JonBenet's neck, pulled off her clothes or some of her clothes, and sexually abused her. At some point she awakened, and, despite the duct tape over her mouth, managed to get off a scream. The murderer instinctively hit her hard on the top of her head with something handy, perhaps the stun gun, thus crushing her skull. He hastily re-applied the duct tape over her mouth, hid JonBenet's body in the adjoining wine cellar, and immediately turned his attention to getting out of the house.

From my standpoint, there are no problems whatsoever with Smit's scenario. There is nothing about it that doesn't sound right, there is nothing about it that is terribly unusual, there is nothing about it that doesn't work. There is a substantial amount of evidence to suggest that this is what happened.

The police scenario, on the other hand, is bizarre, and—my own term—perversely naïve. Naïveté is an unrealistic belief in a highly improbable scenario, based on unquestioning faith. Perverse naïveté is an unrealistic belief in a highly improbable scenario, based on unrestrained cynicism. The belief in the Ramseys' guilt is perversely naïve. The police saw the Ramseys as this too-perfect couple, rich and attractive people who went to church, had lots of energy, got involved in countless activities, and were totally in control of their lives. Being the experienced investigators that they were, they "knew" that every family had secrets, that there was a dark side to the brightest of lives.

The only thing was, they weren't experienced investigators, at all. They were just a bunch of almost-amateur cops who had romanticized their life experiences to convince themselves that they were shrewd and savvy police veterans.

The Lou Smit interpretation of the case is now the mainstream view among those who are still involved in the effort to bring JonBenet's killer to justice. Before the point was reached at which it became the mainstream view, unfortunately, the Ramsey family—on the heels of their tragedy—was hounded by the press, and ridiculed by comedians. It is perhaps the ugliest spectacle in the 200-year history of the American news media. It is my view that *something* had to have happened here which should never be allowed to happen. I wish I could tell you what it was.

Alex Hunter, who was a fine man and an exceptional District Attorney, had a long-standing policy of being open and cooperative with the press. This had always worked for him, dealing with local media; it had given him a reputation for honesty and accessibility, and it had given him some control of the story.

In the opening months of the Ramsey investigation Hunter tried to deal with the tabloid press as an extension of the way he had always dealt with the local press. The national tabloid press was as different from the local media as a tiger is from a housecat, vastly larger, angrier, more aggressive and more cynical. They ate him alive.

John Ramsey, who was a very fine man and an exceptionally competent manager, tried to take control of the situation and "manage" it toward the most successful outcome that was still possible after JonBenet's death. He did this because that was what he did; he took control of things, and steered them toward chosen objectives—but it wasn't appropriate under the circumstances. It wasn't his place to manage the case. To gain control of the case, he had to try to rip the controls out of the hands of the police. The police had no intention of surrendering control over the case and intensely resented the effort to take control away from them, and this triggered a war between Ramsey and the police. Ramsey tried to control—and did control—

when and where and under what conditions the Ramseys gave interviews. He pulled his family out of Boulder to give him control of the situation. He hired investigators, and he hired expensive lawyers who gave him bad advice.

The police—and in particular John Eller, who was the head of the investigation until his career in Boulder was destroyed by it—tried harder than anyone to keep control of the investigation. Eller engaged on the one hand in a tug-of-war with John Ramsey for control of the investigation, on the second hand in a battle with his subordinates (especially Detective Larry Mason) for control of the investigative squad, on the third hand in constant skirmishes with his boss, Chief of Police Tom Koby, on the fourth hand in hostile combat with the media, and on the fifth hand in an extremely unusual if not historically unprecedented War to End All Wars with the District Attorney's office. He didn't have enough hands. Eller was like a man who finds himself locked in a cage with a tiger, a gorilla, a bear and an elephant, but he does have a nightstick. Every time he succeeds in hitting the elephant in the balls with the nightstick, he thinks he's scored a point. The more points Eller scored, the worse his situation became.

The case was lost early because the police *didn't* take control of the things they could have and should have taken control of. It was lost late because Eller was determined to take control of things that he had no chance to control. What Eller needed to do was to go to the District Attorney's office and say, "I need your help. I can't control this situation. It's too big for me; I simply cannot handle it." Instead, in part because he hated the District Attorney's office so much and in part because he had no overview of the situation, no Big Picture, and no experience with any investigation remotely like this, he continued, until he was forced to resign, to flail madly with his nightstick at the bear, the elephant, the tiger and the gorilla.

That's the essential lesson of the Ramsey case: you don't put a choke chain on a tiger. It just pisses him off.

XXXIII

The only thing I know for certain about the JonBenet Ramsey case is that the Ramseys are innocent, and I know that only because the arguments to the contrary are fantastic and irrational. What I have to offer you now is speculation, with which I hope you will be patient. It is my understanding of the rules of fine literature that I am allowed to speculate as long as I have the permission of the audience.

If you make three left turns you have made a right. The experts all assure us that the JonBenet crime scene was "staged" (No Shit, Sherlock), and that the perpetrator was "criminally unsophisticated." He was criminally unsophisticated because he asked for an amount of money that, to the Ramseys, was kind of like asking for a candy bar and a new T-shirt, and also because he made any number of claims that nobody would take seriously, much less believe (i.e., "we represent a small foreign faction"). This is criminally unsophisticated.

Or is it?

The criminal asked for an amount of money that was very small to the Ramseys, yes, but the criminal also knew something. The murderer knew that JonBenet's body was in the basement, where it would be discovered within hours. Therefore, the criminal knew that he had a very short period of time to collect the money. He asked for a small amount of money—small to John Ramsey, but three years' salary for an average person—because he knew that John Ramsey could get that amount of money together *quickly*. John Ramsey could have raised much more than $118,000, true—but not in an hour. As it was, John Ramsey had the money by nine o'clock in the morning.

People assume that the perpetrator had no intention of actually collecting the money; that was all a charade. In fact, I believe that he very probably *did* intend to collect the money—and that he came within a whisker of actually doing so.

The criminal's plan, I think, was this. He would watch the Ramsey house from somewhere in the neighborhood—his apartment, most likely, or a vacant house that he had broken into. He would "monitor" the Ramsey house—as he said in the ransom note that he would—and see if the police were called, and see if the Ramseys were scrambling around to get the money. If Ramsey returned from the bank carrying an attaché case and the police were not in evidence, he would call John Ramsey on a stolen cell phone, and tell Ramsey to take the money and his cell phone and start walking west on Aurora Avenue. When he walked past a certain point—alone—the criminal would call him on the cell phone, and tell him to put down the money and keep walking. In about 300 feet he would find an envelope that would tell him where JonBenet could be picked up.

Three things had to happen for the plan to work:

1) John Ramsey had to get the money together very quickly,
2) JonBenet's body had to be not found for a few hours, and
3) The Ramseys had to not call the police.

Two of the three did happen. John Ramsey did get the money together very quickly, and the body was not found for several hours. The only thing that went wrong was that the police were called. Once the perpetrator saw that every cop in Boulder was going by the Ramsey house, of course, he abandoned his effort to collect the money. But the rest of the plan worked.

The "staging" of the crime scene was not designed to "work"; it was designed to fail. Obviously the crime scene was staged; a fourth-grader could tell you that. Who is *really* going to believe that there is a small foreign terrorist group, the SBTC, that is asking for $118,000 by kidnapping a millionaire's daughter? Nobody is going to believe that; it is intended to be seen as nonsense.

The perpetrator's central goal was to destroy the life of John Ramsey. His secondary goal was to come out of it with $118,000. Suppose that there was a person—an intelligent, organized person, but sick with envy—who hated John Ramsey with an all-consuming passion. He envied Ramsey his money, and his beautiful house, and his beautiful wife, and his beautiful children, and his boats and his airplanes. He hated Ramsey, and he was determined to destroy him.

Such a person would have known that the worst thing that had ever happened to Ramsey was the death of his daughter, and that the worst thing that could ever happen to him would be the death of his other daughter. *I am going to arrange the death of that other daughter*, he thought—*and do it in such a way that the police will think Ramsey did it. I'll make it look like she died in a sex game or something; the police will blame him.*

Is there any way to make this any worse for him? *I know—I'll get his wife, too. I'll make it look like she was involved, fake her handwriting or something. I'll get some of her handwriting, learn to copy it, and make police think she wrote the ransom note.*

What's the worst time you could possibly do something like that to a man? *How about Christmas? I'll do it on Christmas day.*

The ransom letter is directed at John Ramsey. We're assuming that's real.

In all of the books about JonBenet there is this line that comes up over and over again: It had to be an inside job. Somebody had to know things, personal things. OK; let's assume that's true.

One of the things that has to bother you about the case is, the handwriting really is very similar to Patsy's. It *could* be a coincidence, I guess, and it could be Patsy's actual handwriting, but nobody will testify that it is, and I don't believe it is. What it really looks like, to be honest, is somebody *faking* Patsy Ramsey's handwriting. He got most of the letter constructions right, missed on a few of them. Some little things aren't exactly right, and quite a few of the things like how letter combinations are put together aren't right, but there are some words that appear to be exact matches for Patsy Ramsey's handwriting.

What if the killer wrote the ransom letter inside the house precisely because he knew that the police would figure this out and would jump to the conclusion that the Ramseys had staged the scene?

Ordinarily I am suspicious of the theory that the result of a crime was the intention of the criminal. But ordinarily, we at least consider the *possibility* that what happened was what the criminal intended to happen. It seems to me that in this case we have so routinely dismissed the criminal as a blundering incompetent that we have failed to consider the possibility that what he accomplished was exactly what he intended to accomplish: the systematic destruction of John Ramsey's life.

Three left turns. The money was too small; that couldn't be real. The body was in the basement. The crime scene was transparently staged.

But if you put them all together, they all work together. Two wrongs don't make a right, but three lefts will.

We read about crime, we write about crime, we think about crime because we are concerned about crime. To persons who have not been the victims or collateral victims of a serious crime, this concern may seem excessive. To persons who have, the suggestion that we worry too much about it seems preposterous.

As an expert in nothing, I have two suggestions about how our system of justice could be improved. Well . . . I have 250 suggestions about how our system of justice could be improved; I just thought there was some chance you might read two.

First, there is something we could do, as a nation, that would cut our crime rate in half, and incidentally save us some money.

Build smaller prisons.

I hate to sound like I am proposing a panacea, but it is my view there would be wide-ranging benefits to us from getting rid of these huge, horrible prisons that we have become fond of building, and replacing them with a nationwide network of small prisons. My suggestion: A law, applying to every state, every county, every level of government, that no incarceration facility may be used to house more than 24 persons at any time.

Obviously it would take us many years to transition to a system of small prisons, but think about the benefits that it would provide. Large prisons become "violentocracies"—places ruled by violence and by the threat of violence. In a violentocracy, the most violent people rise to the top.

In any prison of any size, the prisoners are going to be pushed toward the level of the most violent persons in the facility. If you have a three-person prison and one guy is a thug, the other two are going to have to defend themselves against the thug. They're going to have to get tougher in order to defend themselves, and by "tougher" what we mean right now is "more inclined to use violence."

But the operation of this "violence virus" in a large prison is very different than it would be or could be in a small prison. In a prison of 3,000 people, the entire prison is pushed toward the level of violence created by the five most violent people in the joint. The most violent person finds the second-most violent person and the third-most violent person, and they form an alliance to exploit the weak. Everyone else is compelled to avoid looking weak.

We are designed by nature to resist violence, and our first instinct is to resist violence with violence. Do you ever watch any of those shows about people locked up in prison? There are a hundred of them. If you watch any of those shows with this thought in mind, it should be obvious to you that the pathologies that breed in these places could not survive and could not exist in a small facility.

Large prisons promote paranoia in the prisoners. You never know who in here is waiting for you with a homemade knife. There are 1500 people here, and 500 of them are crazy people who will kill you because you look at them funny; that's the way a prisoner in a large facility naturally thinks. This paranoia propels the institution toward violence.

A prison of 20 people is, by its very nature, extremely different. You *know* who is in there with you; you know who you have to stay away from. It gives you a measure of control over your environment, which is necessary for mental health. Plus, if you have many small prisons, you can contain the violent people in a limited number of those prisons, thus preventing their violent tendencies from infecting the rest of the prison population.

In a prison of 2,000 prisoners and 250 guards, a canyon develops between the camps. The prisoners develop a way of thinking about the guards; the guards develop a way of thinking about the prisoners. The prisoners develop an ethic about how guards are supposed to be treated; the guards develop an ethic about how the prisoners are supposed to be treated. It is an unhealthy relationship.

In a prison of 24 prisoners and 3 guards, you have a very different inter-personal dynamic. The guard sees and treats each prisoner as an individual. The prisoner sees and treats each guard as he is treated. From a mental health perspective this is a thousand times better.

By transitioning to a system of small prisons, we could also save large amounts of money. In a prison of 1,000 persons there will be 100 or 200 who are determined to escape, 200 or 400 who are determined to get their hands on some drugs, and 100 or 200 who are crazy people who will stab you with an ice pick just to see the blood come out.

A large prison has to assume that *every* prisoner desperately wants to escape, that *every* prisoner is trying to obtain drugs, and that *every* prisoner is a crazy person who will stab you with an ice pick for no reason. The prison has to assume that—but it's not true. This is fantastically inefficient. A large prison spends 50 or 60% of its resources protecting itself against threats that are not real—against the escape risk of prisoners who have little inclination to escape, against the threat of physical violence from people who are not violent or anyway would not be violent were they not incarcerated in a place that was pushing them constantly to become more violent.

What you would do, with a network of small prisons, would be to place each prisoner in a facility that is appropriate to the threat that he represents. You grade the prisoners on the threat of violence that they represent, one through ten. You put the tens with the tens and the ones with the ones.

The "tens"—the most violent prisoners—those guys, obviously, need to be locked in their cells 23 hours a day and closely monitored for the other hour. The "ones"—the most docile prisoners who have no history of violence anywhere, anytime—can be allowed to wander around the facility and interact with guards and other prisoners.

But when you put them all in one large facility, you have to lock them all down 23 hours a day and monitor them all closely the other hour. This is crazy. Plus, when you move to a system in which *some* prisoners have more rights and live in more humane conditions, you create a powerful incentive to get into one of the less restrictive prisons.

In a large and horrible prison, the new prisoner thinks "I've got to show everybody here how tough and vicious I really am, so that nobody will mess with me." But when you put a new prisoner in a 24-man prison with 23 other tough guys, and he knows that there are other prisons that are not like this, his natural thought is "I've got to get out of here. I've got to show these people that I am *not* a crazy, vicious sociopath, so they will move me to some other facility that is not populated by crazy, vicious sociopaths."

With a network of small prisons you can respond to the needs of prisoners in a thousand other ways. If you have intelligent prisoners who want to take college classes, you can move them to a prison with intelligent prisoners where college classes are offered—a prison that is, in essence, a very small college with high walls and a bad basketball team. If you need to protect the child molesters from the general prison population, you can move them to a prison full of short eyes. If you need to protect ex-police officers who are incarcerated, you can move them to a prison with several other ex-police officers. If you need to provide medical assistance to prisoners who are HIV positive, you can house them with other prisoners who are HIV positive.

With a network of small prisons you can break up prison gangs by isolating prisoners from other members of their gang. By doing that—and by forcing prisoners to interact with members of other population groups on a one-on-one basis—you could put the prison gangs out of existence within a few years.

Suppose that there are 6,000 men incarcerated in the state of New Uzbekistan—which would indicate that New Uzbekistan is a very small state—and that, as of now, 3,000 of those are locked up in the New Uzbekistan State Penitentiary, and the other 3,000 are scattered around among 25 other facilities. We replace that with a network of 300 small prisons, each with a capacity of 24 prisoners and averaging about 20.

Those 300 prisons are sorted first into ten types of facilities, with ten different levels of privileges. At a Level One facility, a prisoner is allowed to have *nothing*—no radio, no television, no visitors, no snacks, no pens, no notebooks, no computers, no coffee, no furniture, no playing cards, no wristwatch and no newspaper. He is allowed to have a book of faith, food and drink, and he is allowed to visit his lawyer; that's it.

At a Level Ten facility, a prisoner is allowed to have anything—suits, ties, television, computers with the internet, etc. Obviously he is not allowed to have guns, drugs or violent pornography, but within reason; a Level Ten facility is what we would now call a halfway house.

Between Level One and Level Ten, rights increase gradually as the prisoner moves up. At Level Two, the prisoner is allowed to have a radio. At Level Three, he is allowed to have access to a community television. At Level Four he can have his own television, but no cable. At Level Six he can have basic cable. At Level Eight he can have cable with premium channels if he can pay for them.

At Level One the prisoner can have only a religious volume and whatever access to a law library is required by the courts. At Level Two, he can get a local newspaper; at Level Three, newspapers and magazines. At Level Four the prisoner can have three books in his cell at a time, and he can exchange books once a month; at Level Five, ten books, and he can exchange them once a week. At Level Six he has access to a library; at Level Seven, to a better library.

As the prisoner moves up the ladder the food gets better, and the policies get more lenient. At Level One the lights are on 24 hours a day; at Level Two, they go off from midnight to 6 AM. At Level Seven, you're in your own room and you can turn off the lights whenever you want to. At Level Ten, you can come and go as you please as long as you sign in by 9 o'clock at night.

At Level One you have no access to money. At Level Ten you can hold a job outside the prison. At Level Four you can have a cup of coffee once a day; at Level Five you can have coffee when you want it. At Level Six you can have one soft drink a week if you can pay for it. At Level One you can see no one; at Level Two, you can have three people on your visiting list and they can each visit once a month for one hour. At Level Three, you can have five people on your visitors list, and they can each visit once a week for one hour. At Level One or Two, obviously, you have no pets. At Level Four you can have a goldfish or a hamster; at Level Five, a cat. At Level Six you can have a small dog.

Such a system provides a powerful incentive to the prisoner to buy into the program. If you spend two years at Level Three and move up to Level Four, Level Four seems like heaven; you've got coffee, a television, playing cards, regular visits from your family and a few books. If you're at Level Four, what you think about is how you can get to Level Five, and you *really* don't want to get caught in a violation and get sent back to Level Three. In a large prison nobody can have a pet because it would be crazy if everybody had a pet. In a 24-man prison, eight or ten people might choose to keep pets, and it's not really an issue.

A large prison provides no incentive to the prisoner to buy into the program, and attempts to enforce compliance with the threat of punishment. But since the punishments that can be legally meted out by the prison are trivial compared to the punishments that are meted out by the other prisoners, this is totally ineffective, thus creating a situation in which the *real* rules are the rules created by the prison population. My alternative would provide the state with vastly greater effective control of the prisoner, which is the essential goal of incarceration: to take control of the prisoner's life.

A network of small prisons can be used to set goals for prisoners and push them toward those goals. You want to move to Level Five? OK; we want you to be able to read at a tenth-grade level, we want you to participate actively in anger management therapy, and we want you to select a profession for which you want to train. You meet these goals, we'll talk.

But remember, in New Uzbekistan we don't have *one* Level One prison and one Level Four prison; we have 30 prisons at each level. That means that we can do these things—stratify the privileges—*and* accommodate the needs of prisoners in many other ways. You can have a Level Four prison that operates a small farm, and a Level Five prison that operates a small farm, and a

Level Six prison that operates a small farm. If you have prisoners from a farm background, they can apply to go through that system. You can have a Level Five prison that teaches auto repair, and a Level Seven prison that operates a small auto-repair business, and a Level Six prison that teaches dog grooming and dog obedience, and a Level Eight prison where prisoners teach dog obedience classes. You can have a Level Three prison that teaches upholstery, and a Level Seven prison that has a small business manufacturing couches and chairs.

Much of this is stuff that has existed historically, but has been lost as we have moved toward these large, gruesome, impersonal prisons that offer no opportunities to the imprisoned. And yes, there will be people who will be trapped permanently at the lowest levels of this system, people who have committed crimes so horrible that they will never be allowed to move above a Level Three prison—but those prisoners are not the majority of the system. The majority of prisoners are going to get out.

Many of the problems of the current nightmarish prison system have been created by the NIMBY problem: Not In My Back Yard. It is so hard to find a place to put A prison, in the modern world, that we like to confront that issue as seldom as possible.

But in the prison system that I am advocating, the NIMBY problem goes away because everybody has to understand: There are going to be little prisons *everywhere*. Every town of 3,000 people has a couple of little prisons. If you work in a big office building, the 17th floor may be a prison complex. If you work in a strip mall, the place next door may be a prison.

But that is much less threatening if the prison is small, and if it is generally understood that Charles Manson is not being housed there. The lowest-level prisons are isolated and heavily guarded and the people in the higher-levels prisons are really not that much different from you and me.

Prisons benefit from interaction between the prisoner and the public. Many, many, many people are very willing to go into a prison, and try to help the people who are there make a better life. I am entirely willing to go into a prison and teach a class, and my wife is, and my brother-in-law is. Ministers are almost universally willing to minister to prisoners; many psychologists are willing to donate time to counsel those in need of help. The problem is, that's extremely difficult to arrange if you have a large, hostile prison located in some isolated place as far away as possible from the public.

The better integration of prisons into society would reduce the problem of prisoners getting re-integrated into society. In the current system a prisoner who draws a ten-year sentence might spend 9½ years in what amounts to a Level Four prison, and then has six months in a halfway house—which amounts to a Level Ten prison—to get re-acclimated to society. This system fails a very high percentage of the time, and usually results in the prisoner returning to confinement. By giving the prisoner more contact with more outside citizens as he progresses gradually toward release, the prisoner emerges with many more points of contact.

Here's another benefit that I would predict would follow from a small-prison movement: it would create a generation of professional people who work to create better prisons.

In my youth we were all idealists, and I knew many people who talked about becoming prison reformers. None of them did, because there was nowhere to start. There's no profession there. If you get a job as a prison guard you get $12 an hour and a blue uniform, and after twenty years you've got a job as a prison guard, $18 an hour, a little gold patch on your uniform and you get to go first in choosing your vacation schedule.

With a network of small prisons, if you were hired by a prison you'd be on a staff of four or five people who managed a small prison. With 300 prisons in a state you'd have 300 wardens. You'd have a community of prison wardens. There would be stature in that community. You would have people who were known in that community for their creativity, for their success at helping those they were charged to help. To move up in your profession you could move easily to another prison. If your spouse got a better job, you could move with her or with him. Within a few years, if you did a good job and took the right classes, you could be a prison warden.

Current system, you ain't ever going to be the warden. You get hired as a prison guard, you're a prison guard. It's a train headin' nowhere. This discourages innovation, and it discourages pride in your work. I would predict that a consequence of a small-prison network would be a dramatic increase in the quality and quantity of people who wanted to work in the prison industry—and not money-driven people who wanted to start private prisons, like we had in the 1980s, but quality people who wanted to serve society. Not that there is anything wrong with wanting to do well; actually, a network of small prisons could *be* a network of small, private prisons.

Because the current system discourages innovation, it wastes money. I know that many of you are thinking this system couldn't be run as efficiently as I think, but here's one reason it could. The business of monitoring prisoners is extremely open to electronic innovation—cameras, ankle bracelets, Breathalyzers, voice recognition technology, remote key controls, etc. In the current system, which limits innovation because innovations *have* to work immediately on a large scale, you may need one guard and one other employee for every eight prisoners on average, or something like that.

But in a small-prison network in which small experiments searching for better solutions were easier to attempt, I would predict that we would very quickly reach a point at which one *guard* could safely monitor and control several prisons (higher level prisons), causing the ratio of security to non-security employees to shrink rapidly. Having the prisons privately run, but with standards, could also encourage those innovations. And, of course, we would also save money because we could provide for each prisoner the level of supervision that is necessary for *that* prisoner, rather than the level of supervision that is necessary for the most violent prisoner who represents the greatest threat to the public.

Well . . . that's probably not going to happen tomorrow. A prison of 500 people is vastly better than a prison of 1,000; a prison of 200 people is less evil than a prison of 300. If I can get a few people to see why that is true, I'm happy.

My second suggestion for you is: *please try to stop thinking about issues of criminal justice in conservative and liberal terms.*

Look, what I am essentially arguing above is a liberal agenda: that we are better off, as a society, if we have less harsh prison conditions, that it is *not* a lost cause to try to help people get back on their feet after they go astray, that training and treatment of prisoners is worth the cost, and that people who enter our prisons are by and large, at the time they enter the system, *not* frightening, violent monsters who will take advantage of whoever reaches out to them, but merely young people who have done wrong. At the same time, in advocating this belief, I am merely advocating a return to the mainstream American values of the years 1880 to 1970, when efforts to help prisoners were commonplace.

But it is also my view that 99% of the work of destroying those values was done by liberals. The rights-based agenda of the 1960s and 1970s was poison to progressive prison policy. These huge prisons that we have today . . . do you know why we started building those? You'd never guess.

Law libraries.

One of the chief reasons that we started building these massive dungeons that now house a large percentage of the American prison population was court-mandated access to law libraries. Prisoners are always working on appeals of some kind or another, often doing the work themselves. Beyond that, many prisoners are litigious. As anyone who has ever clerked for a federal judge can tell you, a huge percentage of the lawsuits they see—I've been told 85%—are suits from prisoners protesting that their rights are being violated because the biscuits are burned and the light bulb hums all night and they can't sleep.

In the 1960s and 1970s, numerous judicial rulings established and strengthened the right of prisoners to have access to a law library. Many, many lawsuits were filed by prisoners protesting the inadequacy of the law library. Legal libraries are expensive. If you built 50 small prisons, you had to equip them with 50 law libraries—and I mean 50 first-class law libraries, or you'd get sued. It was much cheaper to bring them all together, and just have one law library. This was probably the second-largest factor, behind the NIMBY syndrome, in the consolidation of prisoners into fewer and larger facilities.

That's behind us now; with the internet you can create one law library and have it wherever you need it. But that's typical of the problem. We had parole, but then prisoners acquired the *right* to make parole, rather than the opportunity to make parole. That killed parole.

In the American political debate as it applies to the justice system, the left's idea of progress is relentlessly expanding the rights of the accused, and the right's idea of progress is longer prison sentences. These are two lousy ideas, and they have resulted in a dysfunctional system.

In a well-functioning family, punishments are so light as to be hardly recognizable as punishments. Supervision is constant, standards are clear, and misbehaviors are corrected with a word, a moment's instruction, an explanation, a hug, and, if need be, with a few minutes in a timeout chair or being grounded for a week.

In a dysfunctional family smaller misbehaviors go unnoticed and uncorrected, standards are unclear, and punishments are harsh. The kid gets by with more and more and more with nobody saying anything, and then he gets slapped, yelled at, humiliated and grounded for a year. This doesn't work.

Our judicial system is, in essence, a dysfunctional family. We ignore small misbehaviors, we let people get by with things that they *shouldn't* get by with—and then we try to play catch-up by handing out harsh punishments for major offenses. It doesn't work.

Who's responsible for that: conservatives or liberals?

Both. The liberals are in charge of insuring that we don't do anything about day-to-day misbehaviors—and the conservatives are in charge of making sure that we act harshly when finally we take action.

Suppose that you tried to keep your yard in order not by mowing it regularly, but by going out once a week and pulling up the biggest weeds. Wouldn't work, would it—but this is essentially what the criminal justice system does. Simple example: bicycle theft.

Routine bicycle theft is, in theory, ridiculously easy to prevent. What you do is, you set up a decoy bicycle with a hidden camera pointed at it and a transmitter hidden in the tubing of the frame, and you wait for somebody to steal it. Then you arrest them, and you put that person in prison for six months. One doesn't get to steal three or four bicycles before you go to prison; one bicycle, six months. You do that regularly, all the time, and after a few months people know better than to steal bicycles.

That's mowing your lawn. Instead, what we do is, we wait until there's an organized ring of bicycle thieves, then we move in on them and send the ringleaders to prison for 20 years. That's pulling up the largest weeds.

Punishment doesn't need to be harsh; it needs to be consistent, and certain. The liberal approach to this problem is to give the bicycle thief every opportunity to straighten himself out before we ruin his life by sending him to jail. The conservative approach is to campaign for much harsher penalties for bicycle theft. Neither one works, and they don't work together worse than they don't work individually.

Criminal justice calls for the careful balancing of competing interests within a complex problem. Liberal/conservative thinking is organized around large principles. It's like trying to fix a pocket watch with a monkey wrench, a hammer and a 16-bit drill. The tools are too large for the problem.

It is my view that the left/right ideological dichotomy does not serve us well with regard to almost any issue—but that about no issue is it more destructive and less useful than about the system of justice. Liberals are hung up on two or three ideas about criminal justice—protecting the rights of the accused, and ending capital punishment, and eliminating prison sentences for non-violent drug offenders—and conservatives are hung up on two or three ideas about criminal justice, such as harsher punishments for repeat offenders, expanding capital punishment, strengthening the hand of prosecutors in dealing with criminals, and making sure nobody passes any new gun laws. One gets the feeling that they fight about these things because they enjoy fighting about these things. It's hard to see what else is being accomplished.

Those who think about criminal justice in political terms have arrived at a stalemate, and this stalemate has lasted for about 30 years at this point. It is to the credit of the constitutional concept that our system of justice has continued to evolve and continued to make progress on many issues despite the political stalemate—yet it is also true that on many issues we have *not* made progress.

I believe in a future with much less crime. I believe in a future of unlocked doors, where bicycles and backpacks may be left unattended because people do not steal them. We're really not that far away from that future. We just need to take a few small, practical steps to get there. Let go of your politics, I am asking, and let us move forward.

XXXIV

I outlined in Chapter X a system of categorizing crime stories by their size and the types of elements that they contain. The murder of JonBenet would be IQBX 9—an innocent-victim story (I), and a mystery (Q for Question Mark) with bizarre overtones (B) and sexual violence (X), very big (9). Despite its popularity with the tabloids, the Ramsey story is not a "tabloid" story in the sense that I intended that phrase, which is a crime story growing out of events in which people take a prurient interest. With the obvious exception of 9/11, no crime since then has been as big a story as that one. There have, however, been many contenders. Let's do a quick survey of some of the biggest crime stories of the last ten years.

Super Bowl XXXIV was played in the Georgia Dome in Atlanta on January 30, 2000. The Baltimore Ravens were not involved in the contest, but late that night a fight developed outside a nightclub between the friends and supporters of *Ray Lewis,* a superstar linebacker for the Ravens, and the entourage of a rapper named Chino Nino. OK, *called* Chino Nino; his name actually is Jeff Gwen.

Anyway, two people were stabbed to death in the fight, and the Atlanta authorities rushed to the conclusion that Ray Lewis had been in the middle of it, kickin' and stabbin' people. In point of fact he had not been. After Ray Lewis was charged with murder all of the people who alleged that they saw Lewis in the melee were exposed as an overexcitable lot who didn't actually know Ray Lewis from Adam. Chino Nino's narrative of the incident was that Lewis 1) had attempted to act as a peacemaker, early on, before the brawl got serious, and 2) had been nowhere around at the time that the violence turned to mayhem. All of the witnesses against Lewis eventually recanted their stories, leaving Atlanta prosecutors with no option but to plead out the case against Lewis as a misdemeanor. Two people were later put on trial for the crime, but no one was convicted.

It is the view of the author that Ray Lewis is a good man who was unjustly accused of crimes of which he was quite clearly not guilty. He was guilty of two things. He was running with a bad crowd, or more accurately, he was allowing a bad crowd to run with him. This was poor judgment, and when it spun out of control he did attempt to orchestrate a cover-up, before he realized that two people had actually been killed in the fracas. But the Atlanta authorities' effort to pin him with a murder rap was unreasonable and irresponsible. We could categorize the event as a CV 6—a celebrity story about a sudden outbreak of violence.

On or about May 1, 2001, *Chandra Levy* was murdered in Rock Creek Park in Washington, DC. Levy, aged 24, had had (or was having) an affair with Gary Condit, a member of the U.S. House of Representatives representing the northern San Joaquin Valley in California. She had interned in his office, and then later, at the time of her death, was an intern in the Bureau of Prisons.

Seeking to draw attention to Levy's disappearance, her family trumpeted the allegations of an affair with Condit. Condit was slow to come clean on the issue and did a poor job of conveying sympathy for the family, and the public grew to suspect that Condit might be involved in Levy's disappearance, although there was never any evidence of that. The disappearance drew little media attention in its first six weeks, but became a major news story in June, 2001, and remained so until buried by the events of September 11. Condit's career was destroyed by the scandal.

We would categorize the story as TPQ 7, a tabloid/political mystery story that was very big for a period of a little less than three months. On November 23, 2010, Ingmar Guandique, an illegal immigrant from El Salvador, was convicted of murdering Levy. The break in this case came from a reporter, Amy Keller of *Roll Call* magazine. When Levy's body was discovered in Rock Creek Park, it occurred to Keller that everybody else might possibly be barking up the wrong tree in hounding Condit, so she went through police reports looking for other attacks on women which had occurred in Rock Creek Park, and encountered the name of Guandique, who had attacked at least two other women in Rock Creek Park in the weeks after the murder of

Levy. When she first wrote about that, people simply thought that she was trying to spin the story away from Condit. It took years for the police to realize that he actually had fingered the right suspect.

On May 4, 2001—three days after the disappearance of Chandra Levy—the wife of actor **Robert Blake** was shot and killed while sitting in a parked car outside an Italian restaurant in Studio City (LA). Blake was arrested in April, 2002, and went on trial for the crime in early 2005. He was acquitted on March 16, 2005, although later found liable for her death in a civil trial. A pure celebrity story; C 6.

In Houston on June 20, 2001, **Andrea Yates** drowned her five children in the bathtub. Originally convicted of capital murder and sentenced to life in prison, Yates' conviction was overturned on appeal, and she was found Not Guilty by reason of insanity in July, 2006.

Yates, born in 1964, was the valedictorian of her high school class. Her husband, Rusty Yates, was a computer programmer for NASA. The couple announced at their wedding in 1993 that, as a consequence of their newfound religious beliefs, they would have as many children as they could have. Rusty Yates, however, did little to help with the child rearing, and the burden that this placed on Andrea was more than she could carry. In 1999 she had a nervous breakdown, and twice attempted suicide. Discharged from a mental hospital in January, 2000, she immediately got pregnant once again, and had a serious relapse after suffering post-partum depression in March, 2001, three months before the murders. Despite doctors' clear warnings that Andrea Yates needed round-the-clock supervision and was not to be left alone, she was left not merely alone but in charge of five young children day after day. I would categorize the story as BI 7—a bizarre story involving the deaths of innocents.

On September 18, 2001—a week after the 9/11 attacks—an unknown person mailed envelopes containing anthrax to several prominent and several less prominent members of the media. Three weeks later there was another round of similar letters mailed to political leaders.

The story of the **anthrax investigation** is extraordinarily complicated. Anthrax is *so* deadly that it would be very, very difficult to put it in an envelope and mail it to someone without killing yourself. If you or I were to get our hands on some anthrax and start to mess around with it, it is extremely likely that we would die a horrible death within the next few weeks. The number of people who have the technical expertise to use anthrax as a murder weapon is very limited, and anthrax itself is extremely difficult to obtain. Only a very limited number of people have any access to it.

So the FBI started the anthrax investigation, so to speak, in field goal range, if not actually in the red zone. On Day One of the investigation they could draw up a list of 60 or 70 names, and feel reasonably confident that the name of the offender was on the list. The FBI, then, started going up and down the list, looking for people who had a widget loose.

After several years the FBI investigation had succeeded in ruining the lives of numerous people by publicly linking them to the investigation. The investigation kept running into state secrets. Any information that anybody has about how to "weaponize" anthrax is, for good reasons, closely guarded. At one point the FBI alienated Congress by telling them that they couldn't give them a complete report on what they were doing to investigate the case, because it involved state secrets. Then, too, early on in the case, persons at the highest levels of the American government wanted the FBI to conclude that the anthrax letters had to have been mailed by someone from Iraq, working in the service of Saddam Hussein. That wasn't true, but persons inside the government leaked bogus secret information suggesting that it was true, anyway, and much of the media was convinced for years—and some people still believe today—that sinister Middle Eastern agents were behind the attacks.

Five people died as a result of the anthrax attacks, and believe me, anthrax is not the way to go. In addition, the costs of cleaning up the buildings and other places that were contaminated by the attacks is estimated to have exceeded $1 billion. The cost of cleaning up and decontaminating the Brentwood mail facility in Washington, DC, where one of the envelopes tore open and killed two employees, was $130 million ($3 million actual cleanup cost; $127 million government waste). The business of the United States Senate was disrupted at a critical moment in history. The anthrax attacks played a significant role in sustaining the paranoia of the post-9/11 era. The investigation into the crime may well be the most expensive criminal investigation in history.

A peculiarity of the case is that whereas ordinarily the forensic scientists are seen as geniuses in white coats, in this case it was extremely difficult to drag the level of the forensic scientists up to the level of the scientists being investigated. One of the first people that the FBI turned to for help in the case was Dr. Bruce Edward Ivins, who was senior biodefense researcher at the United States Army Medical Research Institute of Infectious Diseases in Fort

Detrick, Maryland (known as USAMRIID); in fact, it may well have been Dr. Ivins who generated and then leaked the secret information suggesting that Iraq was behind the attacks. There were people in the FBI as early as 2002 who suspected that Dr. Ivins might not be on the right side of the issue, but the focus in 2002 and for years thereafter was on other scientists. FBI Director Robert Mueller changed the leadership of the team investigating the case in 2006, however, and the new leadership reviewed the candidates and decided to focus on Dr. Ivins. In mid-July, 2008, Dr. Ivins was informed that he was about to be prosecuted as the perpetrator of the anthrax attacks, and on July 27 Dr. Ivins ingested a large quantity of painkillers, putting him in a coma. He died on July 29.

Federal prosecutors and the FBI, days later, announced that Dr. Ivins was the sole perpetrator of the anthrax attacks, and laid out their case against him. However—and this very rarely happens—the community of persons interested in the case by and large has rejected the FBI's arguments against Dr. Ivins, and the debate about his culpability continues. Some experts claim that Dr. Ivins did not have the technical expertise to have committed the crime. The FBI's case against Ivins certainly contains a lot of eyewash. We could categorize the story as QP 8—a mystery story about political issues.

In 2002 *Michael Skakel* was convicted of the October 30, 1975, murder of *Martha Moxley*. Martha Moxley was a distant cousin of my wife; her grandfather was my mother-in-law's first cousin. Of more general interest, Michael Skakel was a cousin of the Kennedys, a nephew of Ethel Kennedy, the widow of RFK. Martha Moxley was an extremely attractive fifteen-year-old girl, while Michael Skakel was (in 1975) a nerdy and depressed fifteen-year-old boy, and they were neighbors in a wealthy gated community in Greenwich, Connecticut. October 30 is "mischief night" or "Hacker night" on the East Coast, and Martha Moxley and some friends were out spraying cars with shaving cream and wrapping trees with toilet paper and stuff. Martha stopped by the Skakel house to see Michael and his much cooler older brother, Tommy. Tommy had had some beers and had gotten into his father's scotch, and Martha was last seen by her friends making out with Tommy outside the Skakel house a little after 9:30 PM. She was within sight of her own home, had it been daylight.

Her body was found about noon the next day, on the tree line of her own property. She had been bludgeoned with a golf club and stabbed with the broken shaft of the club. The club, it was learned, was part of a set that had belonged to Michael and Tommy Skakel's mother, who had died three years earlier. The golf club, however, may have been left lying in the yard before the murder, a weapon of convenience for whoever happened by.

The Greenwich police had the same problems as the Boulder police. They had never actually investigated a homicide before, and they really didn't have much of an idea what they were doing, but they didn't want to admit that and ask for help. They were behind the curve of current best police practices. In the mid- to late 1960s it had become standard police practice to make notes about every interview, to document everything that was said to an investigator as soon as it was said. (For the sake of clarity, Scotland Yard had begun doing this before 1900.) By the mid-1970s many cops still did not do this. The body was not photographed exactly as it was first discovered, and little was done to process the crime scene for evidence.

There were three front-row suspects in the crime: Tommy Skakel, Michael Skakel, and a man who had been employed to tutor and help supervise the Skakel children, and who had moved into the Skakel house on that day, October 30. As little evidence could be developed against anyone, suspicion moved around the neighborhood, eventually visiting a wide variety of people. The investigation stalled.

As did Michael Skakel. A poor student due to severe dyslexia, he had been traumatized by the death of his mother just after his twelfth birthday, and had been poorly parented following her death. His father, who had inherited an immense fortune, was an alcoholic who was off on a hunting trip at the time of the murder, leaving a houseful of unsupervised teenagers. Michael became an alcoholic and drug user with marginal job skills who drifted in and out of rehab.

In the late 1990s Mark Fuhrman wrote a book about the Moxley case. I like Mark Fuhrman; I haven't read the book, but I think Fuhrman has been beaten up enough for his mistakes, and he does good work. Furhman's book re-ignited interest in the Moxley case. Over time, the degeneration of Michael Skakel's life had left him the most vulnerable of the original suspects. It was alleged that he had once confessed to the crime in a group therapy session at a rehab center, and by taking this thing that he had said in 1991 and that remark that he had made in 1984, one could stitch together a case against him.

Not a very good case, but it worked; Skakel was indicted for the murder in January, 2000, and convicted in 2002. We could describe the crime story, I believe, as Q$ 6—a mystery about people with money.

We could describe the case, as well, as being uncannily similar to the murder of **Robin Gilbert**. I could tell the story of Robin Gilbert, but it's the same story I just told. Gilbert was a 14-year-old girl, living in a safe, well-off New England neighborhood, this one in Reading, Massachusetts. On July 2, 1975—less than four months before the murder of Martha Moxley, and less than 170 miles away—Gilbert went for a late-night stroll around the neighborhood. Her body was found the next day, buried under leaves and debris on a golf course near her house. She had probably sneaked out of the house to meet a boy. Inexplicably, the medical examiner ruled that she had died of natural causes—14-year-old girl, her clothes torn open, buried under leaves and debris after 100 feet of drag marks, and the M.E. ruled it was natural causes.

The small-town detectives, as in the Moxley case, talked to everybody but didn't take any notes—plus they were fighting the medical examiner's finding that the girl had died of natural causes. As in the case of Martha Moxley the investigation went nowhere, and the case lay dormant for more than 20 years.

In 1996 the mother of a man named David Allen Jones died of cancer. Before she died she confided to a relative that she had always been afraid that her son was involved in the death of Robin Gilbert. Jones was 16 years old in 1975, and, like Michael Skakel, he had not done well in life. Living in Atlanta and working as a short-order cook, he was arrested in 1997, fought extradition back to Massachusetts, was returned to Massachusetts in 2000 and stood trial in 2004. And . . . here's a little twist for you. On October 26, 2004, a man named David Allen Jones was legally exonerated in California after spending 12 years in custody for a murder he did not commit. On October 28, 2004, a man named David Allen Jones was convicted of manslaughter in Massachusetts for a crime committed 29 years earlier.

Let's face it; the case against Michael Skakel sucks, but I don't understand at all how they convicted David Jones. There's no confession, no physical evidence, no eyewitness to the murder or anything approaching the murder, and the man was not even suspected of the crime at the time that it occurred. A sister of Robin Gilbert claimed that Jones had called the house and talked to Robin on the evening of her disappearance—an unremarkable fact, in that Jones was Gilbert's brother's best friend. Under pressure from police, he "acknowledged" (and later denied) that he had met Robin Gilbert after she snuck out of the house, and they had been making out on the golf course. Combining this with "here's a bad thing he did in 1977—and look, here's another bad thing he did in 1994," prosecutors were able to convince a jury that Jones had strangled Gilbert.

There should be some way to estimate mathematically the probability that two crimes are linked. We have here two young girls of essentially the same age, living in safe neighborhoods, who died under extremely similar circumstances, separated by neither time nor distance of any meaning. Both girls' clothes were torn open, but they were not raped, suggesting an attacker who might be impotent. Is this enough to suggest that the crimes are linked? I don't know. From prison, both Skakel and Jones continue to deny that they had any involvement in the respective crimes.

For three weeks in October, 2002, two men known as the **Beltway Snipers** cruised around Washington, DC, and neighboring cities, murdering people at random with a high-powered rifle. The older of the two, a man named John Muhammad, apparently organized the attacks either as a religious jihad or as a cover for a planned attack against his ex-wife, which would have appeared to be another random shooting. We could categorize the story as KQN 7—a Killer-on-the-Loose Mystery story with a large number of victims, very big for a short period of time.

In January, 2003, **Andrew Luster** was on trial in Ventura, California, facing 87 felony charges connected with a series of date rapes. Luster was an heir to the multi-million-dollar fortune of Max Factor, and, as he had videotaped several of the rapes, he was certain to be convicted.

Luster bolted in mid-trial, and was nowhere to be found. Convicted of the crimes *in absentia*, Luster remained a fugitive until June, 2003. At that point the bounty hunter Duane (Dog) Chapman entered the case, boasting that he was going to find Andrew Luster and haul his sorry ass back to Ventura to face the music. And he did. Very quickly.

Unfortunately, Luster had been hiding out in Mexico, and bounty hunting is not legal in Mexico. Chapman was charged in Mexico with deprivation of liberty, in the unlawful arrest of Andrew Luster. While Luster has been in jail since 2003 and probably will be for the rest of his life, the battle of Chapman versus Mexico dragged on for almost four years. The Mexican government was determined to prosecute Chapman, and the American State Department was fully willing to cooperate in that prosecution. Large numbers of American politicians, however, were appalled at the idea of prosecuting Dog for interfering with the liberty of a scumbag. A battle raged over the issue until the Mexican statute of limitations expired.

This is not a celebrity story because Duane Chapman was not famous before his capture of Andrew Luster. His pursuit and arrest of Andrew Luster was one of the key events that propelled him to fame. The story could be classified as J$P 7—a story about the criminal justice system, centering on money and politics.

On February 3, 2003, the struggling actress Lana Clarkson was found dead in the Los Angeles mansion of legendary record producer *Phil Spector*. Spector, a fantastically successful producer in the 1960s, had become a recluse following a car accident in 1974. That doesn't quite say it; he was an amazingly creepy recluse, albeit an amazingly creepy recluse with a ton of money. He was Dracula with a drug habit. He was *Sunset Boulevard* come to life with amphetamines and painkillers. Spector was convicted of Clarkson's murder in 2009, and is serving 18 years to life. CBT 5; C for Celebrity, B for Bizarre, T for Tabloid.

In 2000 Gavin Arvizo, suffering from cancer, visited *Michael Jackson*'s Neverland Ranch as a part of a "wishes for sick kids" program. Jackson paid for Arvizo's chemotherapy, and became friendly with Arvizo and his family. In 2002 and 2003 Arvizo often stayed at Neverland Ranch, and sometimes slept in Jackson's bed with him. At the time Arvizo and his family insisted there was nothing inappropriate about the relationship, but in subsequent years, following disagreements between the Jackson camp and the Arvizos, their thinking about the relationship changed. Jackson—long suspected of being a pedophile—gave interviews acknowledging that he often shared his bed with young boys, and arguing that this was not inappropriate. As the rumors about Jackson's sexual contact with children mushroomed, Santa Barbara County authorities became increasingly concerned, and eventually Jackson was arrested and charged with molesting Arvizo and related crimes such as holding Arvizo's family at Neverland Ranch against their will.

Jackson stood trial for these charges from January through June, 2005, and was found not guilty of all charges on June 13, 2005—just weeks after the acquittal of Robert Blake. Jackson claimed that he was the victim of a fraud and extortion attempt by the Arvizo family, a claim which, in the view of the author, is almost certainly true. I would classify the story as C F$X 6—a

Celebrity story involving Fraud, Money and seX, big but not all that big out-side of LA. The construction C F$X rather than CF$X is intended to indicate the dominance of celebrity as the driving element of the story.

I am not getting into the issue of whether Michael Jackson was a pedo-phile. I don't know. At the time of the trial reporters would routinely describe Jackson as "the most famous man in the world," a description that beggars the imagination. Michael Jackson was never at any point in his life one of the 100 most famous people in the world. He was one of the 100 most famous people in the Los Angeles celebrity world, which occasionally confuses itself with the real world.

On July 19, 2004, ***Lori Hacking*** disappeared from her home in Salt Lake City, Utah. This was a big story for a few days until it became fairly clear that her husband, Mark Hacking, was responsible for the disappearance. Mark Hacking confessed to her murder in April, 2005, and will be eligible to apply for parole in 2034. M 5.

On February 24, 2005, a nine-year-old girl named ***Jessica Lunsford*** was abducted from her bedroom in Homosassa, Florida. A 47-year-old career criminal and convicted sex offender, John Couey, lived in a trailer near Luns-ford. Couey was convicted of the crime and sentenced to death in 2007. He died in prison of natural causes in 2009. The story could be categorized as MIX 6, a missing person story (M) about sexual violence done to an Inno-cent victim, or perhaps as MIXJ 6, on the theory that the Justice system's failure to deal effectively with John Couey at an earlier date is a central ele-ment of the story.

On May 30, 2005, ***Natalee Holloway*** disappeared during a visit to Aruba. Holloway had graduated from high school in Alabama less than a week earlier; she was on a trip with 100+ classmates to celebrate the graduation. Drinking heavily throughout the trip, she was seen after midnight on May 29 (early hours of May 30) in a car with three locals, who later claimed that they had dropped her off at her hotel.

A prime suspect in the case, although not the only one, was Joran van der Sloot. Exactly five years later (May 30, 2010), van der Sloot murdered a girl in Peru, or at least has confessed to so doing. That finally ended the mystery of what had happened to Natalee, albeit not a legal or satisfactory ending. It's AMQ 8, an adventure/mystery story about a missing girl.

The ***Duke Lacrosse*** non-rape story began on March 13, 2006. Before I say that the lacrosse players were entirely innocent, I should say that they're not *too* innocent. The Duke Lacrosse team on that day had arranged to have a raunchy, drunken party at a private house, and they had hired two strippers to perform at the party. They had requested white strippers, but the women who showed up were black. At least a couple of people made racist remarks, and suggestions were made to the women of such a lewd nature that they caused the performance to be cancelled after a short time.

One of the dancers had been using drugs throughout the evening, and after they left the party the two dancers began to quarrel. The more sober dancer tried to get the stoned one out of her car, and this led to a dispute between the two that was serious enough to result in a 911 call.

Taken into custody for the purposes of getting medical assistance, the inebriated dancer now began to say that she had been raped at the party. This was unmistakably untrue. There was abundant evidence to show that it was untrue. Durham County District Attorney Mike Nifong, however, chose to believe that the allegation was true.

Fair enough—on the first day. People make mistakes; we don't always know who is telling the truth. The story, however, exploded onto the national stage. Durham County is 44% black. Nifong, running for re-election, wanted the black community in Durham to know that he stood solidly with them, which meant that he stood with the dancer making the allegations, rather than with the overprivileged white people who were accused of the crime.

The rapid influx of the media into the story, however, caused more facts to emerge at an unusually fast pace. Over the next two weeks more and more and more information emerged—taxi cab logs, ATM transaction records, time-stamped photographs, cell phone records, DNA tests, medical reports, eyewitness reports from disinterested parties, computer usage records and electronic key signatures, and interviews with the other dancer. These bits of information very quickly made it clear that Nifong was prosecuting people who were not at the house at the time in question for a crime that had never occurred. Nifong illegally suppressed exculpatory evidence, and lied to the court repeatedly in an effort to sustain the prosecution of people who he quite certainly should have known could not have committed the crime.

For his actions in the case, Mike Nifong was removed from office, and was disbarred by the state of North Carolina on June 16, 2007. It was an unusual case, in that the real crime—the unlawful prosecution of innocent people—took place in full view of the public, and after the crime *story* was already underway. I would categorize the crime as JDP 7—J for "Justice System," in that this was a story about the operation of the Justice System, D for "Dreyfus," in that innocent people were prosecuted, and P for "Politics," in that politics were central to the story.

On April 16, 2007, Seung-Hui Cho killed 32 people (33 including himself) on the campus of *Virginia Tech University* in Blacksburg, Virginia. The story could be classified as N 8, a mass-shooting story.

On October 28, 2007, Stacy Peterson was reported missing by her sister, Cassandra Cales. Stacy Peterson had been the fourth wife of *Drew Peterson,* who was a cop in Bolingbrook, Illinois, which is a west-side suburb of Chicago.

Peterson had been a cop for 29 years. The disappearance of Stacy Peterson exploded as a news story on its own, as such disappearances occasionally do for no apparent reason, and then the story flipped up to another level when it was learned that Peterson's previous wife, Kathleen Savio, had died under questionable circumstances in 2004. Although Savio's death had been ruled an accidental drowning, she had been found in a dry bathtub.

What *really* made the story, however, was that Drew Peterson didn't do what everybody else does in those circumstances. He didn't try to hide from the investigation, or from the publicity surrounding it. He hired a publicist. He met with reporters, made jokes about his situation, waved cheerfully sometimes to the people who were staking out his house and sometimes threatened them, and said repeatedly that his wife had left him for another man, and he was sure she would turn up soon. He went on Larry King to talk about the case.

On May 7, 2009, after eighteen months of speculation and investigation, Drew Peterson was indicted and charged with the murder of his third wife, Kathleen Savio. Stacy Peterson is still missing, and Drew Peterson is in jail awaiting trial at this writing. I would classify the case as TMJ 7, a tabloid/missing-persons case involving the integrity of the justice system.

In June, 2008, an adorable two-year-old girl named *Caylee Anthony* disappeared from her home in Orlando, Florida. Her mother, Casey Anthony, did not report Caylee missing until . . . well, ever; eventually Caylee's grandmother called 911, but by that time Caylee had been missing for a month.

Casey Anthony was arrested in October, 2008, went on trial in May, 2011, and was acquitted of the major charges against her (convicted of minor charges) in July, 2011 (I'm guessing you might have heard). It is the view of the author that the Casey Anthony jury did what they had to do. One cannot prove that Caylee Anthony was in fact murdered (rather than that she died in an accident), and, if you can't prove she was murdered, you can't convict somebody of murdering her. The case could be categorized as MIT-9—M for Missing, I for Innocent Victim, T for Tabloid, and 9 to indicate that it was a very, very bit story.

On December 11, 2008, *Bernie Madoff* was arrested for securities fraud. Madoff was a well-respected Wall Street insider, at one time Chairman of the Board of NASDAQ. He had founded his own investment firm in 1960. At some point early in its history this firm became a Ponzi scheme, an investment operation that claimed large non-existent profits and re-paid investors with the money taken in from new investors. Such schemes normally burn out in a year or two, but Madoff was so consistently successful at pulling in new money that he was able to sustain his fraud for almost half a century, eventually defrauding investors of somewhere between $13 billion and $65 billion. The financial panic of late 2008 caused the well of potential investors to dry up, thus exposing the fraud. F$ 7.

On June 25, 2009, pop star *Michael Jackson* died at his home in Los Angeles, apparently as a result of the careless administration of narcotics intended as sleeping aids. It's a Celebrity/Tabloid story, the size of which is yet to be determined at this writing. Jackson's doctor, Dr. Conrad Murray, has been charged with involuntary manslaughter for giving Michael Jackson access to more drugs than anybody needs.

Before I wrap up the book there is an argument I needed to make, having to do with false confessions. I thought I would work this in somewhere in a false-confession story, but I never exactly hit one at the right angle.

In the discussion of a crime story, it is often treated as an extraordinary concept that a person might confess to a murder that he did not commit. It is not uncommon to see otherwise intelligent people debate whether there really are false confessions, in anything other than extraordinary conditions.

In my view, 70 to 90% of confessions to murder *are* false confessions. The confusion has to do with false confessions *that the police believe to be genuine*. Think about it. When the police are investigating a murder, do they share with the public all of the information that they have?

Almost every crime book includes the tidbit that certain information was withheld from the public. Information is withheld from the public, always, in virtually 100% of criminal investigations, precisely in order to help the police distinguish true from false confessions.

The police know that in almost every high-profile murder case, they will at some point have a confession. If it's a *really* high-profile murder case, they will have a dozen confessions. The police, with very few exceptions, do not wish to prosecute innocent people. They hold back information precisely to see that this does not happen. A woman is found murdered in her bathroom with a blue windbreaker tied around her neck. The police will tell the public that the woman was murdered in her bedroom with a red necktie. When somebody comes forward and claims that he murdered the woman in her bedroom with a red necktie, they tell him to go home and stop wasting their time. When somebody tells them that he strangled the woman in her bathroom with a blue windbreaker, they prosecute.

This doesn't happen once in a while. It happens all the time. It happens all the time because the police know perfectly well how to make people confess to something. That's the normal practice. You drag confessions out of people, and then you ignore them if the confessor doesn't come up with the right details. If you include *those* false confessions, that the police have thrown out without action, it becomes obvious that false confessions to murder easily outnumber genuine confessions to murder.

The reason police sometimes turn off the video cameras when they are near a confession is not that they're beating confessions out of people. It is that they don't want a record of a false confession. When the real murderer is eventually identified, they don't want the defense to be able to show a videotape of somebody else confessing to the crime. That's normal practice.

The debate focuses on those few cases in which the normal practice fails. Normally, the nut case who confesses to 22 murders a year because he likes attention can be ignored because he doesn't know the facts. Once in a while, like Henry Lee Lucas, the nut case is canny enough to con the police out of the facts without their realizing they have given them up. Once in a while the false confessor guesses right about something, and the police don't realize it has happened. Once in a while you may get a policeman who

    a) is under great pressure to solve a crime, and

    b) is convinced that his suspect in fact committed the crime.

The police officer may then accidentally or even intentionally let the suspect have the facts that have been withheld from the public, creating a confession which prosecutors incorrectly believe to be valid. The illusion that false confessions are rare comes from focusing on these small number of false confessions that slip through the internal protections of the police investigation.

But debating whether or not there are false confessions to murder is like debating whether there are pigeons in Central Park. The only difference is, there are a lot more false confessions to murder than there are pigeons in Central Park.

To this point, I have not reached a conclusion on perhaps the central issue of the book: Is the phenomenon of Popular Crime a destructive thing that should be disdained and discouraged, or is it a constructive process that merely has more ugly facets than Mike Tyson?

Those who are critical of the prominence of Popular Crime stories in our culture make, I believe, about ten arguments:

1) Crime stories breed cynicism, by engendering in many people a distorted view of the world in which crime is more common than it really is.

2) Crime stories encourage the intervention of the press in the operation of the system of justice.

3) Popular Crime stories coarsen our culture by making entertainment out of the pain and suffering of others.

4) Crime stories enflame the public's emotions about irrelevant and trivial issues.

5) Crime stories feed misinformation to the public about police operations and the criminal justice system.

6) Crime stories violate principles of fair play by leading to the public conviction of people who have not been put on trial.

7) Crime stories are a sort of "near pornography" which excite base emotions by enabling those who take an excessive interest in crimes to wallow in the salacious details of events that are outside the experiences of normal and decent people.

8) Publicity about crimes encourages criminals and creates copycat crimes.

9) An undue focus on horrific events interferes with the development of a sense of inhabiting a secure society.

10) Crime stories detract our attention from more serious issues.

I'll deal with the last item first, as I discussed that briefly in Chapter XVI, in re Julius and Ethel Rosenberg. I question whether anyone understands the world well enough to say reliably what is a serious issue (which will not stop me from doing so in a few minutes).

As adults, we direct the attention of our children and of our students toward issues of significance. But in my view, to try to tell other adults what is or is not a "serious" issue is to step into the role of a "super-adult"—an adult who, by virtue of superior intelligence or greater seriousness, is entitled to sort the interests of others into serious and non-serious pursuits. It's arrogant.

Not everything that is arrogant is untrue. Those who try to tell the rest of us what we *should* be interested in are always arrogant, but they are not always wrong. Probably they are often right.

But I question whether they are *reliably* right, and in particular whether they are right in regard to Popular Crime. Let us suppose, for example, that the Super-Adult is very interested in Saving the Rain Forest, and the Super-Adult's younger brother is just a big dumb sports fan. The Super-Adult regards this as an unworthy use of time.

Well, yes, but people have a legitimate need to enjoy their lives. To pursue the things that make life enjoyable is not un-serious. Suppose that the Super-Adult makes himself miserable and annoys others by worrying at length about the degradation of the Rain Forest—which he is totally unable to prevent. No good whatsoever comes from his concern. Who, then, is the serious man—the younger brother, who enjoys his life, or the Super-Adult older brother, who makes himself miserable worrying about something that he can't do anything about?

It's a debatable point.

It is not clear to me that anyone can say what is or is not a serious subject, and it is my view that the things that people happen to be interested in are as reliable a touchstone as any other to what they *should* be interested in.

Look, I'm like anybody else; I get frustrated with the quality of news. I have several "news" channels on my TV, and I often find myself flipping among them, trying to find the actual news buried behind the clutter. Crime stories, repeated on a thirty-minute loop with lengthy interpretation but no new developments, are among the chief irritants. But when these TV people aren't doing stupid crime stories, what are they doing? Dying movie stars, financial analysts hyping their services with a self-serving interpretation of what's happening on Wall Street, manufactured scandals about sports stars and college basketball coaches, and happy talk by on-air personalities who are fortunate that I lack the capacity to fling them instantly into outer space. Even the "political" news is dominated by distractions that just amount to people screaming at one another about lapses of good manners. One desperately wants to see Walter Cronkite, just giving you the news.

Yes, crime stories are a major irritant when you are trying to find actual news; I can sign on to that. But there's a general problem of the news media prostituting itself in the search for ratings, and losing focus on what people need to know or even want to know. I don't think we can really say that Popular Crime stories are responsible for that. Let us deal systematically with the other nine issues:

1) Crime stories breed cynicism, by engendering in many people a distorted view of the world in which crime is more common than it really is.

Yes, I think that's true, sometimes. I don't think that this is *generally* true, that people are driven toward cynicism by an exaggerated sense of our society's risks, but it is true of some people.

In my view, this comes under the heading of the natural limitations of the human mind. Information about politics often leads to emotional extremism, promoting paranoia and damaging the body politic. Some environmentalists promote paranoia about the environment. Some animal-rights activists are crazy people who get mad at the President for swatting a fly.

It is common, in our society, to exaggerate risks in an effort to prod us toward action. Environmentalists, of course, are the best at it; they have successfully created widespread paranoia about risks that are, in reality, impossibly remote. Top-level environmentalists know perfectly well that they are exaggerating the risks, while rank-and-file activists don't have a clue. What do you want to do; wait until the ozone is gone, and then try to fix it?

Violent crimes are life-altering experiences. An exaggerated fear of crime is not a bad thing, if it merely leads us to redundant security measures. Yes, some people are nutty on the subject, but then, some people are nutty on any and every subject.

2) Crime stories encourage the intervention of the press in the operation of the system of justice.

In my view, the intervention of the press in the operation of the system of justice does a thousand times more good than harm. The news media focuses attention on misconduct by police officers, which the command structure would virtually always prefer to cover up. The news media calls attention to crimes that are difficult to solve, and crimes on which no progress is being made. The news media brings to light cases in which innocent people are convicted of crimes. The news media makes the public aware of crimes, and thus of dangers. The news media gives the public the opportunity to come forward with information about crimes that they might otherwise not realize that they have. Yes, the intervention of the press in the operation of the system of justice does do harm, but it does much, much more good than harm.

3) Popular Crime stories coarsen our culture by making entertainment out of the pain and suffering of others.

Well, yes, that's true. But . . . you know, there are many flaws in our popular culture. Homeless people badgering us for money on the city streets coarsen the culture. Drugs have coarsened our culture, and prostitution, and ubiquitous advertisements screaming for our attention from every corner, and easy access to pornography. We have a pretty coarse culture. I'm not really sure how much responsibility for that is borne by Popular Crime stories or how much better off we would be in this regard without them, but I will agree that Popular Crime stories do make entertainment out of the pain and suffering of others, and that this does contribute to a coarsening of the culture.

4) Crime stories enflame the public's emotions about irrelevant and trivial issues.

Nothing is more dangerous than to have the public's emotions enflamed about *serious* issues. When you have the public's emotions enflamed about a serious issue having direct bearing on their lives, you have a war, and very large numbers of people get killed. When you have the public's emotions enflamed about a trivial issue or an issue that is symbolically important, you get barroom arguments.

5) Crime stories feed misinformation to the public about police operations and the criminal justice system.

Yes, but much more real and valid information than misinformation. The human mind has very wrinkled patterns. We very often misunderstand what we are told, and misinterpret it when we try to repeat it. This has nothing to do with the phenomenon of Popular Crime.

6) Crime stories violate principles of fair play by leading to the public conviction of people who have not been put on trial.

This does happen, and at times with tragic consequences. In some advanced countries, one is not allowed to publish the names of persons accused of a crime until they have a fair trial. This is intended to protect the trial, and this raises two questions:

    1) Whether it is effective in protecting the rights of the accused, and

    2) Whether it is worth the cost to a free press to suppress information.

It seems to me a reasonable practice, but I don't know enough about it to argue it one way or the other. In America we place a very high value on an unregulated press. Crime stories are one of many things that sometimes cause us to wonder about the wisdom of that.

7) Crime stories are a sort of "near pornography" which excite base emotions by enabling those who take an excessive interest in crimes to wallow in the salacious details of events that are outside the experiences of normal and decent people.

There are people who take an unhealthy interest in lurid events; that's a fact.

It is, in my opinion, unfair and inaccurate to characterize the Popular Crime audience by those people. Most of us who read crime books, I would argue, do so out of a desire to better understand the fraying edges of society. That is not unhealthy, and we are not titillated by these events.

8) Publicity about crimes encourages criminals and creates copycat crimes.

Sure, but you have to trade that off against the value of crime stories in making people aware of real dangers in their world. Crime stories remind people to lock their doors, to stay out of dark parking lots at night and to think twice about inviting crazy people into their homes. Crime stories about ATM robberies led banks to surround ATMs with lights and cameras. Publicity about the Tylenol poisonings in 1982 led to tamper-proof packaging of non-prescription drugs. On balance, I have no doubt that the prophylactic value of alerting the public to dangers far outweighs the cost in terms of educating criminals.

9) An undue focus on horrific events interferes with the development of a sense of inhabiting a secure society.

One of our chief assignments, as parents, is to create a safe environment for our children. One of the prime responsibilities of a school or a college is to provide a safe environment for education. One of the basic responsibilities of an employer is to create a safe environment for the workers.

Crime stories certainly interfere with the development of a safe environment, but is it the "story" part that we should blame for that, or the "crime" part? The key there is the word "undue." What is an "undue" focus on a murder?

It is my view that huge Popular Crime cases are "symbolic issues" that society uses to try to think through issues of crime and justice. In the O. J. Simpson case, we were, as a society, trying to confront a series of issues:

How does one deal with a celebrity who is accused of murder?

How do we deal with it when a person who is charming, affable, well-liked and widely admired is accused of a vicious crime?

Is the racism of a police officer relevant to the issue of whether an investigation was properly conducted?

Can a man who is rich and famous still be considered a victim of racism?

Is it proper to sequester jurors for a long period of time, or must we find some alternative to that?

When should society get involved in a domestic-violence situation? Is it sufficient to react to 911 calls about an ex-husband/stalker, or should more be done about that?

We were also educating ourselves about DNA and crime-scene management. At the start of the O. J. Simpson saga most people knew little or nothing about DNA, and I would bet that most people had no idea that there was such a thing as a "crime-scene technologist." Those are meaningful gains for society, but those issues are trivial compared to others. We are thinking about *ourselves*, about our nature. Am *I* capable of a crime like that, under the right circumstances? Is my wife capable of a crime like that, or my husband, or my brother, or my neighbor? How do I know? What can I believe? Would I drive the white SUV for a friend in a situation like this, like A. C. Cowlings did? If O.J. is a bad person, why does he have such wonderful friends? Where does O.J.'s rage come from? Does his anger result from his childhood, from growing up in a racist society, or does it result from the dynamics of his relationship with Nicole? Is this hatred or soured love? Or is hatred merely love gone sour? Or did his actions result from arrogance, from having had too many privileges for too long?

We were, in our involvement in the O. J. Simpson case, asking ourselves very, very serious questions—much *more* serious than the questions that are involved in an election, more serious than the questions so hysterically thrust upon us by environmentalists and obesity researchers who are certain we are all going to die next week because we're overweight and running out of oxygen.

In the case of JonBenet—and in the case of Caylee Anthony, and Jessica Lunsford—we were thinking through issues of crime and punishment, and at the same time very basic issues related to the safety of our children. How did the criminal justice system set loose an unprincipled, dangerous man like the one who killed Jessica? How does that happen? What *should* be done with such people? How do we protect our children from such creatures? Is Aruba a safe place to vacation?

It was easy to believe that John Couey was guilty of murder because he looked like he was auditioning for a part in a zombie movie, but Casey Anthony looks like a goddess, and John Ramsey looks like a pastor. How do we deal with that?

A parent refuses medical treatment for a child for religious reasons, and the child dies. How do we deal with that? Is that murder? A woman encourages her boyfriend to punch an ex-boyfriend's lights out, but the ex-boyfriend dies. Is that murder? *Should* it be murder? How should it be punished?

A person suspected of murder vanishes into the night, and, because there is insufficient evidence to prosecute, the police make little effort to trace him. Is that right or wrong? At what point does a person forfeit the right to drop out of one life and begin a new one?

How do we protect ourselves, and how do we decide what punishment is appropriate? Do we trust our judges? Do we trust our prosecutors? Do we trust our police? If not, how do we fix that?

How do we decide when a missing person may be presumed dead? What may a defense attorney legitimately do, in the defense of a guilty client? Are we doing enough to protect the rights of the accused, or are we doing too much? Are we doing the right things, or the wrong things?

These issues have a clear and present relationship to our real lives. If you take away Popular Crime stories, what involvement does the public have in these discussions? How do we educate the public about these issues, and how do we think through them? Where do we debate them, and, of more relevance, when?

After the Lindbergh case the American media—ashamed of itself for its over-the-top coverage of the crime—made a *de facto* arrangement not to wallow in crime stories. Good enough—but did you ever think that maybe that contributed to the explosion of crime that began about 1963?

Well, it did. It did, in this way. It is one thing to say that no person should be murdered by the state. I am opposed to the death penalty; many of you are opposed to the death penalty.

It is one thing to say that when you are not exposed to pictures of murdered children and stories about convicts who get out of prison and immediately rape and murder a co-ed. It is a very different thing to say that when you are. It is one thing to say that everybody is entitled to a second chance. It is a different thing to say that when you know what the costs are of being too free with second chances. It is one thing to argue for rehabilitation and re-integration of criminals into society, when you are shielded from the costs of their crimes.

The gentleman's agreement not to "exploit" crime stories led gradually to a society that *felt* more safe than it really was. We fell into sloppy attitudes about criminals, attitudes that emphasized the rights of criminals over the protection of society. This led gradually to a criminal justice system that didn't take serious crime seriously enough, and this contributed to an explosion in the crime rate.

We all know that serious crimes result from behaviors that are not criminal. In the same way that a mixture of flour, eggs, sugar, baking powder and a hot oven will result in a cake, a mixture of guns, drugs, prostitution, jealousy and a bad debt will result in a murder. Do you regulate guns to prevent that mix from forming, or drugs, or prostitution, or loan sharking? Or all of them? *How* do you regulate them?

We don't need to think *less* about these issues, as a society; we need to think *more* about them. I acknowledge that there are problems with Popular Crime stories, that there is ugliness to them, that there are victims of the process, that there are distortions of resources that result from them and there are problems in the judicial system that result from the popularization of criminal events.

But we have two choices: we can abandon the criminal justice system to the lawyers—which will result in a justice system that works well for lawyers—or we can involve the public. If we want the public involved, it is Popular Crime stories that are the pathway to their involvement.

Addendum to the Paperback Edition

B efore the publication of the paperback version of this hyar book I have been given the opportunity to include a little bit of new material. This new material consists of three things:

1) Errata,

2) A list of 100 good crime books, and

3) Three new articles.

Errata. All of us who write books make mistakes in our books; we all say things that aren't true. To write a non-fiction book without making any mistakes is entirely impossible. Suppose that you are a realtor. Are you a *perfect* realtor? Do you ask every client every question that should be asked, and none that should not be asked? Do you know every house that is on the market as well as you would like to know it? Is every word that comes out of your mouth always the gospel truth, as honest as you may be, or do you occasionally misunderstand what you have been told, and accidentally mislead the client?

Me, too; I occasionally misunderstand what I read, and pass on to you bad information. I occasionally trust sources that turn out to be unreliable. This happens. I do my best to minimize those events, but . . . it happens.

However, this book has been out for a year, has been read by a dozen or more people in the United States, England and Australia, not counting a couple of hundred reviewers, many of whom have actually read the book, and I have been made aware of only one error in the text. This is very unusual; normally I am bombarded by people who think I have screwed something up—and I've heard from a couple of other people, too, who have objections to things I have written that they believe are wrong, but which I still think are correct. The error has to do with the case of Grace Roberts/Maizie Colbert, which I wrote about in Chapter XI. Somebody who was a distant relative of Ms. Colbert (and no, it *wasn't* Stephen) wrote to me to straighten out some things. He had several points that frankly I couldn't quite grasp, but the two that I did understand were 1) that "Maizie" Colbert was a nickname, not her "real" name, and that she was sometimes called "Grace" by her own family, and 2) that Ms. Colbert's father, who I described as an unskilled laborer, was in fact a relatively skilled worker who provided for his family a comfortable home. That's all I got for errata.

After the book came out I heard from a number of people who asked me, "Why didn't you include a list of the 100 best crime books?" to which I replied, of course, "Why don't you mind your own damned business?" But after I heard this suggestion a couple of dozen times I eventually had to concede that maybe I should have done that, so here it is.

I have to begin by apologizing to the many authors of very good crime books that I have not yet had the time to read, and, more particularly, to the dozen or more authors of very good crime books that I have read, but have forgotten about and overlooked in compiling this list. This is not a list of the 100 Greatest Crime Books; it's just a list of 100 Good Crime Books that I will recommend to you, and then we will assume that there are 1,000 more that I don't know anything about. I've never read anything by Jack Olsen; they tell me he's good, but I've just never gotten to anything. I've never read any of Shana Alexander's books. I bought them, but somehow I never got around to reading them. Maybe they should be on the list. I don't know.

One thing that you probably do know, if you read crime books, is that most books about crimes are terrible. I don't mean to be disrespectful to the people in what is now "my" area, but . . . a lot of books about crimes are just God Awful. None of the books that I will list here are bad; they're all pretty good. I'm going to give them "stars," but I wanted to warn you that I'm grading here on a very, very tough scale; even the one-star books on this list are actually good books. I am recommending all of these books; I am just recommending some of them more highly than others. I will list the books alphabetically by the author and skip the publication data, since many of these books have been re-published numerous times.

1) *Privileged Information*, Tom Alibrandi and Frank H. Armani, 1991 (**).
2) *Bird Man: The Many Faces of Robert Stroud*, Jolene Babyak, 1994 (*).
3) *The Defense Never Rests*, F. Lee Bailey, 1972 (*).
4) *Nightmare in Wichita: The Hunt for the BTK Strangler*, Robert Beattie, 2005 (*).

5) *He Made It Safe to Murder: The Life of Moman Pruiett,* Howard K. Berry, first publication variously reported as 1944 and 1951 (***).

6) *The Murder Trial of Judge Peel,* Jim Bishop, 1962 (**). A monster crime story in its day. So many copies of this book were printed that it turns up in every library book sale ever conducted.

7) *Kansas Charley: The Story of a 19th-Century Boy Murderer,* Joan Jacobs Brumberg, 2003 (***).

8) *The Ice Man: The True Story of a Cold-Blooded Killer,* Anthony Bruno, 1993 (*). There are two books called *The Ice Man,* both of them about Richard Kuklinski. Philip Carlo's book, which was written years later, is probably a little better.

9) *Helter Skelter,* Vincent Bugliosi and Curt Gentry, 1974 (**). Perhaps the only book ever written by a prosecutor in which the cops he worked with are portrayed as bumbling incompetents. He must have been a lot of fun to work with.

10) *In Cold Blood,* Truman Capote, 1965 (*****).

11) *The Ice Man: Confessions of a Mafia Contract Killer,* Philip Carlo, 2006 (**).

12) *The Brothers Bulger: How They Terrorized and Corrupted Boston for a Quarter Century,* Howie Carr, 2006 (***).

13) *Harvard and the Unabomber,* Alston Chase, 2003 (***). One of the problems of crime books is that they are generally intellectual deserts, totally devoid of ideas. The problem with *Harvard and the Unabomber* is exactly the opposite: it is a jungle of ideas. The book is so tightly packed with ideas, theories and arguments that it's difficult to read; you feel like you're hacking your way through the Congo, just trying to track the story. This makes a nice change of pace.

14) *Cell 2455, Death Row,* Caryl Chessman, 1954 (***).

15) *The Face of Justice,* Caryl Chessman, 1957 (*).

16) *The Girl on the Volkswagen Floor,* William Arthur Clark, 1971 (**).

17) *Last Rampage,* James W. Clarke, 1990 (****).

18) *The Murder of Helen Jewett,* Patricia Cline Cohen, 1999 (***).

19) *The Red Ripper,* Peter Conradi, 1992 (**). A book about Andrei Chikatilo, a Russian serial murderer who killed more than 50 victims. Not here to argue, but here's a spectacularly absurd quote from page 57 of this book: "It would be nice to think that in the more open soci-

eties of the West, the first signs of such abnormal behavior would likely have been picked up. Later, if not sooner, Chikatilo would have been obliged to leave teaching, and even be prosecuted. But in the Soviet Union, this simply did not happen."

Here and in numerous other parts of the book, Conradi is suggesting, if not quite arguing, that Chikatilo's sexual dysfunction resulted from the prudishness and lack of sexual openness in Russian society; page 176, "with a kind of naivety that was itself a product of Soviet society's prudish attitudes towards sex, none of the boys seemed to foresee the sexual designs that this apparently normal, elderly man could have upon them." Page 32: if he had been "of another, more liberal generation, in another, more liberal country, Chikatilo would probably have discussed this sadistic streak with his wife, if not with a psychiatrist. With help, maybe he could have found a way to integrate it into his normal sexual life and somehow neutralize it. But this was southern Russia—not southern California—and Chikatilo could not imagine how he could bring up such a delicate matter with his straight-laced wife."

If only Chikatilo had lived in Southern California, he could never have become a serial murderer!

Except, of course, that Southern California has more serial murderers per capita than anyplace else on the planet, except possibly Florida. Openness about sexuality doesn't *protect* us from sexual deviance; it *exposes* us to sexual deviance. The idea that the emancipation of our sexuality will free society of the unfortunate side effects of perverse desires is fifty years behind the curve—and yet we cling to it, as a society, because it was the liberal notion of our youth, and we are afraid to admit that the progressive ideas which we adopted in the best of faith did not turn out to be good investments.

20) *A Grave for Bobby,* James Deakin, 1990 (**). Deakin is a little too clever for his own good. *Zero at the Bone* is a better account of the same case.

21) *The Dungeon Master,* William Dear, 1984 (**).

22) *Please . . . Don't Kill Me: The True Story of the Milo Murder,* William C. Dear and Carlton Stowers, 1989 (*).

23) *I Know My First Name Is Steven,* Mike Echols, 1991 (*).

24) *True Story: Murder, Memoir, Mea Culpa,* Michael Finkel, 2006 (***).
    A very unusual accidental intersection of two unrelated crime sto-
    ries.

25) *The Boston Strangler,* Gerold Frank, 1966 (**).

26) *Birdman of Alcatraz,* Thomas E. Gaddis, 1955 (**).

27) *Killer: A Journal of Murder,* Thomas E. Gaddis, 1970 (**). Based on
    the journals of Carl Panzram, an articulate murderer executed at
    Leavenworth in 1930. You can't believe anything that Panzram says
    (or Gaddis either, for that matter), but Panzram's murderous nihil-
    ism is voyeuristically compelling.

28) *The Court of Last Resort,* Erle Stanley Gardner, 1952 (**).

29) *The Killing of Bonnie Garland,* Willard Gaylin, M.D., 1982 (***).

30) *A Little Girl Is Dead,* Harry Golden, 1965 (***). The murder of Mary
    Phagan.

31) *Stories of Scottsboro,* James Goodman, 1994 (***).

32) *Zodiac,* Robert Graysmith, 1996 (*. OK, maybe **). Graysmith, hav-
    ing written about six or eight books now, still has *no* idea what he
    is doing as a writer, but there is some appeal to his earnest obses-
    siveness.

33) *The Innocent Man: Murder and Injustice in a Small Town,* John
    Grisham, 2006 (**).

34) *The Alice Crimmins Case,* Kenneth Gross, 1975 (***).

35) *Zero at the Bone: The Playboy, the Prostitute, and the Murder of Bobby
    Greenlease,* John Heidenry, 2010 (***). I believe there are six dif-
    ferent crime books named *Zero at the Bone,* but this one is pretty
    decent.

36) *Double Jeopardy,* Bob Hill, 1995 (**). Mel Ignatow.

37) *The Sheppard Murder Case,* Paul Holmes, 1961 (***).

38) *3 Lives for Mississippi,* William Bradford Huie, 1965 (***). Huie was
    a very interesting writer, a Southerner who wrote about the Civil
    Rights cases of the 1950s and 1960s, and did so with quite excep-
    tional integrity. In some cases he takes on the legend of a Civil Rights
    victim, and argues that the supposed victim was in fact a vicious
    criminal. In most cases he is on the side of the Civil Rights move-
    ment, but he doesn't seem to care what you think: He prints the facts
    and lets the chips fall where they may. Huie launched the career of
    William F. Buckley Jr., worked briefly as a butler for Bugsy Siegel,

co-authored a book with Zora Neale Hurston, wrote *The Execution of Private Slovik,* and made Ira Hayes famous (hero of Iwo Jima, portrayed in a film by Tony Curtis, sung about by Johnny Cash). Martin Luther King, Jr.—yes, *that* Martin Luther King, Jr.—wrote the introduction to the second edition of *3 Lives for Mississippi.*

39) *A Death in Belmont,* Sebastian Junger, 2006 (**).

40) *The Boston Stranglers,* Susan Kelly, 1995 (**).

41) *The Michigan Murders,* Edward Keyes, 1976 (**).

42) *Murder One,* Dorothy Kilgallen, 1967 (**).

43) *A Cast of Killers,* Sidney Kirkpatrick, 1986 (**).

44) *The Trial of Levi Weeks,* Estelle Fox Kleiger, 1989 (**).

45) *The Minister and the Choir Singer,* William M. Kunstler, 1964 (**).

46) *The Devil in the White City,* Erik Larson, 2004 (***).

47) *Thunderstruck,* Erik Larson, 2007 (****).

48) *20,000 Years in Sing Sing,* Warden Lawes (Lewis E. Lawes), 1932 (**).

49) *The Falcon and the Snowman,* Robert Lindsey, 1979 (***). The Christopher Boyce spy case.

50) *The Flight of the Falcon,* Robert Lindsey, 1983 (**). Christopher Boyce breaks out of jail and robs banks. This is not fiction.

51) *Irresistible Impulse,* Robert Lindsey, 1992 (**). I think this must be Lindsey's least successful book, but it tells a very interesting story about a California girl who married into the wealthiest family in England, other than the royals.

52) *Where the Money Was,* Ed Linn and Willie Sutton, 1976 (***). Willie Sutton was a famous bank robber of the 1920s, 1930s and 1940s— an entertaining and generally pretty harmless rogue. When asked why he robbed banks, he supposedly said "Because that's where the money was," although in the book he denies that he ever said this. Ed Linn was a wonderful biographer, and I recommend all of his books. This, however, is his only crime book.

53) *The Unspeakable Crimes of Dr. Petiot,* Thomas Maeder, 1980 (*). Petiot was a Frenchman who took advantage of the chaos of World War II. There is also a more recent book about him which I have not yet read.

54) *The Rabbi and the Hit Man,* Arthur J. Magida, 2003 (*).

55) *The Executioner's Song,* Norman Mailer, 1980 (***). Pulitzer Prize, my ass.

56) *Killing for Company: The Story of a Man Addicted to Murder,* Brian Masters, 1993 (**). British serial murderer Dennis Nilsen.

57) *The Dreams of Ada,* Robert Mayer, 1987 (**).

58) *Mortal Error,* Bonar Menninger, 1992 (**). Plodding and almost unreadable at points, but a serious book proposing a serious and credible explanation for the tragedy in Dallas. Who in the hell would name their kid "Bonar"?

59) *The Basement,* Kate Millett, 1979 (*). The story of the abuse to the point of eventual death of Sylvia Likens, a 16-year-old girl who died in a basement in Indianapolis in 1965. Millett spends half the book in stream-of-consciousness rants in which she pretends to be Sylvia, pretends to be her murderer, or pretends to be somebody else. This is maddening, but the case itself is extremely interesting.

60) *The Rose Man of Sing Sing,* James McGrath Morris, 2003 (****).

61) *Torso: Eliot Ness and the Hunt for the Mad Butcher of Kingsbury Run,* Steven Nickel, 1989 (*).

62) *The Wrong Man,* James Neff, 2001 (**). I guess Sheppard was innocent after all.

63) *The Implosion Conspiracy,* Louis Nizer, 1973 (**). The best of the interminable books about the Rosenbergs.

64) *Two of a Kind: The Hillside Stranglers,* Darcy O'Brien, 1985 (**).

65) *The Devil's Rooming House,* M. William Phelps, 2010 (**).

66) *Case Closed,* Gerald Posner, 1993 (***).

67) *The Monster of Florence,* Douglas Preston and Mario Spezi, 2009 (***). A remarkable book badly damaged by the irresponsible accusation of a probably innocent young man.

68) *Courtroom: The Story of Samuel S. Leibowitz,* Quentin Reynolds, 1950 (**).

69) *The Stranger Beside Me,* Ann Rule, 1980 (**). Bundy.

70) *The Want-Ad Killer,* Ann Rule, 1983 (*).

71) *The I-5 Killer,* Ann Rule, 1984 (**).

72) *Homicide!,* Charles W. Sasser, 1990 (**).

73) *Scapegoat,* Anthony Scaduto, 1976 (**).

74) *American Tragedy,* Lawrence Schiller and James Willwerth, 1996 (**). I think I'm required to have one O.J. book on the list.

75) *Perfect Murder, Perfect Town,* Lawrence Schiller, 1999 (**). JonBenet. Schiller is unpretentious, but very professional.

76) *Natural Born Celebrities,* David Frank Schmid, 2006 (**).

77) *Invitation to an Inquest,* Walter and Miriam Schneir, 1965 (*). Rosenbergs.

78) *The Shoemaker: The Anatomy of a Psychotic,* Flora Rheta Schreiber,
1983 (**). Creepy but compelling.

79) *Death Sentence,* Joe Sharkey, 1991 (**). One of several books about
the John List murders; I haven't read the others.

80) *Homicide: A Year on the Killing Streets,* David Simon, 1991 (***).

81) *The Search for the Green River Killer,* Carlton Smith and Tomas Guil-
len, 1991 (*).

82) *And I Don't Want to Live This Life,* Deborah Spungeon, 1983 (***).

83) *Blind Eye,* James B. Stewart, 1999 (****). A scary story about the medical establishment's twenty-plus years of covering up for a murderous doctor.

84) *Final Verdict,* Adela Rogers St. Johns, 1962 (*****).

85) *The Cuckoo's Egg,* Cliff Stoll, 1989 (**).

86) *Twelve Caesars,* Suetonius, written about 115 AD (****). In terms of
violent behavior by crazy people, the Roman emperors were hard
to top. Whereas the other notable Roman historians like to write
about the wars and proclamations of the emperors, Suetonius, who
was a bit of a gossip (while still a very legitimate historian), likes to
write about who they slept with and who they murdered and why.
Extremely entertaining.

87) *The Suspicions of Mr. Whicher,* Kate Summerscale, 2009 (***).

88) *Race Riot,* William M. Tuttle Jr., 1970 (***).

89) *Something Terrible Has Happened,* Peter Van Slingerland, 1966 (**).

90) *Kidnap,* George Waller, 1961 (**). Overlong.

91) *Tears of Rage,* John Walsh with Susan Schindehette, 1997 (**).

92) *The Ultimate Evil,* Maury Terry, 1987 (*). Serious research, seriously
flawed writing.

93) *Murder at Harvard,* Helen Thomson, 1971 (**).

94) *Jury,* Victor Villaseñor, 1977 (***).

95) *The Onion Field,* Joseph Wambaugh, 1973 (****).

96) *Betrayal,* Tim Weiner, David Johnston, and Neil A. Lewis, 1995 (**).
The story of the CIA mole Aldrich Ames.

97) *American Taboo: A Murder in the Peace Corps,* Philip Weiss, 2005
(***).

98) *Bad Company*, Steve Wick, 1991 (**). A serviceable account of a quite remarkable story, the murder of Hollywood producer Roy Radin.

99) *The Black Dahlia Files: The Mob, the Mogul, and the Murder That Transfixed Los Angeles*, Donald H. Wolfe, 2005 (***).

100) *The Newgate Calendar*, original author unknown (****). *The Newgate Calendar* was published repeatedly (in various forms) through the 17th, 18th and 19th centuries, and was one of the most widely read books in the English language for about 200 years, perhaps second only to the Bible, or third behind *Pilgrim's Progress*. Newgate was a large prison in London, where criminals were executed. *The Newgate Calendar* was a collection of short accounts of the lives of famous and terrible criminals. The book was used for generations to teach children about the wages of sin, although it has what we might consider an ambiguous moral tone. Though certainly not reliable, the book is easy to peruse online, and is well worth the investment of a little bit of your time.

While I am in the recommending business here I will also recommend that you explore the website http://law.umkc.edu/faculty/projects, which is a treasure trove of factual information about famous crime cases (Lizzie Borden, the Salem Witchcraft Misunderstanding, Sacco and that other Italian guy, the Sam Sheppard case, etc.). Great admiration for their work.

OK, I had some three other crime stories that I wanted to share with you; these are out of sequence with the narrative, for which I apologize.

On April 10, 1836, a New York City woman working under the name of Helen Jewett was murdered in her brothel. A 19-year-old man named Richard Robinson was arrested and charged with the crime, and was tried but acquitted.

The murder of Helen Jewett occurred at the birth of the modern newspaper industry—a moment very like 1990, the birth of the internet. For a few years newspapers sprouted like dandelions. In a climate of many competing newspapers with small audiences and extraordinarily lax editorial practices, the story of the murder of Helen Jewett emerged as one of the most famous crimes in American history. Patricia Cline Cohen wrote a 1998 book about this case, *The Murder of Helen Jewett*, published by Alfred A. Knopf.

Helen Jewett was a prostitute, yes, but in saying this I am as much misinforming you as the opposite. She was a prostitute, but Robinson and Jewett had an intense, passionate relationship which had been going on for a year before her murder. They wrote one another love letters, dozens or probably hundreds of them. They bought one another gifts; they went to the theater together. They teased one another and fought petty battles that seemed to both of them larger than life. They shared secrets. They carried small, handdrawn pictures of one another. She sewed on his buttons, and mended his shirts. When Robinson had dalliances with other women, she was furious with him, and he had to work his way back into her good graces.

She was, then, more of a surrogate wife or a surrogate girlfriend than she was simply a sex worker, as we think of a prostitute in the 21st century. What is unclear, even having read the book, is to what extent this was unusual in 19th century New York. Jewett had and had had similar relationships with other men, although certainly less intense than her relationship with Robinson.

Ms. Cohen's research is quite remarkable, and the story she tells is twice that remarkable, at least. Helen Jewett's name at the time of her birth was Dorcas Doyen. For several years as a young girl Dorcas worked as a live-in domestic servant with the family of Judge Nathan Weston, in Maine. It's a distinguished family; Judge Weston's grandson became Chief Justice of the United States Supreme Court. In the 1820s there was a woman named Mrs. Anne Royall, who travelled around the United States visiting towns and staying with people and recording her experiences in self-published travelogues that were often petty and vindictive. Ms. Royall visited the Weston house, met Dorcas Doyen briefly, was very much charmed by her, and wrote a couple of very flattering paragraphs about her in one of her nasty little books. No one at the time made any connection between this unnamed servant girl and the woman who, nine years later, became the infamous Helen Jewett, but Ms. Cohen nonetheless finds the passage and uses it effectively to help re-construct Ms. Jewett's early life.

That's remarkable research. There are *many* such discoveries in her book. Nathaniel Hawthorne attended Bowdoin College at the same time as a nephew or cousin or something of Judge Weston, and visited this same small town in Maine for several weeks one summer when he was in college, flirting with a servant girl who worked in his friend's house. Hawthorne wrote about this, and wrote about the family and the little town in letters or journals that still survive, and Ms. Cohen finds these and uses them to re-construct the time and place. The wallpaper in one room of another cousin's house still survives, in an off-the-beaten-track museum somewhere, and Ms. Cohen finds this wallpaper and writes about it. Ms. Jewett, as a prostitute, had several other small run-ins with the police, and was on one occasion profiled in a newspaper by a sympathetic reporter (who was also a client), and Ms. Cohen has found this profile and used it to help re-construct her life—as well as the court records of all of these other little dustups.

She finds letters from one family member to another, discussing social events at which Dorcas Doyen would have worked, and, as Doyen/Jewett was an avid reader and a great lover of books, she finds advertisements in small-town newspapers for books that Doyen might have read and probably read, and she finds articles that appeared in local newspapers that describe events or stories that Doyen would have known about or participated in. She finds descriptions of people that Doyen would have known. She finds court records and census records that make passing reference to Doyen's grandfather or her great-grandmother or her next-door neighbor's dog. She finds the addresses at which Jewett lived in New York, and she finds out who was living next-door and what they did for a living, and who lived in all the houses up and down the street and what the nearby businesses were.

It would be ungracious of me not to mention that, having read countless crime books, I have never before encountered anything remotely like this level of research. By "research" I do not mean hitting Google and Wikipedia. I mean living for weeks in old libraries and dusty courthouses, trying to recognize a name in a stack of 200-year-old property transaction records, and then moving on to the next old library, the next old courthouse or the next university archive or the next small-town museum or the next stack of census reports. I'm a pretty good researcher; I couldn't *begin* to do this.

It would also be gutless of me not to call this what it is. It's academic showboating. In 1804 Jacob Doyen, who was Helen Jewett's grandfather, filed a small-claims court action in Hallowell, Maine, against a man named Stephen Smith, having to do with a $12 debt, and then failed to appear in court when the case was heard. Ms. Cohen finds the record of this action and infers actively from it, but it doesn't actually have a damned thing to do with the story of Helen Jewett; it's just showing off Ms. Cohen's research skills. As much as we might admire her research, it does become tiresome. But I understand; 99.99% of book researchers would never *find* a record like that, and almost all of us, if we did, are damned well going to find some way to get it into the book.

It is showboating and it is tiresome, but it is also this that I most admire about crime books in general: that they preserve an image of the lives that are lost. It is the saving grace of crime stories that details become tremendously important. The controversy of the death, like a cosmic flashbulb, illuminates every crevice of the victim's life and the lives entwined with it, and preserves that record for posterity. Never more than here; Ms. Cohen's over-the-top research preserves snapshots of life in Maine and life in New York that are more vivid than a hundred sober histories of dear and respected citizens. The best source, of course, is their own letters; these star-doomed lovers bounced letters off of one another like tennis balls, often demanding that a same-day response be returned by a private porter. It would be an understatement to say that these were literate people. Here are a few quotes from the letters and journals of Richard Robinson.

> Nell, how pleasant it is to dream, be where you will and as hungry as you will, how supremely happy one is in a little world of our own creation. At best we live but one little hour, strut at our own conceit and die . . . Come will ye embark?—then on we go, gaily, hand in hand, scorning all petty and trivial troubles, eagerly gazing on our rising sun, till the warmth of its beams (i.e. love) causes our sparkling blood to o-erflow and mingle in holy delight.

From another letter:

> I know my letters cannot be very interesting to you, Nell; they are full of oh! how I love you and a piece of other nonsense, exactly what they all write you. They all call you dearest Nelly, so do I. I suppose you think us all alike.

From a journal:

> This is the last day of the races; the day on which they run out all the dregs and draw off the equestrian settlings, the spavined, the ring-boned, the sti-fled, the blind, lame and halt. Friend P. advises me not to bet; he gives me so much advice that, in fact, it would require more wisdom to profit by it than to live without it; his system of morals is like J. R.'s patent dog churn, which was a most excellent machine only it required three hands to tend it.

From another journal:

> It is good policy, in carrying a point against an obstinate adversary, to seem
> to yield, for by this means he is generally disarmed. To convince an obstinate
> and conceited man, it is sometimes necessary to throw arguments around
> him and within his reach, which, though he may not observe it, really go to
> sustain the opinions you wish him to embrace.

These are the words of a 19-year-old store clerk accused of a brutal murder! Actually, when he wrote the journal entries he was 16 or 17, and there
are letters he wrote when he was 15 that are equally striking.

Men of letters in the early 19th century wrote overwrought, self-conscious prose that is today almost unreadable. Thomas Carlyle wrote an 1837
history of the French Revolution (written 1834–1837) which is brilliant and
entertaining if you want to work hard enough to decipher it, but so convoluted with rhetorical flourishes as to be largely unintelligible to a modern
reader. Robinson wrote in that vein, or, if you prefer, vain. Jewett did not;
Jewett responded in clean, clear, unpretentious prose that is as lucid and
graceful today as the day she wrote it:

> My Dear Frank—You have passed your promise by two nights, and yet you
> have not thought proper to send me a single line, even in the shape of an
> excuse. Do you think I will endure this. Shall I who have rejected abundance
> for you sake, sit contented under treatment which seems invented for my
> mortification.

From another letter:

> The day, as you know was extremely cold, so much ice in the Delaware as
> to render it impossible for any boat to take the passengers, therefore, we
> had to make the journey all the way on the railroad, and then had to cross
> from Camden in a small ferry boat, without any cabin or fire, and when we
> arrived, we were nearly perished from the cold, and but for the kindness
> and attention of a gentleman whom I met in the car, I never should have got
> along.

From another letter:

Mr. R. P. Robinson: If you think it requisite that I should remain longer in this most painful suspense, you must pardon me for saying that I think differently. If you were placed in my situation (with all your independence) you would ere this have demanded an explanation . . . I do not ask you to fix upon any time, nor do I ask you to come here if disagreeable to you. But I certainly do ask a note before this night from you, in which you will mention a time and place when I may see you, and you will find me punctual.

From another:

I wish you could have seen me an hour after you left my room. His Grace the Duke, the Captain, Louisa and myself cracked nearly a dozen bottles of champagne; however, this must be uninteresting to you, and having little time to say the much I would say—sum it up in four words, may God bless you.

These letters go on for pages. Her punctuation is at times a little nonstandard, but the message is always crystal clear. These are the words of a destitute shoemaker's daughter, dropped off at age twelve to grow up as a domestic servant to a wealthy family, and given a few months of schooling by her generous masters. I venture to say that, if you took the letters of a murdered 21st century prostitute, you would not be likely to find such eloquence.

In fact, there is a great deal in this story that calls into question the notion of progress. The life of Helen Jewett, apart from its terrible finish at the business end of a small hatchet, seems infinitely better than the life of a modern prostitute, as best I understand that from the images on my television. She did not service a hundred clients a week; more likely five to fifteen. She lived in a large house with beautiful furniture, where sumptuous meals were served as an inducement to the clientele. Paintings hung on the walls that today hang in museums and are well known to art historians. She drank champagne, and she spent her days reading novels and writing letters and making a daily promenade to the post office. She wore beautiful dresses. She went to the theater several times a week. Some of the theaters had special seating areas for the prostitutes. They valued their patronage, because the presence of the glamorous ladies drew out-of-town businessmen into the theater.

She did not have a pimp, or a drug habit. There was a madam who ran the brothel, but the madam worked for the prostitutes as much as the other way around; there was a business arrangement between them, in which the ladies drew in the men who ate the expensive meals and bought the no-doubt-overpriced champagne, and the women paid something more than the standard rent on their rooms, but Helen Jewett was free to leave and go to some other house anytime she was unhappy with the accommodations—and, in fact, she *had* moved several times in the previous three years. There were ruffians who liked to break out the windows of brothels and frighten the women, and I am not suggesting that it was an idyllic lifestyle; merely that it seems quite a bit better than working for a 21st century escort service.

She was, of course, a top-end prostitute; there were also streetwalkers, and there were women working out of houses that were not nearly as clean and comfortable. Helen Jewett was quite attractive, and more than that she was very gracious. She was handy with a needle, a central domestic art of the period, and she could play the piano. (Piano-playing marked a woman as "refined," in that era, because only rich people had pianos.)

It is thus surprising that Robinson, who was living in a rooming house where he shared a bed with another young man and who was working as a clerk in a large dry goods store where he was paid virtually nothing, was able to afford the services of such a lady. In part this may have been because Jewett, who was emotionally involved with Robinson, charged him only what he could afford to pay, and in part it was certainly because Robinson was pilfering from his employer. "Pilfering" is probably not the right word; he appears to have been embezzling at a pretty good pace. His wallet, at the time of his arrest, was found to be stuffed with a thick wad of third-party checks addressed to his employer, and his letters to Jewett allude frequently to clandestine activities of an unknown nature. He may have been selling stuff out the back door; the store where he worked was apparently a pretty big operation.

Robinson, then, was a brilliant young man—and a very capable thief. And handsome; apparently he was stunningly handsome; Jewett's beauty may well have been overstated by the press to sell papers, but there is strong evidence for Robinson's. What is unclear in Ms. Cohen's very detailed re-creation of these remarkable people is exactly to what extent they *were* remarkable, even in their own time, and to what extent they merely seem remarkable to the modern reader, who expects a prostitute and her accused murderer to be grunting savages whose idea of a great day is grabbing three cases of Budweiser and tearing through the backcountry on three-wheeled scooters with mud tires. Ms. Cohen seems to *assume* that these people were as remarkable in their own time as they would be now, but because she assumes this she never demonstrates that this is true, or even says that it is true; it is merely implied. She thinks (and says often) that Robinson was arrogant, which was no doubt true, but he was also a child of the romantic era; all men of substance in that era spoke and wrote and dressed and acted in a way that would seem very unnatural now. To what extent did the young men that Robinson worked with (and lived with—many of the clerks that he worked with also lived in the same rooming house and, now that you mention it, consorted with the same prostitutes) . . . to what extent did these other young men also write and think with the boldness and sophistication of Richard Robinson? We simply don't know; we don't get any clue to that from this book.

Jewett was, to an extent, a con woman, a young woman who acted the part of a devoted girlfriend for any man who would pay her to do so—but at the same time, all of these men knew what she did for a living. To what extent was Jewett truly conning these men, and to what extent were they merely acting out a romantic fantasy in which they all knew the rules? We do not know—and Cohen, intent on tracking down the pedigrees of the most peripheral figures—seems curiously untroubled by the gap. When Robinson strayed, Jewett took offense and demanded penance just as a girlfriend would do, even though she herself was sharing her bed and body with a different man every night. But did she do this because she *truly* expected Robinson to be faithful to her, or because, being a surrogate girlfriend, she was trying to do what a *real* girlfriend would do in the same situation? It is critical to the story to know which—and we simply don't get a clue. Cohen seems to assume, unstated, that those were real emotions. I don't know, but it seems to me more likely that it was part of the game.

Cohen is 100% convinced that Robinson murdered Jewett. I am not saying she is wrong; I am suggesting that the evidence doesn't get you to 100%. Seventy percent, maybe. Near midnight on April 9, 1836, a man knocked on the door of Helen Jewett's brothel, announced himself as "Frank Rivers," and asked to see Helen Jewett. It was a cold, wet Saturday night; he had his cloak pulled up around his face and his hat pulled down low. The madam of the house, Rosina Townsend, looked him over and admitted him to the house, and he went up to Jewett's room. About an hour later she rang for service in the room, and Rosina brought champagne and two glasses. Not long after that the servant girl went into the room and tended the fire.

Sometime well after midnight, Rosina was awakened by a man pounding on her door and demanding to be let out of the house. Rosina told him to have his woman let him out, which was the rule of the house; the women were supposed to escort men to the door, so that they didn't pick something up on the way out. The main doors locked inside and out, and required a key from either side. Rosina went back to sleep.

Sometime later in the night, about 3 AM, she was awakened again by a knock on the front door, a regular customer arriving for a pre-arranged late-night assignation with another prostitute. Stirring through the house, she now noticed things amiss. A back door, which could be opened without a key, was setting wide open, and a lamp that belonged on the second floor had been carried to the first. Escorting the customer to the second floor, Rosina smelled smoke, which she traced to Helen Jewett's room. Entering the room, she found Jewett's body, and found that a candle had been placed in the bed next to her, apparently intended to consume the body in fire and destroy the evidence.

One of the other working girls told police that "Frank Rivers" was a pseudonym used for Richard Robinson, and told them where Robinson lived. Robinson's cloak and the bloody hatchet were found in the alleyway behind the house, along the departure route suggested by the open door. Robinson was arrested the next morning, and over the following two days the case erupted into a huge public sensation. Robinson was put on trial in June, about two months after the murder, and, as I mentioned before, was acquitted.

At this point, as murders will, the story becomes messy and complicated. "Frank Rivers," it turns out, was a code name used not only by Richard Robinson, but also by William Easy, whose name wasn't William Easy, either, it was George Marston. Marston was a co-worker of Robinson's who was Helen Jewett's regular Saturday night client; she had a relationship with him that was not unlike her relationship with Robinson, and the two (Robinson and Marston) apparently regarded one another as romantic rivals.

On this particular Saturday night, however, Rosina Townsend had been instructed to admit the Frank Rivers who was *not* William Easy, so when the man knocked on the door with his cloak up around his face and announced himself as Frank Rivers, Rosina looked to make sure that he was not William Easy, which is to say, not George Marston. Determining that he was not, she admitted him to the house.

The evidence against Robinson consisted of:

• the hatchet, which was taken from Robinson's workplace,

• the cloak, which was identified as Robinson's although it actually belonged to another man, and had been given to Robinson as collateral against a debt,

• the eyewitness identification of Rosina Townsend, who admitted him to the house,

• the eyewitness identification of the servant/maid, and

• some business about a "miniature." A miniature was a small hand-drawn or hand-painted picture, a not-inexpensive treasure in the era before photography. Jewett's miniature was seen in Jewett's room by the maid days before the murder, and was found in the possession of Robinson after the murder, suggesting that he took it with him at the time of the murder.

Patricia Cohen, the author of the book, believes that the testimony of Townsend, the other working girls and the maid (who was black) was discounted because they were women and persons of low social status, and she shares with us a fair amount of feminist outrage over this injustice.

Robinson did not testify on his own behalf. Those who testified on his behalf included

• the owner of a cigar store, who testified that Robinson was in his store at the time that he was supposed to have been admitted to Townsend's house, and for some time thereafter,

• the man with whom Robinson shared a bed in the rooming house (not an unusual practice at that time), who testified that Robinson was in the room and in bed at a normal hour and through the night, and

• the owner of the store where Robinson worked, who was a relative of Robinson's, and who testified to his good character despite the evidence that Robinson was stealing from him.

The most important witness was the owner of the cigar store. He was a well-known businessman, an honest man whose word was given weight, and who was personally acquainted with several members of the jury. He came forward on his own to insist that Robinson was in his store at the time in question, buying cigars and smoking them, which Robinson had never said that he was.

The cigar-store owner was clearly mistaken about the time—probably an honest mistake—and this annoys Cohen, that this man was given credibility, whereas the women were ignored because they were prostitutes and persons of low character although Robinson was engaged in the same behavior that Jewett was engaged in, merely from the other side; you get the drift. Robinson's very good defense attorneys implied that Townsend herself had committed the murder and set the fire in order to collect insurance money, which was a fairly silly argument, but then, that's something defense attorneys do; they put forward whatever silly argument is helpful to their case and cannot be refuted within the confines of the trial.

It seems to me that the case against Robinson is not all that convincing. First, despite Ms. Cohen's objections, a prostitute is by definition a little bit of a con artist, and it seems to me not entirely unreasonable to apply some discount to the testimony of anyone who is a little bit of a con artist.

Second, I can't see that the testimony of Rosina Townsend or the maid is all that compelling. Both of them identified Robinson as the man that they saw there on that night, but both of them did so in an odd, backhanded way. Townsend said that she looked at "Frank Rivers" with his cloak drawn up around his face and determined that he was *not* William Easy (which is to say, not George Marston)—that is to say, not that she observed who it was, but merely that she determined who it was not.

Later, she delivered champagne to Jewett's room, and she saw Robinson again; actually the back of his head: he was propped up in bed on his elbow, reading something, with the covers drawn up around him, and she noticed that he had a big bald spot on the back of his head, which she had never noticed before. That's a pretty unusual identification, isn't it—to say that you noticed something that you had never noticed before? Don't you ordinarily identify someone by saying that you saw the things that you *had* seen before?

The maid came to tend the fire, and she said the same thing; she noticed this big bald spot on Robinson's head, which she had never noticed before.

Robinson was 19 years old. Cohen buys into the "bald spot" theory hook, line and sinker, and attributes Robinson's balding to his hair falling out from the stress of his deceptions and burning the candle at both ends. By the time he went to trial he had shaved his head and was wearing a wig, which Cohen thinks was done to hide his bald spot, although it was a normal practice at the time for a man who wished to appear to be a person of substance to don a wig (remember, all of the founding fathers wore wigs, and this was just one generation later).

Two key questions: how well did Townsend know Robinson, and how dark was the house? We don't know. Cohen says that of course Townsend knew Robinson, he was at the house all the time. This doesn't seem to be necessarily true. Jewett had lived in this house only three months, and Robinson and Jewett were pretty much on the outs through most of that period. There were 11 women who lived in the house, and each of those had a large number of clients. Townsend did not know Robinson's real name; he said that he was "Frank Rivers," and she accepted that although she knew that another man also used the name Frank Rivers.

Robinson and Jewett's letters used code names for everybody they knew. They did this because their relationship was somewhat illicit, and—one suspects—because it made them feel like conspirators to use code names. She sent letters to Robinson at work. If a letter fell into someone else's hands—which no doubt happened—it did not identify either her or him by name. Anyway, the point is that if there were two men using the code name "Frank Rivers," there may very well have been six, and other young men who were involved with Helen Jewett and her co-workers could very probably have been aware of the name.

We don't know how dark the house was and how clearly Townsend could have seen the man who entered, but remember, this was before electricity; after it got dark, a house was dark. Whoever committed the murder apparently carried downstairs with him a lamp which normally stayed upstairs, which strongly suggests that the house was pitch black, and he was afraid of falling down the stairs in the dark. It also suggests that he didn't know the layout of the house all that well, which is relevant to Robinson's defense, for if Robinson had been a frequent visitor to the house as Cohen assumes, then he would have known the layout of the house better, and would have been less likely to go banging on Rosina Townsend's door, asking how to get out.

Cohen puts substantial weight on the miniature. Lovers in this era would exchange miniature portraits. Robinson and Jewett had exchanged miniatures, and when they had fights they would return the portraits, and then they would give them back and promise that they could be kept forever, etc. Robinson had Jewett's miniature after her death, although the maid had seen it in her room just days earlier.

But this, to me, seems like nothing, since a woman in Jewett's position—carrying on make-believe romances with a string of men—might very probably have had several copies of the miniature made, when a normal woman would only have had one.

The hatchet did come from Robinson's place of work, yes, and it was his cloak, yes, but why were these items left in the street or alleyway behind the house? Robinson was an intelligent man, and the murder was obviously pre-planned, witness the bringing of the hatchet. Wouldn't Robinson have known that leaving his cloak near the scene of the crime could help to convict him?

Cohen believes that Robinson set the fire expecting that it would consume the house and kill everybody in the building, thus allowing the murder to go un-detected, but a) this was very far from happening, and b) it doesn't really seem like a reasonable expectation. And c) it directs us back to the issue before: If Robinson expected the fire to destroy the evidence, why did he carry the cloak and hatchet outside the house, and drop them there? For that matter, why would he drop his cloak anyway? It was a cold, wet night. I can understand leaving your coat *inside* the house, in your rush to get away, but why wear it out of the house, on a cold, wet night, and drop it in the street? Doesn't that at least suggest the possibility that Robinson was being framed?

There were several other men who worked at the store where Robinson worked, lived in the rooming house where he lived, and were also involved with Helen Jewett or her co-workers. Those men would have had the same access that he did to the hatchet, and might very easily have taken his cloak.

Cohen gives Robinson a motive for the murder by insisting that Robinson was involved in covert activities—theft and possibly other unknown criminal activities—and that Jewett was threatening to expose him. The letters are full of elliptical references to clandestine activities, but Cohen at times seems to be reading things into the letters that aren't necessarily there.

It may sound as if I am saying that Robinson was innocent, which I am not; I am saying that he was acquitted and that I understand why. At the time of Robinson's trial the public was divided about his guilt. After his trial some letters came out that he had written while in jail, letters which reflected very badly upon his character, and which caused almost everyone to conclude that he had been guilty after all. Perhaps he was.

Not long before her death, Helen Jewett had seen the play *Norman Leslie* and had read the book of the same name, which was a fictionalization of the murder of Elma Sands, a story I told early in this book. In that case the accused murderer, Levi Weeks, was also acquitted although he was certainly guilty. He left town after the murder, moved to Natchez, Mississippi, became a well-known architect, and died at the age of 43. Robinson's fate was similar; he moved to Nacogdoches, Texas, about 200 miles from Natchez; Natchez and Nacogdoches are both just off the Louisiana border, on opposite sides of the state. He adopted the name "Parmalee," which was his mother's name, had a very good and successful career as a rancher, saloonkeeper, and the clerk of the local court. He died in Ohio at the age of 38, attempting to make a trip back east.

Moving ahead now four score and six years.

What must be said about William Desmond Taylor is that he made an exceptionally good impression on those he met. He was handsome, articulate, composed, considerate, and had great dignity. He was able to walk away from extremely good jobs, and walk into better jobs in unrelated fields. Beautiful movie stars half his age fell madly in love with him and wanted to marry him, not once but at least three times. In the early days of Hollywood, when most everybody was a poseur and bullshit was the main credential, he was able to move easily from bit player to movie star to director. He was always able to get the jobs, and the girls, that everybody wanted. At the time of his murder the newspapers said that he had been the world's greatest director.

He was murdered about 7:50 PM on February 1, 1922, in what is called his bungalow. We think of a bungalow as a one-story starter house; this was a nice place. I'm not sure why it is called a bungalow. Anyway, his body was found the next morning by his house servant, Henry Peavey, arriving for work a little less than twelve hours after the killing. The murder was never solved. One newspaper suggested it was called a bungalow because the police had bungled it so badly.

King Vidor was a part of old Hollywood, another director. King was his given name. He had known Taylor, and had worked with him. Not quite a half-century later Vidor decided to figure out who had killed Taylor and to make a movie about it. Vidor was an old man by then; perhaps that would have gone without saying. He had directed the black-and-white scenes in *The Wizard of Oz*. Hollywood had left him behind after a 40-year career, and he was trying to get back in the game. He thought the Taylor story might be his ticket. He worked on it for a year, but the movie never went anywhere and he put it away.

After Vidor's death in 1982, a young writer/director/film student named Sidney Kirkpatrick was working on a biography of him. Fitzpatrick discovered Vidor's cache of notes and tapes about the Taylor case, and decided to turn that into a book. "The Sensational True Story of Hollywood's Most Scandalous Murder," says the cover of *A Cast of Killers,* "Covered Up for Sixty Years and Solved at Last by the Great Film Director King Vidor." (E. P. Dutton, 1986.)

Nathaniel Hawthorne loved the concept of a story within a story. Hawthorne was fond of pretending that his stories were based on some old, dusty manuscript that he had found in the back room of a warehouse. This gave his stories two levels, the first told with the concrete, present-day clarity of events well understood, and the second told through a haze of time and memory, hanging in the air as an ancient myth. This is a story within a story; Kirkpatrick is telling the story of the murder of William Desmond Taylor through the story of King Vidor.

Kirkpatrick is not a bad story teller; he's pretty good. There is a serious problem with the concept of telescoping a crime story inside of another story. A crime story by its nature is particular, specific, tied to its details. The precise sequence of events and observations is the critical essence of the narrative. Relating those events in a jumbled, non-linear sequence, as they are seen through the eyes of the second principal character, is rather like turning the *Mona Lisa* into a kaleidoscope. It's interesting, but I'm not sure that's what Da Vinci intended us to see.

Mary Miles Minter was a silent screen movie star. In 1919, at the age of 16, she was making more than $2,000 a week, perhaps the highest-paid star on the screen for a while there. After the Taylor murder, the *Des Moines Tribune* commented that the great advantage of a murder in Hollywood was that "it was not a difficult matter to get hold of pictures of the various persons involved." By 1922 Minter was 19 years old, and a beautiful, beautiful young woman; Taylor was 49. They weren't exactly engaged, but lingerie was found in his bedroom, embroidered "MMM," and love letters from her. (The *Seattle Star* remarked that every time there was a shooting in Hollywood, "some screen star finds out where the rest of her clothes are.") Minter insisted as long as she lived that she would have married Taylor, had it not been for the tragedy.

The last person to see Taylor alive was Mabel Normand, another young movie star of the era; she had dropped by Taylor's apartment to borrow a book. Like Minter she was poorly educated and naive, and she was being exploited for her beauty, although she was well paid for it. Normand had had drug and alcohol issues. Her account of their relationship was that Taylor was one of the few men she knew who *didn't* try to take advantage of her. An anti-drug activist, he had paid out of his own pocket to get her cleaned up, and he had encouraged her to read and improve herself. Other people have suggested that the relationship was not so innocent, but . . . that was what she said.

Mabel Normand was involved in a period of three years in three separate murder scandals. In none of these does she appear to have done anything wrong. Fatty Arbuckle . . . well, you probably all know the outlines of the Fatty Arbuckle scandal, and if you don't I'm not going to get into it, but it wasn't *exactly* a murder and Arbuckle was, after all, acquitted, and Mabel Normand wasn't anywhere near any of those events, but she and Arbuckle had starred together in several movies, and so her name was tarnished by association. Fatty Arbuckle was on trial at the time that Taylor was murdered, and then, two years later, Normand's chauffeur was so inconsiderate as to shoot somebody with Mabel's pistol. Normand's career was swept away by these scandals, and she died of tuberculosis at the age of 37.

Hundreds of people have been accused over the years of murdering William Taylor, among them Minter and Normand and the drug merchants who were Taylor's sworn enemies. King Vidor's conclusion (spoiler alert) was that Taylor was murdered by Charlotte Shelby, who was an actress herself, but more importantly Mary Minter's mother.

Vidor's argument for this conclusion, however—or at least Kirkpatrick's explanation of it—is so weak that one doesn't even really understand why he believes this to be true. This appears to be one of the critical passages in his argument against Shelby (p. 185):

> Minter was not asked to explain how, if as she claimed she'd never had a physical relationship with Taylor, her nightgown came to be found in his bedroom, or how hair from her head had found its way to Taylor's jacket collar.

OK, two critical facts there: (1) Minter vigorously denied that Taylor had ever given her a monogrammed silk nightie, but such a nightgown was in fact found in his apartment by the police, and (2) two or three hairs identified by police as Minter's were found on Taylor's jacket, the jacket he was wearing at the time of his demise.

But the explanation for the nightie seems stupefyingly obvious to me: Taylor had purchased the nightgown and had it embroidered for Minter, but, as they had not yet consummated their relationship, he had not yet given it to

her at the time of his death. And as to the hairs, which "the police had identified" as Minter's, there was no forensic technique to identify hairs as belonging
to a specific individual until many, many, many years after Taylor's murder.
There not only was no such method in 1922, when Taylor was killed, there
was no such method in 1967, when Vidor was investigating the case. Even in
the 1980s, when Kirkpatrick was writing about Vidor's research, such evidence
was considered speculative. Hair and fiber evidence was introduced in Wayne
Williams' trial in 1981–1982, but it was a fight to get it admitted, and I personally thought that the "hair" portion of it was BS. I believe that the police *thought*
that those were Mary Minter's hairs, but that's as far as I would go with that.

And if they were Mary Minter's hairs, so what? No one denies that there
was some sort of relationship between these two people. It is not unusual
that her hair would be clinging to his jacket. Those facts don't seem to me to
contribute anything toward the case against Shelby, which is, in essence, that
Shelby murdered Taylor because he had chosen her daughter over her.

The time frame surrounding the discovery of Taylor's body is confused
and confusing. Peavey apparently discovered the body about 7:30 AM or earlier, did not realize that there had been a homicide, but immediately called
the police to report the death. But then, not realizing that Taylor had been
murdered, he also called a couple of other people, including Taylor's studio.
Taylor's studio, hoping to avoid another scandal in the midst of the ruinous
Fatty Arbuckle affair, sent people rushing to the bungalow to get anything
out of there that might be considered scandalous. By the time the police
arrived there were eight to twelve other people already on the scene, carrying
out things that might have made Taylor, or Taylor's bosses, look bad.

A bookkeeper claimed (three years after the fact) that Charlotte Shelby
called her on the morning of the murder, about 7:30, and told her about
Taylor's murder. Shelby claimed that a) it was the bookkeeper who called her,
and b) it was more like 9:00.

The police claimed that they were at the bungalow a half-hour after the
call came in. Yeah, right. Some of the people who were at the bungalow by
the time the police arrived reported that they had been roused from their
beds and told to rush to the bungalow. It is virtually impossible to see how
the studio could have responded to a call from Peavey after he had called the
police, called their employees at home, and gotten that many people to the
bungalow in less than half an hour.

The newspapers of the time printed substantially varying reports about the time of the discovery of the body and the time the police responded. Vidor tries to make this into evidence against Shelby by insisting that there is only one timeline—the police timeline—and that that means that Shelby called the bookkeeper about the murder before the police even turned over the body and discovered that Taylor had been shot. What seems much, much more likely is that the police timeline is a fiction designed to make it appear that the police responded much more quickly than they actually did.

Let's face it: Vidor's solution to the mystery is not a *real* solution; it is a Hollywood solution. A movie has to tell a story; I understand that, and I'm not criticizing it. But the fact that Vidor picked this as the story he wanted to tell does not make it true.

On the morning of the murder, Henry Peavey (who discovered the body) was due to appear in court, on a charge of soliciting teen-aged male prostitutes from a nearby park. Taylor was scheduled to appear and speak for him. Vidor believes that Peavey was soliciting prostitutes on Taylor's behalf, that Taylor was a secret homosexual with a taste for young boys.

Vidor has, in my view, no evidence for this whatsoever. He points out that Henry Peavey kept an apartment near Taylor's house, and that Taylor paid for the apartment. Vidor thinks it was a place to take young boys. He quotes several instances of Taylor's lack of interest in young actresses. Page 51, from an interview with an aging co-worker:

> I don't know if Taylor ever slept with [Mabel Normand]. He wasn't the kiss-and-tell type. He didn't even stand in line to peep through the secret holes in the walls of the actress's dressing rooms.

Vidor wonders whether Taylor did not engage in this adolescent sexual behavior because he was not interested in girls. A more plausible explanation is that he was not an adolescent. He was a grown man who understood the process of earning respect by behaving respectfully. Page 185:

> Another Athletic Club member said Taylor himself told of Mary's once bursting into his bungalow, undressing, and begging to be made love to. Taylor again turned her down.

Oh, yeah; that kind of stuff happens all the time. I can't tell you how many times I've had to tell Keira Knightley to put her clothes back on. It reflects poorly on Kirkpatrick's judgment that he finds space for this anecdote, apparently told to Vidor forty years later by someone who claimed to have known Taylor from his athletic club.

I wanted to double back to the issue of the hairs. I would bet that many, many people who read Kirkpatrick's book at the time of its publication in 1986 immediately spotted the problem with Vidor's claim that hairs found on Taylor's jacket were identified by police as Mary Minter's. Anyone who reads crime books would have known that that was impossible, given the forensic science of the time.

The thing is, Kirkpatrick doesn't read crime books. *Many* people who write crime books quite obviously never read crime books. This is obvious first because they often say things like this, which reveal an underlying ignorance of the general subject, and second because they will often spend pages explaining things that, if they read crime books, they would know that almost all of their readers are already familiar with.

This is one of the key reasons that I wrote *Popular Crime*, which I didn't quite get to explain in the first edition: I wrote it in an effort to attack the general, underlying ignorance of the good writers—like Kirkpatrick—who occasionally will whip out a crime book. Think about it: wouldn't it be strange if you had people writing books about physics who never read books about physics? Wouldn't you think it odd if you had people writing books about politics who had quite obviously never read very much about politics?

But that is the real condition of the crime publishing industry: many of the people who write crime books quite obviously never read them. It has to do with how people think about crime books, as a sub-professional diversion. I was trying to elevate the field, just a little bit, by challenging the writers of future crime books to read up on the subject before they dive in.

Regarding the death of Bill Taylor, my instinct is that it was not Charlotte Shelby who killed him. Just a small thing; I would never argue that details like this are persuasive, but . . . just a little thing that bothers me. Taylor was shot in the back while standing with his hands over his head, which we know because the bullet hole in the jacket only lines up with the bullet hole in his body if he had his hands in the air at the time he was shot.

Vidor's argument is that Shelby wanted Taylor for himself, and was furious at him because he rejected her and was trying instead to take her daughter away from her. But if you visualize *that* confrontation, at what point does Shelby say to him, "OK, face the wall and put your hands in the air?" It doesn't happen that way. If he was shot by an angry, jealous woman, he'd have been shot in the chest in the middle of a sentence. When somebody points a gun at you and orders you to face the wall and put your hands in the air, that's not an angry woman; that's an experienced criminal. Just my opinion.

Some information for my discussion of the Taylor case was taken from the website *Taylorology,* and in particular from the article "The Humor of a Hollywood Murder," by Bruce Long.

Moving forward, now, another 40 years. Johnny Cash and Bob Dylan. On February 8, 1963, a heavyset black lady named Hattie Carroll, 52 years old, was working as a serving woman at a party in Baltimore for rich white fops in top hats and tails, the women in finery and lace. It was long past midnight, and many of the rich white fops were as drunk as skunks and acting silly. One of the rich white skunks, twenty-three-year-old William Zantzinger, took offense at something Hattie said, and struck her with his cane, not very hard, and made a vile and racist remark, the transcript of which does not seem to be part of the public record. Overcome with stress and emotion, Hattie became ill almost immediately, and fell into a sickness, which triggered a stroke. She was dead before the morning.

Zantzinger was arrested and charged initially with murder. He was convicted on a lesser charge, and was sentenced to five months in the county jail. The judge who sentenced Zantzinger expressed the concern that giving him any longer term of imprisonment would require him to serve his time in a state prison, and this might ruin his life.

This was never a major national news story, but a few people—some on the left, and more on the right—were outraged at the lenient treatment of a young white man who had caused the death of an entirely innocent black woman, the mother of ten children. Bob Dylan, then 22 years old, wrote a song about it, a very lucid and specific song entitled "The Lonesome Death of Hattie Carroll." The song mentions Zantzinger by name, repeatedly, and denounces the sentence, referring to "you who philosophize disgrace / and criticize all fears."

I revere Bob Dylan, but is that an awful line, or what? Who in the hell philosophizes disgrace? Who does this speak to? Do you think there is anybody in the world who gets up in the morning and says to himself, "I think I'll go philosophize some disgrace today?" What does that even mean? It's not that it is

vague in the sense that Dylan is so often marvelously vague and evocative. It
is more like it is specific but clumsy. It doesn't *sound* good, and Dylan must
repeat this ghastly phrase 40 times during the song. *Yoo-who-phil-osophize-
dis-grace . . . Yoo-who-phil-osophize-dis-grace . . . You-who-phil-osophize-dis-
grace,* over and over. What makes it worse is repeating the You Who sound
(yoo-hoo, yoo-hoo, yoo-hoo). It's awful. It is not a particularly good song,
although Dylan's admirers will soberly insist that it is a great song, and I suppose they are entitled to their opinion.

Anyway, what struck me about this is that Dylan and Johnny Cash were
of course good friends, a 40-year friendship that began when Cash, nine
years older than Dylan and an established star, wrote a friendly note to the
fledgling songwriter on the back of an air sickness bag.

But Dylan, who rarely adopts any comprehensible position except that
the world is a cauldron of injustice and we should all feel bad about it, has,
in this case, adopted a position which is diametrically opposed to a central theme of Cash's career: to wit, that people who commit crimes remain
human in spite of their offense, that they remain within the reach of God's
grace, and that, as much as we can, we should treat them with compassion
and dignity.

So who is right, in this case: Dylan, who argued for a more appropriate sentence, or Cash, who would have liked to go to Zantzinger's cell and
sing him a sad song? Of course five months is a ridiculous sentence under
the circumstances, but the judge who issued the sentence was forced by the
intersections of the law to choose between undue leniency and undue harsh-
ness. The case is a liberal dilemma: do you argue for compassion, or do you
argue for justice for Hattie Carroll?

I would argue that, in the big picture, the judge who sentenced Zantzinger did the right thing. What Zantzinger did was despicable—but it was
not murder. (The blow with the cane was not hard enough to cause a bruise,
let alone hard enough to cause death.) Zantzinger, even drunk, did not
intend to cause Hattie Carroll's death, and he didn't, really; he was the proxi-
mate cause, but not the ultimate cause. It was wiser to give the young fool a
chance to rebuild his life than it would have been to give vent to anger in the
guise of justice.

Zantzinger lived until 2009. He went into the real estate business, wound
up renting inexpensive housing mostly to black people. A young woman
who worked as a housing advocate for the poor, many years later, was aston-

ished to discover that Zantzinger—then facing charges for housing code violations, charges which eventually landed him in jail for longer than the death of Hattie Carroll—was actually a likeable and decent man who was just trying to do what he could to help poor people find housing that they could afford. It is always best, I think, to remember that wickedness is human.

Acknowledgments

My first acknowledgment here should be offered to my longtime friend Mike Kopf, who shares my interest in crime stories, who read this book for me as a favor, who, over the long period of this book's gestation, probably chewed through with me every crime included in here, or nearly every one, and who made numerous other contributions to the book.

Other people were nice enough to read the book and let me know what they thought. Cal Karlin, my friend since college, read through it for me, as did Keith Scherer, Ben McGrath, Bruce Dickson, Chuck Woodling, Matthew Namee, Eddie Epstein and Allen Barra. I much appreciate the insights of each of you, and each of you saved me from saying something stupid somewhere, or showed me a better way to think about something. Steve Moyer, the same for you; I appreciate your reading the manuscript, and letting me know what you thought. It matters.

Actually, I hadn't realized I had asked so many people to read the book; that's certainly a personal record for me—number of people reading the book before it's published. I haven't written about this subject before; I felt like I needed feedback. Or maybe I am becoming needy in my old age.

I have been represented for three decades by Liz Darhansoff and for almost as long by Chuck Verrill; I appreciate your work in helping me get this book to a publisher.

Brant Rumble edited this, so, of course, any mistakes that appear in the book are his fault. Kidding. I gather that I may have a reputation as, um . . . not an easy man to edit. I welcome editorial suggestions with the warmth of an alligator greeting a scuba diver. Brant has made it through two or three books with me now without complaining, which I much appreciate.

We had editorial support, for this effort, from Nan Graham, Scribner's editor in chief, and also from Susan Moldow, our (spoken reverently) publisher. This book has also had the help and support of Roz Lippel (associate publisher), Anna deVries (associate editor), Laura Wise (production editor), Tom Pitoniak (copyeditor), Rex Bonomelli (cover designer), Carla Jayne Jones (interior designer), Alexandra Truitt (photo researcher), Elisa Rivlin (legal reader) and Lauren Lavelle (publicist). I thank you all for your efforts on behalf of the book.

Michael MacCambridge, Joe Posnanski, Josh Levin; I appreciate your interest in the book, your support and your insights.

Dan Okrent helped to launch my writing career, some time in the middle of the last century, and this is still appreciated.

My good wife, Susan McCarthy, has been with me through many books; her love and support are crucial to every one. My children . . . Rachel, Isaac, Reuben. Rachel actually read the book, or tried to, Isaac talked with me about it, Reuben is still here at home with us, and so lived through the book.

The book is dedicated to my mother-in-law, Phyllis McCarthy; I will also acknowledge the help and support of Steve and Patty Metzler, Carol Wells, Georgine Ent and Nell Ritchey, who are relatives.

Mike Webber worked with me during part of the time this book was in progress. I used to say to him, "Mike, there's this book I need; could you find a copy of it?" and he would come in four days later with a copy of the book and say that it had cost him 85 cents on eBay. It's an amazing world we live in. I am not acknowledging eBay; screw 'em.

I am certain I have forgotten someone. I shall remember you next week, and thank you then, but the book will gone and it will be too late, so let me apologize here and thank you later.

Any errors appearing in this book are, of course, the responsibility of the author. Almost all of the people acknowledged here helped to spot errors and remove them, but I make so many mistakes I can defeat a legion of editors, and I am sure that some things slipped through.

I shall resist the impulse to express my gratitude to Richard Hickock and Perry Smith, or even to Truman Capote. I owe so much of my life to the newspapers. I can't say when or why I started reading crime stories; they have just always been a part of me. I grew up sort of in the middle of nowhere, without television or money, cut off from most of the human race by rudeness and fear, obsessing endlessly about the nature of a world that lay outside my reach and my experience, a little bit as if the universe was an unsolved crime and each newspaper was a clue. I remember in the fifth grade I was supposed to prepare a report on current events, which I had forgotten about, but I stood up and chattered about Caryl Chessman until the teacher told me to sit down. My sister Georgine would go to the library and bring home a stack of books, and I would sort through them for the crime books; I should acknowledge Georgine, and the library. Each crime is a clue to human nature—and not always a gloomy one; I still believe this.

Index

abortion, 18–19, 22, 286
Adams, Charles Francis, 29–30
Adams, John, 29
Adams, John Quincy, 29
Adams, Randall Dale, 287, 288, 289, 378
African Americans:
   executions of, 286
   Jewish relations with, 117–18
   murders of, 25, 96
   Southern prejudice against, 116
   see also Scottsboro Boys
Airman and the Carpenter, The
   (Kennedy), 152–53
Alcatraz, 219, 220
Alcott, Bronson, 30
Alexander, Shana, 446
Alibrandi, Tom, 336, 446
Allen, Arthur Leigh, 265, 266, 272
American Tragedy (Schiller and
   Willwerth), 451
America's Most Wanted, 281, 282
Ames, Aldrich, 452
Anastasia, Albert, 140
And I Don't Want to Live This Life
   (Spungen), 310, 452
Andrews, Lowell Lee, 216–17
Anthony, Casey, 434–35, 443
Anthony, Caylee, 434, 435, 443
anthrax investigation, 425–27
Anti-Defamation League, 117
Apronia, 1
Arbuckle, Fatty, 468, 469
Aristotle, 36

Arndt, Linda, 387, 388, 394
Aronson, Harvey, 204, 233
Arran, 33–35
Arts & Entertainment, 7
Arvizo, Gavin, 431
Audubon, John James, 30, 31
automobile industry, 319
Avery, Paul, 266

Babyak, Jolene, 180, 220, 446
Bad Company (Wick), 453
Bailey, F. Lee, 88, 198, 204, 241, 446
   in Boston Strangler case, 228–30,
     232, 233, 234, 235, 236, 239,
     240, 241
   in O.J. Simpson trial, 241
   in Sam Sheppard case, 200, 203,
     241
ballistics, in Kennedy assassination,
   246, 247–53
Barker, Ma, 173
Basement, The (Millett), 451
Baxter, Linda, 386
Beineman, Karen, 258, 260
Bell, Janice, 385
Belli, Melvin, 178, 265
Beltway Snipers, 108, 430
Bembenek, Lawrencia, 317, 374–75
Bening, Annette, 319
Bennett, Glen, 251
Berdella, Bob, 360
Berkowitz, David, 292, 293, 304
Berry, Howard K., 100, 447

Betrayal (Weiner, Johnston and Lewis), 452

Biography, 7

Bird Man: The Many Faces of Robert Stroud (Babyak), 180, 220, 446

Birdman of Alcatraz (film), 108, 220, 223

   see also Stroud, Robert

Birdman of Alcatraz (Gaddis), 108, 219–20, 223, 449

Bishop, Jim, 253, 447

Black Dahlia, 157, 171, 182–86, 241, 352

Black Dahlia Files, The: The Mob, the Mogul, and the Murder That Transfixed Los Angeles (Wolfe), 183–84, 185–86, 453

Blake, Robert, 218, 285, 425

Blind Eye (Stewart), 452

blood spatter, 65, 201, 210, 212

Body Heat (film), 139

Bond, Minnie, 99

Bond, Stanley, 274, 275, 278, 285

Bonnie and Clyde, 96, 108, 173

Borden, Abby, 43, 44, 50, 52, 54, 57–58, 60, 61

Borden, Andrew, 43, 44, 52, 54, 57, 60, 61, 62

Borden, Emma, 56

Borden, Lizzie, 36, 43–44, 49, 50–65, 66–67, 68

Boston, 230

Boston, Mass., 19th century elite in, 30

Boston Cultivator, 23

Boston Globe, 101, 226

Boston Record, 230

Boston Strangler, 226–40, 241, 244, 258, 304, 370

Boston Strangler, The (Frank), 231, 233, 449

Boston Stranglers, The (Kelly), 230, 233, 450

Bosworth, Charles, 398

Bottomly, John S., 227, 230, 244

Bottomly commission, 228, 229, 232, 258

Boyce, Christopher, 450

Boy Next Door, The (Brinck), 349

Bradfield, Bill, 297, 298

Brady v. Maryland (1963), 101, 105

Breckinridge, Henry, 369

Brinck, Gretchen, 349

"Bring Back Our Darling," 38

Brockway, W. H., 38

Broken Vows, 384

Bronx Home News, 146, 156

Brooke, Edward, 227

Brown, Theresa, 355

Browne, Earle, 252–53

Brudos, Jerome, 291

Brumberg, Joan Jacobs, 69, 447

Bruno, Anthony, 326, 447

Brussel, James, 231, 234

BTK murders, 289, 339, 340

Buck, Morris, 75, 81

Buckley, William F., Jr., 449

Buda, Mario, 124–25, 126, 127

Budd, Grace, 301

Bugliosi, Vincent, 447

Bulfinch, Charles, 29

Bullitt, 266

Bundy, Ted, 167, 172, 230, 241, 289, 291–92, 293, 304, 339, 360, 370

Burger, Robert, 345–46

Burger, Warren, 286, 309

Burns Detective Agency, 81

Burr, Aaron, 11, 12, 13, 15

Butcher, Baker: A True Account of a Serial Murderer (Gilmour and Hale), 331

Butler, Joan, 355

Cabell, Mrs. Earle, 252

Cagney, James, 76

Cain, James M., 139

California Supreme Court, 188, 223, 366

Campbell, Ian, 108, 220–21, 222

Canadian Supreme Court, 345

Canfield, Chloe, 75, 80, 81

Canning, Elizabeth, 3–6, 8, 9, 25

capital punishment, *see* death penalty

Capone, Al, 101, 173
Capote, Truman, 217, 218, 344, 447
Carlo, Philip, 447
Carlyle, Thomas, 457
Carpenter, David, 337
Carroll, Hattie, 472, 473, 474
Carter, Jimmy, 241
Casals, Pablo, 187
Case Closed (Posner), 245, 247, 249, 251
Cash, Johnny, 450, 472, 473
Cast of Killers, A (Kirkpatrick), 450,
        467, 468–69, 470–71
CBS, 247, 368
Cell 2455 Death Row (Chessman), 190,
        447
Chandler, Harry, 185
Chaney, James, 118, 243–44
Channing, Stockard, 297
Chapman, Duane (Dog), 430–31
Chase, Alston, 447
Chase, David, 326–27
Chase, Richard, 291, 336
Cher, 255
Chessman, Caryl, 153, 187–93, 447
Chicago, Ill., early 20th century legal
        practices in, 86
Chicago Seven, 87
Chicago Tribune, 40
Chikatilo, Andrei, 163–64, 242–43,
        447–48
children:
    crime stories about, 25
    murders of, 95, 397, 443
    sexual abuse cases involving, 317,
        431, 432
    see also Phagan, Mary; Ramsey,
        JonBenet
Cho, Seung-Hui, 434
Christgen, Eric, 299, 300, 302
Christian Register, 23
civil rights movement, 118, 243–44, 449
Civil War, U.S., 31, 32, 116
Clark, Delores, 282
Clark, Marcia, 45, 46, 371
Clarke, James W., 294, 295, 336, 447

Clarkson, Lana, 431
Claudius, 1
Clemens, Will, 21, 22
Clinton, Bill, 241
Clutter, Herb, 217
Clutter family, 108, 217–18
CNN, 392
Cochran, Johnnie, 84, 241, 371
Colbert, Maizie, 120–22, 445–46
Collins, Joan, 76
Collins, John Norman, 172, 258–61, 291
Colt, Samuel, 32
Compulsion, 223
Condit, Gary, 424, 425
Condon, John F., 145–47, 149, 150,
        151–52, 154, 155, 156, 369
confessions, 47, 221, 236, 240
Congress, U.S., 426
Conley, Jim, 111–13, 114, 115, 116
Connally, John, 247, 249
Conradi, Peter, 447–48
Contract on America, 254
Cook, Richard, 19, 20
Cooper, Cynthia L., 204, 213
Copeland, Faye, 357
Copeland, Ray, 356–58, 360
Copeland Killings, The (Miller), 358
Coppolino, Carl, 240
Corll, Dean, 291
Cormier, Frank, 253
Corona, Juan, 278–81
Corona, Natividad, 279, 280
Corrigan, William, 201–2
Costas, Bob, 195–96
Cotten, Joseph, 269
Couey, John, 432, 443
*Courtroom: The Story of Samuel S.
        Leibowitz* (Reynolds), 101, 451
Coyote, Peter, 297
Crazymaker (O'Donnell), 316
crime books, 7, 9, 99–100, 217–18,
        222, 223, 294–95, 316, 321–22,
        345–46, 384–85
    authors' ignorance of subject matter
        in, 471

crime books (*cont.*)
author's recommended list of,
446–53
"author's solutions" in, 296–97,
468–69, 470–71
on Black Dahlia case, 182–83
on Boston Strangler case, 230, 231,
232–33, 235
on Kennedy assassination, 245, 247,
248, 253–54, 255, 451
on Lindbergh case, 148, 150,
152–56
outlandish theories in, 231, 352,
468–69, 470–71
police in, 349
on Ramsey case, 398–99, 400,
401–3, 405, 451
research in, 455–56
on Rosenberg case, 196–97, 451,
452
on Sam Sheppard case, 199–200,
203, 204–5, 210, 451
about serial murderers, 292–93,
321–22, 331, 335, 336–37,
352–54, 355–56, 359, 447–48,
450, 451
serial murderers' descriptions in,
336–37
sympathy in, 283–84
tangential evidence in, 48
crime rates:
in 18th–19th century New York,
11
historical American, 31–32, 33, 93,
95–96
mid-1960s explosion in, 223, 224,
286, 443–44
crime stories:
academic attitude toward, 2, 7–8,
9, 22
compelling elements of, 8, 24–25,
29, 30, 35–36, 40, 53, 77,
106–10, 113–14, 139, 369–70,
374–75
criticism of, 7–8, 193, 437–42

of early 20th century, 68, 69–79,
139–40, 466–72
endurance of, 2
fictional elements in, 374–75, 382,
386
fictionalization of, 244–45, 345, 368,
465
and justice system, 109, 305, 306,
443, 444
media coverage of, 6, 7, 24, 107,
130, 156–58, 186, 241–44, 293,
365–66, 369, 438–41, 443, 444
in newspapers, 15, 22, 68, 107,
157–58, 173, 453, 467, 469–70
of 19th century, 33, 453
of 1930s, 173–74
politics and, 108, 127, 197
significance of, 8–9, 22, 94, 103,
127–28, 140, 256, 305, 306,
341–42, 439–40, 441–44
songs written on, 472–73
sympathetic suspects in, 316–22
universality of, 6, 7
see also media
criminal profiling:
and Lizzie Borden case, 64
and Mad Butcher of Kingsbury Run
case, 164–72
Croucher, Richard, 13
Crumm, Jimmy, 315, 316
Cuckoo's Egg, The (Stoll), 363, 452
Cunanan, Andrew, 173
Curtis, Tony, 230, 450

Dahmer, Jeffrey, 108, 160, 241, 360
Dalton, Emmett, 41
Dalton, J. Frank, 41
Daniels, Paul Michael, 375, 377, 380
Dannehl, Sean, 348–49
Danson, Ted, 222
Darden, Chris, 372
Darrow, Clarence, 82, 83–88, 110, 122,
174, 241
Darrow (Tierney), 86
D'Autremont, Hugh, 136, 137

D'Autremont, Roy and Ray, 135–37
Davies, John, 347, 348, 349
Day Kennedy Was Shot, The (Bishop), 253
Deadly Lessons (Englade), 367, 368
Deakin, James, 448
Dear, William, 312–13, 314, 448
Death, Dr., 288
Death in Belmont, A (Junger), 233, 234, 235–36, 450
Death of Innocence, The (Ramsey and Ramsey), 398
Death of Old Man Rice, The (Friedland), 74
death penalty, 69, 188, 189–90, 193, 197, 222, 261, 285–86, 288, 342, 345, 422, 444
Death Sentence (Sharkey), 281, 283, 452
Debs, Eugene, 83
Defense Never Rests, The (Bailey and Aronson), 198, 204, 233, 235, 236, 446
DeFreeze, Donald, 277–78
Degnan, Suzanne, 181
DeLorean, John, 318–19
DeMeo, Roy, 324–25, 326
Democratic Convention of 1968, 87
DeSalvo, Albert, 228–40, 241, 275, 304
Des Moines Tribune, 467
detective stories, 18, 22
Devil in the White City, The (Larson), 67–68, 450
Dickens, Charles, 31
Dickinson, Emily, 30
Dietz, Park, 325
Dillard, Tom, 252
Dillinger, John, 108, 173
Dirty Harry, 266
Discovery Channel, 7
DNA, 47–48, 49
Doctorow, E. L., 79
doctors, 168, 352
Dodd, Westley Allan, 331
Dolezal, Frank, 160–61, 163

Donahue, Howard, 245, 247–48, 249, 250–51, 252, 253, 254
Dondoglio, Nestor, 123
Dorsey, Hugh, 114–15
Double Indemnity (Cain), 139
Double Jeopardy (Hill), 365, 449
Douglas, Joe, 38, 39, 40
Douglas, John, 164, 230, 291, 292, 293, 339–40
Doyen, Dorcas, *see* Jewett, Helen
Doyen, Jacob, 455
Dreams of Ada, The (Mayer), 340–41, 451
Dreyfus case, 195
Dreyfus cases, 107, 108, 115, 128, 177
Drimmer, Frederick, 190–92
Dr. Sam: An American Tragedy (Pollack), 204
Ducet, Jeffrey, 319–20
DuClos, Bernard, 331
Duke Lacrosse case, 4, 109, 114, 316, 432–34
Duncan, Ron, 276
Dungeon Master, The (Dear), 314, 448
Dungeons & Dragons, 311
Dunkle, Jon, 305, 347–51
Dwight, John, 26
Dylan, Bob, 472–73

Eastwood, Clint, 266
Eberle, Danny Joe, 335
Eberling, Richard, 204, 205, 206, 210–11, 212, 213
Echoes in the Darkness (Wambaugh), 297–98
Edwards, Willie, 243
Egbert, James Dallas, III, 310–14
Eller, John, 391, 392, 393, 399, 408
Emerson, Ralph Waldo, 30
Endure and Conquer: My Twelve-Year Fight for Vindication (Sheppard), 204
Englade, Ken, 368
Era, 21
Escobedo v. Illinois, 221

Evans, John, 98
evidence, 44–50
  adultery as, 202–3, 380–82
  behavior as, 55–56, 382
  in Boston Strangler case, 231
  in Caryl Chessman case, 192
  in criminal cases, 9, 14, 45–46,
    52–53, 56–57, 59
  financial gain as, 66–67
  in Hall-Mills case, 131, 132
  in Helen Jewett case, 460, 462–65
  in Lindbergh case, 150, 151–52, 156
  in Lizzie Borden case, 49, 50–65
  in Mary Phagan case, 111–13, 115
  misleading, 299–300
  motive, means and opportunity as,
    44, 46–47, 53, 380
  in Neulander case, 378, 379–84, 386
  prior acts as, 45–46, 48, 49–51
  in Ramsey case, 397, 399–405
  repressed memories as, 274
  in Sheppard and Peterson cases, 214
  see also blood spatter; confessions;
    criminal profiling; DNA;
    forensics; identifications
ex-convicts, 41
Eye of Evil (Harrington and Burger),
  345–46
Eyler, Larry, 167, 331

Face of Justice, The (Chessman), 188,
  447
Fair Game (Bernard DuClos), 331
Falco, Edie, 326
Falcon and the Snowman, The (Lindsey),
  450
Family Affairs (Hoffman), 316
Fassitt, Lewis, 26
Fatal Vision (McGinniss), 294, 296, 297
Federal Bureau of Investigation (FBI),
  318, 387, 403, 426–27
Feige, David, 101, 102
Fielding, Henry, 4, 5
Final Verdict (St. Johns), 99–100, 452
Finkel, Michael, 449

Fish, Albert, 301
Fisher, Amy, 139
Fisher, Russell, 248–49
Fletcher, Jaye Slade, 336
Flight of the Falcon, The (Lindsey), 450
Flynn, Billy, 367–68
Fonda, Henry, 230, 244
Ford, Harrison, 215
forensics, 7, 136, 426, 469, 471
  see also blood spatter
Forrest Gump, 255
Fortescue, Grace, 174
Foster, Abby Kelley, 30
Frank, Gerald, 230, 231, 233, 449
Frank, Leo, 106, 107, 111, 112–13,
  114–20
Frankfurter, Felix, 127
Franklin, Bert, 82–83, 86
Franklin, Eileen, 273, 274
Franklin, George, 273–74
Franklin, Leah, 273
Freedom of Information Act (1966), 154
French, Jeanne, 183
French, Rick, 387
Friedland, Martin, 74
Fugitive, The, 203, 204, 215
Fuhrman, Mark, 241, 372, 428
Furman v. Georgia (1972), 286

Gacy, John Wayne, 230, 241, 291, 292,
  293, 351
Gaddis, Thomas, 219, 449
Galleani, Luigi, 123, 124
Gambino crime family, 324–25, 327
Gandolfini, James, 326
Garcetti, Gil, 371
Garland, Bonnie, 307
Garrison, Jim, 246
Garrison, William Lloyd, 30
Gascoyne, Crispe, 5
Gatling, Richard, 32
Gaylin, Willard, 307, 449
Gentry, Curt, 447
Gerber, Samuel, 200
Gibson, Jane, 130–31

Gilbert, Robin, 429–30
Gilmore, Gary, 109
Gilmour, Walter, 331
Gilyard, Lorenzo, 290
Girl in the Red Velvet Swing, The, 76
Goebel, William, 69–71, 78
Goetz, Bernard, 319, 320
Gompers, Samuel, 80
Goodman, Andrew, 118, 243–44
Gore, Thomas P., 99
Gough, Elizabeth, 148
Gow, Betty, 148
Grave for Bobby, A (Deakin), 448
Gray, Henry Judd, 107, 137–39
Graysmith, Robert, 265–66, 268, 269,
    270, 337, 449
Great Depression, 127
Greenawalt, Randy, 291, 294
Green River Killer, 352
Griffin, Will, 247
Griffith, Griffith J., 74–75, 76, 81
Grisham, John, 340, 449
Grissom, Richard, 354–56
Guandique, Ingmar, 424–25
guns, 31–32, 173, 422
Gwen, Jeff, 423
Gyllenhaal, Jake, 265–66

hackers, 362–63
Hacking, Lori, 432
Hacking, Mark, 432
Hackman, Gene, 244
Hale, Leland E., 331
Hall, Edward, 129–34
Hall, Frances Stevens, 129, 130, 131,
    132, 134
Hall, Virtue, 4
Hall-Mills case, 107, 129–35, 139, 157,
    369, 388, 389–90, 394
Halloran, Jack, 177
Hamer, Frank, 96
Hamilton, Alexander, 12, 13, 15
Hansen, Robert, 167, 327–32, 358, 360
Harriman, Job, 81
Harrington, Joseph, 345–46

Harris, David, 287–89
Harris, Jean, 319
Harris, Thomas, 352
Harvard and the Unabomber (Chase),
    447
Harvard murder, 26–31, 67
Hatcher, Charles, 167, 300–304, 331
Hauptmann, Bruno Richard, 107,
    150–56, 157, 318
Hawthorne, Nathaniel, 31, 454–55, 467
Hayes, Ira, 450
Hayes, Susan, 202, 203
Haywood, Big Bill, 75, 83, 87
HBO, 325, 326
Hearst, Patty, 241, 277, 278
Heidenry, John, 449
Heinrich, Edward, 136
Heirens, William, 160, 181
Helter Skelter (Bugliosi and Gentry), 447
He Made It Safe to Murder (Berry), 100,
    102, 447
Henley, Elmer Wayne, 291
Herrin, Richard, 307
Hettinger, Karl, 220, 221, 222
Hickey, George, 247–48, 250, 251, 252,
    254, 255
Hickock, Richard, 217, 218, 332, 344
High Treason, 254
Hill, Anita, 197
Hill, Bob, 365, 449
Hill, Clint, 253
Hillside Stranglers, 291
Hinckley, John, 306, 307, 308
Hitchcock, Alfred, 352
Hobson, Chris, 314–16
Hobson, Sueanne, 315, 316
Hochmuth, Amandus, 151, 369
Hoffman, Andy, 316
Hoffman, Harold, 150
Hoffman, James, 318
Holland, S. M., 251
Holloway, Natalee, 24, 196, 244, 432
Holmes, H. H., 67–69
Holmes, Oliver Wendell, 29, 31, 124
Holmes, Paul, 203, 204, 210, 211, 449

Holt, Frank, *see* Muenter, Erich
Homicide! (Sasser), 337–38, 339, 451
Homicide: A Year on the Killing Streets
    (Simon), 337, 452
Houk, Spencer, 199
Hoverston, Lester, 212, 214
Howard, Jim, 71
Howe, Julia Ward, 30
Huie, William Bradford, 449–50
Hunt, Helen, 349
Hunter, Alex, 392, 393–94, 400, 401, 407
Hurkos, Peter, 258
Hurston, Zora Neale, 450
Hurt, William, 139
Huxley, Aldous, 187
Hyde, B. Clark, 77

I-5 Killer, The (Rule), 336, 451
Ice Man, The (Bruno), 326, 447
Ice Man, The (Carlo), 447
Ice Man, The (film), 326
identifications, 47, 141–44, 463
    in Caryl Chessman case, 190–91
    in Lindbergh case, 149, 151–52,
        155, 156
    see also police sketches
Ignatow, Mel, 363–65
Implosion Conspiracy, The (Nizer), 451
In Broad Daylight (MacLean), 321
In Cold Blood (Capote), 99, 108, 217–18,
    223, 297, 447
Innocent Man, The (Grisham), 340–41,
    449
insanity defense, 216, 228–29, 300–302,
    303, 306–8, 349, 425
intellectualism, 194–95
International Labor Defense Fund, 176
internet, 420
    crime coverage on, 7, 366
In the Company of Darkness, 349
investigative journalism, 153
Irresistible Impulse (Lindsey), 450
Ito, Lance, 372
Ivins, Bruce Edward, 426–27
I Want to Live!, 223

Jackson, Michael, 431–32, 435
Jack the Ripper, 68, 69, 292, 352
    theories about, 10
James, Frank, 41
James, Jesse, 36, 41
James, P. D., 297
Jameson, 395
Jenoff, Len, 375, 376, 377–78, 379–80,
    383, 384–85, 386
Jewett, Helen, 15, 18, 24, 25, 453–65
JFK, 254, 255
Johnson, Lyndon, 253
Johnson-Reed Act (1924), 127
Johnston, David, 452
JonBenet (Thomas), 398, 399, 400,
    401–2, 403, 405
Jones, Charles, 71, 72, 73, 74
Jones, David Allen, 429–30
Jones, Richard Glyn, 139
Jones, Tommy Lee, 215
Joubert, John, 335–36
Judd, Lawrence, 174
Judd, Winnie Ruth, 108, 174, 177–78
Judgment Day: The John List Story, 285
Junger, Sebastian, 233, 234, 235–36,
    240, 450
juries:
    evidence withheld from, 9, 14
    tampering with, 82–83, 85, 86–87,
        98, 101
Jury (Villaseñor), 280–81, 452
justice system, 412–22
    ancient Roman, 2
    and crime stories, 109, 305, 306,
        443, 444
    crime stories' effects on, 8–9
    definition creep in, 261–63
    double jeopardy in, 364
    early 20th century, 73–74, 82–87,
        91, 96–97, 98–99, 101, 119
    evidence in, 9, 14, 44–50, 52–53,
        56–57, 59
    failures of, 241–42, 321, 331–32,
        341–42, 371–73
    false confessions in, 435–37

false prosecutions in, 114
hostile cross-examination in, 385,
   386
insanity defense in, 216, 228–29,
   300–302, 303, 306–8, 349, 425
and juvenile crime, 354
media and, 130, 151, 157, 202, 203,
   241–44, 297, 305, 373, 439–41
19th century, 12, 13, 26, 96
in O. J. Simpson case, 371–73
politics and, 128, 419–22
pretrial discovery in, 101, 102, 105
procedure in, 8–9, 14, 305–6
rights of the accused in, 102, 221,
   223–24, 420, 422
sentencing in, 332–34, 422
in serial murderer cases, 328, 329,
   331–32
Supreme Court decisions on, 101,
   102, 103, 105, 221, 223–24
three strikes in, 262
wrongful convictions in, 116–17,
   287–89, 299, 341, 378–79
see also death penalty; lawyers;
   police; prison reform

Kaczynski, Ted, 270
Kahahawai, Joseph, 174, 175
Kallinger, Joseph, 291, 321–22
Kanarek, Irving, 222
Kansas Charley (Brumberg), 69, 447
Kansas State Prison, 332
Karpis, Alvin (Creepy), 220
Kassab, Freddy, 296
Katf, Michelle, 355
Keers, Christine, 359
Keffer Sheet Music Company, 38
Keller, Amy, 424–25
Kelly, Machine Gun, 173
Kelly, Susan, 230–31, 232, 233, 450
Kemper, Edmund, 291
Kenilworth (Scott), 18
Kennedy, John F., assassination of, 108,
   227, 241, 245–56, 451
Kennedy, Ludovic, 152–53, 155

Kennedy assassination:
   ballistics evidence about, 246,
      247–53
   conspiracy theories about, 246–47,
      254
   cultural significance of, 255–56
Kennedy family, 427
Kent, Saville, 148
Kentucky, early 20th century politics in,
   69–71
Kerr, James, 34, 35
Keyes, Edward, 261, 450
Kidman, Nicole, 368
kidnapping, 37, 40, 98–99, 261
   see also Lindbergh case; Little
      Lindbergh Laws
Kilgallen, Dorothy, 204, 450
Killer (Gaddis), 449
Killing of Bonnie Garland, The (Gaylin),
   307, 449
Killing Season (Smith), 352–54
King, Larry, 434
King, Martin Luther, Jr., 450
Kingsley, Ben, 319
Kinne, Sharon, 291
Kirk, Paul, 200–201, 202, 204, 210, 213
Kirkpatrick, Sidney, 450, 466–67, 468,
   469, 471
Kleiger, Estelle Fox, 12, 14, 450
Knowles, David, 187
Koby, Tom, 391, 392, 393–94, 408
Koch, Ed, 320
Koehler, Arthur, 149, 150, 152, 153, 156
Kraft, Randy, 291
Kuklinski, Richard, 323–27, 447
Ku Klux Klan, 117, 132
Kunstler, William, 131–32, 133, 134,
   296–97, 450
Kurtis, Bill, 293
Kyle sisters, 121

LaBianca family, 289
labor movement, 80, 81, 82, 83, 84, 87,
   96, 122–23, 140
Lake, Leonard, 343–44, 346

Lancaster, Burt, 220, 224
Larson, Erik, 67, 68, 450
Last Rampage (Clarke), 294–95, 336, 447
law, *see* justice system
Lawson, Winston, 251, 252
lawyers, 8
    in Boston Strangler case, 227–28
    early 20th century, 86, 100–101
    judicial procedures exploited by, 14
    see also Bailey, F. Lee; Darrow,
        Clarence; justice system; Moore,
        Fred H.; Pruiett, Moman;
        Rogers, Earl
LBJ: The Way He Was (Cormier), 253
Leavenworth, 178–80, 449
Lee, Harper, 217
Leibowitz, Samuel, 100–101
Leik, David, 259–60
Levin, Peppy, 379–80, 383
Levy, Chandra, 424–25
Lewis, Bernard M., 121–22
Lewis, Neil A., 452
Lewis, Ray, 423–24
Lidd, Ed, 450
Likens, Sylvia, 451
Lindbergh, Anne (Morrow), 144, 145,
    147
Lindbergh, Charles, 144, 146, 147, 156
Lindbergh, Charles, Jr., 148
Lindbergh case, 107, 138–39, 140,
        144–57, 173, 318, 365–66, 369,
        443
Lindbergh Laws, 8
Lindsey, Robert, 450
List, John, 281–85, 295, 452
Littlefield, Ephraim, 27–28
Little Lindbergh Laws, 8, 188, 261
Little Rascals day care case, 317
Livingston, Brockholst, 12, 15
Livingston, John R., 15
Llewellyn Iron Works, 80
Lockhart, Michael Lee, 336
Lodge, Henry Cabot, 29
Loeb and Leopold case, 88, 140, 157
Loggia, Robert, 297

"Lonesome Death of Hattie Carroll,
    The" (Dylan), 472–73
Long, Bruce, 472
Long, Huey, 255
Longfellow, Henry Wadsworth, 30
Los Angeles Police Department, in
    Onion Field case, 221, 222, 223
Los Angeles Times, bombing of, 80–83,
    87, 108
Loss, Fredericka, 17, 18, 19, 20, 21–22
Lowell, James Russell, 30
Lucas, Henry Lee, 436
Lucchese crime family, 325, 327
Lunsford, Jessica, 432, 443
Lusitania, 90
Luster, Andrew, 430–31
Luther, Thomas, 304
Lynch, Jack, 386
lynching, 111, 117, 243
Lyons family, 293–94

McAllister, Ann, 23–24
McCormick, Jack, 357
MacDonald, Jeffrey, 296
McDuff, Kenneth, 167, 337
McElroy, Kenneth, 319, 320–21, 334
McGinniss, Joe, 294, 296, 297
McGovern, Elizabeth, 76
MacLean, Harry N., 274, 321
McManigal, Ortie, 81
McMartin Preschool case, 317
McNamara, James B., 81, 82, 83, 84, 87
McNamara, John J., 81, 82, 83, 84, 87
McQueen, Steve, 266
Mad Butcher of Kingsbury Run, 159–72
Madoff, Bernie, 435
Maeder, Thomas, 450
Magida, Arthur J., 384–85, 450
Mailer, Norman, 76, 450
Malden, Karl, 296
Maness, Terri, 355
Manhattan Company, 11
Mann, Alonzo, 112, 116
Manson, Charles, 108, 222, 224, 256,
    277, 278

Marston, George, 461, 463
Masgay, Louis, 323, 324
Mason, Larry, 408
Massie, Thalia, 156, 157, 174–76, 177
Masters, Edgar Lee, 86
Mathewson, Larry, 258–59
Maul and the Pear Tree, The (James), 297
Mayer, Robert, 340, 451
Mays, Mark, 288, 289
media:
    in anthrax case, 426
    in Boston Strangler case, 226, 227
    changing structure of, 366
    crime coverage in, 6, 7, 24, 107, 130, 156–58, 186, 241–44, 293, 365–66, 369, 438–41, 443, 444
    in Drew Peterson case, 434
    in Duke Lacrosse case, 433
    and justice system, 130, 151, 157, 202, 203, 241–44, 297, 305, 373, 439–41
    in Menendez case, 365, 366, 367
    and Natalee Holloway case, 196
    in O. J. Simpson case, 130, 157, 242, 366, 368–71, 373, 392
    in Pam Smart case, 368
    in Ramsey case, 389, 391–92, 393, 398, 407, 408
    in Ted Bundy case, 292
    see also crime books; movies; newspapers; television
medical malpractice, 96, 108
Melville, Herman, 30
men, crime stories about, 24–25
Mencken, H. L., 157
Menendez, Jose and Kitty, 365
Menendez, Lyle and Erik, 67, 365, 366–67
Menninger, Bonar, 245, 247, 248, 252, 253, 451
Menninger Foundation, 216
Men Who Killed Kennedy, The, 250, 254
Merchants and Manufacturers, 80
Mermaids, 255

Merritt, Gilbert, 21
Metesky, George, 231
Michigan Murders, 257–61, 291
Michigan Murders, The (Keyes), 261, 450
Michigan State University, 310, 311, 312
Milk, Harvey, 306
Milland, Ray, 76
Miller, Austin, 251
Miller, Charley, 69
Miller, Tom, 358
Millett, Kate, 451
Mills, Danny, 135
Mills, Eleanor, 129–35
Mills, James, 129, 133–35
Milo, Dean, 314
Minister and the Choir Singer, The (Kunstler), 132, 296–97, 450
Minnehaha, 92
minorities, crime stories about, 24, 25
Minter, Mary Miles, 467, 468–69, 471
Miranda, Ernesto, 221
Miranda v. Arizona, 221, 223
Missouri, University of, 158
Mitchum, Robert, 298
Mitrione, Dan, 355–56
M'Naghten Rule, 216
Mockery of Justice (Cooper and Sheppard), 204–5, 212–13
Monster of Florence, The (Preston and Spezi), 43, 451
Montgomery, Elizabeth, 63
Mooney v. Holohan (1935), 101
Moore, Fred H., 125, 126–27
Morgan, J. P., 90–92, 93, 124
Morgenthau, Robert, 320
Morris, Errol, 288
Morse, John, 61
Mortal Error (Donahue and Menninger), 245, 247, 248, 253, 255, 451
Moscone, George, 306
Mosher, Bill, 38, 39, 40
"Most Dangerous Game, The," 269

movies:
  crime stories adapted as, 139, 215,
      218, 222, 223, 230, 244–45, 285,
      368, 466
  serial murderers in, 352
Moxley, Martha, 427–28, 429
Mueller, Robert, 427
Muenter, Erich, 75, 76, 89–93, 108,
      110
Muenter, Leone (Krembs), 75–76
Muhammad, John, 430
murder:
  changing definitions of, 95–96
  conviction rates for, 102–3, 104
  premeditated, 261–62
  sentencing for, 332–34
  trial rates for, 101–2
  see also serial murderers
Murder, Inc., 140
Murder at Harvard (Thompson), 28,
      452
Murder in New Hampshire, 368
Murder of Helen Jewett, The (Cohen),
      447, 453–56, 459–60, 462,
      463–65
Murder One (Kilgallen), 204, 450
Murder Trial of Judge Peel, The (Bishop),
      447
Murray, Conrad, 435
My Brother's Keeper (Sheppard and
      Holmes), 204
"Mystery of Marie Roget, The" (Poe),
      17–18

NAACP, 176
Nason, Susan, 273, 274, 303
Nassar, George, 228, 229, 239
National Center for Health Statistics,
      95, 96
Natural Born Celebrities (Schmid), 290,
      452
Natus, Fortune, 4
NBC, 370
Need to Kill, A (Pettit), 335, 336
Neeson, Liam, 244

Neff, James, 204, 211, 451
Nelson, Baby Face, 173
Nero, 2
Nesbit, Evelyn, 76, 78–79
Ness, Eliot, 159, 160, 162, 167
Neulander, Carol, 375–76
Neulander, Fred, 48, 375–86
Newgate Calendar, The, 453
newspapers:
  in Charlie Ross case, 37, 38
  consolidation of, 157–58, 365
  crime stories in, 15, 22, 68, 107,
      157–58, 173, 453, 467, 469–70
  in early 20th century crime cases,
      91, 107, 130, 139–40, 157–58,
      365–66, 466, 467, 469–70
  in Elma Sands case, 12, 13
  in Hall-Mills case, 107, 130, 131,
      369
  in Lindbergh case, 145, 151, 154,
      157, 365–66, 369, 443
  in Mary Phagan case, 107, 111, 114,
      115–16
  in Mary Rogers case, 16
  penny press, 15
  police information in, 199
  in Sacco and Vanzetti case, 107, 125,
      126
  in Sam Sheppard case, 199–200,
      202, 203
  in Snyder-Gray case, 107, 139
Newton, Francis, 232
New York, N.Y.:
  18th–19th century crime rate in, 11
  19th century police in, 17, 18, 22,
      40–41
  population growth in, 15
New York Times, 39
Ng, Charlie Chitat, 343–45, 346
Nickel, Steven, 160, 161, 162, 451
Nifong, Mike, 114, 433
Nilsen, Dennis, 451
Nizer, Louis, 451
No Remorse (Stewart), 337
Normand, Mabel, 467–68, 470

Norman Leslie, 465
Numantina, 1

Oakley, Susan, 340
O'Connor, Sandra Day, 60
O'Donnell, Thomas J., 316
O. J. Simpson case, 368–73, 451
    defense strategy in, 14, 241, 371, 372
    media involvement in, 130, 157,
        242, 366, 368–71, 373, 392
    prosecution mistakes in, 14, 45–46,
        371–72
    significance of, 442–43
Olsen, Jack, 446
Once Upon a Time (MacLean), 274
Onion Field, The (Wambaugh), 108, 222,
        223, 224, 297, 452
Orchard, Harry, 75
organized crime, 108, 140, 173, 324–25
Oswald, Lee Harvey, 245–46, 247, 248,
        249, 252, 253, 254
Otis, Harrison Gray, 80, 81

Palmer, A. Mitchell, 124
Palmer raids, 124
Panzram, Carl, 449
Parker, Ellis, 148
Parkman, George, 26–31, 67
Parton, Margaret, 202
Patrick, Albert, 72–74
Payne, Daniel, 15–16, 17, 19–20
Peavey, Henry, 466, 469, 470
Perfect Gentleman, A (Fletcher), 336
Perfect Murder, Perfect Town (Schiller),
        398–99, 451
Perot, Ross, 255
Perrone, Joseph, 150, 152, 155, 156
Peterson, Drew, 434
Peterson, Laci, 25, 369
Peterson, Scott, 214–15, 369
Peterson, Stacy, 434
Petiot, Marcel, 450
Pettit, Mark, 335, 336
Phagan, Mary, 106, 107, 110–17, 387,
        449

Philadelphia Ledger, 33
Phillips, Nancy, 375, 377–78, 384
"Philosophy for Laymen" (Russell),
        284–85
Physick, Stanley, 91
Pina, Ron, 353, 354
Pinkerton agency, 37, 96
Plauché, Jody, 319, 320
Plauché, Leon Gary, 320
Plautius Silvanus, 1
Poe, Edgar Allan, 17–18, 20, 30
police:
    in American frontier, 32, 41
    in Boston Strangler case, 227–28,
        229, 230–31, 232, 233, 239–40
    in crime books, 349
    crime scene preservation by, 389–91
    in Dunkle case, 348–51
    in 18th century London, 3
    entrapment by, 350
    evidence withholding by, 435–37
    in Hall-Mills case, 130, 135, 388,
        389–90, 394
    in Lake and Ng case, 346
    in Lindbergh case, 148–49, 151
    modern, 102–3, 428
    in movies, 244–45
    murders by, 96
    newspaper information from, 199
    in 19th century New York, 17, 18,
        22, 40–41
    in O. J. Simpson case, 371
    in Ramsey case, 387–88, 389–91,
        392–94, 395–96, 397, 398,
        399–402, 403, 404, 405, 406–8
    in Sam Sheppard case, 199, 201,
        202, 210–11, 212, 213
    and serial murderers, 160, 162, 165,
        183, 186, 230–31, 233, 257–58,
        260, 289–91, 303–5, 330,
        338–39, 353–54, 358–59, 360
    see also justice system; Los Angeles
        Police Department
police sketches, 300, 303–5
Polifrone, Dominick, 325

Polillo, Flo, 161
politics:
    and crime stories, 108, 127, 197
    in early 20th century Kentucky, 69–71
    and justice system, 128, 419–22
Pollack, Jack Harrison, 204
Posner, Gerald, 245, 247, 249, 251, 252
Postman Always Rings Twice, The, 137
Powell, Gregory, 220–22, 224
Power, Katherine Ann, 274–76, 277,
        285, 290, 295
Powers, Caleb, 70–71
Powers, John, 221
Preston, Douglas, 451
Price, Victoria, 177
prison reform, 223, 224–25, 308–9,
        332–34, 412–20, 422
prisons:
    conditions in, 225, 308, 309, 412,
        413–14, 417, 418, 419
    technology and, 419, 420
    see also Alcatraz; Leavenworth
Privileged Information (Alibrandi), 336,
        446
Prongay, Robert, 324
prostitution, in mid-19th century,
        458–60
Pruiett, Moman, 96–99, 100, 101, 109
psychiatric hospitals, 308
Psycho, 352
psychology, 194–95, 306–7, 322

Quincy, Josiah, 26

Rabbi and the Hit Man, The (Magida),
        384–85, 450
racism:
    in crime coverage, 24, 25, 244
    in Mary Phagan case, 116
    in O. J. Simpson case, 372
    see also African Americans
Rader, Dennis, 289, 339
radicalism:
    early 20th century, 77–78, 79, 87,
        122–28, 140, 277

1960's, 78, 79, 87, 122, 123, 255–56,
        275, 277–78
    see also labor movement
Ragtime (Doctorow), 79
Ragtime (film), 76
Ramirez, Richard, 305
Ramsey, Burke, 403
Ramsey, John, 387, 388, 389, 391, 394,
        395, 396–97, 398, 399, 403, 404,
        407–8, 409, 410–11, 443
Ramsey, JonBenet, 25, 241, 242,
        387–408, 423, 443, 451
Ramsey, Patsy, 387, 390, 394, 395–97,
        398, 399–403, 404, 405, 411
Ramsey case:
    alternative theory in, 405–6, 407,
        409–12
    evidence in, 397
    media involvement in, 389, 391–92,
        393, 398, 407, 408
    police mistakes in, 388, 389–91,
        394, 402, 407, 408
    police/prosecutor feud in, 389,
        392–93, 400, 402, 408
    police theory in, 391, 395–96, 397,
        399–402, 403, 404, 405, 406–7
Randall, Pete, 368
Reading Eagle, 37
Reagan, Ronald, 306
Reasonable Doubt, 254
Red Ripper, The (Conradi), 447–48
Reed, John, 87
Rehnquist, William, 60
Reinert, Susan, 297–98
Ressler, Robert, 164, 167, 230, 290, 291,
        292, 293, 335, 336, 339–40
Retrial: Murder and Dr. Sam Sheppard
        (Holmes), 204, 210
Reynolds, Melvin, 299, 302, 304
Reynolds, Quentin, 101, 451
Rice, William Marsh, 71–73
Ridgway, Gary, 270
Riehl, Arthur, 131
Ring, Catherine (Sands), 10, 11
Ring, Elias, 10, 11

Riverside Killer, The (Keers and St.
        Pierre), 358–59
Riverside murder, 266–68
Roberts, Emory, 251
Robey, Ames, 232, 236
Robinson, Richard, 15, 453, 454,
        456–57, 458, 459, 460, 461,
        462–66
Robinson, Robert, 171
Rockefeller, John D., 124
Rogers, Earl, 80–81, 84–85, 99–100,
        101
Rogers, Mary, 15–22, 24, 25
Rollins, Howard, 76
Rome, ancient, 1–2, 452
Roosevelt, Eleanor, 124, 187
Roosevelt, Franklin, 124
Rosenberg, Julius and Ethel, 108, 177,
        187, 193, 196–97, 451, 452
Ross, Charlie, 46–40
Ross, Christian, 36–37, 38, 39, 41
Ross, Walter, 36, 37, 39
Royall, Anne, 454
Ruby, Jack, 246, 254
Rule, Ann, 292–93, 336, 451
Runyon, Damon, 133–34, 139
Rusch, Christine, 355
Russell, Bertrand, 284–85

Sacco and Vanzetti case, 107, 122,
        123–27, 128, 140, 177, 276, 277
St. Johns, Adela Rogers, 99–100, 452
St. Pierre, Dennis, 359
St. Valentine's Day Massacre, 140
Sanborn, F. B., 30
Sands, Elma, 10–14, 18, 24, 25, 465
Sands, Hope, 10, 11
San Francisco Chronicle, 264, 265, 266
San Francisco Examiner, 264
Sasser, Charles W., 337–40, 451
Savage, John, 222
Savio, Kathleen, 434
Saxe, Susan, 274, 275, 276, 278
Scaduto, Anthony, 152, 153, 154–55,
        232, 451

Scapegoat (Scaduto), 152, 153, 232, 451
Schaefer, Brenda, 363–65
Schell, Joan, 259
Schiller, Lawrence, 398–99, 451
Schmid, David Frank, 290, 452
Schreiber, Flora Rheta, 321, 452
Schroeder, Walter, 274
Schwarzkopf, Norman, 147
Schweitzer, Albert, 187
Schwerner, Mickey, 118, 243–44
Scopes Monkey Trial, 88, 140
Scotland Yard, 428
Scottsboro Boys, 101, 117, 174, 176–77
Seales, Franklyn, 222
Search for the Strangler (Sherman), 233
Seattle Star, 467
Secret Service, U.S., 251, 253, 255, 403
Secundus, L. Pedanius, 2
security, 93–94
Sensabaugh, Leone, 89
serial murderers:
        characteristics of, 160, 162, 164–67,
                168–69, 172, 184, 233, 238–39,
                260, 266, 270, 302, 303, 326,
                329–30, 340, 350, 351–52, 355,
                360–61
        crime books about, 292–93, 321–22,
                331, 335, 336–37, 352–54,
                355–56, 359, 447–48, 450, 451
        crime books' descriptions of,
                336–37
        fictional, 351–52
        investigation of, 257–58, 260,
                303–5, 338–39, 353–54, 358–59,
                360
        justice system and, 328, 329, 331–32
        police beliefs about, 160, 162, 165,
                183, 186, 230–31, 289–91,
                338–39
        police sketches of, 303–5
        proliferation of, 291, 327
sexual assault, 20, 235, 263
Sharkey, Joe, 281, 283, 284, 452
Sharpe, Violet, 147, 369
Shawcross, Arthur, 167

Shelby, Charlotte, 468, 469, 470, 471–72
Sheppard, Marilyn, 25, 198, 201, 202, 205, 206, 208, 209, 211, 212, 213, 214
Sheppard, Sam, 157, 198–215, 240, 241, 451
Sheppard, Samuel Reese (Chip), 199, 204–5, 211, 213
Sheppard, Stephen, 199, 204
Sheppard Murder Case, The (Holmes), 203, 204, 210, 449
Sherman, Casey, 233
Shoemaker, The (Schreiber), 321–22, 452
Shore, Mary Ann, 364
Short, Elizabeth, *see* Black Dahlia
Siegel, Bugsy, 185, 449
Silence of the Lambs, The (Harris), 352
Simon, David, 337, 452
Simpson, Alexander, 131
Simpson, Nicole Brown, 108
    see also O.J. Simpson case
Simpson, O. J., *see* O. J. Simpson case
Sins of the Father (Franklin and Wright), 274
60 Minutes, 153, 274
Skakel, Michael, 427–28, 429, 430
Skakel, Tommy, 427, 428
Skelton, Royce, 252
Slaton, John, 111, 116–17
Sleeping Lady, The (Graysmith), 337
Smart, Gregg, 367, 368
Smart, Pam, 367–68
Smit, Lou, 405, 406, 407
Smith, Carlton, 352–54
Smith, Dexter, 38
Smith, Horace, 32
Smith, Jay, 297, 298
Smith, Jimmy, 221–22
Smith, Perry, 217, 218, 332, 344
Smith, Stephen, 455
Smollett, Tobias, 5
Snyder, Albert, 137–38
Snyder, Ruth, 107, 137–39
Sobell, Morton, 220
solitary confinement, 178

Soltysik, Patricia, 277–78
Solved, 139
Something Terrible Has Happened (Van Slingerland), 175, 452
Soncini, Elaine, 375, 378, 379, 381–82, 385
Son of Sam, *see* Berkowitz, David
Sopranos, The, 326–27
Sorrentino, Paul, 314–16
Speck, Richard, 242
Spector, Phil, 431
Spezi, Mario, 451
Spungen, Deborah, 310, 452
Spungen, Nancy, 310
Squires, Mary, 4, 5, 6
Stano, Gerald, 358, 360
Starkweather, Charles, 108
Steele, Michelle, 300, 301
Steenburgen, Mary, 76
Steunenberg, Frank, 75, 108
Stevens, Willie, 129–30
Stewart, Bob, 337
Stewart, James B., 452
Stewart, Martha, 316
Stine, Paul, 264, 266, 272
Stoll, Clifford, 362–63, 452
Stout, Rex, 130
strangulation, 19
Stroud, Elizabeth, 119, 120
Stroud, Robert, 108, 119–20, 178–80, 218–20, 224
Suddenly Gone (Mitrione), 355–56
Suetonius, 452
Suff, William Lester, 358–59, 360
Sullivan, Bridget, 43–44, 52, 61, 62, 63
Supreme Court, U.S.:
    Caryl Chessman's appeals to, 187
    justice system decisions of, 101, 102, 103, 105, 221, 223–24
    1972 death penalty ruling in, 285–86
    and prison reform, 309
    Randall Dale Adams' appeal to, 288
    Robert Stroud's appeals to, 119, 120
    Sam Sheppard's appeal to, 203

Supreme Court of Alaska, 329
Suspense, 269
Sutcliffe, Peter, 304
Sutton, Willie, 450
Swango, Michael, 108
Swope, Thomas Hunton, 76–77

Tacitus, 1
Taken, 244
Tarnower, Herman, 319
Tate, Sharon, 256, 289
Taylor, William, 70–71
Taylor, William Desmond, 466–72
Taylorology (website), 472
television:
    crime coverage on, 7, 366, 368,
        370–71, 438–39
    crime stories adapted for, 215,
        297–98, 326–27
    O. J. Simpson case on, 368–69,
        370–71
    serial murderer stories on, 293,
        351–52
terrorism, 93, 126
    see also radicalism
Terry, Maury, 452
Texas Bankers Association, 96
Texas Court of Criminal Appeals, 289
Thaw, Harry Kendall, 76, 78, 110, 121,
        122
Thebaut, Jim, 325
Thin Blue Line, The, 288
Thomas, Clarence, 197
Thomas, Pat, 335
Thomas, Steve, 389, 392, 393, 398–402,
        403, 405
Thompson, Helen, 28, 452
Thoreau, Henry David, 30
3 Lives for Mississippi (Huie), 449–50
Tiberius, 1
Ticknor, George, 30
Tierney, Kevin, 86
Till, Emmett, 243
Tison, Gary, 293–96, 298, 336
To Die For, 368

Torsney, Robert, 308
*Torso: Eliot Ness and the Hunt for the
    Mad Butcher of Kingsbury Run*
    (Nickel), 160, 171, 451
Toschi, Dave, 265, 266, 268, 269
Townsend, Rosina, 460–61, 462,
    463–64
Train, Arthur, 73–74
Treat, John, 6
Trial of Levi Weeks, The (Kleiger), 12,
    450
Triangle Shirtwaist Factory Fire, 95
Troy, Thomas, 232
True Stories of Crime (Train), 73–74
True Story (Finkel), 449
truTV, 8, 46, 68, 305
Tucker, Preston, 319
Turner, Andrew, 119
Turner, Ted, 293
12 Angry Men, 280
Twelve Caesars (Suetonius), 452

Ultimate Evil, The (Terry), 452
Underwood, Naomi, 280
Unspeakable Crime of Dr. Petiot, The
    (Maeder), 450
Until You Are Dead (Drimmer), 190–91
Urgulania, 1
Urgulanilla, 1

Vallejo Times-Herald, 264
Van Brunt, Charles, 38
Van Brunt, Holmes, 38
van der Sloot, Joran, 432
Van Slingerland, Peter, 175, 176, 452
Versace, Gianni, 173
Vicious, Sid, 310
Vicki, Ms., 385
Vidal, Gore, 99
Vidor, King, 466–67, 468, 469,
    470–71
vigilantes, 319–21
Villaseñor, Victor, 280, 281, 452
Virginia Tech University, 434
Voltaire, 5

Walden, Chris, 335
Walker, Edwin, 245
Wallace, Julia, 107
Walling, Washington, 39, 41
Walsh, John, 281
Wambaugh, Joseph, 222, 297, 452
Wardrip, Faryion, 340
Warren Commission, 227, 228, 247,
    249, 250, 251, 254
Warren Court, 103, 105, 223–24, 309
Washington, George, 11
Watergate, 153
Watt, Robert, 34, 35, 36
Webster, Daniel, 30
Webster, John, 27, 28, 29, 30, 31, 36, 67
Wecht, Cyril, 398
Weeks, Ezra, 12
Weeks, Levi, 11–14, 18, 465
Weiner, Tim, 452
Welles, Orson, 269
Wells, Floyd, 217, 218
Wells, Susannah, 4, 5
Wesson, Daniel, 32
Westervelt, William, 39
Weston, Nathan, 454
Where the Money Was (Linn and
    Sutton), 450
White, Dan, 306–7
White, Fleet, 388, 405
White, Stanford, 76, 78–79, 110, 121,
    122
Whitechapel Club, 68
Whitman, Charles, 242
Whitney, Eli, Jr., 32
Whoever Fights Monsters (Ressler), 167,
    335, 336
Who Killed JonBenet Ramsey?
    (Bosworth and Wecht), 398, 405

Wick, Steve, 453
Wikipedia, 68, 99
"Wild West," 32, 33, 41–42, 78, 135
Williams, Wayne, 172, 317, 318, 469
Willwerth, James, 451
Wilson, Edith, 120, 178
Wilson, Jack, 183
Wilson, Woodrow, 120
Winchester, Oliver, 32
Wizard of Oz, The (film), 466
Wolfe, Donald H., 183–84, 185–86, 453
women, crime stories about, 25
Wood, Richard, 337
Wood, Robert, 287
Woods, James, 222
Woodward, Mary Elizabeth, 252
workplace deaths, 95
World War I, 89–93, 122, 124, 169–70
World War II, 157, 170, 171
Wright, William, 274
Wrong Man, The (film), 223
Wrong Man, The (Neff), 204, 451
Wynn, Keenan, 269

Yale murder, 26, 305
Yarborough, Ralph, 252
Yarros, Victor, 87
Yates, Andrea, 425
Yates, Rusty, 425
Younger, Cole, 32, 41

Zantzinger, William, 472, 473–74
Zapruder film, 249, 250
Zero at the Bone (Heidenry), 448, 449
Zodiac, 25, 264–72, 370
Zodiac (Graysmith), 265, 268, 449
Zodiac Unmasked (Graysmith), 265,
    266